INTRODUCING
The New Testament

JOHN DRANE

LYNX

Text copyright © 1986 John Drane
This edition copyright © 1986 Lion Publishing

Published by
Lynx Communications
Sandy Lane West, Littlemore, Oxford, England
ISBN 0 7459 1168 4
Albatros Books Pty Ltd
PO Box 320, Sutherland, NSW 2232, Australia
ISBN 0 86760 838 2

First edition 1986
Reprinted 1989, 1991, 1992, 1993

British Library Cataloguing in Publication Data
Drane, John W.
    Introducing the New Testament
    1. Bible–N.T.–Criticism, interpretation, etc.
    I. Title
    255.6   BS2361.2
    ISBN 0-7459-1168-4

Printed and bound in Slowenia

INTRODUCING
THE NEW TESTAMENT

John Drane's introductions to both Old and New Testaments have received wide acclaim. The New Testament material has now been thoroughly revised and considerably extended for this new volume: with its awareness of current scholarship, faithfulness to the text and to historical detail, and exciting presentation, this book will be stimulating and informative for both the individual reader and schools and colleges. Dr John Drane is Lecturer in Religious Studies at Stirling University.

For Howard and Joyce Marshall

Contents

5. Into all the world

6. Paul: evangelist extraordinary

7. Paul and the Christian message

8. Unity in diversity

Foreword

The New Testament is one of the most influential books there has ever been. For almost 2000 years it has deeply affected the thinking and lifestyle of people throughout the world. Today it has been translated into more languages and is read by more people than any other book. In the New Testament, we come face to face with one of the world's most powerful opinion-formers – Jesus of Nazareth – and his first followers. And many people find that as they read it, their own lives are challenged and changed by the teaching they find there. For its pages contain a message about human nature and human needs that is still of direct relevance to the concerns of everyday life in the modern world.

At the same time, the New Testament is clearly not a modern book, and it is not always easy to understand. The social background of Jesus and the earliest Christians was vastly different from our own. So was their whole world of ideas. Without some knowledge of its religious and social setting, it is easy to misunderstand what the New Testament is saying.

The aim of this book is to help to set the New Testament in a proper historical and social perspective, and to provide an introduction and guide for the modern reader. The author, John Drane, relates the New Testament to its times; he introduces us to the main characters; he shows the source of their ideas; and he explains how the life of the early church developed in its first generation. In the process, he brings the New Testament to life for a new generation of readers.

John Drane is well equipped for this task. For three years he researched the New Testament and its background at the University of Manchester, particularly Paul's relationship to the developing religion of Gnosticism. Since 1973 he has taught in the Department of Religious Studies of Stirling University. He is familiar enough with the world of academic theology. But he is also concerned to communicate beyond the scholarly world to ordinary readers – and his style and approach will appeal to anyone who wants to know more about the subject.

This book is an expansion and adaptation of three previous books: *Paul, Jesus and the Four Gospels*, and *The Life of the Early Church*. Together with two others, *The Old Testament Story* and *Old Testament Faith*, they form a comprehensive introduction to the Bible which breaks new ground in popular appeal. Written over a period of some ten years, they represent a considerable achievement. The books have been translated into a number of languages and have been well received by a wide cross-section of contemporary opinion.

There is no doubt a common thread running through the whole of the New Testament. Yet it is easy to see why John Drane originally divided the material into the three books which form the basis of this present volume. Paul wrote more than a third of the whole New Testament, including most of its letters. He was the one who took the good news of Jesus beyond its original Jewish base and into the wider Roman world. But precisely because his ideas span these two worlds of thought, they need to be explained very carefully if we are to understand them today. *Jesus and the Four Gospels* is the place where many people begin their Bible reading – yet the Jewish setting of Jesus' life and ministry needs explanation if readers are to grasp the meaning of his teaching fully. Then *The Life of the Early Church*, covering the remaining New Testament books, depicted the story of the developing life of the first Christian communities as they faced the challenge of living for Jesus in a largely hostile environment.

Such a lucid piece of writing on these crucial subjects deserved the best presentation. So the form chosen was the 'illustrated documentary'. Nowadays, most of us take in a large part of our information visually, and the photographs and charts accompanying the text are more than decoration – they are intended to be a part of the communication, giving the feel and impact of the first-century faith.

Some parts of what the author has to say are more complex than others, which is why some of the text is set in special features. In this way the main text can be followed unbroken through the book, with the reader taking in the more specialist detail of the features separately.

This guidebook will be useful in a wide variety of circumstances. University and seminary teachers will find its 25 chapters form the ideal basis for an introductory semester course on the New Testament. Schools and colleges will also find it an invaluable resource. But ordinary readers at home will want to use it too, as an aid to understanding the New Testament and getting to grips with its relevance for their own lives.

ILLYRICUM
& DALMATIA

MOESIA

River Tiber

Rome

Sea of Adria

THRACIA

Neapolis

Appian Way

MACEDONIA

Philippi

Thessalonica

Egnatian Way

Rhegium

Syracuse

ACHAIA

Aegean Sea

Mysia

ASIA

Corinth

Cenchreae
Athens

Ephesus

Malta

CRETE

Fair
Havens

Mediterranean Sea

CYRENAICA

The World of the New Testament

Euxine Sea

BITHYNIA & PONTUS

KINGDOM OF POLEMON

GALATIA

River Halys

CAPPADOCIA

●Colossae
Pisidia

LYCIA

PAMPHYLIA

CILICIA
●Tarsus

Antioch●

River Orontes

SYRIA

CYPRUS

●Damascus

Caesarea●

K'DOM
OF HEROD AGRIPPA

Jerusalem●

NABATAEA

●Memphis

River Nile

EGYPT

1. Setting the scene

Chapter 1 The world of the first Christians

The New Testament tells the story of one of the most remarkable religious and social movements the world has ever seen. Its contents are like a small library, including personal letters as well as books of history and theology. These books were written by many different authors, at different times and places in the Roman empire during the first century AD. But they are all part of the same story, reflecting the fervour and devotion of the first followers of Jesus Christ.

Acts 17:6

In their own day they were accused of turning the world upside down with their message – and they have influenced every subsequent generation in history. Even today in the largely secular cultures of the western world, passages like Jesus' Sermon on the Mount or Paul's great hymn in praise of love are still widely acclaimed.

Matthew 5–7
1 Corinthians 13

No other book from the ancient world has such an impact today. By modern standards its writers were unsophisticated. Yet millions of people read the New Testament regularly and discover in its pages a personal inspiration for their daily living. It was written in a remote corner of the ancient Roman empire – but people in many different cultures still find its message is relevant for all times and places. Men and women will go to amazing lengths to possess a copy. As they read it, they often encounter an overpowering challenge to their thinking and style of life.

In the beginning

Matthew 2:1; Luke 2:1–7

Luke 23:33

All this began with the life of just one remarkable person, Jesus of Nazareth. Born about 4 BC into an ordinary working-class Jewish family, he went on to make a name for himself as a religious teacher. He was in the public gaze for little more than three years before his life was tragically cut short by his execution on a Roman cross. But in that short time he delivered a message about God that was to exert a crucial influence not only on his own people, but on the subsequent course of world history.

No doubt his appearance was not all that remarkable in the context of the Palestinian countryside where he lived and worked. There were hundreds of wandering teachers, or 'rabbis' as they were called – men of exceptional gifts and insight who would

Matthew 10:1–4
Mark 6:30–44; 8:1–9

The Sea of Galilee was the scene of much of Jesus' teaching and healing, and some of his first disciples were fishermen.

gather round them small groups of disciples to perpetuate their teachings after they were gone. The stories about Jesus in the New Testament Gospels tell us how he himself had twelve special followers, though they also report that on more than one occasion thousands of people flocked to hear his teaching. But what really sets Jesus apart from the other Jewish rabbis is the fact that it was not on the shores of the inland Sea of Galilee among simple peasants that his teaching made its greatest impact. For in a very short time after his death, his personality and his beliefs were having a profound effect in places far removed from the shores of Palestine.

A new faith

Within twenty years of his crucifixion, every major centre of Roman civilization could boast at least one group of his followers. There were Christians in Rome, Corinth, Ephesus, Philippi, Antioch in Syria and many other Mediterranean cities – not to

Acts 8:26–39

mention far-flung places such as Alexandria in Egypt, or Ethiopia, or Byzantium. This is not all that surprising when it is realized that the list of people present in Jerusalem to hear Peter's first public sermon reads like a roll-call of most of the cities in the ancient world: 'We are from Parthia, Media, and Elam; from Mesopotamia, Judea, and Cappadocia; from Pontus and Asia, from Phrygia and Pamphylia, from Egypt and the regions of Libya near Cyrene. Some of us are from Rome, both Jews and Gentiles converted to Judaism, and

Acts 2:9–11

some of us are from Crete and Arabia ... ' Presumably not all of them became Christians. But many of them did, and it was not long before these new followers of Jesus began to exert an increasingly powerful influence on life even in Rome itself.

Writing of events in AD 49, less than twenty years after the death of Jesus, the Roman historian Suetonius describes a series of riots that led the emperor Claudius to expel the Jewish population from

Life of Claudius 25.4

the city. And according to him, the cause of all the trouble was a person whom he calls 'Chrestus'. Scholars have debated the precise identity of this person, but there seems little doubt that the events Suetonius records were brought about by arguments over the teaching of those Jews who had become followers of Jesus the Messiah (Latin *Christus*).

Opposition

It was not long before the popular press of the Roman world turned their attention to these followers of Jesus: 'The Christians form among themselves secret societies that exist outside the system of laws ... an obscure and mysterious community founded on revolt and on the advantage that accrues from it ... They form a rabble of profane conspiracy. Their alliance consists in meetings at night with solemn rituals and inhuman revelries ... They despise temples as if they were tombs. They disparage the gods and ridicule our sacred rites ... Just like a rank growth of weeds, the abominable haunts where this impious confederacy meet are multiplying all

Origen, Against Celsus 8.17; 3.14;
Minucius Felix, Octavius 8.4; 9.1–6

over the world ... To venerate an executed criminal and ... the wooden cross on which he was executed is to erect altars which befit lost and depraved wretches.'

Not that the Christians themselves would have agreed with any of this. Far from worshipping 'an executed criminal', these men and women who were causing such social upheaval firmly

Acts 2:32

believed that their Jesus was not dead, but was really and truly alive, and was with them wherever they went. This was the one crucial factor which ensured the lasting success of the whole Christian enterprise. Because they believed that Jesus was not dead, but alive, his first followers were prepared to take the most incredible risks in

Acts 12:1–5; 2 Corinthians 11:23–27

spreading their message. Beatings, imprisonments, shipwrecks, and persecutions of all kinds – even death – were commonplace in the life of the early churches. And the results were spectacular.

Changing the world

Of course, we look back on all this with the wisdom of hindsight. We know that the church did in fact succeed. But if we put ourselves in the position of those first followers of Jesus, we can see that their success was by no means a foregone conclusion. Indeed, quite the opposite. By normal standards everything was against them. Jesus himself was a Jew, as were all his original disciples – and though in some circles in the Roman Empire the Jewish religion was respected, on the whole the Jews living in Palestine were regarded as an incomprehensible, fanatical and unbalanced race. On top of that, neither Jesus nor his followers were of high social standing. They came from the backwoods of rural Palestine. It must have been hard enough for them to gain a hearing even in their own local religious capital, Jerusalem – not to mention the problems of communicating with educated Greeks and Romans in the wider world outside. Yet this is precisely what they did, as a movement that began spontaneously in a country on the edge of Roman civilization suddenly became an important social and political, as well as religious force at the very centre of life in the empire. So what was their secret? What did Jesus and his teaching really mean – and why did his followers feel compelled to take it to the furthest corners of the world they knew? Why did they not stay at home instead, to be a reforming movement in their own Jewish religion? And how did these hill-billies from far away Galilee manage to communicate the message of Jesus so successfully to the cultured inhabitants of ancient cities in Italy and Greece?

To find the answers to these questions, we need first to understand the world where they lived.

The Greek heritage

Alexander the Great's wide conquests spread Greek ways of thought and culture right round the eastern Mediterranean.

There is no such thing as a civilization that comes from nowhere. We are all heirs to the past. In the world of the first Christians, the outward forms of administration and government were those of the Roman empire. But its cultural roots were embedded in a different world altogether. The way people spoke and thought, their aspirations and achievements, and their hopes and fears all went back to pre-Roman times. For the world of the Roman empire had its real origins some three hundred years before the time of Jesus, with one of the first rulers ever to establish a world empire: Alexander the Great (356–323 BC).

Alexander rose to fame almost overnight. He began as the son of a little-known local ruler in Macedonia (the northern part of modern Greece). But he was such a brilliant general that he was able to defeat armies much more prestigious than his own, and establish himself as undisputed emperor of the whole of the world that was then known to people in the Mediterranean lands. The great Persian empire fell to his troops, followed by Egypt, and ultimately by other lands even further to the east. Just ten years after his first major success against the Persians, Alexander died at the age of only 33. But by then his empire stretched from Greece in the west to Pakistan in the east.

Politically, it did not survive his death intact. After much squabbling among Alexander's generals, his territories were divided, and it was nearly three hundred years later that they were finally reunited, when the Roman Octavian (63 BC – AD 14) eventually secured the eastern end of the Mediterranean Sea for his own empire.

Hellenism   Octavian was himself a brilliant strategist. But he owed much of his lasting success to the fact that there was already a far-reaching cultural unity among almost all the nations which he had conquered. In spite of their diverse national traditions, people throughout the Mediterranean world were deeply conscious of being part of a wider world. In east and west, people had common hopes, similar educational opportunities, and much the same way of understanding life. They even spoke the same language: Greek.

All this sprang directly from the genius of Alexander the Great. Unlike many other dictators, Alexander was not addicted to the exercise of power just for its own sake. He was not a brutish, uncultured person. Quite the opposite. In his youth he had been a student of the great Greek philosopher Aristotle, and he never forgot what he had learned from him. Alexander was a fanatic for his own native culture. He was genuinely convinced that civilization had reached its ultimate goal with the Greek way of life. He was determined to share it with the whole world. Greek customs, religion and philosophy – even the Greek language – were all adopted throughout Alexander's domains. Cities were built everywhere in the Greek style, accompanied by Greek temples and sports arenas. And the way of life that resulted – 'Hellenism' – was to last for nearly a thousand years after Alexander's death.

The degree to which any particular nation accepted this Hellenistic culture naturally varied from place to place. Sometimes the changes were only superficial. The names of native gods and goddesses might be changed into Greek forms, but their worship often continued much the same as it had always been. In addition, ordinary working people had little time or opportunity for philosophical debates and sports activities, and it was generally the ruling classes who became most involved in such pursuits. They were also the ones who most often used the Greek language, for it meant they could make international contacts without the tedious necessity of learning foreign languages. But the Greek influence was everywhere, and in one way or another it penetrated to all sections of society.

It was in this Greek dominated world that the earliest Christians proclaimed their new message. For all its size and diversity, it was a world that was easy to reach with the good news about Jesus. There were few language problems; cultural barriers were minimal; and by the Roman age great roads were being built which would make it easy to travel from one part of the empire to another. But these were not the only factors that moulded the world of the first Christians. For by the first century AD many people also had other concerns.

Philosophy

Alexander had been inspired by a love for the great classical Greek philosophers. But by the time of the New Testament, their heyday was long past. Those who succeeded the original generation of creative thinkers were not of the same intellectual calibre, and much philosophy was concerned with detailed arguments about things that to ordinary people seemed trivial and irrelevant. But there were some who tried to keep in touch with the needs of ordinary people.

● *The Stoics* were quite an influential group in the New Testament period. This school of thought was founded by Zeno (335–263 BC). He was a native of Cyprus, but went to Athens and eventually set up his own school in the Stoa Poikile – hence the name 'Stoic'.

Stoic philosophy was based on a belief that both the world and its people ultimately depend on just one principle: 'Reason'. Since the world itself operates by this standard, men and women who want a good life must 'live in harmony with nature'. They could do this primarily through following their conscience, for that itself was also inspired by 'Reason'. This was something people could

The Roman empire contained many religions and philosophies within its boundaries. This gave many people a questioning spirit: could there be truth in some of the new religions?

only do for themselves, and Stoics laid great emphasis on living a life of 'self-sufficiency'. Many of them were widely respected for their high standards of personal morality. It was not uncommon for them to be prepared to commit suicide sooner than lose their self-respect and dignity.

Inevitably, this way of understanding life did not convince everyone – not least because it did not seem to tackle the social realities of the day. If 'Reason' filled and inspired everything, then why were all people not the same? Why were there so many slaves condemned to eke out a wretched existence? The Stoic could reply that, in his mind, the slave was equal to the emperor. But that was not much comfort to the slave!

● *The Epicureans* were another popular philosophical group in the Hellenistic age. They too had an ancient pedigree, tracing their origin back to the Greek Epicurus (341–270 BC). Epicureans adopted a totally different view of life. Though many Greeks had debated what happens at death, they would have none of it. Death is the end, they said, and the only real way to make sense of life is to be as detached as possible from it. A good life consists in 'pleasure'. For Epicurus, this means things like friendship and peace of mind. But many of his followers interpreted it differently, and gained a reputation for reckless living.

These and other philosophical groups had many followers in New Testament times. But they never had much appeal for ordinary people. They were seldom able to stem the fears of the working classes. And in any case, it was time consuming and intellectually demanding to organize one's life this way. As a result, Greek philosophy had few points of contact with the mass of the people, who were not highly intellectual and had little opportunity for the leisurely pursuit of personal morality.

Religion

Many people found it more natural to make sense of life in terms of religion. But for those who took Hellenism seriously, few certainties could remain. While the philosophers had produced systems of thought that were often incomprehensible, they had also questioned many traditional religious beliefs. There were those who still worshipped the old Greek and Roman gods, but they knew that educated people had concluded that such deities did not really exist. International movements of trade and people had also made Europeans more conscious of the existence of other gods and goddesses in the eastern part of the Roman empire. Did they exist – and if so, how could they relate to life in the great urban centres of Greece and Italy?

Such ambiguities eventually led to what has been called 'a failure of nerve' in the Hellenistic world. The philosophers had discredited traditional ways of making sense out of life. But they had failed to establish a plausible alternative. As a result, the majority of people found themselves in a moral and spiritual vacuum. There was no shortage of religious ideas that could fill the gap –

and people throughout the empire were ready to seize anything that might give them new hope in an uncertain world.

Countries on the eastern fringe of the Hellenistic world had their own ancient religions. Westerners had a natural curiosity about them – especially when they seemed to be consistent with the more accessible conclusions of Greek philosophy. Two aspects of western philosophy seemed especially congenial to these eastern cults:

● In order to explain the existence of evil in the world, philosophers had often argued that this world in which we live is not the only world. Nor is it the best. There is, they suggested, another world of goodness and light – and that is the most important sphere of existence. People belong to it because they have a 'soul' – a spark of light that is related not to bodily existence in this world, but to spiritual existence in the other world. Our brief existence here is merely an unfortunate encumbrance, and to find true meaning and fulfilment we need to escape the body ('the prison of the soul', according to Pythagoras).

● Alongside the moral philosophy of people like Plato, another major strand in Greek thinking had been concerned with natural philosophy – working out how things work, and how the universe fits together. As Roman and Greek thinkers explored the mysteries of the universe, they were often impressed by the movements of the planets and the stars. They seemed to operate with such precision and regularity that many believed the key to the whole of life was somehow locked up within them.

So the way was prepared for the penetration of many oriental religions into the Roman empire. For a long time astrology had been of great interest to eastern sages. So had the possibility of reincarnation. It was not long before these speculations were combined with the conclusions of Greek scientists to produce a new kind of religious movement in the Hellenistic world.

● **Gnosticism** is a term often used to describe this movement today. There is a good deal of uncertainty about its precise origins, and a lot of disagreement as to whether it existed in the earliest Christian generations, or whether it developed only later as a result of the spread of the Christian message itself. We have positive evidence of its existence in the second and third centuries AD, both from Gnostic documents and also from the writings of church leaders who wrote to denounce it. At that time it was obviously a widespread religious movement.

It is unlikely that there was such an organised group in the New Testament period. But we can be sure that these later groups built their systems out of materials that had been in circulation for a long time. Several New Testament books seem to refer to notions that later became central to such Gnostic thinking, and it is obvious that such ideas were floating around independently in the religious atmosphere of the earlier Hellenistic age.

Gnostic thinking was based on the belief that there are two worlds: the world of spirit, where God is, which is pure and holy;

and the world of matter, where we are, which is evil and corrupted. If God is holy and pure, Gnostics said, then he can have nothing to do with our own world. Salvation therefore cannot be relevant here, and a person's best chance is to escape to the spiritual world and find true fulfilment there.

For most Gnostics, this chance to escape came at death, when the soul left the body behind. But not everyone would be automatically qualified to reach the world of spirit. To do so, a person must have a divine 'spark' embedded in their nature, otherwise they simply return to this world to start another meaningless round of bodily existence. Even those who have the 'spark' can never be certain of finding ultimate release, for the evil creator of this world (the *Demiurge*) and his accomplices (the *Archons*) jealously guard every entrance to the world of spirit. To get past them, the spark must be enlightened about its own nature and the nature of true salvation. For this, it requires 'knowledge' (Greek *gnosis*). When Gnostics spoke of 'knowledge' they did not have in mind an intellectual knowledge of theology or science. They thought of a mystical experience, a direct 'knowing' of the supreme God.

In practical terms, this kind of belief could lead to two quite different extremes. Some argued that their aim of complete liberation from the grasp of the material world could best be achieved by a rigorous asceticism which would effectively deny the reality of their bodily human existence. But there were others who believed they had already been released from all material ties. So what they did in their present life was totally irrelevant to their ultimate spiritual destiny. They saw it as their duty to spoil everything connected with life in the world – including its standards of morality. And so they indulged in all sorts of undisciplined behaviour.

It is not difficult to trace connexions between this and various groups who are mentioned in the New Testament, though we must remember there is no evidence that it had all been worked into a comprehensive system at this period. Nevertheless, Paul's letters to the church in Corinth often seem to be criticizing views that would certainly be congenial to later Gnostics. Colossians, 1 John and Revelation also seem to be correcting people who thought like this.

● **Mystery religions** Direct emotional experience of God also played a key role in the various mystery religions which sprang up in the Roman empire. Mithraism was one of the best known of these, but there were many others, associated with the gods of Asia Minor and Egypt as well as traditional Greek practices. Like Gnosticism, these groups were by definition secret societies, and our specific knowledge of them is therefore inevitably limited. It seems likely however that many of them arose as developments from the various fertility religions which had been popular for thousands of years throughout the ancient Middle East. Their mythologies certainly seem to reflect the cycle of the seasons, as the new life of spring follows the barrenness of winter, all of it symbolized by the death and rebirth of the gods of fertility. The ancient

The background to Christianity's spread in the Mediterranean world was the Hellenistic culture. Buildings, thought-forms, and even language were Greek, and this gave a uniform cultural setting for the growing Christian church.

religions of Egypt and Palestine had generally depicted all this through annual festivals in which priests and priestesses would act out the role of the gods, usually in rituals with strong sexual overtones.

In the Hellenistic mysteries, such rituals became mystical experiences for the individual worshipper. Their original mythology was transferred from the ongoing life of nature into the experience of individual people, who themselves spoke of undergoing the death and rebirth that had been so important to the prosperity of the ancient farmer.

A person could gain access to this mystical experience by way of an initiation ceremony. One account of the consecration of a priest tells how the subject was placed in a pit in the ground, covered with a wicker framework. On this a bull (symbol of life and virility) was slaughtered, and its blood ran down and soaked the initiate. When the priest emerged, those around would fall down and worship him, for he himself had now been made divine through being drenched in the life of the bull.

Prudentius, *Peristephanon.* X.1011–50

No doubt the initiation of a priest differed in some details from that of an ordinary person. But a similar pattern would be followed, often accompanied by more overtly sexual rites as well.

The Mysteries gave a sense of hope and security to their initiates, in both personal and social terms. Individuals gained a sense of personal meaning and purpose in life. They also became part of a distinctive group, which often operated as a mutual aid society in times of difficulty or hardship.

● **Judaism** Surprisingly enough, Judaism was also very popular in the Hellenistic world. There were a number of reasons for this – not least the fact that large numbers of Jews lived in most of the major towns and cities of the Roman empire. Wherever they went, they took their distinctive religion and life style with them. They were always conscious of a deep difference between themselves and their non-Jewish neighbours, but they were also happy for others to join them. And many Greeks and Romans were attracted.

From the perspective of the west, Judaism itself was an eastern religion, and held all the attractions of mystery and intrigue that such an origin provoked. But unlike the esoteric mystery cults, Judaism was easy for outsiders to understand. They could see its practical outcome in the life of their Jewish friends. More important, they could read the Jewish scriptures – the Old Testament – in their own Greek language.

This opened up a wide range of possibilities for communicating the faith to those who were not of the Jewish race. And Jewish teachers were not slow to take advantage of the opportunity. Jesus himself spoke of the persistence and enthusiasm of Jewish rabbis in sharing their faith with others, crossing land and sea to do so. Moreover, the Jewish emphasis on rigorous standards of personal and social morality found a warm reception among many thinking Greeks and Romans, who were dissatisfied with the permissiveness of their own culture. Some of them became full members of

Matthew 23:15

Acts 10:1–48

the Jewish faith, accepting all the demands of the Old Testament law to become 'proselytes'. Others merely accepted the Old Testament's moral teaching, and were given a lesser status as 'God fearers'. These groups played a significant role in the developing life of the early Christian church. One of the first non-Jewish Christians mentioned in the New Testament – Cornelius, the Roman centurion – was a 'God fearer'. As Paul and others took the good news about Jesus into the wider Roman empire, they often found an enthusiastic response among such people. Indeed, Paul felt it was so important to share the message with these people that he made it a specific policy always to go first to the Jewish community in every town he visited.

Jews and Judaism in the Roman Empire

The Jewish 'diaspora', or dispersion, was crucial in forming beliefs and in the rise of the synagogue. Israelites were exiled to the city of Babylon in the time of Nebuchadnezzar. One of Babylon's many splendid buildings, the Ishtar Gate rose 50 feet/15 metres above a sacred processional way leading into the city.

Most of us today think of Palestine as the land of the Jews in New Testament times. But in fact there were probably more Jews living in a city like Alexandria in Egypt than there were in Jerusalem itself. Josephus quotes the Latin author Strabo, who said that the Jewish nation 'has already made its way into every city, and it is not easy to find any place in the habitable world which has not received this nation, and in which it has not made its power felt' (*Antiquities of the Jews* 14.7.2).

In Old Testament times, the land and people of Israel had been a self-contained geographical and national entity. Indeed, the Old Testament story is largely concerned with how Israel's ancestors had been gathered from various parts of the Middle East, to be united in their common heritage, the promised land of Canaan. But by the time of Jesus the process was working in reverse, and the Jewish people were living all over the world. This scattering, or 'Dispersion' as it is sometimes called, had begun many centuries before in 586 BC. That was the year when Nebuchadnezzar, king of Babylon, invaded the Old Testament kingdom of Judah. So that he could control the conquered nation, he took all the most gifted and influential inhabitants of Jerusalem off to a new life in Babylon. This was a disaster of immense proportions for the Jewish people. Politically, of course, it was the final catastrophe, for never again were the Jewish people to enjoy an independent existence. Yet in spite of that, this Jewish exile in Babylon was to become one of the most creative forces in the whole of Jewish religion.

In the heyday of Old Testament religion, the worship of the temple in Jerusalem had been of central importance. It was by regular visits to the temple and the offering of sacrifices there that a person declared his loyalty to the God of Israel and his obedience to the Law. But Nebuchadnezzar destroyed the temple, and though the remnants of the population who were left in Jerusalem still continued to worship in its ruins, even that consolation was not possible for those who had been removed to Babylon. Their feelings were expressed most movingly in words from Psalm 137: 'By the rivers of Babylon we sat down; there we wept when we remembered Zion. On the willows near by we hung up our

Opposite, above: Jews in Alexandria had to face up to the problem of working out their beliefs in everyday life in a new situation. As a centre of Hellenistic thinking, Alexandria confronted Judaism – and later Christianity – with relating faith and philosophy. Here too the Old Testament was translated into Greek.

Opposite, below: Jews across the empire

harps. Those who captured us told us to sing; they told us to entertain them: "Sing us a song about Zion." But how can we sing to the Lord in a foreign land? May I never be able to play the harp again if I forget you, O Jerusalem!'

In the event, Jerusalem was not forgotten, and it was not long before the exiles discovered that though at first it seemed inconceivable, they could indeed sing the Lord's songs in a foreign land. It was in the synagogue that they did so. In a different social setting, some things just had to be different, and the local synagogue was not a replica of the temple back in Jerusalem. Worship in Jerusalem had been concerned with sacrifices, but this was no longer possible, and in the worship at the synagogue the central place of sacrifice had to be filled by something else. So a form of worship developed which had no place for sacrifice. Instead, the emphasis was now laid on those things that Jews could do anywhere: prayer, the reading of the Torah, keeping the sabbath day, circumcision, and the observance of the Old Testament food laws.

This adaptation of traditional Jewish worship was so successful that when Jews from Babylon were eventually able to return to their homeland, they took it with them. And when, following the conquests of Alexander the Great, other enterprising Jews decided to emigrate voluntarily to different parts of the Mediterranean world, it was natural that they should adopt the synagogue as the central expression of their religious and national allegiance. By the time the first Christian missionaries were beginning to travel the roads of the Roman Empire with the good news about Jesus, there was an extensive network of Jewish synagogues spread the length and breadth of the entire empire.

Not all synagogues were exactly the same, of course. In earlier times, the temple in Jerusalem had imposed a certain degree of central control over religious beliefs and practices – and it continued to do so in Palestine until its final destruction in AD 70. But the synagogues were much freer to develop their own ways of thinking. The problems of being a Jew in Babylon were quite different from the problems facing Jews in Rome, while the Egyptian city of Alexandria was different again. So in each local centre, Jewish people had to work out for themselves how best to face up to the challenge of their new environments. Even within the same locality, different synagogues could give different

responses. In Rome, for example, some Jews were quite happy to go along with many aspects of pagan society, even giving their children Latin or Greek names, and adopting the art-forms of Roman civilization. But others in the same city deplored what they saw as a dilution and betrayal of their ancestral faith, and stuck rigidly to a more traditional understanding of the Old Testament Law.

We also know of Jews who became deeply interested in the study of Greek philosophy. The most famous of these was Philo, a Jew from the Egyptian city of Alexandria. We know few details of his life, but he must have been born some time before Jesus, and probably lived until the mid-forties of the first century AD. He was a member of an influential Jewish family, and some of his relatives became deeply involved in politics both in Egypt and elsewhere. But Philo was most interested in explaining the thinking of Greek writers, especially the Stoics. He found many of their ideas congenial, and set out to show how the Old Testament and Greek philosophy were really saying the same things in their own distinctive ways. In order to demonstrate this, he had to regard much of the Old Testament as a kind of allegorical or symbolic presentation of the truths expounded by the philosophers.

Orthodox Jews elsewhere in the empire would certainly have regarded Philo as a traitor to his religion. But he was convinced that he was a faithful interpreter of the Old Testament. He was proud of his ancestral traditions, and had no doubt that what he was doing was both worthwhile and necessary.

There was, however, one thing on which all the synagogues of the Roman world were united. This was in their use of the Greek language. As one generation succeeded another it was not long before the vast majority of Jews in the Mediterranean world could speak no other language, and so it became important that the ancient Jewish scriptures, originally written in Hebrew, should be translated into the language that most Jews now spoke and understood best.

The actual origins of the Greek Bible that was produced are shrouded in obscurity. According to one ancient legend, the Jews of Egypt managed to persuade the Egyptian king, Ptolemy II Philadelphus (285–247 BC) to sponsor the project. He sent to Jerusalem for seventy men who knew both Hebrew and Greek, and locked them up in seventy cells while each one produced

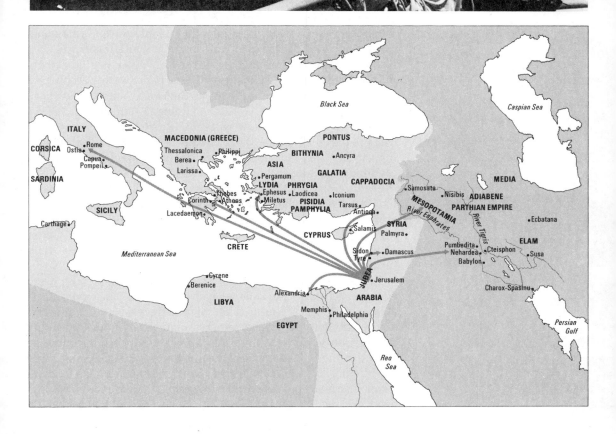

his own translation. When their work was finished, to everyone's amazement the seventy men not only expressed the same ideas, but also used the very same Greek words to do so – whereupon Ptolemy was so impressed, that he was immediately convinced of the divine origins of their work! Not everyone believed that sort of story even in the ancient world, and another ancient source, 'The Letter of Aristeas', suggests that the translators set the precedent for all modern translations, and worked as a committee.

Probably neither of these stories by itself reflects what actually happened, and many scholars now believe that the Greek Septuagint version of the Old Testament (the LXX) just evolved gradually over many generations. But wherever it came from, it had enormous influence and importance. It was widely used not only by Jews all over the Roman Empire, but it was also read by intelligent Romans who wanted to know more about the Jewish faith – and it also became the Bible of the first Christian churches.

● **Christianity** This, then, was the world into which the first Christians brought their message about Jesus. It was a world that had been cut adrift from its roots. A world that was in search of a new self-understanding. And a world full of competing sects and ideologies, all of them claiming to have the answers to the big questions of the day.

There are many ways in which we can try to explain the phenomenal success of the Christian faith in this context. But the simple fact is that the good news about Jesus was directly relevant to the Roman world. As the original followers of Jesus moved from their homeland on the fringes of the empire into the large urban centres of the west, they met people at their point of need. Not only were they able to answer the questions that people were asking on an intellectual level. But the groups of Christians which they established throughout the empire demonstrated in a practical way the sense of purpose and meaning in life for which so many were searching.

Jesus' claim to be the fulfilment of the Old Testament faith gave his followers a head start. Greeks and Romans – and expatriate Jews – naturally wanted to know what the Christians had to say. And because the Old Testament had already been translated into Greek, the earliest Christian missionaries had no difficulty at all in explaining their message in specific terms.

In addition, Christianity had a certain curiosity value to the western city dwellers. For it was one of the many religions that were moving in from the east. Palestine itself was widely regarded as the very edge of the civilised land, and anything from that quarter would at least command a hearing from those who were disillusioned with their own religious heritage.

The early Christians could also appeal to those who were attracted to Gnosticism and the mystery religions. The whole thrust of Jesus' teaching was quite different from these world-denying systems of thought. But for that very reason it gave a more convincing explanation of life as it is in this world, rather than encouraging people to opt out and dream of the possibilities of life in some other world. The Christian message was firmly based on events that had taken place in the real world of everyday experience – the life, death and resurrection of Jesus. But it also affirmed that a good life could not be achieved by human ingenuity – not even by the exercise of 'Reason'. It did however offer the prospect of a new, close relationship with God himself to those who were prepared to commit themselves to Jesus and allow his Spirit to remake their lives. In addition, Christians found themselves part of a new social grouping – the church – that could offer corporate as well as personal benefits.

It is not difficult to see why and how the early Christians were able to fill the spiritual vacuum of the Hellenistic world so successfully. But the story of their faith is much more than just a haphazard coincidence of social factors in the ancient world. Indeed, it was not in this predominantly Greek world at all that the story had its beginnings, but in the much more complex world of Jewish history and religion.

Palestine and its people

When Alexander conquered the ancient world, most of its nations went along with his policy of Hellenization. In many instances they accepted it only grudgingly. Quite often, Hellenism made little impact on native customs. National institutions would be adjusted to conform with the Greek style, and the ruling classes in particular often found it advantageous to adopt Greek habits. But in many lands the life of ordinary people was almost untouched by the Greek influence.

Most nations around the Mediterranean world would have preferred to retain full control over their own lives. But they knew well enough that the realities of international politics obliged them to go along with the superpowers of the day. And for many centuries, subject nations had demonstrated their subordination by accepting the culture of their conquerors. It was taken for granted that this would include at least a token allegiance to the religions of their overlords. Modern states change the image on their postage stamps when a new ruler comes to power. In the ancient world, they changed the statues and altars in their temples. So no one can have been surprised to discover that under Greek rulers they would be expected to find a place for the Greek gods.

Most were willing to do so. But not the Jews of Palestine. For them, practical politics and deeply held religious convictions could never be reconciled quite so easily. For one thing, their ancestral faith had always insisted that there is just one God, and that he must be worshipped without idols, and according to carefully prescribed regulations. Other nations could declare their allegiance to Zeus simply by worshipping him alongside their own gods and goddesses. But Israel could never do this. It would have meant the complete denial of some of the most cherished aspects of the Old Testament faith.

Hellenism and Judaism

All these problems came to a head long after Alexander's death, under the Greek ruler of Palestine, Antiochus IV Epiphanes (175–164 BC). Antiochus was a member of the Seleucid dynasty, and his predecessors had always allowed the high priestly rulers in Jerusalem a good deal of independence. Unfortunately, the high priesthood itself became the subject of an internal power struggle at exactly the same moment as Antiochus suffered a humiliating defeat in Egypt at the hands of the Romans (168 BC). This hurt Antiochus's pride, and he was determined to reassert his authority. He marched on Jerusalem, bent on showing who was in charge. Antiochus could see that the problem was not purely political: it was also a dispute among the Jews themselves about their own religion. This was something he neither understood nor cared for. But if it was causing trouble, its power would have to be diminished.

Antiochus responded by inaugurating a thoroughgoing policy of enforced Hellenization. All the things that were most distinctive about Jewish life were banned, including circumcision, keeping the sabbath day, and reading the Old Testament. Even worse, Antiochus decreed that the temple in Jerusalem, the focal point of traditional Jewish worship, should be given over to the worship of the Greek god Zeus. And, to rub salt into the wounds, he opened the temple up to the whole population of the land, which included people who were not themselves Jews.

This kind of cultural integration had always been desirable to the Greek rulers of Palestine. But Antiochus believed it was now essential for his own political survival. Whether they liked it or not, everyone in the land would be united under the Greek religion in a thoroughly Greek way of life.

But Antiochus had seriously underestimated the strength of Jewish religious feeling. It was one thing to erect altars to Greek gods – but it would be another thing altogether to persuade the Jews to worship at them. Antiochus's efforts to force them only increased their determination to fight back. It was not long before an armed resistance movement was established by Mattathias, a priest from the village of Modein, along with his five sons. They came to be known as the 'Maccabees', and their freedom fighters were so successful that it took only three years for Antiochus's troops to be defeated and for his policies to be reversed.

Jews and Romans

All this took place nearly 200 years before the time of Jesus. In the meantime the Greeks had been replaced by the Romans as the dominant superpower. But the Jews of Palestine never lost their firm determination to resist religious compromise and, if possible, to preserve their own rights to political self-determination.

Their fiercely independent posture was largely the result of their belief that they had been specially chosen by God to rule the world under the leadership of God's promised deliverer, whom they called the 'Messiah'. At one time it had been possible for them to expect that this would happen in the normal course of history. In the days of David and Solomon, almost a thousand years before the birth of Jesus, they had been one of the great world powers. Their more recent successes against Antiochus had shown that they were still a force to be reckoned with. But it was obvious to most Jews living in Palestine in Jesus' day that something of almost supernatural proportions would have to take place if they were ever to be released from the iron grip of Rome.

At the same time, not all Jews wanted to be freed from Roman rule. There were some sections of society in Palestine who found it was comfortable to be friendly with the Romans. And even among those who saw freedom as an ideal, there were not many who were prepared to take practical action to secure it.

The Romans had an unenviable task in Palestine. For in addition, it was a frontier post of their whole empire, and its continuing security was essential. But they were on occasion prepared to make allowances for Jewish scruples. When they appointed Herod the Great as ruler of Judea in 37 BC, they hoped he would be acceptable to Jewish public opinion. Naturally, the Romans felt they could trust him. But he was also half Jewish, and they believed this could help to overcome resistance to foreign rule.

Herod the Great

Matthew 2:16

The story of Herod's rise to power, and indeed of the rest of his reign, is a classic tale of intrigue and ruthlessness. As a king he combined a strange mixture of diplomatic brilliance with almost unbelievable stupidity. The story of how he murdered the children of Bethlehem after Jesus was born (although we have no record of it in any other documents) fits in perfectly well with all that we know of his character and behaviour. Anyone who opposed his policies could expect a violent death. Like many other tyrants, he never thought twice about killing even his own family. One of his wives, Mariamne, was executed on his orders; and he was involved in the murder of two of his own sons, Alexander and Aristobulus. Only five days before he died in 4 BC, he ordered the execution of yet another of his sons, Antipater, who was expected to succeed him.

Yet Herod the Great was not called 'Great' for nothing. In contrast to previous rulers Herod maintained peace and order throughout his territory. He was also responsible for a massive building programme. It was Herod the Great who began building the temple at Jerusalem, which was still not finished during the lifetime of Jesus. He also built many other magnificent buildings in Jerusalem and Caesarea, and even in other Roman cities outside his own territory.

The three Herods

When Herod the Great died in 4 BC the Romans divided his kingdom among his three remaining sons. With one possible exception, none of them was any better than his father.

● Judea, the part of Palestine that included Jerusalem, was given to his son Archelaus. He was not allowed to call himself 'king' of Judea, as his father had been, but was called 'ethnarch'

The Herodium is a fortress 7 m/12 km south of Jerusalem. Built by Herod the Great between 24 and 15 BC, it stands on the spot where he achieved one of his most important victories over the Hasmoneans in 40 BC.

The land of Jesus and the Gospels

Many of the places associated with Jesus were not very large or important, and some names have changed since the first century. No indication is given here of the relative sizes of towns and villages. Sites not definitely known are indicated with a question mark (?) and alternative names are in brackets. Some of the places here are not directly associated with Jesus but are known from other parts of the New Testament.

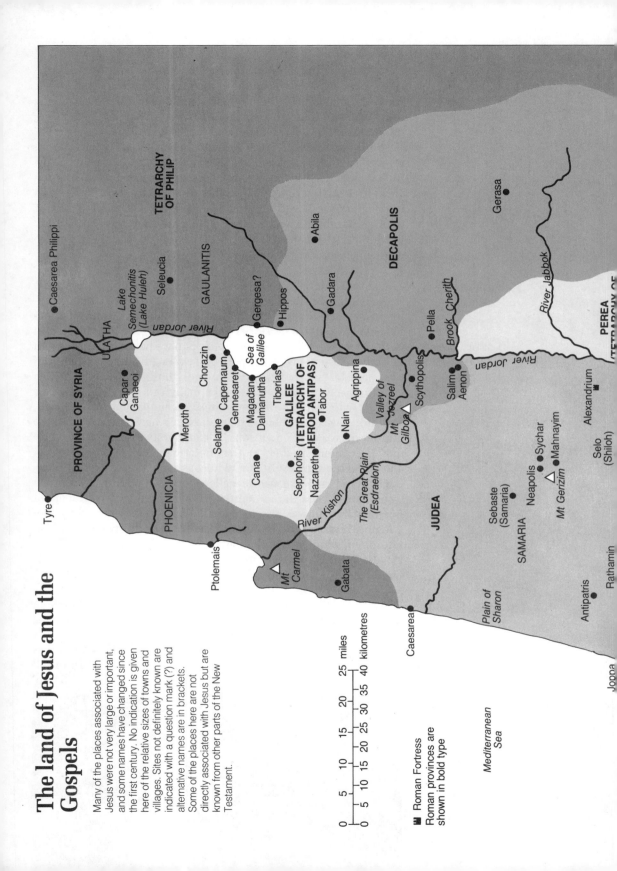

■ Roman Fortress
Roman provinces are shown in bold type

```
0    5   10   15   20   25 miles
|----|----|----|----|----|
0  5  10 15 20 25 30 35 40 kilometres
```

Tyre

PROVINCE OF SYRIA

Caesarea Philippi

ULATHA

Lake Semechonitis (Lake Huleh)

TETRARCHY OF PHILIP

Seleucia

GAULANITIS

River Jordan

Capar Ganaeoi

PHOENICIA

Chorazin

Capernaum

Gennesaret

Sea of Galilee

Gergesa?

Hippos

Abila

DECAPOLIS

Gerasa

Meroth

Selame

Magadan
Dalmanutha

Tiberias

GALILEE (TETRARCHY OF HEROD ANTIPAS)

Gadara

Pella

Brook Cherith

River Jabbok

Ptolemais

Cana

Sepphoris
Nazareth

Tabor

Agrippina

Valley of Jezreel

Mt Tabor

Nain

Scythopolis

Salim
Aenon

River Jordan

PEREA (TETRARCHY OF

Mt Carmel

Gabata

River Kishon

The Great Plain (Esdraelon)

Mt Gilboa

Sebaste (Samaria)

Neapolis

SAMARIA

Sychar

Mahnayim

Mt Gerizim

Alexandrium

Selo (Shiloh)

JUDEA

Plain of Sharon

Antipatris

Rathamin

Caesarea

Mediterranean Sea

Joppa

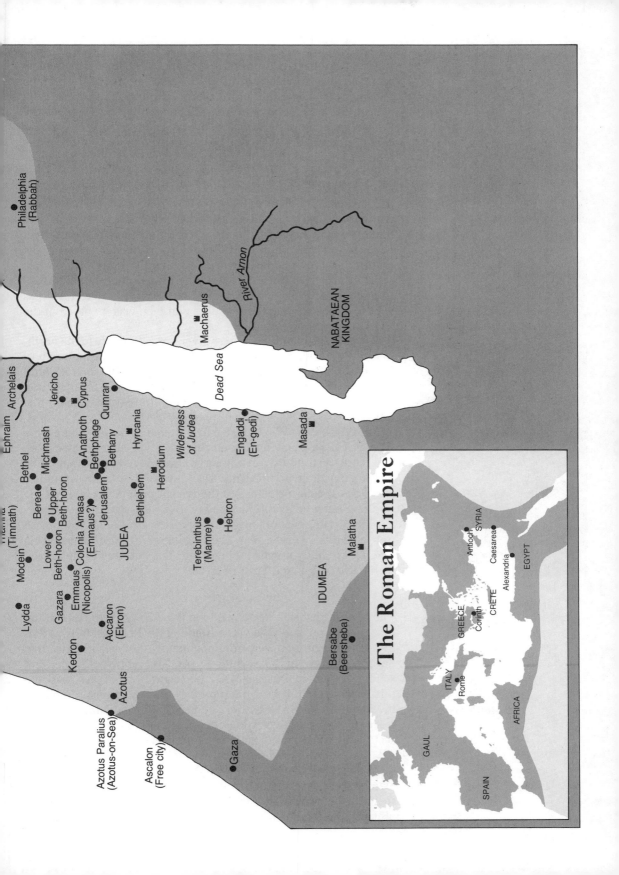

Philadelphia
(Rabbah)

River Arnon

Machaerus

NABATAEAN
KINGDOM

Dead Sea

Ephraim
Archelais

Jericho

Cyprus

Bethel

Michmash

Anathoth

Qumran

Berea

Upper

Bethphage

Hyrcania

Lower Beth-horon

Bethany

Beth-horon

Wilderness
of Judea

(Timnath)

Engaddi
(En-gedi)

Modein

Colonia Amasa

Jerusalem

Herodium

Masada

Gazara

Emmaus
(Nicopolis)

(Emmaus?)

JUDEA

Bethlehem

Lydda

Accaron
(Ekron)

Terebinthus
(Mamre)

Hebron

Kedron

Azotus

IDUMEA

Malatha

Azotus Paralius
(Azotus-on-Sea)

Bersabe
(Beersheba)

Ascalon
(Free city)

Gaza

The Roman Empire

GAUL

SPAIN

ITALY
Rome

AFRICA

GREECE

Corinth

CRETE

Antioch

SYRIA

Caesarea

Alexandria

EGYPT

instead. He lasted for only ten years, and then the Romans removed him from office. In AD 6 Judea became a third-grade province of the Roman Empire, under an officer of the upper class equestrian rank, who was himself under the command of the Roman governor of Syria. These Roman rulers of Judea were later called 'procurators'. The one best-known to us is Pontius Pilate, who governed Judea from AD 26 to 36.

● The northern part of Palestine was given to Antipas, another son of Herod. He was known as the 'tetrarch' of Galilee and Perea. His territory included the village of Nazareth where Jesus grew up. Antipas was very much like his father. He was a crafty man who liked living in luxury. To make a name for himself he took great pride in erecting public buildings. One of his projects was the rebuilding of Sepphoris, a town only four miles from Nazareth. He also built the new town of Tiberias by Lake Galilee, and named it in honour of the Roman Emperor Tiberius. It was Herod Antipas who had John the Baptist executed and who was involved in the trials of Jesus.

● A third brother, Philip, was given some territory to the north-east of Palestine when his father died. He founded the town of Caesarea Philippi at the foot of Mt Hermon. Of all the sons of Herod the Great, Philip was the only one who proved to be a balanced and humane ruler. He survived as 'tetrarch of Iturea and Trachonitis' until the year AD 34.

After Archelaus was replaced by a Roman governor, there were many revolts against the Romans in Judea. The Jews became more and more frustrated at not having control of their own affairs. The Romans for their part became less interested in trying to understand the special problems of the Jewish people. As a result the oppression and corruption of many of the Roman rulers, encouraged by a rising tide of Jewish nationalism, continued to increase until eventually in the year AD 66 a general revolt broke out. This revolt was finally crushed when Jerusalem was largely destroyed by the Roman general Titus in AD 70.

The ruins of Masada, the last Jewish stronghold to resist the Romans in AD 70. It is near the southern end of the Dead Sea.

Mark 6:17–29
Luke 23:6–12

Religious loyalties

The Jewish historian Josephus, who lived towards the end of the first century AD, and who was a friend of the Romans, tells us that three main opinions were common among the Jews in Palestine: 'Jewish philosophy takes three forms. The followers of the first school are called Pharisees, of the second Sadducees, and the third sect, which has a reputation for being more disciplined, is the Essenes.' He also mentions a fourth group, called Zealots. But since he does not always include these among the philosophical sects, they must have formed a much looser kind of association. All these groups had their origins in the years following the Maccabean Revolt. Obviously not all the Jewish people were members of one group or another, just as not everyone in our own society is a member of a political party. Each of the four groups probably had quite a small membership, though the ordinary

Jewish Wars 2.8.2

Jewish Wars 4.3.9

person in the street would look to one of them for leadership. We meet three of these groups in the New Testament: the Sadducees, the Pharisees and the Zealots.

● **The Sadducees** are often mentioned along with the Pharisees, but in fact the two groups were quite separate and held opposite opinions on almost everything. The Sadducees were only a small group, but they were very influential. They consisted mainly of the more important priests in the temple at Jerusalem, and included only the most well-to-do classes of Jewish society. They were extreme conservatives in everything and disliked changes of any kind, especially changes which could affect their own dominant position in society. Even if they believed theoretically in the coming of a Messiah, they generally had nothing to do with political protests. That would only cause trouble with the Romans.

The name 'Sadducee' probably means 'son of Zadok', although the Sadducees were certainly not direct descendants of the Zadok mentioned in the Old Testament. Other meanings for the name have also been suggested: either from a Hebrew word that means 'moral integrity' or 'righteousness' (*sadiq*); or from the Greek word *syndicoi*, which could mean 'members of the council' – and it is certainly true that the Jewish council of seventy (the Sanhedrin) had many Sadducees among its members.

If the Sadducees are to be regarded as political conservatives, their understanding of the Jewish religion can only be called reactionary. They held that the only religious teaching with any authority was the Law given by Moses in the first five books of the Old Testament (the Pentateuch or *Torah*). They had no time either for the rest of the Old Testament, or for anyone who tried to reinterpret it or to apply it in a more direct way to their own situation. This meant that they did not share with other Jews some of the beliefs of Judaism that were not very explicit in the *Torah*. Sadducees did not believe that God had a purpose behind the events of history, and matters such as belief in a future life, resurrection, or a final judgement were to them simply irrelevant.

● **The Pharisees** were a much larger group; there may have been as many as 6,000 of them at the time of Jesus. Many of them were professional students of the Old Testament, but others had ordinary jobs. They were a national organization, with a large number of local groups. Each group had its own officials and rules, and groups were to be found in most towns and villages throughout Palestine. Religiously, they were probably the most important people in Judaism during Jesus' lifetime. The Sadducees disliked them because they believed and did things that a literal understanding of the Law of Moses could not really allow. But most ordinary people had a great respect for them.

The Sadducees' chief complaint against the Pharisees was that they had amassed a whole lot of rules and regulations to explain the Law of the Old Testament. Though the Pharisees

2 Samuel 15:24–29

Exodus 20:8

regarded the Old Testament as their supreme rule of life and belief, they also realized that it had no direct application to the kind of society they lived in. To be relevant, it needed to be explained in new ways. For example, the Ten Commandments instructed people to keep the sabbath day holy. But what did that really mean in everyday terms? What should the pious Jew do and not do on the sabbath day? The Pharisees had a list of rules to answer that question in practical terms.

One of their writings, the *Pirke Aboth*, opens with the saying 'make a fence for the Law'. This meant 'protect it by surrounding it with cautionary rules to act as a warning notice to stop people before they get within breaking distance of the God-given Law itself'. This intention was praiseworthy enough. But there can be no doubt that eventually it led the Pharisees to make so many absurd rules that the Law became a moral millstone to the pious, rather than a gift from God. And to unbelievers much of it was simply nonsense. A tailor, for example, was not allowed to go out carrying his needle late in the day before the sabbath, in case it was still in his pocket when the sabbath began. But he, like everyone else, could go for a walk on the sabbath day – though not further than 2,000 cubits, two-thirds of a mile, the distance between the people of Israel and their holy ark when they first

Joshua 3:4

A street scene in present-day Bethlehem. While things have changed in the Middle East, as everywhere else, since Jesus' time, many customs and clothes remain very similar to those he would have known or worn.

entered Canaan! This became known as the 'sabbath day's journey' and is mentioned in the Gospels.

In spite of the absurdity of some of their standards, there can be no doubt that many Pharisees did actually keep these rules. Josephus says that 'the people of the cities hold them in the highest esteem, because they both preach and practise the very highest moral ideas'. But Jesus denounced them as hypocrites. He could see that the keeping of their own sectarian rules and regulations had become far too important.

Jewish Antiquities 18.1.3
Matthew 23:13, 15

Like many others since, they came to equate knowing God with being a member of their group – a Pharisee. To be a member of the sect was ultimately more important than knowing and understanding the will of God himself. Though they often claimed to be keeping God's Law, they were in fact only drawing attention to their own moral achievements.

In Jesus' view what was really wrong with the Pharisees was that they believed God was only concerned with the demands of the Law. The theology of the Pharisees had no room for the kind of God whom Jesus knew as his Father – a God who was kind and loving, and more concerned for prostitutes and beggars in their need than for those who were conventionally religious. No Pharisee could ever say with Jesus: 'I came not to call the righteous but sinners.'

Mark 2:17

The Pharisees had distinctive views on other subjects, of course. They accepted the authority of the whole of the Old Testament, and not just the Law of Moses. Unlike the Sadducees they had no difficulty in believing that there was a life after death. They may well have expected a Messiah to come and right the wrongs of their people – and though they themselves never took part in a revolt against the Romans they probably admired those people who did.

● **The Zealots** were the people who became most involved in direct action against the Romans. They probably shared many of the religious beliefs of the Pharisees. But their overriding conviction was that they could have no master but God, and so the Romans must be driven out at all costs. According to Josephus, their founder was a man called Judas, a Galilean who led a revolt in AD 6 at about the same time as Archelaus was removed from office by the Romans. He also tells us that 'these men agree in everything with the opinions of the Pharisees, but they have an insatiable passion for liberty; and they are convinced that God alone is to be their only master and Lord ... no fear can compel them to give this title to anyone else ...'

Jewish Wars 2.8.1

Jewish Antiquities 18.1.6

The Zealots continued as a guerilla movement until the siege of Jerusalem in AD 70, and perhaps even after that. At least one of Jesus' disciples, a man called Simon, was a Zealot, and it is often thought that Judas Iscariot was, too. But the more typical Zealots seem to have been men such as Barabbas, whom the crowd chose to liberate in preference to Jesus, and the trouble-maker with whom Paul was once confused.

Mark 3:18

Mark 15:6–15
Acts 21:37–39

Herod's Temple

Herod the Great began building the temple in Jerusalem in 19 BC. The main building was complete by AD 9 but work continued on it for many years. It was twice as high as Solomon's temple had been, and shone with gold decoration. This is an artist's impression of what it looked like.

The Holy of Holies, divided from the Holy Place by a curtain which Matthew's Gospel says split from top to bottom when Jesus died. The ark of the covenant stood here in Solomon's day but no longer existed in Jesus' time

The Holy Place, where the priests regularly burnt incense

A bowl for ritual washings

The altar where animals were sacrificed. Jesus was described by John the Baptist as being 'the lamb of God that takes away the sin of the world'

The court of the Gentiles. This was the only part in which non-Jews were allowed. The traders and money-changers worked here, and were turned out by Jesus

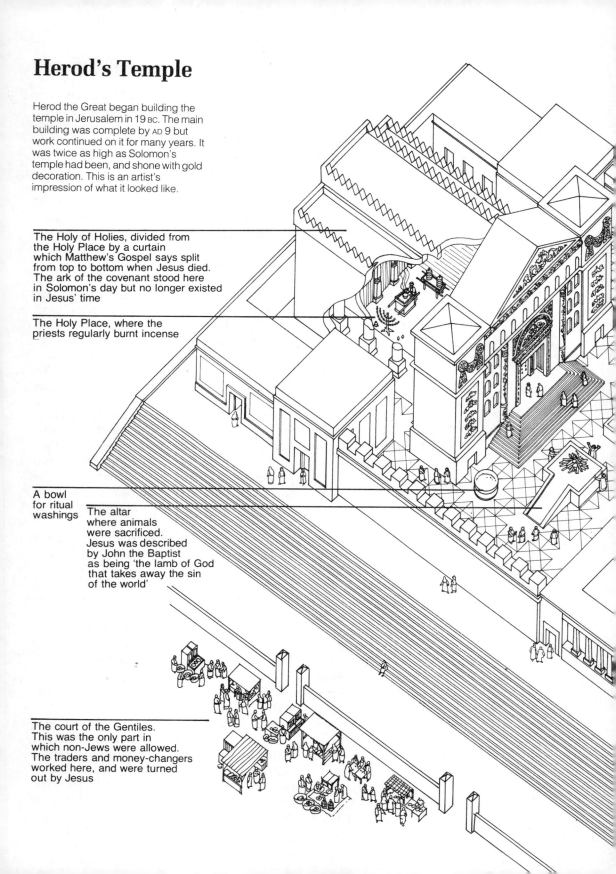

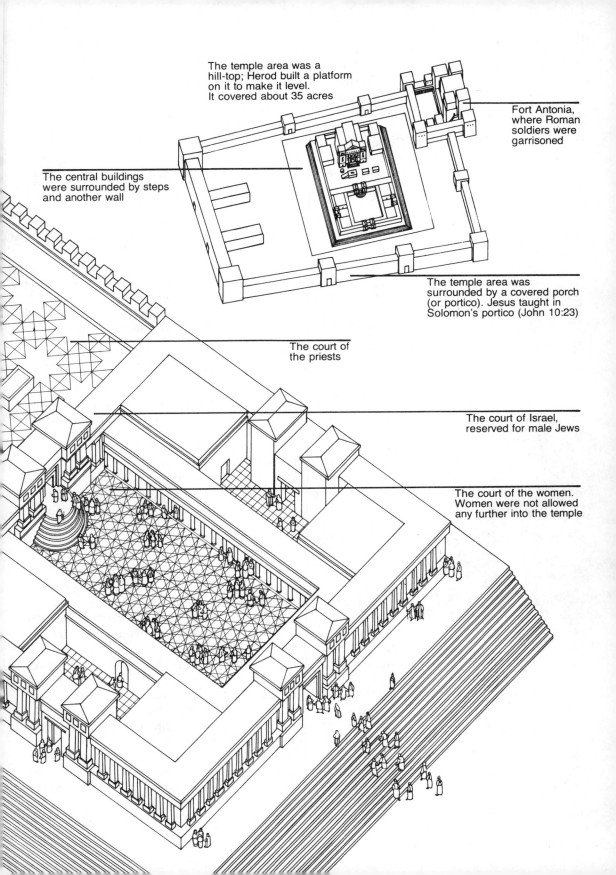

The temple area was a hill-top; Herod built a platform on it to make it level. It covered about 35 acres

Fort Antonia, where Roman soldiers were garrisoned

The central buildings were surrounded by steps and another wall

The temple area was surrounded by a covered porch (or portico). Jesus taught in Solomon's portico (John 10:23)

The court of the priests

The court of Israel, reserved for male Jews

The court of the women. Women were not allowed any further into the temple

● **The Essenes** are spoken of by several writers. Philo (a Jew from Alexandria in Egypt, who wrote in Greek), the Latin author Pliny, and Josephus all mention them. They are not explicitly mentioned by any of the New Testament writers.

Many people believe that one section of the Essenes wrote the documents known as the Dead Sea Scrolls. This group had their headquarters at Qumran near the north-west corner of the Dead Sea. The people of Qumran probably had their origins among the religious supporters of the Maccabees. But they became disenchanted with the corruption of their successors. So they had withdrawn from normal life and lived in a commune in the desert, trying to preserve the traditions of religious and moral purity which they believed they could find in the Old Testament.

But not all the Essenes lived in this way, for Josephus says that the Essenes 'occupy no one city, but settle in large numbers in every town'. He also speaks of others who, unlike the monastic groups, were married – though he goes to some pains to make it clear that they looked on this only as a means of continuing the human race. We also have written evidence that another group lived in the desert near Damascus; their organization was slightly different from the group at Qumran.

Jewish Wars 2.8.2–13

No one really knows the relationship between these groups nor how they were related to the Essenes scattered throughout Palestine. We know most about the community at Qumran, because of the discovery of their writings, and at most points these documents support the account given by Josephus.

From the Dead Sea Scrolls we know that the people of this community regarded themselves as the minority in Israel who were faithful to God's covenant. They regarded the Jewish nation as a whole, and even the temple and the priests in Jerusalem, as unfaithful. Only their own leader, the 'Teacher of Righteousness', and his faithful followers could fathom the mysteries of the Old Testament.

Like some of the other sects, the Essenes looked forward to a day of crisis in history. At this time God would assert his sovereignty over the world by defeating the native-born heretics as well as foreign enemies such as the Romans. Then the members of the sect, and not the whole Jewish nation, would be recognized as God's chosen people. They would take over and put right the worship of God at the temple in Jerusalem. They expected three leaders to appear: the coming prophet who had been predicted by Moses; a royal Messiah who would be a descendant of King David; and a priest Messiah who would be the most important.

Deuteronomy 18:18–19

So that they might be in a constant state of readiness for these events, the Essenes of Qumran went through many ritual washings. Everything they did had some religious significance. Even their daily meals were an anticipation of the heavenly banquet which they believed would take place at the end of the age.

With the possible exception of the Sadducees, then, all the dominant religious groups in Palestine at the time of Jesus were

Armed resistance to the Romans was the aim of the Zealots in the first century. Guerilla warfare is still a feature of the Middle East; here young Palestinian boys train with rifles.

hoping and praying that God would do something in the life of their people. They all had their own ideas about what he should do, and when and how he should do it. Some, for example the Zealots, were prepared to give God a helping hand when they thought it necessary. Others, such as the Pharisees and Essenes, believed that God had his predetermined plan which could be neither changed nor enforced by human intervention. But we can be sure that there were many ordinary people who were interested neither in political manoeuvring nor in theological disputes. They simply knew that they needed God to do something for them. Their only desire was to be in the right place and frame of mind when God's promised deliverer arrived.

A modern orthodox Jew praying on a roof-top. The phylactery on his forehead contains extracts from the Old Testament Law.

The apocalyptists

The future expectations of the Jewish people found their fullest expression in the work of the 'apocalyptists' which literally means 'people who reveal secret things'. The books they wrote are 'revelations of secrets', 'apocalypses'. The exact significance of these people is uncertain, since we know of them only through their writings. It is not clear whether they formed any sort of sectarian group, or whether they were individuals belonging to any of the various religious sects. It is unlikely that any of the apocalyptists were Sadducees, since they claimed to receive new revelations from God (Sadducees could not accept that any revelation had been given since the time of Moses). In some ways their beliefs are similar to those of the Pharisees, for they placed great emphasis on God's predetermined plan for the history of the world.

Whatever the apocalyptists may have been, their writings have a number of unusual characteristics which make them readily recognizable.

● They have a strong emphasis on the life of heaven rather than the everyday world of human experience. Though events in this world are mentioned, they are important only in so far as they reveal something about events taking place in the spiritual world. One apocalyptic writer states that 'the Most High has made not one world but two' (2 Esdras 7:50), and this viewpoint would be shared by many apocalyptists. It was their job to reveal what was happening in God's world, and to assure their readers that they had a central position in God's activities.

● This means that the apocalyptic writings also emphasize dreams, visions and communications through angels. Since God is remote in his own world ('heaven'), he needs to use go-betweens in dealing with men and women. A typical apocalypse is an extended report of how its writer received speculative visions and messages revealing what is happening in heaven.

● Corresponding with this is an unusual literary form. For the visions are not described in straightforward terms, but use a kind of special coded language. There are often many references to the books of the prophets in the Old Testament, and mythological beasts and symbolic numbers are used to stand for nations or individuals.

● Apocalypses were normally written under the name of a great figure of the past. Enoch, Noah, Adam, Moses, Ezra and a number of other outstanding Old Testament characters all had apocalyptic works attributed to them. This may have been necessary because it was widely thought by the Jews that the time of genuine prophecy had passed. Any contemporary seer who wanted to get a hearing for his message therefore had to attribute his work to somebody who had actually lived in the age of the Old Testament. Revelation, the only New Testament book to use extensive apocalyptic imagery, is quite different in this respect. The book of Revelation is not ascribed to some ancient figure; its author is identified as John, a contemporary and friend of his readers (Revelation 1:1–9).

Why did this kind of writing become so popular in the centuries immediately before the birth of Jesus? An attractive answer is that apocalyptic writing was a response to the difficult realities of life in Palestine at the time. The Old Testament prophets had often suggested that the course of Israel's history somehow depended on their attitude to God. If they were obedient they prospered; if not, they could expect hard times.

These hard times had culminated in the capture of Jerusalem by Nebuchadnezzar in 586 BC, and the exile of its population to Babylon. After only a short time in exile, the Jews had been allowed to return to their homeland, and those who returned were determined that they would not make the same mistakes as their ancestors. So they went out of their way to try to keep every detail of the Old Testament laws.

Yet, as things turned out, they did not prosper either. As time went on the way to prosperity seemed to lie more in collaboration with outsiders such as the Romans than in remaining faithful to their own religion. Those who tried to keep the Old Testament faith alive found themselves more and more in a minority, and those who prospered often did so by sitting loosely to their fathers' faith, or even abandoning it altogether.

Apocalyptic writing may well have begun as an answer to this problem. Why did faithfulness not lead to prosperity? Why were good people suffering? Why did God not put an end to the power of evil forces? To these questions the apocalyptists answered that the present difficulties were only relative. Seen in the light of God's working throughout history, the good would eventually triumph and the oppressive domination of evil would soon be relaxed.

It is often asked whether Jesus had any connection with these apocalyptists and their visions of the heavenly world. Albert Schweitzer certainly thought so, as we shall see later in this book. There is also a good deal of evidence to show that Jesus was familiar with the ideas that the apocalyptists put forward. Much of the imagery and language Jesus used in his own teaching on the future is similar to that of the apocalypses (Mark 13, Matthew 24–25, Luke 21). But there are some important differences.

● Apocalyptic literature is always the report of visions and other insights into the heavenly world given to men through some special means. But Jesus did not base his teaching on visions and revelations of this kind. He spoke on his own authority, and his main concern was not with the affairs of some other, heavenly, world, but with life in this world. He did not reveal secrets; he made disciples and reminded them of their responsibilities to God.

● The apocalyptists were always concerned to encourage and comfort their readers by demonstrating that they were in the right, and their enemies would soon be overcome. But Jesus' teaching, even in what are called the 'apocalyptic discourses', was never designed to comfort his disciples. Nor does he suggest that they will automatically triumph over their enemies. Quite the opposite is the case, for Jesus makes his teaching on the future an occasion to challenge his disciples' attitude to life; and he makes it clear that when God inter- venes in human affairs it is a time of judgement for those who are his dis- ciples as much as for everyone else.

● There is no systematic view of the future in Jesus' teaching. This is quite different from the apocalyptic outlook, in which every detail of the future has already been mapped out in advance. It is all in God's predetermined plan, and those who hold the key to the coded language can know precisely what the future holds. Some New Testament interpreters have, of course, tried to find such a system in Jesus' teaching. But the great variety of systems they have produced shows their lack of success. Nor can we expect them to be successful, for Jesus himself stated that 'No one knows ... when that day and hour will come – neither the angels in heaven, nor the Son; the Father alone knows' (Matthew 24:36, Mark 13:32). No apocalyptist could ever have said that.

● Apocalyptic writers were almost invariably pessimistic about the world and its history. Unlike the Old Testament prophets, they despaired of God ever being able to work in the world. The forces of evil seemed too strong for that, and they saw the world running headlong to a final and tragic end. There was no point in trying to discover God at work in the midst of such evil, for he was not there. This is all in strong contrast to the outlook of Jesus. He made it abundantly plain that the new society which he had come to inaugurate would affect the everyday life of ordinary people in this world (Luke 4:16–21). By both precept and example, he declared that God's will was not just something to be done 'in heaven', but must have its effect on the social and political realities of life here and now (Matthew 6:10).

In view of the fundamental differences between Jesus and the apocalyptists, it is clear that he cannot simply be classed with them. He did not have an apocalyptic outlook on life. To be sure, he did occasionally give his teaching in the language and imagery of the Jewish apocalyptists – just as he referred to the 'Golden Rule' of the rabbis (Matthew 7:12). As a good teacher he realized that he needed to speak the language of his hearers, and it may well have been that many of the ordinary people of Palestine were most familiar with apocalyptic language. But, characteristically, Jesus took these familiar concepts and gave them a new meaning. On his lips they were not platitudes to compliment the pious, but a devastating challenge to commitment applied to disciples and sinners alike.

2. Jesus: God's promised deliverer

Chapter 2

Jesus' birth and early years

The stories of how Jesus was born show that it was the ordinary people and not the religious experts who first recognized God's promised deliverer when he came. The first chapter of Luke's Gospel paints a vivid picture of the little-known priest Zechariah and his wife Elizabeth waiting for God to deliver their people, and being rewarded for their vigilance by the announcement of the birth of their own son, known as 'John the Baptist'. Mary, the mother of Jesus, belonged to the same family. From the stirring poetry of Mary's hymn of praise, the Magnificat, we can see just how eagerly these people were waiting for God to act in their lives. Mary and her friends were really excited that God was going to act in a new and fresh way.

The same themes are emphasized throughout the familiar stories of that first Christmas. The first people to hear the good news that God's promises had been fulfilled with the birth of Jesus were some shepherds in the Judean hills, then Simeon and Anna in the temple. None of these people were of any significance to the world at large. The stories in the first chapters of Luke's Gospel emphasize that officialdom – whether political or religious – had no eyes with which to recognize Jesus. This lesson is repeated throughout the story of Jesus' life, as it becomes clear that to have a real understanding of God's actions in Christ even the most important people must become like little children.

Luke 1:5–28, 57–80

Luke 1:46–55

Luke 2:8–20
Luke 2:25–38

Luke 18:17

Bethlehem, where Jesus was born, is a small town south-east of Jerusalem. Matthew's Gospel quotes the prophet Micah who emphasized the apparent unimportance of Bethlehem (Matthew 2:6).

When was Jesus born?

The Emperor Tiberius is portrayed in this statue at the Vatican museum.

Deciding exactly when the birth of Jesus took place is not as simple a matter as we might think. The obvious thing to suppose is that Jesus was born between 1 BC and 1 AD. But this has been known to be untrue for a long time, because of mistakes made as long ago as the sixth century in calculating the extent of the Christian era. There are four pieces of evidence to be considered.

● According to Matthew, Jesus was born 'in Bethlehem of Judea in the reign of Herod the king' (2:1) – that is, before the death of Herod the Great in 4 BC.

● Luke was much more interested in placing his story in the wider context of affairs in the Roman Empire, and he says that Jesus was born during 'the first enrolment, when Quirinius was governor of Syria' (2:2). Josephus tells us that a man called Quirinius was indeed sent to Syria and Judea to take a census just after the beginning of the Christian era (*Jewish Antiquities* 18.1). But this census was part of the clearing-up operation after Herod the Great's son Archelaus had been deposed. It must have been in the year AD 6 or 7, and could not have been before the death of Herod the Great in 4 BC.

Because of this, some people have suggested that the man Luke calls 'Quirinius' was in fact Saturninus, the imperial legate in Syria, who took a census in 6 BC. However, we have no evidence at all to show how Luke could have confused the two men. In the rest of his Gospel, and also in his second volume, the book of Acts, he is extremely careful, and also very accurate, in his use of the names and titles of Roman officials. In any case, we have no absolutely conclusive evidence that this man Saturninus did actually take a census.

● At the same time, Luke makes other statements about the date of important events in the life of Jesus. He tells us, for example, that Jesus was about thirty years old when he was baptized, and that this was 'in the fifteenth year of the reign of Tiberius Caesar' (3:1). Tiberius became ruler of the Roman Empire in AD 14, and so the fifteenth year of his reign would be AD 28. But in fact, Tiberius had shared power with his predecessor Augustus from about AD 11, so although he only became emperor after Augustus died in AD 14 he had

been in power for the previous three years. It is likely that Luke was reckoning the fifteenth year of Tiberius from AD 11, and this means Jesus would be thirty years old in AD 25–26. This means, in turn, that he must have been born in 5 or 4 BC, and so before the death of Herod the Great.

● Some people have tried to be more specific by calculating that there was a conjunction of certain planets about 6 BC, and that this astronomical event could explain the bright star mentioned in Matthew's Gospel. But this kind of argument requires a lot of imagination to be convincing.

We can see from this that there are two pieces of evidence pointing to a date for Jesus' birth round about 4 BC, and another piece of information given by Luke about the census under Quirinius which does not seem to agree with this dating. There are three possible explanations of this problem.

● Luke has been misunderstood. A number of scholars have argued that the problem as we have presented it simply does not exist. They point out that it is possible from a grammatical point of view to translate Luke 2:2, 'This enrolment was before that made when Quirinius was governor of Syria', instead of the usual translation, 'This was the first enrolment, when Quirinius was governor of Syria'. This understanding is certainly possible, though it is by no means the most obvious meaning of the statement, and it does involve an implicit emendation of the text. Some notable New Testament scholars have supported it, and continue to do so, but this explanation of the matter is by no means universally held.

● Luke made a mistake. Most scholars are in fact inclined to dismiss the information given in Luke 2:2 as erroneous. This is an easy way out of the problem. But it also leaves some difficulties. We have already remarked that in other places in his Gospel and the book of Acts where Luke is concerned with people and events in the Roman Empire, he shows himself to be a very trustworthy historian. It is therefore rather unlikely that he would have made such a specific reference here unless he had good reasons for doing so. We have also seen that his statement about the date when Jesus was baptized by John fits in with the assumption that Jesus was born in the reign of Herod the Great, something like ten years before the rule of the Quirinius whom Josephus mentions. It is certainly unlikely that any intelligent historian would have made two contradictory statements in such a short space within his narrative. If we assume that Luke used his sources carefully and wrote with discrimination and insight there are a number of important difficulties involved in simply saying that he was wrong about the census under Quirinius.

● Luke does not tell the whole story. A rather better explanation can be found if we consider the practical realities of life in the Roman Empire. Ruling Judea from Rome in AD 7 was not the same thing as it would be today. Nowadays we have instant communications between different parts of the world. The United Nations in New York can take a decision affecting a country on the other side of the world, and its decision can be delivered there within a matter of minutes. But in ancient Rome things were different. Even in ideal conditions, it could take months for a decree signed by the emperor in Rome to be delivered to a distant province like Judea – and there was always the possibility that the messenger could be shipwrecked, and the emperor's orders delayed even further or lost altogether. At a later period, for example, the Emperor Caligula sent orders that his own statue should be erected in the temple at Jerusalem. The local governor was wiser than the emperor, and realized that this would create great resistance from the Jews. So he wrote and asked the emperor to think again. But Caligula insisted on his plan going ahead,

and wrote to the governor to tell him so. The ship carrying his message took three months to make the voyage from Rome to Judea. But in the meantime Caligula was assassinated, and another ship that left Rome much later bringing the news of his death and the end of his policies, arrived twenty-seven days earlier than the first one!

When we think of the practical details involved in taking a census in an empire with such problems of communication and government, we can see that the difficulty over the exact date of Quirinius's census is nothing like as great as we would think if we looked at it only in a modern context. It is a well-known fact that the Roman enrolments (carried out for tax purposes) were often resisted in many parts of the Empire. One such census in Gaul, for example, was so resisted by the people that it took forty years to complete! Add to that the communication problems, and it is clear that a census completed by Quirinius in AD 6 or 7 must have been based on information collected much earlier.

The Emperor Augustus was very keen on gathering statistics, and he may well have persuaded Herod the Great to carry out a census. Quirinius was sent in AD 6 to clear up the mess left by Archelaus, and it is quite possible that he would use information gathered earlier rather than beginning the tedious process all over again. If this is the case, then there is no real reason to suppose that Luke's information about the census is necessarily contradictory to the rest of the evidence suggesting that Jesus was born about 5 BC. In any case he was far more interested in telling of the birth of Jesus than explaining the complexities of Judean politics which surrounded it.

A bronze head of the Emperor Augustus, who shared power with Tiberius from AD 11 until his death in AD 14.

Jesus grows up

We know very little about Jesus' life as a child. His home was presumably the typical flat-roofed, one-roomed house of the time, built of clay. Joseph probably carried on his business, assisted by Jesus, from his house. They would make agricultural tools, furniture, and perhaps also worked on building projects. Every small village the size of Nazareth would have its joiner, who was probably a kind of odd job man as well as being a skilled craftsman in wood. The pictures we sometimes see of Jesus as a boy making smooth yokes for the backs of oxen certainly do not represent all that he would do, and we can be sure that he must have been as adept at plastering walls as he would have been at planing wood.

Yet in spite of the relative simplicity of his home life, Jesus must have had a good education. He was considered a suitable person to read the Old Testament in Hebrew in the synagogue at Nazareth, and by no means every person of his age could read Hebrew, even though they may have been able to speak in that language. Jewish boys were usually educated in the local synagogue, and Jesus must have been one of the brighter ones in his class.

Luke 4:16–20

Nazareth itself would be an especially stimulating place for a bright boy to grow up in. It is true that it was not a very important place. It is never mentioned in the rest of the Bible, or in any other contemporary literature. But that is probably because the very strictest Jews felt that the people of Galilee, of which Nazareth was a part, had too much contact with non-Jewish people. Galilee itself was often called 'Galilee of the Gentiles', because there were more non-Jews than Jewish people living there. The people in the southern province of Judea, on the other hand, were isolated from all but their own society, and so they became introverted and self-centred, as well as being self-righteous and hypocritical. But Galilee was quite different. The great roads that brought oriental traders from the East and Roman soldiers from the West passed through Galilee. In Nazareth Jesus would meet and mix with many people who were not Jewish, and he no doubt spent much of his time thinking and talking about the ideas of the Greeks and Romans as well as the religious heritage of his own people.

One of the special advantages of growing up in Galilee was that Jesus would be able to speak three languages. We have noticed already that he could speak and read Hebrew. But that was no longer the normal language of the Jewish people. For several centuries before his time the Jews had used another language similar to Hebrew, called Aramaic. This is the language Jesus would speak in his home and among his friends. Since there were so many non-Jewish people in Galilee, he probably spoke Greek as well, for this was the international language used everywhere throughout the whole of the Roman Empire.

Apart from what we can infer from our knowledge of the kind of society in which Jesus was brought up, the New Testament tells us virtually nothing about his life before he was thirty years old. Christian writers in the second century thought there was something wrong and unnatural about this, and they lost no time in compensating for what they saw as a deficiency in the New Testament. We have a number of accounts of the childhood of Jesus, stories with titles such as *The Gospel of the Nativity of Mary*, *The History of Joseph the Carpenter*, or *The Childhood Gospel of Thomas*. There is no need to take seriously any of the stories about Jesus' childhood that we find in these so-called 'gospels'. They are all just the kind of legends that often grow

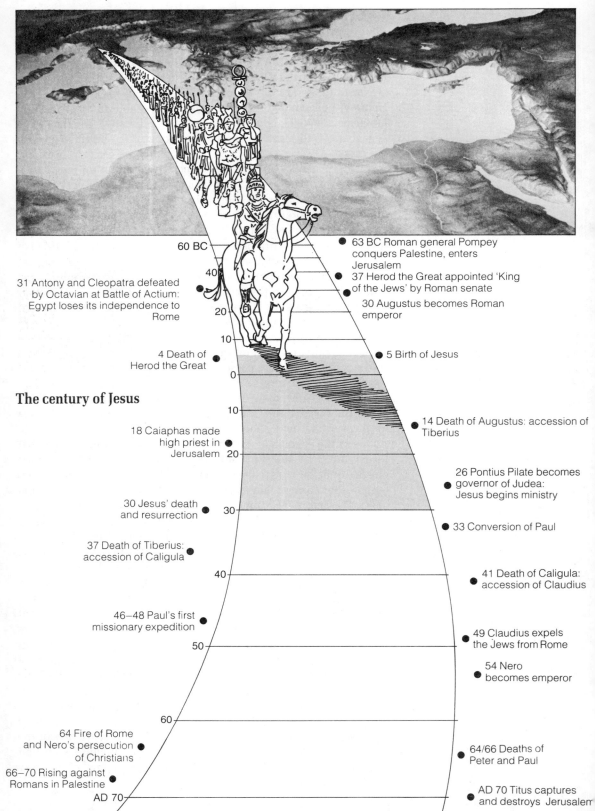

60 BC

63 BC Roman general Pompey conquers Palestine, enters Jerusalem

40

37 Herod the Great appointed 'King of the Jews' by Roman senate

31 Antony and Cleopatra defeated by Octavian at Battle of Actium: Egypt loses its independence to Rome

30 Augustus becomes Roman emperor

20

10

4 Death of Herod the Great

5 Birth of Jesus

0

The century of Jesus

10

14 Death of Augustus: accession of Tiberius

18 Caiaphas made high priest in Jerusalem

20

26 Pontius Pilate becomes governor of Judea: Jesus begins ministry

30 Jesus' death and resurrection

30

33 Conversion of Paul

37 Death of Tiberius: accession of Caligula

41 Death of Caligula: accession of Claudius

40

46–48 Paul's first missionary expedition

49 Claudius expels the Jews from Rome

50

54 Nero becomes emperor

60

64 Fire of Rome and Nero's persecution of Christians

64/66 Deaths of Peter and Paul

66–70 Rising against Romans in Palestine

AD 70

AD 70 Titus captures and destroys Jerusalem

Little is known about Jesus' boyhood except that he was brought up in an orthodox Jewish home and was well educated.

up around an important person when those who actually knew him have died. But there are some second-century writings often called 'apocryphal gospels' that may contain authentic sayings of Jesus, writings such as the *Gospel of Thomas* and the *Gospel of Philip*. These are considered in more detail in a later chapter.

Luke 2:40

Luke describes Jesus' childhood very simply by saying that he 'grew and became strong' like any other boy. But he goes on to add that Jesus was also 'filled with wisdom; and the favour of God was upon him'. And he then tells just one story as an illustration of what he meant.

Luke 2:41–52

The story tells how Jesus was lost in Jerusalem when he was twelve years old. He had gone there on a religious pilgrimage with Mary and Joseph to take part in one of the great Jewish festivals. When his parents eventually found him in the temple, he asked them: 'Did you not know that I must be in my Father's house?' Even at this age, Jesus was growing not just physically and mentally, but also in a spiritual dimension. He had an unusual sense of the presence of God in his life. God was his Father, and this relationship was more important to him than anything else.

The next we hear of Jesus is when he was about thirty years old. His cousin, John the Baptist, had started a religious movement and had attracted quite a following. John lived a simple kind of life in the Judean desert. His clothes were made of camel's hair, and he ate only the food of the desert, 'locusts and wild honey'.

Mark 1:6

John was by no means the only wandering prophet at that time. Many people were talking about the coming of God's promised deliverer to inaugurate some kind of new society. Further south in the same desert the people of Qumran were talking about similar things. And, even later, many rabble-rousers and prophets made a name for themselves in the same place.

But the difference about John was that he did not want to make a name for himself. Palestine had more than its share of crackpots, each claiming to be God's promised deliverer appointed to get rid of the political and social injustices of the time and with the authority to set up a new society. But John made no such claims. He claimed only to be 'a messenger', 'a voice' sent to bring the good news that the new society was about to begin.

Mark 1:2–3

Those Jews who were looking for God's new society had learned from the Old Testament to expect such a messenger, who would be like the Old Testament prophet Elijah. The Gospel writers leave us in no doubt that they saw John the Baptist as this very person. Their description of his way of life and of his message is closely modelled on the stories of Elijah in the Old Testament book of Kings.

Malachi 4:5

1 Kings 17–19

Josephus, *Jewish Antiquities*, 18.5.2

The New Testament and the Jewish writer Josephus both describe John's work as a call to the Jews to put their lives in order so that they would be morally fit to meet the person who was to establish the new society. The prophets whose sayings are preserved in the Old Testament had often seen that though the Jews were God's people they were in no fit state to meet their God. If God was ever to work in their lives, his coming would have to begin with judgement – and the judgement would be most severe for those who had had the greatest privilege.

Jesus came to be baptized by John the Baptist in the Jordan Valley.

John's message was exactly the same. He called on the Jewish people to be prepared to change their way of life, so that they would be fit to meet their God. Those who were ready to face up to the challenge showed their willingness to change by being 'baptized'. The Greek word from which we get the word 'baptize' simply means 'to dip'. It was often used, for example, of the dyeing of clothes as they were immersed in a bath or tub. 'Baptism' in the religious sense was just the same, except that it was people who were immersed, and they were dipped not in dye but in clean water. John presumably used the River Jordan as a handy source of water.

Most Jews would know what baptism was. It may have been used as a means of admitting non-Jews into the Jewish religion. It was certainly used in this way later. There is also ample evidence from the Dead Sea Scrolls that the Essenes used baptism regularly as a way of preserving their moral and religious purity.

A Bedouin tent in the Judean desert, the area in which John the Baptist lived.

One of the most conspicuous features of the ruins of the monastery at Qumran is the incredibly complicated system of aqueducts and water tanks that provided enough water in the desert for people of the community to undergo their baptismal rites. Of course, the rituals of people like the Essenes were not quite the same as the baptism of non-Jews into the Jewish religion. Ceremonial baptisms and washings were repeated over and over again at Qumran. But baptism of converts into Judaism was a once-for-all event.

It is difficult to decide whether the background of John's ritual is to be found in repeated washings, like those of the Essenes, or in the once-only baptism of Gentile converts. The radical nature of John's message and the opposition he provoked would certainly be easier to understand if he was calling Jews to take part in something that had been designed not for God's chosen people but for pagans. John saw that if the Jews were to have any part in the new society that was about to come they too would need to begin all over again, just as if they were Gentile pagans getting to know God for the first time.

Yet John did not see the full implications of that new society. He was standing in a kind of no-man's land between the promises of God in the Old Testament and the fulfilment of those promises that was about to take place. He saw the coming of the Messiah in the conventional terms of judgement and condemnation. He describes God's promised deliverer as a person who would chop down fruit trees that gave no fruit and burn the chaff away from the wheat. Admittedly, he saw much more clearly than the Pharisees or the Zealots. They thought that the objects of God's damnation would be the Romans, but John insisted instead that God would judge his own people – with the Pharisees first in line.

At the same time, he did not fully appreciate the true character of the society God was about to introduce. For God's new society would be based not on damnation and judgement but on love, forgiveness and a personal concern for all people. This was the one thing that the Jewish people found most difficult to understand. Even later, Jesus' disciples did not fully understand him when he spoke of the society coming through service and suffering. The precise nature of God's activities was not clear until after the death and resurrection of Jesus.

Luke 3:7–17

Mark 8: 31–33

Jesus is baptized

Matthew 3:15

Jesus came to John and asked to be baptized. At first John did not want to allow Jesus to share in this symbol of repentance. After all, if Jesus really did have the special relationship with God which John believed he did, what could he possibly have to repent of? But Jesus assured John that he must take part in it. He told him: '...in this way we shall do all that God requires.'

What did Jesus mean by saying this? The simple explanation is that Jesus felt he must identify himself with those repenting sinners who would be his own first disciples. Far from separating him from other people, the special relationship he felt he had with God was a powerful reason for becoming completely involved in the lives of the most ordinary of folk. But some have suggested there is even more than that implied in these words. They suggest that Jesus regarded his baptism as the first step on the road to the cross, which he saw as the climax and goal of his whole life. It is certainly true that he later called his death a 'baptism', and that in it he really and truly fulfilled God's will.

Mark 10:38

It was probably in the experience of being baptized that Jesus first began to understand the precise nature of his special relationship with God. According to Mark, Jesus heard the words: 'You are my own dear Son. I am pleased with you.' This is a combination of statements found in two passages in the Old Testament. On the one hand there is an echo of Psalm 2:7, 'You are my son, today I have become your father.' In its original context, this statement referred to the kings of ancient Judah. By the time of Jesus it was widely regarded as a prediction of the coming Messiah. On the other hand, there is also a clear allusion to the poem of the suffering servant in Isaiah, where the servant is described as 'the one I have chosen, with whom I am pleased'. This idea of the servant was never connected with the expectation of a Messiah before the time of Jesus.

Mark 1:11

Isaiah 42:1

It therefore seems likely that at his baptism Jesus learned two lessons: he was reassured of his own special relationship with God as the person who had been specially chosen to inaugurate God's new society; and he was also reminded that to be God's promised deliverer meant something very different from what most people expected. It meant the acceptance of suffering and service as an essential part of his life. This was very difficult, as Jesus was soon to discover. But he faced the problem with the power of God himself – something of which he was reminded when the Holy Spirit symbolically came to him in the form of a dove.

Jesus decides his priorities

The Gospels tell how, immediately after he was baptized, Jesus was challenged to get his priorities right as God's promised deliverer, the Messiah. Each of the temptations he faced was a temptation to be that deliverer in a way which would not involve the suffering and humble service that Jesus knew to be God's will.

Luke 4:1–4

● First of all came the temptation to bring in the new society by economic means, to make stones into bread. There were certainly plenty of hungry people in the world who would have welcomed bread from any source. Jesus himself was in the desert, and must have been hungry enough at the time. In addition, the Old Testament had often pictured the new society as a time of great material prosperity when the hungry would be fed and everyone's needs would be satisfied. So there were plenty of good reasons why Jesus should be concerned with such matters. But he knew that the fame and popularity of an economic miracle-worker

Isaiah 25:6–8; 49:9–10
Ezekiel 39:17–20

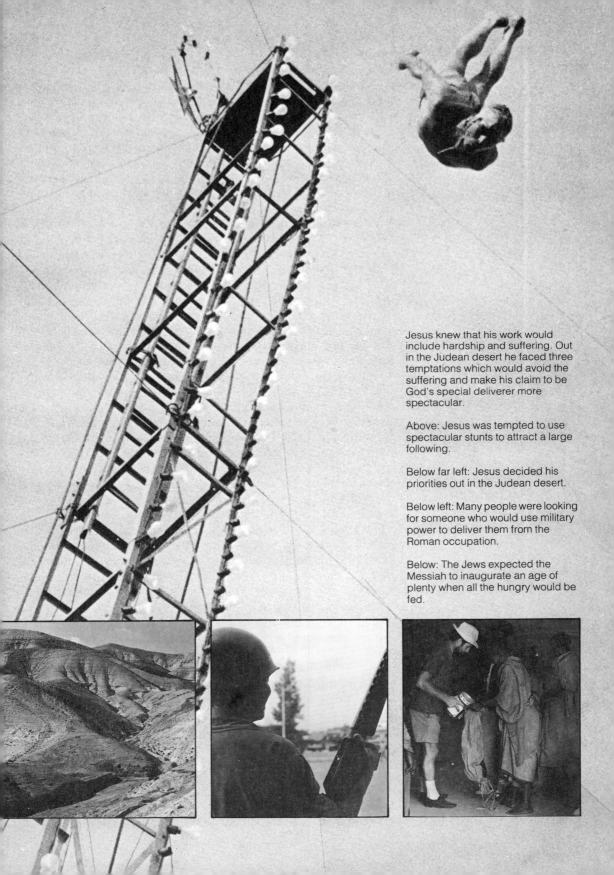

Jesus knew that his work would include hardship and suffering. Out in the Judean desert he faced three temptations which would avoid the suffering and make his claim to be God's special deliverer more spectacular.

Above: Jesus was tempted to use spectacular stunts to attract a large following.

Below far left: Jesus decided his priorities out in the Judean desert.

Below left: Many people were looking for someone who would use military power to deliver them from the Roman occupation.

Below: The Jews expected the Messiah to inaugurate an age of plenty when all the hungry would be fed.

was not the same as suffering and service.

A word of God to the people of Israel at a crucial moment in their past history helped him to overcome the temptation: 'Man shall not live by bread alone'. It was not that Jesus failed to recognize that people had economic needs. Rather, he recognized, on the one hand, that this was not their deepest need and, on the other, that this was not what God intended to be the main emphasis of his work. As a matter of fact, Jesus did later produce food for hungry people. But he knew this was not to be his main purpose in life.

Deuteronomy 8:3

Mark 6:30–44

● A second temptation was to throw himself down from the tower of the temple into the crowded courtyard below without injuring himself. It would have been an easy thing to show that he was the Messiah by working miracles, because the miraculous and unusual had a special kind of appeal to the people whom Jesus knew best. Paul, who knew Judaism better than most, said it was characteristic of the Jews to 'demand signs'. Even in our sophisticated scientific age, most of us are still drawn by the strange and spectacular, and anyone who claims to be able to perform wonders has no difficulty in attracting followers.

Luke 4:9–12

1 Corinthians 1:22

Here again, there was more to this temptation than just the logic of the situation. For there was actually a prophecy in the Old Testament about the Messiah suddenly appearing in a dramatic way in the temple. There was also a promise in Psalm 91 to the effect that God would protect those who put him to the test. Was this not the time to put God to the test? If Jesus was really God's Messiah, then surely he could expect God to honour his promises. A very attractive thought. But the answer to it came from the same crucial time in the experience of the people of Israel: 'You shall not put the Lord your God to the test.' The context of God's promise in Psalm 91 makes it clear that it was valid only to those who were living in obedient service to God's will. And for Jesus to do God's will meant service and suffering, and not the arbitrary use of God's promises for his own selfish ends.

Malachi 3:1

Deuteronomy 6:16

So Jesus rejected the temptation to be known as God's promised deliverer by a display of miraculous power. He did, of course, perform miracles. But, as we shall see later, he also made it clear that the miracles were living signs of his message: they were not the message itself.

● The third temptation was to be a political Messiah. Luke places this one second, but Matthew puts it last. He probably does this to emphasize its importance. There is no doubt that this must have been the strongest of all temptations. After all, this was precisely what most Jews expected the Messiah to be. They also commonly believed that they would rule all the other nations in the new age that was coming – and Jesus was tempted to accept the authority of Satan in order to gain power over the world. The idea was made even more vivid by a vision of the splendour of the world's kingdoms. But Jesus realized again that

Matthew 4:8–10

this was far different from the kind of new society that he was to inaugurate. Not that Jesus was unsympathetic to the deeply felt desire of his people for freedom. After all, he had himself lived under the tyranny of Rome. He had worked with his own hands to produce enough to pay Roman taxes. He knew well enough the miserable condition of his countrymen.

But he rejected political messiahship for two reasons. First, he rejected the terms on which the devil offered it to him. According to the Gospel narratives the devil offered to share sovereignty with Jesus. If Jesus accepted that the devil had authority over the universe as a whole, then he would be given limited political authority in exchange. That was something Jesus could not accept. His own commitment, and the commitment that he later demanded of his followers, was exclusively to God as sovereign and Lord. To acknowledge the devil's power in any area of life would have been to deny God's ultimate authority.

But in addition, Jesus was offered the possibility of ruling by the 'authority' and 'glory' of an empire like that of the Romans. And he knew that this was not his job. He knew that God's rule in men's lives and in society could never be imposed from outside. If there was one lesson to be learned from the history of his people, this was it. They had all the rules, in the Old Testament, but time and again they had been quite incapable of putting them into operation. Jesus saw that what men needed was to give their will and free obedience to God, and so be given the moral freedom to create the kind of new society that God wanted them to have.

This third temptation, then, was certainly the strongest and the most pressing. And it was also rejected in the most decisive fashion: 'Begone Satan!' Jesus would not try to impose a new authoritarianism on the world to replace the old authoritarianism of Rome. His new society was not to be a rule of tyranny and cruelty such as many Jews envisaged, but something that would spring from the new, inner nature of those who were a part of it, as they served and worshipped God alone.

Matthew 4:10

The stories of Jesus' birth

The stories of how Jesus was born are certainly not the easiest parts of the Gospels to understand. We have already seen that even the date of Jesus' birth presents a number of problems. But that difficulty is overshadowed by much larger questions about the whole nature of the stories. We have assumed so far that the Gospel narratives provide sufficient reliable information for us to uncover at least the bare outline of events. But some scholars have tended to ignore altogether the stories told about Jesus' birth by Matthew and Luke.

They regard these stories as later narratives produced by the early church to portray Jesus as the kind of person they saw him to be after the events of the first Easter, rather than as the kind of person the 'historical Jesus' really was.

To the first Christians, Jesus was their risen Lord and the Son of God. He was not just the son of Mary and Joseph, a joiner from Nazareth. He was none other than God himself. The argument goes that because of their beliefs, the first Christians realized that such a person could not have had an

Jesus was born in the stables off a courtyard such as this ancient one behind an inn in Bethlehem.

ordinary birth – and so they produced the stories we now have in the Gospels. The problem about these stories centres on the statements by both Matthew and Luke that Mary and Joseph had never had a sexual relationship at the time when Jesus was conceived (Matthew 1:18; Luke 1:26–27). Since this is something we know from our own experience to be impossible, many people, both Christian and non-Christian, have denied that there is any historical truth in these stories. Instead they have often seen them as symbolic attempts to convey religious truths – a poetic, picturesque way to emphasize that Jesus had a special relationship with God right from the very beginning of his human existence, and even before that.

The answer to questions such as these will depend ultimately on our own basic attitudes and presuppositions in understanding the New Testament. Those who see these stories as religious rather than historical truth begin from the fact that we can never have children unless we have sexual intercourse with another person of the opposite sex. Therefore, they say, it can never have happened differently: things just don't work that way. If we start out from the basic position that anything contrary to our own experience of life cannot exist, then

of course we must conclude that the stories about Jesus' birth in the New Testament are legendary additions to the authentic stories of Jesus' life and teachings. It seems to me, however, that this is not the most useful way to approach the problem.

None of us finds it easy to believe in, still less to understand, miracles and the supernatural. But the sensible question to ask is surely not whether our own experience leads us to believe that miracles can happen, but whether the evidence we have leads to the conclusion that in a given case what we call a miracle has taken place. This means that the question of the birth of Jesus without human intervention (the 'virgin birth') must be approached by asking: Does the evidence of the Gospels make good sense as historical evidence? If the answer to that question turns out to be 'No', then we must regard the stories told by Matthew and Luke as later attempts to show how a miraculous birth would be appropriate for a remarkable person. If the answer turns out to be 'Yes', then similarly we must be prepared to come to terms with what the evidence suggests.

Now this is not the same as saying that we should naïvely accept as historical fact every statement made in the whole of the Gospel narratives. What I am saying is that we must be prepared to examine every piece of evidence on its own merits – and if we find that there is good historical evidence which points to something 'supernatural', then it should not be dismissed as irrelevant.

As it happens, the stories of Jesus' virgin birth give us a particularly good example of the kind of issues with which we have to deal. Several arguments are involved here:

● Except in the first few chapters of Matthew and Luke there is no explicit statement in the whole of the rest of the New Testament that Jesus was virgin born. There is no mention of it in the accounts of the preaching of the first disciples in the book of Acts. Paul never mentions it. Nor is it found in the Gospels of Mark and John – though, of course, neither of those Gospels mentions Jesus' birth at all. It therefore seems certain that it was possible for the earliest Christians to have a complete understanding of what God had done for them through Jesus Christ without any mention of the virgin birth. Later Christian writers have often tried to argue that the virgin birth is essential if Christians are to believe that Jesus was sinless, and that he was both human and divine. But Paul, amongst others, believed all these things without ever basing his arguments on the particular way that Jesus was born.

This may appear to be a very strong argument for suspecting the authenticity of the stories in Matthew and Luke. But in fact it is a double-edged argument. Since the idea of a virgin birth was not essential for a complete understanding of the precise nature of Jesus' person, why would Matthew and Luke want to invent it? This is an especially pressing question, since no theological points are explicitly made in the stories that describe Jesus' birth. Neither Matthew nor Luke ever say, for example, that Jesus was sinless because he was born in this way, or that this made him the Son of God as well as being a human person. They simply present it as a factual statement about the way Jesus was born. It is very difficult to find any

The Gospels record that shepherds from near Bethlehem were among the first people to see the newly-born Jesus.

religious motive for the fabrication of such stories. It is in fact far easier to suppose that Matthew and Luke had access to historical traditions of some kind which contained these stories of Jesus' birth, and that they both incorporated their own rather different stories into their respective Gospels.

● In certain passages of the Gospels, Jesus is referred to as 'the son of Joseph' (Luke 4:22; John 1:45; 6:42), and the lists in both Matthew (1:2–16) and Luke (3:23–38) trace his ancestry through Joseph. It is therefore sometimes suggested that even within the Gospels themselves there is no consistency. For how could Joseph be Jesus' father if Mary was a virgin when Jesus was conceived? This is not as serious an objection as it appears to be. When Joseph married Mary he would be, in the eyes of both public opinion and of the Jewish law, the legal father of Jesus. Besides, there is no word for foster-father in either Hebrew or Greek, and so the Gospel writers were probably just recording the common description of Jesus as 'Jesus son of Joseph'. Luke certainly thought this was what he was doing (3:23). It is in any case unlikely that either Gospel writer would have contradicted himself in so obvious a fashion.

● It has sometimes been suggested that the idea of the virgin birth was derived from Greek or oriental stories about the gods having intercourse with human women and producing children. This is not a very serious argument, and the stories of the Gospels move in a very different atmosphere from the stories told of the Greek gods. We need only to read the account of the announcement of Jesus' birth to Mary (Luke 1:26–38) and compare it with the licentious stories of Greek mythology to realize that there can be little contact between them. In addition, the whole of Luke 1–2 has a very primitive character by comparison with the rest of Luke's writing. Though some scholars believe this to be a deliberate device used by Luke in imitation of the style of the Greek Old Testament (the Septuagint), others have argued that Luke's Greek is of a sufficiently consistent character to suggest that he is here quoting or depending on an Aramaic source. If that is true, then he must have obtained these stories of Jesus' birth from the very earliest

group of Christians in Palestine itself, the only Christians ever to speak Aramaic.

● Matthew's account presents a problem of a rather different kind. In support of his story he quotes from the Old Testament: 'All this took place to fulfil what the Lord had spoken by the prophet: "Behold, a virgin shall conceive and bear a son, and his name shall be called Emmanuel" ...' (1:22–23). What is more, this passage from the Old Testament prophet Isaiah has a very different meaning in the Greek version of the Old Testament from that which it had in the original Hebrew text. Matthew quotes from the Greek version. But in the Hebrew text of Isaiah 7:14 the mother of Emmanuel is said to be a 'young woman'; she is not called by the technical term for a 'virgin'. Some have therefore argued that the whole idea of the virgin birth was manufactured out of this unfortunate mistranslation of a passage from Isaiah in the Septuagint. Three things need to be noted here.

In the first place this argument can apply only to Matthew since Luke does not quote the Old Testament in support of his story of the virgin birth. So, even supposing this argument is correct, it can dispose only of Matthew's account, and not of Luke's.

Then it is undoubtedly true that Matthew's sole reason for accepting and using the Greek version instead of the Hebrew text was that it was appropriate to his purpose in a way that the Hebrew was not. But this is a common feature of Matthew's Gospel. Matthew often selects Old Testament texts and says they have been fulfilled in Jesus' life and ministry in a way that to us seems irrelevant and trivial. This was almost certainly because he was writing mainly for Jewish readers. The Jews believed that God's Messiah would fulfil certain promises made in the Old Testament, and so Matthew refers to the Old Testament far more than the other Gospel writers, to convince Jewish readers that Jesus was indeed their expected Messiah.

Thirdly it is quite likely that it was not the actual author of the Gospel of Matthew who selected this particular version of the text from Isaiah. There is considerable evidence to suggest that at a very early stage of its existence the church began to gather together Old Testament texts which seemed to them to predict or forecast some aspect of Jesus' life. These are the collections of texts often called *testimonia* by New Testament scholars. There were probably several different collections in existence not long after Jesus' death. The concept of a virgin birth was quite unacceptable in any form to orthodox Jews, and we know that many of the members of the first churches remained good Jews as well as being Christians. Since no one but convinced Jews would be interested in proving that Jesus fulfilled the prophecies of the Old Testament, it is highly unlikely that they would have discovered such an idea there unless they knew of some historical foundation for it.

What then are we to conclude about Jesus' birth from these stories in Matthew and Luke? We can certainly see that when we apply the normal rules of historical investigation to them, the issue is not quite as straightforward as it appears to be when we look at it from a philosophical standpoint and simply ask: Is it possible that such a miracle could have taken place? It is clear that Matthew and Luke have rather different traditions about the birth of Jesus. Yet they are both agreed that Mary was a virgin when he was conceived, and we should not forget that the other two Gospels make no mention of Jesus' birth at all. No theological claims are made in the stories, and though the idea of a virgin birth is mentioned nowhere else in the New Testament, there is nothing elsewhere that contradicts it.

In addition, the whole tradition of the Christian church from the second century onwards supports the belief that Jesus was virgin born, and even in the apocryphal gospels of a later age there is no other account of the birth of Jesus. It therefore seems that the majority of attempts to deny any historical character to the Gospel narratives at this point rest on presuppositions that do not allow for the supernatural, rather than on a scientific and historical examination of the evidence on its own terms.

Have we taken a long time to prove nothing? If the only outcome of our investigation is to show that Jesus was born without the benefit of a human father, then we have not said anything very profound or relevant. But the first Christians wanted to say much more than that. And Jesus himself wanted to say a great deal more, as we shall see in the next chapter.

Was John a member of the commune at Qumran?

In view of the similarities between what we know of John the Baptist and the activities of the commune at Qumran, it is inevitable that we should ask if there was any connection between them. There are two main similarities between them that we need to consider.

In the Judean desert

According to Luke, John the Baptist lived in the desert until he began his public work (1:80; 3:2). Since his baptizing took place in the River Jordan, it is natural to assume that the desert in question was the Judean desert surrounding the Dead Sea, into which the River Jordan flows. This means he was probably living in the same desert as the Qumran people, and at about the same time. Since their monastery must have been one of the few places where it was possible to live in the desert, it is suggested that John may well have known them, even that he may have been a member of their commune.

It is certainly not difficult to believe that John would know of the existence of the monastery at Qumran. But some people have suggested that he was a member of the group, and that he was brought up by them from an early age. They base this argument on the statement in Luke 1:80 that as a child John 'grew and developed in body and spirit. He lived in the desert until the day when he appeared publicly to the people of Israel.' This statement can be put together with a piece of information given about the Essenes by Josephus. He says that they often adopted other people's children in order to indoctrinate them with the ideas of their sect (*Jewish Wars* 2.8.2). This is an attractive theory, but there are many problems about it.

● The Greek words used in Luke 1:80 and 3:2 do not necessarily suggest that John was actually brought up as a child in the desert. It is certainly implied that he was in the desert thinking about his life's work immediately before he began baptizing people – but the natural implication of the story about his birth is that he was brought up in the normal way by his parents.

Facing page: One of the most exciting and extensive discoveries of ancient Bible documents was made in some caves at Qumran near the Dead Sea. A chance discovery by a shepherd boy led archaeologists to the area and excavations began in 1947. Over 400 manuscripts dating from the first century have been discovered. All the books of the Old Testament except Esther have been found there. The manual which contained the rules and beliefs of the Essene community who lived there at the time of Jesus has also been found. The community had separated itself from other Jewish groups to form its monastery. The scrolls were hidden in jars in the caves to protect them from the Roman Army which was attacking Jews in AD 68.
Background picture: The entrance to Cave 4, where most of the scrolls were found.
Top left: The caves at Qumran.
Bottom left: Tourists today can visit the excavated buildings where the Essenes lived.
Centre: Two jars which contained scrolls. They are the only complete ones of their kind in the world.
Right: Part of a scroll of the book of Deuteronomy.

Baptism was seen by John as a symbol of repentance. It is still used by Christians today to signify faith in Christ, whether of children or adult converts.

● It is also unlikely that his parents would have allowed a group like the people of Qumran to adopt their child. Not only were they longing to have this son, but John's father Zechariah was a priest – and one of the distinctive beliefs of the Qumran group was that the Jerusalem priests were corrupt. It is difficult to think that John's parents would have given their child to a group who were so hostile to all that they themselves stood for.

● We must also remember that the Judean desert was a big place, and by no means everyone who lived there would need to live at Qumran. The shores around the Dead Sea are full of caves that would make ideal lodgings for hermits, as they did for the Zealots who resisted Rome after the destruction of Jerusalem in AD 70. Even Josephus tells us how he once joined a man called Bannus who was living a solitary life in the desert (*Life of Josephus* 2). The appeal of this kind of life has always been strong to people of a particular disposition, and we can be quite sure there must have been plenty of individuals living like this in the desert surrounding the Dead Sea.

Baptism

If it is difficult to make any direct connection between John and the Essenes through their style of life, it is certainly no easier to do it through their religious rituals. We know that both John and the Qumran people made use of water in their religious rites, but there is little we can say beyond that. There are in fact several striking differences between John's concept of baptism and the ritual washings that went on at Qumran:

●The people who took part were different. John baptized people who wanted to change their way of life. The community at Qumran accepted only those who could prove that they had already changed their way of life. An initiate often had to wait for a year or two before being allowed to take part in the ritual washings at Qumran, whereas John was prepared to baptize immediately anyone who was willing to repent.

●The character of the ritual was different. A person baptized by John was baptized once and for all. But at Qumran the ritual washings were repeated over and over again. Indeed, Professor H.H. Rowley has pointed out that 'baptism' in the sense we usually understand it is not really the right word to describe what went on at Qumran. The Essene 'baptisms' were a means of effecting a ritual purification in the lives of those who were members, rather than being a rite of admission to the sect.

●The meaning of the ritual was different. John's baptisms were carried out as part of the preparations for the arrival of God's expected Messiah. But the Qumran washings were not connected with the expectation of a Messiah, or of anyone else. They were simply means of expressing in symbol the moral and spiritual purity which the community hoped to preserve among its members.

So, was John a member of the Dead Sea sect? The best answer seems to be that if he had at any time been a member, he had certainly changed his outlook quite radically by the time he began his public work. But arguments in favour are not very strong, and we would certainly need further evidence if they were ever to be conclusively shown to be correct.

Chapter 3   Who was Jesus?

John 1:38; 3:2; 9:2

Mark 1:21; Luke 4:16; 6:6; Mark 1:16–20

Matthew 7:29

Mark 2:7

After he had met John and been baptized, most of Jesus' life was spent as a religious teacher. It was quite normal for Jewish religious teachers, or rabbis as they were called, to live an itinerant life, wandering about from place to place, often accompanied by their disciples. Jesus plainly fitted into this pattern. He had his disciples, and he was often called 'Rabbi' or 'Teacher'. Like the other Jewish teachers he carried out much of his work in the synagogue, the place where Jews met for worship each sabbath day. He also spoke with people wherever he met them. He called his first disciples from their fishing boats, and often taught out in the open countryside where large crowds could gather round him.

It was Jesus' teaching that really caught the imagination of the people. For as they listened to him they realized that this was no ordinary rabbi. He was not just someone else's disciple passing on what he had heard from others. He was saying totally new things about men and women and their relationship with God. And he was saying them in such a way that no one could escape making a decision about him. One had to accept either the verdict of many ordinary people that 'he taught them as one who had authority', or the opinion of the Pharisees that he was the worst kind of religious pretender.

The teaching that caused such a sharp division among his hearers was on just two subjects. On the one hand Jesus made many bold claims about his own person and significance. He clearly believed that he himself was the promised deliverer whom the Jews were expecting to be sent from God. He alone was the Messiah who could establish the new society. On the other hand, alongside Jesus' claims about his own destiny and importance, we have statements about the exact nature and meaning of the new society Jesus believed he had come to inaugurate. We will be looking at some of Jesus' statements about the new society in a later chapter. It is important that we look first of all at Jesus' claims about himself. For his ideas about God's new society and its place in the lives of men and women are meaningless unless we have understood what Jesus claimed about his own significance in God's plan.

The Son of man

So far we have seen how the Jewish people were looking for God to send a promised deliverer, the Messiah, who would inaugurate the new society. Of course, the term 'God's promised deliverer' is not used in the Gospels: I have used it here to try to convey in everyday language something of what the Jewish people understood by the word 'Messiah'.

But it is surprising to look at the Gospels and see how few times even the word 'Messiah' (or its Greek translation, 'Christ') is used there to describe Jesus. Take Mark's Gospel, for example. This was perhaps the first Gospel to be written, and the word for 'Messiah' or 'Christ' is used only seven times. One of these is in the title of the Gospel, and of the other six only three could be taken as a reference to Jesus being the Messiah or Christ. And in only one does Jesus himself make a direct claim to be the Messiah. It is also striking that in the only passage where Jesus does directly claim to be the Messiah, he at once goes on to speak of a different figure, and identifies the Messiah with someone he calls 'the Son of man'.

So who was the Son of man? It is impossible to read far through any of the stories of Jesus' life without realizing that this 'Son of man' was a very important concept for Jesus. The actual term is used fourteen times in Mark's Gospel; in the longer account of Matthew it occurs no less than thirty-one times. 'Son of man' is in fact the term that Jesus used most often to describe himself and his work. So what did it mean?

Some people would say that when Jesus spoke of himself as 'the Son of man' he was simply wanting to emphasize that one part of his nature was ordinary and human, while another side of his character could be described by the term 'Son of God'. But the phrase 'Son of man' must mean more than this. Jesus speaks, for example, of 'the Son of man coming in clouds with great power and glory', or 'seated at the right hand of the power of God'. Claims like that can hardly have been intended to emphasize Jesus' human character over against his claims to have a special significance in the plans of God!

Mark 1:1

Mark 8:29; 9:41; 14:61–62

Mark 14:61–62

Mark 14:62

Mark 13:26

Luke 22:69

The meaning of 'Son of man'

The *exact* meaning of the term 'Son of man' is one of the most hotly disputed subjects in modern study of the New Testament. What we can say here is only the barest summary of what some of the scholars are saying.

One point on which all scholars are agreed is that the most helpful question to ask is: What would come into the minds of those people who actually knew Jesus when they heard him use the term 'Son of man'? Since his first hearers were Jews, it would be best to look to the Jewish religion for the answer.

It is always helpful to look first at the Old Testament. Here we find that the expression 'Son of man' is used in two ways.

More often than not, it simply means man as distinct from God. In this context, it usually emphasizes the weakness and poverty of human beings in contrast to the might and power of God himself (Numbers 23:19; Job 25:6; Psalm 8:4; 146:3; Isaiah 51:12). One or two of the Old Testament prophets were addressed by God as 'son of man', and this was a means of emphasizing the difference between them and their Master (Ezekiel 2:1; Daniel 8:17).

But the term is also used in a

It is not possible to compile a complete calendar of the events in Jesus' life. This table lists the main events of his life as they are recorded in the Gospels.

quite different way in Daniel 7:13–14. Far from indicating the weakness of men and women as opposed to the greatness of God, 'one like a son of man' here 'came to the Ancient of Days and was presented before him. And to him was given dominion and glory and kingdom, that all peoples, nations and languages should serve him.' And 'his dominion is an everlasting dominion, which shall not pass away, and his kingdom one that shall not be destroyed'.

Some experts also believe that important clues can be found in some of the apocalyptic books that may have been current at the time of Jesus. In *The Similitudes of Enoch*, 'the Son of man' again appears as a supernatural figure sent from God as the future judge of humanity (1 Enoch 37–71). And 'the Man' of 2

The life of Jesus
recorded in the synoptic Gospels

	Matthew	Mark	Luke
BIRTH AND CHILDHOOD			
Jesus' ancestors	1:1–17		3:23–28
The promise of Jesus' birth to Mary			1:26–38
The birth of Jesus	1:18–25		2:1–20
Visitors from the East	2:1–12		
Jesus' circumcision			2:21–40
Jesus' parents escape to Egypt	2:13–23		
Twelve-year-old Jesus in the temple			2:41–52
IN AND AROUND GALILEE			
Jesus' baptism	3:13–17	1:9–11	3:21–22
The temptation	4:1–11	1:12–13	4:1–13
First preaching in Galilee	4:12–17	1:14–15	4:14–15
Jesus rejected by people in Nazareth			4:16–30
The call of the first disciples	4:18–22	1:16–20	
Teaching and healing in Capernaum		1:21–38	4:31–43
Miraculous catch of fish			5:1–11
The Sermon on the Mount	5:1 — 7:29		
Jesus heals a leper	8:1–4	1:40–45	5:12–16
Healing the sick and calming the storm	8:5–34		
Healing a paralysed man	9:1–8	2:1–12	5:17–26
Matthew called to be a disciple	9:9–13	2:13–17	5:27–32
Discussion about fasting	9:14–17	2:18–22	5:33–39
Jairus' daughter and a woman healed	9:18–26	5:21–43	8:40–56
Two blind men and a dumb man healed	9:27–34		
The twelve commissioned and instructed	9:35 — 10:42	6:6–13	9:1–6
Jesus talks about John the Baptist	11:1–19		7:18–35
Teaching about the sabbath	12:1–14		
The sermon on the plain			6:20–49
A slave healed and a boy brought back to life			7:1–17
The women who served Jesus			7:36 — 8:3
Jesus debates with the religious leaders	12:22–50	3:20–35	
Parables of the kingdom	13:1–58	4:1–41	8:4–25
The Gerasene demoniac		5:1–20	8:26–39
Jesus feeds 5,000 people	14:13–21	6:30–44	9:10–17
Jesus walks on the water	14:22–33	6:45–52	

	Matthew	Mark	Luke
Teaching on religious traditions	15:1–20	7:1–23	
Jesus heals many who are ill	15:21–31	7:24–37	
Jesus feeds 4,000 people	15:32— 16:12	8:1–21	
He predicts his death	16:13–28	8:27–37	9:18–27
The transfiguration	17:1–27	9:2–32	9:28–45
Jesus sends out seventy helpers			10:1–24
Teaching on love, prayer and materialism			10:25— 12:59
Healings and parables			13:1–30
Jesus leaves Galilee			13:31–35
Some well-known parables			14:15— 16:31
Ten lepers healed			17:11–19
JESUS GOES TO JERUSALEM			
Jesus predicts his death again	20:17–19	10:32–34	18:31–34
The sons of Zebedee seek privilege	20:20–38	10:35–45	
The healing of blind Bartimaeus	20:29–34	10:46–52	18:35–43
Zacchaeus meets Jesus			19:1–10
Jesus enters Jerusalem like a king	21:1–9	11:1–10	19:28–44
He turns out the traders from the temple	21:10–22	11:11–26	19:45–48
More parables	21:28— 22:14		
Indictment of the Pharisees	23:1–36	12:37–40	20:45–47
Jesus predicts the destruction of the temple	24:1–3	13:1–4	21:5–7
Teaching on the future	24:4–36	13:5–37	21:8–36
DEATH AND RESURRECTION			
The conspiracy against Jesus	26:1–5	14:1–2	22:1–2
Judas betrays Jesus	26:14–16	14:10–11	22:3–6
The disciples prepare for the Passover	26:17–19	14:12–16	22:7–13
The last supper	26:20–29	14:17–25	22:15–38
Jesus is captured	26:30–56	14:26–52	22:39–53
The trials of Jesus	26:57— 27:26	14:53— 15:15	22:54— 23:25
The crucifixion	27:27–44	15:16–32	23:26–43
Jesus dies	27:45–56	15:33–41	23:44–49
Jesus is buried	27:57–66	15:42–47	23:50–56
The empty tomb	28:1–10	16:1–8	24:1–12
Jesus appears alive to his followers	28:11–20		24:13–53

One interpretation of Jesus' title 'Son of man' is that it emphasizes the weakness of people compared with the greatness of God. To Jesus, God was the provider of everything people enjoyed.

Jewish apocalypses, the 'son of man' was a transcendent, heavenly figure who shared in God's own power.

It is quite likely that all these facts are relevant. If the term 'Son of man' had no very clearly definable meaning in the Aramaic that Jesus spoke, he may have chosen to use it simply because he was free to make it mean exactly what he wanted it to mean. If he had used the term 'Messiah' it would not have been easy for him to explain precisely what he understood his role to be, since people had so many preconceived ideas. By using the ambiguous term 'Son of man' he avoided such problems.

At the same time, for those with the perception to see it, the background of the term provided some very important clues to the things Jesus wanted to say about himself. For he wanted to claim both that he was an ordinary human being, and that he was specially sent from God himself – and both these ideas could be found in the Old Testament use of the 'Son of man'.

Jesus actually uses the name in three rather different ways which illustrate this.

● Quite often, he uses the term 'Son of man' instead of the personal pronoun 'I', simply as a means of describing his ordinary human existence. At those points where the different Gospels have the same sayings, one Gospel often uses 'Son of man' where another writer uses the pronoun 'I'. Compare, for example, Mark 10:45 and Luke 22:27; or Mark 8:27 and Matthew 16:13; or Matthew 19:28 and Luke 22:30.

● At other times, Jesus uses the title 'Son of man' with reference to his future coming on the clouds of heaven and to his exaltation at God's right hand (Matthew 24:27, 37; Luke 17:30; 18:8; 21:36; 22:69). This is the same use as in Daniel 7.

● But most often it is used in a new and different way, with some reference to the suffering and death that Jesus expected to be part of his experience. In nine out of the fourteen uses in Mark, the term 'Son of man' is used by Jesus to refer to his coming death (Mark 8:31; 9:9; 14:21; Matthew 26:2). It is at this point that he has given an entirely new meaning to what may well have been a little-known idea before his time. And it is characteristic of him that he should have talked about himself most often as a suffering Son of man.

Esdras 13 may carry the same connotations.

Unfortunately, we cannot be sure that either of these books was actually in writing by the time of Jesus. In addition, our only knowledge of them is through relatively late texts, that have no direct connexions with Hebrew or Aramaic originals, and may well have been corrupted in any case. It is therefore difficult to use them with any confidence to claim that the term 'Son of man' was a recognized title of any sort in the time of Jesus.

Some scholars contend that the Aramaic word *barnasha* would not usually be a title anyway, but was a perfectly normal way of referring to 'man' in a generic sense rather than an individual sense.

So we have three facts to consider before we can decide what Jesus meant by calling himself the Son of man:

● The actual Aramaic words 'son of man' may well have had no specific meaning, but were probably just a longer (tautological) phrase for 'man'.

● In the Old Testament, the term 'son of man' had been used to describe human beings and their difference from God.

● In the book of Daniel and other

The Messiah

Mark 9:41

We need not spend long thinking about Jesus' claims to be the Messiah. It was not a title Jesus used for himself. In Mark, the first Gospel to be written, there is only one instance where he may have been doing so. There are, however, four very significant occasions when other people called Jesus 'the Messiah', and he apparently accepted the title.

Jesus' 'Son of man' sayings occur most often in the context of his suffering and death. He identified most readily with the poor and needy; like these Asian refugees he had no permanent home of his own.

● When Peter finally realized the truth about who Jesus claimed to be, and told him 'You are the Christ', Jesus replied that he was 'blessed' to have received such a special insight.

Matthew 16:16–17

● Another occasion was during his trial before the Jewish authorities, when Jesus acknowledged to the high priest that he was the Messiah.

Mark 14:61–62

● There is also the story of how Jesus healed a man who was thought to be possessed by demons. Not only did he allow this man to address him as 'Son of the Most High God'; he also told him, 'Go home to your friends, and tell them how much the Lord has done for you'.

Mark 5:1–20

● On another occasion Jesus was going along a road near Jericho when a blind beggar called Bartimaeus shouted out and addressed him as 'Son of David'. Though others who were standing around evidently told the man to be silent, Jesus did not do so, and therefore seems to have accepted this title for himself.

Mark 10:46–52

From these four instances it is clear that Jesus did not have the same attitude towards the claim that he was the Messiah, 'the Son of David', on each occasion. By the time he appeared before the high priest it was obvious that he was to be condemned anyway, and so he had no qualms about claiming to be the Messiah. Though even here he at once went on to re-define the concept of 'the Messiah' in terms of his own favourite name 'the Son of man'. But at an earlier stage, when Peter confessed that he was the Messiah, Jesus told him and the other disciples not to tell anyone about it, but to keep it secret. On the other two occasions he apparently accepted a Messianic title from other people without saying anything about it – and in the case of the man possessed with demons he told him to share his experience with his friends and relatives. It is obvious that Jesus' attitude to letting people know he was the Messiah varied according to the circumstances, and was partly dependent on the question of whether or not this claim should be publicized. What are we to make of all this? Two explanations seem possible.

● Jesus never claimed to be the Messiah. One way to solve the problem is to say that Jesus never in fact claimed to be the Messiah at all, and that Mark and the other Gospel writers have written their stories of Jesus' life and teaching with an eye more to what they believed about Jesus than to what he claimed for himself. They believed he was the Messiah because they were living after the resurrection. From this new perspective they came to see that it was fitting to think of Jesus as the person who had fulfilled God's promises made in the Old Testament. When they came to write their Gospels, however, they wanted to make it perfectly clear that Jesus was actually the promised Messiah. So they bridged the gap between their own beliefs and what they knew to be the historical truth by inventing the idea of 'the messianic secret'. This is a phrase first coined by a German scholar, William Wrede, to explain why it is that whenever Jesus is depicted talking to his disciples about his position as Messiah he always tells them to keep it a secret. Wrede thought that the whole idea of this 'messianic secret' was the invention of Mark, the writer of the earliest Gospel.

The difficulty with his suggestion is that although it fits in with some of the evidence, there are other pieces of information which do not fit. There are, for example, the incidents involving the demon-possessed man at Gerasa and Bartimaeus at Jericho. Then there is also the undeniable fact that Jesus was actually condemned to death because he claimed to be 'king of the Jews', that is, their Messiah. It is difficult to see how Mark could have left these stories in his narrative in this form if he had been so intent on making the idea of the 'messianic secret' convincing.

● Jesus believed, but never claimed, he was the Messiah. We seem to be left with the implication that Jesus thought he was the Messiah, but that he did not explicitly claim he was. But how can we explain such an odd state of affairs? Three things can be said about it.

First, we have to remember that the Gospels were written not so much to preserve the story of Jesus' life and teaching as to be helpful to Christians later in the first century. And the Christians who first read the Gospels had the same perspective as we have now. They knew of the resurrection of Jesus and the coming of God's power into their own lives. On that account they had no difficulty in recognizing that Jesus must be the Messiah, God's promised deliverer sent to inaugurate the new society. How could they have any doubt, since they themselves were members of this new society? Gradually, the word 'Messiah' or 'Christ' came to be used as a kind of second name for Jesus, and it is still used in this way today. This perhaps explains why the word 'Christ' is used so many times in John's Gospel, whereas it is hardly ever used in the other three. It is generally thought that John was writing later than the others, and by that time the word had become almost a surname for Jesus.

Then the Gospels themselves make it clear that Jesus and his contemporaries were at cross-purposes when they spoke of the Messiah. To the Jews, the Messiah was to be a political king. For Jesus, being the Messiah meant humble service and obedience to God's will. And for him to have spoken openly of being the Messiah would have concealed the real meaning of his coming, and brought about an early encounter with the Romans. Even the disciples, including Peter who declared that Jesus was the Messiah, did not fully understand who Jesus was until after the resurrection. Despite their close relationship with Jesus, they displayed their ignorance of his intentions on more than one occasion. And we can be quite sure that this is an accurate historical picture, for when the Gospels were written the disciples were the church's heroes, and no one would have made up stories that portrayed them in a bad light.

Mark 8:14–21; 9:30–32;
10:35–45

There were many beggars in the streets of Israel during Jesus' lifetime; one of them, Bartimaeus, addressed him as the Messiah, the 'Son of David'.

Thirdly, it seems certain that Jesus' attitude did in fact vary, and that his whole life and work was a mixture of revelation and secrecy. This comes out in the way he liked to call himself 'the Son of man', which had no ready-made meaning. To those who were not prepared to think very deeply about it, it was a name that could only confuse them and conceal Jesus' claims rather than reveal them. At the same time, many incidents in Jesus' life – including the miracles, but also occasions such as his baptism, his temptations and his entry into Jerusalem – would lose their meaning if Jesus was not claiming to be the Messiah.

Mark 1:9–11
Luke 4:1–13
Mark 11:1–11

Many of the things he did and said were exactly the things that the Messiah was expected to do and say when he came.

The best conclusion seems to be that Jesus did not use the word 'Messiah' of himself because he knew that it would suggest to his hearers an earthly king and a new political state. Jesus certainly had no intention of being that kind of 'Messiah'. He had already decisively rejected the idea in the temptations. So he cast his whole ministry in a mould that would conceal his claim to be Messiah from those who did not want to understand it in the same way as he did, but that would reveal his true identity to those who really wanted to know.

The Son of God

The belief of the Christian church from the very earliest times has always included the statement that Jesus was 'the Son of God'. This too was an expression that would be familiar to the people of Jesus' day. Greek-speaking people often used the phrase to indicate some heroic human figure. When the Roman centurion at the cross said of Jesus, 'Truly this was the son of God', all he probably meant was that Jesus was a great man. Indeed, Luke's account clearly suggests this, for there the centurion says, 'Certainly this man was innocent'.

Matthew 27:54

Luke 23:47

Like the terms 'Son of man' and 'Messiah', the term 'Son of God' had also been used in the Old Testament. The nation of Israel was often called 'God's son'. The kings of Israel, especially those who were descendants of David, also had this title. Many of the psalms refer to the king as God's son – though the Jews soon came to regard such passages as references to the coming Messiah.

Hosea 11:1

But there can be no question that in the Gospels the phrase 'Son of God' was used to indicate that Jesus claimed a special relationship with God himself. Jesus was very conscious of a close spiritual relationship with God as his Father. Even at the early age of twelve he regarded the temple at Jerusalem as 'my Father's house'. And in the story about the wicked tenants of the vineyard he made it clear that he himself was the son whom the owner had sent to put things in order.

Luke 2:49

Mark 12:1–11

The claims that are implied in these stories were also made very explicitly by Jesus. Take, for example, this statement recorded by both Matthew and Luke: 'All things have been delivered to me by my Father; and no one knows the Son except the Father, and no one knows the Father except the Son and any one to whom the Son chooses to reveal him.' It is clear that Jesus was claiming a unique relationship with God, and his claim is of such a character that it leaves very little room for misunderstanding.

Matthew 11:27; Luke 10:22

There is certainly no place for saying, as many non-Christians do, that Jesus was a good man who did not in fact claim to be divine. If Jesus' claims were not true, he was either a deliberate impostor or a deluded imbecile – and neither the evidence of the

Facing page: The crowds that thronged the narrow streets of Jerusalem nearly two thousand years ago were expecting a political leader to deliver them from the Romans. Even some of Jesus' closest followers thought he would be this kind of Messiah.

Gospels, nor common historical opinion, pictures him in either of these roles.

So what did Jesus mean when he claimed to be 'the Son of God'? This is, of course, one of the great questions that theologians have thought and talked about for centuries. So nothing we can say here is likely to be the full and final answer to the question! But there are at least three essential facts to note if we are ever to have any intelligent understanding of what Jesus and the first Christians were saying when they used this term.

● We must never forget that when we describe Jesus as 'the Son of God' we are using pictorial language to describe something that is in principle indescribable. Jesus was using an analogy. He took the human relationship of child to parent, and said: 'My relationship with God is rather like that.' He did not mean us to take the analogy literally. Nor was he suggesting that every aspect of our own relationship to our parents fits exactly the relationship between Jesus and God. Not everyone has a happy relationship with their parents. And although many people may be able to say truthfully, 'He who hates me hates my Father also', no human could ever say 'I and my Father are one'. Indeed, the whole of Jesus' teaching, especially in John's Gospel, makes it clear that this relationship between Father and Son was unique. It existed long before Jesus was born in Bethlehem: Jesus was 'in the beginning with God'.

John 15:23
John 10:30

John 1:2

● Like all the other titles we have looked at here, this one had also been used in the Old Testament. The term 'son of ...' was a common idiom of the Hebrew language. For example, in the Old Testament the Israelites are often called 'sons' or 'children' of Israel, though modern translations have disguised the wording. Wicked people are often called 'sons of wickedness' or 'sons of Belial'. And the Hebrew for our word 'human beings' is 'sons of men'.

Deuteronomy 1:1;
Judges 1:1

Deuteronomy 13:13;
1 Samuel 2:12

Now if we described ourselves as 'sons of men' we would be saying that we share precisely the same characteristics and nature as the whole of the human race before us. So when the New Testament says that Jesus is 'the Son of God' it is stating that Jesus shared the characteristics and nature of God himself. He was claiming to be really and truly divine. Some people, the Jehovah's Witnesses for example, have been unable to see this because they have forgotten that Jesus was using an analogy when he described himself as 'Son of God'. And they have also ignored the real meaning of the term 'the son of ...' in the language that Jesus was speaking.

● In the first chapter of John's Gospel, and in Revelation, this relationship between Jesus and God is expressed in another way. There Jesus is called the 'word' or *logos* of God. God's word is, of course, the way that God communicates. But when the New Testament calls Jesus 'the word' it says something more than that. For John says that 'the Word was God' – that is, God's message to mankind was not just written in a book, it was

John 1:1–18;
Revelation 19:13

John 1:1

John 1:14

displayed in the person of God himself. He also says that 'the Word became a human being': God himself was embodied in 'the Word', in Jesus.

So when Jesus claimed to be the 'Son of God', and when the New Testament writers described this in terms of 'the Word of God', they were all saying that because of Jesus we can truly know what God is like. Jesus himself said: 'He who has seen me has seen the Father.' We all have our ideas of what God is like, ideas formed according to our own prejudices and preconceptions. But if Jesus' claims are correct, we can now substitute God as he really is for our imaginary pictures of him. That is why it is so important for us to get back to what Jesus was actually saying and doing, for in his life and teaching we can see and hear what God is really like.

John 14:9

Jesus told his followers, 'I am among you as one who serves'. The idea was familiar to them; there were many servants and slaves in contemporary Palestine.

The servant

Isaiah 52:13–53:12

Mark 1:11; Isaiah 42:1

Perhaps we discover what God is really like most adequately in this final title – 'the servant' – that Jesus seems to have applied to himself and his work. It is true that nowhere in the Gospels do we find Jesus using of himself the title 'the servant of God'. Yet we have seen already that it was just because he lived and died in the way predicted of the suffering servant in Isaiah that his concept of what it meant to be Messiah was so very different from the kind of Messiah expected by the Jews of his time. We also have many references to Jesus' conviction that it was to be his lot to suffer and, as we have noticed, the most distinctive use of the term 'Son of man' was in connection with Jesus' statements about his own suffering and death.

From the time he was baptized, and perhaps before that, Jesus saw that the course of his life was to be one of suffering. The voice he heard at his baptism, echoing words from one of the passages in Isaiah about the suffering servant, made it clear to him that his life's work was to consist of humble self-denial, and this conviction was vigorously reiterated in his reactions to the

Many Jewish religious customs have continued almost unchanged since Old Testament times. A series of festivals throughout the year, celebrated by whole families, remind them of the great events in their past history. The Passover is held each spring as a reminder of the 'exodus' or escape of the Israelites from Egypt. For the family above, the Passover they are celebrating is their first one since they settled in modern Israel.

The Passover plate (centre left) contains foods symbolizing different aspects of the event: a boiled egg; a shankbone of lamb; parsley dipped in salt water; horse-radish and bitter herbs; a mixture of chopped fruit and nuts.

Centre right: A Jewish rabbi wearing traditional costume. Over his head and shoulders is a tallith, or prayer shawl, and attached to his forehead and left arm are phylacteries containing short portions of the Jewish scriptures.

The wailing wall (bottom) in Jerusalem is a place where Jews frequently go to pray. It is part of the original wall which protected the temple court in the first century.

temptation experience. According to Mark, Jesus warned his disciples at a very early stage in his ministry that the day was near when he, the bridegroom, would be taken away from his friends. Immediately after Peter declared his belief that Jesus was the Messiah, Jesus again repeated that 'the Son of Man must suffer many things'. A great purpose was to be accomplished by his service and suffering: 'the Son of Man also came ... to give his life as a ransom for many.'

Mark 2:20

Mark 8:31

Mark 10:45

We have spent a lot of time looking at the various titles that Jesus used to describe himself. Most of them are difficult to understand in detail. But all have one very clear implication. There is no doubt that by using them Jesus was claiming a unique relationship with God, and a unique authority. We find this authority expressed in his claim to forgive the sins of other people. The Jewish religious experts saw quite correctly that this was a claim to exercise power that belongs only to God. He also demanded from his followers a loyalty and devotion that no ordinary human being could ever have the right to claim. He told would-be followers: 'Whoever does not bear his own cross and come after me, cannot be my disciple.'

Mark 2:1–12

Luke 14:27

This claim to a unique relationship with God is expressed in John's Gospel in terms of a complete identification between Jesus and God: 'I and the Father are one ... whoever has seen me has seen the Father.' And we find exactly the same claims in the Gospels of Matthew and Luke.

John 10:30, 14:9
Matthew 11:27;
Luke 10:22

Despite this we are often told by secular historians that Jesus lived as a wandering Jewish teacher, that he may not even have claimed to be a prophet, and that it was the early church, especially Paul, who first made him divine. But the claims Jesus made for himself are clearly expressed in the very earliest records about him, and we must not forget that by comparison with other historical writings of that age, the Gospels were written down a very short time after the events that they describe. What is more, the work of scholars who have investigated the way the Gospels actually came to be written, the Form Critics, has shown that there is no trace anywhere in the New Testament of a Jesus who did not make supernatural claims for himself. It really is quite impossible to separate the purely human figure, the 'Jesus of history', from the Christ and risen Lord who is equal with God in early Christian theology.

If Jesus' claims were false, we are left not with a pious Jewish rabbi, as some historians like to imagine, but with either a man suffering from delusions, or a self-conscious fraud. In either case, Jesus could only be classified with the other 'Messiahs' who appeared sporadically in the first century, whose influence was short-lived, and who are now mostly forgotten. But Jesus was not forgotten and, if his followers later made any new claims about his importance, these claims were firmly grounded in his own teaching about himself and his place in the plans of God.

Chapter 4 Why did Jesus die?

Why did Jesus die? Of all the questions we can ask about Jesus, perhaps no other can be answered in so many different ways. To a certain extent, the answer we give depends on the way we approach the question. We can see this quite clearly, even in books written as long ago as the first century AD.

Take Josephus, for example. He says very little about Jesus. But he does say that 'he was the Messiah; and when Pilate heard him accused by the most highly respected men amongst us, he *Jewish Antiquities* 18.3.3 condemned him to be crucified'. He was obviously convinced that Jesus died as a result of political intrigue and collaboration between Pilate, the Roman prefect of Judea, and the leaders of the Jewish people. This is also clearly stated in the stories of Jesus' death in the Gospels.

But if we look at some other parts of the New Testament and ask, 'Why did Jesus die?', we find a slightly different emphasis in some of the answers. According to the book of Acts, Peter said on the day of Pentecost that though Jesus was 'crucified and killed by the hands of lawless men', he was also 'delivered up Acts 2:23 according to the definite plan and foreknowledge of God'. Paul expresses the same point. In explaining his most deeply held convictions to the Christians in the Greek city of Corinth, he 1 Corinthians 15:3 said that 'Christ died for our sins in accordance with the scriptures'.

So in the New Testament itself the question, 'Why did Jesus die?' is given two kinds of answer. One is based on the historical facts that brought about Jesus' death. The other is based on the claims Jesus made about himself, and on the beliefs of the early church about his significance in God's plan for humanity. We are, then, dealing with a subject that can be understood in two ways. Jesus' death can be understood as a simple matter of history. But at the same time, we can never forget that in the last analysis Jesus' death can only be fully understood as part of God's plan. Luke 19:10 In the light of what Jesus himself claimed, we must give some sort of explanation of his execution as a common criminal.

History and the death of Jesus

A question that is often asked about the Gospels today is whether they intended to give any sort of chronological outline of Jesus' life, or whether the individual stories and sayings were strung together by the Gospel writers in the way that would best suit their own purposes in writing. We shall look at this question in some greater detail in Chapter 10, when we consider the way the Gospels were written.

The course of Jesus' life

Regardless of our detailed answer to the question, it is obvious that we must be able to make certain assumptions about Jesus' career. We can, for example, assume that his baptism by John did take place near the beginning of his ministry. We can assume too, that his ministry took place not only in Galilee, his own home territory, but also in Judea, the area surrounding Jerusalem. Then there is also the indisputable fact that Jesus was crucified in Jerusalem; so we can assume that at some stage immediately before his death he had spent some time teaching in and around Jerusalem itself.

Stories telling of Jesus' work in all these areas show that from the start Jesus' presence created divisions among those who met him. John explains this in a theological way by saying that when Jesus came, God's light had come into the world. Faced with this revelation of God, men and women must make a decision. They

John 3:16–21

must be on one side or the other: on God's side, or against him. Jesus put it like this: 'No one can serve two masters; for either he will hate the one and love the other, or he will be devoted to the one and despise the other. You cannot serve God and mammon.'

Matthew 6:24

And there are many stories about Jesus which show how he enjoyed great popularity as a teacher and healer, but was also opposed by the religious and civil authorities of the day.

The Roman rulers of Palestine were always suspicious of anyone who made a following for himself, just as we are often suspicious of bureaucrats who have too much power in their own hands. According to Josephus, Herod Antipas got rid of John the Baptist because he was afraid of political revolts. It must have been difficult for the authorities not to think of Jesus in the same way. After all, he attracted very large crowds of people, and on at least one occasion a crowd of 5,000 wanted him to become their

The Jewish and Roman calendars

There are a number of references to special days and festivals in the Gospels. John, for instance, records how Jesus went to the feast of Tabernacles, and his death took place at Passover time. Some of the festivals, such as the Passover itself, were memorials of great events in the history of Israel. Others, such as the feast of Firstfruits, were associated with events in the agricultural calendar.

Agricultural events		Flax harvest		Cereal/ Barley harvest	Vine tending	First-ripe grapes		Summer fruit
	Later rains			DRY SEASON				
Jewish religious festivals			21 Firstfruits ●			6 Weeks/ Pentecost ●		
		14 Passover ●	15–21 Unleavened Bread					
			Seven weeks					
Months of the Jewish calendar	1 NISAN		2 IYYAR		3 SIVAN		4 TAMMUZ	5 AB
Months of the Roman calendar		APRIL		MAY		JUNE	JULY	A

John 6:15   king and lead a revolt against the Romans.

The Gospels show Jesus resisting such political power time and again. But they also show that he had no such qualms about getting on the wrong side of the Jewish religious authorities. Right from the very start, the crowds declared that his teaching was

Mark 1:22   different from that of their own religious experts. And Jesus accepted this. What is more, he had no hesitation in condemning the Pharisees and Sadducees outright. They were 'blind leaders

Matthew 23:16–24   of the blind', men who had perverted and denied the word of God. Though they appeared to be very religious and holy, he said that deep down inside they were as rotten and worthless as a

Matthew 23:27   grave full of old bones!

What is more, Jesus' criticism of these people appears to have been a deliberately planned policy. Though Jesus is portrayed spending a short time in more remote areas teaching his disciples,

Mark 10:32–34; Matthew 20:17–19;   all the Gospels suggest that there was a specific moment at which
Luke 18:31–34; John 11:55–57   he decided the time had come to confront the Jewish authorities in Jerusalem itself. Different explanations have been given of this step.

● The oldest view is that Jesus realized the time for his death had come, and so he set himself to go to Jerusalem to fulfil God's will. This is clearly implied in what Jesus said to his disciples according to Luke's account: 'Behold, we are going up to Jerusalem, and everything that is written of the Son of man by

Luke 18:31   the prophets will be accomplished.'

● Albert Schweitzer argued that Jesus made a deliberate gamble that did not pay off. According to Schweitzer, Jesus expected God to intervene in history in a dramatic and more or less immediate way, and his visit to Jerusalem was an attempt to force God's hand. But God did not act, and Jesus found himself unexpectedly dying on the cross.

● Others have suggested that Jesus went to Jerusalem simply because he had been to most other parts of Palestine and he wanted to continue his teaching in the religious capital. The fact that he became involved with the political authorities there was just an unexpected and unfortunate miscarriage of justice.

Albert Schweitzer's theory is considered separately later, in chapter six. The other two explanations of Jesus' visit to Jerusalem probably both have some truth in them. No doubt Jesus did want to share his teaching with the people of Judea as well as those in other parts of Palestine – though according to John's Gospel, he may well have done so on more than one occasion before his final visit there. But if we admit that Jesus was aware of his unique relationship with God, we must recognize that he cannot have been ignorant of the growing opposition he was arousing among the religious leaders of his people. A visit to Jerusalem was bound to bring him into direct confrontation with them.

Shortly before his trial and death, Jesus' disciples borrowed a donkey for him to ride into Jerusalem. The cheering crowds who lined the route spread palm leaves on the path and hailed Jesus as king.

If there had previously been any doubt as to who Jesus was claiming to be, his entry into the holy city made it plain. For Jesus entered Jerusalem in a way that amounted to an open declaration that he was the Messiah. He came on an ass, in accordance with a prophecy in the Old Testament book of Zechariah, and the crowd accepted him as their king entering his capital city. Immediately after this he went to the temple. The Messiah was popularly expected to drive the Gentiles out of Jerusalem. Instead Jesus made a symbolic attempt to restore to the Gentiles the only court of the temple in which they were allowed to worship, by throwing out the Jewish bankers who used it as a place of business.

Zechariah 9:9

Mark 11:10;
John 12:12–19

Mark 11:15–17

Jesus obviously knew what he was doing, and he can hardly have been surprised to discover that the Jewish leaders soon put a price on his head. He does not even appear to have been surprised when one of his own followers, Judas Iscariot, picked up the money offered by the high priests. He was betrayed by one of his own disciples, arrested, and put on trial for his life.

Mark 14:43–52

Jesus on trial

The Gospels appear to report two different trials of Jesus. One was before the Jewish authorities, when he was charged with a religious offence. The other was before the Roman prefect Pontius Pilate, where he was charged with a political offence. Probably the Jews had no authority to carry out a death sentence themselves, and this was why they needed the support of the Roman prefect. But scholars disagree about this, and also about the precise relationship of the different trials to one another. It certainly makes good sense to suppose that Jesus' enemies would make much of the charge of blasphemy before a Jewish court, and then change to a charge of political revolt as the one most likely to secure the death sentence from a Roman official.

According to John's Gospel the trial began in the house of Annas, father-in-law of Caiaphas, the high priest. Annas had no official position, but he was a former high priest and a leading Sadducee. He was obviously a man of great influence. Perhaps this trial was an informal investigation held to formulate proper charges. The supreme Jewish court of seventy members, the Sanhedrin, could not officially meet until daylight, but as soon as it was morning the members were summoned to Caiaphas's house.

John 18:12–14

Mark 14:53–15:1;
John 18:15–27

After Jesus had refused to answer questions about his teaching, and the witnesses had failed to agree in their evidence, Caiaphas asked Jesus a direct question under oath: 'Are you the Christ, the Son of the Blessed?' To this Jesus not only replied 'I am', but added 'and you will see the Son of man sitting at the right hand of Power, and coming with the clouds of heaven'. This confession convinced the whole Sanhedrin that Jesus was guilty. But it can hardly have been the actual claim to be Messiah that condemned him in their eyes, for many of them would certainly have welcomed a political leader who would strike a blow against

Mark 14:61

Mark 14:62

the Romans. What they found shocking and blasphemous was the kind of Messiah Jesus claimed to be: the Son of God coming on the clouds of heaven.

The next step was to bring Jesus before Pilate. Here the charge of blasphemy was dropped. A charge based on Jewish religious scruples would never have appealed to a Roman official. It appears that Jesus' accusers first tried to get Pilate to confirm the Jewish sentence without stating a charge at all. But when Pilate insisted on a charge, three accusations were made:

John 18:28–30
Luke 23:1–2

● Jesus was perverting the Jewish nation. The Jewish leaders, of course, thought of this in terms of perverting the nation from their own brand of Judaism. But they wanted Pilate to think of it in terms of perverting the nation from their loyalty to the emperor.

● Jesus had forbidden the payment of taxes. This was the usual charge made against Zealots.

● Jesus had claimed the title 'king' – something that only the Roman senate could give.

After Pilate had interviewed Jesus, he realized that though Jesus may have upset the sensitivities of the Jews he was not really guilty of any crime under Roman law. If he had claimed to be a king, he was certainly not the kind who could rob Caesar of his power. But Pilate also realized that to upset the Jews was a very serious thing. Pilate was caught in a cleverly contrived trap. On the one hand he could acquit Jesus and risk a riot – which would be looked upon very seriously by his own superiors. On the other hand, he could condemn Jesus – and have to live with a guilty conscience for the rest of his life. It was the fear of Jewish riots that eventually forced his hand, as the crowd told him: 'If you let this man go you are no friend of Caesar's.' That was the last thing Pilate could face. He did not want any bad reports of his conduct going to Rome.

Luke 23:13–16

John 19:12

John 19:19

So Jesus was crucified. As usual in such cases, a placard was nailed to the cross to show his offence. It said: 'Jesus of Nazareth, the King of the Jews.' The Jews were satisfied that the claim to be king meant a claim to be the Messiah. The Romans were satisfied that Jesus was worthy of death as a revolutionary opposed to their own power. To both crucifixion was a daily occurrence. The only difference between Jesus and the thousands of others who had died that way was that his death took perhaps a little less time, only six hours. It was just as well, for the Jews needed to get rid of his body as fast as they could in order to be ritually pure for the sabbath day, which began at sunset. As soon as he was sealed in a grave they could get back to normal, giving thanks to God that yet another disturbing influence had been removed from their lives.

Or had he? We have gone as far as we can in understanding the crucifixion in purely historical terms. But for the earliest Christians it was an event of tremendous religious significance as well.

A model of Fort Antonia, which was adjacent to the temple in Jerusalem. It is traditionally believed that Jesus appeared before Pilate here.

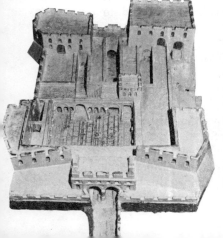

Understanding the death of Jesus

The first generation of Christians, like all Christians ever since, were convinced that Jesus' death on the cross had a profound effect on their own lives. They claimed that their own lives had become meaningful in a new and fresh way because of what Jesus did on the cross. They expressed it in many different ways. Some said their sins had been forgiven. Others that they had found peace of mind, or that they had been reconciled to God. But all of them were convinced that what had happened to them as a result of Jesus' death was real – as real as the fact that Jesus had died. Indeed, in one way they knew it better. For whereas they knew about Jesus' death from hearing the reports of other people, each one of them had personally experienced this dynamic change in his or her own life.

But how could such a thing be explained in terms that other people would understand? For if Jesus really was the Son of God, as he claimed to be, there must be something profound and mysterious about such a person dying at all – let alone dying on a cross between two common criminals. This was not something that could be analysed scientifically. It was an event that needed to be described and talked about in pictorial language, using the familiar and ordinary to describe something that was quite extraordinary. So the New Testament uses many different figures of speech to describe what Jesus was actually doing when he died on the cross. He was sacrificed for us. He took the punishment for our sins. He ransomed us. He justified us. Each of these statements, and many others, brings out some of the things the early Christians understood about Jesus' death. But in talking about them we must remember two things.

1 Corinthians 5:7
1 Corinthians 15:3
1 Timothy 2:6
Galatians 2:16

● We must remember that they are pictures, or analogies. Just as it was important not to press too literally the metaphors and images that Jesus used in talking about his own person, so it is important that we recognize the essentially illustrative nature of the New Testament language of his death. Otherwise we can end up in absurdity.

● We must also remember that the theology of the New Testament is more like a landscape than a portrait. Just as a landscape is made up of any number of different items, so the New Testament's explanation of Jesus' death is made up of many different images. We can, if we wish, consider certain parts of the landscape separately and in greater detail than others. But it is always important that we view each detail in its context, in the total picture. Every one of the metaphors used in the New Testament to describe Jesus' death contains an indispensable element of truth. But not one of them by itself contains the whole truth. For that we need to look at the New Testament as a whole, and consider the entire experience and theological understanding of the early church.

It is particularly important for us to try to understand at least five things that the New Testament says about Jesus' death on the cross.

Jesus' death was a battle

The Gospels show the whole of Jesus' life and ministry as a battle against the forces of evil. In his temptations Jesus faced God's enemy, the devil. His miracles were often concerned with releasing men and women from the power of evil. And Jesus saw his whole life as an effort to win a victory over the evil powers that dominate the world, over suffering, sin and death. Paul also regarded the cross as the final and decisive struggle against the powers of evil. In spite of Jesus' apparent defeat, this struggle resulted in a complete victory over sin and death in the resurrection.

Luke 11:21ff.

Colossians 2:8–15

Jesus himself certainly shared this view, for he said of his death: 'Now shall the ruler of this world be cast out.' The picture of the cross as a battle with the forces of evil is one that often appears in Easter hymns. But to understand Jesus' death only in these terms leaves unanswered a very important question. If Jesus triumphed over sin in his cross and resurrection, why is there still so much evil in the world today?

John 12:31

The French theologian Oscar Cullmann has to some extent given an answer to this question by using yet another military picture. He points out that in a war there is usually a decisive moment that settles the outcome (D-Day), but that the final day of victory (V-Day) can often be much later. He describes the day of Jesus' crucifixion as the D-Day of God's warfare against sin. But the V-Day is still to come, at a future date when all things will be subject to Jesus and evil will finally be conquered. This is not the full answer to the problem of evil, as we shall see. But it is a partial answer to it when we think of Jesus' death in terms of a battle.

Jesus' death was an example

Many of the best-known Christian hymns look at Jesus' death as an example. It is based on the fact that on the cross Jesus revealed God's love for the world. Jesus himself never spoke of the cross as a revelation of God's love, but both Paul and John do. They also suggest that as we consider Jesus' sufferings, we ought to be challenged to share such sufferings ourselves. The writer of 1 Peter used this as a powerful motive to encourage Christians who were being persecuted for their beliefs: '...to this you have been called, because Christ also suffered for you, leaving you an example, that you should follow in his steps.'

Romans 5:8; 1 John 4:10

1 Peter 2:21

This is a concept we find quite easy to understand and accept. We can think of many people who have selflessly given their lives for a good cause. We admire and respect them, and we may even be moved to take up their cause ourselves. But this is obviously not the whole truth about Jesus' death. For the New Testament makes it plain that he was not simply an innocent man dying for a good cause. And if it was in some sense God who was there on the cross, then there is only a very limited sense in which we can take up and share that experience. It is this that makes the death of Jesus quite different from that of all other martyrs.

Jesus' death was a sacrifice

John 1:29

1 Corinthians 5:7

1 Peter 1:19

Leviticus 5:17–19

Exodus 12

Mark 14:22–25

It was natural for Jewish people to use the picture of sacrifice. Animals were sacrificed as part of their own religious ritual. Sacrificial language is used in connection with the death of Jesus throughout the New Testament. John the Baptist exclaimed when he saw Jesus: 'Behold the lamb of God...' Paul speaks of 'Christ our Passover lamb'. Peter describes Jesus as 'like a lamb without blemish or spot' – and the writer of Hebrews goes to great pains to show that Jesus' death was the fulfilment of the whole sacrificial ritual of Judaism.

Two questions about this picture naturally arise in our minds today: First of all, what was 'the lamb' Jesus was compared with?

Since the New Testament writers were conscious that their sins had been removed through Jesus' death, it is natural to see the background to this language in the 'sin offerings' of the Old Testament. We read about this in the book of Leviticus. But there was also the well-known event of the first Passover, at which the people of Israel were delivered from slavery in Egypt, and in which the sacrifice of a lamb played a large part. Jesus himself seems to have made a deliberate connection between his own death and the annual death of the Passover lambs (see the note on the Last Supper). He reminded his disciples that what he was to do on the cross was to be as great a turning-point in their own lives as the Passover had been in the experience of their nation. So when the New Testament describes Jesus' death in terms of a lamb being sacrificed, there were probably these two images in view: the lamb of the sin offering, and the lamb of the Passover.

The second question is even more important: What did the act of sacrifice mean?

Most of us will never have seen an animal sacrifice. It is something that plays no part in our lives today, and we tend to think of it as a rather barbarous ritual from an uncivilized past. But, however crude it may have been, the important thing to notice is that for people who practise sacrifice its real importance lies in what it represents or symbolizes rather than in what takes place.

Worshippers who made a sacrifice in ancient Israel did so out of a consciousness of being alienated from God because of sin and disobedience. They knew they needed to be put right with God before life could be full and free. The first step in this process of reconciliation was for the sinner to approach the altar of God with the sacrifice, hand laid on the animal's head. This identified the worshipper with the animal. So what happened physically and outwardly to the animal was to happen to the sinner inwardly and spiritually. Four things then took place:

● The animal was killed. In this action the sinner was reminded of the consequence of sin: evil results in death, which is to be separated from fellowship with God who can know no evil. Sinners deserve death themselves.

● The priest then took the blood of the sacrifice (which now represented the sinner's life given up to God) to the altar. This was the act of reconciliation, or 'atonement' as it is sometimes

Jerusalem

Herod the Great transformed
Jerusalem from a well-populated but
unspectacular centre of religion to an
important provincial city. He built many
public amenities, including an
amphitheatre, and reconstructed the
temple. This is a reconstruction of the
city in the first century, based on
archaeological excavations.

The Pool of Siloam.
Jesus sent a
blind man to wash
here after he
had been healed

Herod's
Palace

The Hinnom valley,
a smouldering
rubbish tip which
sometimes featured
in Jesus' teaching

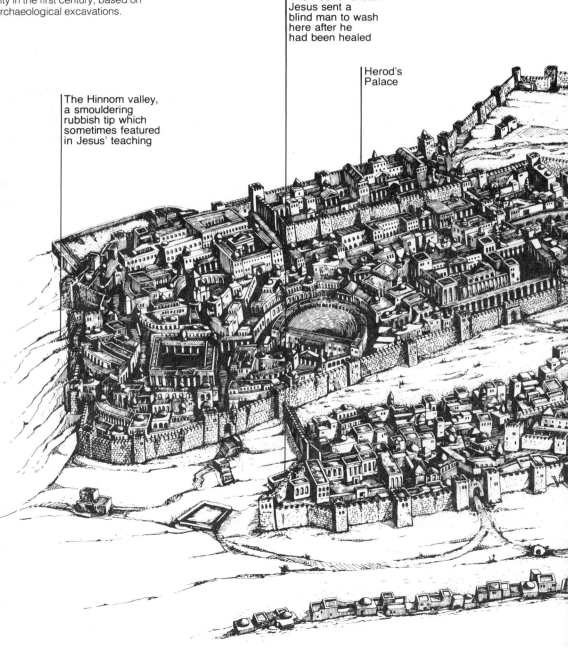

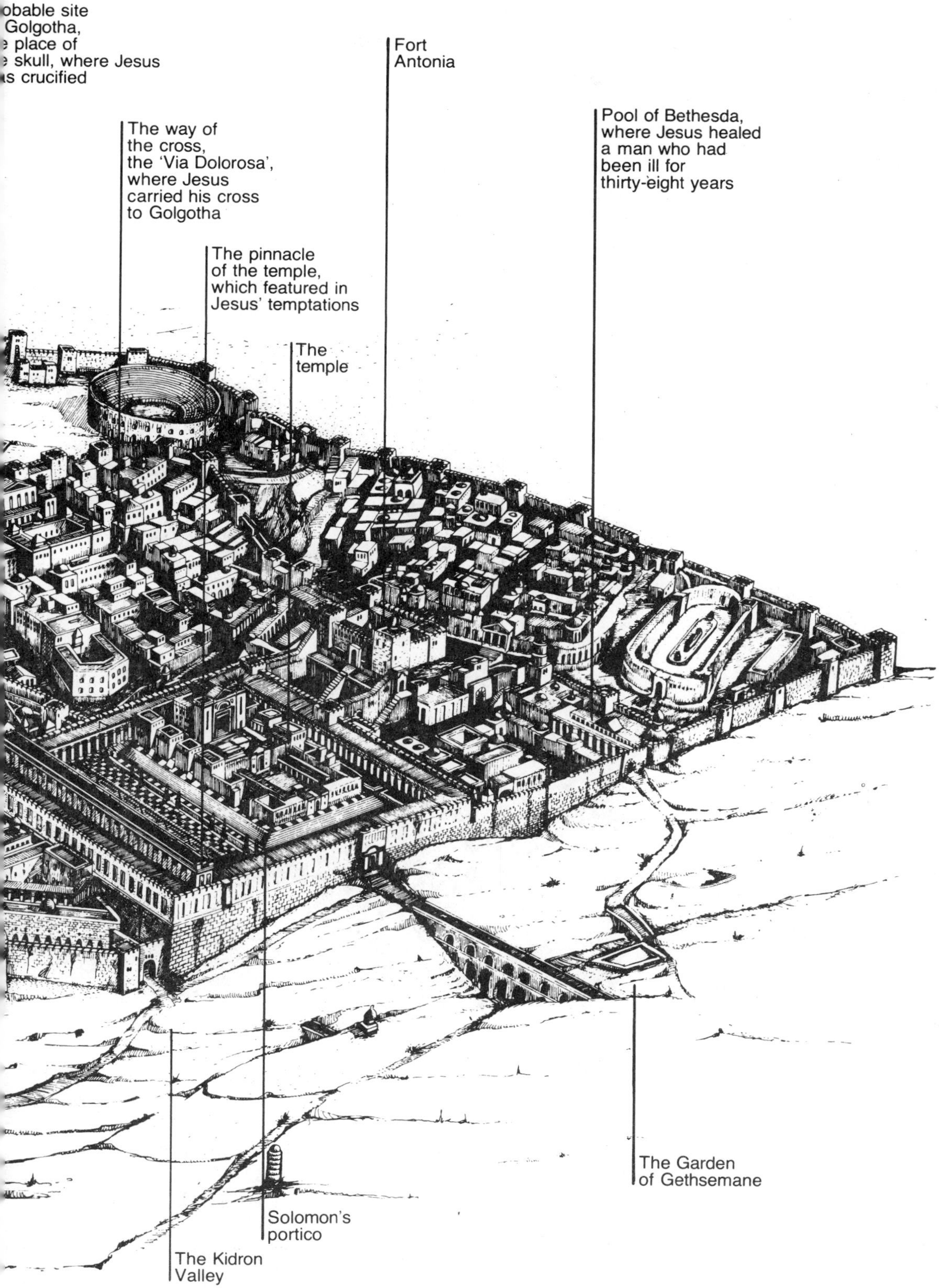

...obable site
...Golgotha,
...e place of
...e skull, where Jesus
...is crucified

The way of
the cross,
the 'Via Dolorosa',
where Jesus
carried his cross
to Golgotha

Fort
Antonia

Pool of Bethesda,
where Jesus healed
a man who had
been ill for
thirty-eight years

The pinnacle
of the temple,
which featured in
Jesus' temptations

The
temple

Solomon's
portico

The Garden
of Gethsemane

The Kidron
Valley

J JAARTSVELD '74

called. The sin had been dealt with, and God and the sinner had been reunited in fellowship.

● After this, the animal's body was placed on the altar in the temple, as a sign that the forgiven sinners were offering their whole being to God.

● Then, finally, some of the meat still left was eaten in a meal. This indicated that the sinner had been reconciled not only to God but also to other human beings. Fellowship – with people and God – had been restored.

John the Baptist described Jesus as 'the Lamb of God that takes away the sin of the world'. The sacrificial lamb, in Old Testament thought, was a means of removing people's guilt and restoring their relationships with God but the New Testament writers believed that Jesus' death rendered such sacrifices unnecessary. Animal sacrifices are still a feature of some religions: this is a sheep killed for a Moslem festival in Pakistan.

So in the Old Testament the ritual of sacrifice was a symbolic means through which a sinner could be reconciled to God. And this is what the New Testament means by describing Jesus' death as a 'sacrifice'. Indeed, the writer of Hebrews went so far as to say that there was some logical connection between the Old Testament concept and the death of Jesus. The death of Jesus was, he said, the true fulfilment of the Old Testament symbol. His death was the reality, the sacrifices the picture. In Jesus,

Christians can know that they are reconciled to God. He has suffered the ultimate alienation from God that sin brings. Now, too, as people 'made new', Christians must offer themselves to God. This is what Paul meant when he urged Christians 'to present your bodies as a living sacrifice, holy and acceptable to God'.

Romans 12:1

Jesus' death was a ransom

Mark 10:45

Jesus himself explicitly said that his intention was to be 'a ransom'. This is a figure of speech that we find much easier to understand. We all know of cases where one group of people has been kidnapped by others, and a third party has been forced to pay a ransom to have them released.

The background to this picture in the New Testament was not, of course, the hijacking of aeroplanes or the kidnapping of rich businessmen. The 'ransom' was the price paid to set a slave free. This ransom was often paid by a third party. In the Roman world, the slave and the person who was to pay the ransom went along to the shrine of their local god, and in a religious ceremony the ransom was paid to the slave's owner. Legally, this ceremony was meant to indicate that the slave had been bought by the god, and so could no longer be owned by another person.

This is certainly a very appropriate picture of Jesus' death, for a person set free by Jesus is set free really and truly to belong to God. Throughout the New Testament, it is emphasized that Christians are the property of God. They have been 'ransomed from...futile ways'. And Paul often reminds his readers: 'you are not your own; you were bought with a price, so glorify God in your body.' This then is perhaps the most comprehensive of all the pictures used in the New Testament to describe what Jesus did on the cross: he paid the price of sin.

1 Peter 1:18

1 Corinthians 6:19–20

Jesus died in our place

1 Peter 2:24

Mark 10:45

To say that Jesus died as a sacrifice, or to pay our ransom, is basically to say that he died in our place. On the cross he did something for us that we are unable to do for ourselves. In 1 Peter, for instance, we are told that Jesus 'bore our sins in his body ... that we might die to sin and live to righteousness'. And Jesus' statement that he came 'to give his life as a ransom for many' can hardly have any other meaning. But it is important to clarify what we mean by saying that Jesus suffered in our place, for it is so easy to interpret the pictorial language of the New Testament in such a way that it simply does not make sense.

Opponents of the Christian faith have often taken this picture of Jesus' death to imply that we are talking about a kind of celestial law court. In the chair is God the Father, a harsh, authoritarian figure, like Shylock in Shakespeare's *Merchant of Venice*, demanding his pound of flesh. We ought to be in the dock, and because we are alienated from God through our disobedience we deserve the death penalty. But instead Jesus is in the dock, and despite his own perfect obedience he is to become the unfortunate victim of God's harsh and unbending demand that justice

The cross was used by the Romans to execute criminals. It has become the central symbol of Christianity because Jesus was put to death on a cross. This is a reconstruction of the scene from the film *Jesus Christ Superstar*.

must be done.

If we think of the picture in this way, then it is very difficult to accept it as an adequate account of what Jesus did on the cross. Can we, for example, accept that God is less just than a human judge – and how many of us would consider justice to be satisfied if an innocent person were punished in place of a guilty one? How many of us would even say that it is always good for a repenting sinner to escape all punishment? And how can we reconcile this with the fact that God does sometimes allow us to suffer the consequences of our misdeeds – indeed, that we sometimes suffer for no apparent reason at all?

The fact is that if we think about Jesus' death in our place in the context of a law court we have missed the point of much of what Jesus was trying to say. The Jews often regarded God as a terrible and awesome figure, certainly remote from their own lives, and generally more interested in punishment than in forgiveness. But Jesus described God on more than one occasion as a loving Father who cares for every member of the human race. So, when we talk about Jesus suffering instead of us, we should be talking not in the context of a law court but in the context of a family. Jesus' suffering for our sins was not something imposed by a stern judge to fulfil the demands of justice. It was suffering in the way that a person suffers for the wrongdoing of a member of his family. God's justice in dealing with sin is not so much the justice of a judge imposing a sentence in court: it is the justice of a father who is brokenhearted and eager to restore his children to their proper place.

Even so, this picture leaves much unexplained, and the analogy is ultimately inadequate. When one person suffers for another's wrong, his suffering does not blot out or cancel that wrong. But the New Testament is insistent that Jesus' death does in a very real way cancel out sin, so that by it we can be forgiven.

Each of these five ways of talking about Jesus' death has its inadequacies, for they are all only pictures, and to most of us the cross still remains a great mystery. But, despite that, the mystery of Jesus' death and its exact significance does tell us two very important things about God and his relationship with men and women.

● For many people, one of the most pressing problems in life is the problem of evil. If God is really loving and forgiving, why is there so much evil in the world? If God is a forgiving God, we say, then surely he would arrange the universe differently so that the misdeeds of his silly creatures would not cause so much suffering to themselves and to other people. There is no easy answer to such questions. Indeed, I doubt if there is any answer at all. They are part of the frustration of a world that has been so spoiled by sin that Paul could speak of 'the whole creation ... groaning in travail' as it waits to be released from its suffering. But the cross shows us that, even if God does not remove the

Romans 8:18–25

suffering that followed human sin and is now so inherent in life, he certainly shares it with us. God was not a harsh judge passing an unreasonable sentence on the innocent Jesus. God himself was actually sharing in the cross the final and extreme consequence of our sinfulness.

● The cross shows us what God's forgiveness costs. It often costs a lot for us to forgive another person, even someone in our own family. Yet many people forget that' when they talk about God's forgiveness. The nineteenth-century German poet Heinrich Heine said as he was dying: 'God will forgive me. It's his trade.' And that absurd statement seems to sum up the attitude of many people, who take it for granted that God must automatically forgive them in the end. But forgiveness is not God's trade: it was his crucifixion. God cannot forgive arbitrarily. If he were simply to overlook evil that would deny his very nature. It costs him a lot to forgive even one sinner, and the cost of our forgiveness is seen in the cross.

All these statements are figures of speech, pictures, metaphors, analogies. From our twentieth-century perspective they may seem remote, even irrelevant. We naturally ask ourselves: Why did the first Christians come to think of Jesus' death in these terms? Why couldn't they be content to regard him as a good man dying a bad death? Why did they have to 'theologize' the whole thing, and make it so complicated?

The answer to questions like that is to be found in what they believed to have happened three days after the cross. For they were convinced that Jesus came to life again. If they had not believed that, then the cross would have meant nothing to them. But because of their belief in the resurrection and their experience of the risen Christ at work in their own lives the earliest Christians were totally convinced that Jesus really was who he had claimed to be. On the cross he had fought and won the decisive battle against evil. He had made it possible for God to pardon sinful men and women and receive them into his family. And he was offering them the possibility of a life filled with the reality of God's own presence.

But were they right? This is the crucial question for us today, and one that we must now look at in some detail.

Did the Jews condemn Jesus?

Some people have doubted whether what we have called Jesus' Jewish trial was really a trial at all. The problem is that we have no contemporary evidence about Jewish customs and practice at this time. Our only knowledge of the subject comes from the Jewish law book, the *Mishnah*, which dates in its present form from about AD 200. The *Mishnah* contains traditions that are much earlier than the time when it was written down, but it is impossible to know how far these regulations were in force at the time of Jesus.

Judged according to these later standards, we would certainly have to conclude that a trial such as that which the Gospels describe was very irregular. The leading members of the Sanhedrin were the prosecution as well as the judges, and they had already been involved in the plot to have Jesus arrested. The trial appears to have begun with no definite charges, and no evidence was called for the defence even though the prosecution witnesses contradicted each other. Moreover, two very important rules of later Jewish law were ignored completely. These laid down that twenty-four hours had to elapse between a death sentence and its execution; and that a trial should not be held on the day before the Jewish holy day, the sabbath.

Because of these irregularities most Jewish writers have insisted that there is no historical truth in the Gospel narratives at this point. But there is no convincing reason

why we should regard this trial as fiction. Though the Jews had very little real influence over their political society, we know that they were always keen to apply their own law whenever they could. This was not only a kind of psychological prop to the Jewish leaders: it was also a useful means of gaining the support of the mass of the Jewish people for their policies. A death sentence passed on Jesus under Jewish law by a religious court would certainly have influenced the ordinary people against him, and it might even have been expected to exert a certain moral pressure on the Roman judge who was to have the final word.

It is, however, not very likely that this Jewish trial was as illegal as it can be made to appear if compared with the rules of the

This slave chain dates from Roman times. One of the images used in the Gospels to explain Jesus' death is that he 'redeemed' those who were 'enslaved' to their wrong ways of living.

Mishnah. We have already seen that we cannot be sure that these rules were in operation at the time. But it is also significant that, of all the charges made by the first Christians against the Jews, they never accused them of breaking the law in order to have Jesus executed. There is also the fact that the members of the Sanhedrin were not, by and large, rogues and scoundrels. Most of them would be men of high moral ideals – people such as Paul before his conversion. Perhaps they met with their minds already made up, and to that extent were unable to give Jesus a fair trial. But they were genuinely convinced that their view of things was right, and that Jesus was nothing but a messianic pretender and a trouble-maker.

The Last Supper

All four Gospels give an account of what is generally called the 'Last Supper' of Jesus. They relate how Jesus acted as host to his disciples in a room loaned by a friend in Jerusalem, on the evening before he was crucified (Matthew 26:20–30; Mark 14:12–26; Luke 22:7–39; John 13:1–30). The first written account of this meal is contained not in the Gospels but in the writings of Paul in 1 Corinthians 11:23–26. But his account of the Last Supper agrees in its main details with the stories told in the synoptic Gospels – Matthew, Mark and Luke. John's Gospel gives a fuller account of some aspects of the meal, and includes the story – not mentioned by the other Gospel writers – of how Jesus washed his disciples' feet. At the same time, John omits to mention the central feature of the other accounts, the institution of the Lord's Supper.

At this last meal with his disciples, Jesus followed the normal Jewish custom and gave thanks to God for the meal. He then proceeded to break the bread that was on the table, and handed it to his disciples, saying, 'This is my body which is for you. Do this in remembrance of me' (1 Corinthians 11:24; compare Matthew 26:26; Mark 14:22; Luke 22:19). Then he handed them a cup of wine, telling them: 'This cup is the new covenant in my blood. Do this, as often as you drink it, in remembrance of me' (1 Corinthians 11:25; compare Matthew 26:27–28; Mark 14:24; Luke 22:20).

The new covenant

The disciples, like all other Jews, would be quite familiar with the idea of a 'covenant'. The Last Supper took place at about the same time as the Jewish people were preparing to celebrate one of their most important religious festivals, the Passover. In the Passover festival, the Jews celebrated and recalled the inauguration of God's 'covenant' with their ancestors. They remembered how, long ago, God had delivered Israel from slavery in Egypt, and in gratitude for his deliverance Israel had given her obedience and devotion to God (Exodus 12–23). Ever since that time they had regarded themselves as 'the people of the covenant'. And the 'covenant' was simply the fact that God had done something for his people, and they had responded in love and obedience.

When Jesus compared his own death to the inauguration of a 'new covenant', he was saying to his disciples that through him God was performing a new act of deliverance, and that a similar promise of loyalty and devotion would be required of those who share in its benefits. The new society makes demands of those who enjoy it, and Paul says that Christians ought to repeat this meal regularly as a constant reminder of the fact that their new life of freedom was won by Jesus on the cross. Because of that, they owe him their unfailing loyalty and obedience.

Paul, of course, was not intending to give a historical account of the Last Supper; he mentions it more or less incidentally. His main intention was to emphasize that the Lord's Supper (as it came to be called) was a continuing reminder to Christians of how much they owe to God. But in the case of the Gospel accounts of the Last Supper, the matter is much more complex. They were intending to give some sort of historical explanation of the Last Supper, and we are therefore justified in asking historical questions of them. The most important of these is the question of whether the Last Supper was a celebration of the Jewish Passover, or whether Jesus was observing some other kind of feast with his disciples.

Two main questions are involved. First: *Do Jesus' actions at the Last Supper suggest that he was observing the Passover with his disciples?*

Here we shall restrict our discussion to what Jesus and his disciples actually did. The question of what the Gospel writers *thought* he was doing is dealt with separately.

Within the Gospel stories it is possible to find arguments both for and against the idea that Jesus was observing the Jewish Passover. The following facts seem to be in favour.

● The meal of the Last Supper was eaten in Jerusalem, and not at Bethany where Jesus was staying (Mark 14:13; Luke 22:10). With growing opposition from the Jewish religious leaders, this can hardly have been a sensible time for Jesus to make unnecessary excursions into Jerusalem. But if Jesus was intending to share in the Passover Festival, he would have to do so, since the Passover feast could only be eaten within the walls of the city. This could explain the emphasis on the disciples' concern to find a room in a suitably located house (Matthew 26:17–19; Mark 14:12–16; Luke 22:7–13).

● According to John 13:23–25, Jesus and the disciples took their meal reclining on couches. This was not the invariable Jewish custom, but it was obligatory at the celebration of the Passover. The instructions for the Passover (the Passover *Haggadah*) say: 'On all other nights we eat and drink either sitting or reclining, but on this night we all recline.' The *Mishnah* adds that even the poorest person in Israel must not eat the Passover feast except while reclining (*Pes.* 10:1).

● The meal took place at night. This was also a distinctive custom associated with the Passover. The usual custom was to eat the main meal of the day in the late afternoon. But the Passover was always at night, the time when the events it commemorated had taken place.

● The dipping of pieces of food into a sauce (Mark 14:20; John 13:26) was definitely a custom used only at the Passover. The Passover *Haggadah* does not refer to bread being served in this way. But it does say: 'all other nights we do not dip ... even once, but on this night twice.'

● The disciples sang a hymn before they left the room (Mark 14:26). And the singing of the so-called 'Hallel' psalms (Psalms 113–18) was a special feature that marked the end of the Passover meal.

Despite all these similarities between the Last Supper and the Passover, however, there are other parts of the Gospel stories that suggest the Last Supper was not a Passover feast:

● It is most unlikely that Jesus would have been judged, condemned and crucified in the middle of such an important feast as the Passover. In particular, it is unlikely that a Roman governor would have been so foolish as to take the great risk involved in the public execution of a popular figure at a time when Jerusalem was crowded with pilgrims. To have done so would have defiled the day of the great festival, and could easily have sparked off a riot among the Jews.

● It would have been against Jewish Passover laws for Jesus to be tried in the middle of a festival. All forms of work were prohibited on the Passover, and this included the work of the Sanhedrin. In addition, the Jewish leaders would have risked ritual defilement by having anything to do with Pilate at this time (John 18:28). The whole business of the trials, and especially the element of urgency about them, is better explained if the Passover was about to begin than if it was already taking place.

● A number of circumstantial details do not seem to fit in with the assumption that Jesus was keeping the Passover. There is, for example, no mention of a lamb or of unleavened bread, though these were the most important items of the Passover meal. It would also be surprising to find Simon of Cyrene coming in from the fields at the height of such an important festival when work was strictly forbidden (Mark 15:21). It is also surely significant that the earliest Christians observed the Lord's Supper once a week and not annually, as we may have expected them to do had it originally been a Passover celebration. Taken by themselves small details like this would not prove very much. But when considered along with the other evidence they can be given some weight in the argument.

Faced with these apparently conflicting pieces of evidence, equally reputable scholars have made different judgements. The German theologian Joachim Jeremias, for example, has argued strongly in favour of the view that Jesus was actually keeping the

Jewish Passover. Others have argued just as strongly that Jesus was not keeping the Passover. They suggest it was a *Kiddush*, a type of feast with which pious Jews often approached the beginning of the weekly sabbath. It has also been understood as a feast of a more general nature known as a *Haburah*. Such feasts are well-known in later Judaism, and still form a part of modern Jewish observances. But we have very little evidence to show that such feasts existed at the time of Jesus, and even less to show what may have taken place at them.

So the problem remains. If we were to make a judgement solely on the basis of the evidence we have reviewed so far, the balance of the argument seems to be slightly in favour of the view that the Last Supper was not a Passover meal.

But before we claim this as the final answer to the problem, we need to ask another crucial question: *Did the Gospel writers think Jesus was observing the Passover with his disciples?*

This is the really awkward question, for the three synoptic Gospels say quite definitely that the Last Supper was a Passover meal – though, as we have seen, not every detail of their description of the meal fits in with this assumption (Matthew 26:18; Mark 14:12; Luke 22:15). On the other hand, John says equally clearly that the Last Supper was not the Passover, but took place on the day before the Jewish festival – yet here, again, not every part of his description of the supper fits in with this statement (John 13:1, 18:28).

This is one of the most difficult questions that New Testament scholars have had to try to resolve, and it is not possible to give any simple answer. There is no possibility of explaining it from the text of the Gospels themselves, for Matthew, Mark and Luke all say quite categorically that Jesus was keeping the Passover, and John says quite clearly that he was not.

Twenty years ago it would have been easy for scholars to solve the problem simply by saying that John made a mistake – and there are some scholars who still take that approach today. But they are now very much in the minority. For it is increasingly recognized that even if John's Gospel was one of the latest books of the New Testament to be written, it is by no means a later fabrication of the life and teachings of Jesus. Indeed, as we shall see in chapter 11, the accounts preserved by John are now generally believed to contain authentic, reliable and early traditions.

What, then, can we say about a problem like this? First of all it will be helpful for us to understand the precise nature of the difficulty. Jewish chronology is notoriously difficult to understand, and in this case the matter is made more complex for us by the fact that the Jewish day begins at sunset, whereas the Roman day (like our own) began at midnight. So, for example, the weekly Jewish sabbath begins at sunset on Friday evening and ends at sunset on Saturday evening. But for the sake of convenience we would normally say that Saturday is the Jewish sabbath.

Now the Gospels all agree that

This stepped road in Jerusalem dates from the century before Jesus, and leads to the garden of Gethsemane.

Jesus was crucified on a Friday afternoon, and his resurrection from the grave was discovered on the Sunday morning. In between this was the sabbath, which was always a holy day for the Jews. But on the particular week that Jesus was crucified, the Passover was also being celebrated, and this in itself was a specially holy day. Putting together this information with what we learn from the Gospels, it seems that the synoptic writers thought that the Friday was the Passover Festival, whereas John believed that the Passover fell on the sabbath in that particular year. So there is no problem with the

One of the most striking differences between the Essenes of Qumran and the Pharisees in Jerusalem, for example, was on the question of their religious calendar. The normal Jewish calendar was based on calculations related to the movements of the moon, whereas the commune at Qumran appears to have used another calendar as well, based on calculations about the movements of the sun.

The same calendar features in the Jewish *Book of Jubilees*, and according to it the Passover meal was *always* on the day that began in the Tuesday evening. If Jesus used this same calendar, then he could

	Synoptics	John
Thursday evening	Passover Last Supper Arrest	Last Supper Arrest
Friday morning afternoon evening	Trials and crucifixion Beginning of sabbath	Trials and crucifixion Beginning of sabbath and Passover
Saturday	Sabbath	Sabbath and Passover
Sunday	Resurrection	Resurrection

statements made about Jesus himself. The difficulty is concerned with the chronology of the Jewish religious festivals.

We must beware of giving too easy an answer to this question. There is no answer that could claim to be the generally accepted consensus of opinion. But a number of scholars have recently tried to explain the awkward distinction between John and the synoptics by supposing that the two traditions were using different calendars, and that what was in one calendar the day of the Passover would be another day in a different calendar.

Nowadays we would find it impossible to believe that there could be different opinions about something as basic as the date. But in the context of first-century Judaism this is not such a far-fetched explanation as it sounds. The Jews were constantly speculating on calendrical calculations, and their differing outlooks on the matter are to a large extent reflected in the existence of the various sectarian movements within first-century Judaism.

have celebrated a real Passover with his disciples on the *Tuesday* evening, but still have been crucified as the official Passover was about to begin on the Friday evening. This is the ingenious solution proposed by the French scholar Annie Jaubert. But it still leaves unanswered a number of vital questions:

● We have no reason to suppose that Jesus did in fact use anything other than the official calendar. He appears to have moved in the mainstream of Judaism rather than in any sectarian movements, and is often depicted taking part in the worship of the synagogue. If, as John suggests, he had often attended the great Jewish religious festivals in Jerusalem, it would be more natural to suppose that he kept the same calendar as the Jerusalem authorities – otherwise he would not have attended the festivals at the right times (John 7:1–39). What is more, Jesus often appears to have been in conflict with the Pharisees about the observance of religious festivals like the sabbath. He was often accused of doing things that were not allowed on the sabbath. Yet he never claimed that he did them because he used a different calendar. He explained his actions by reference to the fact that he believed himself to be 'lord even of the sabbath' (Mark 2:28).

● The Passover lambs had to be ritually slaughtered in the temple, and this would obviously be done according to the official calendar. It is therefore difficult to see how the disciples could have had a lamb available in Jerusalem on the Tuesday evening – yet without the lamb, there could be no Passover meal.

● This alternative calendar would mean that Jesus was held in custody for two days before his crucifixion. It is difficult to reconcile this with the unanimous testimony of all four Gospels that the trials took place in a hurry so that Jesus could be condemned and executed before the beginning of the Jewish sabbath.

It therefore seems to me that this theory rests on rather shaky foundations. It may well be, of course, that new evidence to strengthen it could be discovered in the Qumran texts or elsewhere. But in the present state of our knowledge it is difficult to accept this explanation of the difference between the synoptic Gospels and John.

It is more likely that John's Gospel was written from the perspective of the Jews of Palestine, and that they celebrated the Passover on the sabbath in the year in question. Mark, however, followed by Matthew and Luke, was following the customs of the Jews of the Dispersion, and on their reckoning the Passover was held on the Friday in the year that Jesus died.

Many more speculative theories have been advanced on the matter, and it could be that the wisest answer to the problem is that given by the Australian scholar Dr Leon Morris, who writes: 'I do not see how with our present knowledge we can be dogmatic. But on the whole it seems most probable that the explanation is to be found in calendrical confusion.'

Of course, we must not allow this one detail to hide the fact that all four Gospels are in complete agreement on everything else. Nor must we conclude that because we

know of no answer at present, that means there is no answer. But if an explanation lies in the speculations of the Jewish leaders about their calendar, it will be a long and tedious process before a widely acceptable answer is found.

In any case, we will never find a full explanation of the Last Supper if we only ask what sort of Jewish feast Jesus was keeping. What Jesus was doing at the Last Supper fits in with many Jewish customs. We would expect that anyway, since he and his disciples were Jews. But the precise nature of what he was doing cannot be fitted exactly into any specific occasion in the Jewish religious calendar. It seems unlikely, for the reasons already given, that the disciples were celebrating the Jewish Passover. But at the same time it seems obvious that their Last Supper with Jesus followed fairly closely the formal setting of the Passover meal.

Perhaps we ought to leave a little more room for the creative originality of Jesus himself than most scholars are prepared to do. In the nature of the case the Passover lamb was absent, but in this supper that was of little importance. Jesus knew that God was already providing a lamb, and he was here offering himself in symbol to his disciples as 'the Lamb of God who takes away the sin of the world' (John 1:29). The lamb of God was Jesus himself, and he knew that he was to be crucified for the sin of the world. It was no coincidence that he was crucified at the very same time as the symbols of God's past deliverance were being sacrificed in the temple courts.

But what Jesus did on the cross was not merely a re-interpretation of an ancient ritual. God was about to do something quite different and revolutionary, that would both sum up and supersede the events associated with the first Passover. The new society was being inaugurated and in the Last Supper, surrounded by the nucleus of this society, Jesus was symbolically offering himself for their freedom in the bread and the wine. And so these things became within the church the external symbols of that deliverance from sin and its consequences which Jesus' death as God's chosen Son was to accomplish.

Chapter 5 The resurrection

Jesus prayed in the garden of Gethsemane shortly before his arrest.

All the New Testament writers agree that Jesus was raised to life on the third day after his death. Our reaction to this claim will of course depend to a large extent on our basic presuppositions about the supernatural. If we believe that such things as the renewal of a dead person are impossible, we will have to find some other explanation for what the first Christians thought was the resurrection of Jesus. If we are willing to accept the possibility of supernatural occurrences, we will think it worthwhile to examine critically some of the claims of the New Testament.

In this book we have taken the statements made in the documents as they stand; we have taken belief in the supernatural as a viable option. This does not of course mean that we necessarily assume that everything claimed about Jesus can simply be accepted by reference to our presuppositions. But it does mean that we can examine the evidence without any fear of being embarrassed by the results of our investigation – whatever those results may turn out to be.

In the case of the resurrection, the most striking thing about it is that the earliest Christians were completely convinced that the resurrection event, or complex of events, was a real, historical happening that had taken place in their own world, and which had made a profound influence on their own lives. We have already seen that it is not easy to know just how widespread was belief in the virgin birth of Jesus. We do not know, for instance, what Paul knew about it. We certainly do know that neither he nor anyone else ever claimed that belief in the virgin birth was an indispensable part of being a Christian.

But the resurrection was a different matter altogether. Paul spoke for the whole of the early church when he declared that if the reality of Jesus' resurrection was denied the Christian faith would be emptied of its meaning: 'If Christ has not been raised, 1 Corinthians 15:17 your faith is futile and you are still in your sins.' Because of this conviction, Paul goes on in the same passage to give a list of witnesses who could verify that Jesus had come to life again. He obviously thought of the resurrection event as something that could be attested by witnesses – an outward, public happening rather than a private religious experience. Yet it is very striking that the New Testament nowhere provides witnesses to the actual act of rising again, only to the results of that act in the appearances of the risen Jesus, and the fact that his tomb was found empty.

The evidence itself can be arranged in four parts.

The belief of the early church

The earliest evidence we have for the resurrection almost certainly goes back to the time immediately after the resurrection event is alleged to have taken place. This is the evidence contained in the early sermons in the Acts of the Apostles. Of course, these are now contained in a document that was compiled in its present form at least thirty years after the death of Jesus, and perhaps as much as fifty years later. But there can be no doubt that in the first few chapters of Acts its author has preserved material from very early sources.

Scholars have discovered that the language used in speaking about Jesus in these early speeches in Acts is quite different from that used at the time when the book was compiled in its final form. It is also quite different from even the letters of Paul, which were certainly written long before the book of Acts. So we may be reasonably certain that here we have very early sources.

The early speeches show a largely Jewish type of Christianity, holding a set of simply expressed beliefs about Jesus, and providing a generally accurate picture of what really happened in the first days of the church. According to this picture, the central feature of the message of the early Christian church was the story of Jesus himself – how he had come to fulfil God's promises, how he had died on the cross, and how he had come back to life again. The message of the first Christians was so consistent that Professor C.H. Dodd was able to find a regular pattern of statements that were made about Jesus from the very earliest times. He called this pattern of statements the *kerygma*, a Greek word meaning 'the declaration'. Every authentic account of the Christian message contained these statements:

- Jesus has fulfilled the Old Testament promises.
- God was at work in his life, death and resurrection.
- Jesus has now been exalted to heaven.
- The Holy Spirit has been given to the church.
- Jesus will soon return in glory.
- Men and women who hear the message must respond to its challenge.

If we removed the resurrection from this *kerygma*, most of it would no longer make sense. The whole existence of the early church was based on the belief that Jesus was no longer dead, but was alive.

It also seems likely from the evidence in Paul's letters as well as from Acts, that the recognized qualification for an apostolic preacher was that he had seen the risen Jesus. This was explicitly

Acts 1:21–22

Galatians 1:11–17

made a condition when the apostles came to appoint a successor to Judas Iscariot, and Paul also claimed that his own vision of Jesus on the road to Damascus gave him the same status as that of the older apostles.

The evidence of Paul

1 Corinthians 15

The second main piece of evidence for the resurrection of Jesus is given to us by Paul himself. If there is room for differing opinions on the importance of the evidence of Acts, there is no such room in the case of Paul's evidence. He was certainly writing his letter no more than twenty-five years after Jesus was crucified, and his statements may well form the earliest piece of evidence for belief that Jesus had risen again. If we read 1 Corinthians 15, and look at its context, we see that Paul's main intention there was not to give a reasoned argument for believing in the resurrection of Jesus. He was in fact trying to help his Christian readers to overcome a specific set of problems that had arisen in their local church. The information he gives us about how Jesus rose from the dead is more or less accidental. This makes it all the more impressive, for he reminds the Corinthians that what he says is something they have always known. And even though he does so in just a few sentences, he shows that at a very early date Christians, even in Greece, were quite familiar with the full story of how Jesus had died and come back to life again.

In this account Paul refers to an occasion when the risen Jesus was seen by more than 500 disciples at one time, most of whom were still alive when he wrote and could confirm what he said.

1 Corinthians 15:6

1 Corinthians 15:7–8

He also mentions an appearance to James, the brother of Jesus, and includes his own conversion encounter with the risen Lord among these resurrection appearances. The Gospels say nothing about any of these appearances of the risen Jesus. Yet they were probably written later than Paul's letter to Corinth! The fact of Jesus' resurrection must have been considered to be so widely believed that the people who wrote the Gospel stories did not

Paul wrote to the Christians at Corinth about twenty-five years after Jesus' death, explaining the significance of the resurrection.

even think it important to marshal *all* the evidence for it. As with the rest of the narratives, they used only a small selection of the material that was at their disposal.

The Gospel traditions

When we think of the resurrection, we naturally think first of the stories found at the end of each of the four Gospels. There are certain distinctive features about these stories.

● They all emphasize two main facts: that the grave of Jesus was found empty, and that the risen Jesus was seen by different people on several different occasions. Both these pieces of evidence are important. By itself, the fact of the empty grave would prove nothing except that Jesus' body was not there. Without the empty grave, the visions would prove nothing objective, though they might tell us something about the psychology of the disciples. But the combination of the two facts, if they are indeed correct, would be strong evidence in support of the claim that Jesus was alive.

● If we read right through the Gospels, we notice that by comparison with many of the other stories about Jesus, the stories about his resurrection are told very simply. They contain no symbolism requiring special insight to understand. There are no allusions to the Old Testament. Nor do they make any attempt to bring out the theological significance of the events they describe. If we compare them in this respect with, say, the accounts of how Jesus was baptized, the contrast is very marked indeed.

Why do the accounts differ?

Despite the fact that the information given in the Gospels is told in a simple way, the Gospel accounts are not easy to reconcile with one another. Though many people have tried, no one has really been successful in producing an 'agreed version' of how it all happened. It is unlikely that anyone ever will. Throughout their work, the Gospel writers were selective. They used only those stories and teachings of Jesus that would be helpful to their first readers. That is one of the reasons why we have four different Gospels. This process of selection was clearly applied to the resurrection stories, as we can see from the fact that Paul had some pieces of information not mentioned by any of the Gospels.

At first sight, this may appear to be an argument against the resurrection having happened at all. But in fact it is a strong argument on the other side. Eye witnesses often give very different accounts of what they have seen, especially when they see things that do not fit in with their concept of life. The disciples themselves no more expected a dead person to come to life again than you or I would. According to Mark 9:9–10 they had no idea what 'resurrection' could possibly mean: it was something quite alien to their way of thinking. So we need not be surprised that the disciples did not tell a logical and coherent story. The story of someone rising from the dead would be much more difficult to believe if all four Gospels had given exactly the same account. Yet despite minor discrepancies in detail, all our accounts are agreed on the main parts of the story. In all of them the tomb is empty and Jesus appears to the disciples.

In Mark, the earliest Gospel, the account ends at 16:8, and what follows in some English versions as 16:9–20 is generally considered to be a later addition to an originally mutilated or unfinished book. In this account, we are told that some women who came to the grave on the Sunday morning to finish the process of embalming Jesus' body found that the stone slab used as a door to the rock tomb had been rolled back. They were terrified by the sight of a young man in white sitting inside. This 'young man' said, 'Do not be amazed; you seek Jesus of Nazareth, who was crucified. He has risen, he is not here; see the place where they laid him. But go, tell his disciples and Peter that he is going before you to Galilee; there you will see him, as he told you' (Mark 16:6–7). The women ran terrified from the graveyard, and because of their fear

After his crucifixion, Jesus was placed in a tomb carved from the solid rock. Tombs of this kind often had a heavy stone which could be rolled across the entrance.

they told no one of what they had seen and heard.

In Luke, two disciples walking home to the village of Emmaus met the risen Jesus without recognizing him. They spoke of women visiting the grave and seeing a vision of angels who assured them that Jesus was alive (Luke 24:22–24). No reference is made there to the message about Galilee. Perhaps the women did not deliver the message about Galilee for the simple reason stated by Mark: they were afraid to go back there, for they thought that the king of that area, Herod Antipas, would now be ready to get rid of any of Jesus' followers who

were found there.

Matthew repeats Mark's account with some additional details, such as the great earthquake on the Sunday morning, and the terror of the guards at the graveyard (Matthew 28:1–4). The women left the grave in a mixed mood of fear and joy, and they were met by Jesus himself, who repeated the message about going to Galilee (Matthew 28:5–10). According to Matthew, the disciples appear to have obeyed this instruction at once, and on a mountain in Galilee Jesus gave them the commission to preach the gospel to all nations and to make them his disciples (Matthew 28:16–20). This appearance of Jesus does not seem to be the same as the ascension story told by Luke. Though Jesus made some similar statements, the ascension took place not in Galilee but in or near Jerusalem (Luke 24:44–53, Acts 1:6–11). Matthew brings the story begun by Mark to its logical conclusion: Jesus' appearance in Galilee and commission to the disciples to proclaim the good news about him.

Luke's story has certain differences from Mark's: there were two angels in the tomb, and Galilee is mentioned, not as the place where Jesus would meet the disciples later, but as the place where he had originally foretold his death and resurrection (Luke 24:1–11). When the women told the disciples their story, it was not believed. In some old manuscripts of Luke, there is at this point a story of how Peter and John visited the tomb to confirm what the women reported. But this is probably only a later effort to harmonize Luke's story with the incident recorded in John 20:1–10. After telling of how Jesus met the two disciples on the road to Emmaus, and then all the disciples in a room in Jerusalem (Luke 24:13–43), Luke goes on to record the ascension on the road to Bethany, as if it followed immediately after the resurrection (Luke 24:44–53). But in Acts he makes it clear that the ascension took place after an interval of forty days (Acts 1:3). He does not mention an appearance in Galilee.

John's Gospel, on the other hand, describes appearances of Jesus both in Jerusalem and in Galilee. Of the women described in the other Gospels as having discovered the empty grave, only Mary Magdalene is mentioned in John (20:1). But the fact that she uses the plural pronoun 'we' in describing the event to Peter suggests that others may have been with her (John 20:2). They found the tomb empty and returned to tell the disciples. Peter and John then went to the tomb and found the grave clothes lying undisturbed – proof that the tomb had not been robbed (John 20:3–10). At this point Mary saw two angels in the tomb and was greeted by Jesus, whom she mistook for the gardener (John 20:11–18). An account follows of two appearances to the disciples in Jerusalem. During the first of these appearances Jesus breathed on them and gave them the Holy Spirit (John 20:19–29). The last chapter of John, which many scholars regard as a later addition, though by the same author, describes Jesus' appearance to the disciples on the shore of Lake Galilee and how he had breakfast with them before re-commissioning Peter.

The disciples

The fourth, and final piece of evidence for the resurrection event is the indisputable fact that a thoroughly disheartened band of disciples, who should by all the rules of historical probability have been depressed and disillusioned by their master's crucifixion, were in the space of seven weeks transformed into a strong band of courageous witnesses, and the nucleus of a constantly growing church. The central fact of their witness was that Jesus was alive and active, and they had no hesitation in attributing the change in themselves to what had happened as a result of his rising from the dead. They themselves were obviously convinced that this was what had actually happened. For the resurrection was not just something they talked about: it was something they were willing to die for. And men and women are not prepared to die for something unless they are totally convinced of its truth.

Facts and faith about the resurrection

So much, then, for the evidence. What are we to make of it? To understand its importance, we must remember three things.

● There is no evidence that the risen Jesus appeared to anyone apart from his own followers, though it is possible that he may have done so. Those who wrote the Gospels were writing for a specific readership – in every case a Christian readership. Their first interest was in what happened when Christians met their risen Lord.

● Evidence about somebody who appeared and disappeared in a room with closed doors is obviously not the kind of evidence that historians are used to dealing with, and it does not fit into the ordinary rules of evidence.

● The fact that Mary Magdalene, the two disciples on the road to Emmaus, and the disciples in the boat on Lake Galilee failed to recognize Jesus, though they knew him well and had seen him only a few days before, suggests that his physical appearance must have changed in a way that would certainly be confusing to any ordinary witness in giving evidence.

What, then, has our examination of the evidence established? We can say with absolute certainty that the earliest church believed that Jesus had come back to life again. The disciples and their followers knew that something had happened to change their lives after the crucifixion of their master, and they explained this change by the fact that he had risen from the dead. Every reader of the New Testament must accept this, for the fact of the change in the disciples' lives is established beyond all reasonable doubt. But to speak of the 'resurrection faith' is one thing; to speak of a 'resurrection fact' is quite another. The relationship of facts to faith is discussed more fully in chapter 12. Here we need only note that there must have been *something* we can call 'the resurrection fact' that created the disciples' 'resurrection faith'. But what was this? Several possible explanations spring to mind.

The Mount of Olives overlooked the city of Jerusalem. It was the site of Jesus' last resurrection appearance, his ascension.

The 'resurrection fact' was a subjective experience

Our natural reaction to the evidence about the resurrection is to suppose that the so-called 'resurrection appearances' were purely subjective. The pious might call them visions; psychologists would be more inclined to call them hallucinations. If we could assume that this is what happened, it would solve the problem.

But there are many facts against such an explanation.

● The fact that the tomb was empty, and that neither friend nor enemy produced the body of Jesus is so strongly emphasized in the Gospels that it must be accounted for. The Jews and Romans obviously had a vested interest in producing a body, for that would have squashed the Christian message once and for all. So presumably they had not taken it. The disciples, on the other hand, were prepared to stake their lives on the fact that Jesus was alive – and it would have been psychologically impossible for them to do that if they had themselves taken the body away and buried it somewhere else.

● Although an individual experience like that of Peter or James might reasonably be regarded as subjective, and an appearance to a crowd of 500 might sound like a mass hallucination, an encounter such as that on the road to Emmaus, with the absence of excitement and the gradual recognition of the stranger by two people, has all the marks of an authentic account. The statements that the risen body could be touched, that the risen Jesus ate food with his disciples, and that he breathed on them, show that the disciples were convinced that they were in contact with a real physical body and not a vision.

● Unlike the other disciples, Paul was what we might call psychically experienced. He writes of having had visions and revelations of an ecstatic nature on several occasions. But he placed his Damascus road experience in a different category altogether. It was quite distinctive, to be compared only with the appearances of the risen Jesus to the other disciples. Encounters with the risen Jesus were apparently a unique kind of experience – neither purely subjective like dreams, nor purely objective like the facts observed by scientists, but with some of the characteristics of both.

1 Corinthians 14:18;
2 Corinthians 12:1–4

The 'resurrection fact' was a theological invention

It has been argued that the 'resurrection faith' arose because the disciples saw some theological reason that required it. Because they believed Jesus to be God's Messiah it would be natural for someone who claimed this position to rise from the dead. But this explanation cannot be accepted either.

● For one thing, we have no evidence from any source at all to suggest that the Messiah was expected to rise from the dead. The Jews expected the Messiah to kill other people! If he suffered and died himself, then he was not the kind of Messiah most Jews wanted to know about.

● The Old Testament expresses a very negative attitude to the idea of resurrection, and many Jews simply did not believe it was possible. The disciples themselves appear not to have known what it was earlier in the ministry of Jesus.

Mark 9:9–10

● It is also difficult to see how the idea of resurrection can have come from an interpretation of Old Testament expectations, since the resurrection stories are completely lacking in Old Testament quotations. In this respect there is a sharp contrast with

Disheartened and upset by Jesus' sudden trial and execution, some of his closest followers went back to Galilee, and returned to their old job of fishing. They used nets cast from a boat; here a modern Galilean fisherman draws in the nets he has thrown from the shore.

the stories of the crucifixion, which are full of such quotations.

Many other more fanciful suggestions have been made from time to time to account for the 'resurrection fact'. But the overwhelming weight of all the evidence suggests that, however it might be described in scientific language, the 'resurrection fact' was a real, historical event. No other hypothesis gives an adequate account of *all* the evidence.

What does the resurrection mean?

To talk of describing the 'resurrection fact' in scientific language takes us beyond the categories of thought of the first disciples. One of the most striking things about the evidence of the New Testament is that the disciples had no interest at all in probing the whys and wherefores of the 'resurrection fact'. They knew that it was a real fact, because of their own experience of Jesus Christ and the evidence of the empty tomb – and that was all they needed to know. So we have no description in any of our records of *how* the resurrection actually took place. Some Christians in the second century regarded this as a deficiency in the

New Testament, and produced their own vivid descriptions of what the body of Jesus looked like, how it came out of the grave, and how those who saw it were affected.

But for the first witnesses such details were not the main focus of interest. For them, the resurrection was not just a happy ending to the story of Jesus. It was the natural climax of the whole of his life, and the vindication of the high claims he had made for himself during his ministry. It was also a guarantee that the life and teaching of Jesus was not just an interesting chapter in the history of human thought, but was the way through which men and women could come to know God. This is why the fact that Jesus was alive became the central part of the message the disciples declared throughout the known world.

But why was it so very important? Why did Paul claim that without the resurrection of Jesus the whole of the Christian message would be meaningless?

The best way to answer this question is to put it the other way round. Rather than asking negatively what would be lost if the resurrection could be disproved, we should ask what positive place the resurrection held in the beliefs of the first Christians. When we ask this, we find that three things are said about the meaning of the resurrection in the New Testament.

● By the resurrection, Jesus' claims to be the Son of God were shown to be true. Peter said on the Day of Pentecost that the resurrection was a clear proof that 'God has made this Jesus, whom you crucified, both Lord and Messiah'. Paul wrote to the Christians of Rome that Jesus was 'declared Son of God by a mighty act in that he rose from the dead'. In spite of Jesus' sinlessness, in spite of the authority he displayed in his teaching and actions, and in spite of his miracles and clearly expressed claims about his central role in God's plan, if it had not been for the resurrection he might have been thought of simply as a great and good man. But after he had risen from the grave, his followers knew for certain that he was who he had claimed to be. They could now see and appreciate his whole life on earth in a new and fuller way, as the life of God himself living among men and women.

Acts 2:36

Romans 1:4

John's Gospel records that when the fishermen came ashore, Jesus had a fire burning over which they cooked some fish for breakfast.

● But the resurrection was more than just a new light on the crucified Jesus. It is emphasized throughout the New Testament, and especially by Paul, that the resurrection, as well as the cross, was an indispensable part of God's action in bringing in the new society.

The first Christians were practical people before they were theologians. What they wanted was something that would work in real life. They were longing for a relationship with God in which their whole existence would be revolutionized. They wanted to be reconciled with God, and delivered from their self-centredness so that they could be better people. And they realized that they could not achieve this either by religious observance or by their own efforts at self-improvement. The only thing that can truly transform the human personality is a new centre and a new life-force.

Paul found this new life-force in Jesus – the Jesus who had risen from the dead, was alive in the real world and living dynamically in Paul's own life. This was such a striking reality in his everyday life that Paul could even say, 'It is no longer I who live, but Christ who lives in me'. This was not just pious religiosity. Paul really meant what he said: Jesus was now living in him in the most literal sense. So much so that even the details of Paul's life were directed not by him but by his living Lord.

Galatians 2:20

In trying to express what he meant, Paul used a picture in which he compared the baptism of Christians with the death and resurrection of Jesus. He said that when Christians are

Romans 6:1–11

covered with water at their baptism, and subsequently emerge from the water, this is a physical picture of something that should happen to them inwardly and spiritually. Being drenched with water is like being buried (as Jesus was). Coming out of the water is like being raised again (as Jesus was). And the essence of Paul's understanding of these events was that to become a Christian a person must first be willing to 'die', to get rid of their old self-centred existence. Then they can be 'raised' again and receive a new existence, the life of Jesus Christ himself living within them.

So the resurrection of Jesus was crucial. If Jesus had only died on the cross, he might well have done all the things the theologians claimed. He might well have died as a punishment for sin, or to pay the ransom for our freedom. But in that case his suffering would have no power to affect our lives. Paul was quite sure that without the resurrection, the cross would have been nothing more than an interesting theological talking-point. It would have been powerless to have any lasting effect on the lives of ordinary people. But because of the resurrection, Paul had discovered Philippians 1:21 a new life: 'For to me, life is Christ.' And he was confident that this was to be the normal experience of everyone who was a Christian: Jesus Christ actually living in those who commit themselves to him.

● But the resurrection of Jesus has a further implication for those who already have Christ's life within them. An important part of Jesus' teaching was that his followers would share in John 3:15, 4:14, 17:3 'eternal life'. This 'eternal life' includes two things. On the one hand, the phrase indicates that Christians are to enjoy a new quality of life. 'Eternal life' is God's life. And when Paul wrote of his own Christian experience as an experience of Christ living within him, he was faithfully interpreting the teaching of Jesus himself.

But to have the kind of life that God has does not just mean that Christians have a new dynamic for life in this world. It also means that Christians have a life that will never end. This is another part of Jesus' teaching that is reinforced and emphasized by Paul when 1 Corinthians 15:20 he says that the resurrected Jesus is 'the first fruits of those who have fallen asleep'. By this he means that the rising again of Jesus is a pledge and a promise that his followers, too, will survive death. Those people who share in Christ's sufferings and resurrection in a spiritual sense have the assurance of a life beyond the grave which, like their present life, will be dominated by the presence of God. But it will also be distinctive and new, for Christians can expect to share the full reality of the kind of life that Jesus now has – a life in which death and sin are for ever destroyed, and replaced by the victory which God has given them 'through our 1 Corinthians 15:57 Lord Jesus Christ'.

And in order-to understand the full implications of that, we must now consider Jesus' teaching about the nature of God's new society, 'the kingdom of God'.

3. The kingdom is here

Chapter 6

What is God's kingdom?

So far we have talked of Jesus' coming in terms of a new society that the people of his day were expecting to arrive. They anticipated it as a time when the promises of the Old Testament concerning the place of Israel in God's plan would be fulfilled in a dramatic way, and the hated Romans would once and for all be driven out of their land.

It is no wonder, then, that when Jesus emerged as a travelling prophet after his baptism and the temptations, and declared that

Mark 1:15 'the time is fulfilled and the kingdom of God is at hand', people of all kinds showed great interest in what he had to say. This was what they were waiting for. A new kingdom of God that would finally crush the old kingdom of Rome. And they fully expected that they, the Jewish people, would have a prominent part in this coming kingdom under the leadership of their Messiah.

The kingdom of God

But what did Jesus mean when he spoke about 'the kingdom of God'? What would we mean by such a phrase? My dictionary defines a 'kingdom' as 'the state or territory ruled by a king'. Perhaps then Jesus' contemporaries weren't so far wrong after all: God was going to set up a new state and rule it himself.

Or was he? Is that what Jesus really meant? Did he talk about a new state – or a new society? The difference is quite obvious. If Jesus was talking about a new state he must have seen himself as the agent of a new political dynasty, a Zealot. If he was talking about a new society, then he must have regarded his work as being concerned chiefly with the quality of life that his people enjoyed. A new state would simply replace the old authoritarianism with a new one. A new society would give to people a new and fresh reality of freedom, justice and the presence of God in their lives.

So what was Jesus really talking about? Many Christians have thought that he was mainly concerned with starting a society that was to be ruled by God, as distinct from political states that are ruled by men and women. Many theologians of the Middle Ages, for example, followed St Augustine in thinking that the kingdom of God Jesus was talking about was the organized society we call

Jesus taught that the kingdom of God was radically different from other ways of life. This girl, tattooed as a child in a cruel ceremony, has since become a follower of Jesus.

the church. Even in our own day, Christian preachers often speak as if 'the kingdom' is just another word for 'the church', and others talk of the kingdom of God as if it is a new kind of political manifesto. But it is now widely recognized by those who study the New Testament that, whatever Jesus meant by his term 'the kingdom of God', it was not any of these things.

Kingdom and new society

One clue to what Jesus really meant can be found in the language that he spoke. Although Jesus may well have been able to speak two or three languages, it is likely that most of his teaching was given in Aramaic, the language that most people in Palestine knew best. The Gospels were written in Greek, of course, like the rest of the New Testament, and we therefore have no direct record of the actual Aramaic words used by Jesus. But even the Greek word that is translated into English as 'kingdom' (*basileia*), more often means the activity of a king rather than the territory he rules. And the Aramaic word which most scholars think Jesus himself used (*malkutha*) certainly has that meaning. So we are justified in supposing that Jesus was talking about what we might call 'the kingship of God', rather than his 'kingdom'. That is why we have thought of his message here in terms of 'the new society'. For Jesus was concerned more than anything else about the quality of human life, and the relationship of men and women with God and with each other.

This helps to explain some of the more difficult things that Jesus said. For example, he told the Pharisees, 'The kingdom of God does not come in such a way as to be seen ... because the kingdom of God is within you'. On another occasion he told his disciples, 'Whoever does not receive the kingdom of God like a child shall not enter it'. It is obvious that a political territory could hardly exist in the lives of individual people. They could not 'receive' a state, nor could it be 'within them'. But Jesus was saying that from the moment God is in charge of someone's life, the new society has really arrived. He could say that God's society was 'among' his hearers, because he himself was there – and God was in complete control of his life.

Professor W.G. Kümmel helpfully draws attention to the way Jesus says that 'entering the kingdom' means 'entering into life'. Those people who 'inherit the kingdom' also 'inherit eternal life', and the gate leading to the kingdom is 'the way that leads to life'. The well-known story of the son who ran away from home also emphasizes the fact that to be a member of the kingdom is to share in God's life, and to know him as Father. In the same way, Paul reminded his Christian readers in Corinth that 'the kingdom of God does not consist in talk but in power' – the power of God at work in the lives of men and women whose only allegiance is to him. God's new society is already present in the lives of those who have committed themselves to God's direction.

At the same time, we would be wrong to place all the emphasis on the new society as part of an individual relationship between ourselves and God. There are many statements in the Gospels which show that Jesus regarded the kingdom of God as a tangible, real society as well as the inward rule of God in the lives of his followers. For example, he said that people will 'come from east and west, and from north and south, and sit at table in the kingdom of God'. At the Last Supper Jesus told his disciples: 'From now on I shall not drink of the fruit of the vine until the kingdom of God comes'. And Matthew records him saying that his followers will 'inherit the kingdom prepared ... from the foundation of the world'.

It therefore seems that Jesus understood the new society in two ways. On the one hand it is God's rule over the lives of men and women who commit themselves to him. On the other hand God's rule is something that can and will be demonstrated to the world at large.

Both of these concepts were a true reflection of the expectations of the Old Testament. It is important to remember that not all the Old Testament writers had seen God's future intervention in human affairs in the self-centred, nationalistic terms that some of Jesus' contemporaries did. It is true that in parts of the Old Testament we find an overwhelming consciousness that

Luke 17:20–21

Mark 10:15

Mark 9:43–47
Matthew 25:34–46;
Mark 10:17–23
Matthew 7:14

Luke 15:11–32

1 Corinthians 4:20

Luke 13:29

Luke 22:18

Matthew 25:34

God's sovereignty over men and women would be displayed in the form of an organized kingdom that would replace the empires of the world.

This is, especially, the outlook of the apocalyptic sections of the Old Testament. In Daniel, for example, 'the saints of the most high', represented by 'a figure like the Son of Man', receive the kingdom of God and possess it for ever. This kind of expectation was heightened and magnified a thousand times by other, later apocalyptic writers, some of them contemporaries of Jesus. It was an outlook expressed by some of Jesus' followers when they wanted to make him their king after the miraculous feeding of the 5,000. And it was an attitude that was found even among the disciples. When James and John tried to claim the chief places on either side of Jesus' throne they were obviously thinking in crude political terms.

Though Jesus rebuked them on that occasion, he never denied that God's kingdom would in some way affect society in a political sense. He sometimes suggested that it would do so in relatively undramatic ways – as yeast makes bread rise, or as a mustard seed quietly grows into a large tree. But he was also quite convinced that God would act decisively and directly, not just in the lives of individuals, but also in the political and economic life of nations.

This tension, or paradox, between the rule of God's new society in the lives of individuals and the outward expression of it in tangible political forces had existed in Old Testament days. God had been regarded as Israel's 'king' right from the time of the Judges, and perhaps even before that. The psalms are full of expressions that emphasize God's sovereignty over the course of history.

Daniel 7:13–18

John 6:15

Mark 10:35–45

Matthew 13:33
Matthew 13:31–32

Mark 13

Judges 8:22–23

Psalms 96:10, 99:1, 146:10

Many people believed that the kingdom of God would consist of a specific territory and political organization. But Jesus taught that it would transcend geographical and cultural boundaries.

At the time of Jesus, many of the rabbis were emphasizing that God's kingship over Israel was already in existence, even under the Roman rule, and that it operated through the Torah or Law. The rabbis sometimes referred to people 'taking upon themselves the kingdom of God', and by this they meant accepting and obeying the Torah as the instrument of God's rule over his people.

If we look carefully at other parts of the New Testament we can see that this tension between what God can do now in those who accept his rule over their lives, and what he will ultimately do through them in society at large, is always present. Paul, for example, says that 'the kingdom of God is not concerned with material things like food and drink, but with goodness and peace and joy in the Holy Spirit.' And since these are things that Christians already have, to be a part of God's kingdom must mean allowing God to exercise his ultimate sovereignty over our lives.

Romans 14:17

Yet, at the same time, Paul elsewhere connects the arrival of God's kingdom with the events surrounding the end of the world: 'The end comes when Jesus delivers the kingdom to God the Father after destroying every other rule and authority and power.' He clearly expected that God would break into history and alter its course – and this was to be in some way connected with the coming of God's new society, 'the kingdom'. This is made quite explicit in the book of Revelation, where 'The kingdom of the world has become the kingdom of our Lord and of his Christ, and he shall reign for ever and ever'. It is also an important element of the teaching of Jesus himself.

1 Corinthians 15:24

Revelation 11:15

'Eschatology' and the new society

This whole question of the different things we mean when we speak of God's new society is called 'eschatology'. The actual word 'eschatology' comes from some Greek words which mean 'ideas about the end'. But eschatology is not just concerned with what may happen at the end of the world. It is essentially concerned with God's kingship, and with all the different ways that God's new society makes itself felt, whether in the lives of individual people, or in society, or in the final winding up of things.

In the last seventy years or so, three main suggestions have been made about the real meaning of Jesus' teaching about the new society, or 'kingdom of God'.

'Futurist eschatology'

The first of these views Jesus' teaching as part of a 'futurist eschatology'. When we use the word 'futurist' here, we mean in the future from Jesus' point of view, and not from the standpoint of the present day. There are many Christians today who have a 'futurist eschatology' in the sense that they expect God's kingdom to come in a tangible form at a time that is still in the future. They usually identify the coming of God's kingdom in this way with the second coming (or *parousia*) of Jesus himself. But when scholars talk of the Gospel traditions, they reserve the term 'futurist' for Jesus' own expectations about the new society, and not the expectations of modern Christians.

It was Albert Schweitzer, the German theologian who became a medical missionary in Africa, who first popularized the idea that Jesus had a futurist eschatology. He meant that Jesus held the same expectations as many Jewish apocalyptic writers of his day. He suggested that Jesus believed God was about to intervene immediately and dramatically in the affairs of humanity, and that his own life's work was to be the decisive climax of history – a climax that would therefore come within Jesus' own lifetime. This, said Schweitzer, is what Jesus meant

Albert Schweitzer was a doctor in Africa. His ideas about the kingdom have been widely influential.

and a cry of despair from the cross, as Jesus realized that the God he served had abandoned him. As Schweitzer put it: 'The wheel of fate would not turn, so Jesus flung himself upon it and is left there hanging still.'

Yet, though Jesus' hopes ended in apparent failure, Schweitzer claimed that an even greater power resulted from this incredible act of misplaced confidence than would have been the case if the expected apocalyptic kingdom had actually arrived. For the example of Jesus is something that can still exert a dynamic moral and spiritual influence over those who are willing to be obedient. And Schweitzer himself certainly put into practice the lessons he saw there. Not that he took Jesus' actual teaching very seriously, for he regarded even the Sermon on the Mount as an 'interim ethic', intended to apply only to a very short time during the ministry of Jesus. Instead, he attached the greatest importance to Jesus' faithfulness to his convictions. This, he said, is something that must have its effect on everyone who thinks seriously about it.

Schweitzer's views were published in a remarkable book that first appeared in English in 1909, under the title *The Quest of the Historical Jesus*. It is still regarded as one of the great theological classics. Many aspects of Schweitzer's argument are still widely regarded as valid even today. Hardly anyone would disagree with his view that Jesus' teaching about the new society must have seemed very similar to the apocalyptic expectations of the people of his time. It certainly had more in common with their expectations than with the ideas medieval churchmen developed about the kingdom and the church. Schweitzer was also undoubtedly correct in seeing that Jesus' life's work, and especially his death, were an absolutely essential part of God's intervention in the lives of ordinary people.

There are, however, many difficulties involved in accepting this as an explanation of the whole of Jesus' life and teaching. For one thing, Schweitzer consistently ignored the claim that Jesus undoubtedly made about his own

when he declared that 'the kingdom of God is at hand'.

Jesus pictured himself as 'the Messiah designate', who would assume a position of full authority once the kingdom had actually arrived. But, like many other visionaries both before and after him, Jesus found the reality of life rather different from these idealistic dreams. Gradually, as life went on very much as before, it began to seem as if the dream had been only an illusion.

Early in the course of his work, said Schweitzer, Jesus was sufficiently confident to tell his disciples that the Son of man was about to appear in glory – so soon that they could expect his arrival in the course of a few days (Matthew 10:23). But it never happened, and so Jesus decided to try to force God's hand by going to Jerusalem and pressing the issue with the authorities there. The result was that Jesus was arrested, tried and tragically sentenced to death. Even this astonishing act of faith did not bring about the desired result. Instead it ended with defeat significance, and he confined his attention almost exclusively to Jesus' statements about the kingdom of God. We have already seen that these two parts of Jesus' teaching must be understood together. It is impossible to understand what he meant about God's new society without taking full account of his claim to have a special relationship with God himself.

Unless we are prepared to deny all historical credibility to the Gospel narratives, it is hard to believe that Jesus realized the importance of dying at Jerusalem only after the failure of all his previous efforts to bring about the new society. Nor do we need to believe with Schweitzer that Jesus' death also failed in its intended purpose, and left only a vague spiritual influence to affect the lives of those who take time to think about it.

Schweitzer made much of statements such as Jesus' words to his disciples just before his transfiguration: 'There are some standing here who will not taste death before they see the kingdom of God come with power' (Mark 9:1). According to Schweitzer's theory, this never happened. But he reached this conclusion only because of his sceptical attitude to the evidence of the New Testament. For the whole conviction of the early church was that God *did* truly intervene in human affairs in a powerful and dramatic way with the resurrection of Jesus and the gift of the Holy Spirit to his followers, and that both of these were the direct outcome of Jesus' death on the cross. And when we recall that much of the New Testament was written less than a generation after these events took place, it is clear that its evidence cannot be brushed aside quite as easily as Schweitzer thought.

'Realized eschatology'

The exact opposite of Schweitzer's theory is Professor C.H. Dodd's idea that Jesus had what he calls a 'realized eschatology'. According to Dodd, what Jesus was really saying was that the new society had already arrived in his own person. So we could say that the coming of Jesus was itself the coming of God's reign. Though the new society may need to grow and develop, the ultimate and decisive act had already taken place.

This is an attractive view, especially to people of a modern scientific age. The thought patterns familiar to first-century Jewish apocalyptists are strange to us. Most of us find it easier to think that Jesus' coming was the arrival of the new age, rather than to become involved in the bizarre and fruitless speculations about the future that even today still occupy the attention of some fringe Christian groups.

The idea that Jesus saw his own life and work as the coming of God's new society also helps us to understand more clearly the exact nature of some of the incidents recorded in the Gospels. The miracles, for example,

are much easier to understand if we regard them as signs and demonstrations that God was really at work in creating a new society than they would be if we regarded them in the traditional way as 'proofs' of Jesus' divine nature.

Dodd recognizes, of course, that not all the Gospel materials can be easily understood in the context of a realized eschatology. What are we to make, for instance, of the pictures and parables that appear to be concerned with the last judgement and some kind of future winding-up of things – parables like the story of the ten bridesmaids or the sheep and the goats (Matthew 25:1–13, 31–46)? Dodd interprets these as pictures, not of a final judgement to come at the end of the world, but of the kind of challenge that comes to all people whenever they are confronted with the message about Jesus and God's new society.

There is certainly plenty of evidence that Jesus regarded the

C.H. Dodd, the British theologian who developed the idea of 'realized eschatology'.

declaration of his message as in some sense a judgement on those who heard it and did not respond. The terms in which Jesus condemned the Pharisees often seem to imply that they were beyond being saved (Mark 3:28–30; Matthew 23); and the author of the fourth Gospel is surely giving an accurate representation of at least part of Jesus' message when he comments that 'He who believes in him is not condemned; he who does not believe is condemned already, because he has not believed in the name of the only Son of God. And this is the judgement, that the light has come into the world, and men loved darkness rather than light, because their deeds were evil' (John 3:18–19).

So it is not difficult to find passages in Jesus' teaching that can give some support to Dodd's theory. But the theory cannot explain every detailed bit of the evidence. There are two major stumbling-blocks:

● Although there are many passages in Jesus' teaching which support the theory, there are a good many more which do not. In many cases Jesus refers to the Son of man coming 'with the clouds of heaven', and his whole outlook was undoubtedly coloured by the kind of apocalyptic imagery to which Schweitzer so strikingly drew attention.

● We also have to consider what the rest of the New Testament tells us about the beliefs of the first Christians. And we find there a mixture of a 'futuristic' type of eschatology and a 'realized' type.

In the letters that Paul wrote to the church in the Greek city of Thessalonica in the early fifties of the first century we find great emphasis on the expectation of the early Christians that Jesus would again return in glory. Paul himself obviously shared this expectation, though not in the same extreme fashion as the Thessalonians (1 Thessalonians 4:13–5:11; 2 Thessalonians 2:1–12). In Corinth, on the other hand, Paul met some people who believed that the conventional descriptions of the end of things were to be taken as symbols of their own spiritual experience – and to them Paul again emphasized his own belief that Jesus would come again in the future (1 Corinthians 15:3–57).

But Paul himself was not totally one-sided in the matter, for in

Galatians, probably his earliest letter, he suggests that in a very real sense the fullness of God's new society has come and is already at work in those who are Christians.

Now, if Dodd's theory was completely correct and Jesus did actually think that the new society had already arrived in its final form, it is hard to see how and why the first Christians should have forgotten this emphasis so soon and turned instead to speculations about the future. This is an especially important question, since so many of these Christians were not Jews, and they would not naturally think

of the future in terms of Jewish apocalyptic. We must also bear in mind that the Gospel traditions themselves were preserved in the churches, and for the churches' use, and it is surely unlikely that such a glaring inconsistency between the teaching of Jesus and the actual beliefs of the church would have gone unnoticed.

'Inaugurated eschatology'

Because of the difficulties involved in both the futuristic and the realized views of Jesus' eschatology, there is considerable support today for a view

The kingdom of God, in Jesus' view, would consist of people from every generation and of every nationality.

that tries to take the best from both of them. This view recognizes that in a sense God's new society did actually come in the person of Jesus, but its complete fulfilment was still seen in the future. Thus Jesus' teaching is what we might call an 'inaugurated eschatology'.

This seems to me to be the best explanation of the matter. It is essential that we recognize with Schweitzer that Jesus' background was that of first-century Judaism, and his teaching included a complete view of the future course of events, including last judgement and final resurrection, as part of the consummation of God's new society. It is also important to recognize that Jesus claimed that the new society had arrived already in his own person, and so men and women must make their own response to God's demands upon them here and now.

We can perhaps summarize this rather complex subject by saying that there are four points which seem to be basic to understanding what Jesus has to say about the coming of the new society.

● Jesus certainly used the language and perhaps to some extent shared the views of those who expected the imminent arrival of the new society through a direct intervention of God in human affairs.

● Jesus believed that the fundamental nature of the new society was being revealed in his own life and work. It is clear from the Gospels that this proved to be very different from what most Jews expected. The society was revealed not as a tyrannical political force that would take over from Rome, but as a loving community of those whose only allegiance was to God himself.

● God's direct intervention is to be seen not only in the life and teaching of Jesus, but also in his death, in the resurrection and the gift of the Holy Spirit to his church. It may well be that it was in these events that some of Jesus' own predictions about the last things were fulfilled – for example, the statement that some of his disciples would see the new society coming with power before they died (Mark 9:1).

● There is so much variety in the language used by Jesus to describe the new society that it is likely to be almost impossible to understand it by any but the most comprehensive outlook. It can arrive secretly, like the yeast working in the dough (Matthew 13:33); or it can come by the sudden appearance of Christ in glory as at the expected second coming (Mark 13).

Jesus said that the demands of his kingdom were very great. 'Anyone who starts to plough and then keeps looking back is of no use for the kingdom of God' he told a would-be follower.

The kingdom of God and the kingdom of heaven

One of the striking facts about the Gospel of Matthew is that it consistently uses the term 'kingdom of heaven' to describe the subject of Jesus' teaching. The only exceptions to this are in Matthew 12:28, 19:24, 21:31 and 21:43, where we find the term 'kingdom of God', which is used throughout Mark and Luke.

On the basis of this distinction, some people have thought they can distinguish two quite separate phases in Jesus' teaching. But in fact there can be no doubt that the two terms refer to the same thing. This can be demonstrated quite easily by comparing the same statements in Matthew and in the other two synoptic Gospels. For example, when Mark summarizes Jesus' message as 'the kingdom of God is at hand; repent ...' (Mark 1:15), Matthew has, 'Repent, for the kingdom of heaven is at hand' (Matthew 4:17). The two statements appear in exactly the same context (the beginning of Jesus' teaching ministry), and it is obvious that they are different versions of the same saying. There are many other examples of the same process throughout the rest of the Gospels.

The explanation of this variety of expression is the fact that Matthew was writing for Jewish readers, whereas Mark and Luke were both writing for a predominantly non-Jewish readership. The Jews had never liked to use the name of God, in case they should unwittingly find themselves breaking the commandment, 'You shall not take the name of the Lord your God in vain ...' (Exodus 20:7). So they often used other terms instead, and 'heaven' was a favourite alternative. Matthew therefore speaks of 'the kingdom of heaven' in order to avoid offence to his readers. But non-Jews had no such reservations, and to them a term like 'kingdom of heaven' would have been unnecessarily complicated, if not altogether meaningless. So Mark and Luke use the term 'kingdom of God' instead.

It might be thought that since 'kingdom of heaven' was the Jewish term, this must have been the one originally used by Jesus himself, later adapted for non-Jews by Mark and Luke. But the likelihood is that Jesus actually spoke of the 'kingdom of God', and it is Matthew who has adapted this to 'kingdom of heaven' for his own purposes. There are two reasons for thinking this.

● Jesus never showed any reticence in speaking about God. Not only did he claim to know God in a close and personal way – he even dared to call God his 'Father'.

● There are, as we have seen, four instances in Matthew where the term 'kingdom of God' is used. This can readily be understood if we suppose that Matthew overlooked these four occurrences of the word, but it is really impossible to think that in just these four cases he changed an original 'kingdom of heaven' into 'kingdom of God' for the benefit of his Jewish readers.

Perhaps the bewildering variety of ways in which the new society is described was designed to teach us one very important lesson about it: that what God can do among men and women through Jesus Christ is something far greater than any of us can fully understand. When God works he does it in a big way. He also does it in a simple way, so that everyone can understand enough about it to be able to respond to the challenge. That is why Jesus gave so much of his teaching in parables or simple pictures. And before we can get much further in understanding God's new society we shall have to look at some of these.

Chapter 7 Pictures of the kingdom

Luke 10:25–37
Matthew 18:12–14;
Luke 15:1–7
Matthew 13:1–9;
Mark 4:1–9; Luke 8:4–8

Some of the stories of Jesus which are best-known are the 'parables': stories such as the good Samaritan, or the lost sheep, or the sower spreading seed in his field. But if we go through the Gospels and list the different parts of Jesus' teaching that are described as parables, we discover that they include not only these story parables but also other sayings that we would more naturally classify as metaphors, similes, proverbs, allegories, or even riddles.

The pictures and their meaning

Luke 4:23
Mark 7:15–16
Matthew 5–7

John 10:1–18
John 15:1–11
John 4:31–38
John 6:35
John 7:37–39

A popular proverb such as 'Physician, heal yourself' is called a 'parable'. So is the more or less factual statement, 'there is nothing that goes into a person from the outside which can make him ritually unclean. Rather, it is what comes out of a person that makes him unclean.' Some of the statements in the Sermon on the Mount are also of the same type, drawing a vivid picture of something familiar – salt, light, or a city – by means of which Jesus explains his message. Many of Jesus' pictures in John's Gospel also use the same kind of imagery to drive home their message. There, Jesus describes himself as 'the good shepherd', or 'the true vine'. He compares the disciples' task with the reaping of a harvest, and himself with bread and life-giving water.

Jesus' teaching is full of 'parable' sayings like this. But in discussing Jesus' teaching it is usual and convenient to reserve the word 'parable' for actual stories that Jesus told.

Parable or allegory?

The traditional way of understanding these story parables has been to regard them as 'allegories'. An allegory is a detailed account of a subject, written in such a way that it appears to be about something altogether different. John Bunyan's *Pilgrim's Progress* is a well-known example of this kind of writing. In this book Bunyan *seems* to be telling the story of a man on a journey. But the journey is so extraordinary, and the characters so much larger than life, that it soon becomes obvious he is not really writing about a journey at all. He is describing the things that happen in the life of a Christian, from the time when he first becomes a Christian through to the end of his life.

We find this kind of teaching in some parts of the New Testament. In John's Gospel, for example, there is the allegory of the vine and its branches. In this story Jesus is ostensibly explaining the means by which a vine bears grapes on its branches. But when he begins to talk about the branch of a vine deciding to cut itself off from the main stem of the plant, it becomes obvious that he is not really giving a lesson on how to grow grapes, but talking about what it means to be one of his disciples.

John 15:1–11

Though there are a few examples of allegories in the Gospels, in most cases this method of understanding the parables is neither faithful to the original intention of Jesus' teaching, nor is it very helpful. Take, for example, the parable of the good Samaritan. According to Luke, this story was told by Jesus in answer to the question, 'Who is my neighbour?' At the end, Jesus told his questioner to behave as the Samaritan had done in the story. Yet within a very short time Christians were applying an allegorical interpretation to the story, losing sight of the fact that it was an answer to a practical question.

Luke 10:25–37

Many of Jesus' pictures were drawn from agricultural life. One parable describes a vineyard owner whose tenants refused to share the crop with him.

Where to find some of Jesus' parables

	Matthew	Mark	Luke
The Sower	13:1–23	4:1–20	8:4–15
The weeds in the field	13:2443		
The mustard seed	13:31–32	4:30–32	13:18–19
The hidden treasure	13:44–46		
The unforgiving servant	18:23–35		
The good Samaritan			10:25–37
The friend at midnight			11:5–8
The rich fool			12:13–21
The great feast			14:15–24
The lost sheep	18:12–14		15:1–10
The prodigal son			15:11–32
The unjust servant			16:1–13
The rich man and Lazarus			16:19–31
The unjust judge			18:1–8
The Pharisee and the tax collector			18:9–14

	Matthew	Mark	Luke
The workers in the vineyard	20:1–16		
The pounds			19:11–27
The wicked tenants	21:33–46	12:1–12	20:9–19
The wedding feast	22:1–14		
The faithful servant	24:45–51		
The ten maidens	25:1–13		
The talents	25:14–30		

Some of the 'I am' sayings of John's Gospel are similar to parables:

The bread of life	John 6:35–40
The light of the world	8:12–13
The door	10:7–10
The good shepherd	10:11–18
The resurrection and the life	11:17–27
The way, truth and life	14:1–7
The true vine	15:1–11

According to the fourth-century thinker Augustine, the man who went down from Jerusalem to Jericho was Adam. Jerusalem represented the heavenly city of peace from which he fell, and Jericho was the human mortality that he inherited as a result of his fall. The robbers were the devil and his angels, who stripped him of his immortality. The priest and the Levite who passed by on the other side were the priesthood and ministry of the Old Testament, which could not save him. The good Samaritan was Christ himself, and his binding of the traveller's wounds was the restraint of sin. The oil and wine that he poured in were the comfort of hope and encouragement to work hard. The beast was the flesh in which Christ came to earth; the inn was the church, and the innkeeper the apostle Paul. The two pence he was paid are the commandments to love God and love our neighbour.

Augustine, Quaestiones Evangeliorum 2.19

Now this is undoubtedly an ingenious account of the whole story of salvation – and, to be fair, we should remember that Augustine tells us that he thoroughly enjoyed thinking up this kind of thing. But in the final analysis we must admit that such an interpretation is quite unrelated to the story of the good Samaritan. These 'spiritual meanings' are read into the story rather than coming out of it. In Augustine's version, the original question of Jesus' hearer is not answered at all!

The point of the parables

We may find it somewhat surprising to discover that it was not until the end of the nineteenth century that the futility of this method of interpretation was finally realized. When scholars began to read the New Testament as a historical document, they realized that Jesus probably used parables in much the same way as other teachers in the ancient world. After comparing Jesus' methods of teaching with the way parables are used in Greek literature, a German scholar, Adolf Jülicher, suggested that Jesus used parables in the same way as a modern preacher uses illustrations. They were not intended to convey a hidden meaning in every detail, but simply to illustrate and drive home a particular point.

So in the parable of the good Samaritan, the main point is that the person who proved to be a real neighbour was not a religious Jew, but one of the despised and hated Samaritans. All the other details in the story, about the ass and the inn, the oil and wine, were simply an imaginative description of the scene to make the story realistic and interesting. They had no connection with the main point of what Jesus was trying to say.

Once this fact was realized, it soon disposed of some real problems of interpretation. For in some parables the main characters are not the kind of people whose actions Christians have ever felt they ought to copy. There is the unjust steward, for example, who gained his master's approval by manipulating the accounts to his own advantage. Was Jesus really commending this sort of behaviour? Of course not. And when we appreciate that the main point of the parable is that we should copy his far-sighted

Luke 16:1–8

Today, as in Jesus' time, sheep and goats often graze together. He used the picture of a shepherd dividing the sheep from the goats to illustrate the last judgement.

determination to be ready for a crisis in life, we can see that the rest of the story is simply a realistic portrayal of an imaginary situation.

Following on from the important insights of Jülicher, other scholars set out to discover the real meaning of Jesus' parables, notably Professor C.H. Dodd in England and Professor Joachim Jeremias in Germany. Both agreed with Jülicher that a parable generally has only one lesson to teach – though they also saw that the subject of the parables is not generalized moral truth (as Jülicher had thought) but the coming of God's new society. However, Dodd and Jeremias took over from Jülicher certain assumptions that have recently been questioned by other students of the New Testament:

● Though it is true, in general, that each of the parables of Jesus has only one main point, it can be misleading to insist that no parable can ever have more than one main point. Some of them quite obviously do have more than one lesson to teach.

In the parable of the talents, for example, at least two simple points seem to be made. The story tells of a man who is going away and divides his money among his servants for safe keeping. When he returns he rewards the servants in different ways, according to the different uses to which they have put his money. Now the main point of this story must be to emphasize the connection between individual responsibility and ultimate judgement. But there is another emphasis that may be just as important, for the master went far beyond either his legal or his moral obligation by generously entrusting his property to his servants. The parable of the wedding feast seems to make exactly the same two points, and of course both were important parts of Jesus' teaching about the nature of his Father.

Matthew 25:14–30;
Luke 19:11–27

Matthew 22:1–14;
Luke 14:15–24

Matthew 13:1–9;
Mark 4:1–9; Luke 8:4–8

Matthew 13:18–23;
Mark 4:13–20;
Luke 8:11–15

Matthew 21:33–45;
Mark 12:1–12;
Luke 20:9–19

In the parable of the sower Jesus compared the response of his hearers to the growth of seed, some of which was sown on stony ground.

● Though most of the parables are not to be given an allegorical interpretation, many scholars now recognize that this does not apply to all of them. The parable of the sower incorporates an allegorical meaning: the different kinds of ground are said to correspond to different types of people hearing Jesus' message. It is often argued that this explanation does not go back to Jesus himself, but originated in the early church, at a time when Christians were trying to explain why only a few people responded to their preaching. There is no doubt that this parable would help to answer a question like that. But if we omit this interpretation of the parable as being only a secondary meaning, perhaps added later, we are still left with the problem of explaining the main point as Jesus first told it. And the fact is that it is very difficult to see what other meaning it could possibly have.

There is an even more striking example of this in the case of the parable of the wicked tenants. The story concerns a man who let out his vineyard to some tenants for a rent that included part of the annual crop of grapes. Yet, when he sent his servants to collect his share of the crop, they were beaten and killed. After this had happened several times the man sent his son, thinking that he would command greater respect. But exactly the same thing happened to him. So when the owner himself finally comes to the vineyard it is inevitable that the tenants will be put out and destroyed. In this story, an allegorical interpretation seems to be the only meaning possible. If Israel was not the vineyard, and the prophets were not the servants sent by the master (God), and Jesus himself was not the Son, then the whole parable loses its point.

So it seems wise to adopt a more flexible approach, and to recognize that although the parables do not normally need an allegorical interpretation, some of them may.

● Dodd and Jeremias emphasized the importance of understanding the parables in their original historical context. Because they insisted on this point they made a great effort to try to discover the original meaning of the parables for Jesus' hearers, and later for the Christians who first wrote them down. But other scholars are now beginning to realize that there is a hidden dimension in the parables which gives them a distinctive appeal not found in the rest of the New Testament.

It is generally true to say that before we can be sure what the New Testament means for us today, we need to know what it meant to those who first read it. But this is not really the case with the parables. They are more like the work of a great artist than a self-conscious theologian, and their characters and situations have a correspondingly universal quality that can be understood by anyone, for they deal with the basic needs of human beings. We do not need any special insights to understand the parable of the lost son, or the talents, or the workers in the vineyard. Their meaning and their challenge is self-evident as we read them.

The pictures and their message

Matthew 13:24, 31, 33, 44

But what is the message and the challenge of the parables? In the widest sense, the subject of the parables is the coming of God's new society, or 'kingdom'. This is clearly indicated by the many parables which start with the words, 'The kingdom of God is like ...' Because of this, the exact meaning that we see in the parables will to some extent depend on what we believe the new society to be. If, with Albert Schweitzer, we think that the spectacular and immediate intervention of God in the affairs of human society is the most important thing about it, then we will naturally want to understand the teaching of the parables in that context. If, on the other hand, we follow C.H. Dodd, we will have no difficulty in finding traces of a realized eschatology in the parables.

But the real message of the parables is rather more complex than either of these alternatives suggests. When we consider them all as a group, their message seems to be concerned with four main subjects, each of them explaining some important facts about God's society and the effect it has in the lives of those who are a part of it.

The society and its Sovereign

Luke 15:1–7;
Matthew 18:12–14

Luke 15:8–10
Luke 15:11–32

Matthew 20:1–16

Most communities are strongly influenced by the character of their leader or leaders. A harsh, authoritarian ruler will not have too much difficulty in persuading his people to adopt the same attitudes. And the example of a liberal, humane ruler will usually encourage his people to share a similar viewpoint. The new society that God has founded is no exception to this. It takes its character and form from the God who is its Sovereign.

So we are not surprised to find that several of the parables tell us important things about the nature of God himself. The story of the lost sheep explains the fundamental fact that he is a God of grace: he takes the initiative in finding and restoring those who because of sin are out of harmony with his will. He is concerned when even one of his creatures has lost his way in life, and must go after that lost one to restore him. The other parables in Luke 15 – the lost coin and the lost son – also emphasize God's love for sinful men and women. His undeserved love is so great that God will do all he can to find us and he will not be satisfied until, like the lost son, we have been fully restored.

The precise extent of God's generosity is illustrated in the story about the workers in the vineyard. Here Jesus tells of a master who hired men to work in his vineyard. They started work at different times of the day, so that when the time came for them to receive their wages some of them had only worked for an hour, while others had worked the whole day. But the master gave them all the same wages! He was not cheating anyone, because those who started early in the day had agreed in advance what their pay should be. But the master was generous to those who began late in the day. He gave them as much as if they had been there from the start. This, said Jesus, is what the kingdom of heaven is like. God, of course, is the Sovereign of the kingdom,

The story of the good Samaritan referred to the notorious Jericho road. It passes through desolate country making an ideal hideout for robbers.

and he is overwhelmingly generous. Those who join his society at the last minute are given as big a welcome as those who are first in at the door.

This may seem to suggest that God is a little unfair, for surely those who arrived early *did* deserve more than those who came to work late in the day. This is the kind of question Jülicher was trying to answer when he suggested that a parable normally has only one point – and in the case of this parable he was undoubtedly correct. For there are many other sayings of Jesus which show that God is overwhelmingly responsive to the needs of all his people. There is, for example, the story of the friend who requested food at midnight, which is used by Luke to emphasize that God is only too willing to answer our prayers: 'Ask, and you will receive; seek, and you will find; knock, and the door will be opened to you.' Another example is the story of the unjust judge, which emphasizes a similar point.

Then there are the statements in the Sermon on the Mount which, though not story parables, are certainly parables in the wider meaning of the word. 'Look at the birds of the air; they neither sow nor reap nor gather into barns, and yet your heavenly Father feeds them. Are you not of more value than they? ... And why are you anxious about clothing? Consider the lilies ... how they grow; they neither toil nor spin; ... if God so clothes the grass of the field ... will he not much more clothe you, O men of little faith?' God cares about his people, and he cares about even the smallest details. He is their 'Father'.

This emphasis on the close personal relationship that exists between God and those who acknowledge his sovereignty over their lives is one of the most strikingly original parts of Jesus' teaching. Jesus himself addressed God as his Father. In John's Gospel, God's relationship to Jesus as Father to Son is often used to emphasize Jesus' divine nature. But in the other three Gospels it is the character of the relationship that is more often emphasized. As Jesus' Father God can be addressed and known in the same intimate way as a human father is addressed by his child. Jesus spoke like that to God. He called him 'Abba', the

Luke 11:5–8

Luke 11:9
Luke 18:1–8

Matthew 6:26–30

Mark 14:32–36

John 1:14, 18; 5:43; 8:19

Matthew 6:9; Luke 11:2

Aramaic word for father used in the home, and he allowed his disciples to do the same when speaking to God in prayer.

This way of addressing God was quite new. Though the Jews did occasionally address God as 'Father', they did not use the familiar language Jesus used, and they normally qualified it by some reference to God's holiness and majesty.

But the God of Jesus' parables is not remote and out of contact with the real world. To be sure, he is 'holy': he is completely different in character from men and women. But he is a God whom we can know in a personal relationship as our Father. What is more, he is a loving Father. He watches over all those who belong to him, and cares about the very smallest detail of their lives.

The society and the individual

To be a part of the new society that Jesus talks about not only gives us the privilege of knowing God in an intimate and personal way, it also imposes certain responsibilities on us. A number of the stories Jesus told emphasize the kind of response that is required if we are to 'enter the kingdom'.

Mark 1:15

At the beginning of Mark, the main thrust of Jesus' teaching is summed up in the slogan, 'Repent and believe in the Gospel', and many of the stories told by Jesus emphasize the importance of turning away from sin ('repenting') in order to become a member

Luke 15:11–32

of God's society. The story of the lost son, for instance, not only emphasizes the goodness and generosity of the father: it also underlines the importance of the son realizing his foolishness and being willing to change his way of life.

Repentance has never been a popular idea, for it involves us in recognizing that we have done wrong. It means a certain loss of face and loss of moral credibility. But Jesus made it quite plain that those who are not prepared to accept this loss of face can never have a living relationship with God. There is the story of the Pharisee and the tax collector, who went to pray in the

Luke 18:9–14

temple at the same time. The Pharisee prided himself on his moral and religious attainments – and told God so. The tax collector, on the other hand, was so conscious of his own unworthiness to speak to God at all that he could only cry out, 'God, have pity on me, a sinner.' But, said Jesus, 'the tax collector, and not the Pharisee, was in the right with God when he went home', because he recognized his own sinfulness and came to God with no spiritual pretensions.

Jesus makes a similar point in the story of the rich fool, who thought that his wealth would place him in good standing with

Luke 12:13–21

God. And he made the teaching of these parables quite explicit in his statement that God's rule over our lives is to be accepted in an attitude of childlike trust: 'Whoever does not receive the

Luke 18:17; Mark 10:15

kingdom of God like a child will never enter it.'

But repentance and forgiveness are not the end of the matter. Indeed, they are only the beginning of a life lived under the rule of God himself. For in God's new society we enjoy a new kind of life – 'eternal life' or 'abundant life' as Jesus calls it in some of the sayings recorded in John's Gospel. Life in God's society means a life which is directed and controlled by God. Those who have entered the kingdom by repentance and forgiveness of their sins must love God with all their energy. They must serve him as their only true master, even to the point of giving him absolute control of their lives. For those who do this, there are important practical consequences in the way they live day by day.

John 3:15; 6:54; 10:28; 17:3

Matthew 22:37–38; Mark 12:29–30 Matthew 6:24; Luke 16:13 Matthew 16:24–26; Luke 9:23–25

● For one thing, they are far more concerned with what God thinks about them than what other people may think. This comes out especially in their attitudes to religious matters. Though some may accept God's rule over their lives rather reluctantly, their devotion is preferable to that of someone who makes a great show of serving God but who in reality does nothing about it. God's people must serve him in the spirit of the widow who secretly put her last penny into the offering-box at the temple. They will not behave ostentatiously so that others will see them and know of their goodness. They will pray and fast in secret and 'your Father who sees what you do in private, will reward you'.

Matthew 21:28–32

Mark 12:41–44; Luke 21:1–4

Matthew 6:5–6; 16–18

Matthew 6:4

● But this is not an excuse for doing nothing. Those who accept God's rule in their lives must make good use of God's provision for them. They must act responsibly, using the resources God has given them, and like the unjust steward, they should always be ready to face their master.

Matthew 25:14–30; Luke 19:11–27 Luke 16:1–8

● Indeed, their main ambition in life must be to learn more of God and his ways. Two of the shortest parables illustrate this – the stories about the hidden treasure and the pearl. A man who finds a field full of treasure will have no hesitation in selling all his goods to buy that field. Or, similarly, if he is looking for fine pearls and comes across an especially good specimen, he will sacrifice everything to own it. God's kingdom is like that. It is worth sacrificing all we have to be able to enjoy the reality of God working in our lives.

Matthew 13:44

Matthew 13:45

This is what Jesus meant when he said to his disciples, 'the kingdom of God is within you'. God is already exercising his sovereign rule in the lives of those who know him as Father. The new society can be present in the experience of just one person who recognizes God's claims on his life.

Luke 17:21

The society and the community

At the same time, we would be wrong to think that Jesus' message was restricted to the purely personal, individual aspects of religious life and belief. A large part of his teaching concerns the relationship of God's people to the world at large, and to one another. Indeed in the parable of the unforgiving servant, Jesus seems to suggest that the way God deals with us will in some way depend on the way we deal with other people. Then there is also the statement of Jesus that loving our neighbour comes second in importance to loving God.

Matthew 18:21–35

Matthew 22:39; Mark 12:31

What this means is that those people who accept God's rule

Shepherds in Israel's rough hill-country protected their flocks from wild animals and thieves. Jesus called himself the good shepherd who cared so much for his sheep that he was willing to die for them.

over their lives must behave in the same way as their Father in heaven. God's generosity extends even to the outcasts of society, and his followers should be no different. They are to behave like the good Samaritan in the parable. Jesus put this into practice himself, by taking God's message to the outcasts of society. That was what made the disciples realize that the kingdom of God was actually present in his person, and that they could share in its blessings here and now.

Luke 10:25–37

For those who were willing to accept God's claims over their lives, this new experience was in store. Not only did they share a new relationship with God himself; they were also bound to one another in a new community of caring service and mutual love.

The society and the future

Finally, a number of parables refer to the coming of God's kingdom in the future. They refer to Jesus coming as the heavenly, supernatural Son of man, and speak of the final judgement of men and women.

Some have thought that this was just a picturesque way of presenting the challenge of Jesus' message as it came to his hearers when they first heard it. But, in view of the strongly apocalyptic tone of much of the language that is used, it is hard to escape the conclusion that Jesus was thinking of some future time when God would assert his authority and kingship in a visible way.

At this time there will be a great day of reckoning. Those who merely profess to serve God but do not actually do so will be sorted out from those who really carry out God's will. This is the main lesson of the parables about the fishing-net, the corn and the weeds, and the sheep and the goats.

Matthew 13:47–50
Matthew 13:24–30

Matthew 25:31–33

In other parables the future climax of the kingdom is depicted as a feast. This kind of imagery was often used by the Jews to describe the coming blessings of the messianic age. But Jesus' pictures of it make it clear that not everyone will gain admission. Indeed, the parable of the great supper suggests that the conventionally religious will have no place in it at all. Those who share in its blessings will come in from the streets rather than from the sanctuaries.

Matthew 22:1–14; Luke 14:15–24

In Matthew's Gospel great emphasis is laid on the responsibilities that all this places on those who profess to be God's people. Since no one knows the day or the hour when this will take place, we must be in a state of constant readiness – like the bridesmaids who waited for the bridegroom to arrive at a wedding.

Matthew 24:36–44, cf. Mark 13:32–37

Matthew 25:1–13

This element in Jesus' teaching transcends the sharp distinctions we like to draw between what will happen in the future and what is already present. Because Jesus has come, God's new society has already arrived. Those who are willing to accept God's authority are even now a part of his kingdom. Whatever else may be revealed in the future will be, not so much a new beginning, as the final working out of all the implications of something that, in its essence, is already here. Though God's new society had had small and insignificant beginnings, it is the kind of beginning that must inevitably produce spectacular growth. Its development is like that of the mustard seed, 'the smallest seed in the world' which grows up into one of the biggest plants of all.

Matthew 13:31–32; Mark 4:30–34; Luke 13:18–19

The pictures and their hearers

Some scholars have spent a lot of time trying to discover the exact 'life situation' (*Sitz im Leben*) of the various parables, thinking that if they do so their immediate meaning will be easier to grasp. But in most cases it is not possible to discover the precise situations in which Jesus told particular stories. For, like the other parts of the Gospels, the parables have been recorded not as part of a biography of Jesus, arranged chronologically, but as a message explaining Jesus' teaching and its continuing relevance to the needs of the world and the church.

Very occasionally the parables have a story attached to them, and this perhaps gives some indication of their original life setting in the ministry of Jesus. Probably no one would doubt that the parable of the good Samaritan was given in answer to the question 'Who is my neighbour?' addressed to Jesus by a Jewish religious leader. Similarly, the parable about the unforgiving servant was told in reply to Peter's question about how often he should forgive someone who was offending him. Or again, Jesus told the story of the rich fool in answer to a question about the best way of dividing a legacy.

Matthew 18:21–35

Luke 12:13–21

Some of the parables are told in different contexts in different Gospels. The parable of the lost sheep appears in Luke along with the parables of the lost coin and lost son as an answer to the Pharisees' complaints about the bad company Jesus was keeping. In Matthew the same parable is told as an encouragement to the

Luke 15:1–7

Matthew 18:12–14

disciples to be faithful 'shepherds' of the church. It is of course not inconceivable that Jesus may have told the same story more than once, and drawn different lessons on each occasion. Many preachers re-use a good illustration.

But the fact is that these parables are exceptional in having any background information at all attached to them. We know nothing about the circumstances in which Jesus first told most of the parables. This is emphasized by the way they are collected together in blocks in the various Gospels. Matthew has a complete section of his Gospel devoted entirely to parables. Mark contains a similar (though not identical) collection, while Luke also has a long section predominantly composed of parables.

Matthew 13
Mark 4
Luke 13:18 – 16:31

Nor is it really profitable to try to discover the use to which the parables were put in the early church. Students of what is called 'redaction criticism' have examined the ways in which different parables are used in different Gospels. For example, we can see that Matthew has a number of parables that refer to the coming of God's kingdom in the future – and we may surmise that this subject was of some importance in the churches for which Matthew was writing. Luke, on the other hand, preserves a number of parables, not found in the other Gospels, concerned with the place of non-Jewish people (Gentiles) in God's new society. Observations of this kind can tell us valuable things about Matthew and Luke and their respective readerships. But ultimately they tell us very little about either the origins or the meaning of the parables themselves.

The real meaning of the parables must be inextricably bound up with the challenge they bring to those who read or hear them. They give us a picture of God and of his new society, and they challenge us to commit ourselves unconditionally to accept his will. It is only as we identify ourselves with the lost sheep, the wicked tenants, or the man who discovers a field of hidden treasure, that their full impact is felt. In the last analysis, the parables are nothing less than God's claim on the lives of men and women. They require both the disposition to understand and the will to obey.

To make his message clear to people who came to listen to him, Jesus used many illustrations from everyday life.

Why did Jesus teach in parables?

There is a statement in Mark 4:11–12 which seems to suggest that Jesus told parables with the deliberate intention of making his teaching obscure to those who were not already his disciples, so that, echoing the words of Isaiah, 'they may indeed see but not perceive, and may indeed hear but not understand; lest they should turn again, and be forgiven'. Such an idea is so contrary to all we know of Jesus that some explanation seems to be required. Many suggestions

have been put forward, of which we mention two:

● According to C.H. Dodd (and a number of others who follow his views), this is not a genuine saying of Jesus. It was inserted by the early church to explain why the Jewish people had rejected Jesus. It was, they said, a part of the providential wisdom of God himself, who had always intended this to happen. There are, however, two arguments against this view.

First, it was probably only the

first generation of Christians who were deeply concerned that the Jews had rejected Jesus. The church was Jewish only at a very early stage of its development, and after the destruction of Jerusalem by the Romans in AD 70 Jewish Christianity almost ceased to exist. It certainly had little influence on the church at large. This means that the problem was most acute not long after the events of Jesus' own lifetime – and the nearer we are in time to Jesus himself, the less room there must be for the church making additions and alterations to his teaching.

Secondly, Matthew's Gospel has a similar saying, quoting the same passage from Isaiah. Since we know Matthew was specially interested in the relative status of Jews and Christians, we would expect him to have preserved exactly the same words as Mark, if this statement was indeed concerned with the Jewish rejection of Jesus. But in fact the statement in Matthew's Gospel has a slightly different implication. Here Jesus says: 'This is why I speak to them in parables, because seeing they do not see, and hearing they do not hear, nor do they understand' (Matthew 13:13).

● A second suggested explanation fits in with this statement in Matthew. On this understanding we need to suppose that the word translated *so that* ... they may see' in Mark is actually meant to be the beginning of a factual statement, much as it is in Matthew. Evidence for this view can be drawn from a comparison of the Greek that Mark wrote with the Aramaic statements that probably lay at the back of it. Thus the statement describes, not the *purpose* of teaching in parables, but the inevitable *consequences* of doing so. Jesus was pointing out that the parables will inevitably separate those who listen to them with spiritual insight from those who are spiritually blind.

This explanation is the more likely. It fits in with what we saw in a previous chapter about Jesus' attitude to keeping his messiahship secret. It also fits well with the nature of the parables themselves. Though they do not require great mental effort, a certain degree of commitment is called for in order to understand what Jesus is saying. The parables are not a philosophical statement of the truths about God. There *is* a sense in which the truth is 'hidden', for the parables challenge Jesus' hearers to think out for themselves what the implications of his message must be. Those who were not specially interested could no doubt listen to a parable and see nothing in it but a story. But with a little careful thought, the same story can become a picture of God and his dealings with men and women in the new society that Jesus had come to inaugurate.

Did Jesus intend to found the church?

People have often asked whether Jesus intended to found a church. We do have in Matthew's Gospel two statements that seem to suggest that he did (Matthew 16:18–20; 18:17). But some scholars believe these statements come from Matthew himself, and not directly from the teaching of Jesus. Albert Schweitzer, for example, found it impossible to think that Jesus intended to found a church, for he believed that Jesus expected the immediate end of the world. But even those who do not share this opinion have often rejected the notion that Jesus was intent on starting a church. Adolf von Harnack and the theological liberals viewed Jesus as a simple ethical teacher. Because they regarded the concept of a church as inconsistent with this, they concluded that it was a later, alien intrusion into the originally simple Gospel.

Though very few people today would agree with this point of view, it does draw our attention to two important facts that need to be borne in mind whenever we talk about Jesus and the church:

● 'The church' need not imply the kind of religious hierarchy that evolved in the second century and that is familiar to us in institutionalized Christianity today. Jesus spoke of two or three people gathered in his name (Matthew 18:20).

● In the strict sense it is probably anachronistic to speak of the existence of 'the church' in the lifetime of Jesus. The church in the New Testament is not simply a collection of like-minded people organized as a religious society. It is a living fellowship of those who share in the salvation that God has provided through the life, death and resurrection of Jesus himself. There is a sense therefore in which the church came into existence only *after* Jesus' death and resurrection. The New Testament depicts the pouring out of the Holy Spirit on the day of Pentecost as the real 'founding' of the church (Acts 1:8; 2:1–4).

We therefore need to qualify any statement that we make about Jesus 'founding' the church. But at the same time, there are strong indications in the Gospels that he certainly intended to form a community of those who followed him.

● All the Gospels depict Jesus as the person in whom the messianic promises of the Old Testament have

The early followers of Jesus were not organized into any church structures, but the gathering of Christians together for worship and instruction has been called a 'church' from New Testament times.

been fulfilled. The Messiah of whom the Old Testament speaks had come in Jesus. A significant element in the Old Testament expectation was the belief that when the Messiah came he would set up a new community, and in this community God's people would enjoy a new and close relationship with their master and with one another. As we have seen, there is good reason to believe that at least the core of Jesus' claims to be Messiah can be traced back to the teaching of Jesus himself – and if he viewed himself as Messiah, it would be only natural for him to envisage the foundation of some kind of community among his followers. The name that Jesus

regularly used for himself, Son of man, also contains this implication. It is probably incorrect to say, as some do, that every time Jesus used this name he meant to include his disciples along with himself. But there is no doubt that in the Old Testament book of Daniel the Son of man was not simply an individual; he was a representative member of 'the saints of the most high' (Daniel 7:13–18).

● When we consider the ways in which Jesus describes his own work and the work of God's kingdom, his words often suggest that he is talking about a group of people linked not only to God, but to one another. For example, he talks of himself as a shepherd, implying that he must have a flock (John 10:1–18; Luke 12:32). When he compares himself to a vine and his disciples to its branches, it is obvious that he is meaning to suggest that the branches have some kind of connection with each other as well as with the main stem (John 15:1–11). Many of the things Jesus says about the kingdom would be difficult to understand without assuming that he had some kind of visible society in mind (Matthew 23:13; Luke 16:16). And his ethical teaching is invariably concerned with life among his followers within a community (Matthew 5:22; 7:3–5).

● More striking is the fact that some of the parables suggest that the kingdom of God is to be not only a new society but also a visible society. Parables like the mustard seed (Mark 4:30–32), the corn and the weeds (Matthew 13:24–30), the fishing-net (Matthew 13:47–50), the workers in the vineyard (Matthew 20:1–16) and the wedding feast (Matthew 22:1–14) clearly suggest an organized society.

So it seems reasonable to conclude that Jesus did have in mind a continuing community of his followers, and that the kind of churches spoken of in the rest of the New Testament gave form to the community Jesus intended to found.

Chapter 8

The power of the kingdom

Mark 1:29–34
Mark 4:35–41
Mark 5:21–43;
Luke 7:11–17;
John 11:1–44

Some of the most striking parts of the Gospels are the stories about Jesus performing what we call miracles. He healed the sick, he exercised authority over the forces of nature, and on occasion he even raised the dead. Of all the subjects mentioned in the Gospels, this is the one that presents most problems for us today.

We usually have no real difficulty in understanding Jesus' teaching about God and his new society. Even people who are unable to accept Jesus' teaching as the full and final truth about God and the world can still respect his ideals, and many people who are not Christians make a genuine effort to put some of them into practice. But when it comes to the miracles, things are very different. Most people, including a number of Christians, find it hard to believe that the miracles recorded in the Gospels actually took place. They may be old superstitions, or even fairy tales, but there is a widespread feeling that it is quite impossible for modern people to accept them as literal facts.

We have already noticed in dealing with subjects such as the birth of Jesus that it is all too easy to make presuppositions of this kind an excuse for failing to take serious account of the nature of the actual evidence for remarkable events. A great many people find it difficult to conceive the possibility of super-natural intervention in the natural world. But the question posed

Some of Jesus' miracles reported in the Gospels

	Matthew	Mark	Luke	John		Matthew	Mark	Luke	John
Healing of Peter's mother-in-law	8:14–15	1:29–31	4:38–39		Feeding the 5,000	14:13–21	6:30–44	9:10–17	6:1–14
Turning water into wine				2:1–11	Walking on the water	14:22–33	6:45–52		
Miraculous catch of fish			5:1–11		Feeding the 4,000	15:32–39	8:1–10		
Healing the centurion's servant	8:5–13		7:1–10		Healing a blind man at Bethsaida		8:22–26		
Calming the storm	8:22–37	4:35–41	8:22–25		Healing a man blind from birth				9:1–12
The Gerasene demoniac healed	8:28–34	5:1–20	8:26–39		The epileptic boy healed	17:14–21	9:14–29	9:37–43	
Healing a paralysed man	9:1–8	2:1–12	5:17–26		Healing ten lepers			17:11–19	
Jairus' daughter healed	9:18–26	5:21–43	8:40–56		Lazarus raised from the dead				11:1–44
Widow's son raised from the dead			7:11–17		Blind Bartimaeus healed	20:29–34	10:46–52	18:35–43	

by the miracles of Jesus can hardly be answered simply by reference to our own disposition not to believe in miracles. Two other considerations are also important.

First of all we must ask ourselves whether the miracle stories are consistent with the teaching of Jesus himself, especially the teaching he gave about his own person. There can be no doubt that if the claims we examined in section one are in fact correct, we will not find it so difficult to accept the trustworthiness of the miracle stories. Not that this will solve the whole problem, of course. Believers can no more prove the truth of the miracles simply by reference to their presuppositions, than unbelievers can disprove them by reference to their own rather different preconceptions. It is essential to take full account of the evidence itself.

We must also remember that it is not always clear what people mean when they speak of a 'miracle'. Someone might say a miracle is anything that goes against the 'laws of nature'. But another person may point out that there are no such things as fixed 'laws of nature', and what we call 'laws' are in fact only a rationalisation of how things usually happen. Someone in a primitive tribe might see a modern invention like television and regard it as a miracle, whereas another will know how it works and describe it differently. A mother with a long history of miscarriages and stillbirths has a healthy baby, and regards it as a miracle. Someone else can point to the statistics, and say it was bound to happen sooner or later.

People can look at the same event, and depending on their perspective, make rather different assessments of what has taken place. If we bring a modern rationalist perspective to the Gospels, and ask their writers only twentieth-century 'scientific' questions, then we are unlikely to get very helpful answers. Even if it were possible for two modern scientists to be whisked back to the time of Jesus in a time machine, they might not agree on what they saw. The Gospel writers began from the assumption that, if God was truly at work in the life of Jesus, then it was reasonable to expect Jesus' actions to demonstrate the reality of God's presence. And this he did in the miracles. When John the Baptist sent to ask Jesus

Jesus' miracles were intended to be a call to faith. He rejected the temptation to turn stones into bread, but used five loaves and two fishes to feed a crowd of 5,000 who had been listening to him all day.

if he really was the expected Messiah, and if God's new society had at last arrived, Jesus replied that the miracles, amongst other things, provided striking evidence for the truth of both these claims.

Luke 7:18–23

The miracles and the evidence

It is obviously important to look critically at all our sources of information before we even begin to consider the more general problems involved in understanding what we call 'miracles'. For if it can be shown that there is no good evidence for the belief that Jesus did in fact perform these deeds, we can forget all our other questions about the miracles.

When we look into ancient history it is striking to find that its evidence unambiguously supports the belief that Jesus was widely thought to have performed remarkable deeds of the kind mentioned in the Gospels. This evidence comes not only from the Gospels themselves, but also from non-Christian historical sources.

Jewish history

Josephus makes the following statement about Jesus: 'About this time arose Jesus, a wise man, if indeed it be lawful to call him a man. For he was a doer of wonderful deeds, and a teacher of men who gladly receive the truth. He drew to himself many both of the Jews and of the Gentiles. He was the Christ; and when Pilate, on the indictment of the principal men among us, had condemned him to the cross, those who had loved him at the first did not cease to do so, for he appeared to them again alive on the third day, the divine prophets having foretold these and ten thousand other wonderful things about him. And even to this day the race of Christians, who are named from him, has not died out.'

Antiquities of the Jews 18.3.3

This passage poses a certain problem, and scholars have different opinions as to how much of it was written directly by Josephus himself. The problem is that the passage says explicitly of Jesus that 'he was the Christ'. But of course we know that Josephus was not a Christian, and it would be remarkable for a Jew – even a renegade one – to make such an unequivocal statement. Perhaps this phrase has been inserted into Josephus's work by a later Christian editor. Or Josephus may originally have written that Jesus was 'called the Christ', and the text has subsequently been amended to make his reference more specific. But, in spite of this, most scholars have no doubts about the authenticity of the rest of Josephus's description of Jesus, which contains the statement that he was 'a doer of wonderful deeds.'

More evidence from a Jewish source is contained in the Babylonian Talmud (tractate *Sanhedrin* 43a) which reports that Jesus was executed because he practised 'sorcery' and misled the people. This is an interesting parallel to the evidence from the Gospels, which suggest that the Jews had no quarrel with Jesus over the *fact* of his miraculous power to heal, but only over the *source* of it. His Jewish opponents believed he was operating under the control of the devil, 'Beelzebub' – but they apparently had no reason to doubt the reality of what he was doing.

Matthew 12:22–28; Luke 11:14–23

Early Christian preaching

A second source of information is the (admittedly slight) evidence provided by the *kerygma* of the early church, as reconstructed by Professor C.H. Dodd. One of the elements of this early statement of Christian belief was that the promises of the Old Testament had come true in the life, death and resurrection of Jesus. And in several places the ministry of Jesus is explicitly described in terms of miracle working. On the day of Pentecost, for example, Peter is reported as speaking of the 'mighty works and wonders and signs which God did through Jesus'. Again, in the sermon to Cornelius and his household, there is a mention of how Jesus 'went everywhere, doing good and healing all who were under the power of the devil, for God was with him'.

Acts 2:22

Acts 10:38

We need not enter here into the complex subject of the authenticity of these sermons attributed to Peter, for regardless of whether they come directly from him, they do suggest that at an early stage Christians believed that Jesus had performed miracles. They could also appeal to non-Christians on the basis of these miracles. If we take this together with the evidence from Jewish sources, it seems clear that most people who knew anything at all about Jesus' ministry believed that he had done remarkable deeds – and this belief was independent of whether or not they were themselves Christians.

Jesus was out on the Lake of Galilee with his disciples when a storm arose. The disciples' fear turned to amazement when they saw Jesus calm the storm – his first miracle over the forces of nature.

Miracle stories in the Gospels

It is when we come to the Gospels themselves that we encounter some of the most formidable problems about Jesus' miracles. Three main questions need to be considered here.

● Some form critics, scholars who study how the Gospels were written, have shown that in their literary form the miracle stories of the Gospels are often similar to stories found in Hellenistic literature. A number of scholars have drawn particular attention to the parallels between the Gospel accounts and the stories of a first-century Cappadocian seer and wonder-worker found in the *Life of Apollonius*, written by the third-century author Philostratus. This of course is what we might expect, for the stories of Jesus' miracles were first written down by Greek-speaking people, who would naturally use the literary forms and conventions that were most familiar to them. It is hardly surprising that authors writing about the same kind of incidents in the same cultural situation should use similar language.

In addition, the 'parallels' drawn between Apollonius and Jesus favour the originality of the Gospel traditions. Not only are the Hellenistic stories of much later date than the New Testament, but they were published with the express purpose of disputing the Christian claims about Jesus. If there is any question of 'dependence' by either account on the other, it could more

easily be supposed that later writers consciously modelled their stories on the Gospel accounts than the other way round. In any case, similarity of literary form can really tell us nothing at all about the historical facts. (See the fuller discussion in chapter 10.)

● It is a well-known fact of history that as time goes on, miracles tend to be attached to people who are highly regarded for other reasons. We can see this tendency at work in the legends that have been gathered around the lives of so many of the medieval saints. It is undeniable that the same thing happened to the stories of Jesus. We can see this from the so-called 'apocryphal gospels' which were written in the second century. They relate all kinds of bizarre miracle stories about Jesus. There are also certain miracle stories in the New Testament Gospels of Matthew and John that some scholars have compared with the

stories in these apocryphal gospels. But on the whole there is compelling evidence to suggest that the central miraculous element of the New Testament Gospels does not derive from this kind of speculation.

In the first place, according to some recent datings of the Gospels, the earliest written records about the life of Jesus may be as early as AD 45, which is only fifteen years after his death. Even the more conventional dating of Mark to about AD 65–70 takes us only thirty-five years beyond the events recorded in the Gospels. A conscious mythologizing process would certainly need longer than that to develop, and at the time the Gospels were taking shape there must have been many surviving eye-witnesses of the events they describe. They could no doubt have corrected any stories that were out of character with Jesus as they remembered him.

Then there is also a striking difference between the miracle stories of the New Testament Gospels and the stories told about Hellenistic 'divine men', or medieval saints, or even about Jesus himself in the apocryphal gospels. There is, for example, nothing in the New Testament to compare with the grotesque tale told in the *Arabic Infancy Gospel*, according to which Jesus produced three children out of some goats he found in an oven. And even the story found in the *Infancy Gospel of Thomas* about Jesus turning twelve clay birds into real sparrows on the sabbath is of quite a different character from the stories told in the New Testament. Legendary tales of miracles are almost always concerned with the ostentatious display of special powers. But in the four Gospels there is none of this. Indeed it is made quite clear that the miracles Jesus performed were not concerned with satisfying idle speculation about the supernatural. When the Pharisees asked Jesus to perform a miracle to satisfy their curiosity, he told them in no uncertain terms that this kind of spectacle was quite alien to his work (Matthew 12:38–42; Mark 8:11–12; Luke 11:29–32).

It is also significant that Jesus is portrayed as a worker of miracles in even the very earliest strands of the Gospel traditions that we can trace. The Gospel source Q (see chapter 10) is generally thought to have been an early collection of Jesus' sayings, but this material also reports one

Jesus' ability to heal became so well known that crowds followed him wherever he went. Healing services and medical missions have remained an important part of Christian activity.

miracle, the healing of the Roman centurion's servant (Matthew 8:5–13; Luke 7:1–10). It also states that Jesus was in the habit of doing miracles. It is in Q that John's disciples are told to report the miracles they have seen (Matthew 11:1–19; Luke 7:18–35), and the cities of Galilee are condemned because they have not repented in spite of the miracles done in them (Matthew 11:20–24; Luke 10:13–15).

Perhaps the strongest reason for distinguishing the Gospel miracles from both pagan and later Christian stories is the fact that in the New Testament the miracles mean something. They are not just demonstrations of the supernatural for its own sake. Rather they are an essential part of Jesus' message about the arrival of God's new society.

● There is, however, yet another aspect. It is often pointed out by sceptics that in at least two of his temptations Jesus decisively rejected the temptation to perform miracles (Matthew 4:1–11; Luke 4:1–13). He was tempted to turn stones into bread and to throw himself from the temple without injury, and he refused to do either. Is it then likely that he would perform in the course of his ministry such a miracle as the feeding of the 5,000, which apparently resulted in the crowd trying to make him their king? (See John 6:1–15; Matthew 14:13–21; Mark 6:30–44; Luke 9:10–17).

This is not such a problem as it appears at first sight. Indeed it only arises if we regard Jesus first and foremost as a wonder-worker. The ancient world was full of magicians who practised their art as a means of displaying their own special powers and significance. But the whole tone of the Gospel stories is quite different. Jesus' work is characterized not by a quest for power, but by humble service of God and man. In the temptations he rejected the possibility of commanding the obedience of men and women by working wonders, and the Gospels show how even his miracles were subordinated to that intention. For the miracles, like his teaching and preaching, were a call for faith and obedience from those who experienced or witnessed them.

It seems therefore that the various pieces of evidence all have the same implication. Both Jewish and Christian sources suggest that Jesus did perform remarkable deeds. Though there is obviously room for making different judgements about different miracles, we cannot reasonably dispose of the whole of the miraculous element in the Gospel traditions. At the same time, we must resist the temptation to regard the miracles as an end in themselves. Like so many other parts of Jesus' ministry, their real importance lies in what they teach us about God.

The miracles and their meaning

To understand fully what the miracles mean, we have to set them in their proper context in the whole of Jesus' ministry. The Gospels view the life and work of Jesus against the background of God's promises in the Old Testament. These promises are being fulfilled in Jesus, and the long-awaited new society, or kingdom, has arrived.

This means that we need to begin our understanding of the precise significance of most of Jesus' teaching by looking at the Old Testament. For example, his self-designation as 'Son of man' would be difficult if not impossible to understand without our knowledge of its Old Testament meaning in the book of Daniel. Jesus' message about the kingdom of God would also be rather obscure if we did not link it with the Old Testament promises. The same is true of the miracles.

In the Old Testament, miracles invariably meant something. What God says is often associated with what he does. Indeed, in Hebrew the word *dabar* can mean both a word and an action, and the two were very closely linked together in Hebrew thought. God's actions could be regarded as an extension of his words. What

Magdala was once a fishing town on the western shore of Lake Galilee. Mary Magdalene, one of many people whom Jesus released from the power of evil, came from this region.

Exodus 10:1–2

Isaiah 20:1–6

Ezekiel 4:1–3

he does is essentially identical with what he says. So, for example, at the time of the exodus the remarkable deeds performed by Moses before Pharaoh were not just wonders performed for effect. They were themselves the vehicle of God's message, living signs of the truth of God's words.

This idea was taken up especially by the prophets of the Old Testament, who often performed symbolic actions to illustrate and enforce their message. Isaiah, for example, walked round Jerusalem naked and barefoot as a symbol of his belief that Judah's allies would soon be destroyed by their enemies. Ezekiel drew a picture of a besieged city on a tile, as a picture of what was going to happen to his own city of Jerusalem. Yet these actions were more than just symbols or illustrations. They were a part of God's message through the prophets, and were closely bound up with the meaning of God's activities in the history of his people.

When the New Testament calls Jesus' miracles 'signs', it is probably this kind of 'dynamic illustration' that is in mind. Our English word 'sign' implies merely a symptom or an indication, and so it is easy for us to suppose that the miracles were nothing more than artificially contrived indications to prove that Jesus was the Messiah, or that the new society had come. But they are more than that. Like the 'signs' given by the prophets, the miracles are part of Jesus' message. They are an extension in actions of the teaching given in the parables. Like that teaching, they describe God's new society and present its challenge to men and women.

When we consider the miracles in this light we can see that they draw attention to three aspects of the new society, or 'kingdom of God'.

The arrival of the kingdom

When Jesus began his teaching ministry, the main content of his message was the declaration that 'the kingdom of God is at hand'.

The precise meaning that we give to the phrase 'at hand' will depend on our view of Jesus' eschatology. But most scholars agree that at least one implication of the statement is that the kingdom has already come into existence with the coming of Jesus himself. This is brought out quite clearly in Jesus' miracles, where the arrival of God's kingdom is both declared and explained.

Mark 1:15

On one occasion John the Baptist sent some of his disciples to ask Jesus whether he was indeed the Messiah who was to inaugurate God's new society. And the answer that Jesus gave was as follows: 'Go and tell John what you hear and see: the blind receive their sight and the lame walk, lepers are cleansed and the deaf hear, and the dead are raised up, and the poor have good news preached to them.' These words in which Jesus addressed John were a quotation from the Old Testament book of Isaiah, and were generally believed to be a reference to the future messianic age. Jesus was telling John that his miracles were a sign that ancient promises were coming true.

Matthew 11:4–5; Luke 7:22

Isaiah 35:5–6

In John's Gospel the miracles are actually called 'signs'. Through the miracles men and women realize not only that the new society has come, but that Jesus is its central figure. In the first miracle recorded in John (the changing of water into wine) Jesus 'revealed his glory, and his disciples believed in him'. Later on, the raising of Lazarus is 'the means by which the Son of God will receive glory'. Yet Jesus did not use miracles for personal gain. In the prologue to John's Gospel we are reminded that Jesus' glory was not his own. It was the glory of God, which he shared as God's Son. The same theme comes out in a number of the miracle stories, where Jesus requires praise to be given to God and not to himself. In the miracles, God was demonstrating his own power so that men and women would realize that his long awaited kingdom had arrived with the coming of Jesus.

John 2:11

John 11:4

John 1:14

Luke 17:11–19; John 11:4

The scope of the kingdom

The miracles not only announce the arrival of the kingdom in a general sense: their message also parallels Jesus' explicit teaching in many more detailed ways. It is not difficult to see how the various types of miracle that Jesus performed were meant to emphasize in a striking way the different things he said in the parables about the new society. The miracles fall into three main groups, each group expressing a different aspect of Jesus' teaching. They declare the meaning of the kingdom for individual men and women, for the world as a whole, and in the future.

● *The kingdom and the individual.* In one of his temptations, the devil had claimed that *he* was the master of the world's kingdoms. Many people in the time of Jesus would have agreed with him. As they looked at their own lives and the lives of other people, they saw suffering and illness and death as signs that their lives were influenced by the operation of evil forces in the world. It was commonly believed that disease was caused by the demonic members of an evil spiritual world operating in the natural, physical world. Sin and evil caused disease – not in the personal sense implied by those Pharisees who suggested that because a

Matthew 4:8–10; Luke 4:5–7

John 9:1–12

person was blind he and his family must be great sinners, but in a cosmic sense, so that human illness was seen as a part of the total fallenness of God's creation.

We have seen that an important part of Jesus' teaching was that men and women could be set free from the mastery of sin in their lives. In the casting out of demons and in the other healing miracles, Jesus made this announcement in the most dramatic way possible. He also underlined another part of his teaching, for the miracles more often than not involved those who were the outcasts of society – lepers, whom no one would touch for fear of religious impurity; a Roman centurion, whom many Jews must have hated; those who were past helping themselves. Those were the people to whom Jesus' message and miracles were of most value.

Matthew 8:1–4;
Luke 17:11–19
Matthew 8:5–13;
Luke 7:1–10
Mark 5:21–43

● *The kingdom and the world.* If the healing miracles show Jesus releasing individual people from the power of sin, the 'nature miracles' show Jesus doing the same for the whole of creation. The devil's power had affected not just the lives of individuals, but the life of nature as well. There was a real sense in which Satan *was* the ruler of the world, and Jesus had come to cast him out of every part of his dominion. So he 'rebukes' the wind and the waves in the same way as he 'rebukes' the demons that have such a harmful effect in the lives of men and women.

John 12:31
Mark 4:39
Mark 1:25

It was an important part of Jesus' message that he had come to save men and women in their whole environment, and in the nature miracles we have a striking declaration of the global scope of Jesus' work.

● *The kingdom in the future.* It is interesting that the future dimension of Jesus' teaching about the new society is also pre-

Bethany was the home town of Mary Martha and Lazarus. Here Jesus brought Lazarus back to life – a miracle that caused such a stir that the Jewish leaders began plotting to kill Jesus.

served in the miracles. In Jewish thought the future kingdom of God was often pictured as a meal, and Jesus himself described it in terms of a banquet. The miraculous feedings of the 5,000 and of the 4,000 are an acting out of this picture, in which Jesus showed himself as God's Messiah feeding God's people. According to one account of the feeding of the 5,000, the people were so impressed by what took place that they thought Jesus was meaning to imply that they should make him their king there and then.

Matthew 8:11; Luke 22:30; 14:15–24

Matthew 14:13–21; Mark 6:30–44; Luke 9:10–17; Matthew 15:32–39; Mark 8:1–10

John 6:14–15

There are also three instances in which Jesus restored to life people who were dead. These miracles are an expression in action of his teaching that his followers would have 'eternal life', by which they could anticipate in the present the future blessings of the messianic kingdom.

Mark 5:21–43; Luke 7:11–17; John 11:1–44

The challenge of the kingdom

When we dealt with the parables, we saw that they were a way of making people think out the full implications of God's new society in their own lives, and we noticed that without repentance and faith the full meaning of many of the parables would be hidden. The challenge of God's rule is presented in exactly the same terms in the miracle stories.

Faith seems to have been important in Jesus' cures. On three occasions Jesus says, 'Your faith has made you well' and according to Mark the absence of faith was a hindrance to performing miracles. Indeed without faith it was not possible to realize that the miracles were a sign of God at work, and unbelief led to the conclusion that Jesus was in league with Satan.

Mark 5:34; 10:52; Luke 17:19

Mark 6:5

Matthew 12:24

Some students of the New Testament point out that in modern psychiatry 'faith' is often an important part of a cure, and they

suggest that this may offer some sort of explanation of the healings Jesus performed. There is no doubt that observations of this kind have helped many people to accept the truth of the Gospel accounts. And there is equally no reason to suppose that Jesus, who knew what was in the heart of men and women, could not have anticipated some of the methods of modern psychology.

John 2:23–25

But the faith that Jesus required was really rather different from the kind of faith the psychiatrist asks for. What Jesus demanded was not a predisposition to be healed, but an unconditional acceptance of God's rule. To ask Jesus for healing was a sign of this kind of faith, that is, faith in the sense that it appears in the parables – implicit trust in God and in Jesus as his Son, so that we may share in the benefits of his new society.

Matthew 8:13; 15:28

The purpose of the miracles can therefore be helpfully compared with the purpose of the parables. To those who are willing to trust God they are the vehicle of revelation. But to those whose minds are closed not even a miracle will bring the possibility of enlightenment.

Luke 16:19–31

Chapter 9

God's kingdom in action

Mark 2:27

Much of Jesus' teaching was in the open air, on the hills and in the crowded market places. Christians have often followed his example and proclaimed their faith in public places.

Every society, no matter how primitive or how civilized, needs rules and regulations to govern the conduct of its members. Often these rules are simply the result of what experience has taught about the best ways of doing things. Sometimes, as in a few of the law codes of the ancient Middle East, the rules stem from a system of religious beliefs.

Occasionally, as in the Old Testament, we find a mixture of both. Not that the Old Testament seemed quite that simple to the people who were trying to follow it in Jesus' day. For by then the relatively straightforward laws of the Old Testament had been complicated by the addition of detailed interpretations and applications – so much so that one needed to be a theologian even to understand them, let alone to keep them.

Jesus' attitude to behaviour was quite different from that. On several occasions he directly challenged the rules laid down by the Pharisees. On the question of the sabbath day, for example, Jesus declared his belief that 'the sabbath was made for man, not man for the sabbath'. It was a day for men and women to use and enjoy rather than a dull and dreary day to be spent trying desperately not to profane it. The Pharisees were naturally distressed at this setting aside of their law, for after all its avowed purpose was to help men and women to please God – and how else could they do that except by obeying his requirements?

As we read the Gospels it is clear that Jesus, too, was intending to help people to know God. But the God of whom he spoke was pictured rather differently. He was not a God who required the observance of a lot of impossible regulations, but a God with whom one could have a personal relationship as Father. Jesus' Father was a forgiving God, one who cared about people even in their moral imperfection. But he was concerned that they should get to know him better so that his power might be set loose to transform their lives.

We have seen the implications of all this in the parables that Jesus told, and we have also noticed some of the ethical consequences of his teaching. Those who live in fellowship with God must also love their neighbours. They must care for the

The synagogue

Synagogues were the local centre of Jewish worship, and many were also schools. The drawing is an artist's impression of what such a building would have looked like in Jesus' time, based on the ruins at Capernaum. Many synagogues were not so lavish as this, however. The photograph shows the ruins of the synagogue at Capernaum. The building probably dates from the end of the second century AD, but is almost certainly on the same site as the synagogue in which Jesus taught.

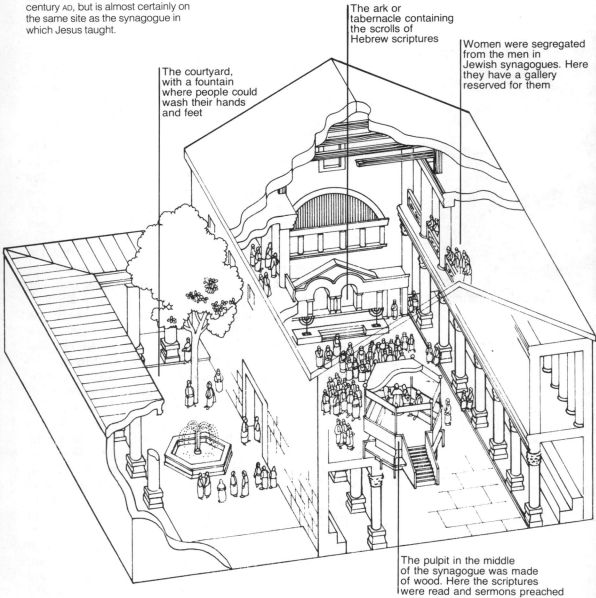

The ark or tabernacle containing the scrolls of Hebrew scriptures

Women were segregated from the men in Jewish synagogues. Here they have a gallery reserved for them

The courtyard, with a fountain where people could wash their hands and feet

The pulpit in the middle of the synagogue was made of wood. Here the scriptures were read and sermons preached

Jesus told his hearers to be careful of false teachers, who would betray themselves by the way they lived. 'A healthy tree cannot bear bad fruit, and a poor tree cannot bear good fruit,' he said. Fruit trees – these are figs – grow abundantly in Israel.

Matthew 5–7

outcasts of society, and be concerned for one another's welfare. But why should God's people act like this? What is the basis for the ethical teaching – the teaching about behaviour – that Jesus gave, and how can we understand it? These are the questions that we shall try to answer in this chapter.

It is of course not very easy to speak of Jesus' ethics in isolation from the rest of his teaching. All his teaching about God and his new society has an ethical dimension to it. And the Sermon on the Mount, which is generally taken to be the most comprehensive collection of ethical teachings in the Gospels, is also full of theology. Nevertheless, this sermon does give us a good idea of the place of ethics in the new society that Jesus had come to inaugurate.

Before we look at the actual content of the Sermon on the Mount, we first need to consider the best way of understanding what Jesus says in it. This is an important question, for it is obvious that the way Jesus gives his teaching here is quite different from the approach of modern ethics textbooks, and even quite different from the ways ordinary people would express the same ideas. As a good teacher, Jesus naturally used forms of language and expression that would mean something to those who first heard him. There are at least three distinctive devices used in putting over his teaching.

● Much of the sermon is poetry, though until it is pointed out to us we probably would not recognize it as such. English poetry depends for its effect on rhyme or stress. But Hebrew poetry was rather different. It depended for its effect on a correspondence of thought, and there could be two basic kinds of poetry depending on whether the correspondence was one of similarity or of difference. Take, for example, the following statement from Matthew. This can be arranged poetically as follows:

'Do not give dogs what is holy;
Matthew 7:6   and do not throw your pearls before swine.'

What we have here is genuine Hebrew poetry, in which the second line repeats the thought of the first line, but using different imagery. This is called 'synonymous parallelism', and there are many examples of it in the psalms and other poetic sections of the Old Testament.

Another type of Hebrew poetry was what we call 'antithetical parallelism'. Again there is an example of this in Matthew:

'Every sound tree bears good fruit,
Matthew 7:17   but the bad tree bears bad fruit.'

A similar lesson is being taught in each line, but the thought is expressed by the use of exactly opposite concepts. This technique also occurs frequently in the Old Testament.

Matthew 6:9–13 Even the Lord's Prayer can be arranged poetically. Professor A.M. Hunter sets it out like this:

'Our father in heaven	hallowed be thy name,
Thy kingdom come;	Thy will be done;
As in the heavens,	so on earth.
Our daily bread	give us today
And forgive us our debts,	as we forgive our debtors;
And lead us not into temptation,	but deliver us from evil.'

● Another common feature of Jesus' teaching is the use of pictures. Sometimes they take the form of story-parables; on other occasions they are simply vivid illustrations from everyday life. Many of the parables do of course teach moral lessons, but the Sermon on the Mount makes much use of pictures from real life. This is quite different from the way we tend to moralize today. We speak of ethics in an abstract way, but Jesus always dealt with concrete things. For example, we might say, 'Materialism can be a hindrance to spiritual growth'. Jesus said, 'No one can be a slave of two masters... You cannot serve both
Matthew 6:24   God and money.'

● Jesus stated things in a vivid way. He often used extreme

Matthew 5:29

exaggeration to make his point. For example, he said that it is better to pull one's eye out rather than to commit adultery, or better to cut one's hand off rather than displease God. He was obviously not meaning to suggest that we should do either of these things, but he used this extravagant language to impress on his hearers the seriousness of his message.

As we read the Sermon on the Mount, we need to look out for these different techniques that Jesus used to put over his message. Recognizing the different forms will often help us to understand what Jesus was meaning to say.

What sort of ethic, then, did Jesus put forward? What principles of action should guide those who accept God's sovereignty in their lives? There are three things that distinguish the ethic of God's new society from most other ethical systems.

Jesus declares God's standards

Jesus' ethical teaching is quite inseparable from his teaching about God's sovereignty in the lives of men and women. Without understanding this, it is very difficult to make sense of the Sermon on the Mount.

All ethical systems have a basic premise from which everything else is developed. Jesus' ethical teaching is based on the declaration that the God who created all things and who acted in history in the experience of Israel recorded in the Old Testament can be known in a realistic and personal way. The behaviour of his followers is a natural outcome of their personal association with God, their Father.

This principle had always had a central place in Judaism. The Old Testament itself was based on two simple premises that are also basic to Jesus' teaching in the New Testament.

Human goodness takes its character from God

Leviticus 19:2

The central part of one section of the Old Testament law is the statement, 'You shall be holy; for I the Lord your God am holy'. The ethical standards which God's people were required to achieve were nothing less than a reflection of the character of God himself. One scholar sums it up by describing biblical ethics as 'the science of human conduct, as it is determined by divine conduct'. Men and women should behave as God behaves.

One of the most characteristic of God's activities in the experience of Israel had been his willingness to care for people who had no thought for him. Abraham was called from Mesopotamia and given a new homeland not because of any moral or spiritual superiority that he may have possessed, but simply because God's affection was centred on him. Israel subsequently emerged from the shattering experiences of the exodus and what followed, not because of their own moral perfection but simply through the care of a loving God. On the basis of these undeserved acts of kindness, God had made certain demands of his people.

The Ten Commandments begin with the statement, 'I am the Lord your God, who brought you out of the land of Egypt,

Exodus 20:2

out of the house of bondage...' This is the presupposition on which the commandments are based. Because God has done something for his people, they are to respond in love and obedience to him. The same pattern is found elsewhere in the law of the Old Testament: 'You shall remember that you were a slave in the land of Egypt, and the Lord your God redeemed you;

Deuteronomy 15:15

therefore I command you today...'

The ethic of the New Testament has exactly the same basis of action. It is striking, for instance, that when Paul wanted to stop the quarrelling that was going on in the church at Philippi, he appealed not to ordinary common sense to solve the problem, but to just this very aspect of God's character that we have seen in the Old Testament. He takes the example of the way God gave himself for our salvation in Christ and makes this the basis of his moral appeal to his readers. Because Jesus gave up everything for us, we ought to be willing to sacrifice our self-centredness in order to please him.

Philippians 2:5–11

The fact that God's character as a holy God and as a loving Father underlies all the Bible's teaching on behaviour has at least three important practical consequences...

● It has given to both Jews and Christians a greater sense of the seriousness of sin. When people are faced with a holy God who was willing to give himself entirely in love for the benefit of those who neither cared for him nor respected him, they recognize how different their own character is from the character of their God. When Isaiah, for instance, had been impressed with the true meaning of God's holiness, his immediate reaction was to appreciate, perhaps for the first time, the full extent of his own sinfulness. The same must have been true of most people who met Jesus. In many cases Jesus forgave the sins of those who came to him – and he reminds us himself that only those who recognize their need can be forgiven.

Isaiah 6:1–8

Jesus said that his teaching was not intended to replace the Old Testament law but to make it come true. This Hebrew scroll is part of the Torah, or Law.

● Christian goodness has a numinous, other-worldly quality that goes beyond the demands of common sense. The character of God as revealed by Jesus shows his self-giving love, and this is recommended in practical action over and over again in Jesus' teaching. The rich man was told to '... go, sell what you have,

Mark 10:21

and give to the poor...' In the Sermon on the Mount Jesus tells his disciples to go two miles if the Roman troops force them to carry their bags for one. They are to 'turn the other cheek' and

Matthew 5:38–42

return good for evil. These things often seem quite unreasonable to us, perhaps even absurd. But when we view them in the light of what God has been willing to sacrifice for us, they take on a different appearance.

● The overwhelming desire of God's people should be to please God and to respond to his love in ways that reflect his own character. This is their motivation to obey Jesus' commands. We are to love our enemies not in order to draw attention to ourselves, but 'so that you may become sons of your

Matthew 5:45

Father in heaven'.

Christian goodness and the community

The central theme of the Old Testament is the belief that God had acted decisively in the history of his people Israel and had entered into an intimate relationship with them through the making of a covenant. This meant that the individual Israelite was never simply an individual, but a member of the people of God. As a result of this the goodness that God required was to be demonstrated not simply in pious individuals but in the institutions of national life.

In the same way Jesus declared that he had come to establish God's kingship in the lives of his followers, and not only in their lives as individuals, but in their corporate life together. One of the two great commandments was that men and women should love their neighbour as themselves. And those who were willing to accept God's rule over their lives were given a new commandment that was to be the basis of the Christian community: 'that you love one another; even as I have loved you, that you also love one another. By this all men will know that you are my disciples, if you have love for one another.'

Matthew 22:34–40;
Mark 12:28–34;
Luke 10:25–28

John 13:34–35

Jesus' ethic demands commitment

Jesus' teaching was intended as a way of life only for those people who subjected their lives to God's rule. This is the point at which Jesus' ethic has most frequently been misunderstood. People who claim to be able to accept the Sermon on the Mount but not the claims that Jesus made about his own person have misunderstood the essential character of Jesus' teaching. It is quite impossible to isolate his theology from his ethics, and to do so destroys both.

In his introduction to the Sermon on the Mount Matthew tells us it was the disciples who formed the audience for the sermon; and the various elements of it are clearly directed to certain committed people, not to all and sundry. This was clearly understood by the earliest Christians. The sermon was almost certainly used in the form we know it to instruct new converts in the churches with which Matthew was associated in the first century. Both in the context of Jesus' life and in the context of the early church, the ethical instruction of the sermon was preceded by the preaching and acceptance of the Christian message.

C.H.Dodd has demonstrated that two strands of early Christian teaching can be distinguished in the New Testament, and it is interesting to find that they correspond to the general pattern we have noticed in the ethics of the Old Testament. On the one hand there is the kind of teaching that he calls *kerygma*. This was essentially a declaration of what God had done for men and women in the life, death and resurrection of Jesus.

This was comparable to the way Abraham and his descendants had been called and established as a nation in the Old Testament. God had acted through Jesus not because of any moral value in the people who became his followers, but out of his own undeserved love – what Christians call 'grace'. As Israel

Jesus could be stern as well as thoughtful. On one occasion he said that if a man caused a child 'to lose his faith in me' it would be better for him 'to have a large millstone tied round his neck and be drowned in the deep sea'.

had been called to obey the Law on the basis of what God had done, so too the early Christians could be given moral and spiritual exhortations.

Professor Dodd called this *didache*, or 'teaching'. We can see this distinction most clearly in some of the letters of Paul, which often deal with theological matters first and then make practical appeals to Christians on the basis of theological arguments. But the distinction is not terribly important, and in reality both *kerygma* and *didache* tend to run into one another, for the ethic of the New Testament is not some rule imposed from outside, but a new quality of life given to Christians through what Jesus has done for them.

We can illustrate this from some of the individual sayings of the Sermon on the Mount, none of which can be understood apart from the belief that in Jesus God had broken into history in a decisive way. When Jesus says to his disciples, 'forgive

'Do not save riches for yourselves here on earth, where moths and rust destroy,' Jesus said. His ethical teaching has been a source of inspiration to many people. The way of life of individuals and whole societies has been transformed by its application by dedicated Christians.

William Wilberforce was a nineteenth-century Christian politician who campaigned for many years for the abolition of the slave trade.

The Earl of Shaftesbury also campaigned during the last century for shorter working hours and better conditions in Victorian mines and factories.

Matthew 6:14–15
Matthew 5:44

others the wrongs they have done to you', it is because they themselves are receiving God's forgiveness. When they are called to love their enemies we call to mind the dynamic of God's own love, shown to them when they had no regard for him. In each case God's gift, his free grace, comes before his demand for action. Even the missionary work of the disciples was to be carried out on the same basis. Jesus told them that since 'You have received without paying, so give without being paid'.

Matthew 10:8

Jesus teaches an ethic of freedom

One of the greatest temptations to all readers of the Sermon on the Mount has always been to try to interpret it as a set of rules and regulations – a new law for Christians, to replace the old law of the Old Testament. This was something that emerged very early in the church's history, and some scholars believe that even Matthew himself considered it to be a 'new law' delivered

Mother Teresa has lived for many years in Calcutta caring for the sick and orphaned. Jesus specifically commanded his followers to care for the needy.

Jesus also warned his followers that some of them would be persecuted for their faith. Archbishop Janani Luwum is believed to have been murdered by the Ugandan authorities for speaking out against injustice.

by Jesus on a mountain in Galilee, comparable to the 'old law' delivered by Moses on Mt Sinai.

But the ethical teaching of Jesus was never intended to be a 'law' in any sense at all.

● The teaching of the Sermon on the Mount is quite different from what we normally understand by 'law'. Most laws are based on calculations of how the majority of people can reasonably be expected to behave. A law that cannot be kept is a bad law, and it is no use making a law to put pressure on men and

In the Sermon on the Mount Jesus spoke of those whose faith did not stretch to trusting God for everyday things. 'Look how the wild flowers grow,' he said. 'It is God who clothes the wild grass. Won't he be all the more sure to clothe you?'

women to become what they are not. But this, of course, is essentially what Jesus' teaching does: it asks us to be different from what we would naturally be. It is therefore inadequate to regard it as a 'new law', because its requirements are not the kind that anyone could keep simply by making the effort.

● Throughout the course of his ministry Jesus was in conflict with the Pharisees, the law-makers of the Jewish nation. They were concerned with actions that could be governed by rules. But Jesus had a different approach altogether. He was most concerned with people and principles. For him the secret of goodness was to be found not in obedience to rules, but in the spontaneous activities of a transformed character. 'A sound tree cannot bear evil fruit, nor can a bad tree bear good fruit.'

Matthew 7:18

Jesus' teaching is not a law. It is an ethic of freedom. Those who accept God's sovereignty within his new society enjoy the freedom to know him in the context of a living relationship as their Father. Jesus' Sermon on the Mount does not give rules and regulations. It sets out principles, and the principles are more concerned with what people are than with what they do. Not that actions are unimportant. But Jesus realized that the way we behave depends on the kind of people we are. Without the right internal disposition and motivation, we cannot even begin to understand Jesus' ethical teaching. For, as T.W.Manson succinctly put it, Jesus' teaching is 'a compass rather than an ordnance map; it gives direction rather than directions'.

Did Jesus abolish the Old Testament Law?

One statement found in the Sermon on the Mount often causes some difficulty. This is the saying, in Matthew 5:17–18, 'Think not that I have come to abolish the law and the prophets; I have come not to abolish them but to fulfil them. For truly, I say to you, till heaven and earth pass away, not an iota, not a dot, will pass from the law until all is accomplished.'

Several explanations have been suggested for this statement.

● The simplest of them is to argue that this saying is not in fact original to Jesus, but has come into the sermon later and reflects a situation in the Jewish Christian churches for whom Matthew was writing his Gospel. Matthew may have had in mind the chaos that had been caused in some churches as a result of misunderstanding Paul's teaching about freedom from the restraint of the law, and perhaps he wished to pre-empt any similar movement by the Christians he knew. This may appear to be a drastic solution, but these verses are so out of character with the whole of the rest of Jesus' teaching that many

scholars believe it to be the best answer.

● It has also been suggested that when Jesus speaks of 'fulfilling the law' he may have meant something rather different from what we imagine him to mean. The new society that Jesus talks about is usually depicted as the fulfilment of the Old Testament, and an important element in the Old Testament was the belief that God's people could enjoy a living relationship with him. Though the scribes and Pharisees had externalized and legalized this relationship, Jesus could have been referring to its original intention, which called for a person's life to be right before God: 'what does the Lord require of you but to do justice, and to love kindness, and to walk humbly with your God?' (Micah 6:8).

● It is also possible that what Jesus says about the Law's permanence is not to be taken literally. Like so much of his teaching, it could be an exaggerated way of emphasizing that his whole mission and message were firmly grounded in the Old Testament revelation.

4. Knowing about Jesus

Chapter 10 Understanding the Gospels

Ruins of the forum in Rome
(associated with Luke and Mark).

In the first three sections of this book, we have said a great deal about the life and teachings of Jesus, but very little about how we have come to know about him. Naturally, our picture of Jesus has been based on those parts of the New Testament which tell of his life and work – the four books we call 'Gospels', and commonly associate with the names of Matthew, Mark, Luke and John.

Yet it must by now be obvious that in understanding the Gospels we have made a number of assumptions about them that, in one way or another, have coloured the picture of Jesus presented here. For example, we have assumed that the Gospels are not so much biographies of Jesus, as selective presentations of those aspects of his life and teaching which seemed most important to the people who first wrote them down. In addition, we have assumed that there is a good deal of overlap and repetition in the various accounts of Jesus' life, so that one Gospel may be used to elaborate or clarify the teaching contained in another. Then we have also implied that it is actually possible to know something about Jesus from the study of the Gospels – that, although they are indeed the products of the early church, they tell us not only about their writers but about Jesus himself.

The time has now come to examine some of these assumptions in greater detail, to explain the reasons for holding them, and to explore their implications.

What is a Gospel?

The modern reader approaching one of the Gospels for the first time may think it looks very much like a biography of Jesus. But a quick glance through any one of them will show that it is hardly that. A good biography usually begins with an account of the subject's childhood years, and progresses consecutively through adolescence and adulthood to show how the mature person has developed in response to the various influences of early life and environment. By contrast, the main emphasis in the Gospels is not on the course of Jesus' life, but on the events of the last week or so. This is prefaced by reports of Jesus' teaching and accounts of a few incidents from the three years immediately preceding his death, with virtually no mention at all of his childhood and adolescence. If this is biography, then it is certainly no ordinary biography.

We can most easily find out what it is by turning to the Gospels themselves. Rather than trying to classify them as a modern librarian would, we should ask what their authors thought they were doing as they wrote. Take Mark, for instance, the Gospel commonly thought to be the earliest of the four. The author describes his work in the opening sentence as 'The beginning

Mark 1:1

of the gospel of Jesus Christ'. This statement stands as a kind of title or heading to what follows, and two words are important here for an understanding of the purpose of the Gospel: the words 'beginning' and 'gospel'. 'Gospel' is simply the English equivalent of Mark's Greek word *euangelion*, and it was originally chosen because the two words had the same meaning: 'good news'. Mark, then, was writing about 'the beginning of the good news'.

What does this mean? Mark and the other Gospel writers had heard the 'good news' about Jesus. They had accepted its authority and recognized Jesus as Lord of their lives. Mark himself had subsequently become deeply involved in the work of the church,

Acts 12:25–13:13; 15:36–40;
Colossians 4:10; 2 Timothy 4:11

and an important part of this work was preaching and teaching the message that had changed his own life. This preaching and teaching is recorded in the New Testament. In its most basic form it consisted of the statements summed up by C.H. Dodd in his definition of the earliest *kerygma*. For Mark and his contemporaries this message was not just a bare statement of the facts about the Christian faith: it was also in an important sense the 'good news' of their faith, because as they accepted its challenge to repentance they found it a life-changing experience.

So when Mark describes his Gospel as 'the beginning of the good news', he is saying that his purpose is to describe the first stage in the development of the message to which he and others had responded. The story he tells was an integral and important part of their own story and experience as Christians. Luke had a similar intention: he writes so that his readers may know the full implications of the Christian message which they had heard so

Luke 1:4

often. Indeed, Luke felt it necessary to emphasize the continuity of the life of the church with the life of Jesus by writing a second volume (the Acts of the Apostles) to bring the story more fully up to date.

When we call the writers of the Gospels 'evangelists' we are therefore accurately describing their intention. For they were primarily concerned to deliver the message about Jesus to their own contemporaries, and only secondarily, if at all, with the normal interests of a biographer. This fact has at least three important consequences for our understanding of the Gospels they wrote.

● We must regard the Gospels as a *selective* account of the life and teachings of Jesus. In their preaching of the message the apostles and others no doubt spoke of incidents from Jesus' life in much the same way as a modern preacher may use appropriate illustrations to explain his theological points. Mark and the

Quoted in Eusebius, *Ecclesiastical History*, III.39.15

other evangelists had no doubt heard these incidents used to illustrate many a sermon, and they incorporated them into their Gospels for broadly similar purposes. Indeed Papias, one of the Fathers of the early church, claimed that Mark's Gospel consists of material extracted from the preaching of none other than Peter himself.

The fact that the information contained in the Gospels was first used to illustrate the message of the church also explains some of the difficulties we often feel about the apparent incompleteness of the Gospel accounts. All four of them put together would hardly contain enough information to document three years of anyone's life, let alone someone as active as Jesus. But when we realize that the information we have has been preserved because of its relevance to the life of the earliest churches, we can readily understand why so much that we would like to know has been left out.

This probably explains why we find no mention in the New Testament of the early childhood of Jesus, nor for that matter any descriptions of what he looked like, or the kind of person he was. Had the evangelists been writing merely to satisfy people's curiosity about Jesus, they would have included that sort of information. But that was not their intention. They were primarily concerned to win other people to faith in their Lord and Master, and for this purpose such details were quite irrelevant.

● If the Gospels are illustrations of the apostolic preaching, this means that we cannot regard their contents as simple stories about Jesus. They must be closely related to the theology of the evangelists. At one time it was fashionable to suppose that it was possible to recover from the Gospels a picture of a simple Galilean teacher which had later been altered by Paul and others into a theological message about the Son of God. But it is now widely recognized that the Gospels are themselves among the most important theological documents of the early church, and we can never in fact discover a picture of Jesus as a simple Galilean teacher. As far back as we can go, the Jesus whom we find in the pages of the New Testament is always a person who makes great claims for himself and utters definitive pronouncements on the relationship of men and women to God. All his teaching and every incident recorded in the Gospels has something specifically theological to tell us.

● If, as we have suggested, the authors selected their materials to serve their own purposes in writing, it follows that we can probably discover something about them and their readers by comparing their relative selection and use of information about Jesus. In the case of the first three Gospels we can do this quite easily, for they tell roughly the same story in the same order, and each of them repeats large sections of the material that is found in the others. By comparing the different ways that Matthew, Mark and Luke have used the deeds and teaching of Jesus in their narratives, we can readily learn something about them and the situation in which they lived and worked.

So to understand the Gospels fully is a rather complex business. We need to know why the evangelists wrote as and when they did. Then we need to try to understand the way they assembled their material, and why they used it in one particular way rather than another. And always we need to bear in mind that their Gospels were intended to serve the preaching ministry of the church: they were not written as biography, history, or even theology in the usual sense.

Preaching and writing

An obvious question to ask about the Gospels is: Where did the evangelists get their information, and what did they do with it? This may seem at first to be a rather irrelevant question, a kind of theologian's 'Everest', demanding to be conquered just because it happens to be there. But it is a helpful question for a satisfactory understanding of the nature of the Gospels. Tracing an author's sources and investigating his method of using them can be an important part of understanding what he is saying. If we know what he is doing, then we can understand more clearly what he may be getting at. And if we misunderstand his method, it is quite likely that we will also fail to grasp his essential message.

Since the Gospels almost certainly developed in the context of the preaching of the early church, we may expect to find some clues to their origin by examining the church's message. This

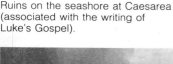

Ruins on the seashore at Caesarea (associated with the writing of Luke's Gospel).

essentially contains three major themes. First, the Christian gospel was connected with the promises of the Old Testament. Then came a series of statements about Jesus and his significance. Finally there was a challenge to men and women to repent and accept the message.

Old Testament texts

The message began with the statement that the promises of the Old Testament had been fulfilled in the life of Jesus. In the New Testament summaries of the preaching this statement is often made in a rather generalized way. But of course in real life situations it must have been a more specific declaration. For anyone familiar with the Old Testament would not be content until they had found out just which prophecies Jesus was supposed to have fulfilled. We know from other evidence that one of the favourite occupations of the Jews was the compilation of lists of Old Testament passages which the Messiah would fulfil when he came. The people at Qumran, for example, kept such lists, and so did other Jewish groups. These lists are generally referred to by scholars as *testimonia*.

There are a number of indications in the New Testament that these text-lists were probably in regular use amongst Christians from the earliest times. In both Matthew and John a great number of texts from the Old Testament are cited, with an indication that they were fulfilled in some particular incident in the life of Jesus. Yet it is striking that they hardly ever used the same passages. This may well have been because they were using different collections of *testimonia*.

In some of Paul's letters, too, we find Old Testament texts strung together in continuous passages in what often seems to be a rather arbitrary fashion. Again, it is reasonable to think that Paul originally found these grouped together under the same heading in his collection of Old Testament texts. It may well be that the collection of these texts from the Old Testament was the very earliest form of literary activity in the Christian church. They would be assembled for the convenience of Christian preachers, so that they could cite specific examples to support their claim that Jesus had fulfilled the Old Testament promises concerning the Messiah.

Words of Jesus

But the central element in the *kerygma* was the series of statements about Jesus himself. No doubt in the very earliest days of the church's existence it would be possible to proclaim the message with no more than a passing reference to Jesus' life and teachings. For most Christians were Jews and the church was still a local Palestinian sect, and many people in Palestine must have known something about Jesus, however little. But it was not very long before Christian missionaries were spreading out far beyond Palestine and carrying their teaching to parts of the Roman Empire where Jesus was quite unknown. It must have been essential at this stage for the preachers of the good news to include in their message some kind of factual information about

Jesus himself, if only the account of the events of his death and resurrection.

Once people had become Christians they would require further instruction in their new faith. This instruction would include information about Christian beliefs, as well as the kind of advice about Christian behaviour often found in the New Testament letters. One obvious and important source of such teaching must have been the remembered statements of Jesus himself. This would not necessarily be given as information about Jesus, as we can see from Paul's advice in Romans 12–14. Much of what he says there is so close to Jesus' teaching in the Sermon on the

A street in old Jerusalem (associated with John).

Matthew 5–7 Mount that it is hard to believe that the two do not derive from the same source. Yet Paul never identifies his advice with the teaching of Jesus himself. Other parts of Paul's writings also show that the traditions of Jesus' teaching were familiar to the early

1 Corinthians 7:10–11 Gentile churches.

It is therefore quite likely that long before the Gospels were written in their present form the sayings of Jesus would be collected together as a kind of manual for the guidance of teachers in the early church. No doubt there would be a number of such collections of Jesus' teaching, made for different purposes and occasions in the church's life. Scholars often call these collections of sayings by the name *logia*.

In addition to the general considerations already mentioned, there are several more substantial reasons for believing that this was one of the earliest types of Christian writing about Jesus.

● We know that there were later collections of this kind, even long after the writing of the New Testament Gospels. A number of papyrus fragments dating from the third century AD, found at Oxyrhynchus in Egypt, contain sayings of Jesus, some of them different from those found in the Gospels. A whole book of such sayings written in Coptic has also been found in Egypt. This is known as the *Gospel of Thomas*. It contains sayings of Jesus not found in the New Testament, some of which could be authentic. Whether or not they are genuine, however, these documents do show quite clearly that it was the custom of the early church to make such collections of the sayings of Jesus.

● About AD 130–40 Papias, the bishop of Hierapolis, wrote a five-volume *Exposition of the Oracles of the Lord*. Though most of this work is now lost, we do possess a few fragments of it in the form of quotations given in the writings of other people. Writing of Matthew, Papias says that he 'compiled the *logia* in

Nazareth was Jesus' home town. But he said the people's lack of faith there prevented him from doing many great works. This picture was taken looking across the valley of Jezreel from Nazareth. It shows the site of Megiddo where many Old Testament battles were fought. 'Armageddon' (the hill of Megiddo) became a symbol in apocalyptic literature of the final battle between good and evil.

Quoted in Eusebius, *Ecclesiastical History*, III.39

the Hebrew language, and each one interpreted it as he could'. The precise implication of this statement is uncertain, but most scholars believe that the *logia* to which Papias refers is a collection of the sayings of Jesus rather than the book we know as the Gospel of Matthew.

● The organization of the material in the Gospels often seems to suggest that Jesus' sayings had been grouped together before they were placed in their present context. There are many groups of sayings which are only loosely linked together and do not form any kind of consecutive argument. For example, the

Mark 9:49–50

sayings about salt in Mark really seem to be quite different from each other, and may well have been put together in a collection simply because they all mention salt.

Matthew 5–7

Then there is the whole of the Sermon on the Mount. Anyone who has ever tried to discover the argument of the sermon will realize the impossibility of the task, for there is no consecutive argument. What we have is a body of Jesus' teachings collected together because they all deal with ethical issues. But they hardly follow on in the same way as a modern sermon is expected to do. According to Professor Jeremias, the reason for this is that the sermon originally formed a collection of sayings of Jesus strung together to make them easily accessible to new converts to the Christian faith.

● A strong reason for assuming the existence of collections of Jesus' sayings early in the church's history is the fact that Matthew and Luke have a large amount of material that is common to both their Gospels, but which is altogether absent from Mark's Gospel. This material consists almost entirely of Jesus' teachings, but it also includes the story of his baptism and temptations and the story of one miracle, the healing of the centurion's servant. The generally accepted explanation of this common material is that Matthew and Luke both used the same collection of Jesus' sayings and incorporated it into their respective Gospels.

Scholars call this supposed sayings collection Q. It may have been a written document, or perhaps a body of oral tradition. Its existence in some form is certainly credible, especially since its alleged contents are closely parallel to the collections of prophetic oracles that we find in the Old Testament. In addition to the prophet's words gathered together and edited by his disciples, the prophetic books also often contain an account of the prophet's call and one or two incidents in his life. This is precisely what we get in the tradition called Q: an account of the baptism and temptation of Jesus (which can reasonably be equated with his call), and an illustration of the most typical of his activities: a healing miracle. But the main emphasis is on his teaching.

From the evidence assembled so far, we may conclude that from the very earliest times the church's main interest was in two kinds of literature: the *testimonia*, and the *logia* of Jesus. They may also have had a commonly agreed outline of the course of Jesus' life and teaching. But before too long it began to be necessary to gather all this material together in a more permanent form. This process did not of course take place overnight. Indeed it may not really be a separate process at all, but just the natural extension and completion of the work already begun in making collections of *testimonia* and *logia*. But the end product was to be the four documents we now know as the Gospels of Matthew, Mark, Luke and John.

Putting the Gospels together

The first three Gospels are called the synoptics because they are so much alike; and the precise way in which their writers transformed *logia* into Gospel is at the centre of the 'Synoptic problem'.

These Gospels are in effect three different editions of what is more or less the same basic material. Much of their resemblance can of course be explained by the assumption that these evangelists may have been using the same collections of sayings that had been circulating among different groups of Christians.

Matthew 3:13–4:11;
Luke 3:21–22; 4:1–13
Matthew 8:5–13; Luke 7:1–10

But the resemblances are more complex than that, for there are so many instances where the three Gospels use precisely the same language, vocabulary and grammatical constructions that most scholars believe they must have shared written sources.

As early as the fourth century AD, Augustine believed that Matthew must have been written first, and Mark later made a summary of it. Then Luke came along and wrote his Gospel on the basis of both Matthew and Mark. Until almost the beginning of the twentieth century, this was the most widely held view. There were of course variations on it. One of them – the 'Griesbach hypothesis' (put forward by the German J.J. Griesbach, 1745–1812) – has recently been the subject of much interest by contemporary scholars. Griesbach agreed with Augustine that Matthew was the first Gospel to be written, but he believed that Luke came next, and that Mark later used both Matthew and Luke as a basis for his work.

There are a number of difficulties with this view:

● Why would anyone have wanted to condense Matthew and Luke in order to make a Gospel like Mark? Compared with the two longer Gospels, Mark's short narrative can hardly be regarded as comprehensive. It has no mention at all of Jesus' birth or childhood, comparatively little about some of his most distinctive teaching, and only a very abbreviated account of the resurrection. We have already seen that the Gospel writers selected their materials

The closest followers of Jesus were mostly working people. Peter, who is believed to have supplied the author of Mark with stories of Jesus, was a fisherman, as were his brother Andrew, and James and John.

according to the interests and concerns of their readers. So in principle, there would be no reason why an abbreviated version of Matthew and Luke should not have been produced. But given the absolute centrality of precisely those elements which are either missed out or underplayed in Mark, it is virtually impossible to envisage a Christian group that would have been satisfied with Mark's account of Jesus if they already had access to Matthew and Luke. Indeed, it was not long before Christians almost universally preferred Matthew and Luke for this very reason. If Mark was written last, in full knowledge of the other two synoptic Gospels, it is very difficult to explain why it was written at all.

● Much of Mark's language seems to point to the same conclusion. If Mark used the polished accounts of Matthew and Luke, why did he so often write Greek that is virtually unintelligible?

Mark 4:30–32; Luke 13:18–19; Matthew 13:31–32

The parable of the Mustard Seed is a good example here. Both Matthew and Luke use eloquent expressions, which are quite similar to each other. Mark, by contrast, has a complicated Greek sentence without any verb in it, that really makes imperfect sense. If he was copying Matthew's or Luke's account, then it looks as if he went out of his way to avoid using their words – and it is very difficult to think of a good reason for doing that!

● It is almost as difficult to believe that Luke read and used Matthew's Gospel. If he did, then here again he must have adopted some rather strange literary procedures. Matthew contains one of the greatest masterpieces in any of the Gospels, the Sermon on the Mount. If Luke had that before him as he wrote, why did he break it all up – using some of it in his own Sermon on the Plain, but scattering the rest of it in small sections all over his own Gospel?

There are many other examples of the same problems at other points in these three Gospels. This is why most modern scholars have preferred a rather different explanation of their relationships with each other.

The more generally accepted explanation of the resemblances between the synoptic Gospels is that Matthew and Luke both used two source documents in writing their own accounts of Jesus' life and teaching. These were the sources we now know as Mark's Gospel and the hypothetical document Q. It is, of course, certain that Luke, at least, used a variety of sources in composing his Gospel, for he explicitly says that he has sifted through the work of other people, selecting those parts of their record that were suitable for his own purpose in writing. In view of the close literary connections with Mark and Luke, it seems certain that the author of Matthew used the same method in his work.

In reaching the conclusion that Matthew and Luke used Mark, New Testament scholars have analysed the text of the three synoptic Gospels using at least five different criteria.

● *Wording*. A comparison of the words used in different texts is a very simple way of determining their literary connections. More than half of Mark's actual vocabulary is contained in Matthew and Luke, and both of them have identical sections not found in Mark. So it seems that there was one source known to them all, and another source used only by Matthew and Luke.

● *Order*. If the order of events in a narrative contained in more than one Gospel also corresponds with those sections that have the same wording, we can go a step further and assume a common source whose order as well as wording has been substantially reproduced by all three evangelists. Again, there is much evidence for this. Matthew, Mark and Luke all follow the same general order of events. They begin with John the Baptist's ministry, then go on to tell of Jesus' baptism and temptations. Following this comes a ministry of miracle working and teaching in Galilee, which begins to arouse opposition from the Jewish leaders. Then Jesus makes journeys in the north to give teaching privately to his disciples. Finally they go to Jerusalem, and we have the account of Jesus' last days there, his trials, crucifixion and resurrection.

Within this general framework, particular incidents are also often recorded in the same order.

This feature of the synoptic Gospels is best explained if we suppose that Matthew and Luke were using Mark, and not the other way round. For it is striking that when Matthew departs from Mark's order, Luke has the same order as Mark; and when Luke departs from Mark's order, Matthew follows Mark. There is only one incident which both of them place differently from Mark: the appointment of the twelve disciples. Sometimes Matthew or Luke will leave the pattern of Mark's narrative in order to add something new, but after their addition they usually go back to the point in Mark at which they left off. This is one of the strongest arguments to support the belief that Matthew and Luke copied Mark, and not the other way round.

Mark 3:13–19;
Matthew 10:1–4;
Luke 6:12–16

● *Contents*. An analysis of the contents of the narratives also reveals the use of different sources. If one writer records the same story in the same words and order as another author, then we can suppose either that both have used the same source, or that one has used the work of the other. This is what happened in the case of the synoptic Gospels; of the 661 verses in Mark, 606 are found in Matthew in a virtually identical form, and about half of them are also contained in Luke.

● *Style*. This is a very difficult criterion to use satisfactorily. An author's style can depend on so many things: the situation in which he is writing, the readership he has in mind, whether or not he uses a secretary, and so on.

There certainly are marked stylistic differences between Mark and the other two synoptists, and on the whole Mark's Gospel is written in a poorer Greek than the other two. For example, he very often describes incidents in the historic present tense (using the present tense to speak of something that happened in the past). Matthew and Luke however always have a past tense, which is, of course, the correct literary form. This is one of the weaker arguments, for it depends on the assumption that the evangelists used their sources in a rather wooden way, simply copying out word for word what they had before them. But not many authors would follow a source closely enough for its style to obscure their own. If Mark was poor at writing Greek, then his grammar would tend to be poor whether or not he was copying from some other source.

We are on firmer ground when we observe that in eight cases where Mark records sayings of Jesus in Aramaic there is no trace of this in Luke, and only one example in Matthew. It would certainly be more likely that Matthew and Luke have omitted the Aramaic sayings than that Mark had deliberately introduced them.

● *Ideas and theology.* If it could be shown that one Gospel narrative contains a more developed theology than another, then it may seem reasonable to regard it as the later of the two. This appears to be a simple test, but again it is not so easy to apply in practice. It is often hard to be sure that an apparent difference in attitude is a real one. And, in any event, who is to define what is a 'developed' theology, and how can we be sure that this must be later in time than a 'primitive' outlook? When we remember that the highly developed theology of Paul was certainly in existence at the time the Gospels were taking shape we can see that the definition of such differences, and their chronological relationship to one another, must be a very subjective matter.

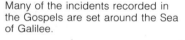
Many of the incidents recorded in the Gospels are set around the Sea of Galilee.

There are, of course, a number of different emphases in the Gospels. But it is difficult to know for certain what their signifi-

cance is for the composition of the Gospels. For example, Matthew and Luke appear to have modified or omitted certain statements in Mark that could be thought dishonouring to Jesus. Mark's blunt statement that in Nazareth Jesus 'could do no mighty work' appears in Matthew as 'he did not do many mighty works there', and Luke omits it altogether. Similarly, Jesus' question in Mark, 'Why do you call me good?' appears in Matthew as, 'Why do you ask me about what is good?'

Mark 6:5
Matthew 13:58
Mark 10:18
Matthew 19:17

Not all of these five points are of equal importance. There are difficulties in assessing the value of at least two of them. But taken together the cumulative effect of their evidence is most easily explained if we suppose that Matthew and Luke used Mark's account, rather than that Matthew was the original Gospel which Mark summarized and from which Luke made selective extracts.

The first Christians travelled widely in the years after the death of Jesus, partly as a result of opposition in Jerusalem. They took with them the stories of Jesus which in time were written down.

Two sources or four?

What has been said so far about the way the Gospels came to be written can be taken as the almost universally held view of New Testament scholars. Though there may be differences of opinion on points of detail, by far the majority of experts are agreed on the broad outline of the facts.

But in addition to the idea that the synoptic Gospels depend mainly on the two sources Mark and Q, it has been suggested that these are not the only sources we can trace behind our Gospels. B.H. Streeter was one of the first British scholars to set out the arguments for the idea that Matthew and Luke both used Mark's Gospel. But he went further than that, and suggested that in order to understand every detail of the synoptic Gospels we need to have a slightly more sophisticated theory, dealing with not two but four basic sources. Besides Mark and Q, he defined sources which he called M and L. In effect this material is simply what is left of the accounts of Matthew and Luke when the Marcan and Q material has been removed. But Streeter believed that these two collections of material were themselves separate and coherent sources of independent origin.

Proto-Luke

Streeter began his observations from the fact that Matthew and Luke each seem to use Mark in rather different ways. Matthew follows Mark's order and general framework very closely, though at the same time he frequently rewrites the actual material, and often condenses material from Mark to make more room for additional information. The result is that Matthew's Gospel looks rather like a new and enlarged edition of Mark. But Luke is rather different. Whereas Matthew makes use of almost all the material contained in Mark, Luke's Gospel contains only about half of Mark's material. What is more, Streeter discovered that if we remove all the Marcan material from Matthew, what is left has no coherence. The book simply falls to pieces. But if we do the same thing with Luke, we are left with a reasonably consistent and continuous story. This is particularly true of the stories of Jesus' death and resurrection in Luke, which seem to have been supplemented by information from Mark, rather than being based on Mark's story.

Streeter therefore suggested that before Mark was written, Luke wrote a first draft of his Gospel, based on the sayings collection Q and the material labelled L, which he had learned from the church at Caesarea where he stayed while Paul was in prison (Acts 23:23–27:2). Streeter called this first draft of the Gospel 'Proto-Luke'. Then, he suggested, when Luke was living in Rome at a slightly later date he got to know of Mark's Gospel, which had been written in the intervening years, and he fitted extracts from it into his own already existing Proto-Luke. At the same time, he may also have added the preface (Luke 1:1–4) and the stories of Jesus' birth in chapters one and two.

There are a number of facts which fit well into this theory. For example, Luke often gives a quite different version of a story from Mark's. The story of Jesus' rejection at Nazareth is a good example (Mark 6:1–6; Luke 4:16–30). It is obvious that both evangelists are reporting the same incident, but Luke's account is so much fuller that it is clear he must have had a different source of information. Then there is the way that small sections of Mark's narrative, often in Mark's exact wording, have been inserted into the middle of other material in Luke – almost as if they had been put in later. It is also striking that a great deal of information contained in Mark is simply omitted in Luke. Streeter argued that if Luke had known of Mark's work when he made the first draft of his own Gospel, he would have included more of Mark's material in it.

It has also often been noticed that Luke's Gospel seems to have two beginnings. There is its present beginning at 1:1–4, but then, after the stories of Jesus' birth, it seems to begin over again in 3:1, with Luke's careful dating of the opening of Jesus' ministry, followed by the list of his ancestors in 3:23–38. Streeter explained this unusual feature by supposing that 3:1 was the original beginning of Proto-Luke, to which Luke later prefaced what is now chapters 1 and 2 of his Gospel.

The importance of Streeter's theory about the way Luke wrote his Gospel lies in the fact that if there was ever a Proto-Luke this would form another independent and early source of our knowledge of the life and teachings of Jesus. It has not, however, commanded anything like universal assent – though a number of recent writers on Luke have accepted it in some form or another.

Perhaps one of its weakest points is the assumption that is made about the nature of the Gospel traditions in the early churches. For Streeter assumed that we are dealing with a neatly definable literary process. He tended to think of the evangelists as newspaper editors, sitting down with a number of written sources in front of them and extracting various sections from the different documents. This was a popular concept at the time Streeter wrote (1924), and was widely applied to the study of both Old and New Testaments. But subsequent research has shown that this is an over-simplification of the matter, and it could well be that Luke was familiar with the Marcan material, but not through Mark's Gospel in its present form.

This is also a weakness in other suggestions that Streeter put forward. He argued not only that four identifiable sources can be traced behind our synoptic Gospels, but that each of them represented the traditions of the life and teaching of Jesus as they had been preserved in the four most important centres of early Christianity: Mark was written in Rome, Q in Antioch, M in Jerusalem and L in Caesarea. There are, however, a number of difficulties with this view.

● Streeter assumed that M and L were coherent documents. But this is very hard to maintain. When the Marcan and Q material is taken away from Matthew, what is left is not a coherent collection at all. And the same is true to a lesser extent of L, which is just Luke's Gospel minus the Q and Marcan material.

● This theory seems to assume a

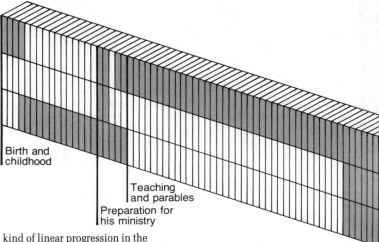

Matthew

Mark

Luke

Birth and
childhood

Teaching
and parables

Preparation for
his ministry

kind of linear progression in the development of the Gospels, whereby the tradition proceeded from more or less primitive forms to the compilation of our present Gospels by a purely literary development. But it is now being widely recognized that we can no longer speak with much confidence of this kind of development from primitive accounts to more sophisticated ones.

New light on old problems

Much of the emphasis in New Testament scholarship is now moving away from a 'mechanical' analysis of the Gospels. Though the two-source theory of Gospel origins is still widely accepted, a number of new questions are being asked, some of which may well have a decisive influence on our understanding of the way the New Testament came to be written.

● Questions continue to be asked about the two-source hypothesis itself. Was Mark really the first Gospel to be written? Did Q ever exist independently as yet another 'gospel'? If so, why was it originally written, and what was its distinctive message? And is it really necessary to suppose that Q represents a fixed collection of *logia* rather than just a looser collection of traditions known by both Matthew and Luke? Debates that seemed to have been settled 50 years ago are now being reopened, and much of the evidence for the two-source theory is being looked at again. We can now see that the way a question is posed can have important effects on the answers that are produced. For instance, the order of events in the Gospel narratives has generally been held to prove conclusively that Mark was written first. But if we analyse not the order of events, but the order of words within specific sections of the narratives, then even this evidence can be interpreted differently. Yet despite all this, the balance of probability still suggests that Mark was written first and that Q had a more or less fixed form. If we accept the suggestion that Q had a form similar to that of the Old Testament prophetic literature, then its form may well have been a written form too.

● The older idea of a linear development from *testimonia*, *logia* and *kerygma* through to a finished Gospel is now being questioned. What we know of the earliest churches suggests they were for the most part independent of one another. Churches in different parts of the Roman Empire would therefore develop at their own rate, and it is quite likely that Christians in different geographical locations would not be at the same stage of development at the same time. This means that it is unrealistic to suppose that in the collection of traditions about Jesus there was a period when all the interest was in collecting *logia*, and this was then followed by a period of intense literary activity during which the Gospels came to be written. It may well be that the type of information about Jesus current in any given church varied according to the needs of the particular congregation.

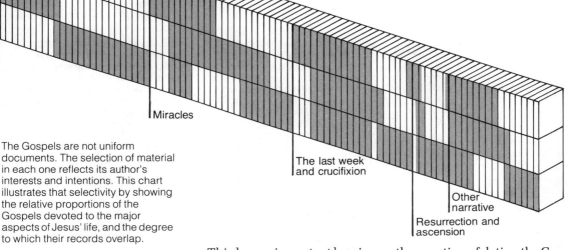

Miracles

The last week and crucifixion

Other narrative

Resurrection and ascension

The Gospels are not uniform documents. The selection of material in each one reflects its author's interests and intentions. This chart illustrates that selectivity by showing the relative proportions of the Gospels devoted to the major aspects of Jesus' life, and the degree to which their records overlap.

This has an important bearing on the question of dating the Gospels. If it is necessary to suppose a long history of development from *logia* to Gospel, then we need to allow time for this in our dating of the Gospels. But if *logia* and Gospel were both being formed at the same time, to meet the requirements of different churches, then there is no reason why we cannot date the Gospels somewhat earlier than is usually done.

● A similar point has been made with regard to the 'theological development' some suggest can be traced within the Gospels. In his book *Redating the New Testament*, Dr John Robinson has pointed out that a sophisticated theology does not necessarily indicate a later date than a primitive theology. For example, Mark's Gospel is undoubtedly less sophisticated than John's Gospel – and this has been one reason (though not the only one) why Mark has generally been dated first, and John last. But of course this assumes a direct evolutionary progression working through all the Gospels. If, however, the different Gospels were written to serve the needs of independent churches in different places, it is not difficult to believe that churches with a primitive theology could have existed at the same time as churches with a more sophisticated belief – and so 'theological development' is not necessarily a very useful concept in studying the Gospels we now have.

So there are a number of new questions being asked about the Gospels today, and they are of a rather different kind from those asked by earlier generations. It is now widely recognized that, wherever the information actually came from, each evangelist has written what is essentially an original work, distinctive in important respects from the work of any of the others. Much of our interest is now focussed on *what* the evangelists were doing, rather than on finding out *how* they were doing it. And that is a question that calls for a theological answer to supplement the earlier findings of the literary critics.

Form criticism

Once the two-source theory had been widely accepted as the most likely explanation of the 'mechanics' of Gospel writing, a whole series of new questions began to present themselves. For the isolation of the various sources used by the evangelists in composing their accounts of Jesus' life and teaching only answers the question, where did the Gospels come from? But there is also the further question, where did their sources come from? What was happening to the traditions about Jesus between his death and resurrection and their preservation in writing in the Gospels?

These questions had occurred to a number of scholars in Germany even before Streeter had published his great work on Gospel origins. In trying to answer them, they used a new method of analysing the Bible literature. They called it *Formgeschichte*, which literally means 'form history', but it is usually referred to in English as 'form criticism'. This technique was first applied to the Old Testament by the German scholar Hermann Gunkel, though some outstanding New Testament scholars were quick to appreciate its relevance to the study of the Gospels. The most prominent of these were K.L. Schmidt, M. Dibelius and R. Bultmann.

These scholars began from the observation that ancient literature generally assumed a particular literary form, depending on what kind of literature it was. This principle had been explored most thoroughly in the study of the traditional folk literature of northern Europe, which could be classified into fairy tales, history, biography,

saga, and so on, simply by observing the way it was written. The form critics assumed that the same was true of the New Testament. The units of tradition from which the evangelists composed their Gospels had, they said, assumed particular literary forms according to the 'life situation' (*Sitz im Leben*) in which they were used in the early church. So, by examining the literary form of a story, they claimed to be able to discover the original use to which it was put in the teaching ministry of the earliest churches.

If this could be done successfully, it would of course be an invaluable aid to our understanding of the Gospels. For if we can know something of the use to which the gospel traditions were put in the early church, we are in a good position to understand their relevance to the church's life, and hence to discover their essential meaning. Unfortunately, however, those who have studied the Gospels by this method have failed to agree at one crucial point. There is no widely accepted agreement on what formal types can actually be found in the Gospels. Martin Dibelius claimed to be able to distinguish five different forms, each corresponding to a specific situation in the life of the early church. But only two of these five forms have been at all widely recognized by other scholars: paradigms and tales.

Paradigms were called 'pronouncement stories' by the English form critic, Vincent Taylor. This term more accurately reflects their contents, for they are generally brief stories culminating in a striking statement made by, or about, Jesus.

According to Dibelius this form originated in the earliest Christian preaching, in which such stories were used as examples and illustrations. A typical pronouncement story would be the incident in which Jesus picked corn on the sabbath day, and explained his actions to the Jews by saying, 'The sabbath was made for the good of man; man was not made for the sabbath. So the Son of man is Lord even of the sabbath' (Mark 2:23–28; Matthew 12:1–8; Luke 6:1–5). Stories like this would often have been told in preaching long before they were written down in the Gospels.

Form critics generally distinguish

Other stories besides those contained in the four Gospels were circulated during the first two centuries, most of which are probably legend and fantasy. This is a fragment of an unknown 'Gospel' from the second century.

two main characteristics of such stories:

● They always end with a striking saying of Jesus. According to some, this was a favourite device of early Christian preachers. Whereas a modern preacher usually begins with his text, the apostles may have kept theirs to the end, to serve as a natural climax to what had gone before.

● These stories contain very little descriptive information. Just a bare minimum of fact is given to set the scene for the most important element, which is the saying of Jesus. When a story is handed on by word of mouth, two things may happen to it. Either it can be worn down by frequent repetition, so that nothing remains except the most essential facts expressed in a succinct and striking way. Or it can be elaborated as it is told, with extra details being added to make it more realistic and interesting. According to most form critics, the pronouncement stories have been worn down to their bare essentials, rather than being elaborated as they were handed on.

Tales were called 'miracle stories' by Taylor, though not all of them are

concerned with miracles. According to Dibelius the distinctive feature of these stories is that they have been elaborated rather than worn down in the course of their transmission. Indeed he suggested that these stories may have been put into their present form by a special class of person in the early church – the story-tellers, whose job was to cast stories about Jesus into the same form as the stories of the Greek gods. They were stories designed to win converts to the Christian faith by demonstrating that Jesus was superior to other deities.

There is of course no trace of such people in the New Testament. It is especially striking that Paul, who gives more than one list of people who have special functions in the church, never mentions story-tellers (1 Corinthians 12:1–11, 28–30; Romans 12:6–8; Ephesians 4:11). It may well be that the vivid details in these stories derive from an entirely different source. Perhaps they were told by eye-witnesses, who actually remembered all the details of the incidents they were describing. In view of the fact that the Gospels themselves were written down in something less than a generation after the events they describe, it is very difficult to believe that professional story-tellers could have freely invented fictitious details at a time when many eye-witnesses of the life of Jesus were still alive.

Dibelius identified three other forms of story in the Gospels, but not many other scholars have accepted his opinion at this point. These forms are:

Legends, which Dibelius compared with the stories often connected with the medieval saints. He defined them as 'religious narratives of a saintly man in whose works and fate interest is taken ... They are intended to give a basis for honouring the saint'. Such stories need not necessarily be fabricated, though according to Dibelius they most often are. Their function is to glorify the person they describe, rather than to report any factual information about him.

Myth was the name Dibelius gave to any narrative involving supernatural personalities or events. Stories such as the baptism, the temptations and the transfiguration came into this category.

Exhortations were essentially the teaching contained in the Gospels, used to instruct converts in the early church.

The study of the forms of the Gospel narratives has been pursued by others since the pioneering work of Dibelius, and it has undoubtedly shed some light on the origins of the Gospels. There are a number of outstanding insights which we now take for granted that have been a direct result of the work of the form critics.

● We can now see that the Gospels are not meant to be biographies of Jesus. They are selective accounts of certain parts of his life and teaching, preserved because of their usefulness to the ministry of the earliest churches.

● Because of this, it is now recognized that the interpretation of the Gospels is intimately bound up with our whole understanding of the early church. In order to appreciate the relevance and meaning of the Gospels we need to have a sympathetic understanding of the people who produced them.

● This process has in turn led to a positive, tentative understanding of what was going on in the period before any of the New Testament documents were written, as the teaching of Jesus was applied and interpreted to new situations in the life of his followers.

These insights are undoubtedly valuable, and their importance must not be underestimated – especially the first one, which has radically affected our whole approach to the Gospels. There are, however, a number of points at which the work of the form critics has been less useful. Three major criticisms can be made of their work, especially in the early days.

● *Form and content*. Many of the classifications made by Dibelius really depended, not on literary form, but on content. For example, there is no purely formal reason why stories including supernatural persons should be put into a different category from other stories. In making distinctions of this kind some form critics were too often influenced by their own rationalistic presuppositions. As we have noticed, only two of Dibelius's forms have been at all widely recognized, and some scholars have doubted whether even these are really all that obvious. There are many instances where there is no very clear-cut distinction between paradigms and tales, and much of the Gospel material is difficult to categorize. When there is so little agreement on what the forms actually are, we cannot have much confidence in the constructions placed upon them.

● *Tradition and Gospel*. Another basic problem is that form criticism was based on the assumption that the development of New Testament literature was similar to the development of folklore in northern Europe. But there are important differences between the two. The early church saw its main job as the preaching of the good news about Jesus, not the handing on of traditional stories. They were more concerned with the present than with the past. And in so far as the past did concern them, it was the immediate past and not, as in the case of the European traditions, a long-forgotten past. The church's knowledge of Jesus did not come from traditional tales handed on for generations, but from the immediate experience of some of its own members. This means that the actual scope for the traditions to develop into standardized forms must have been very limited indeed.

● *Forms and facts*. Many form critics have not been content to make observations on the literary form of the Gospels, but have proceeded to make historical judgements about their contents on the basis of form criticism. Referring to the earlier form critics, Professor Ernst Käsemann writes that their main work 'was designed to show that the message of Jesus as given to us by the synoptists is, for the most part, not authentic but was minted by the faith of the primitive Christian community in its various stages'. This aim is clear even from the names given by Dibelius to some of the forms he discovered. 'Myth' and 'legend' are loaded terms – and even in his discussion of 'tales' it is almost a basic axiom that because there are literary similarities with stories told of pagan gods, this is the ultimate origin of the stories about Jesus.

But two important criticisms can be made of this procedure:

● Evidence drawn from literary 'form' is of no value at all in formulating historical judgements. This becomes quite clear if we take an example. Nowadays we do not generally distinguish different types of narrative by giving them special literary forms. Professor F.F. Bruce has drawn a helpful parallel with the one place where a story still usually does have a specified form. This is in the law court.

When a policeman gives evidence in court, he does not give an eloquent, literary account of what he has seen. Instead he sticks as closely as possible to a prescribed form – so much so that, apart from the alteration of various details, a description of one road accident will sound more or less the same as a description of any other. The hope is that by using a stereotyped formula the most important facts can be summarized as accurately as possible.

No sensible person would believe that because a policeman describes two incidents in identical language, he was giving variant accounts of one and the same incident; still less that neither of them actually happened, and the accounts had been fabricated out of a familiar legal formula. Whether or not the incident took place would depend on criteria of a totally different kind. And the same thing is true of the Gospels. We simply cannot make a judgement about their historical reliability on the basis of their literary form.

● There are also a number of other good reasons for doubting that the early church freely invented stories about Jesus, as some form critics have alleged.

First, there is the question of eye-witnesses, many of whom must have been alive at the time the Gospels were written, and who could have challenged the wholesale fabrication of 'events' in Jesus' life.

Second, a basic assumption of Dibelius and Bultmann was that the early church made no effort to distinguish its own teaching from that of Jesus. After all, they argue, Jesus' spirit was thought to be active in the church, and what the apostles said in his name was therefore just as much a word of Jesus as anything he said during his ministry. But this inference is not supported by the New Testament itself. For in many instances its writers show that they did distinguish between their own teaching and that of Jesus. The most striking example of this is in 1 Corinthians 7, where Paul goes out of his way to distinguish his own opinions from the words of Jesus. But even in the Gospels themselves there are instances where editorial comments made by the evangelists

Newsmen put their own different angles on the same story. In a similar way, the Gospel writers bring their different areas of interest to the incidents of Jesus' life.

are clearly distinguished from the teaching of Jesus himself (Mark 7:19).

Another fact which points in the same direction is the difference between the Gospels and the rest of the New Testament. For example, Jesus is called 'Son of man' in the Gospels, though with one exception this title is found nowhere else in the New Testament. Moreover, the questions dealt with in the Gospels are not the same as those that troubled the writers of the letters. Take the question of the relationship between Jews and non-Jews, for example. This was a pressing problem in the early church, but it is not really touched upon anywhere in the Gospels. These facts suggest that the church did not feel at all free to place its own ideas into the mouth of Jesus, but was to a considerable extent consciously preserving traditions handed down from an earlier period.

More recent form critics have taken account of these problems in the work of their predecessors, and the discipline is now much more narrowly concerned with formal literary questions. The question of the Gospels' reliability is gradually being separated altogether from form criticism. Then there has been a further development which is in some ways the successor of the earlier form criticism. This is the discipline known as redaction criticism.

With the recognition that the history of the Gospels was not quite comparable with the history of European folklore, it became clear that the most useful question we can ask of the Gospels must concern the actual use the evangelists made of their source materials. What were these people doing as they wrote their Gospels? Why did they need to write four, instead of just one agreed account? And what were the special circumstances in their churches which led them to write in the particular ways they did? These are the questions that redaction criticism is trying to answer. It is a relatively recent development in the study of the Gospels, and there are by no means any agreed results as yet. But many of its insights will be of value in our next task, which is to discover the meaning and significance of the various Gospels.

Chapter 11

Four portraits of Jesus

Mark

Mark's Gospel is considered first because it is now recognized as a basic source for the other two synoptic Gospels. It is, however, only in fairly recent times that Mark has received careful attention. It was generally neglected by the church from quite early times, in favour of the longer accounts of Matthew and Luke. This is hardly surprising, for they contain most of Mark's information and a lot more as well, and so Mark soon came to be regarded as an abbreviated version of Matthew. But the situation has now changed and, with the knowledge that Mark's Gospel was almost certainly the first to be written, it has achieved an eminence it has probably never enjoyed since the time of its first compilation.

There is, however, some evidence to show that it was valued in certain Christian circles not long after its composition. Papias, for example, writing about AD 140 but quoting an earlier source, identifies Mark as 'Peter's interpreter', and says that 'he wrote down accurately, but not in order, as much as he could remember of the things said and done by Christ'. Irenaeus and Clement of Alexandria also associate Mark's Gospel with Peter's preaching, and in recent times the contents of the Gospel have often been

Quoted in Eusebius, *Ecclesiastical History* III.39.15
Irenaeus, *Against Heretics* I.1.1.
Clement of Alexandria, quoted in Eusebius, *Ecclesiastical History* VI.14.6ff.

Mark's Gospel was probably written in Rome, during the time the Emperor Nero tried to blame Christians for setting fire to the city. These ruins are of the Colosseum in Rome, the arena where many Christians later suffered and died for their faith.

thought to support the belief that Peter was the source of much of it.

A number of stories are told with such vivid details that it is natural to regard them as first-hand accounts of the events they describe. The story of Peter's call and of Jesus' first sabbath in Capernaum, when Peter's mother-in-law was healed, are good examples of this. In addition, some of the references to the disciples, and to Peter in particular, are highly unfavourable. The disciples are consistently portrayed as ignorant, obtuse men who failed to understand what Jesus was trying to teach them. In Mark's Gospel the disciples are not at all the kind of people the later church liked to think they were. It is therefore unlikely that they would have been depicted in such an unfavourable light had Mark not had good information, perhaps coming from Peter himself, to support such a picture.

Mark 1:14–20
Mark 1:29–34

Mark 4:35–41; 5:25–34; 6:37–38; 8:14–21, 31–33; 9:2–6, 32; 10:35–45

The author

But who was Mark? Mark, or Marcus, was of course a very common name, and he could have been anybody. In considering this question we need to remember that none of the Gospels actually names its author. John's Gospel comes nearest to doing so, but even there we have only an enigmatic reference to a witness to the crucifixion. Though this person is often identified with the 'beloved disciple', it is far from clear who that might have been. In this respect the Gospels are quite different from most of the rest of the New Testament, for they are presented to us as anonymous writings. The traditional ascriptions to Matthew, Mark, Luke and John were of course added at an early stage, but they represent the opinions of the early church about the authors of the Gospels, rather than any sort of claim by the authors.

John 19:35

It is clear from the evidence that the author of the second Gospel was generally associated by the early church with a man called John Mark who is known from other parts of the New Testament. According to Acts, a group of Christians regularly met in his mother's house in Jerusalem, and John Mark himself is named as the companion of Paul and Barnabas in their earliest missionary work. Though Mark deserted them, Paul mentions him favourably in two of his later letters, so the two men must have patched up their differences. He is also spoken of with affection in 1 Peter and that (depending on one's view of the authorship of 1 Peter) may be taken as evidence for associating him with Peter as well as with Paul.

Acts 12:12

Acts 12:25; 15:37–41
Colossians 4:10; Philemon 24

1 Peter 5:13

It is more difficult to be certain that this same Mark was actually the author of the Gospel. But in view of the tendency of second-century Christians to associate books of the New Testament with key figures in the early church, it may well be that the tradition connecting Mark with the second Gospel is not altogether untrustworthy. John Mark whom we meet in the New Testament is a very insignificant person, and not the kind of individual who would be credited with writing a Gospel unless there was good reason to believe that he did in fact do so.

The readers

It is generally thought that Mark's Gospel was written in Rome, to serve the needs of the church there. Irenaeus and Clement of Alexandria disagree on the precise circumstances of its composition, but both agree it was written in Rome. If the author of the Gospel was indeed John Mark, then references to him in the New Testament also place him in Rome.

The Gospel was certainly written for a non-Jewish readership.

Mark 5:41; 7:34

Aramaic phrases such as *talitha*, *koum* or *ephphatha* are translated into Greek for the benefit of Mark's readers. Jewish customs

Mark 7:3–4

are also explained in a way that suggests they were unfamiliar. Then there are also a number of Latin technical terms in Mark,

Mark 4:21; 12:42; 14:65; 15:19

which suggests that the Gospel originated in a part of the Roman Empire where Latin was spoken. In view of all these pieces of evidence Rome certainly seems to be a plausible place of composition.

The first Christians in Jerusalem used to meet at a house owned by the mother of John Mark. He may have been the author of Mark's Gospel. The picture is of a street in old Jerusalem.

The date

Dating the Gospel, however, is not so easy, for a number of reasons.

● The evidence of the church Fathers is contradictory. Clement of Alexandria says that Mark wrote the Gospel under Peter's dictation, and that the final draft of it was approved by Peter himself. But Irenaeus says that the Gospel was not written until after the deaths of both Peter and Paul. This means that we have to try to decide from the evidence of the Gospel itself when it may have been written, and this is no easy task.

● It is often thought that the many references to trials and persecutions in Mark suggest that his readers were suffering for

Mark 8:34–38; 10:33–34, 45; 13:8–13

their faith in Christ. If this is so, it could date the Gospel somewhere between AD 60 and 70, during which period Nero tried to blame the Christians for the firing of Rome. But of course, persecution was such a common feature of church life in the first century that it is not essential to connect Mark's Gospel with one of the more well-known persecutions. There must have been many local persecutions that we know nothing of, though they would be real enough to those who had to suffer them.

● Then there is the question of whether the apocalyptic section in Mark presupposes that Jerusalem had already fallen to the Romans. Since this took place in AD 70, an answer to this question would at least date the Gospel on one side or the other of that event. But here again opinion is divided. J.A.T.Robinson has argued that Mark was certainly written before AD 70 (along with the rest of the New Testament), and in his view was in existence a long time before that date. He accordingly places its composition in the period AD 45–60. Other scholars, however, continue to date it between AD 60 and 70, and one or two later still.

Mark 13:1–37

Mark's reasons for writing

Mark's intention in writing as he did is easier to define.

● If, as the early traditions suggest, Mark's Gospel has some connection with Peter, one reason for its composition could well have been the desire to preserve Peter's reminiscences as a lasting testimony for the church. This would be especially easy to understand if Mark wrote at a time immediately preceding, or just after, Peter's death.

● But this Gospel was also written with some specific situation in view. There are a number of striking and distinctive aspects to the portrait of Jesus in Mark. He is presented here as a very human figure. Jesus is angry on occasions; he is unable to perform miracles if the appropriate conditions of faith are absent; and he suffers physically in a way that might be thought incompatible with his position as the Son of God. At one time these things were thought to be signs of Mark's 'primitive' theology. But there may well be another explanation for them.

Mark 1:43; 3:5; 8:12; 8:33; 10:14
Mark 6:1–6

Mark 8:31–33; 9:31

Many Christians found it difficult to reconcile the idea of Jesus' divinity with the fact that he was also fully human. So they suggested that the divine Christ only came into the human Jesus at his baptism, and left him again before the crucifixion. We call these people Docetists, because they held that Jesus only seemed to be human (from the Greek verb *dokeō*, 'to seem'). The writer of 1 John was concerned to correct such people, and John's Gospel may also have them in view. But Mark's Gospel too may well have been a corrective to this idea. In reply to those who were asserting that Jesus' humanity was illusory, Mark emphasizes its reality by depicting Jesus as the divine Messiah whose origin and significance is both hidden and revealed in the life of a truly human person.

Luke

Traditions associating the third Gospel with a person called Luke date from as early as the second century. The Muratorian Canon and the anti-Marcionite Prologue to Luke, as well as Irenaeus, Clement of Alexandria, Origen and Tertullian, all identify Luke as its author. The exact value of these traditions is, however, uncertain, since most of what they contain could just as easily have been deduced from the New Testament itself, and so they are not necessarily of any independent worth. The evidence of the New Testament is in fact more useful in identifying the author of this Gospel.

● A distinctive feature of this Gospel is that it is not complete in itself: it is the first volume of the two-volume history of early Christianity which is continued in the Acts of the Apostles. The style and language of these two books is so similar that there can be no doubt that they are both the product of one writer. Both are addressed to the same person, whose name is given as Theophilus.

Luke 1:1–4; Acts 1:1

● In Acts there are certain passages known as the 'we passages'. They are given this name because at these points the narrative changes from using 'they' and 'he' to the pronoun 'we'. Though it is never clearly stated who the 'we' are, the use of this pronoun clearly implies that the writer was present on these occasions, and therefore was a companion of Paul. Since the style of these passages is the same as that of the book as a whole, it seems likely that the author has used his own travel diary as a source of information. A careful scrutiny of the narratives shows that Luke is the person who best fits in.

Acts 16:10–17; 20:5–15; 21:1–18; 27:1—28:16

● This Luke is identified as a doctor by Paul, and it has often been thought that the author of Luke-Acts displays a certain degree of specialized knowledge of medical language, and an interest in the diagnosis of illness. This point has often been given too much emphasis, and it is likely that the limited medical terminology used would be familiar to any intelligent person in the Roman world. But there are one or two points in the Gospel at which Luke seems to show himself to be more sympathetic than Mark to the work of doctors. This comes out very noticeably in the story of how Jesus healed a woman with an incurable haemorrhage. Mark records the fact that she had been treated by many doctors, and then comments, somewhat cynically, 'She had spent all her money, but instead of getting better she got worse all the time'. Luke, on the other hand, simply comments that 'no one had been able to cure her'.

A Roman corn ship similar to the ships Paul and Luke would have sailed in.

Mark 5:26
Luke 8:43

Luke is mentioned three times in the New Testament. On each occasion he is said to be a companion of Paul, and in Colossians Paul says that he was not a Jew. If he is indeed the writer of Luke and Acts he is probably the only non-Jewish writer of the New Testament. The Greek style of these writings certainly suggests that their author could have been a native Greek speaker.

Colossians 4:14; Philemon 24; 2 Timothy 4:11

According to Eusebius Luke came from Antioch in Syria, and one ancient manuscript of the book of Acts implies that he was in Antioch when the church there received news of the impending famine. But the generally accepted text of Acts has Luke join Paul when he enters Europe for the first time. He also accompanied Paul on his final journey to Jerusalem, and then on to

Ecclesiastical History II.4.6

Acts 11:28

Rome itself. According to Streeter and others, Luke may have collected some material for his Gospel during this period from the church at Caesarea – though his final version of it may well have been written in Rome.

The date

It is not possible to be certain of the exact date when Luke finished his Gospel. Since he incorporates in his own account some material from Mark, he must have written the final draft of his own book after the Gospel of Mark was written and in circulation. So the date we give to Luke will depend to some extent on the date we assign to Mark. It has been suggested that Luke displays a knowledge of the fall of Jerusalem to the Romans in AD 70, and if this is so we would need to date the finished Gospel some time after that. But others see no reason to support this idea, and date the Gospel earlier, some as early as AD 57–60.

Luke 21:5–24

Luke's reasons for writing

Why did Luke write his Gospel? This has been one of the more hotly debated issues in recent New Testament scholarship, and a large number of suggestions have been made. A few of the more important ones are worth mentioning.

Luke 1:1–4

● It must not be forgotten that Luke does tell us something of his purpose in the prologue to the Gospel. He says he is writing for a person called Theophilus, 'so that you will know the full truth about everything which you have been taught'. He also says that he did his work in a consciously literary manner: he studied the accounts written by other people, and on the basis of those decided to write 'an orderly account'.

A number of things are clear from this. On the one hand it seems obvious that Theophilus (whoever he was) was a Christian. Luke wrote his Gospel to help him and other believers to a better understanding of the Christian faith. But the author also suggests that in his view the best way to achieve this was to set out as much as could be known of the life and teaching of Jesus himself. So he also had a historical interest in discovering the facts about Jesus. Like the other evangelists, he did not set out to write a biography of Jesus in the technical sense. But at the same time, he realized that if his message to Theophilus was going to carry much weight then it needed to be firmly anchored to the facts of history.

● Because of this, Luke begins his story of Jesus with Judaism. In the first two chapters of his Gospel he demonstrates the continuity of Christianity with Judaism and the Old Testament. At the same time he emphasizes that Jesus is the fulfilment of all God's promises, and so the religion of the Old Testament is now redundant. The relationship of Jews and Christians was of course an important question in the earliest churches, as we can see from the letters of Paul. And Luke emphasizes at the very beginning of his Gospel that those who follow Jesus do not first need to become Jews in order to be Christians. Rather, Jesus had come to be 'a light ... to the Gentiles'.

Luke 2:32

● By the time Luke wrote, the events of Jesus' life were in the past. This fact has often led later generations of Christians to be more interested in the history of the first century than in the events of their own day. But in his account of Jesus' life and ministry, Luke emphasizes that there is an important connection between the events of Jesus' life and life in the contemporary church. He does this by stressing that the life-force of Jesus' presence in the church, the Holy Spirit, had also played a central role in the ministry of Jesus.

At many important points Luke draws out clearly what is

Luke is traditionally believed to have been a doctor because of the familiarity of his Gospel with medical terms.

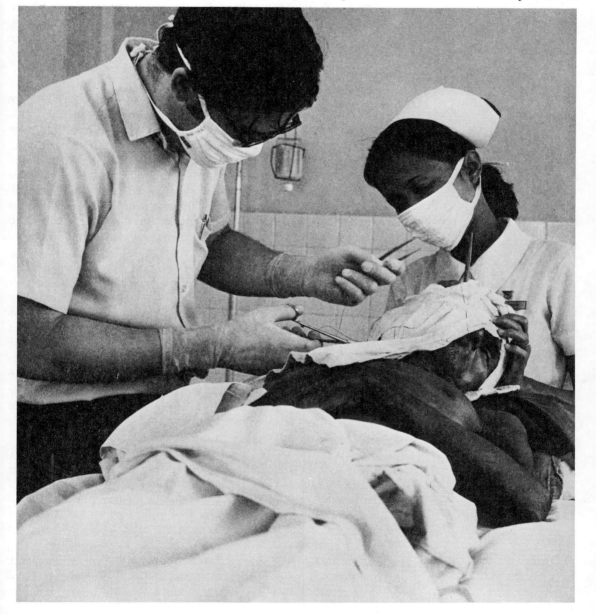

Luke 1:35; 3:22; 4:1, 14

Luke 24:49

only implicit in Matthew and Mark. The Holy Spirit is involved in Jesus' birth, baptism and ministry. And at the end of the Gospel the disciples are told to wait in Jerusalem until they too receive the gift of the Spirit. It may be that Luke emphasized the continuing presence of Jesus with his followers as a corrective to some of his contemporaries who were becoming impatient because the second coming of Jesus, the *parousia*, had not yet taken place. He reminds them that although his final appearance in glory is yet in the future, Jesus is with his people in a real way through the presence of the Holy Spirit in their lives.

● Another notable feature of Luke's Gospel is its emphasis on the fact that the Christian message is for everyone. This is something that is obvious to us today, but it was not at all obvious to the first few generations of Christians. One of the greatest contributions of Paul was to show that God's love extends to the very lowest classes of society. In his Gospel Luke demonstrates that this was also the message of Jesus' life and teaching. When he tells the story of the infant Jesus, he includes the statement that

Luke 2:32

Luke 3:28–38
Matthew 1:1–17

Luke 4:16–30

Luke 9:51–56; 10:25–37; 17:11–19

he is to be 'a light to reveal God's will to the Gentiles'. In tracing Jesus' ancestry, Luke goes back to Adam, the common ancestor of all, whereas Matthew traces it back only to Abraham, the father of the Jewish race. In Luke's account of the sermon in the synagogue at Nazareth, Jesus' message is concerned with the Gentiles. And Luke also tells of Jesus' special interest even in the Samaritans, whom the Jews hated more even than the Romans. Throughout this Gospel Jesus is characteristically presented as the friend of the outcasts of society.

Luke 2:10

Luke 24:52

Luke 15:1–7; Luke 15:11–32

These are the people whom God is happy to welcome; and his pleasure in accepting people like this into his kingdom is also shared by Jesus' followers. The happiness of being a Christian is emphasized over and over again. Luke's account begins with the angels telling 'glad tidings of great joy', and ends with the disciples returning to Jerusalem after the ascension 'with great joy'. In between these events, many of the most appealing of Jesus' parables end on the same note of happiness. The lost sheep, the lost son, and many others emphasize the joy that is given to Jesus' disciples – a joy based on God's forgiving love shown to them when they were themselves outcasts and sinners.

Probably no other book in the whole New Testament depicts Jesus so vividly as the friend and saviour of men and women. And this is exactly what Luke intended. For it was important that the church of his own day should realize how their own mission to the whole world was firmly grounded in the teaching and example of Jesus himself.

Matthew

Matthew's Gospel is very different from either Mark or Luke, and there are a number of special characteristics that need to be considered before we can say anything about its origin, date or authorship.

● This Gospel has a very well organized arrangement of the material, which is set out in topics. It is possible to divide it up in a number of different ways. One outline that has been widely used in the past treats the Gospel as a series of five blocks or 'books' of material, arranged between the prologue of the birth stories and the epilogue of the passion narrative. Each of these sections of the Gospel can be seen to have a well-balanced combination of narrative and teaching material, as follows:

Matthew 1:1 – 2:23
Matthew 26:1 – 28:20

Luke's Gospel emphasizes the concern of Jesus for the underprivileged. These people, victims of an earthquake in Guatemala, are queuing for food.

Matthew 7:28; 11:1; 13:53; 19:1; 26:1

1 The new law
Narrative (Galilean ministry)	3:1–4:25
Teaching (Sermon on the Mount)	5:1–7:29

2 Christian discipleship
Narrative	8:1–9:34
Teaching	9:35–10:42

3 The meaning of the kingdom
Narrative	11:1–12:50
Teaching (parables)	13:1–52

4 The church
Narrative	13:53–17:27
Teaching (order, discipline, worship)	18:1–35

5 Judgement
Narrative (controversies in Jerusalem)	19:1–22:46
Teaching (judgement on the Pharisees, apocalyptic teachings)	23:1–25:46

It was suggested by B.W. Bacon that Matthew uses this scheme to present Jesus to his readers as the new Moses, and the five-fold division of his Gospel is a conscious parallel to the five books of the Law in the Old Testament. But this is difficult to prove. Nowhere does Matthew say that Jesus is the 'second Moses', nor do the individual sections of the Gospel really correspond to the five books of the Pentateuch. The only thing common to both is the number five.

Indeed it is not even certain that there are five sections in the Gospel. The main reason for dividing it up like this was the fact that the statement 'When Jesus had finished saying these things ...' is found five times in the Gospel, at points corresponding to the alleged end of these sections. But if we analyse the Gospel according to its contents, rather than using this criterion of literary style, we may reach different conclusions altogether. Professor J.D. Kingsbury has suggested that there are not five divisions in Matthew, but only three. He argues that Matthew's main concern was to show how Jesus was God's Son and Messiah, and that the Gospel is arranged topically around this theme:

1 The person of Jesus as Messiah and Son of God (1:1–4:16)

2 The proclamation of Jesus' message (4:17–16:20)

3 The suffering, death and resurrection of the Messiah and
Son of God (16:21–28:20)

A number of more speculative attempts have also been made to
explain the structure of the Gospel by means of Jewish lec-
tionaries, or various linguistic and mathematical formulae. It is
of course true that the Gospel's teaching is often grouped in
series of threes and sevens, but this may have been intended as
an aid to Christians who wished to memorize Jesus' sayings,
rather than as a cryptic clue to the organization of its material.

● Matthew also places a special emphasis on the Old Testament. The life and teaching of Jesus are presented as the fulfilment of the promises made by God to Israel. This is stated not
just in the general sense that Jesus is 'the son of David', but more
often with specific reference to Old Testament texts. The author
was convinced that Jesus had fulfilled in his experience all that
happened to Israel. To prove it he often quotes Old Testament
texts in ways that to us may seem a little strange. For example,
when Matthew tells of Jesus returning from Egypt to his homeland as a baby, he quotes Hosea's statement about the exodus of
Israel from Egypt: 'Out of Egypt have I called my son.' But his
message is clear: everything that was central in the relationship of
God with his people Israel finds its true and final expression in
the life of Jesus.

Matthew 2:15; Hosea 11:1

● It is therefore rather surprising to find that alongside this
strong Jewish interest there is a great emphasis on the universal-
ity of the Christian message. The faults of Judaism are not passed
over in silence. It is in Matthew that we find the most
scathing criticisms of the hypocrisy of the Pharisees, and there are
a number of indications that Israel's day as God's people has
now passed. This is balanced by a striking emphasis on the missionary work of the church. It becomes most explicit in the great
missionary commission given by Jesus to his disciples at
the end of the Gospel. But it is implied right from the very
beginning, when the non-Jewish wise men join in worship of the
infant Jesus.

Matthew 23:1–36

Matthew 8:10–12; 21:43

Matthew 28:16–20

Matthew 2:1–12

●There is also a distinct interest in eschatology here, and the
teaching on this subject in chapters 24 and 25 is considerably
fuller than the corresponding sections of the other synoptic
Gospels. Matthew has a number of parables on the subjects of the
second coming and last judgement that are not found in the other
Gospels. Most of them are concerned to encourage Christians to
live in a state of constant readiness for Jesus' return, because
'you do not know the day or the hour'. Perhaps some members
of Matthew's church were beginning to doubt that Jesus would
return; parables like that of the ten bridesmaids emphasize that
with such an attitude Christians can never be in a fit state to meet
their Lord.

Matthew 25:13

● Another important characteristic of Matthew's Gospel is its
concern with the church. Indeed it is the only Gospel where the

Matthew 16:18; 18:17

The author

Matthew's Gospel reveals a strongly Jewish background and a concern with Old Testament law.

actual word church (*ekklesia*) is used. This fact almost certainly contains the clue to the whole Gospel. Matthew was making a collection of Jesus' teachings in a form that could be directly utilized in the ongoing life of the church. It was a compendium of authoritative advice for both new converts and older believers as they tried to put their Christian faith into practice in their everyday lives.

Matthew undoubtedly succeeded in this last aim, for it was not very long before his Gospel was the most widely used and respected. It contained Jesus' teaching in a form that could easily be understood by new converts, and so this Gospel could provide the basis of their instruction in the Christian faith. It also demonstrated the continuity between Jesus and the Old Testament in a very direct way, and so could be a useful handbook for dealing with questions raised by enquiring Jews. It had the added advantage of being the most comprehensive of all the synoptic Gospels. Since it contained almost all of Mark, and much of Luke, its position as the most important Gospel was soon assured in the early church.

The author

There is no widespread agreement on who wrote the Gospel, and when. Many scholars today find no difficulty in accepting the early Christian traditions that identify Mark and Luke with the other two synoptics. But with Matthew the position is rather different. For the Matthew whose name is associated with this Gospel by the church Fathers was a disciple of Jesus, and therefore an eye-witness of the events he describes. It is not easy to see why one of the twelve disciples should have relied so heavily on the Gospel of Mark, which was written by someone who was not a witness of the events of Jesus' life.

The question of the actual authorship of the Gospel is of course not crucial for our understanding of it. The book itself is anonymous, and makes no claim at all about its author. He may well have been associated with the apostle Matthew, but at what stage or in what way is impossible to say with certainty.

The date

The date of the Gospel is also in doubt, and depends on the answer we give to a number of other questions.

● It must presumably have been written after Mark, and after the collection of sayings known as Q was in existence. But we have already seen the problems involved in giving firm dates to these materials.

● Many scholars believe that Matthew was written later than Luke, because the Gospel appears to contain direct references to the fall of Jerusalem in AD 70. Again, this does not necessarily mean that the Gospel was written after the event. The assumption that it was is largely based on the belief that there is no such thing as genuine predictive prophecy, and so if Jesus appears to have predicted an event in the future this means the early church must have rewritten the tradition in the light of later circum-

Matthew 22:7; 24:3–28

stances. But Robinson has rightly pointed out the naïveté of such an assumption, and argues for a much earlier date mainly on that basis.

● It has also been argued that the type of church organization envisaged in Matthew is well developed, and therefore reflects a stage very late in the first century. But this is not easy to substantiate. When we compare the details of this Gospel's teaching on the church with, say, Paul's letters to the church at Corinth in the mid-fifties of the first century, it is very difficult to see any real differences between the two.

Depending on how we answer these questions, the Gospel can be dated either in the period AD 80–100 (with the majority of scholars), or pre-AD 70, perhaps as early as AD 40–60 (with Robinson, Guthrie and one or two German writers).

John

With only one or two minor exceptions, almost everything that has been said here about the synoptic Gospels represents a consensus of opinion that has existed among New Testament scholars for a very considerable time. In most important respects relatively little has changed since Streeter's monumental work of fifty years ago. Here and there new and different emphases have been made as the newer disciplines of form and redaction criticism have been explored – though even this is a natural development from the work of previous generations.

But in the case of the fourth Gospel, John, matters are now very different. Streeter wrote of this Gospel that it derives 'not from the original authorities, but from the vivid picture ... reconstructed by [the author's] own imagination on the basis of contemporary apologetic'. A majority of his contemporaries shared this view. They regarded John as a second-century theological interpretation of the life of Jesus using the language and thought-forms of Hellenistic philosophy. They thought of it as a kind of extended sermon, with no real connection with reliable traditions about Jesus as he actually lived and taught.

Recent developments, however, have shattered this picture of the fourth Gospel once and for all. Whereas twenty or thirty years ago John was often regarded as a fabricated misinterpretation of the synoptic Gospels, many competent scholars are now prepared to regard it as an early, independent source of knowledge about Jesus' life and teaching, and of equal value with the synoptic Gospels. We can trace three main reasons for this radical change of opinion.

John and the synoptic Gospels

John 6:1–15; Mark 6:30–44
Matthew 14:13–21; Luke 9:10–17
John 12:1–8; Mark 14:3–9;
Matthew 26:6–13

Fifty years ago it was widely assumed that the author of John's Gospel knew the synoptic Gospels. The reason for this was the number of stories common to both. The story of how Jesus fed the 5,000 and the story of his anointing at Bethany are examples. It was therefore supposed that John was writing a kind of 'theological' interpretation of the 'factual' stories of the synoptic Gospels.

This inevitably led to the conclusion that the fourth Gospel must be late in date and inferior in quality to the synoptic Gospels.

This assumption has, however, been questioned at two points. First of all, it is now widely recognized that it is not possible to set the 'history' of the synoptics over against the 'theology' of John. The synoptic writers were themselves theologians. They did not write their Gospels for purely biographical reasons, but because they had a message for their readers. It has also been demonstrated that the fourth Gospel is not really dependent on the other three, and indeed its author may well have written his work without any knowledge of the writings of the other evangelists.

The thought-forms used by John in his Gospel were those of the Hellenistic world. The author was associated with the city of Ephesus, now on the west coast of Turkey.

Closer examination of these stories found in all four Gospels shows that though there are similarities, there are also a number of differences in John's account, and these differences are not the kind that can easily be explained on theological grounds. John's variations are in fact much easier to understand if we assume that he had access to different reports of the incidents known also to the synoptic writers. When this hypothesis is tested in detail, it can be seen not only that John's account comes from a different source, but also that there are a number of pieces of information in John which can be used to supplement the information of the other Gospels. These help to make the whole story of Jesus' life and ministry more understandable.

For example, John tells us that some of Jesus' disciples had previously been followers of John the Baptist. This helps to explain the exact nature of the Baptist's witness to Jesus in the synoptics, and especially the emphasis placed there on his role in 'preparing the way of the Lord'. John's account also helps to answer the question (not obvious from the synoptics) of what Jesus was doing between his baptism and the arrest of John the Baptist. The synoptics report that Jesus began his ministry in Galilee after John's arrest. This is the only ministry recorded in the synoptic Gospels. But during his last visit to Jerusalem Matthew and Luke (Q) report that Jesus said of its inhabitants, 'How often would I have gathered your children together ...'

John 1:35–42

Mark 1:14; Matthew 4:12; Luke 4:14–15

Matthew 23:37; Luke 13:34

This suggests that Jesus had visited Jerusalem on a number of previous occasions. John tells of just such an occasion, right at the beginning of Jesus' ministry, when he worked alongside John the Baptist in Judea before going back to Galilee when John was arrested.

John 2:13—4:3

John's Gospel fills out the synoptic material at a later point, when it records another visit by Jesus to Jerusalem some six months before his entry on Palm Sunday. John records how Jesus left Galilee and went to Jerusalem for the Feast of Tabernacles (September) and stayed there until the Feast of Dedication (December). Then, because of growing hostility, he returned to the area where John the Baptist had worked, and only made a brief visit to Bethany when he heard that Lazarus had died. A little later, six days before the Passover (April) he returned for his final visit to Jerusalem. This is the only one recorded in any detail in Mark, though the others are perhaps implied by Mark's summary statement: 'he left [Galilee] and went to the region of Judea and beyond the Jordan.'

John 7:1–10:42

John 10:40
John 11:1–54

John 12:1, 12

Mark 10:1

There are also a number of smaller details provided by John's Gospel which help to explain and clarify some points in the synoptic narratives. There is, for example, the feeding of the 5,000. At the end of the story in Mark we are told that Jesus compelled his disciples to escape on a boat while he himself dismissed the crowd. John's independent tradition fills in some of the detail, explaining that Jesus had to take this action because the crowd were eager to kidnap him and make him their king. We have already noticed in an earlier chapter how the stories of the Last Supper and of Jesus' trials can be fully understood only in the light of information contained in John's Gospel.

Mark 6:45

John 6:14–15

In view of evidence of this sort, it is now coming to be realized that John's Gospel is a source in its own right. The information it contains is independent of that in the synoptic Gospels, but at many crucial points John complements the other three.

The background of John in Judaism

It is also becoming recognized that the background of much of John's Gospel is Jewish, and not exclusively Greek. Early traditions place the origin of this Gospel in Ephesus. It was therefore natural that scholars should look for a Hellenistic background,

Medieval etchings represent some of the great scholars of the early church who wrote about the Gospels: (left to right) Tertullian of Carthage, Clement of Alexandria, Irenaeus of Lyons, Origen of Alexandria.

John 1:1–18

especially in view of the Gospel's prologue which explains the incarnation in terms of the word or *logos*. These church traditions are of course not always reliable. In the case of John's Gospel it is interesting to note that, if we remove the prologue from the Gospel, there is little in the rest of it that demands a Greek background. Quite the reverse, in fact. The evangelist states his purpose in writing in a very Jewish form: 'these things are written that you may believe that Jesus is the Christ (Messiah), the Son of God.' There is also an emphasis throughout the Gospel on the fulfilment of Old Testament sayings which again suggests a Jewish background.

John 20:31

This impression is confirmed by a closer analysis of the actual language of the Gospel, for at many points the Greek language shows a close connection with Aramaic sources. The writer often uses Aramaic words – for example, *Cephas*, *Gabbatha*, or *Rabboni*, and then explains them for the benefit of his Greek readers. Even the meaning of the word Messiah is given a careful explanation.

John 1:42; 19:13; 20:16

John 1:41

More significantly, there are also a number of points at which the Greek of the Gospel follows the rules of Aramaic grammar. An instance of this occurs when John the Baptist says of Jesus, 'I am not worthy *that I should untie* the thong of his sandals.' Though the distinction is not made in our English versions, the other Gospels have a different, and correct Greek expression, 'to untie'. But the unusual form of the statement in John is a regular idiom of the Aramaic language.

John 1:27

Then we also find Jesus' sayings in John expressed in the typical parallelism of Semitic poetry, and other sections of his teaching can be retranslated into Aramaic to form completely realistic Aramaic poetry.

John 12:25; 13:16, 20

John 3:29–30

It is not likely that John is a direct translation of an Aramaic document, though some have suggested this. But these facts do suggest that the teaching in John has the same Palestinian background as the material of the synoptic gospels; and the curious use of Aramaic grammar in Greek writing may well suggest that Aramaic was the author's native language.

Archaeological discoveries

In addition to the internal evidence, there is also a considerable and important body of evidence drawn from archaeology which makes the old idea that John was a late Hellenistic Gospel now untenable. Three main pieces of evidence are important here.

● The Dead Sea Scrolls have shown that the odd combination of Greek and Jewish ideas which we find in John was current not only in Greek cities like Ephesus in the second century AD, but also in Palestine itself, in strict Jewish circles, in the pre-Christian era. Many phrases familiar from John are also found in the scrolls. 'Doing the truth', 'walking in darkness', 'sons of the light', 'the Spirit of truth' and many more expressions are as typical of the Qumran community as they are of John's Gospel. Moreover, the contrasts made in John between light and darkness, truth and error, are also typical of the Qumran scrolls. And in both contexts this dualism between light and darkness, truth and error is an *ethical* dualism, in contrast to the metaphysical emphasis of most Greek and Gnostic philosophies.

John 3:21; 12:35
John 12:36; 14:17

Archaeology has shown that John is more accurate than was once thought. The pool of Bethesda, a gathering place for the ill and disabled where Jesus once healed a man, was discovered only in this century.

● Another discovery, of equal importance, and made at about the same time as the Dead Sea Scrolls, is the Coptic Gnostic library found at Nag Hammadi in upper Egypt. Prior to the discovery of these documents our knowledge of Gnosticism was based largely on information given by a number of church historians and theologians who wrote books to refute it. From their statements it was not too difficult to imagine that John's Gospel could have been written in the second century as a part of the battle between Gnostic and 'orthodox' Christians. But with our new knowledge derived from the writings of Gnostic teachers, it has become quite clear that there is a vast difference between the world of John's Gospel and the world of classical Gnosticism.

● Archaeological excavations in Jerusalem have also provided evidence to illuminate the traditions of John's Gospel. One of the unusual features of this Gospel is its proliferation of names and descriptions of places. It was widely thought at one time that these names were introduced either as a theological device (as symbols), or to give the impression of authenticity in otherwise fabricated accounts. But it is now clear that most of this geographical information rests on real knowledge of the city as it was before AD 70. In that year the Romans completely destroyed Jerusalem, and after that time it would have been impossible to observe the ruins and imagine what the city must have been like beforehand. Excavations in Jerusalem have now shown that descriptions of the Pool of Bethesda, for example, or 'the Pavement' where Jesus met Pilate are based on intimate knowledge of the city at the time of Jesus.

John 5:1–18
John 19:13

The author and date of writing

The cumulative effect of all these converging lines of investigation has been to reinstate John's Gospel as a credible source of the life and teaching of Jesus. It has also re-opened the question of the authorship and date of this Gospel. The question of authorship has always been a rather confused one, not least because the church traditions mention two Johns in connection with the Gospel: the apostle, and a John whom they call 'the Elder'. Then there is the fact that the 'beloved disciple' seems to be portrayed in the Gospel itself as a source of some of the information. Here again it is far from clear who this person was. Irenaeus identifies the beloved disciple with John the apostle. But many scholars believe he may just be an ideal figure, symbolic of the true follower of Christ. He has even been identified with Lazarus who is, after all, the only person of whom it is consistently said that Jesus loved him.

John 21:24
Against Heresies I.1.1

John 11:5, 36

An attractive hypothesis that may explain the new facts now coming to light about John is the idea that this Gospel has gone through two editions. We have already seen that apart from the prologue the Gospel seems to be a very Jewish book, but with the prologue it takes on the appearance of a book more suited to the Greek world. It is therefore possible that the prologue was added after the completion of the original work, to commend the Gospel to a new readership.

This possibility is also supported by the odd connection between chapters 20 and 21. The last verse of chapter 20 appears to be the logical conclusion of the book, but this is then followed by the post-resurrection instructions of Jesus to Peter in chapter 21. This final chapter could also have been added at the time when the book was sent off to serve the needs of a new group of people, though its style and language is so close to that of the rest of the Gospel that it must have been added by the same person.

It seems possible that the Gospel was first written in Palestine, to demonstrate that 'Jesus is the Christ'. The author may have had in view sectarian Jews influenced by ideas like those of the Qumran community. Then, when the same teaching was seen to be relevant to people elsewhere in the Roman Empire, the Gospel was revised: Jewish customs and expressions were explained, and the prologue and epilogue added. The advice to church leaders in chapter 21 suggests that the final form of the Gospel may then have been directed to a Jewish Christian congregation somewhere in the Hellenistic world, perhaps at Ephesus.

John 20:31

Another place mentioned by John is 'the pavement' where Jesus was tried before Pilate. It may have been part of the Antonia Fortress. The scratch marks on the ancient stones are part of a game played by Roman soldiers.

The question of the date of the Gospel is really wide open, because we have no other evidence against which to set it. The church Fathers imply that it was written by John the apostle at the end of a long life, and most scholars continue to date it somewhere between AD 70 and 100. It must certainly not be dated later than the end of the first century, but there is no real evidence for dating it towards the end of that period. Robinson has argued with some force that it could well be the earliest of all the Gospels, and he places its composition in the period AD 40–65. If this is corect, John's Gospel could well be a contemporary of the synoptic Gospels, and such a date would effectively remove any barrier to viewing John the apostle as the author of the Gospel which now bears his name.

Chapter 12 Can we trust the Gospels?

In our study of the life and teaching of Jesus, we have taken it for granted that we can actually learn something about him from the Gospels of the New Testament. We have recognized that the Gospels are not so much biographies of Jesus, as selective accounts of his words and actions compiled because of their usefulness in the preaching ministry of the earliest churches. But we have not taken that fact as a reason to doubt the general reliability of their account of Jesus' life and teaching. At most points we have felt justified in treating these records as a picture of Jesus as he really was, rather than regarding them as psychological case studies of the Christians who first wrote about him.

It must be frankly admitted, however, that this assumption has been called into question from a number of different directions. We do not need to take seriously those writers who occasionally claim that Jesus never existed at all, for we have clear evidence to the contrary from a number of Jewish, Latin and Islamic sources. But when people who have studied the New Testament for a lifetime claim that the Gospels reveal nothing of importance about Jesus, then we need to take serious account of their arguments.

Perhaps the most radical expression of this viewpoint in our generation has been associated with the name of Rudolf Bultmann. In a book first published in 1934, he made the remarkable statement: 'I do indeed think that we can now know almost nothing concerning the life and personality of Jesus.' The precise implication of what Bultmann meant by that must be decided in the light of some of his other writings, where he makes it clear that he does believe certain elements of Jesus' teaching as found in the Gospels to be original to Jesus himself. But to his dying day Bultmann remained sceptical about both the possibility and the value of knowledge about 'the historical Jesus'.

Not all Bultmann's followers have been quite as sceptical as he was. We can see this clearly enough from Gunther Bornkamm's book, *Jesus of Nazareth*, which shows that even from a radical form-critical standpoint there is still a good deal that can confidently be known about Jesus. But, for all that, those scholars who have been most influenced by Bultmann and his form-critical approach to the Gospels have generally taken it for granted that the Gospels are primarily a record of the beliefs of the early church about Jesus, rather than any sort of account of Jesus as he actually was.

Clearly, our knowledge of Jesus is not the same as our knowledge of, say, Winston Churchill, or Martin Luther, or even of Paul. For we can know these people through their writings and recorded utterances. Indeed, in the case of Luther and Paul, the main source of our information about them is the books that they themselves wrote. But Jesus did not write a book. He spent his brief life as a wandering teacher, working in a more or less remote corner of the Roman Empire, among people who were probably not very interested in literary matters.

It is quite unlikely that Jesus' words and actions had ever been written down, either by himself or by any of his contemporaries. Furthermore we know that Jesus lived in a society whose main language was Aramaic, and yet our knowledge of his teaching comes from documents written in Greek. It is possible that Greek may have been familiar to someone brought up in Galilee. But it is certain that most of Jesus' teachings were not originally given in this language, and that the Gospels are therefore a

There were no reporters with notebooks and tape-recorders following Jesus from place to place recording his words and actions. The story of Jesus was mostly passed on by personal conversation and public preaching for some years before the Gospels were written.

translation of the words of Jesus into the major language of the Roman Empire.

Moreover, one of the consequences of handing on Jesus' sayings in Greek is that we now have variant accounts in our Gospels of what is obviously the same basic tradition. If we take the Lord's Prayer, for example, we find that Matthew and Luke preserve different versions. The similarities are so close that there can be no doubt we are dealing with the same basic tradition. But the differences are too striking to be explained merely as variant translations. The same observations could be made at many other points in the Gospels, and they are the basic facts with which source, form and redaction critics are concerned.

Matthew 6:9–13; Luke 11:2–4

We must not exaggerate the problems. Many generations of Gospel readers ignorant of the findings of modern scholars have found little difficulty in dealing with such matters. For all the distinctiveness of the various stories about Jesus and the reports of his teaching, there is clearly an inner coherence in the Gospels as a whole. It is not difficult to gather together an account of what the Gospels collectively present to us as 'the teaching of Jesus' – and the basic elements of that teaching are the same in all four Gospels.

Identifying the authentic words of Jesus

Jesus spoke Aramaic, and some Aramaic words are retained in the Gospels. But they were largely written in Greek. Left is an example of Aramaic from a fifth-century papyrus; right the Greek text of a first-century letter.

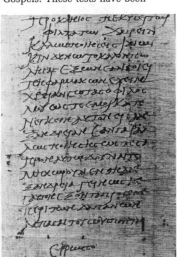

But how can we be sure that the Gospels contain the teaching of Jesus himself, and not the impressions of the early church about Jesus? This question has been the subject of a very considerable debate among New Testament scholars for the past decade or so, and it still continues. As a possible answer, a number of tests have been devised which are often claimed as a reliable means of identifying the authentic teaching of Jesus in the Gospels. These tests have been applied most comprehensively to the synoptic Gospels by Professor Norman Perrin. He outlines three separate tests, or criteria, and on the basis of these he argues that at least three areas of Jesus' teaching in the Gospels can be shown to be authentic: the parables, the teaching on the kingdom of God, and the themes mentioned in the Lord's Prayer.

The test of distinctiveness

The test of distinctiveness had already been used by Bultmann himself, in his book *The History of the Synoptic Tradition*. It is based on the assumption that anything in Jesus' teaching that can be paralleled in either the teaching of Judaism or the theology of the early church is of doubtful authenticity, for it could have come into the Gospels from either of those two sources rather than from an authentic reminiscence of Jesus. So at those points where Jesus' teaching is totally unique and distinctive we may be sure that we are in direct contact with Jesus himself. We could give as examples Jesus' use of the word *Abba*, 'Father', in his address to God, and his characteristic way of beginning important statements with the word *Amen*. As far as we know, neither of these devices was used by the Jewish rabbis or by the early church.

Many scholars would agree with Professor Perrin when he claims that information retrieved from the Gospels by this means represents 'an irreducible minimum of historical knowledge' about Jesus.

But when we examine it more carefully, it is doubtful whether even this modest claim can be fully justified on the basis of this particular method. For its successful use depends entirely on the further assumption that our present knowledge of both Judaism and the early church is more or less complete. The fact is, however, that we know very little about the form of Judaism at the time of Jesus. New information is constantly being discovered and assessed – and with it new parallels to the teaching of Jesus are certain to emerge. As a method, therefore, the criterion of distinctiveness is a counsel of despair. It can only be a matter of time before the logical outcome is reached, that nothing certain can be known about Jesus. Besides this weakness in method, there are two other major problems with this particular approach.

● Even the limited picture of Jesus produced by this means is bound to be unreal and untrue to life, for it presupposes a Jesus who was completely isolated from his environment. The old adage that 'a text without a context is a pretext' is as true here as it often is in modern sermons. Jesus *must* have had a context – and it is certain that his context was Judaism. It is equally certain that there must have been *some* continuity between Jesus and the early church. A Jesus who is unique in the sense that his teaching is totally detached from both Judaism and the church is unlikely to be the real Jesus. And if this test cannot uncover him it must be judged to be a failure.

● There are large and important areas of the Gospels where this method is of no use at all. Take the question of Jesus' teaching about himself. On this subject the test of distinctiveness leads to completely negative results on all the major titles ascribed to Jesus. 'Messiah', 'Son of God', 'Son of man' were all used by some in the early church, and the application of this test therefore leads to the conclusion that Jesus gave no teaching about his own destiny and person. The same happens with his eschatology, for that can be paralleled in Jewish

and early Christian sources. Even the distinctive teaching of the Sermon on the Mount would have to be jettisoned for the same reasons, for Paul shows a clear knowledge of that in Romans 12–14. There is therefore a basic fault in the whole concept of this approach. It must inevitably lead, both theoretically and practically, to the claim that nothing useful can be known about Jesus from the Gospels.

The test of 'coherence'

Those who use these tests are not unaware of the problems involved with the test of distinctiveness. Perrin therefore puts forward another one which can be used in conjunction with it. This is the test of coherence. It is based on the assumption that any material in the Gospels that is compatible with the teaching which passes the distinctiveness test can also be counted as a genuine statement of what Jesus said and did.

On the face of it, this further test seems promising. But of course it is very heavily dependent on a successful application of the first test. We have already seen the difficulties involved in this, and if it leads to no sure results then this second test is also useless. In any case it is very difficult to judge what is 'coherent' and what is not. Even supposing we can make our own judgement on the matter, there is no guarantee that what seems coherent to us would have seemed so to the early church. So we are once more faced with serious practical difficulties in applying this test to the Gospel traditions.

The test of more than one source

A third criterion often used for assessing the traditions about Jesus is not directly dependent on the other two. It was widely used by T.W. Manson, who had little time for the approach of the form critics.

On this test, teaching mentioned in the Gospels is genuinely from Jesus if it is found in more than one Gospel source. This is a useful test as far as it goes, for if Mark and Q give us a similar impression of the content of Jesus' teaching, then it is reasonable to believe that it is an authentic impression.

But this test for authenticity also meets a number of difficulties, though they are not as great as the problems involved in operating the other two.

● It is not possible by this means to say anything about specific statements attributed to Jesus, for there are very few stories or sayings that are contained in more than one of the Gospel sources. Indeed this fact is one of the foundations of the whole source-critical approach to the Gospels. If the same teaching was represented everywhere, it would not have been possible for Streeter to formulate his hypothesis on Gospel origins. This means that the most this method can discover is the general tone of Jesus' teaching, rather than a detailed account of it.

● It also has another built-in limitation, for it would presumably dismiss as not authentic those parts of Jesus' teaching that are found in only one Gospel source. Yet this is the case with some of the most characteristic parts of Jesus' teaching. Using this test, stories such as the good Samaritan (Luke 10:25–37) or the lost son (Luke 15:11–32) would be excluded altogether from an account of Jesus' life and teaching, because they are found only in Luke's Gospel.

● When Manson and others applied this test to the Gospels, they could assume a fairly rigid distinction between the various Gospel sources, for at the time Streeter's hypothesis was widely held by British scholars in more or less its original form. But more recent study has shown that the question of the relationships between the Gospels and their sources is far more complex than Streeter thought. We can no longer assume as a matter of course the simple division into the four independent sources, Mark, Q, M and L.

A basic flaw

There are clearly many serious problems involved in using these tests to identify the authentic words of Jesus within the Gospels. So it is perhaps not too surprising that some scholars should have reached rather negative conclusions. It is hard to see how they could do otherwise. There is in fact a basic flaw in the whole method represented by these tests. They all begin from the basic assumption that the Gospels mostly contain the beliefs of the early church, and only a very little, if anything at all, that comes directly from Jesus himself. Professor Perrin gives two main

reasons to justify this built-in pessimism.

● 'The early Church,' he writes, 'made no attempt to distinguish between the words the earthly Jesus had spoken and those spoken by the risen Lord through a prophet in the community, nor between the original teaching of Jesus and the new understanding and reformulation of that teaching reached in ... the Church under the guidance of the Lord of the Church.'

The starting-point of this argument is the fact that the earliest Christians clearly believed that the risen Jesus was present and active among his followers in the church. He was, of course, no longer physically present, and so his word could be communicated to Christians only indirectly. An example of how this could happen is said to be found in the first three chapters of the book of Revelation. There the Christian prophet John delivers messages from the heavenly Christ to seven churches in Asia Minor. Paul also mentions prophets working in the church (1 Corinthians 12:27–31), and it is often argued that their main function was to issue 'sayings of Jesus' to meet some specific need in the church's life.

Though this argument is widely accepted by New Testament scholars, it is highly questionable. A number of very serious objections can be made against it.

First, it is based on very precarious evidence. Though it is often confidently stated that the role of the Christian prophet was to invent sayings of Jesus, we have in fact no real evidence to show what the prophets did in the early church. The messages to the seven churches in the book of Revelation are quite irrelevant, for a clear distinction is made there between the experience and words of the writer of the book and the message of the risen Christ. In any case he claims to have received them in a vision, and we can say that he made them up only if we make the further questionable assumption that visions never happen. The only direct evidence in the New Testament of the function of these prophets is in Acts 13:1–3 where they give instructions regarding the missionary work of Paul and Barnabas. Even these instructions are given, not in the name of Jesus, but with the authority of the Holy

Spirit. This kind of evidence is so slight that it can give us only the vaguest indication of the precise work of the prophets in the life of the church.

Secondly, the assumption that prophets could freely invent 'sayings of Jesus' also assumes that the first Christians made no clear distinction between Jesus' teaching and their own. But this is quite

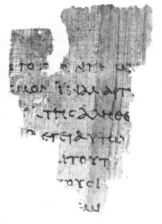

A very early fragment of John's Gospel, dating from about AD 130.

untrue. Paradoxically, our evidence for this is clearest in the writings of Paul, and for that reason it is all the more striking. For, of all the New Testament writers, Paul is the one most often accused of sitting loosely to the teachings of Jesus. He also claimed more than once to have a greater measure of God's special gifts than most of his contemporaries (1 Corinthians 14: 18–19; 2 Corinthians 12:1–10). These two facts alone would make him an ideal candidate to have been a purveyor of 'sayings of Jesus'. We would expect his letters to be full of such sayings, manufactured by himself under the influence of the Holy Spirit for the purpose of giving advice to his readers. But in fact we find quite the opposite. In 1 Corinthians 7, for example, he goes out of his way to distinguish between his own opinions and the teaching of Jesus.

Thirdly, another problem with the assumption that the early church freely manufactured sayings of Jesus is its illogicality. The only 'evidence' that the prophets formulated such sayings is the notion that the Gospel traditions

had their origin in the early church and not in the ministry of Jesus. A hypothetical life-setting has been imagined for the Gospels; then the Gospels are interpreted in the light of the hypothesis. This is a very uncertain procedure, not least because it is a circular argument with no external support. It is not surprising that on this basis the Gospels can be demonstrated to be products of the pious imagination of the early church; the evidence has been put into them at the outset of the investigation.

● Professor Perrin's second reason for scepticism has a firmer foundation. He asserts, quite correctly, that the primary aim of the Gospels was not to give historical or biographical information about Jesus, but to edify their readers. Everything in the Gospels is there because it served a particular purpose in the church's life. But he goes on to say that this fact of itself excludes the possibility that the Gospels contain historical reminiscences of Jesus as he actually was. This is another argument that is often asserted but seldom supported.

There is, however, no logical reason at all why a story or piece of teaching that conveys a practical or theological message has to be historically false. For example, I have often preached sermons on Paul's statement that in Christ 'There is neither Jew nor Greek, there is neither slave nor free, there is neither male nor female; for you are all one ...' (Galatians 3:28). No doubt many sermons have been preached on that theme, relating it to our modern problems of inequality and injustice. It is certainly highly relevant to such issues. But the fact that I preach a sermon on that text and relate it to twentieth-century problems would not normally lead people to conclude that I made it up myself and Paul never wrote Galatians, or even that he never existed at all. That would be absurd. Yet this is precisely the kind of reasoning that some scholars apply to the Gospels when they argue that, because their contents were relevant to life in the middle of the first century, they can have had no historical context in the times of Jesus himself. It is an assertion that simply does not make sense.

A positive approach to the Gospels

Many scholars find the scepticism of Bultmann and his followers quite unacceptable. They argue instead that there are a number or good reasons for starting from the assumption that the Gospels are reliable, rather than unreliable, as records of Jesus as he actually was. A number of important arguments point in this direction.

● To begin at the most general level, we must not forget that ancient writers were not on the whole either fools or frauds. Many modern theologians (though not as many historians) speak so disparagingly of the historians of the Roman world that we are often given the impression that the concept of accurate history writing was quite unknown to them. It is of course true that the ancient historian did not have at his disposal all the modern aids we have today. But that is not to say he simply invented his stories. Both Latin and Greek historians had high standards, and though they did not always keep to them, it was certainly not for lack of trying. The principles outlined by people like Lucian and Thucydides make it quite clear that they operated within guidelines that would not be out of place even today.

Whatever else may be said about the people who wrote the Gospels, it is clear that they thought they were working within this kind of historical tradition. Luke explicitly says that he sifted all his sources of information and carefully compiled his story on that basis. Since the other synoptic writers used a more or less similar technique in dealing with their sources, it is natural to suppose that they also worked on the same lines. Certainly they all thought they were giving actual information about a person who had really lived in the way they described. They were not conscious of reporting sayings made up by their contemporaries and attributed to Jesus. They believed that their risen Lord was actually a Galilean rabbi, and that as a wandering teacher he lived and spoke as they depicted him.

Luke 1:1–4

● This argument is of course not very strong by itself, for the evangelists could have been mistaken and deluded. But it gains considerable added force when we discover that the details of their accounts do actually give an authentic picture of life in Palestine at the time of which they purport to write. When we recall that they all wrote in Greek for a more or less non-Jewish readership, and that at least two of them were not living in Palestine when they wrote, this is all the more remarkable. At point after point we find that the background of the Gospels is authentic. Moreover, at places where their record was once believed to be mistaken (as in the case of John's Gospel), subsequent discoveries of new information have often shown that the Gospels preserve reliable accounts of a number of important geographical and social details.

● The Gospels have also been firmly rooted in a Jewish context by the work of two Scandinavian scholars, Harald Riesenfeld and his pupil Birger Gerhardsson. Gerhardsson has put forward the view that the teaching of Jesus was very similar in form to that of the Jewish rabbis, and in an extended analysis of their teaching methods he has shown how the rabbis took great pains to ensure that their sayings were accurately remembered and passed on by word of mouth to their followers. Gerhardsson suggests that Jesus adopted the same methods, and that he formulated his teaching with a view to his disciples learning it by heart so that they could pass it on to their own followers in the same easily memorized form. It is suggested that the teaching of Jesus was handed on in this way as 'holy word' in the early church, and that the Gospels represent the writing down of accurately transmitted traditions going right back to Jesus himself.

We have no evidence that the early Christians regarded themselves as the transmitters of tradition, however. They were preachers of the good news, explaining how the life and message of Jesus was relevant to the needs of their own generation. We also have the unanimous testimony of the Gospels that Jesus was **Mark 1:22** quite different from the Jewish rabbis. He taught 'with authority', and did not simply hand on memorized sayings from one group of disciples to another.

Yet, though the case of Riesenfeld and Gerhardsson may be exaggerated, they have reminded us that Jesus' teaching was given in a Jewish context, and in that context the teaching of an authoritative leader was treated with great respect. Even if the earliest disciples did not learn Jesus' sayings by heart, they would certainly have a high regard for them.

There is also ample evidence for the reliable oral preservation of stories in the wider Hellenistic world. Take the *Life of Apollonius of Tyana*, which we have mentioned in an earlier chapter. This man Apollonius was a contemporary of Jesus, though he

The Bible has been subjected to close scholarly scrutiny over the past two centuries. This group of people organized the translation of the New English Bible. Their task took twelve years.

lived on into old age and died towards the end of the first century. The account of his life, however, was not written down until the beginning of the third century. Though the author collected the stories of his life from a number of different sources, and though he was not an impartial biographer, very few ancient historians would have serious doubts about the reliability of the main outline of his account. In the case of the Gospels we are dealing with documents that were written down very shortly after the events of which they speak. To most ordinary people it would seem absurd to assume that such accounts are useless for the purpose of knowing something of Jesus himself.

● According to the German scholar Joachim Jeremias, the Gospels do indeed bring us into close contact with Jesus as he actually was. Jeremias has scrutinized the linguistic and grammatical features of the Gospels, and argues that in them we can discover the authentic voice of Jesus.

Occasionally we come across actual Aramaic words, even in the Greek text of the Gospels. In many other cases there are passages where an idiomatic Aramaic construction has been used in the writing of the Gospels in Greek. Jeremias also outlines a number of ways of speaking which he says were characteristically used by Jesus. Much of his teaching is given in the form of Aramaic poetry, recognizable even in an English translation. At other points, as we have already said, it has been shown that when sayings attributed to Jesus are translated back into Aramaic, they often assume a typically Semitic form, and even display alliteration and assonance that could have had meaning only in Aramaic. Then there are the parables, which are quite different from the teaching of the rabbis; and Jesus' special use of the words *Amen* and *Abba*.

Features such as these do not themselves prove that the Gospel traditions go back to Jesus. Strictly speaking, the most they can show is that they go back to a form in which they were preserved by Aramaic-speaking Palestinian Christians. But when we get back into that context we are also back to a time shortly after the

Mark 5:41; Matthew 27:46; John 19:13

The Gospels – and most of the Bible – have been translated into many languages. Some tribal languages first have to be reduced to writing before the translation can begin.

events of Jesus' life, death and resurrection. At this time many eye-witnesses must still have been alive to challenge any accounts which were pure fiction.

These facts therefore favour the authenticity of the Gospel accounts of Jesus' teaching. Jeremias for one has no doubt that they place the burden of proof squarely on those who would dispute their accuracy: 'In the synoptic tradition it is the inauthenticity, and not the authenticity, of the sayings of Jesus that must be demonstrated.'

● Another consideration that gives us confidence in accepting the Gospels as generally authentic records of Jesus' life and teaching is the fact that they are so different from what we know of the life and concerns of the early non-Jewish churches. It is wrong to imagine that, because the Gospels were written to serve the needs of the churches, they are little more than a mirror reflecting the life of the early church. The rest of the New Testament shows that the church had many needs that are not even remotely met in the Gospels.

There is, for example, no real teaching on the church itself in the Gospels. This is so obvious a gap that we found it necessary to ask in an earlier chapter whether Jesus was interested in founding a church at all. It was suggested there that the emergence of the church was by no means incompatible with Jesus' teaching, but we still need to admit that there is virtually no specific guidance on the subject in the Gospels. Even baptism, which very soon became the rite of initiation into the Christian fellowship, is never mentioned by Jesus, apart from one isolated

Matthew 28:19   instance. Jesus himself did not baptize, nor did he make baptism a central part of his teaching. Yet this was a matter of great importance to the early church. If they did indeed make a regular practice of manufacturing 'sayings of Jesus' to meet their needs, they certainly missed an important opportunity here.

We find the same lack of specific guidance on other crucial topics. The question of Jews and non-Jews, for example, is not really dealt with in the Gospels, though we know from the rest of the New Testament that it soon became one of the most important matters of all.

In other places the Gospels make quite a different emphasis from the rest of the New Testament. The term 'Son of man', for instance, is the most widely used name for Jesus in the Gospels, but it hardly appears anywhere else. Likewise, 'the kingdom of God', which was the heart of Jesus' teaching, is hardly mentioned in the rest of the New Testament.

The fact is that if we were to try to reconstruct the church's life-situation from the Gospels, we would never arrive at the kind of picture we know to be true from the New Testament letters. For there are so many features of the Gospel stories about Jesus that are quite different from the life and concerns of the early church.

In the light of facts such as these, it seems reasonable to conclude that there are good reasons for supposing the Gospels preserve authentic reminiscences of Jesus as he actually was. The whole character of their picture of Jesus is such that we would need very strong and coherent arguments to show that they are fundamentally mistaken.

This assumption does not of course mean that we can adopt a naïve and uncritical attitude. The evangelists were not mere recorders of tradition. They were interpreters of the facts handed on to them, and we need to scrutinize their work carefully in order to understand the precise nature of what they were doing. But it does give us confidence in thinking that the tradition they interpreted for their first readers was itself authentic, and that in general terms they have preserved a realistic account of the life and teaching of Jesus. Whether they have done so in specific instances must naturally be determined by a literary and historical approach to particular sections of their work.

God's revelation and history

In view of the many reasons that lead us to presume the authenticity of the Gospels as records of Jesus' teaching, we might well be surprised that so many scholars have adopted such a negative attitude towards them. One basic reason for this is almost certainly to be found not so much in their historical and literary approach to the Gospels themselves, as in their total understanding of the whole question of revelation and the knowledge of God.

To understand this, we need to go back to the work of Friedrich Schleiermacher (1768–1834), the so-called 'father of modern theology'. In trying to deal with the great upsurge of rationalism that came with the European Enlightenment, Schleiermacher reasoned that if religious belief was to retain any validity for modern Western people, it would need to be removed altogether from the realm of rational investigation. For the historical science of his day was totally sceptical of the whole idea that God could make himself known in history through the kind of events recorded in the Bible.

Schleiermacher therefore aimed to rescue religious belief from what he thought would be its inevitable suffocation in this sceptical atmosphere. He argued that the essence of faith is quite different from the essence of either morality, which directs the practical side of life, or science, which is concerned with rational thought processes. Faith, he said, is pure feeling, and this means that religious belief can be valid quite independently of anything that can be interpreted scientifically.

This idea has been challenged and modified at many points by later thinkers. But Schleiermacher's general distinction between religion and reason has been decisive for the subsequent development of theological thought in much of the Western world. In the study of the Gospels it is expressed by the acceptance of two principles which dominate the thinking of many scholars.

Friedrich Schleiermacher (1768–1834), the German thinker, was the father of one school of modern theology.

● *The supernatural and history*. Many theologians, especially those who, like Bultmann, stand in a German Lutheran tradition, believe that the universe is a closed system, operating according to rigidly structured 'laws of nature' which cannot be broken. When taken to its logical conclusion, this belief means that it is impossible to accommodate any kind of miraculous or unique occurrence in our concept of history. If the workings of the world are totally predictable then, by definition, the unpredictable cannot take place. On this view it therefore becomes inevitable that the Gospels should be seen as something other than history, for they do contain accounts of a number of unique happenings which appear to violate the 'laws of nature' as we know them.

Various arguments may be brought against this kind of view of the world and its workings. For one thing, it is outdated. It is interesting to note that, at this point, the assumptions of some philosophers and theologians are much less flexible than the views of many modern scientists. The discoveries made by twentieth-century physicists, for example, have shown at many points how tenuous the concept of the universe as a closed system really is, and many scientists now recognize that there is more to its workings than just the mechanical operation of laws of cause and effect.

Then, from another standpoint, the belief that the universe is a closed system can too easily become a means of avoiding the need to take serious account of the actual evidence of history. If we are to allow ourselves room to consider the full implications of the Gospel accounts, or indeed of history as a whole, we must in principle be prepared to operate on a wider definition of history and reality than is allowed by many modern theologians. To say that unique events cannot happen, or that the supernatural does not exist, is no kind of answer to the questions raised by history. It merely begs larger and more important questions.

● *Facts and faith*. Another assumption often made by theologians is that facts and faith are unconnected, and that religious belief cannot be founded on the facts of history. There is a problem with Christianity at this point. For no matter what we say about Christian belief it is somehow connected with the Jesus who lived and died in first-century Palestine. In some sense, therefore, it must be a 'historical' faith. But what do we mean when we say that?

When we speak of 'history' or of 'historical events', we can mean two things. On the one hand, 'history' can mean 'the past'. It is what really happened on a given occasion: what we would have seen with our own eyes and heard with our own ears had we been there. This is the kind of 'history' the nineteenth-century rationalists were trying to discover in their quest for the historical Jesus. But we can also use the word 'history' to mean 'referring to the past' – what we might call 'history-as-story' rather than 'history-as-fact'. In the one case we are dealing with the actual things that happened, and nothing else. In the other, we consider the events in their proper context and in the light of their ultimate significance for our own existence.

A number of German theologians have seized upon this technical distinction as a means of separating the Jesus of Christian faith (the risen Lord) from the Jesus of history. They use two different German words to describe the two kinds of history: *Historie* to denote 'history-as-fact', and *Geschichte* to denote 'history-as-story'. And, they say, it is only the latter that is really important to Christian faith. It is the *significance* of history as it affects us that matters, not the history itself. This means that knowledge of Jesus himself as a historical person is irrelevant to faith. What really matters is the Christian's beliefs about Jesus.

This kind of assertion is gravely inadequate, both as a statement about theology in general, and as a statement about the Gospel accounts of Jesus' life and teaching. The sharp distinction made between *Historie* and *Geschichte* is based on a misunderstanding of the true nature of history-as-fact and history-as-story. For the two things are very closely related, and it is quite impossible to think of one of them without also presupposing the other. Nobody would ever write history-as-story unless he was convinced that something had actually happened that was important enough to be worth writing about. And, similarly, we can gain access to 'what actually happened' only through the medium of stories and records that tell of them in their context and over-all significance.

It is therefore logically inevitable that when we speak of 'history', whether in general or in relation to the New Testament, we should include something of both meanings. It is also highly desirable that we should do so. If we confine our attention to the meaning of history we are in a very precarious position, for if an event did not actually take place then any interpretation we place upon it is bound to be completely meaningless. It would, for example, be pointless to convince myself that Jesus died for my sins if, as a matter of historical fact, he never died at all. To say that faith is important and facts are not is naïve. It leads away from objectivity in historical understanding, and represents a religious faith that is both irrational and subjective.

The writers of the New Testament were not unaware of these questions, and they provide their own answers to them. In his important account of the resurrection of Jesus and its meaning, Paul emphasizes very strongly the importance of facts as an indispensable element in his own Christian faith. Though he himself became a Christian through a direct encounter with the risen Christ, he sets his theology very firmly in the context of a historical event that he believed could be verified in the normal way by the report of witnesses. And he has no hesitation in saying that if the witnesses were wrong, and 'if Christ has not been raised, then your faith is a delusion...'

1 Corinthians 15:17

The various accounts of the early Christian preaching also emphasize that history is important, and much of the *kerygma* as outlined by C.H. Dodd is a recital of facts about Jesus. The Jesus who confronts us in the New Testament, and supremely in the Gospels, is not a phantom figure whose only importance is his meaning. He is a real person who can be relevant to our world because he has lived in it.

But the good news does not demand that we become ancient historians in order to be Christians. The facts require us to take action, to exercise faith. If Jesus rose from the dead, then we must face the implications, the need to submit to the risen Lord and his demands over our lives. But it also assures us that both his demands and his promises are reasonable, fair, and true because they can be vindicated by reference to the events of history.

In the final analysis, the Jesus of history can only be the Jesus of the church's faith. For it was in the events of the life, death and resurrection of this person that God was at work, revealing his own character and reconciling the world to himself.

Although the Gospels have presented scholars with many questions, people of every race and generation have found in them a source of inspiration and hope.

Sayings of Jesus outside the New Testament

At various points we have referred to traditions about Jesus' life and teaching that are not found in the New Testament. A number of 'gospels' written in the second century purport to tell of the early childhood of Jesus. Then we have also mentioned collections of Jesus' sayings, such as the *Gospel of Thomas*. A very

considerable number of such traditions about Jesus are known to us (see the book list).

These documents are not the only sources which contain information about Jesus not found in the New Testament Gospels. Some of the church Fathers preserve a few fragments of teaching which they say was first given by Jesus, and of course in other parts of the New Testament itself we occasionally find references to sayings of Jesus not found in the Gospels. For example, at the end of his message to the elders of the Ephesian church, Paul sums up by quoting what he says are the words of Jesus, that 'It is more blessed to give than to receive' (Acts 20:35). Yet no such saying of Jesus is recorded anywhere in the Gospels.

The material preserved in the second-century sources is of a remarkably varied character. Much of it, especially in the infancy stories, is clearly legendary. It was written to fill in the gaps that are left by the New Testament Gospels, for they tell us nothing at all of Jesus' childhood. Many of the stories of these apocryphal infancy gospels are so unreal and pointless that one only need read them to realize that they are of a quite different character from the New Testament accounts of Jesus.

Other questions are raised, however, by the collections of Jesus' sayings found in such documents as the Gospels of Philip and Thomas, or the various papyri discovered at Oxyrhynchus in upper Egypt. Most of these documents were written for sectarian purposes, and many of them emanate from the various Gnostic groups that were prevalent in the second century and after.

The *Gospel of Thomas* in its present form was compiled for the purpose of supporting the life of an esoteric group in the church. Scholars are uncertain as to whether it was a Gnostic group, or perhaps some other kind of group connected to Jewish Christianity, but they are unanimous in regarding it as a document produced to uphold the beliefs of a particular sect. Many of its sayings are taken from the New Testament, but presented with a Gnostic slant. Others have probably come in direct from some other Gnostic source.

But, besides these, there are still some others which appear to be of independent origin. For example, logion 82 of *Thomas* reads as follows: 'Jesus said, He who is near me is near the fire; he who is far from me is far from the kingdom.' This particular saying was also known to the church Father Origen (AD 185–254), and there may be allusions to it in other early Christian writers. It is certainly

characteristic of the kind of sayings of Jesus recorded in the New Testament and, in addition, it has the form of Aramaic poetry, which again is a regular feature of Jesus' teaching in the four Gospels.

There are a number of such sayings scattered about in the literature of the early church. When they do not teach any specially sectarian doctrine, and when they are in general agreement with the teaching of Jesus found in the New Testament, there seems to be no real reason for doubting that they could go back to authentic traditions about Jesus. If, as in the example we quoted, they also have the form of Semitic poetry, that is a further indication of their primitive character.

In his book *Unknown Sayings of Jesus*, Professor Jeremias has isolated a number of such fragments of teaching, and a few stories told about Jesus, that he considers may be genuine reminiscences of the life and teaching of Jesus himself. Some of them undoubtedly do have the marks of authenticity. The fact that such information should have been preserved outside the New Testament need not surprise us. The writer of John's Gospel mentions many accounts of Jesus' life and teaching known to him, but which he did not use in his own Gospel (John 20:30–31). But we can be sure that they would not be entirely lost to the church. No doubt they were remembered and repeated, and perhaps some of them ended up in the various documents we have mentioned here.

But it is important to notice that by comparison with the vast number of apocryphal traditions about Jesus, only a tiny proportion have even a slight claim to being genuine. The vast majority of the material is quite worthless as a historical source for knowledge of Jesus. Professor Jeremias is undoubtedly correct when he comments that 'The real value of the tradition outside the Gospels is that it throws into sharp relief the unique value of the canonical Gospels themselves. If we would learn about the life and message of Jesus, we shall find what we want *only* in the four canonical Gospels. The lost dominical sayings may supplement our knowledge here and there in important and valuable ways, but they cannot do more than that.'

5. Into all the world

Chapter 13 Confronting the ancient world

After the resurrection of Jesus, his followers were faced with some hard choices. The previous two or three years had been the most exciting time of their lives. They had listened with wonder to his teaching, and watched with growing expectancy as Jesus' actions made it plain that God's long-awaited new society had really and truly arrived. The kingdom was here, because Jesus was the king! Then came the crucifixion, and with it all they had hoped for seemed doomed to certain failure. Even the resurrection left them afraid and disillusioned, and when they realised that Jesus would no longer be physically present with them they must have been under intense pressure simply to forget him. Not to forget him entirely, perhaps – but to write off those three years as an experience which had taught them a lot, but which was no longer of immediate concern to their continuing life style.

It must have been a great temptation for them to drift back home and pick up the threads of their working lives where they had left off before they joined Jesus. There, they could still share their memories of him – and perhaps even try to put some of his teaching into practice in the local synagogues of rural Palestine.

Yet the more they thought about Jesus, the more they knew how impossible such a reaction would be. Jesus had demanded their radical and wholehearted obedience when they first met him. And his final message to them was just as challenging and uncompromising: 'Go, then, to all peoples everywhere and make them my disciples ... you will be witnesses for me in Jerusalem, in all Judea and Samaria, and to the ends of the earth...'

Matthew 28:19, Acts 1:8

Back to Jesus

Luke 9:25; 19:18, 39

Mark 1:22

Jesus had never really been an establishment figure. People who met him often recognized him as a 'rabbi', and gave him that title. But right from the very beginning, they all knew that he was different and that his message was distinctive. In his very first report of Jesus' public teaching, Mark comments: 'The people who heard him were amazed at the way he taught, for he wasn't like the teachers of the Law; instead, he taught with authority.'

That does not mean to say that his teaching was completely new and unique. Many Jewish writers have rightly pointed out that almost everything in Jesus' teaching had been said before him by the Jewish rabbis. Since both Jesus and the rabbis were setting out to explain the significance of the Old Testament for their own generation, it is hardly surprising that they sometimes reached the same conclusions. But what was so different about Jesus – and what was to set his followers radically apart from Judaism – was the framework in which he set his teaching. For on two basic issues Jesus adopted a fundamentally different stance from the other Jewish teachers of his day.

Keeping the Law
Genesis – Deuteronomy

The Law, or Torah (the first five books of the Old Testament), was central to the Jewish faith. By keeping the Law in all its details a person demonstrated his or her obedience and faithful response to God. It is often difficult for a non-Jew today to understand the almost mystical significance of the Law for a faithful Jewish believer in the time of Jesus. For instance, it has been shown recently that some of the most influential Protestant biblical

The Law still has great significance for the orthodox Jew. Here a rabbi holds the Sefer Torah, or scroll of the Law.

scholars of the last 100 years or so have been guilty of gross misrepresentation of the Jewish attitude to law-keeping. Judaism was not the rigid, legalistic system that many people imagine. Pious Jews in the time of Jesus must have had a far more positive understanding of their faith than the kind of blind obedience credited to them by some Christians writers in modern times. But no matter what their motivation, keeping the law and its precepts has always been a central plank of Judaism. To be a good person, one must keep the Law.

But there was more than one way to do that. As long as 700 years before the time of Jesus, the prophet Amos had condemned his contemporaries for their eagerness to keep the minute details of the ritual and ceremonial regulations, while ignoring the central moral requirements that were also laid down in the Torah. And things were no different in Jesus' day. His condemnation of the Pharisees is strongly reminiscent of Amos's warnings: 'You hypocrites! You give to God a tenth even of the seasoning herbs, such as mint, dill and cumin, but you neglect to obey the really important teachings of the Law, such as justice and mercy and honesty.' The problem was obviously widespread, for when Jesus was asked why his disciples did not keep every detailed requirement of the Old Testament Law, he pointed out to his questioners their own inconsistency in avoiding moral obligations to their parents by using a legal loophole to use their wealth for more 'religious' purposes. 'And,' added Jesus, 'there are many other things like this that you do.'

Jesus never denied the validity of the Old Testament Law, nor did he deny that it had been given by God. But he did suggest that with his own coming, its day was finished. More than that, in a series of remarkable statements he contrasts his own teaching with that of the Torah, and elevates his own authority to a higher status than that of Moses, the great Old Testament law-giver: 'You have heard that people were told in the past [by Moses] but now I tell you...' It is also significant that according to Mark's account of his trial before the Sanhedrin, Jesus was first charged with blasphemy against the temple. The charge failed, but from the authorities' viewpoint it was not totally without foundation, as we can see from his statement in Matthew's Gospel: 'I tell you that there is something here greater than the temple.'

It is therefore not surprising that, though Jesus seemed to be an ordinary Jewish rabbi, he was soon outlawed by the Jewish religious establishment. This radical teaching about the Law and the temple was striking at the very foundations of their most firmly-held convictions. Of course, many rabbis had asked awkward questions before – and if Jesus' teaching had been restricted to theoretical debate about the Law, perhaps the system could have coped with it. It had survived many changes before, and was to assimilate many others after the time of Jesus. But Jesus was not content to be just a propounder of theories, and the way he behaved was, if anything, even more scandalous than his teaching.

Mark tells how he and his disciples disregarded the Jewish laws

Amos 5:21–24

Matthew 23:23

Mark 7:1–13

Luke 16:16

Matthew 5:21–22, 27–28, 31–47

Mark 14:57–59

Matthew 12:6

Mark 2:23–28   about the sabbath day, picking grain as they walked through the fields – actions that were regarded as harvesting by pious believers. Jesus' reply to the Pharisees' criticism of this behaviour was to dismiss their concern for the keeping of the Law with the declaration that 'the Sabbath was made for the good of man; man was not made for the Sabbath'. Then when he was asked why his disciples

Mark 7:1–15   disregarded the regulations about ritual washing before eating a meal, he dismissed the criticism by appeal to a higher principle: 'There is nothing that goes into a person from the outside which can make him ritually unclean. Rather, it is what comes out of a person that makes him unclean ... evil ideas which lead him to do

Mark 7:21–22   immoral things, to rob, kill, commit adultery, be greedy...'

In addition to all this, Jesus insisted on taking his message to all sorts of people who were regarded as unclean by pious Jews. Lepers, prostitutes, tax gatherers (Roman collaborators) – all of them figure prominently in the Gospels, and Jesus himself was described as 'a glutton and a drinker, a friend of tax collectors and other

Matthew 11:19   outcasts'. Instead of making his friends among the conventionally religious, Jesus chose those who were despised for their inability to keep the Law. Indeed, he made a virtue out of it, reminding his questioners on one occasion that 'I have not come to call respect-

Mark 2:17   able people, but outcasts'.

A number of stories in the gospels explain why Jesus felt like that, but perhaps none has a greater impact than the parable of the Pharisee and the tax collector who went to pray in the temple at the

Luke 18:9–14   same time. The Pharisee prided himself on his moral and religious attainments – and told God so. The tax collector, on the other hand, was so conscious of his own unworthiness to speak to God at all that he could only cry out, 'God, have pity on me, a sinner'. 'But,' said Jesus, 'the tax collector, and not the Pharisee, was in the right with God when he went home,' because he recognized his own sinfulness and came to God with no spiritual pretensions.

The Pharisees were laying all the stress on external actions that could be assessed and regulated by rules. Jesus believed it was possible to keep all the rules, and yet not please God. And so in all his teaching, Jesus was much more concerned with what a person *is* than with what he or she *does*. Not that he believed actions to be unimportant. But Jesus realized that the way we behave depends on the kind of people we are. And for him, the secret of goodness was to be found not in obedience to rules, but in the spontaneous activities of a transformed character: 'A sound tree cannot bear evil

Matthew 7:18   fruit, nor can a bad tree bear good fruit.'

Religion and race

But there was another element in Jesus' conflicts with the Jewish establishment. Many people in the Roman Empire admired the moral precepts of the Old Testament. The principles enshrined in the Ten Commandments and other parts of the Torah commanded the respect of many upright Romans and Greeks. But admiring the Law was not quite the same thing as pleasing God, and before they could be fully accepted as part of God's people, Jews demanded that non-Jews must be circumcised and be prepared to keep every detailed regulation of the Old Testament Law. In a word, they had to become Jews – for the Jewish people believed that they, and they alone, were the people of God, and others had no chance of being accepted by God unless they too accepted all the burdens of the Law. This did not stop the Pharisees and others from engaging in missionary activity among non-Jews. Indeed, Jesus himself commended them for their enthusiasm. But he did not approve of their insistence that in order to please God such people should accept all the detailed regulations of the Old Testament Law.

Matthew 23:15

The precise extent of Jesus' own involvement in a mission to those who were not Jews is somewhat unclear. He certainly made no concerted effort to preach the good news to non-Jews (Gentiles). But at the same time, all four Gospels show him accepting and respecting the faith of such people whenever he met them. He was not unwilling even to assist a Roman officer, remarking in the process that 'I have never found anyone in Israel with faith like this'. Then a number of incidents show his acceptance of various foreign groups within Palestinian society, while one of his best-known parables extols the virtues of a Samaritan, the race that was despised perhaps more than any other by pious Jews.

Matthew 8:5–13

Mark 5:1–20; 7:24–30

Luke 10:25–37

Some readers of the Gospels have found a difficulty in Jesus' instruction to his disciples in Matthew 10:5–6, 'Do not go to any Gentile territory or any Samaritan towns. Instead, you are to go to those lost sheep, the people of Israel.' But this advice was given in respect of a limited mission tour which the disciples were to undertake for a short period only, during Jesus' own lifetime. Matthew himself certainly did not believe it to be binding advice for all time, for he is the only Gospel writer to record the great

Jesus said that the way people live shows what they are really like, just as a healthy tree naturally produces good fruit.

Matthew 28:19
Matthew 8:10–12; 21:43

Acts 1:8

commission of Jesus, exhorting his disciples to 'Go ... to all peoples everywhere and make them my disciples ...' Other passages in Matthew's Gospel make the same point, as do many passages in the Gospel of Luke. The best way to understand the advice of Matthew 10:5 is to set it alongside another commission given, according to Luke, after the resurrection: '... you will be witnesses for me in Jerusalem, in all Judea and Samaria, and to the ends of the earth.' For Jesus, evangelism, like charity, must begin at home.

The church is born

Christians are actively involved in sharing their faith today in obedience to Jesus' command to be his witnesses.

As they met behind closed doors in Jerusalem in those early days after Jesus' resurrection, the disciples knew that it was easier to talk about changing the world than it was to go out and do it. But it was not long before something happened that not only altered their thinking, but gave them a courage and boldness to share their faith that was to send shockwaves throughout the Roman world.

Only fifty days after the death of Jesus, Peter found himself standing before a large crowd in the streets of Jerusalem, fearlessly proclaiming that God's kingdom had arrived, and that Jesus was its

king and Messiah. At the time Jerusalem was full of pilgrims who had come from all parts of the empire for the Festival of Pentecost – and as Peter spoke they not only understood his message, but responded to it in amazing numbers. When Peter declared that they too should become disciples of Jesus by turning from their sin and accepting the new life that God would give them, 3000 accepted his challenge and committed their lives to Jesus.

Acts 2:14–42

What had happened to bring about such a transformation in the lives of Jesus' followers? The answer to that is contained in the opening section of Peter's address. For as he stood up to speak to the crowd, he reminded them of an Old Testament passage that had described the coming new age as a time when God's Spirit would work in an exciting new way in the lives of men and women. As the Old Testament prophets had looked to the future, some of them realized that the human predicament would never be resolved until a new relationship was set up between people and God. Human sin and disobedience had made such a mess of things, but in the new age God would not just ask for obedience – he would actually give people a new moral power that would enable them to be what they were intended to be. In the prophecy of Joel, this new power for living had been associated with the gift of God's Spirit – and Peter took this passage as his text, claiming that it was now coming true in the experience of Jesus' disciples. Through Jesus' death and resurrection, men and women could now have a new relationship with God himself. From his own experience, Peter knew it was all true.

Jeremiah 31:31–34

Joel 2:28–32

The Roman Empire at its widest extent in AD 117.

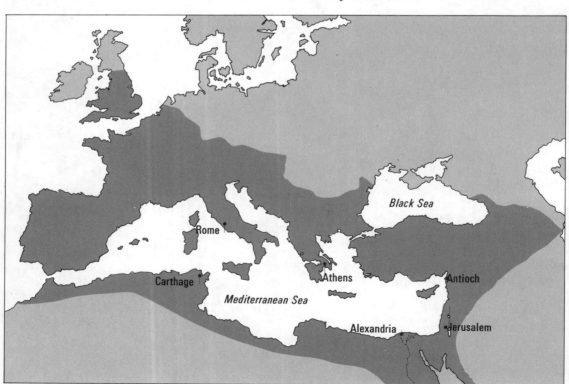

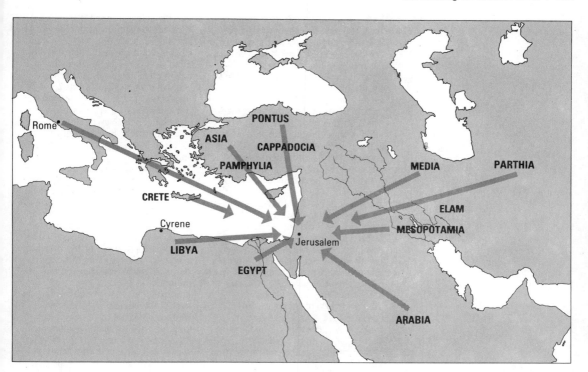

Peter's audience on the Day of Pentecost.

For Peter and the others, that day had begun like any other. But as they faced the enormity – and the impossibility – of the task Jesus had left them, they were taken by surprise as a new life-giving power burst into their lives. It was a moral and spiritual dynamic that equipped them to bear witness to their new faith – a power that would make them like Jesus. It was the power of the Holy Spirit. It is not easy to describe in words exactly what their experience was. But as a result of it, their hesitating and uncertain trust in Jesus and his promises was remarkably confirmed. From this moment onwards, they were certain that God's promises in the Old Testament were coming true in their own lives – and they were quite sure that the presence of the living Jesus was with them in a unique way. The church had been born.

Their whole life was revolutionized in such a way that they needed no further argument to persuade them that their everyday experience was a direct result of the power and presence of Jesus in their own lives. Peter, John and others had the power to perform remarkable deeds in the name of Jesus – and, of course, Peter himself was given the unexpected ability to speak in a powerful way to the crowds gathered in Jerusalem.

Acts 2:43; 3:1–10

Acts 2:14–39

The Day of Pentecost

The precise nature of the disciples' experience on the Day of Pentecost has been much discussed. Indeed, some scholars believe that it never happened, and that the whole of the story in Acts chapter 2 was intended by Luke to convey some theological lesson rather than to report an actual incident. In his commentary on Acts, Ernst Haenchen suggests that the key to understanding

Luke's purpose here is to be found in the fact that Jewish rabbis linked the festival of Pentecost with the giving of the Old Testament Law at Mt Sinai. According to the late second-century Rabbi Johanan, the one voice of God at the giving of the Law had divided into seven voices, and these had then spoken in seventy different languages. That, together with the fact that wind and fire were present both at Sinai and at the events of Pentecost, is said to be enough to explain the picturesque language used by Luke.

But there is no reason to accept this kind of rationalistic explanation of the story in Acts. For one thing, we have no evidence at all to show that the Jewish rabbis linked Sinai and Pentecost before the second century – and that was long after either the alleged event itself or the lifetime of Luke. In any case, it is inherently probable that the disciples would have been in Jerusalem at the time, and that after the unexpected events of the previous Passover they would have gathered in the way Luke describes, apprehensive about what might happen next.

Perhaps they were naively expecting that, after the death and resurrection of Jesus, there was nothing else left except the end of the world. If so, they were in for a surprise. For the new age of which Jesus had spoken did indeed dawn – but not in the way they expected. The life of God himself broke into their own lives, and they were never to be the same again. Speaking of this experience, Peter had no doubt that what had happened to them was what the Old Testament prophet Joel had expected in 'the last days' (Acts 2:17–18).

We cannot of course penetrate the exact nature of their experience. It certainly had some of the common features of visions, as the disciples saw 'what looked like tongues of fire' (but were not fire), and heard 'a noise from the sky which sounded like a strong wind blowing' (but was not the wind). But the result of this experience was clear for others to see: 'They were all filled with the Holy Spirit and began to talk in other languages, as the Spirit enabled them to speak' (Acts 2:1–4). Speaking in tongues, or 'glossolalia' as it is sometimes called, is mentioned elsewhere in the New Testament as one of the gifts of the Spirit (1 Corinthians 12:10; 14:5–25). It is also widely known and practised today. But it is generally agreed that such speaking in tongues is not the speaking of foreign languages otherwise unknown to the speaker, so much as a kind of ecstatic speech, quite different from the form and content of actual languages. Paul contrasted the speaking of ordinary languages with what he called speaking 'the language of angels' (1 Corinthians 13:1), which suggests that he was aware of this difference.

Some scholars, however, have argued that the experience of the Day of Pentecost was not the speaking of tongues, but the speaking of foreign languages. But if that was the case, it is hard to see why some who heard it should have concluded that the disciples were drunk (Acts 2:13), while others heard God speaking to them quite clearly in terms that they could understand. No doubt the explanation for this lies in the fact that what Luke reported he had learned from others who had been there, and whose lives had been changed as a result of what they had heard. And for them, whatever kind of inspired speech the apostles were expressing, there could be no doubt that they were speaking in terms that could easily be understood. For though they began as interested bystanders, these people were themselves caught up by the power of the Spirit and incorporated into this new and dynamic Christian movement.

As a result of all this, the apostles and their converts were so totally dominated by their love for the living Jesus and their desire to serve him that the humdrum concerns of everyday life were forgotten. Instead, the Christians 'spent their time in learning from the apostles, taking part in the fellowship, and sharing in the fellowship meals and prayers'. They even sold their goods, and pooled the proceeds so they could live as a true community of Jesus' followers. Making money was no longer the most important thing in life. The only things that really mattered were praising God, and taking their life-changing message to other people.

Acts 2:42

Acts 2:44–47; 4:32–35

The church grows

During these early days in Jerusalem, the open friendship and simple life style of the early church must indeed have seemed like the dawning of a new age. But it was not long before other more complex questions reminded Peter and the others that God's kingdom had not yet arrived in all its fullness. Their new-found fellowship with one another was certainly proof that the new society was here. But as time passed, that tension between present and future that was so fundamental in Jesus' teaching was to have disturbing repercussions for the ongoing life of the developing Christian community. During the lifetime of Jesus, the new Messianic movement which he founded was for the most part a local sect in Palestinian Judaism. All the disciples were Jews, and, though both the logic of Jesus' message and the example of his own practice made it clear that Gentiles were not to be excluded, the issue simply did not arise to any great extent. Those Gentiles whom Jesus encountered himself were isolated individuals. There were not many of them, and in any case many of them were probably adherents in the local synagogues, if not actual converts to Judaism.

Mark 7:24–30; Luke 7:1–10

But it was not long before the followers of Jesus were forced to give considerable attention to the whole question of the relationship between Jewish and Gentile believers. Though they did not realize it at the time, the events of the Day of Pentecost recorded at the beginning of the book of Acts were to be a watershed in the life of the infant church. For when Peter stood up to explain the Christian message to the crowds in Jerusalem, he was facing a very cosmopolitan audience of 'religious men who had come from every country of the world'. Naturally, they must all have been interested in Judaism, or they would not have travelled to Jerusalem for a religious festival. But not all the Gentiles among them would be full converts who had accepted the whole Jewish Law – while even those who were from Jewish families in various parts of the Roman Empire must have had a rather different background and outlook from those Jews who had been born and bred in Palestine itself. The majority of those who heard Peter's sermon on the Day of Pentecost were probably Greek-speaking Jews who had made a pilgrimage to Jerusalem for this great religious festival. Many of them would have been visiting Jerusalem for the first time. Though their homes were far away, they always had a warm regard for Jerusalem and its temple. This was the central shrine of their faith, just as it was for Jews who lived much nearer to it. Peter and the other disciples had no doubt that the good news about Jesus must also be shared with people like this. Indeed, they had much in common. The disciples themselves were regular supporters of the synagogue services. They too observed the great Jewish festivals, and on occasions they could even be found preaching within the temple precincts. This was something that Jesus himself had not been able to do without fear of the consequences, and though Peter and John were subsequently arrested and charged before the Jewish council, they were soon released, and the only restriction imposed on them was

Acts 2

Acts 2:5

Acts 3:1–26

Acts 4:18

that 'on no condition were they to speak or to teach in the name of Jesus'. Apart from their curious belief in Jesus, their behaviour was generally quite acceptable to the Jewish authorities.

The conflict begins

Acts 6:1

The Western ('Wailing') Wall in Jerusalem is the only remaining part of the ancient temple and, as such, is a special place of prayer and devotion for Jews.

But it was not long before all this was to change, for an argument arose between some Jews who spoke Greek (Hellenists) and others whose main language was Hebrew or Aramaic (Hebrew). They had all become Christians, perhaps on the Day of Pentecost, and some of these 'Hellenist' Christians were probably visitors to Jerusalem from other parts of the Roman Empire. But of course many Jews in Palestine also spoke Greek, and some of them may well have been permanent residents. At any event, those whose main language was Greek felt they were getting an unfair deal in the distribution of funds within the church. So alongside the twelve apostles who had

Acts 6:2–6

the care of the more conservative Hebrew Christians, seven other men were appointed to supervise the arrangements for the Hellenistic Christians. Though most of them are just names to us, one of them – Stephen – soon demonstrated that he was at least as gifted in theological argument as he was in the administration of funds.

According to Acts, it all started as an argument within the 'synagogue of the Freedmen' in Jerusalem. It is not certain just who these 'Freedmen' were, but they were probably Jews who had come from other parts of the Roman Empire, released from some form of slavery, and had then formed their own synagogue in Jerusalem. Acts says that this synagogue congregation 'included Jews from Cyrene and Alexandria', and that they sided with others 'from the provinces of Cilicia and Asia' in debates with Stephen. Stephen himself was presumably a member of this synagogue, and no doubt he supposed that by sharing his new insights with other members of the synagogue he would be able to help them in the same belief in Jesus as he himself had reached. But it was not to be. Far from convincing his fellow Hellenists of the truth of the Christian claims, all he managed to do was to convince them that he was himself a

Acts 6:8–15

heretic. And so they dragged him before the Jewish council, the Sanhedrin.

The story of Acts suggests that in order to bring effective charges, Stephen's accusers had to tell lies: 'This man,' they said, 'is always talking against our sacred Temple and the Law of Moses. We heard him say that this Jesus of Nazareth will tear down the Temple and

Acts 6:13–14

change all the customs which have come down to us from Moses!' There is a familiar ring about all this, for according to Mark this was

Mark 14:57–59

one of the charges brought against Jesus at his trial. But whereas on that occasion the false witnesses failed to agree, and so other charges had to be found, in the case of Stephen he went on to condemn himself out of his own mouth.

Stephen's speech

The speech of Stephen before the Sanhedrin (Acts 7:1–53) is one of the longest speeches reported anywhere in the New Testament, and many people have found it difficult to see how it can be regarded as any sort of response to the charges that had been made against him. Because of this, some scholars have suggested that what we now have in Acts 7 was simply composed by the author of Acts as an appropriate theological explanation of why the Hellenist Christians began to move away from Jerusalem and to break their allegiance to Judaism. This question is not of course restricted to the story of Stephen: it is also relevant to the speeches allegedly delivered by Peter, Paul and others elsewhere in Acts. Were these speeches based on verbatim reports that were handed down to the author of Acts? Or did he follow the example of a writer like Josephus, who

seems to have inserted speeches at will into the mouths of those whose exploits he describes? A number of points are relevant to this question:

● Obviously, none of the speeches reported in Acts can be verbatim accounts. They are far too short for that, and in any case people in the ancient world were not obsessed with the desire for accurate quotation which is so important to us today. We can see this quite clearly in the way some New Testament writers refer even to the Old Testament. Though it had supreme authority for them, they often do not quote it from any known version, but simply refer to it from memory – and often do so inaccurately as a result! In the case of Stephen's trial, it is unlikely that anyone would have taken down extensive notes of what was actually said. The impression one gets is that the whole thing took place with great

The Greek historian Thucydides.

Stephen brought down the full wrath of the Sanhedrin on his head by attacking the most precious and revered Jewish institution – the Jerusalem temple. He was taken outside the city wall and stoned.

urgency, quite unlike a major trial today.

● At the same time, we also need to note that not all ancient historians were like Josephus. Josephus was a Jew. But the Greek tradition of history-writing is better represented by someone like Thucydides. He also felt that the inclusion of speeches at appropriate points in his narrative would help to highlight the important points. But he was not in the habit of simply inventing such speeches, as he explains in the beginning of his *History of the Peloponnesian War* (1.22.1): '... some speeches I heard myself, others I got from various quarters; it was in all cases difficult to carry them word for word in one's memory, so my habit has been to make the speakers say what was in my opinion demanded of them by the various occasions, of course adhering as closely as possible to the general sense of what they really said.'

● On more general grounds, Acts would appear to fit into the Thucydidean mould rather than following the traditions of a person like Josephus. Though its story of early Christianity is undoubtedly selective, when it can be tested against external

evidence from the Roman Empire, it appears to be generally trustworthy.

● All the speeches in Acts at least have the appearance of authenticity. In subject matter, language and style they are varied to suit the people who make them. Certainly, so far as the Stephen speech is concerned, the content of the speech does fit in admirably with the kind of occasion that is described. Whenever dissidents of any kind are on trial for their lives, they often choose to defend not themselves, but the ideals for which they stand. And this is precisely what Stephen does. No doubt he had argued like this many times before within the synagogue itself, and no doubt others would repeat the arguments after him. To that extent, his speech is a confession of faith. It is not unrealistic to imagine that he would be determined to take his own last chance of standing before the highest Jewish authority and making sure his message was heard there too. It is certainly the sort of thing one can imagine having taken place – and in this respect it is quite different from the verbose and often irrelevant speeches which Josephus inserted into the mouths of many of his characters.

In his long speech before the Sanhedrin, Stephen not only admitted the truthfulness of the vague accusations made against him by the witnesses; he also went on to make very specific statements about the subjects in dispute. With a carefully detailed survey of the history of Israel, he argued that the temple ought never to have existed at all. With copious quotations from and allusions to the Old Testament, he pointed out how a simple tent of worship had been given to Moses by God as the place where he should be worshipped – and this had continued even long after the desert wanderings were over. It was only with the accession of Solomon to the throne of Israel that things started to change. With increased wealth and a new international political stature, Solomon had decided to build a central sanctuary in Jerusalem. The Old Testament suggests that he had divine approval for his actions, though strenuous religious and moral conditions were also imposed to ensure the continued existence of the temple. But Stephen was quite sure that the temple had been a mistake from the start. Quoting the prophet Isaiah to support his argument, he asserted quite categorically that 'The Most High God does not live in houses built by men'. He then went on to accuse the Jewish leaders of wholesale disobedience to the very Law that they professed to uphold.

Acts 7:1–53

1 Kings 5:4–5

1 Kings 9:1–9

Isaiah 66:1–2

Acts 7:48

Acts 7:53

Not surprisingly, all this was too much for them. And when Stephen committed what they regarded as the final blasphemy by asserting that he could 'see heaven opened, and the Son of Man standing at the right hand side of God', he can hardly have been taken aback when he was dragged out of the council chamber and stoned to death.

Acts 7:56

Acts 7:57–60

Stephen's speech is almost unique in the New Testament. With the exception of Hebrews (see chapter 24 below), no other New Testament person or book has much to say about the temple and its services. But outside the New Testament, we have evidence of others who disapproved of what was going on there. At a much later date, the so-called *Epistle of Barnabas* adopts a very similar radical position on the Jewish temple – though there can be no question of Stephen having been familiar with that document, for it was not written until the early second century. Some of its strongly anti-Jewish sentiments could perhaps have been inspired by the story of Stephen in the New Testament.

But some scholars have suggested that Stephen's thinking could have been influenced by two religious groups in Palestine who did exist at the same time as him, and who also rejected the temple in Jerusalem. These were the people of Qumran, who wrote the Dead Sea Scrolls, and the Samaritans. Neither of them took part in the worship at the temple, though their reasons for not doing so were rather different from the convictions that Stephen apparently held.

The Qumran community had imposed on themselves an enforced isolation from Jerusalem. Believing the temple and its priesthood to be corrupt, they had moved out to establish their own monastic commune by the shores of the Dead Sea. But they fervently believed that this state of affairs was only temporary. They were expecting the Messianic Age to come very soon, and then they themselves would be able to return to Jerusalem and restore the temple and its worship to its original purity. They did not despise the temple as an institution, as did Stephen. Instead, they deplored what they regarded as its temporary corruption.

The Samaritans were also unable to take part in the temple worship at Jerusalem, though for rather different reasons. It is not altogether clear just who the Samaritans of New Testament times actually were. It may be that they were descendants of people like Sanballat and Tobiah, who during and after the time of the Jewish exile in Babylon had collaborated with the foreign rulers of Palestine. If so, pious Jews would naturally regard them as half-breeds and traitors – certainly unfit to worship in Jerusalem. On the other hand, it is quite likely that they had no connection at all with such people, and had arisen as a new Jewish sect of some kind in the years just before the beginning of the Christian era. In any event, they had their own sanctuary on Mt Gerizim and their own version of the Old Testament, which was substantially shorter than that used by the Jews themselves. The fact that they worshipped at Gerizim rather than Jerusalem formed the basis of the conversation between Jesus and a Samaritan woman, and it is interesting to see how that conversation ends on a note that was not altogether out of harmony either with Samaritan thinking or with the speech of Stephen: 'Jesus said, "...the time will come when people will not worship the Father either on this mountain or in Jerusalem ... the time is coming and is already here, when by the power of God's Spirit people will worship the Father as he really is, offering him the true worship that he wants."'

Nehemiah 6

John 4:19–24

John 4:21, 23

There are obvious similarities between the thinking of the Qumran community and the Samaritans and Stephen, and the way that Stephen expounded the Old Testament is not unlike the way some of these other sects understood it. But it is highly unlikely that Stephen had ever been a member of either group. If he had been, it is hard to see how and why he could have been in Jerusalem in the first place.

It is more likely that his thinking on the temple, which was derived from the Old Testament, was brought out spontaneously as a result of the events of the Day of Pentecost and what followed. Through the presence and power of the Holy Spirit in the church, Christian believers now had direct access to God himself – and so the temple was redundant. It was at best an indirect means of worshipping God, and when men and women had direct access to him, then the temple became an unnecessary stumbling-block to those who were following Jesus.

Stephen's death

Did the Jewish Sanhedrin have the right to execute Stephen in the way they did? At the time, Judea was a Roman province, and in Roman provinces generally the right to execute even convicted criminals was reserved for the Roman governor and no one else. This point is brought out quite clearly in the stories of Jesus' trials and execution in the Gospels. According to John 18:31, the same Jewish leaders who were involved in Stephen's death had been forced to admit earlier to Pilate that 'we are not allowed to put anyone to death'.

This was not strictly accurate, for there was just one instance when the Sanhedrin was allowed to carry out a death sentence without reference to the Roman authorities. This was in the case of a person who violated the sanctity of the temple at Jerusalem. Anyone, even a Roman, who entered the temple unlawfully could be executed on the orders of the Sanhedrin (Josephus, *Jewish Wars* 6.2.4). But this was a special arrangement, which simply serves to emphasize the general powerlessness of the Sanhedrin. For if it already had general powers of jurisdiction in such cases, it would not have required this kind of special dispensation.

In view of the way that Stephen had spoken out against the temple, it is always possible that he may have been deemed to have violated the temple and its rights in some way. But it is more likely that his death was not the result of a formal sentence, so much as a mob lynching. Acts 7:54–60 does not suggest that any legal verdict was given, but rather that the Jewish leaders spontaneously stoned him in their fury. We do know of at least one other example of such behaviour, namely the execution of James of Jerusalem in AD 62.

The death of Stephen was undoubtedly one of the crucial events in the life of the early church, and its effects were soon to be felt not only in Jerusalem but throughout the rest of Palestine, and ultimately throughout the Roman Empire.

Persecution

One of its immediate consequences was a widespread persecution of the Christians in Jerusalem. Not many of them had adopted the same radical attitude towards the temple as Stephen. But it was inevitable that people should suppose that most, if not all Christians would think like him. And the Jews disliked it intensely, for Stephen was striking at the very roots of their most treasured beliefs. But persecution inevitably led to the dispersal of Christians from Jerusalem itself, especially those who were most sympathetic to the message of Stephen. Caesarea, Antioch and Damascus – not to mention other, more far-flung cities from which the Hellenist Christians had originally come – all witnessed a remarkable influx of these people. They were not just the first Christian refugees: they were also to be the first Christian missionaries. Though it was hardly what was intended, the Jewish persecutors of the church in Jerusalem were only encouraging it to spread to other parts of the land.

Acts 8:4

Not everyone had to leave Jerusalem. According to Acts, those who had shown themselves faithful to the principles of Judaism

Acts 8:1

were able to stay, even in the face of such intense opposition. Luke mentions by name only the apostles, but it is certain that others must have stayed behind too – and all of them would be committed to some degree to Judaism as well as to their new faith in Jesus as the Messiah. This inevitably meant that the church in Jerusalem became more conservative and more rigidly Jewish, a fact that in due course led to its demise and the extinction of all Jewish forms of Christianity.

But Acts has very little to say about the church in Jerusalem at this time. Instead the attention shifts to the exploits of various Christian leaders elsewhere in Palestine.

Into Judea and Samaria

Acts 21:8–9

Acts 8:4–25

Acts 8:26–40

Tarsus •

• Antioch in Syria

CYPRUS

SYRIA

Damascus •

Caesarea

to Alexandria

• Samaria

Joppa

Jerusalem

JUDEA

The church reaches out.

Acts 8:14–17

Acts 8:25

Acts 9:32–10:48

Widening outreach

Philip is one of the Hellenist Christian leaders singled out for special mention in Acts, and he was no doubt typical of many others. We know comparatively little about him, but he was obviously very successful in communicating the Christian message to the inhabitants of other parts of Palestine, especially in Hellenistic cities like Caesarea. Some years later, he and his daughters were leading figures in a prosperous Christian community there. But before settling in Caesarea, he had a successful mission among the Samaritans too. We also have the story of how Philip met and baptized an African. This man was an Ethiopian bureaucrat, who was presumably an adherent of Judaism, since he was on his way home from visiting the temple in Jerusalem when Philip came across him in the desert. After an extended conversation about the meaning of the Old Testament, the man declared his faith in Jesus as the Messiah, and was baptized there and then.

Philip had little choice but to take his message outside Jerusalem. As one of the seven men appointed to oversee the funds for Hellenist Christians, he had been a close associate of Stephen, and it was no longer safe for him to stay in Jerusalem. But it was not long before some of the original disciples of Jesus also began to tour the countryside of Palestine with their message. We should not be surprised that men like Peter and John should have decided to leave Jerusalem. They were themselves countrymen, and Jerusalem was not their home. Moreover, though Jesus had no doubt visited Jerusalem on several occasions during his own lifetime, the main centre of his activity was not among the conventionally religious people there, but among the beggars and peasants of rural Palestine. So when Peter and John moved on to other areas, they were just following in their master's footsteps.

But they were clearly doing more than that. For the two of them together visited the Samaritans who had come to believe in Jesus as a result of Philip's preaching. It is easy to gain the impression from Acts that this was a kind of 'official inspection' of Philip's work – Peter and John giving the stamp of Jerusalem's approval to what he was doing. But a closer reading suggests that there was more to it than just that. For Peter and John were not afraid to identify themselves publicly with the work that Philip was doing. Not only did they accept his Samaritan converts as true Christians, but they also engaged in preaching among the Samaritans on their own initiative. And it was not long before Peter became involved in a travelling ministry over a wide area of the Palestinian countryside. Lydda, Joppa and even Caesarea itself were all on his itinerary.

It was in the course of such travelling that Peter was to become convinced of the importance of non-Jewish people for the future of the Christian church. Of course, he himself had probably never been as conservative and traditionally Jewish as some of the church members whom he left behind in Jerusalem. The very fact that he was prepared to take his message to the more Hellenistic parts of Palestine is itself evidence of that. Then it is not insignificant that in the

Acs 9:43

Mishnah, *Kelia* 26. 1–9

Luke 15:1–2

course of this tour, 'Peter stayed in Joppa for many days with a leather-worker named Simon'. No strictly orthodox Jew would have been prepared to do that, for workers in leather were generally regarded as being ritually unclean, since they were in constant contact with the skins of dead animals. But in this case, Peter was simply following the example of Jesus himself, who was not afraid to have close dealings with all kinds of outcasts of Jewish society.

While he was staying with this man, Peter had an experience that

Acts 10:1–23

Joppa, modern-day Jaffa, was the scene of a radical about-turn in Peter's attitude to preaching the gospel to non-Jews.

Acts 10:9–16

Mark 7:14–23

was to change his life. In a dream, he saw a large sheet full of 'all kinds of animals, reptiles and wild birds', many of them ritually unclean by the standards of the Old Testament food laws. So when a voice told him to help himself to some of these creatures, he naturally stated his unwillingness to do so – only to be rebuked by the voice, which he now recognized to be God's voice, telling him 'Do not consider unclean anything that God has declared clean'. This was another lesson that Peter must have heard from the lips of Jesus himself. But in the tense atmosphere of Jerusalem after the death of Stephen, that can hardly have seemed an important principle, and Peter had adopted the more expedient course of following normal Jewish practices. But he was now to become caught up in something far larger than arguments about food, and what followed was to have far-reaching implications for the rest of his life's work.

No sooner had he woken from his dream than messengers arrived at the door of the house asking that he go to their master,

Acts 10:17—22

The message of Jesus was shown to be relevant for everyone, whether they lived in rural areas or sophisticated Hellenistic cities.

Acts 10:24—48

Cornelius. This man was a Roman centurion in the main Roman garrison town, Caesarea, and Peter must have realized the serious implications of going there. But after his vision he had no choice, and so he entered Cornelius's house and accepted the Roman's hospitality — something that was quite unthinkable to the Jewish Christians back in Jerusalem, whether on political or religious grounds. But as Peter spoke with these people, it became obvious that they were deeply interested in the Christian faith. As they listened, they responded to his message and Peter had to accept that they were true believers in Jesus, for they began to share in the same experience of the Holy Spirit as the first converts on the Day of Pentecost. At that, he was quite convinced that they should be baptized and accepted into the church; and as if to underline his own acceptance of them, Peter stayed in their home for a few days, no doubt instructing them further in their new faith.

This was a turning-point for Peter. When he got back to Jerusalem, his more conservative Jewish Christian friends were not at all pleased. Though his own account of the affair gave them some reassurance, it is obvious from the rest of Acts that this incident had a deep and lasting effect on Peter's relationship with the church at Jerusalem. For it was not long before a man who had not been one of the original twelve disciples became the acknowledged leader of the church there: James, the brother of Jesus. In addition, it was not long after Peter's visit to Caesarea that Herod Agrippa I, the ruler of Palestine at the time, instituted an official persecution of the Christians in Jerusalem. As a result of this James, the brother of John, was martyred, and Peter himself put into prison. It may well have been that Peter's willingness to reach out to Gentiles with the Christian message gave Agrippa just the opportunity he was looking for to gain the sympathetic support of pious Jews for his actions

Acts 11:1–3

Acts 12:1–5

against the church. If so, that would be an added reason why Peter soon fell from prominence among the Jewish Christians.

We know very little in detail about Peter's activities after this point. But what we do know connects him not with the Jewish churches in Palestine, but with the Hellenistic churches scattered throughout the Roman Empire. We know of an occasion when he visited Antioch in Syria, and he also seems to have had some kind of contact with the church in the Greek city of Corinth. He clearly travelled far and wide in the service of the gospel, often accompanied by his wife on his travels. And, according to well-attested traditions, he had strong connections with the church at Rome, and it was there that he was martyred for his faith in the persecution of Nero about AD 64.

Galatians 2:11–14
1 Corinthians 1–4

1 Corinthians 9:5

The church in Galilee

Apart from occasional visits to Jerusalem, Jesus spent most of his life in Galilee. The majority of his followers must have lived there – many thousands of them, according to the Gospels. Yet Galilee is hardly ever mentioned in the story of early Christianity. Instead, the New Testament lays all the emphasis on the followers of Jesus in Jerusalem and in the Gentile cities of the Roman Empire.

It is not difficult to see the reasons for this. Luke is the only New Testament writer to produce anything like a history of the church, and he himself was probably a Gentile. His own main interest was therefore in the work of Paul and others who took the gospel to people like himself. For Luke and his readers, Palestine was a remote outpost of the empire, and small internal distinctions, like the difference between Galilee and Judea, were

insignificant to people who scarcely knew the location of either of them. In his Gospel, we can see how Luke does not always distinguish the two quite as carefully as the other Gospel writers, and in his history of early Christianity the only real division he makes is that between Jewish Christians and Gentile Christians. But a native of Palestine would not have seen it like that. The Judeans had no time for the people of Galilee. It was too open to Gentile influences for their liking, and the fact that Jesus originated there was to many people a good reason for paying no attention to him (John 1:46).

But in spite of the fact that followers of Jesus in Galilee would tend to be ignored by Gentile Christians and despised by those from Jerusalem, they must nevertheless have continued to flourish. Great movements like that built up by Jesus do not vanish

Christians in the early church had to confront the power of Hellenistic culture and thought. This fragment from a second-century Christian sarcophagus shows a philosophical discussion in progress.

overnight, especially in a rural area. So what happened to his followers in Galilee? Some have suggested that they simply faded away. Some of them had no doubt gone to Jerusalem with Jesus, expecting him to set up a new nationalist government to overthrow the Roman rule, and when he died in apparent defeat they went back home to look for another leader. There must have been some who thought like that: Judas Iscariot may have been one of them. But not all Jesus' followers went with him on his last journey to Jerusalem, and not all of them had an exclusively political view of his message. No doubt these others would continue the work that Jesus had started in Galilee, perhaps developing their own churches in complete independence of what was going on in Jerusalem. A number of facts seem to support such a view:

● Galilee had always been quite different from Jerusalem. It had its own ways of doing things, and its own religious traditions, most of which were despised by the more orthodox and conservative Jews in Jerusalem. It is unlikely therefore that the church in Jerusalem would have wanted any involvement in affairs in Galilee, and still less probable that the Galilean followers of Jesus would have been prepared to accept the authority of the Jerusalem church and its leaders.

● The very character of these leaders must have been an influential factor in the development of the Galilean church. After the expulsion of the Hellenists, the church in Jerusalem seems to have adopted a very conservative Jewish outlook. The priests and Pharisees whom Jesus had strongly opposed soon rose to positions of authority even in the church (Acts 6:7; 15:5), and it is quite likely that James, the main Jerusalem leader, was himself a Pharisee. They were now Christians, of course, and accepted Jesus as their Messiah. But that seems to have made little difference to their outlook and behaviour. They still held that the Jewish Law and customs were of special importance, as we can see from their attitude to Peter after he had stayed with Cornelius (Acts 11:1–4). It was no coincidence that Peter and the other original disciples did not stay long in Jerusalem. Persecution from the authorities and opposition from the Jerusalem church soon forced them to leave the city – and most of them must have gone back home, to Galilee.

● This also fits in with what we know about Peter, and enables us to guess at what he was doing between the time when he left Jerusalem and the

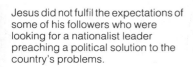

Jesus did not fulfil the expectations of some of his followers who were looking for a nationalist leader preaching a political solution to the country's problems.

time when we find him travelling the Roman Empire with the message of Jesus. Perhaps it was in Galilee that he was able to give more time and thought to this whole question of non-Jewish followers of Jesus. According to early church traditions, the Gospel of Mark contains the kind of things that Peter used to tell people about Jesus, and it is interesting to note how Mark's Gospel always shows the people of Galilee responding to the Christian message, while Jerusalem rejects it. Perhaps this reflects Peter's thinking about the development of the church at Jerusalem at this period.

● Two other New Testament books have also been connected with the Galilean churches: James and Hebrews. Both of them have clear Jewish connections, but are difficult to identify with the kind of beliefs that were held in the church at Jerusalem. James has a very simple view of the Christian message – very similar to the message of Jesus himself as we know it from the Gospels, while Hebrews also has many references to the teachings of Jesus. It also sets out to show that Jerusalem and its temple are irrelevant – something that would be welcomed by Galileans. Both these books are discussed in more detail in chapter 24.

We can never be sure exactly what happened to the followers of Jesus in Galilee, for no one wrote down their story. But there is enough evidence to suggest that the movement started there by Jesus did not die out, but probably grew and flourished at least for the lifetime of his original disciples.

The Acts of the Apostles

Every book of the New Testament tells us something about the history of the early church. The letters written by Paul and other Christian leaders are the kind of information which modern social historians would use and value, while even the Gospels tell us a great deal about their first readers. But the book of Acts tries to set out the early history of Christianity in some kind of orderly way. It is the sequel to the Gospel of Luke, and the two books belong together. They were both written to the same person, 'Theophilus', the Gospel to tell the story of the life and teaching of Jesus, and the book of Acts to tell how the work of this one person had developed into a worldwide Christian movement.

Acts does not in fact tell the story of all the apostles. Only some of them are mentioned extensively, and the book has most to say about Peter and Paul, together with a few incidents from the lives of other early Christian leaders such as Philip, John, James the brother of Jesus, and Stephen. The story is told in two parts. The first is concerned mainly with events in Jerusalem and elsewhere in Palestine, and here Peter is the leading character (chapters 1–12). The second section of the book tells the remarkable story of Paul (chapters 13–28). The two stories are not entirely unconnected. Paul makes his first appearance at the stoning of Stephen (Acts 7:58), while Peter is still involved at the time of the so-called Council of Jerusalem, which is essentially a part of the story of Paul (Acts 15:7–11).

The author

Who wrote the book of Acts? Or, to put the question more accurately, who wrote the two volumes, Luke and Acts? There is no doubt they were both written by the same person. They are both addressed to Theophilus, and their style and language are identical. All the evidence points to Luke, the Gentile doctor who accompanied Paul on some of his travels.

The date

The date of Acts is a more controversial issue, and three main suggestions have been put forward:

The Second Century. The Tübingen School of F.C. Baur believed that Acts must have been written sometime after AD 100, and this view has been revived in recent years by the American scholar, Professor John Knox. Two main arguments are put forward to support this:

● Acts 5:36–37 refers to two individuals called Theudas and Judas, and 21:38 mentions an Egyptian troublemaker. Since Josephus' *Antiquities of the Jews* 20.5.1 seems to describe the same events, and since this was not published until AD 93, Acts, it is claimed, must have been written later than that. But there is no evidence to support the idea that Luke had actually read Josephus' stories. In fact, his description of these people is different from what Josephus says, and it is only possible to connect the two by supposing that Luke misunderstood Josephus' story when he read it.

● It is also suggested that Acts was written in about the middle of the second century to counteract the influence of the heretic Marcion. Among other things, Marcion was suggesting that the first disciples of Jesus had misunderstood the point of his teaching, and that Paul was the only true interpreter of Jesus. It is certainly true that Acts was read with renewed interest at the time of Marcion, for its story shows little sign of the kind of misunderstanding that Marcion emphasized. But there is no real trace of second-century concerns in the book – while there is plenty of evidence to connect it with the period that it purports to describe.

AD **62–70.** At the opposite extreme, other scholars suggest that Acts was written almost at the same time as the events it describes – either immediately after the arrival of Paul in Rome (62–64, according to F.F. Bruce and J.A.T. Robinson), or shortly after his death (66–70, in the view of T.W. Manson and, hesitatingly, C.S.C. Williams). The following arguments are said to favour such an early date:

● By any standards, Acts ends very abruptly. Paul arrives in Rome, and the last we see of him he is 'teaching about the Lord Jesus Christ quite openly and unhindered' (Acts 28:31). It must be said, however, that this is the natural climax of Luke's story. He said at the outset that he would relate the progress of the gospel from Jerusalem to Rome (Acts 1:8), so perhaps nothing further needed to be said. But the modern reader is inevitably curious to know whether Paul appeared before the emperor's court, and if so what happened to him. We are not the first ones to ask these questions, and there are ancient traditions claiming to give us the answers. Eusebius, one of the early church historians, says that 'after defending himself the apostle was sent again on his ministry of preaching, and coming a second time to the same city, suffered martyrdom under Nero' (*Ecclesiastical History* 2.22). A statement in 1 Clement 5 (written about AD 95) suggests that Paul visited Spain during this short time of freedom, while some modern scholars would like us to think that it was during this time that Paul penned the so-called Pastoral Epistles (1 and 2 Timothy and Titus). We do not really know whether Paul went on such further travels. But there is no reason to doubt that he ultimately died as a martyr in Rome during the persecution ordered by Nero in AD 64.

Because of this, it is suggested that if Acts was written after Paul was dead, then the statement about him preaching openly and unhindered is an odd note on which to finish the story of his life. But this kind of argument is double-edged. Since Paul is Luke's

Nero ruled from AD 54 to 68 and was the first Roman emperor to persecute the Christians.

hero, surely it would be at least as likely that he would present his life ending in the triumph of his preaching in Rome as that he would finish his story with the apparent defeat of martyrdom. It is always haphazard to try and guess what this or that ancient writer may or may not have written in given circumstances. We can really only guess at what we might have written ourselves had we been there – and even then we cannot be sure, since at this distance from the events we do not know all the facts. So this argument in favour of an early date for Acts really carries very little objective weight.

● A more substantial argument is that the book of Acts has a generally favourable attitude to the Roman authorities. Paul's Roman citizenship is an asset to him, giving him freedom to travel in peace all over the empire. When he meets Roman officials, they are always on his side: Sergius Paulus, the proconsul of Cyprus who became a Christian (Acts 13:6–12); Gallio, the proconsul in Corinth who gave him a fair hearing (Acts 18:12–17); even the Roman commander in Jerusalem who rescued him from a hostile Jewish mob (Acts 21:31–40). They all look favourably on Paul's mission, and the impression is given that, if the empire is not exactly supporting the church, it certainly is not at enmity with it. But of course all that changed in AD 64, with the great persecution instituted by Nero, and official persecution of one sort or another was to continue spasmodically right through to the end of the first century. So again it is argued that Acts must have been written prior to AD 64. But again this is a subjective judgement, for it implies that the events of the author's own day would colour his historical judgement. But if Acts can be regarded as a reasonably faithful presentation of the period it describes, then its apparent pro-Roman bias may simply reflect the facts of the situation.

● Acts does not seem to give any hint of the Fall of Jerusalem, which took place in AD 70, and if Jerusalem had been destroyed before Acts was written, it is claimed that we would have expected a mention of the fact. For it would have been a striking vindication of Luke's viewpoint on Judaism and indeed on Jewish Christianity. Again, this argument depends on the assumption that we can know precisely what was in the mind of an ancient author, and what he might be expected to write in given circumstances.

● Another relevant fact is that Acts makes no mention at all of the letters that Paul wrote to his churches. So far as the date of Acts is concerned, this undoubtedly suggests that it was written before the letters were collected together and circulated, and so Acts must be earlier than a writing like 2 Peter, which mentions Paul's letters as a part of sacred Scripture (2 Peter 3:16).

AD **80–85.** Many scholars feel that there is no justification for either a very late second-century date for Acts, or a very early date in the sixties of the first century. Instead, they prefer to date it sometime in the eighties of the first century. Two substantial reasons have been put forward for this:

● Acts begins with the words: 'In my first book I wrote about all the things which Jesus did and taught' (Acts 1:1). This 'first book' was Luke's Gospel. But we know that when he wrote this, Luke incorporated stories and sayings of Jesus that he took from the Gospel that had already been written by Mark. And since Mark seems to have written his Gospel sometime between 60 and 65, this means that we can hardly date Luke's first volume much earlier than about 65–70. This in turn means that Acts, as the second volume, cannot have been written as early as 62–64.

This is a persuasive argument, though it is not absolutely convincing. It has at least two weak spots. First, it depends on the date we give to Mark. But we have no absolutely certain indications of when that Gospel was written. The general consensus may be right. On the other hand, it may not, and when John Robinson, for instance, urges a much earlier date for Mark, he does have some evidence in his favour. Second, it is also possible that the prologues of both Luke and Acts were added last, when the two books were in their final form. Many competent scholars believe that Luke's Gospel originally existed in a shorter version before Luke came across Mark's work ('Proto-Luke'), and Acts could also have been written in stages. The passages where Luke uses 'we' rather than 'they' may have been just the first of several editions of Luke's story of the early church. This original account may later have been expanded to include stories about the early Jerusalem church, perhaps brought to Luke's attention during his stay in Caesarea while Paul was in prison there. So it is always possible that the basic core of Acts could have been written before the Gospel, with only the prologue being added later to commend it to Theophilus.

● But there is a more substantial reason for dating Acts later than the lifetime of Paul. Luke's writing often seems to show signs of attitudes and beliefs which were common in the post-apostolic age. Indeed, Luke and Acts together are sometimes regarded as a kind of manifesto of what scholars refer to as 'early catholicism'. This subject is dealt with in some detail in chapter 25. It is argued there that the emergence of so-called 'catholic Christianity' was a natural, almost imperceptible development of certain elements within the teaching of the apostles themselves. Here we should simply note that Luke does have a distinctive outlook, and that in some respects this outlook corresponds to the development of early catholic thinking.

For instance, reading only Acts one might well get the impression that the early church had a largely uncontroversial existence. But as we read Paul's letters, it becomes obvious that there is another side to the picture. No doubt it was a part of Luke's intention to stress that there was fundamental agreement between all sections of the early church. And, up to a point, Paul himself accepted this, for he goes out of his way to emphasize his own continuity with the earliest disciples. But it is only part of the picture. For Paul's letters also show that he often had profound disagreements not only with his enemies, but with his friends as well. Paul often emerges from his letters as a very impulsive person, and it is quite possible that some of the issues he wrote about with such passion were not in fact as serious as he thought at the time. But Luke, writing some time later, could take a more detached view of these things, and see them in their proper perspective, both in the life of Paul and in the ongoing experience of the church.

This does not mean that Luke was any less a friend or even a disciple of Paul. A good teacher does not turn out students who are detailed replicas of himself. Instead, he aims to encourage them to develop their own distinctive thinking. And, as we shall see below, the positions that Luke adopts in Acts differ from Paul in the details rather than on the fundamentals.

The real choice for the date of Acts is between the sixties and the eighties of the first century. But the evidence on the one side is as problematic as that on the other, though the balance of probability seems to favour a date in the eighties, perhaps around AD 85.

The value of Acts

What sort of a book is the Acts of the Apostles? We have occasionally referred to it as a history of the early church, but of course it is not a comprehensive history. There are so many things it does not tell us that it is clearly not the full story of early Christianity. Instead, it is a selective story, drawing attention to those people and movements which Luke believed to be especially significant. In writing his Gospel, Luke had adopted exactly the same procedure. Indeed, none of the New Testament Gospels is a comprehensive account of the whole of Jesus' life. In his Gospel Luke selected those aspects of the life and teaching of Jesus which meant most to him, and in Acts he did the same thing, picking out those incidents which for him typified the trend of events among the first Christians. He wanted to show how Christianity spread from Jerusalem to Rome, and everything that he records is intended to illuminate that transition. In the process, he omits many things we would like to know. What happened to Peter? And how did James get on in the church at Jerusalem? Or what did the

other apostles do? Luke simply ignores these questions because they were not relevant to his purpose.

This means that his story is also an interpretation of the progress of the early church. All history, of course, is an interpretation of past events. When you read the newspaper, you are not getting a 'factual' account of what it describes: you are getting the facts as they were understood by a reporter who was there. Even watching events on television does not enable you to see and to hear exactly what you might have seen and heard had you actually been there, for you can only see and hear what the camera is aiming at. There could well be other things taking place just out of sight which would radically alter your whole perception of what was going on. But you have to depend on what the television technicians and editors have decided is important. So when we say that Luke gives us his interpretation of early church history we are not saying anything that would not be true of any

On film or television, what we see is dictated by the editorial decision of the person directing the camera. It reflects what he judges to be of significance. Similarly, in the book of Acts, Luke recounts the events which he considers important in the development of the early church.

kind of second-hand knowledge we may have. We are not suggesting, for example, that Luke simply invented his stories. Indeed, if nothing had happened, there would have been nothing to interpret! But what we have in Acts is the way that Luke, from his own presuppositions and background, saw the history of the early church.

There are in fact a number of reasons for thinking that the picture which we have in Acts is an essentially authentic reproduction of life in the period which it describes:

● In the prologue to his Gospel (Luke 1:1–4) Luke tells us how he worked: he read all that he could find, sifted

character than the theology either of Paul or of the church later in the first century. For example, Jesus is still referred to as 'the Messiah' (Christ) in Acts 2:36; 3:20; 4:27, and he can be called 'the Servant of God' (Acts 3:13, 26; 4:25–30), or even in one instance, 'the Son of Man' (a title much used by Jesus himself but found nowhere in the rest of the New Testament except Acts 7:56). The Christians are called simply 'disciples' (for example, in Acts 6:1–7; 9:1, 25–26), and the church itself is 'the Way' (Acts 9:2; 19:9, 23; 24:14, 22). Professor Norman Perrin describes all this as 'extraordinarily realistic ... the narratives of Acts are full of elements

The Roman emperors exacted heavy taxes from both their own people and those in subject provinces. This third-century relief shows the payment of *tributum*, a tax on land and personal property.

through it and then wrote his own considered account of what had happened. In the case of the Gospel, we can see how he went about it, for we possess at least one of his source documents (Mark). The way he uses Mark shows that he was a very careful writer, aware of the need to reproduce his sources accurately and without distortion. We have no direct knowledge of his sources for Acts, though it is widely supposed that he relied on written information for his story of early events in Jerusalem and Samaria (chapters 1–9). If so, he would probably take the same care in compiling his story in Acts as he had previously taken with the Gospel. In addition to that, he was himself personally present for at least some of the events in Acts (the 'we passages').

● The picture Luke paints of life in the earliest Palestinian churches is consistent with what we would expect. Much of the theology which he attributes to those earliest Christian believers has a far less sophisticated

taken directly from the life and experience of the church'.

● This same realism can be seen in Luke's description of the Roman world and its officials. He always uses the right word to describe Roman administrators, and sometimes uses words that would only be familiar to people living in particular cities. Sergius Paulus and Gallio are correctly designated 'proconsuls' (Acts 13:7–8; 18:12). Philippi is accurately described as a Roman colony, ruled by the *Stratēgoi* (Praetors). This is an unusual word to find in a literary source, but it has been discovered on inscriptions, showing that it was the colloquial term used in Philippi itself (Acts 16:12, 20–22). Thessalonica also has its own name for its rulers, who are called 'politarchs' (Acts 17:8). This title was once thought to be a mistake, because it is not found in Latin or Greek literature. But subsequent archaeological discoveries have shown that Luke was right to describe the authorities at Thessalonica in this way. There are also many other points at which Luke's stories can be shown to depend on direct and reliable knowledge of the Roman world as it actually was at the time he is describing.

● The same concern for authenticity can also be seen in Luke's presentation of the problems of the early church. The only real controversy that appears in Acts is concerned with the relationship of Jewish and Gentile Christians. But this argument soon became less important, and after AD 70 it was of no importance at all, except on a theoretical level. At the time when Luke was writing, other issues were far more prominent: heresy and orthodoxy, and false teaching of various kinds. But he never tries to import the problems of a later day into the story of Acts.

● There is just one point which may at first sight appear to contradict our generally positive evaluation of Luke's trustworthiness as a historian. This is his treatment of Paul. It has been suggested, especially by the German scholar Philipp Vielhauer, that as we read Paul's own letters we sometimes get a different view of Paul's life and teaching from the picture in Acts. And of course Acts does not even mention the fact that Paul wrote letters at all! A number of points need to be mentioned here:

Firstly, Luke's failure to mention Paul's letters is not all that serious. He may quite possibly have regarded them as personal letters, and therefore of no great importance for his own purpose. We must also remember that though we regard Paul's letters as primary evidence for his activity, they are to some extent evidence without a context, and it is therefore easy for us to overestimate their original significance.

More seriously, however, it is pointed out that the sort of things Paul concerns himself with in Acts are usually significantly different from his normal concerns in his letters. But again this is not specially surprising. When Paul wrote letters, he was writing to Christians. But when he speaks in Acts he is usually addressing non-Christians. There has been plenty of speculation about the content of Paul's initial preaching to the Galatians, Corinthians, Thessalonians and others, but we cannot know for certain what he told them. We can be sure that he would present his message in a different way to engage the attention of the unconverted than he did when trying to correct the errors of those who were already Christians. It is noteworthy that in the only instance

when Acts gives us an address to Christians by Paul (Acts 20:17–38), the substance of his message is not materially different from the typical content of his letters. Even the sermon at Athens (Acts 17:22–31) is not significantly different from what he wrote on the same subject in Romans 1:18–2:16.

A third consideration, however, is that significant differences are said to emerge when we get down to what many believe to have been the central feature of Paul's thinking: 'justification by faith'. But this is not a strong argument. It depends on the assumption that 'justification' was in fact the centre of Paul's thinking. Many readers of the New Testament – especially those of the Lutheran tradition – regard this as beyond question. But does the legal theory of justification by faith as conventionally understood really occupy the centre of Paul's thinking? It assumes such large importance in letters like Galatians and Romans only because, either really or potentially, Jewish opponents were in view. But quite apart from that, 'justification' does in fact appear on the lips of Paul in Acts 13:39 (the sermon in the synagogue at Antioch in Pisidia). And though what is said there is certainly not as fully worked out as Paul's arguments in Galatians or Romans, it is not out of keeping with them. Paul's statements are in any case the work of a trained rabbinic theologian. Luke's report of Paul's thinking is the work of an interested layperson. Though it is fashionable nowadays to speak of Luke as a 'theologian', he was not a professional, and he would not have had the same concern for detail that Paul himself no doubt had. John Robinson has rightly drawn attention to the fact that the kind of theology Luke attributes to Paul is exactly what we would expect in the circumstances. He shows his knowledge of key phrases and ideas that Paul used, though he is less interested than Paul in the detailed arguments that could be brought out in their support.

The purpose of Acts

Though he does not address their problems directly, Luke must have hoped that his first readers would learn something from his story to help their own Christian thinking. He may therefore have had at least three primary aims in view:

● Perhaps the main thing that comes out clearly from Acts is the conviction that Christianity is a faith with the potential to change the world. Indeed, through Paul and others it *did* change the world, and the secret of its success was the way in which these first Christians had the power of the Holy Spirit working within them. Luke encourages his readers to follow the example of those who had been Christians before them, and to do for their generation what Paul had achieved in his.

● But then Luke also seems to go out of his way to emphasize that Christianity can have good relationships with the Roman Empire. On the one hand, he commends the Christians to Rome itself, as he stresses that their faith is the true successor of Judaism – and Judaism, of course, was a recognized religion with the empire. But he also encourages his readers themselves to take a positive attitude towards the empire. He emphasizes that its officials are good and upright men, and by implication suggests that a maniac like Nero was the exception rather than the rule.

● In view of what he says at the beginning of his Gospel, we must also take seriously the fact that Luke claimed to be the first historian of Christianity. His two books are addressed to Theophilus in order that he might know the facts about the Christian faith. And the procedure that Luke adopted for compiling his story does suggest that he had a historian's interest in finding out about the past for its own sake. As the church became established as a significant institution in the Roman world, it was important for its members to know their origins and history, and Luke was perhaps the first person to set some of it out in a systematic form.

The presence of uniformed soldiers was a constant reminder to occupied nations of Roman power. Despite the resentment this could cause, Luke advocated a positive attitude towards the empire and its administrators.

The missing apostles

All three synoptic Gospels, together with Acts, list twelve special disciples of Jesus. Yet apart from Peter, James, John and Judas Iscariot, none of them feature prominently in the Gospels, and they are not mentioned at all in the rest of the New Testament. We do not really know what happened to these people, but there are a number of stories about them in early Christian writings outside the New Testament.

Thomas supposedly went to India, where he died as a Christian martyr – though not before he had persuaded a notable Indian ruler and his family to believe in Jesus. The Mar Thomas church in southern India claims that he was its founder, but it is more likely that it was established by other missionaries from the church in Edessa, by the banks of the River Euphrates. Eusebius says that Thomas himself went to India, and perhaps that is why the Indian Christians regard him as their patron saint (Eusebius, *Ecclesiastical History* III.1.1).

Andrew is said to have travelled extensively throughout Greece and Asia Minor, even crossing to the northern shore of the Black Sea. His life was allegedly characterized by miraculous deeds, including the resurrection of thirty-nine dead sailors washed up from a shipwreck! But when the proconsul's wife in the Greek city of Patrae became a Christian, her husband was so enraged that he had Andrew crucified on a cross shaped like the letter X. Other legends claim that sometime between the fourth and ninth centuries, his arm-bone was taken by Regulus to Scotland, where Andrew became the patron saint and his cross the national flag.

Thaddaeus is mentioned in the New Testament only by Matthew and Mark. According to Eusebius (*Ecclesiastical History* 1.13), a man of that name was connected with the establishment of the church in Edessa. The story tells how Agbar, king of Edessa, had written a letter to Jesus asking that he be healed

Argentinian evangelist Luis Palau travels worldwide preaching to thousands about the new life that Jesus Christ offers.

of a disease. Jesus replied that after his ascension, Thaddaeus would be sent to heal him. But other traditions connect Thaddaeus with Africa.

Philip and *Bartholomew* feature in stories about their travels around Asia Minor, accompanied by Philip's sister Mariamne. The *Acts of Philip* tell of encounters with dragons and beasts who speak to them, with Philip finally being martyred in Heirapolis. But Clement of Alexandria suggests that he lived to old age. Bartholomew has also been connected with a mission to India.

Matthew is said to have preached in Judea for eight years after the ascension, before going off to Ethiopia and Arabia. According to Papias, he had something to do with the Gospel of Matthew.

James the son of Alphaeus is mentioned in Spanish traditions that tell how Theodorus, Bishop of Iria, discovered his tomb at Santiago in 835, apparently guided there by a star.

Simon the Zealot travelled to England, according to some stories, together with Lazarus and Joseph of Arimathea.

We cannot trust any of these traditions about the 'unknown' apostles. Some of them may conceivably be based on vague recollections of their exploits, but on the whole their stories are just designed to fill in the gaps in the New Testament story, and have no historical value.

6. Paul: evangelist extraordinary

Chapter 14   Who was Paul?

Acts 15:5

Acts 22:3, 27

In the New Testament, the centre of interest moves away from Peter and the other disciples of Jesus to another important figure in the life of the early church – Paul, the Pharisee. He was not the only Pharisee to become a Christian, but he was certainly the best-known of them. Unlike many other Jewish Christians, Paul was not born in Palestine. Like many of the converts on the Day of Pentecost, he was a Hellenistic Jew. His home was in the city of Tarsus in the Roman province of Cilicia, and he was also a Roman citizen.

Paul's early life

Acts 9:30

There were probably two distinct periods in Paul's early life: his childhood, spent in Tarsus, and his youth and early manhood, spent in Jerusalem. The words translated 'brought up' in Acts 22:3 could indicate that Paul was only a baby when he moved from Tarsus to Jerusalem. But most scholars think they refer only to his education. Since he went back to Tarsus after he became a Christian, this seems the most obvious meaning of the expression.

First and foremost, Paul was a Jew, and proud of it. He was also proud of Tarsus, which was a university town and centre of government and trade. But he had no real affection for its culture, which was Greek and pagan. Paul's parents were good Jews, as well as being Roman citizens. Though they tried to shield him from the pagan influences of a city like Tarsus while he was a boy, it was the kind of place where any bright child would be bound to pick up some of the language and ideas of pagan Greek culture. The general influence of this kind of city is probably enough to explain the three references to Greek literature which we find in Paul's letters and sermons: references to the poets Epimenides, Aratus, and Menander.

Acts 17:28
Titus 1:12
1 Corinthians 15:33

Paul the student

Quite early in life, Paul's parents decided that he should become a student and teacher of the Jewish Law. As a small child in Tarsus, he learned the traditions of the Jewish people through regular instruction at the local synagogue. His first Bible was probably the

Paul's early life was spent in Tarsus. These Turkish schoolchildren of modern Tarsus stand in front of one of the few structures remaining from Paul's time.

Greek edition of the Old Testament, the Septuagint.

While he lived in Tarsus, Paul also learned the art of tent-making, for every student of the Jewish Law was expected to learn a practical trade as well as doing his studies. This was something that was of great value to Paul later in his life, for it enabled him to earn his own living while he was engaged in his missionary work.

Paul was soon sent away from Tarsus to the centre of the Jewish world, Jerusalem. Here he became a student of the learned Rabbi (or teacher) Gamaliel, who was the grandson and successor of the great Rabbi Hillel (about 60 BC–AD 20). Hillel had taught a more advanced and liberal form of Judaism than his rival, Shammai. What Jesus

Mark 10:1–12   said about divorce may have been provoked by the arguments of the followers of these two rabbis. Hillel declared that a man could divorce his wife if she displeased him in any way – even if she burned his dinner! But Shammai took the view that divorce was

Herod's Temple in Jerusalem was the focus of Jewish religious activity. In the outer area, the 'Court of the Gentiles' (on the left), was a thriving market in sacrificial animals; and in the porticos men would gather to listen to religious teachers. Inside the 'wall of partition', beyond which only Jews could pass, the daily pattern of worship and sacrifice was continued by priests and Temple servants. In this reconstruction of Herod's Temple the details of decoration are mainly guesswork.

Galatians 1:14

Acts 26:10

justified only in the event of some serious moral sin. What Paul himself later wrote on this subject shows that he must have changed his mind after he became a Christian.

Yet Paul did gain at least one great benefit from his education in the tradition of Hillel. Shammai had refused to see any place for the Gentiles in the purposes of God. His rival, however, had not only welcomed them, but positively set out to evangelize them. No doubt it was from Gamaliel that Paul first learned what a great job was waiting to be done among the non-Jewish people of the Roman Empire.

Paul progressed well in his studies at Jerusalem. On his own account, he was a highly successful student. He became so important that when Christians were being tried for their faith, he was in a position to 'cast his vote' against them, either in a synagogue assembly or in the supreme council of the Jews, the Sanhedrin.

So much for what we know about Paul's background and education. We have sketched briefly the main outline of events almost up to the time when he became a Christian. Now we must dig beneath the surface, and see what we can discover in his early life that will help us to understand his complex personality and some of the darker corners of his letters.

Paul's life and writings

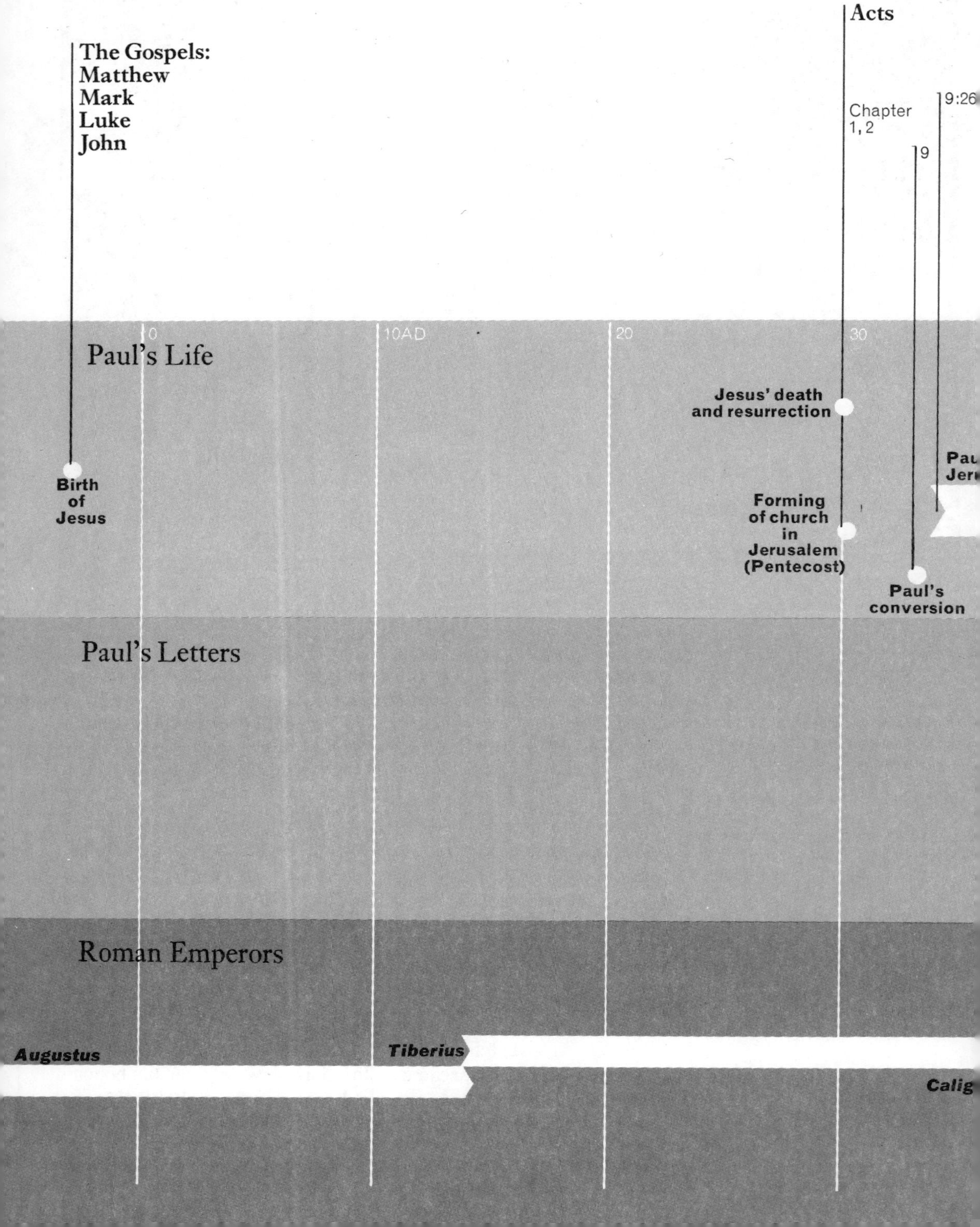

Acts

The Gospels:
Matthew
Mark
Luke
John

Chapter 1, 2

9:26

9

Paul's Life

0   10AD   20   30

Jesus' death
and resurrection

Birth
of
Jesus

Forming
of church
in
Jerusalem
(Pentecost)

Pau
Jeru

Paul's
conversion

Paul's Letters

Roman Emperors

Augustus

Tiberius

Calig

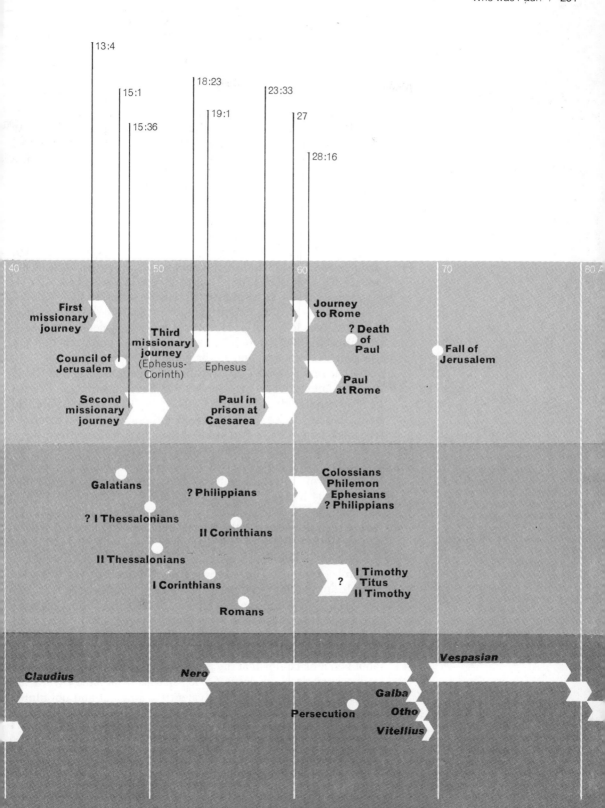

Three main influences must have been at work on the young Paul's mind: Judaism, Greek philosophy and the Mystery Religions.

Paul and the Jews

Paul himself never mentions Greek or pagan influences, but he makes many statements about his Jewish background and upbringing. He makes a great deal of the fact that he was a good Pharisee. As we read the letters he wrote as a Christian, it is obvious that he still retained the best beliefs of his teachers. One of the main rivals of the Pharisees was a group called the Sadducees. The two groups represented, respectively, the liberal and the conservative wings of Judaism. At every point of dispute between the two groups, Paul takes up and often improves the Pharisees' viewpoint:

● Pharisees believed that history had a goal and a purpose. They held that God was ordering events according to his own plan, which would culminate in the coming of a Messiah to lead his people. This was something Paul could readily accept as a Christian. In Romans 9–11 he argues that God is ordering the course of history with a view to the ultimate incorporation of the Jews into the Christian fellowship. He is arguing like a good Pharisee – though at the same time he went further, for Paul knew that the Messiah had already come, in the person of Jesus Christ.

● Pharisees believed in a future life. Paul stressed this to his own advantage when on trial before the Sanhedrin, and again before Herod Agrippa II. But as a Christian Paul went further. He knew that no one could guarantee that there would be a resurrection apart from the fact that Jesus Christ had risen from the dead.

Acts 23:6–10
Acts 26:6–8

● Pharisees believed in the existence of angels and demons. The Sadducees did not. Again, Paul retained this belief as a Christian, but transformed it in the light of his experience of Christ. On the cross, Christ had conquered the powers of evil. Because of this, Christians are 'more than conquerors through him who loved us'. No angel could ever rival the risen Lord whom Paul served, and in whom 'all the fullness of God was pleased to dwell'.

Romans 8:37

Colossians 1:19

It was not only in terms of belief that Paul continued to show his Jewish background. The very way he writes, using the Old Testament to 'prove' his theological points, is taken directly from his training as a Pharisee. No one who reads his letter to the Galatians can fail to be amazed, and sometimes amused, by the way Paul draws very unusual meanings from what to us are quite straightforward Old Testament passages. For instance, he argues like a Jewish rabbi when he claims that the promises made to Abraham referred to one single person, Jesus Christ, because the Greek word for 'offspring' (like its English equivalent!) is singular and not plural in form. Like the rabbis, Paul argues from single isolated texts, and can link up texts taken from completely different, and unrelated, parts of the Old Testament.

Galatians 3:16

Yet there was one crucial point at which Paul departed from his Jewish heritage. The Pharisees were legalists. They insisted on a detailed observance not only of the written Law of the Old Testament, but of traditional laws and customs for which there was no biblical authority. What is more, they claimed that those who did not observe all of these in every particular, could never attain to full salvation. Paul had been driven to the depths of despair as he vainly tried to be a good Pharisee and keep all the Law. He knew he could never do it. Therefore he could never truly know God. In an optimistic moment he once said that 'as to righteousness under the Law' he was 'blameless'. But at heart he knew that there was a greater power than his own at work to prevent him from ever keeping the whole Law. Even the success he did manage to achieve was far from adequate: 'I do not understand my own actions. For I do not do what I want, but I do the very thing I hate.' The more Paul tried to do good, the more impossible he found it.

It was only because he was such a faithful Pharisee that he was able to appreciate the importance of what God had done for humans in Jesus Christ. Pharisaism was a mirror in which Paul saw his own shortcomings so clearly revealed that he seemed to be 'the foremost of sinners'. But in Jesus Christ he saw a reflection of what he could become by the free grace of God: 'God has done what the law ... could not do: sending his own Son in the likeness of sinful flesh and for sin, he condemned sin in the flesh ... So then ... if by the Spirit

Philippians 3:6

Romans 7:14–15

1 Timothy 1:15

An orthodox Jew reads the Law (or *Torah*) at the Wailing Wall in modern Jerusalem. Some of the stones in the Wall formed part of the structure of Herod's Temple.

A strict observer of Judaism in modern Israel. The box tied to his forehead is called a phylactery, and contains passages from the Jewish Law (see Deuteronomy 6:8).

Romans 8:3, 12, 13, 26

you put to death the deeds of the body you will live ... the Spirit helps us in our weakness.'

Paul and the philosophers

The synagogue was of great importance in Jewish life. It formed the centre of worship, education and government of the civil life of the local Jewish community. This reconstruction of a synagogue of Paul's time shows the Scriptures in a prominent position, symbolizing their importance for the Jews.

Colossians 1:16–17

Acts 17:28

Of the many philosophical schools of the time, **Stoicism** was probably the most congenial to Paul. One or two of the great Stoics came from Tarsus, and Paul may have remembered something about their teachings from his youth.

Some scholars have suggested that Paul's acquaintance with Stoic philosophy was closer than this. In 1910 Rudolf Bultmann pointed out that Paul's reasoning sometimes resembles the Stoics' arguments. Both use rhetorical questions, short disconnected statements, an imaginary opponent to raise questions, and frequent illustrations drawn from athletics, building, and life in general. It is even possible to find phrases in Paul's teaching which could be taken to support Stoic doctrine; for example the statement that 'all things were created through him and for him. He is before all things, and in him all things hold together'. There is also the fact that in his sermon at Athens, Luke reports that Paul had actually quoted from Aratus, who was a well-known Stoic poet. Some of

Paul's letters also often reflect Stoic terminology – as when he describes morality in terms of what is 'fitting' or 'not fitting'. No doubt Paul would know and sympathize with many Stoic ideals. But there are outstanding and quite fundamental differences between Paul's Christianity and Stoicism:

Colossians 3:18; Ephesians 5:3–4

● Stoicism was based on philosophical speculations about the nature of the world and people. Its real 'god' was abstract human reason. Christianity is quite different. It is based firmly on the historical facts of the life, death and resurrection of Jesus Christ.

1 Corinthians 15:3–11

● The Stoic 'god' was an ill-defined abstraction, sometimes associated with the whole universe, sometimes with Reason, and sometimes even with the element of fire: 'What god we know not, yet a god there dwells.' Paul's God, on the other hand, was a personal Being revealed in Christ: 'In him all the fullness of God was pleased to dwell.'

Seneca, *Letters* 41.2, quoting Virgil

Colossians 1:19

● Stoics found 'salvation' in self-sufficiency. They sought to win mastery of themselves so they could live in harmony with nature. 'The end of life is to act in conformity with nature, that is, at once with the nature which is in us and with the nature of the universe ... Thus the life according to nature is that virtuous and blessed flow of existence, which is enjoyed only by one who always acts so as to maintain the harmony between the daemon within the individual and the will of the Power that orders the universe.' For Paul salvation was completely different from this. He found it not in dependence on himself, but in submission to Jesus Christ: 'I have been crucified with Christ; it is no longer I who live, but Christ who lives in me; and the life I now live in the flesh I live by faith in the Son of God, who loved me and gave himself for me.'

Diogenes Laertius vii.1.53

Galatians 2:20

● Stoicism had no future: it was a religion of hopelessness. Most people were considered incapable of reaching any moral maturity. They were destined to be destroyed as one cycle of the world's history followed another, only to be reborn, or reincarnated, again so that the whole cycle could be repeated. But Christianity contrasted with this, asserting that the world as we know it would end decisively with the future personal intervention of Christ himself. Then a completely new world order would emerge.

1 Corinthians 15:20–28

The influence of the Stoics on Paul must be reckoned to be minimal. None of us can escape using words and phrases, even religious ones, with which we are familiar in other contexts. But if Paul ever used the language of the Stoics, he gave it a new meaning. For his own message of salvation through Christ was a long way from the Stoic message of salvation through self-discipline.

Paul and the mystery religions

There are several superficial resemblances between the mystery religions and the Christian faith. Both came to Rome from the east. Both offered 'salvation' to their followers. Both used initiation rites (Christian baptism) and a sacramental meal (the Christian communion). Both referred to their saviour god as 'lord'. The two often became intertwined as converts from the mysteries entered the

Mithraism was the most powerful mystery religion in the Roman Empire in Paul's time. Worshippers believed that the god Mithras would save the faithful and help them reach heaven. Here Mithras, a Persian god, is killing the bull as a sacrifice.

church, sometimes bringing their mystery beliefs with them. It was probably an event like this that was the cause of much of the trouble in the church at Corinth, about which Paul wrote in his letters to the Corinthians (see also chapter 18).

Because of these resemblances between Christianity and the mysteries, some scholars have thought that what Paul did was to change the simple ethical teaching of Jesus into a kind of mystery religion. No one today holds this view. There is no real historical evidence to support it. What evidence there is tends to show quite the opposite:

● The mysteries were always ready, and even eager, to combine with other religions. This was something that Christians always rejected, believing that they alone had the full truth revealed to them by Christ.

● Much of the evidence that was claimed to show that Paul was a mystery adherent is now seen to be false. For instance, the title 'lord' applied to Jesus is now known to come not from mystery religions, but from the Old Testament. The Christian confession of faith 'may our Lord come' (recorded in its Aramaic form, *Maranatha*) shows that the very earliest church in Jerusalem, the only one to speak Aramaic, must have given Jesus that title long before Paul came on the scene.

1 Corinthians 16:22

● What impressed the pagan world was not the similarity of Christianity to other religions, but its difference from them. The accusation most often made against Christians was of atheism, because they would not admit even the possibility that other gods could exist.

No doubt Paul knew of the mystery religions and their resemblances to Christianity. They told of gods coming down in the form of men; of salvation as 'dying' to the old life; of a god giving immortal life; and of the saviour god being called 'lord'. It is possible that Paul, who was ready to be 'all things to all men', sometimes deliberately used their language. But it is more likely that he used it unconsciously. For educated people in his day would use the language of the mystery religions as easily and as uncommittedly as we often use the language of popular astrology today. Paul shows no detailed knowledge of the mystery religions. He makes no clear reference to any of their ceremonies.

1 Corinthians 9:22

Paul's background included three worlds of thought: the Jewish, the Greek and the mystery. Each one of these can shed a certain amount of light on his personality and his teaching. But we would be foolish to regard Paul as merely the natural product of his cultural surroundings. He regarded himself supremely as 'a man in Christ'. Whatever he may have gained from these other sources, he recognized in his new Lord a power greater than them all, and someone for whom he counted everything else as 'refuse'.

2 Corinthians 12:2

Philippians 3:8

Paul and the earliest church

But what about Paul's relationship to the other leaders of the early church? When we read the New Testament, it is not difficult to get the impression that only two people really mattered in the early church: Jesus himself, and Paul. For the stories of Jesus in the Gospels and the writings of Paul together account for something like three-quarters of the whole New Testament. We occasionally meet Peter, James and other lesser characters such as Silas or Timothy on the pages of Paul's letters. But even in Acts, they seem to take a back seat to Paul himself. Of course, there are reasons for this, no doubt connected with the purpose for which Acts was written in the first place. It is on any account a selective story of the beginnings of Christianity. For example, if we only had Acts to go by, we might suppose that Paul was the first Christian to take the gospel to Rome. But we know from his letter to the church in that city that a large and thriving Christian fellowship existed there long before he visited Italy. So Paul's work, though of fundamental importance, was clearly complementary to that of many other figures in the early church, whose names and exploits have not been recorded for us.

Romans 1:6–7

But was Paul's work really complementary to that of Peter and other early Christian leaders – or was he instead establishing a different brand of Christianity altogether, different from the original church at Jerusalem not only in character, but in belief as well?

That was the suggestion put forward in the middle of the nineteenth century by the members of the so-called 'Tübingen School' in Germany. Influenced by the great New Testament scholar, Ferdinand Christian Baur, they argued that there was a vast difference between Paul's type of Christianity and the sort of churches

The religion of Mithras was tough. It involved tests like being walled up for several days, and appealed particularly to soldiers. However women were not allowed to participate, and its limited appeal weakened its resistance to Christianity. This little temple of Mithras was discovered at Walbrook, London.

founded by Jewish Christians such as Peter, or James of Jerusalem. They saw the whole of the first generation of Christianity as a conflict between these rival forms of Christian belief – a conflict that was resolved only with the emergence of the catholic church in the second century. This was not a new idea. Even in the second century, the anonymous authors of the *Clementine Homilies* and *Recognitions* were suggesting that there were irreconcilable differences between Paul and the original apostles.

But is this a fair picture, either of Paul or of the others? Was he really independent of the Jewish base of the church in Jerusalem? Or do we today just like to think that he was, perhaps because his more open-minded view of the gospel is, in general, more acceptable to our own modern outlook?

When we examine the New Testament closely, whether in Paul's own writings or in the stories of Acts, it soon becomes clear that Paul was much more conscious of his own Jewish origins and background than many modern scholars are prepared to allow. At a number of points he goes out of his way to establish some sort of continuity between his own Gentile churches on the one hand, and the earliest Jewish church, and even Judaism itself, on the other.

Christians and the Old Testament

It is significant that when Paul defines Christian faith, he consistently does so in relation to Judaism. Take his letter to the Galatians, for example, the argument of which is also closely followed in Romans. The Galatian churches were being infiltrated by people claiming that in order to be a Christian one also needed to be a Jew (either by being born one or by accepting circumcision and the Old Testament Law). Paul found that quite abhorrent for, he claimed, a living relationship to God through Jesus Christ depended on simple *Galatians 2:15* trust ('faith'). And, he argued, it had always been so. Long before the Old Testament Law had even come into existence, Israel's ancestor Abraham had trusted God's promises, and had found fellowship with God on that basis. Therefore, anyone who wanted to be a part *Galatians 3:6–9* of God's covenant people needed only to follow the example of Abraham, and trust God. The Law was in some ways an aberration from the original simplicity of the relationship between Abraham and God.

To us today, the argument of Galatians can be somewhat difficult to read and understand. But it is occasionally obscure to us precisely because of its Jewish nature. Though Paul disagreed with the argument that in order to please God a person needed to accept the Jewish Law and customs, nevertheless he accepted without question the more basic premise that in order to please God a person must become a part of the covenant nation which had its historical origins in the Old Testament stories of the call of Abraham. In a sense, he was agreeing with those Jewish Christians who said that Gentiles must become Jews in order to be Christians. But, while they supposed that obedience to the Law was the hallmark of the real Jew, Paul redefined 'Jewishness' to lay all the emphasis instead on continuity with Abraham. To be a child of God was to be a *Galatians 3:6–25; 4:21–31* member of Abraham's family – and to join that, faith in God was the only required qualification.

Paul continued this line of argument in his letter to the church at Rome. Indeed, there he added the comment that 'the real Jew is the person who is a Jew on the inside ... and this is the work of God's *Romans 2:29* Spirit, not of the written Law'. In saying this, he stands in the same tradition as Stephen, and the Old Testament prophets before him. Racial pedigree was not the most important thing, but obedience to God's will. But we should notice here that, no matter how he redefined the Old Testament faith in relation to the Judaism of his own day, Paul always felt it important that Christians, whether Jews or Gentiles, should be seen within the context of the continuing actions of God in history that had begun with Abraham, and would receive their final fulfilment and consummation at some future *Galatians 3:29* time. Unlike some of his later admirers, Paul never suggested that the Old Testament was irrelevant for the Christian. Instead, he saw even Gentile Christians as part of a great line of faith stemming from Abraham himself, and this qualified them to be a part of 'the Israel

Galatians 6:16

of God'. This line of argument has close similarities to the thinking of Peter, as we shall see in chapter 23 below.

The church and Israel

The most difficult passage in the whole of Paul's writings makes all this even more explicit. This is what he writes in Romans chapters 9–11. Scholars are undecided as to how this section of Romans fits into its context. Some argue that this is the key that unlocks the door to the whole of the rest of the letter. Others believe it was an afterthought, representing Paul's uncertain speculations on the fate of the Jewish people, rather than any kind of carefully developed thinking on the subject. Whichever view we take, there can be no doubt about what Paul actually says here. For whatever reason, he quite clearly asserts that to be born a Jew still carries a distinct advantage. He compares the whole 'people of God' (the Israelites of the Old Testament, together with the Gentile Christians) to an olive

Romans 11:13–24

tree. The roots of this tree go down deep into the Old Testament, and Gentile Christians have been grafted like a new branch onto this plant. In the meantime, some of the original (Jewish) branches have been broken off. But they will in due course be restored, says Paul. Indeed, the present situation is a temporary one. Though it may seem to some that 'the people of God' are now the Gentile Christians, God has allowed them to come in only to encourage the Jewish people to further obedience: 'Because they sinned, salvation has come to the Gentiles, to make the Jews jealous of them ... but the stubbornness of the people of Israel is not permanent, but will last only until the complete number of Gentiles cries to God. And this

Romans 11:11, 25–26

is how all Israel will be saved.'

This Jewish boy has portions of the Law in tiny leather 'phylacteries', in literal obedience to the instruction in Deuteronomy 6:8 to tie the commands of the Lord 'on your arms and wear them on your foreheads'.

On that rather cryptic note, Paul leaves his discussion of the subject. There are many difficulties in understanding precisely what he meant. But however he thought this was to be accomplished, Paul clearly believed that the Jews had an important part to play in the whole history of salvation – and this in itself suggests that he was by no means as implacably anti-Jewish as some have suggested.

To the Jews first

Acts 13:14; 14:1; 17:1–2

When we examine his practice, we find the same emphasis. Whenever he went to a new town in some hitherto unvisited part of the Roman world, Paul always went first to the Jewish synagogue. Of course, there would be good tactical reasons for doing so. Since he was concerned to declare that Jesus was the Messiah, it was only natural that he should speak first to people who had some notion of who and what the Messiah might be. The fact that they had rather different expectations from Paul himself usually became clear fairly quickly, as he was thrown out of one synagogue after another. But that did not stop him following the practice. Indeed, he makes it clear in Romans that, in addition to the practical advantages, he also had a strong theological reason for working like this: '... the gospel ... is God's power to save all who believe, first the Jews and also the Gentiles.'

Romans 1:16

Jews and Gentiles

Galatians 2:7–9

Despite this, Paul believed he was specifically called to take the good news about Jesus to Gentiles rather than Jews. According to his letter to the Galatians, this special commission was recognized by the Jewish church leaders in Jerusalem: Paul would go to

Paul uses the imagery of an olive tree to describe the Jewish nation, onto which Gentile Christians have been 'grafted'.

Gentiles, they to Jews. Inevitably, this was not a hard and fast rule. Paul often met and spoke with Jews, while Peter in particular was to become involved in missionary activity among Gentiles. But as a rough arrangement, it was a satisfactory division of labour. It may well have been agreed for social and economic reasons rather than for purely theological ones. Paul, as an unmarried person, was singularly well fitted to long and arduous journeys in a way that the Palestinian apostles were not. They had wives and families, and needed to depend for their support on the regular generosity of the churches, whereas Paul could move about the empire quite freely, finding casual work to support himself as the need arose.

Acts 18:3; 2 Thessalonians 3:8

There are many complex problems involved in understanding the accounts of Paul's dealings with the leaders of the Jerusalem church. But the fact remains that Paul evidently had regular and not unfriendly contacts with the leaders of the church there.

Paul and Jerusalem

But was it more than that? Was Paul, as some have argued, almost under the control of the Jerusalem leaders? Do his letters conceal the truth in some way, making him appear much more independent than he actually was? This suggestion has gained some support from the fact that towards the end of his third missionary tour, Paul put a great deal of effort and energy into taking a collection among the Gentile Christians of Greece and Asia Minor, which was to be for the benefit of the church in Judea. We know from other sources that Hellenistic Jews throughout the empire sent an annual temple tax to the authorities in Jerusalem, to support the temple and its services there. So could the Jerusalem church exercise some kind of central control on the whole Christian movement by imposing a similar burden on the churches of Gentile believers founded by Paul?

1 Corinthians 16:1–7

It seems unlikely. In Romans, Paul outlines his own understanding of the collection: '... the churches in Macedonia and Achaia have freely decided to give an offering to help the poor among God's people in Jerusalem. That decision was their own ...' He goes on to add, however, that 'as a matter of fact, they have an obligation to help them. Since the Jews shared their spiritual blessings with the Gentiles, the Gentiles ought to use their material blessings to help the Jews'. In other words, conscious of his own deep indebtedness to the Jewish Christian church, Paul had organized this collection as a kind of thank-offering and spontaneous expression of love for the Christians in Jerusalem. Of course, the Jewish Christians may well have seen it in a different light. It has been suggested that they would think of it as the fulfilment of the ancient prophecies of Isaiah, which speak of 'the wealth of the nations' being brought to Jerusalem, and its Gentile bearers 'bowing down to show their respect'.

Romans 15:26–27

2 Corinthians 8:8–14

Isaiah 60

If that were the case, however, we might expect them to have received Paul and his Gentile Christian companions with open arms. But in fact it is not clear what happened to the collection when it finally arrived in Jerusalem. It has been suggested that the

Acts 21:27–40

The dramatic events of AD 70, when the Roman armies destroyed Jerusalem and plundered the temple, are depicted on the Titus Arch in Rome.

Jewish Christians actually refused to accept it. And it is certainly striking that when Paul was subsequently arrested in the Temple at Jerusalem, his fellow Jewish Christians did not spring to his defence. That was left to a Roman. Perhaps the Jewish Christians had not gone so far as to lead him into some sort of trap, but at least they were not sorry to see the last of him. The same cannot, however, be said of Paul's attitude to them. The very fact that he had made the effort to return to Jerusalem at this time shows his deep and lasting indebtedness to the leaders of the first Christian church.

Paul and the teaching of Jesus

This indebtedness also comes out in the way Paul often displays knowledge of and familiarity with the teachings of Jesus himself. One of the most intriguing features of Paul's letters is the complete

absence from them of any direct references to the life and teaching of Jesus. At one time it was fashionable to suggest that Paul had no time for Jesus, and that his own brand of Christianity was based instead on Greek and Roman concepts. But this kind of argument does not square with the facts.

While Paul very rarely makes a direct reference to Jesus' teaching, there are several sections of his writings which bear a remarkable similarity to what we find in the Gospels. Occasionally, Paul does say that he is quoting from or referring to 'words of the Lord'. But there are many other places where his own advice is so close to the teaching of Jesus as we know it from the Gospels that Paul must have been referring to it – for example, in the practical advice given to the church in Rome.

1 Corinthians 7:10; 9:14;
1 Thessalonians 4:15

- Love your enemies — Matthew 5:43–48 / Romans 12:14–21

- Love God and your neighbour — Mark 12:29–31 / Romans 13:8–10

- Teaching on 'clean' and 'unclean' foods — Mark 7:14–23 / Romans 14:14

- Responsibility to state authorities — Mark 12:13–17 / Romans 13:1–7

Paul's knowledge of the words and deeds of Jesus had not come from personal contact with Jesus, but from those who had been Jesus' first disciples – especially, perhaps, from Peter with whom Paul spent two full weeks after his conversion. Paul must have known a great deal more about Jesus' teaching than we would guess from his letters. But there are reasons for his apparent silence on the matter. For one thing, his letters are occasional writings rather than considered and carefully worked out accounts of his whole theology. And then, it is also likely that his readers already knew a lot about the life and teaching of Jesus. Paul must have told them about this when he first told them the good news of the Christian message. He could not have spoken meaningfully about Jesus either to Gentiles or to Hellenist Jews without at the same time giving them some explanation about who Jesus was! And to be able to do that, he needed the co-operation and friendship of the original Jewish disciples.

Galatians 1:18

Taken together, these six points suggest that, far from being an odd man out, Paul was part and parcel of the Christian movement as it began among the first Jewish disciples of Jesus.

But we have already anticipated much of Paul's life. Before we go any further, we must pause and ask how and why Paul the Pharisee became a Christian in the first place.

Chapter 15 Paul the persecutor

One of the most cherished beliefs of the Jews, and one that Paul no doubt shared, was that God would soon intervene in history to rescue his chosen people Israel from the domination of alien political forces. They believed that God would set them up as one of the great nations of the world by the arrival of the 'Messiah' or 'Christ'. Both words mean 'anointed one': 'Messiah' is Hebrew, and 'Christ' is Greek. He would arrive in dramatic fashion, a royal figure of the ancient house of David. He would march on Jerusalem with his followers, enter the Temple and drive the hated Romans from the land.

Luke 1 and 2; John 1:46
Matthew 5:38–42
Mark 11:1–19; Zechariah 9:9

So when Jesus of Nazareth appeared evidently claiming to be the Messiah, it was not surprising that the Jews did not recognize him as the kind of deliverer they were looking for. Far from being royal his birth took place in obscurity. He had no army, and often spoke in terms that showed his contempt for physical violence. When he entered the Temple in fulfilment of the prophecy of Zechariah, it heralded not victory over the Romans but humiliation and death at their hands.

Paul shared the contempt felt by the Jewish leaders for this crucified 'Messiah'. He despised even more the activities of the followers of this pseudo-Christ. For they were claiming that after his degrading execution he had risen from the dead, and that God had recognized him as the true Messiah by giving him a place of high

Acts 2:22–24

honour.

Now Paul could conceivably have had some respect for Jesus himself. After all, he had been an ethical teacher, and said many things with which the Jewish rabbis could agree. But his followers

Acts 4:13

had nothing to commend them at all. They were ignorant and uneducated. What right had they to tell the religious leaders of the day that they had been mistaken, that they had demanded the death of none other than God's own Son?

Persecution

Acts 7:2–53

When Stephen dared to say in public that the days of the Jewish religion and its Temple were finished, Paul and his fellow-Pharisees knew that the time had come for action. No longer was it enough to regard these followers of 'the Way', as they called themselves, as amiable cranks. They posed a dangerous threat to the Jewish religious system.

So Stephen was stoned to death by a Jerusalem mob. Paul himself stood by, happy to guard the coats of the executioners while they did their evil work.

Acts 7:54–8:1

But Paul was more than just a coat-minder. He was a crafty man, and an influential Pharisee. When he saw that the Christians were beginning to move out of Jerusalem to other places, he realized that, far from having solved the problem, the way the Jews were persecuting Stephen and the others was only helping the Christian cause to spread to other parts of the Roman Empire.

One of the places where these fanatics were congregating was Damascus, an independent city within the Nabatean kingdom. At the time Aretas IV (9 BC–AD 40) ruled over the Nabatean kingdom,

2 Corinthians 11:32–33

though he had no direct authority over Damascus itself. This was not the first time that Damascus had served as a haven for religious refugees from Judea. According to the *Zadokite Fragments* (documents which stem from a Jewish sect associated with the people who wrote the Dead Sea Scrolls) a large number of Jews had fled there just before 130 BC. Since these people had been able to live independently of the authorities in Jerusalem, no doubt the early Christians thought they could do the same. In addition, the Jewish communities formed by these earlier immigrants would provide an ideal audience to which to proclaim the message of Jesus as Messiah.

But the Christians had reckoned without Paul. He remembered that earlier in his nation's history the Romans had given to the high priest in Jerusalem the right to have Jewish criminals extradited

1 Maccabees 15:15–24

from other parts of the empire. So he went to the high priest to ask for a letter authorizing him to pursue the Christians to Damascus, and bring them back to Jerusalem for trial and sentence. It was

Acts 9:1–2

while doing so that Paul had a remarkable experience which was to alter the course of his whole life.

Paul meets Jesus

This experience is described in detail in three different places in the book of the Acts, which shows just how important it was not only in Paul's life, but in the entire history of the early church. In Acts 9:3–19 we have Luke's summary account of what happened; in 22:6–16 we have a personal account given by Paul when defending himself before a Jewish mob in Jerusalem; and in 26:9–23 we have another account given by Paul, this time in his defence before Herod Agrippa II.

The three accounts build up a composite picture rather than agreeing precisely in every detail. Two of them were from Paul himself; the other is Luke's own summary of what happened. Luke was simply recounting the broad outline of what took place; Paul on each occasion had particular reasons for expressing himself as he did.

Stephen was stoned after attempting to defend himself against the charge of blasphemy in a Jewish court. The execution may have taken place outside St Stephen's Gate, Jerusalem, viewed here from the Mount of Olives.

The different accounts of Paul's conversion

There are three main differences in points of detail in the accounts of Paul's conversion.

● In Acts 9:7 Paul's companions heard the voice of the risen Christ, but saw no *person*. They may have seen the bright light. In 22:9 Paul says they 'saw the light but did not hear the voice of the one who was speaking to me'. What they heard was presumably a sound, but not an intelligible voice. The account in chapter 26 does not refer to the companions either seeing or hearing.

● In Acts 9:4 and 22:7 the only person mentioned as falling to the ground is Paul, the central figure in the drama. But this need not exclude the possibility that the others fell to the ground, as in 26:14.

● In Acts 9:6 and 22:10 Paul is told to go on to Damascus, where he will be told what to do. In 26:16 his commission to be an apostle is given at the time of the vision. Possibly Paul did not wish to bore Agrippa with the details of his story, and so compressed it into this form.

These distinctions are not of great importance, and can easily be explained by the different purpose of the narrative in each case. Indeed the fact that these variations in emphasis have been preserved by Luke gives us greater confidence in him as a credible historian. If he had invented the story, he would have been more likely to have made sure that each account of it was identical with the others in form and language.

Acts 26:13

Acts 9:4; 22:7; 26:14

In all essential points, the three accounts are agreed. Paul was travelling along the road to Damascus, bent on wiping out the Christians there, when 'a light from heaven, brighter than the sun' shone down on him, and he was challenged by the voice of the risen Christ, 'Why do you persecute me?' Paul's life was to take a radical about-turn. He immediately realized that the hopes he had previously entertained as a Jew were false. Jesus of Nazareth, whom, along with his followers, Paul had so despised, was standing before him as the Son of God and Lord of all, demanding that he should recognize Christ's rule over his nation, and over Paul's own life. And Paul responded by accepting these demands. The Pharisee who had hated the Christian faith was to become its greatest advocate. Though he might have boasted about his great achievements in Judaism, from now on his life was totally dominated by the risen Christ who appeared to him on the Damascus road, and revolutionized his life and thinking.

Paul gives several accounts of the decisive events on the Damascus Road, when the risen Christ spoke to him. The encounter meant a radical change in Paul's life.

Yet Paul's remarkable conversion did not spring from nothing. No doubt he already knew a great deal about the life and teachings of Jesus of Nazareth. Indeed, some suggest that he may have been personally acquainted with Jesus. But that is unlikely. What is certain, however, is that he must have taken a considerable interest in the kind of interpretation being placed on the Old Testament by Hellenist Jewish Christians like Stephen. Perhaps the very fact that he did not himself take part in the stoning of Stephen may suggest that he had an uncertain sympathy with what was being said. There can be little doubt that such thinking had an enormous and profound influence on his own life, for in many respects the teaching of Paul on the place of the Old Testament Law and covenants in the Christian life is but a logical extension of the teaching of those Hellenist Jews who were Christians before him. As a Christian, Paul was not much interested in the ritual and ceremonial aspects of the Old Testament Law. He was much more concerned about the Law as a source of morality – no doubt because of his own background as a Pharisee. But what he wrote about the temporary and passing nature of the Law in Galatians bears a striking similarity to Stephen's arguments about the Law and the temple in Acts.

2 Corinthians 5:16

Galatians 3:1–25

Paul at Damascus

Acts 9:9

Acts 9:10–19; 22:12–16

When he arrived in Damascus after his remarkable experience, Paul was still overwhelmed, and was unable to eat or drink for three days. But God had a plan for Paul's life that covered the details as well as the broad outline – and so Ananias, a Christian living in Damascus, came to visit Paul. He was able to restore Paul's sight, and at that Paul was baptized and spent some time with the Christians in Damascus. Like Peter in the household of Cornelius, Paul was now to discover that within the fellowship of the Christian church he could be united with men and women who on any other ground would have been abhorrent to him. But his experience was even more radical than that of Peter. For these people who had

The good news about Jesus Christ has been taken 'to the ends of the earth'. Here, Christians in Papua New Guinea celebrate the dedication of their first New Testament.

accepted him so generously were the very ones whom he had been intent on hounding to death. Instead of that, they now became his closest friends. It is hardly surprising that when he later wrote a letter to the churches of Galatia, the central burden of his message should be the conviction that men and women of different social and religious backgrounds could come together only through a

Paul travelled along the Egnatian Way, a busy Roman road between Philippi and Thessalonica.

living relationship with Jesus Christ: 'There is no difference between Jews and Gentiles, between slaves and free men, between men and women; you are all one in Christ Jesus.'

Galatians 3:28

It was this burning conviction that later inspired Paul to carry the Christian message not only to the cities of Palestine – places like Damascus itself, Antioch, and even Jerusalem – but also to the furthest corners of the known world. In doing so, he displayed an amazing vitality, and through the letters he wrote to many of his churches he has left us a priceless insight into what it must have been like to be a Christian in the wider Roman world of the first century AD. It was not all easy going, even for an apostle. Paul's long journeys must have been physically exhausting and highly

2 Corinthians 11:25–27

When he arrived at Damascus, Paul lodged with a man named Judas who lived in Straight Street, which is today a busy shop-lined road. A Roman gateway and parts of the city walls of Paul's time still stand in modern Damascus.

dangerous. But Paul was undaunted. He was quite convinced that he was not alone in his endeavours. Indeed, they were not really *his* endeavours at all, for he was conscious of the living Christ of the Damascus road continuing to live within him throughout his life. From that moment onwards, his life was dominated by the desire to please his risen Lord, and everything else was trivial by comparison. Writing towards the end of his life, he put it like this: 'I count everything as loss because of the surpassing worth of knowing Christ Jesus my Lord.'

Galatians 2:20; Philippians 1:21

Philippians 3:8

Paul did not forget his original purpose in coming to Damascus, which was to visit the Jewish synagogues of the city. He went straight to the Jews, who were no doubt expecting his arrival. But his message was most unexpected. Instead of denouncing the Christian faith he proclaimed it, and made known his new allegiance to Jesus the Messiah.

Acts 9:20–25

In Galatians 1:17 Paul mentions a brief visit to a place called 'Arabia' (probably an area near Damascus) before returning to

Acts 9:23

Damascus for three years. This is not inconsistent with Acts, where it is stated that he remained in Damascus for 'many days'. He may have gone to 'Arabia' immediately after meeting Ananias, or he may have gone there after some initial preaching in the Jewish synagogues.

2 Corinthians 11:32
Acts 9:23–25

Eventually, Paul found it impossible to stay any longer in the city of Damascus. Both the Jews and the city authorities were eager to get rid of him, so his friends secretly let him down over the city wall in a basket.

Paul and the Jewish Christians

Acts 9:26–30

Paul now paid a visit to Jerusalem, probably the one described in Galatians 1:18–24. Paul struck terror into the disciples in Jerusalem until Barnabas, one of the leaders of the church, told them of Paul's conversion and witness in Damascus. After this, Paul went out and preached so boldly in Jerusalem itself that the Jews wanted to do away with him. The apostles sent him away to Caesarea for safety, and from there he returned to his original home, in Tarsus. In Galatians Paul explains that his main motive for visiting Jerusalem at this time was to meet Peter, with whom he stayed for fifteen days.

Paul's movements between the time of his Damascus road experience and the Council of Jerusalem.

A Jerusalem to Damascus

B Damascus to 'Arabia'

C Damascus to Jerusalem to Caesarea to Tarsus

D Next 11 years in Cilicia and Syria

E Antioch to Jerusalem

Galatians 1:18–19

Galatians 1:22–24

He also met James, the brother of Jesus. But he did not meet many of the Christians, and most churches in the area only knew of him by reputation. Paul spent the next eleven years in Cilicia and Syria, probably still unknown to many of the Christians.

Acts 11:19–26

Acts 11:27–30

Galatians 2:1–10
Galatians 2:2

Though the Christians in Jerusalem might justifiably have forgotten Paul, Barnabas did not. When he found himself involved in the work of the church in Antioch, in the Roman province of Syria, he sent for Paul and brought him back from Tarsus to help. Paul and Barnabas had been working together for about a year in the church at Antioch when a prophet named Agabus arrived from Jerusalem and declared to the church that a great famine was coming which would affect the Christians in Jerusalem. The church in Antioch decided to send aid to their fellow believers. Barnabas and Paul were to take the relief fund in person. According to Luke, this visit to Jerusalem probably took place in AD 43, when the persecution of Christians in Jerusalem begun by Herod Agrippa I in AD 42 was still going on. It was probably this visit that Paul referred to in Galatians, where the 'revelation' of which

Antioch, on the River Orontes, was the third largest city in the Roman world. It was the capital of the Roman province of Syria, and an important centre of commerce. The church at Antioch was fast-growing and dynamic. The town is now Antakya in south-east Turkey.

he speaks was presumably the prophetic message of Agabus about the famine. Paul says that on this visit he saw the church leaders privately, which is easy to understand if there was persecution going on at the time.

Who were the prophets?

As third largest city of the Roman Empire, Antioch built a reputation for its cultural achievements. The Seleucids and Romans built impressive temples and monuments: this Roman head from Antioch dates from the second century AD.

When Paul was giving advice to the Christians at Corinth about the use of spiritual gifts (*charismata* in Greek) within their church, he advised them to desire all the gifts that had appeared among them, but especially 'prophecy' (1 Corinthians 14:1–5; 12:4–11). What was this prophecy, which we find mentioned in 1 Corinthians and throughout the book of Acts?

It is clear that there was in the early church an important group of men and women known as prophets. They are frequently listed immediately after the apostles (1 Corinthians 12:28–29; Ephesians 2:20; 3:5; 4:11), while what appear to us to be the more ordinary tasks of evangelist, pastor and teacher are placed after the prophets in order of importance (1 Corinthians 12:28–29; Ephesians 4:11; Acts 13:1; Romans 12:6–8).

These prophets were men and women who had a specially close access to God's will. They could not only forecast certain specific events in the future (as Agabus did, Acts 11:28; 21:10–11; see also Revelation 22:6), but they could also deliver an authentic and authoritative message for a contemporary situation. In Acts 13:1–4, the prophets of the church at Antioch, inspired by the Holy Spirit, gave directions that Paul and Barnabas should be 'set apart ... for the work to

which I have called them'. In the church at Caesarea, the four daughters of Philip the evangelist regularly acted as prophets (Acts 21:8–9). Prophecy also had some connection with the appointment of Timothy (1 Timothy 1:18; 4:14). We also find prophets rebuking Christians who are lazy and encouraging Christians under attack (see for example 1 Corinthians 14:3; Acts 15:32).

Besides such practical activities within the Christian community, the prophet also had an important theological task. In 1 Corinthians 13:2, being a prophet is equated with understanding 'all mysteries and all knowledge'; while Ephesians 3:5–6 makes it clear that the prophet could have a special understanding of God's purposes for the salvation of the Gentiles.

It is difficult for us to appreciate the exact function of these men and women, for we have little with which to compare them. Although there are churches which claim to have prophets today, they usually have different functions from those of New Testament prophets. But it is clear that local congregations of the first century highly regarded the prophets as people who lived in close contact with God, and through whom God could make his will known to the church.

Jews and Gentiles
Galatians 2:1–10

Paul makes it clear that this meeting with the leaders of the Jerusalem church was crucial for his own ministry. At this time the Jerusalem apostles were willing to recognize his mission to the Gentiles as a valid extension of the Christian message. This was an important issue for the early church.

Some Jews, mostly those living in scattered communities in other countries (known as Jews of the 'Dispersion') and Pharisees of the more liberal school of Hillel, had shown considerable missionary zeal in winning converts to Judaism. The Pharisees were great evangelists, willing to 'traverse sea and land to make a single proselyte'. But these converts were required to obey the whole Jewish Law, both ritual and moral. Part of the condition for their full admission to the Jewish faith was the rite of circumcision. (Though it was possible to join in Jewish worship as 'God-fearers' – Cornelius was one of these – without taking upon themselves the

Matthew 23:15

Acts 10:22

whole burden of the Jewish Law.) Naturally the church leaders in Jerusalem, who were still practising Jews, supposed that any Gentiles who wished to become Christians should first become Jews, by being circumcised.

Acts 10:1–11:18

The experience of Peter with Cornelius had convinced them that it was possible for a Gentile to be converted and receive the power of the Holy Spirit. But when Paul and Barnabas had a successful mission among the Gentiles in Antioch it was a different matter. For one thing, Cornelius had been an adherent of the Jewish religion as a 'God-fearer', though not as a full proselyte; his case was therefore different from that of complete pagans. In addition, there does not appear to have been a widespread Christian movement connected with Cornelius at the time of Peter's visit; whereas in Antioch a church of Gentile believers was formed. The Jewish Christian leaders were willing to recognize that Paul and Barnabas were engaged in a commendable enterprise, but they refused to accept any responsibility for it.

When Peter later visited Antioch, he at first followed the custom established by Paul, and ate with the Gentile converts. This was something no Jew would normally do, though Peter himself had previously eaten with the family of Cornelius. But when more rigid Jews came from Judea, he gave it up and persuaded Barnabas to do

Galatians 2:11–14

the same. This inconsistency led to a severe rebuke from Paul.

This incident is the first example known to us of something that was to trouble Paul throughout his ministry. Although he knew that his own special mission was to Gentiles, Paul could never forget his own race. He was proud of being a Jew. Wherever he went, his first approach was always to the Jews and to those who accepted Judaism. On more than one occasion he raised money for the underprivileged Jewish Christians in Jerusalem. When he came to consider the position of the Jewish race as God's own people, he felt so passionately that he could write: 'I could wish that I myself were

Romans 9:3

accursed and cut off from Christ for the sake of my brethren, my kinsmen by race.' Yet in his heart he knew that the Jews were wrong; they had not recognized God's chosen Messiah.

From the beginning of his ministry Paul was an individualist. His commission was unique, just as his conversion had been. But the rumblings of discord first heard in Antioch were to develop into a full peal of thunder in a very short time, as Paul began to fulfil the terms of his calling.

What happened after Paul's conversion?

In our account of what happened after Paul's conversion on the Damascus road, we have taken information from Acts and from Paul's letter to the Galatians. By combining the two sources the order of events emerges as follows:

● Paul's conversion (Acts 9:3–19; 22:6–16; 26:9–18; compare with Galatians 1:11–17).

● A brief stay in Damascus (Acts 9:19b)
● A visit to 'Arabia' (Galatians 1:17).
● Work in Damascus for something like three years (Galatians 1:17; possibly Acts 9:20–22).
● Paul's first visit to Jerusalem after his conversion (Acts 9:26–30; Galatians 1:18–24).
● Paul's stay in Tarsus (Acts 9:30;

Today orthodox Jews still observe detailed regulations concerning food, clothing and Sabbath activity. These male members of a Russian Jewish congregation talk with their Rabbi over cakes and wine.

Opposite. The church at Antioch sent Paul and Barnabas with relief funds to help the Christians in Jerusalem. This early Byzantine structure in Antioch has been claimed as the first Christian church building.

11:25; Galatians 1:21).
● Barnabas joins the Christian movement among the Gentiles in Antioch (Acts 11:20–24).
● Paul joins Barnabas in Antioch (Acts 11:25 –26).
● Paul and Barnabas visit Jerusalem with famine relief for the church there, fourteen years after Paul's conversion (Acts 11:29–30; 12:25; Galatians 2:1–10).

The view that we have taken here is by no means universally accepted, especially by German scholars. The question is: Can Paul's own account of his contact with the Jerusalem apostles be reconciled with the account in Acts?

Paul lays great emphasis on the visit which he speaks of in Galatians 2:1–10. He suggests that it was crucial for his entire ministry to the Gentiles. If we look in the book of Acts for an account of a visit which had such significance for Paul's ministry to the Gentiles, the occasion which immediately seems to meet this requirement is the one recorded in Acts 15:1–29, when Paul and Barnabas met in council with the other apostles and church leaders to decide once and for all what was to be required of Gentile Christians in relation to the Jewish Law (this is often known as 'the Council of Jerusalem'). The traditional view has therefore been to regard Acts 15:1–29 as an account of the same meeting as Galatians 2:1–10. If this view is accepted, however, two major problems present themselves:

First, according to Acts 15:1–29, the council visit resulted in a thorough and wide-ranging discussion of the very issues with which Paul was dealing when he wrote Galatians. The Council debated the question of Gentile Christians and the Law of the Old Testament. In Acts 15:28–29 we have the details of an agreement worked out by the Council with Paul and Barnabas, and apparently accepted by all as a basis for the admission of Gentiles to the Christian church. Yet in Galatians 2:1–10 Paul makes no reference to any such agreement, even though it would have been crucial in this defence of his own position. In Galatians 2:6 he declares that the Jerusalem church leaders 'added nothing to me', which is a very different story from that in Acts 15, where they insisted that he should conform to the rules they laid down.

Secondly, if Acts 15:1–29 refers to the same events as Galatians 2:1–10, there is a historical discrepancy between the account in Acts and that in Galatians. For between Paul's conversion and the council visit Acts tells of two earlier visits to Jerusalem (Acts 9:26; 11:30; 12:25), while Paul mentions only one (Galatians 1:18). It is inconceivable that Paul could have been mistaken, for the whole of his argument in Galatians would be made invalid if he had omitted to mention even a single meeting. It would therefore be necessary to suppose that Luke must have been mistaken in his account in Acts, either by describing the same incident twice, or out of sheer ignorance of what really happened.

Besides these difficulties in accepting the association of Acts 15:1–29 with Galatians 2:1–10, several smaller points also suggest that in fact these two accounts are not describing the same meeting:

● In Acts 15:2, Paul and Barnabas were 'appointed' by the church at Antioch to go to Jerusalem and meet with 'the apostles and elders'. In Galatians, on the other hand, Paul says that he 'went up by revelation' (Galatians 2:2).

● The conference of Acts 15:1–29 was a semi-public affair, with the apostles and elders and 'the whole church' (15:22). In Galatians, however, Paul makes a special point of mentioning that the meeting was held in private (Galatians 2:2); and only James, Cephas (Peter) and John are mentioned (2:9).

● The outcome of the meeting of Acts 15:1–29 was a decision ('the Apostolic Decree') allowing Gentile converts to remain uncircumcised. It also insisted that they ought to observe certain Jewish dietary customs that would make it easier for Jews to enjoy fellowship with them (Acts 15:28–29). The outcome of the Galatians conference was a mutual recognition of Paul and Barnabas as apostles to the Gentiles, and of Peter and the others as apostles to the Jews (Galatians 2:9–10).

In view of these differences between Acts 15:1–29 and Galatians 2:1–10, it seems better to suppose that Galatians 2:1–10 records the same events as Acts 11:29–30; 12:25. There are at least four factors in favour of this:

● According to Galatians 2:2, Paul went to Jerusalem 'by revelation'. This expression could well have been intended to denote the prophecy of the famine by Agabus (Acts 11:28).

● Galatians 2:2 suggests that the meeting with the church leaders was a private one. Since Acts dates the famine either during, or shortly after, the persecution of Herod Agrippa I, this could easily explain such secrecy. The absence of James and other Christians from the meeting mentioned in Acts 12:17, which took place during this visit, also supports this reconstruction.

● It is possible to translate Galatians 2:10 as follows: 'Only they asked us to go on remembering the poor, and in fact I had made a special point of doing this very thing.' If this translation is accepted, Paul was in fact making a direct allusion to some such visit as is recorded in Acts 11:25.

● Since Paul obviously intended to recount every visit he made to Jerusalem from the time of his conversion to the time he was writing, if Acts 11:29–30 refers to the same events as Galatians 2:1–10 we can easily explain why he did not mention the Apostolic Decree (which would have been so relevant to his argument in Galatians). The simple fact was that the Apostolic Council had not yet taken place.

On this interpretation, Paul's letter to the Galatians must have been written sometime between the events of Acts 12:25 and Acts 15:1–29. This in turn raises other important questions about the date of Galatians (see chapter 16).

Chapter 16   Into all the world

Not long after they had returned from Jerusalem to Antioch, Paul and Barnabas entered a new phase of the work. The Gentile church there, under the guidance of the Holy Spirit, set the two friends Acts 13:1–3 apart and sent them off on their first real missionary expedition.

Cyprus

Acts 13:6–12

When they left Antioch, they first went to Cyprus, which was Barnabas' home country. It was there at Paphos, in the record of his interview with the Roman proconsul Sergius Paulus, that we first hear of Paul bringing the Christian message to a Roman official. From this point in Acts, he is always given his Roman name Paul rather than his Hebrew name Saul.

Acts 13:13–14

Acts 13:51–14:7

From Cyprus they sailed to the south coast of Asia Minor, and then crossed the mountains into Pisidia, to another town called Antioch. They then pressed on eastwards to a region called Lycaonia, part of the Roman province of Galatia. After successful

Paul's first missionary journey.

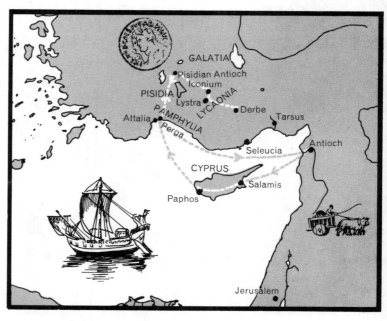

Paul and Barnabas' first visit on Cyprus was to Salamis. They started as they meant to continue by preaching first at the Jewish synagogue. The ruins of Salamis, which is near modern Famagusta, include a Roman theatre, harbour and a gymnasium, pictured here.

Opposite: Antioch in Pisidia, high in what is now central Turkey, was a Roman city with a strong Hellenistic Greek and Jewish culture – just the sort of place Paul chose for his visits. The aqueduct once carried by these arches provided Antioch's water-supply.

At Paphos Paul brought the Christian message to the Roman proconsul. These remains may have formed part of his residence, or the forum.

Acts 14:7–20   missionary work in several towns there they returned to Antioch in Syria by roughly the same route, except that they did not visit
Acts 14:21–28   Cyprus again.

In each town the apostles began their work in connection with the Jewish synagogue. Probably they felt that in this context they were likely to meet the kind of Gentile 'God-fearers' who would be most open to their message. On the return journey, Paul and Barnabas made a point of revisiting each new congregation of Christians that had been formed, consolidating them in their new
Acts 14:21–23   faith and appointing elders to be in charge of them.
Galatians 4:13–15   At some stage during this expedition Paul fell ill. He refers to a disease which gave him a repulsive appearance when he was visiting the Galatians. We also know that he suffered from a 'thorn in the
2 Corinthians 12:7   flesh', which is sometimes thought to have been epilepsy. But there is no real evidence that Paul was an epileptic, and the reference in Galatians may well suggest that he had some kind of eye disease.

The first Gentile churches

As a result of Paul's visits, both 'God-fearers' and complete pagans were converted to belief in Jesus Christ. Paul began to realize just how important his own call had been. His experiences at this time

also convinced him that Gentile believers should be admitted to the Christian fellowship, without being obliged to be circumcised or to observe other regulations of the Jewish Law. Paul had discovered after his own conversion that his new relationship to Jesus Christ also established a new relationship with other people – including those whom he would otherwise have despised. So now he found that, though he himself had been among the strictest of the Jews, he was united in a new and deeper way with non-Jewish pagans once they too had accepted the claims that Jesus Christ made on their lives. After his experience on the Damascus road, this was what Paul had come to expect. It had been made clear to him then that he was to fulfil a very special role in spreading the Christian message throughout the world. When Paul and Barnabas returned to Syrian Antioch, they found that the church there agreed with them on this point, and welcomed their success in evangelizing the peoples of southern Asia Minor.

Acts 14:27–28

Jews and Gentiles

Galatians 2:11–14

But this happy situation did not last long. Messengers from the Jerusalem church soon arrived in Antioch with a very different attitude. What was worse, they also visited the new congregations of Christians which Paul and Barnabas had just formed on their first missionary expedition. They began to cause havoc among these new Christians by telling them that Paul had only told them half the Christian message. According to Paul, if Gentiles were willing to accept the claims of Christ over their lives they would be given power by the Holy Spirit working within them to live the kind of life that was pleasing to God. To many Jewish Christians, this idea was blasphemous. They believed that God had revealed his will in the Old Testament, where it was clearly taught that in order to be a part of the divine community a person must be circumcised and observe many other regulations. How could Paul claim that these Gentiles were proper Christians when they had never even considered the full implications of God's Old Testament revelation?

It was through country like this that Paul and Barnabas travelled during their first missionary journey. This part of the Turkish central highlands is near Pisidian Antioch.

How dare he suggest that Christian morality could be attained by any means other than a strict application of Jewish rules and regulations to the life of the Christian?

The new converts were thrown into confusion by such teaching. All they knew was that they had accepted the message Paul declared; that their lives had been revolutionized by the same Lord whom Paul had met on the Damascus road; and that they were to trust that Lord to help them live lives that were pleasing to God. Many of them had never been followers of the Jewish religion, and had no idea what was in the Old Testament. Paul had given them no indication that it was necessary for them to find out in order to be acceptable to God.

But when these new Christians began to read the Old Testament under the guidance of these Jewish Christians, they found themselves faced with a mass of rules and regulations which they knew they could never hope to fulfil, even if it was necessary to do so for salvation. Some of them decided to make a brave attempt, and began by keeping the Jewish sabbath and possibly certain other Jewish festivals as well. A large number of them began to think about being circumcised, in order to fulfil what seemed to be the requirements of the Old Testament. But the great majority simply did not know what to do.

Galatians 4:8–11

Galatians 5:2–12

It was at this point that news of the situation reached Paul. He was naturally infuriated by what he heard. It was impossible for him to visit these churches again just at that time, so in the heat of the moment he decided that he must write a letter to them. This was the letter known to us as the letter to the Galatians.

Paul the letter writer

Acts 23:26–30

When Paul wrote letters to the Christians who were under his care, he naturally followed the common style of the day. We have an example in Claudias Lysias' letter to Felix. An ancient letter usually followed a more or less set pattern:

● It always began with the name of the writer, and then named the person it was sent to. Paul follows this quite closely.

● Then follows the greeting, usually a single word. But Paul often expanded this to include the traditional Hebrew greeting (*shalōm*, 'peace') together with a new, Christian greeting ('grace' – in Greek very similar to the normal everyday greeting).

● The third part of a Greek letter was a polite expression of thanks for the good health of the person addressed. This is usually expanded by Paul into a general thanksgiving to God for all that was praiseworthy in his readers.

● Next followed the main body of the letter. In Paul's letters this is often divided into two parts: doctrinal teaching (often in response to questions raised by his readers) and then advice on Christian living.

● Personal news and greetings came next. In Paul's case this is more often news of the churches and prominent individuals in them.

● There is often also in Paul's letters a note of exhortation or blessing in his own handwriting, as a kind of guarantee of the genuine and personal nature of the letter.

● Finally, ancient letters often ended with a single word of farewell. Paul almost always expands this into a full blessing and prayer for his readers.

Paul writes to the Galatian churches

After preaching in Perga, Paul and Barnabas completed their first missionary journey by sailing back from Attalia to Syrian Antioch. There they recounted their experiences to the church which had commissioned them. Attalia is now the modern resort of Antalya in southern Turkey.

A quick look at Galatians will show us just how closely Paul kept to this pattern, even when he was writing what must have been a very hurried letter. He begins by giving his own name: 'Paul an apostle', and he associates with his letter 'all the brethren who are with me'.

The people to whom he was writing are then named, in this case a group of churches: 'the churches of Galatia'. The greeting follows, 'grace ... and peace', and is expanded into a brief sentence of praise to God.

Galatians 1:1–2
Galatians 1:3
Galatians 1:4–5

One very significant omission is to be noted at this point. Nowhere in Galatians does Paul give thanks for the spiritual condition of his readers. There was nothing to be thankful for. They had not been Christians long enough for Paul to be able to refer to praiseworthy deeds done in the past (as he does, for example, in Philippians 1:3–11). And their condition at the moment of writing certainly gave Paul no cause for thanksgiving.

The main body of the letter now follows. It is divided roughly

Paul wrote to many of the churches which he had founded or visited. This example of a letter on papyrus was written in Greek in the first century AD and opens, 'Prokleios to his good friend Pekysis, greetings.'

Galatians 6:11–17

Galatians 6:18

into a doctrinal and theoretical section, from 1:6 to 4:31; and a practical description of Christian living from 5:1 to 6:10. No personal news and greetings finish this letter. Paul had no time for such pleasantries. But he does make a final appeal in his own handwriting. This supplies the interesting information that his own writing was much larger than that of the secretary who had written most of the letter – an observation which, incidentally, gives added probability to the suggestion that Paul may have suffered from bad eyesight. Paul ends his letter with a blessing which was also a prayer for his readers, and assures them that a power greater than their own is ready to their hand: 'The grace of our Lord Jesus Christ be with your spirit, brethren, Amen.'

Who were the Galatians?

In our earlier discussion of the order of events following Paul's conversion, it was suggested that the letter to the Galatians is to be dated about AD 48, written just before the visit of Paul and Barnabas to Jerusalem for the Apostolic Council. The arguments set out there are solid evidence for accepting this early date. On this reckoning Galatians would be the first letter that Paul ever wrote, and probably therefore the first part of the New Testament to be written. But what we have said so far is only half the story.

In addressing the letter, Paul says he is writing 'to the churches of Galatia'

(Galatians 1:2); and he calls his readers Galatians (3:1). Now the mention of people who could be called 'Galatians' would most naturally suggest the Celtic people of that name who lived in the region of Ankara in present-day Turkey, and who gave their name to an ancient kingdom there. The problem is that if these are the people referred to, we know from Acts that Paul did not visit them until his second and third missionary expeditions (Acts 16:6; 18:23). In that case he could not have written to them as early as AD 48.

It has also been argued that Paul's teaching in Galatians closely resembles

The location of Galatia.

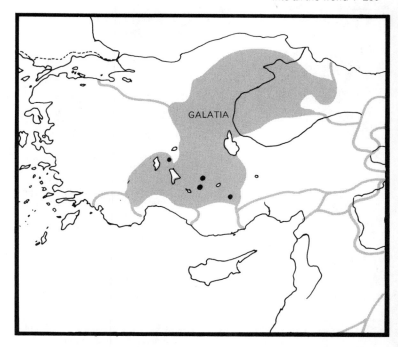

what he says in Romans, and without doubt Romans was written towards the end of his third missionary tour. Is it not therefore more reasonable to suppose that this letter was written to the people of north Galatia some time between AD 56 and 58? This view is in fact widely held, and the dating suggested in this book is a minority view, though one that has been, and continues to be, held by many very eminent scholars.

Sir William Ramsay was the first scholar of any importance to put forward the view adopted here. At the beginning of this century, he engaged in extensive archaeological investigations in the very areas of Asia Minor of which we are speaking. In the course of his work he discovered that the *Roman province* of Galatia included not only the ancient kingdom of the Galatians in the north of Asia Minor, but also the

southern region of Lycaonia ('south Galatia'), in which Paul had preached during his first missionary expedition and where he had established churches at Lystra, Derbe and Iconium. If we accept Ramsay's evidence, we have strong support for the viewpoint adopted here – that Galatians was written about AD 48 to the churches Paul had visited on his first missionary expedition.

The other argument put forward to support a later date for the letter (that it is similar to Romans) is weak. It is based on the subjective comparison of two documents. The evidence which led the great nineteenth-century scholar, J.B. Lightfoot, to give a late date to Galatians can just as easily be interpreted in a completely different way to support an early date for the letter!

Galatians

That has covered only the bare bones of the letter. The more important question is, what was Paul actually saying? Though Galatians is not an especially long and involved letter, it is not always very easy to understand Paul's meaning. This is partly because the letter was written hastily in the middle of a raging controversy. In such circumstances people do not express themselves in the ordered way they would in calmer moments. The

complexity of his expression also stems partly from the subject-matter. For Paul was as much at home in the Old Testament as we are in our daily newspapers. He quotes it with great freedom as he sets out to expound the twin principles of liberty and equality within the Christian fellowship.

Paul's letter falls conveniently into three main sections. He deals in turn with three false ideas that had been propounded by the Jewish Christians

('Judaizers') who had visited the Galatian churches.

Did Paul have any authority?

The first thing the Judaizers had said was that Paul was not a proper apostle. Because he had not been accredited by the original apostles in Jerusalem, he had no right to give any directions to new Christians, nor ought they to pay attention to what he said. We find Paul's reply to all this in Galatians 1:10–2:21. He makes it quite clear that he needed no authorization from Jerusalem or anywhere else, since he had himself met with the risen Christ.

The other apostles (except James, who had a similar experience to Paul, see 1 Corinthians 15:7) had all been disciples of Jesus during his ministry. But Paul was not inferior on that account, for he too had a face-to-face encounter with Jesus. It was this meeting that gave him his authorization as an apostle (Galatians 1:11–12). He had indeed visited Jerusalem on several occasions, but on none of them had he felt it necessary to obtain the permission of the original disciples to carry on his work, nor had they suggested that he needed such permission (1:18–2:10).

In fact, quite the opposite was the case; for, Paul says, 'when they saw that I had been entrusted with the gospel to the uncircumcised (or non-Jews), just as Peter had been entrusted with the gospel to the circumcision (the Jews) ... and when they perceived the grace that was given to me (by my encounter with the risen Christ), James and Cephas and John ... gave to me and Barnabas the right hand of fellowship, that we should go to the Gentiles and they to the circumcised' (Galatians 2:7–9).

The events at Antioch proved conclusively that Paul was in no way inferior to Peter (Cephas), commonly reckoned to be the greatest of the apostles. When Peter had broken off eating with Gentile Christians at Antioch, merely because some Jewish believers arrived from Jerusalem, Paul had no hesitation in opposing him 'to his face' (2:11). So far as we know Peter accepted the rebuke delivered to him on that occasion.

Christians and the Old Testament

After he has dealt with this malicious attack on his own credentials, Paul appeals briefly to the Galatians' own experience before going on to deal with the second piece of false teaching propounded by the Jewish intruders.

What they knew of Christ ought to have shown them that they had received the Holy Spirit (the mark of the true Christian, Romans 8:9) not because they had obeyed the Old Testament Law, but because they had exercised faith in Jesus (Galatians 3:1–5).

This leads straight into an attack on another part of their teachings. In the Old Testament the promise of the Messianic kingdom was given to Abraham and his descendants (Genesis 17:7–8). Therefore the Judaizers argued that anyone who wished to be in the Messianic kingdom must become members of Abraham's family by circumcision and continued obedience to the Old Testament Law (Genesis 17:9–14). Paul answers this in three ways, by appealing to the Old Testament itself:

● In Galatians 3:6–14, he points out that the blessings promised to Abraham belong to 'all who believe' (verse 9). Abraham had faith in God, and this faith was the basis of his acceptance by God (Genesis 12:1–4; see also Hebrews 11:8–12, 17–18). At the same time, 'all who rely on works of the law are under a curse' (verse 10). Everyday experience and the Old Testament both proved that in practice it was impossible to be justified in God's sight by keeping the Law.

● But was not the Law God's highest revelation in the Old Testament, surpassing all that had gone before it? No, says Paul. Since the Law (or Torah) came into effect long after Abraham's time, it could not possibly alter a direct promise made to him by God. The 'inheritance' promised to Abraham could not be obtainable by both Law and promise (verse 18). The Law had a rather different purpose in God's plan:

First, the Law served to show up sin as a transgression against God (Galatians 3:19; see also Romans 4:15; 5:13). Before it was given, the only law that humans had was the 'law of nature' expressing itself through their own conscience. After the Law was given by Moses, people saw wrongdoing for what it really was – defiance against God's will.

Secondly, the Law was given to be a teacher 'until Christ came, that we might be justified by faith' (Galatians 3:24). As people tried to gain salvation by their own efforts at keeping the Law, they realized that it was an impossible task. So the way was prepared for God's new act of grace in Jesus Christ.

● Paul now takes the argument to its logical conclusion (Galatians 3:25–4:7). The Old Testament Law was only effective 'till the offspring should come to whom the promise had been made' (verse 19). The 'offspring' *had* come in Jesus Christ. So the era of the Law was now finished, and to those who had faith in him, Christ would give freedom from the Law. Before they had been slaves to 'the elemental spirits of the universe' (which included the Law, 4:3). Now they were sons and heirs of the promise made to Abraham (4:4–7).

Freedom and legalism

By trying to put themselves under the Law and keeping the Jewish holy days, the Galatians were really trying to undo what God had already done for them in Christ. Paul was fearful that if they did this, he had laboured over them in vain (4:8–11). So he goes on to deal with another argument put forward by the Judaizing teachers. They had given 'scriptural' reasons to suggest that Christians ought to keep the Torah and to be circumcised. Paul answers in three ways:

● Paul looks again at the status of the Law (4:21–5:1). Again he appeals to the story of Abraham, this time using the incident of Sarah (a free woman) driving out Hagar the slave. This, he says, is an allegory of the superior position of the good news in Christ over against the legalism of the Jewish Law.

● Paul answers the queries about circumcision (5:2–12). He makes it clear that circumcision is of no value either way to Christians. It makes no difference whether Christians are circumcised or not. Their standing before God depends not on this kind of external sign but on 'faith working through love' (5:6). In the case of people like the Galatians, to submit to circumcision would actually be a denial of what Christ had done for them (5:2). In any case to be circumcised also obliged people to observe the whole of the Jewish Law (5:3). This was the very thing that Paul had just rejected, and which experience showed to be impossible anyway. The freedom that Christ brings is clearly incompatible with the 'yoke of slavery' (5:1) brought by circumcision and the Law.

● Paul deals with the problem of Christian behaviour (Galatians 5:13–6:10). One thing that marked the Jews off from other peoples in the ancient world was their very high moral standards, which came as a result of their close adherence to the Old Testament Law. The false teachers who visited Galatia had argued that if Christians did not follow the Jewish Law, they would have no guide for their conduct. They would be indistinguishable from the pagans around them. This was an important question, and one that was not easy to answer.

Paul had told the Galatian Christians that, if they accepted the risen Christ as Lord over their lives, the Holy Spirit would reproduce within them the life of Christ himself. This is the kind of thing he indicated in 2:20: 'I have been crucified with Christ; it is no longer I who live, but Christ who lives in me; and the life I now live in the flesh I live by faith in the Son of God who loved me and gave himself for me.'

Paul deals with the accusations of the Judaizers on this score by making four important statements:

First (5:13–15), 'freedom' in Christ does not mean a freedom to do what we like. It is a freedom to serve one another in love. Since the Holy Spirit aims to produce in Christians a Christ-like character, their freedom should obviously be demonstrated in ways that are consistent with this.

Secondly (5:16–26), though the Christian gospel does not lay down a list of do's and don'ts, 'those who belong to Christ Jesus have crucified the flesh with its passions and desires' (5:24). So the Christian's life will be marked out by the fruit of the Spirit. The demands of Christ are far more radical than those of a religion that only imposes rules and regulations from the outside. The Christian's whole personality has been revolutionized. Attitudes and behaviour have been changed from within. This was the same lesson that Jesus himself had taught: 'A sound tree cannot bear evil fruit, nor can a bad tree bear good fruit' (Matthew 7:18).

Thirdly (6:1–6), Christians should beware of judging others. They ought to recognize that they themselves could have no moral strength to do what was right, apart from the power of the Holy Spirit. They are to 'fulfil the law of Christ' by bearing 'one another's burdens' (6:2). This is very different from keeping externally imposed rules and regulations by their own efforts.

Fourthly (6:7–10), Paul sums up his advice. In order to reap the harvest of eternal life, they must sow not to the flesh – their own self-gratification – but to the Spirit – their new life given by Jesus Christ.

Then, finally, in Galatians 6:11–18, Paul makes his last appeal to his readers. He makes two further points against his opponents; then he makes two balancing statements of his own belief and practice.

His opponents, in spite of their high

pretensions, were in fact spiritually bankrupt (6:12). They 'want to make a good showing in the flesh', the very thing that Paul had denounced in the previous section of his argument (Galatians 6:8: 'he who sows to his own flesh will from the flesh reap corruption'). They are also inconsistent, even with their own starting-points; though they emphasize the outward sign of circumcision they are not willing to accept the spiritual discipline involved in keeping the Old Testament Law.

Paul knew that the truth revealed to him by the risen Christ was greater than anything else. So he says finally that the only real cause of boasting before God is that the Christian has been crucified to the world, through the cross of Christ.

When someone spoke of a cross in the first century, he meant only one thing – death. That is what Paul means when he writes of Christians sharing in the cross of Christ (Galatians 2:20). He is not urging them to be martyrs. But he is saying that Christians must die to themselves. They must give up their claims over their lives, and accept Jesus Christ as Saviour and Lord over every aspect of life. This kind of 'new creation' is the only thing of any value in the sight of God, and forms the sole qualifying mark of 'the Israel of God' (Galatians 6:14–16). Paul himself may be criticized because he is a Jewish deserter. But he has the mark of true spirituality before God: 'I bear on my body the marks of Jesus' (6:17).

This, then, is how Paul dealt with the problems of the churches of Galatia. If we want a slogan to sum it all up, and indeed to sum up the whole of Paul's conviction, we can find it in Galatians 6:15: 'in Christ, it is not circumcision or uncircumcision that counts, but the power of a new birth.'

The Apostolic Council

Acts 15:6–21
Acts 15:6–11

No doubt it was in this fashion that Paul set out his arguments at the Council of Jerusalem in AD 49. According to Acts even James, probably the most Jewish of the Jerusalem leaders, had to accept the truth of the main part of Paul's argument. The Jerusalem apostles agreed that there was no great doctrinal principle involved. But there was still the simple, practical problem of how Jews and Gentiles could meet together at the same table (including the communion table).

In order to make this possible the Jewish leaders suggested that Gentile converts should abstain from those activities that were particularly offensive to Jewish Christians: things like eating food that had been offered in pagan sacrifices, eating meat from which the blood had not been drained, or practising pagan marriage habits which did not accord with the Jewish Law and custom.

Acts 15:19–21, 28–29

This arrangement was accepted by Paul. But it was a compromise, and a compromise solution is hardly ever very successful. This one appears to have been no exception, for when Paul came to face the same problems over again in Corinth, he did not refer to the terms of the Apostolic Decree at all, but argued once more from the basic principles involved in the matter.

1 Corinthians 8:1–13; 10:19–11:1

Why did Paul accept the Council's decree?

There is another problem with the Apostolic Decree, however, which is not explained quite so easily. We must face the fact that if Paul had written Galatians just before he went to the Council, the narrative of Acts 15 depicts him accepting something that he had vehemently rejected in Galatians – the application of some sort of 'law' to Gentile Christians.

One solution to this problem has been *to suppose that the Apostolic Council never actually happened*. This view suggests it was invented by Luke for the purpose of showing that both Jewish and Gentile sections of the church were united in the early years of its history. It is largely the result of supposing that the narrative of Acts cannot be reconciled with Galatians 1–2. We have already seen that this is no real difficulty. So we need not suppose that Luke was either unknowingly or deliberately falsifying the record when he wrote of the Council. We have also noticed that in those areas where his story can be tested by external evidence, Luke emerges as a first-class historian. We have no reason to suspect his reliability at this point on general historical grounds.

Another possibility is *to suppose that the Apostolic Decree was in fact addressed to just a small and relatively local group of churches*, namely those mentioned in Acts 15:36–16:5. If this was the case, there would be no difficulty over the fact that Paul did not quote the Decree in 1 Corinthians.

Perhaps a better explanation is simply that *Paul was at heart a conciliatory sort of man*. Having said his piece in Galatians, and having won the theological debate in Jerusalem, he was content to accept that regardless of theological difficulties Jews and Gentiles had to live together within the local church, and the acceptance of these guidelines was a simple means of achieving this.

As we go on to look at Paul's experiences in other churches, we will see that time and again he bent over backwards to accommodate people whose viewpoint was different from his own (see also 1 Corinthians 9:19–23). He realized that a divided church was a poor witness to the non-Christian world, and at this stage of his ministry the Apostolic Decree seemed the best solution to a pressing problem.

Chapter 17 Paul the missionary

Back to Galatia

After his crucial meeting with the leaders of the Jerusalem church, Paul went off again into the Gentile world fired with a new enthusiasm. He was determined to revolutionize the Roman Empire in the name of Jesus Christ.

He began his second expedition with a new companion. Barnabas did not go along because Paul was unwilling to give a second chance to John Mark, Barnabas' cousin who had deserted them during their first expedition. But Paul found a keen helper in Silas, one of the men sent to Antioch to explain the decisions of the Jerusalem Council to the church there. In the course of his expedition, he was to acquire two other companions in addition to Silas: Timothy, who joined them at Lystra, and Luke who joined them at Troas.

Acts 15:36–40

Acts 15:30–33

Acts 16:1–3
Acts 16:10–12

The first thing Paul did on this tour was to revisit some of the congregations which he had founded in south Galatia during his first expedition from Antioch. He had been wanting to see them ever since he heard of the interference of the Judaizers in their congregations. During this further visit he no doubt explained that, although as Christians they were free from all the legal requirements of the Jewish Law, it would be desirable if they could agree

Paul was summoned to Europe by a dream in which a Macedonian (a man from northern Greece) appealed to him. This Latin inscription from Philippi includes the name of the Roman province of Macedonia.

to accept the arrangement that had been worked out in Jerusalem. In this way Jewish Christians could feel free to meet with them.

Acts 16:4

After this, Paul and Silas went on with Timothy, who had joined them in Lystra, through Phrygia and Galatia – perhaps this time north Galatia. Paul had planned to go to the Roman province of Asia, the area round Ephesus in the west of Asia Minor, and also into Bithynia, the province to the north which adjoined the Black Sea. But both these intentions were expressly forbidden by the Holy Spirit (we do not know by what means). So Paul and his companions went on into Troas, ancient Troy, in the part of Asia Minor nearest to Europe.

Acts 16:6

Acts 16:6–7

During the night Paul had a dream of a Macedonian appealing for help. This was recognized by Paul as a directive from God to cross the Aegean Sea into Europe. This was not the first time that Christian missionaries had gone into Europe, for at a later date Paul wrote to a large and flourishing church at Rome, which had not been founded by his own efforts. But Paul's entry into Europe at this point was a distinct step forward in the achievement of his desire to spread the good news of Jesus throughout the whole of the Roman Empire.

Acts 16:9–10

Paul's second missionary journey.

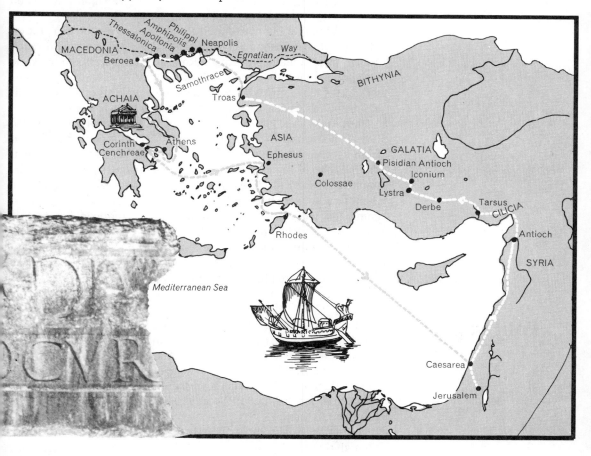

Philippi

Acts 16:13

The first town the missionaries visited was Philippi. This was a Roman colony in the north-east corner of Macedonia, largely populated by retired soldiers from the Roman army. Although the city had such a large Gentile population, Paul still followed his earlier custom of first going to the Jews at their usual meeting-place, in this case simply called 'a place of prayer' by the riverside. There were so few Jews in Philippi that they did not even have a synagogue building.

Among Paul's hearers at this place of prayer was Lydia, and she was the first one to become a Christian in Philippi. If Paul had any doubts about abandoning his earlier plans and moving instead into Europe, they must have disappeared with the conversion of this woman. She was a native of Thyatira, a city in the very area of Asia Minor where Paul had been intending to go. She may well have been the one who first took the Christian message to her home town,

Revelation 2:18–29

where there was soon a large Christian church. In any event, her belief in Jesus Christ clearly made a revolutionary change in her life. Though she was a woman of some importance, her own home was soon opened to Paul and his friends and became the headquarters of their activity. Once again it was demonstrated that belief in Jesus Christ created a unity of fellowship between men and women that overthrew all normal social and racial barriers.

One thing that happened at Philippi gives us a good illustration of some of the reasons why the Christian faith aroused so much antagonism in many parts of the Roman Empire at this time. As he was going about his evangelistic work, Paul was continually pestered by a slave girl who, by means of some kind of second sight exercised in trances, had brought a large income to her owners.

Luke 4:16–21

Paul knew that Jesus had promised to give 'release to the captives'; and he had declared clearly that Christians could be released from captivity to the Jewish Law, and from bondage to the social distinctions of the day. Surely Christ's apostles should act in his name to release a girl like this from slavery to her owners and to the demons who were believed to possess her? Jesus had already overcome the very powers of evil which had reduced her to this condition. So Paul cured her of the spirit of divination in the name

Acts 16:16–18

of Christ. At this, her owners were so angry that they accused Paul and Silas of creating a public disturbance by recommending

Acts 16:19–21

customs that were unlawful for Roman citizens.

Paul in prison

Accusing someone of causing a public nuisance could always be guaranteed to arouse a Roman official to some sort of action. This occasion was no exception. Paul and Silas were flogged and thrown into prison. They had shown a slave girl the way to a new freedom in Christ, only to lose their own freedom. Not that they worried about that, for they spent the night singing praises to God for his goodness to them.

During the night an earthquake broke open the prison doors. Though they could have escaped, they chose to remain, along with

As Roman colonists, the Philippians had the same rights and privileges as the Italians themselves. This Latin inscription includes the city's name.

the rest of the prisoners. Their jailor was ready to kill himself, thinking they had already escaped. But when confronted with the messengers of Christ he realized that they were men with an inner dynamic he did not possess. He immediately asked the secret of their power, and became a Christian himself, along with his family.

After the conversion of this man Paul knew that there was no need for him to remain in prison. In fact he ought never to have been there in the first place, for he was a Roman citizen. Paul therefore claimed his rights as a citizen, demanding from the city authorities an apology for the illegal beating he had suffered. Then he left the city of Philippi altogether.

Acts 16:22–40

Luke stayed in Philippi to look after the new Christians. They came from all levels of society and included a prominent local trader, a soothsayer who looked for business in the main streets, and the town's jailor and his family. Small wonder that at one of the next places they visited Paul, Silas and Timothy were described as 'men who have turned the world upside down'.

Acts 17:6

The great Roman roads were of vital military and commercial importance. The stone slabs of the Egnatian Way were worn down by the heavy traffic. Paul's group used this route to travel on from Philippi to Thessalonica.

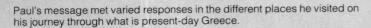

Paul's message met varied responses in the different places he visited on his journey through what is present-day Greece.

During his second missionary journey Paul revisited many of the places where he had previously been, and travelled hundreds of miles across the mountains of what is now central Turkey.

Paul first set foot in Europe at Neapolis, the modern port of Kavalla in northern Greece. Neapolis stood at the terminus of the Egnatian Way, the military road connecting Rome with the east. From Neapolis he went to Philippi, leading city of the district.

Athens symbolized the tradition of classical learning. The Acropolis, on which the Parthenon was built as a temple to the goddess Athene, served as both a focus of worship and a defensive stronghold.

Philippi was an important Roman colony standing on the Egnatian Way. Its citizens fostered great civic pride. It was a largely Gentile city, and in Paul's time the 'God-fearers' used to meet by the river bank.

Corinth, like Athens, was dominated by a stonghold built on a steep rock above the city. In the foreground is the Tribunal, near to which stood the other principal public buildings, including the theatre and *agora*.

The next towns the three friends came to were Thessalonica and Beroea, in both of which there were large Jewish communities. In both places many converts were made, and in both there was severe opposition from the Jews. This seems to have been directed specifically at Paul himself, as a former Pharisee, since Silas and Timothy were able to stay on there when Paul went on to Athens.

Acts 17:4–15

Athens

So Paul arrived in Athens, the intellectual centre of the ancient world. By this time it had lost its former claims to political greatness. But it was still a university town to which many young Romans were sent to study philosophy or to be initiated into one of the many oriental mystery religions which found a home there. The Athenians still liked to have a good debate. When the news got around that the teacher of a new religion had arrived from the east, Paul was called before the court of the Areopagus, which evidently believed that taking an interest in philosophy was part of its job of ruling the city.

In speaking at Athens to people who had no Jewish or biblical background at all, Paul adopted a completely different approach from his earlier work. However, it is comparable with the way he had addressed pagans in Lystra. When addressing Jews and Gentile

Acts 17:22–31
Acts 14:15–17

'God-fearers', Paul could begin from the Old Testament and point out how the promises made there had been fulfilled in the life, death and resurrection of Jesus. At Athens, he began from the Greek view of God as creator, benefactor and 'presence' within the universe. He then went on to speak of the human search for God, who is 'not far from each one of us', a statement which he supported by quotations from the Greek poets Epimenides and Aratus.

Acts 17:27

Paul condemned as a form of ignorance the idolatry which he saw in Athens, with arguments that had been used in philosophical Greek thought since the days of Xenophanes in the sixth century BC. The same kind of arguments had also been used by Jewish missionaries when they spoke in support of their own faith in one God, and we can see here several resemblances to the teaching of the early Christian evangelist Stephen.

Acts 17:29–31

Acts 7:48–50

Having condemned idolatry, Paul went on to call his hearers to repentance and the worship of the one true God. So far every-

Acts 17:30

Paul opened his address to the Court of the Areopagus by referring to an altar dedicated to an 'unknown god'. This example of a similar altar stands in the Palatine Gardens, Rome, and dates from the period of the Roman Republic in the century before Christ.

Opposite. The Court of the Areopagus, where Paul was called on to speak, met in one of the colonnaded buildings surrounding the market-place (*agora*) in the foreground. Overlooking the *agora* are the Acropolis (centre) and Areopagus (sometimes known as Mars Hill) from which the court took its name.

thing would be received sympathetically by many of his Greek audience. In concluding his address, Paul referred to the coming judgement of the world, of which he said an assurance had been given in the fact that God raised Jesus from the dead. At this point, the Athenians were either amused or annoyed by what he said. It

Acts 17:34

was not the Platonic doctrine of the immortality of the soul that Paul was preaching, but the Jewish belief in the resurrection of the body, something absurd and abhorrent to intelligent Greeks. Even so there were a few converts at Athens.

Corinth

Acts 18:11

Acts 18:7

Acts 18:8

Paul now pressed on to Corinth, an ancient Greek city that had been rebuilt as a Roman colony in 46 BC. It was a prosperous trading centre, and also had a name for permitting vice of every kind.

Paul made Corinth the headquarters of his work for Christ for the next eighteen months. While he was there he made friends with Aquila and his wife Priscilla who, like himself, were tent-makers. As before, he began his work in the Jewish synagogue, but left when he met the usual Jewish opposition, dramatically shaking out his clothes before doing so. He then started preaching from the home of a new Christian, Titius Justus, who lived next door to the synagogue. As a result of Paul's work, many inhabitants of Corinth became Christians, including Crispus, one of the synagogue rulers. A very large and influential Christian congregation was established in the city.

We can date Paul's eighteen-month stay in Corinth by this inscription from Delphi. It shows that Gallio, who was magistrate at the time of Paul's visit, came to Corinth as proconsul in AD 51 or 52.

After Paul had been there for about eighteen months, the Jews decided to make a concerted effort to have him convicted of some crime. There was a new Roman magistrate, the proconsul Gallio, who was brother of the Roman poet-philosopher, Seneca. The charge failed, because Gallio would not judge Paul under the Jewish Law, and according to Roman law he had committed no crime. This is one of the incidents in Paul's life which we can date fairly precisely. The period of Gallio's office in Corinth is recorded

This inscription, from one of Thessalonica's gates, mentions the rulers of the city as 'politarchs' – the term used in the account of Paul's visit in Acts. It helps reinforce the authenticity of the account in the Bible.

in a copy of a letter sent from the emperor and preserved on a stone inscription: it suggests that Gallio's year of office must have been either AD 51–52 or AD 52–53.

More letters

At an early point in Paul's stay in Corinth, Silas and Timothy, who had stayed in Thessalonica, arrived with news of the church there. In the period of about six months since their conversion, the Thessalonian Christians had lived up to their responsibilities so well that the Christian message had been spread by their example through the whole of the surrounding area. But there were also some problems in the church. There had been attacks by the Jews, and maybe a more general persecution. There was perhaps some sexual immorality, possibly a failure to respect the leaders of the church, and a curiosity about the state of Christians who died. So Paul wrote to encourage them in their difficulties and to give them direct guidance on their particular problems. His letter is preserved for us in the New Testament as 1 Thessalonians.

1 Thessalonians 1:1–10

1 Thessalonians 1:6
1 Thessalonians 4:3–8
1 Thessalonians 5:12–13

1 Thessalonians

After his usual introduction, Paul began by commending his readers for their faithfulness to the Christian message. Paul had told them how the risen and living Christ had revolutionized his own life, and he had challenged them with the fact that Christ could do the same for them by the power of the Holy Spirit. The Thessalonians had fully accepted this message, and the result had been that a strong church had been established. In addition, by the example of their changed lives, the Christian message had been commended to the pagan world around them. So much for the accusation flung against Paul in Galatia, that his message of freedom in Christ would lead to low moral standards! Quite the reverse had happened here, as the whole of Macedonia and Achaia saw the difference that the Christian faith made to the way of life of these believers (1 Thessalonians 1:2–10).

Paul and his converts

This, as Paul explains, was exactly what he and his helpers had hoped would happen. When they first visited Thessalonica with the Christian message they had been careful not to advertise themselves, but to draw attention to what they knew the risen Christ could do in the lives of the Thessalonians. Though they had been sent out on the authority of God himself, and with the approval of the Jewish churches, they followed the example of their Lord and Master, taking a low place as the servants of all: 'we were gentle among you, like a nurse taking care of her children ... we were ready to share with you not only the gospel of God but also our own selves' (2:7–8).

For this they had been well rewarded. The Thessalonians responded to the word of God. They recognized it as the means whereby they could enter into the full reality of life: 'when you received the word of God which you heard from us, you accepted it not as the word of men, but as what it really is, the word of God, which is at work in you believers' (2:13). This, and the news brought by Silas and Timothy, proved a great encouragement to Paul as he worked in difficult conditions in Corinth (2:17–3:8).

Nevertheless, there was something lacking in their faith (3:10). So Paul set out to try to give good advice on the difficulties which Timothy had reported to him.

How should Christians behave?

One thing that often posed the greatest problem for converted pagans was the question of personal morality. In the pagan society of the day immorality of all kinds was normal. From what Paul says in chapter 1 of his letter, it is clear that the majority of the Thessalonian Christians had been enabled by the power of the Holy Spirit to overcome the pressure to be like their fellow citizens in this respect. But it was still necessary to reinforce what he had no doubt told them when he founded their church (4:1–8).

This was a subject that naturally led Paul to think of what he had written earlier in Galatians on the same matter: 'you were called to freedom ... only do not use your freedom as an opportunity for the flesh, but through love be servants of one another' (Galatians 5:13). The Thessalonians had learnt this lesson well: 'you yourselves have been taught by God to love one another; and indeed you do love all the brethren throughout Macedonia' (1 Thessalonians 4:9–10).

It was a lesson that could never be over-emphasized. In a world in which the established order was rapidly changing, and in which men and women were frantically grasping at whatever religion came their way, one of the most important things the church could do was to display the love of Christ (4:9–12). Was not this what Jesus himself had taught? 'By this all men will know that you are my disciples, if you have love for one another' (John 13:35). The advice is here repeated and reinforced by Paul.

What about the future?

One thing above all was troubling the church at Thessalonica. They understood well the relationship that ought to exist among the members of their church. But what about those Christians who had died shortly after Paul's departure from the city? Paul found the answer to that in his conviction that the Lord he knew was present in the church by the operation of the Holy Spirit would one day come back openly and triumphantly (4:13–18). Meanwhile, the Thessalonian Christians should not worry unduly about loved ones who had died: 'since we believe that Jesus died and rose again, even so, through Jesus, God will bring with him those who have fallen asleep' (4:14).

Paul realized the possible trap in emphasizing what God would do in the future. So he went on to remind the Thessalonian Christians that their belief in the future return (or *parousia*) of Jesus was no excuse for inactivity in the present. Though some people would not be prepared for 'the day of the Lord', Christians ought to be. Their business was not to try and calculate 'the times and the seasons' (5:1), but to 'encourage one another and build one another up' (5:11).

Living the Christian life

Finally, Paul gave some advice to his readers on a number of topics, summarizing all that he had said before (5:12–21):

● In the church, the Christians should:
respect those who laboured among them – the elders whom Paul had presumably appointed in their church; be at peace among themselves (a repetition and reinforcement of what he had said in 4:9–12); encourage one another in their faith in Christ (5:14).

● In their everyday life, the Christians should:
return good for evil (5:15) – one of the most characteristic marks of the Christian (see also Matthew 5:44); 'rejoice always' (5:16).

● In their individual relationship to God, the Christians must:
live in an attitude of prayer (5:17);
allow the Holy Spirit to direct their lives (5:19–20).
Paul signs off with his usual blessing and greeting, making a last appeal and promise to his readers. He knew that the secret of the Christian faith was the work of the living Lord operating in the lives of his followers. This was what he wanted them to keep in the forefront of their minds: 'He who calls you is faithful, and he will do it' (5:24).

But the Thessalonians were soon diverted away from the importance of God's faithfulness. They began instead to speculate on what Paul had said about the state of Christians who died, and the expected return (*parousia*) of Jesus. It was not long before Paul had to write another letter to help sort out the difficulties which, to some extent, the Thessalonian Christians seem to have invented for themselves out of certain parts of his first letter. Paul's second letter, known as 2 Thessalonians, is found alongside his first in our New Testament.

2 Thessalonians

In this second, shorter letter to the Thessalonians Paul clarifies three main points:

The church and its enemies

From what he says in 2 Thessalonians 1:5–12 it appears that the church had come under increasingly fierce persecution. This was to be expected; for the more widely known their love and Christian character became, the more could their enemies be expected to increase. The Jews and Romans never bothered about a religious faith that meant nothing to those holding it; but the revolutionary character of the life of the Thessalonian church naturally drew their attention to what was going on. It would be impossible to turn the world upside down without provoking some reaction from that world. Paul reminds these Christians that though for the moment things may be difficult, God is on their side. He will ultimately vindicate them.

The church and the future

A more subtle form of 'persecution' had also come into the church, with the appearance of letters claiming to be written by Paul and his associates (2 Thessalonians 2:1–12). Fanatics of some kind had taken advantage of Paul's mention of the *parousia* of Jesus in his earlier letter, and used the occasion to put their own point of view on the subject.
    Paul had to warn the Thessalonian Christians 'not to be quickly shaken in mind or excited, either by spirit or by word, or by letter purporting to be from us, to the effect that the day of the Lord has come' (2:2). The precise meaning of the suggestion that 'the day of the Lord has come' is difficult to establish. In 1 Corinthians we find mention of people who thought that the resurrection (which was associated with the end of things, and the *parousia* of Christ) had already taken place. On the basis of this belief they indulged in all kinds of immoral practices (1 Corinthians 15:12–58). But it is difficult to connect the two groups of people in any direct way. In any event, Paul goes on to emphasize here that in his view the *parousia* of Jesus and all that it entails was not an event that could take place invisibly or mystically (which would need to be the case if it had already happened). On the contrary, he fixes his own hope firmly in history by making it clear that certain historical events connected with 'the man of lawlessness' (2:3–12), would herald the return of Christ.

The church and society

The outcome of the interest in future events that had arisen in Thessalonica was that some of the Christians had stopped living a normal life. They had opted out of society and were idly waiting for Christ to return, an attitude which Paul criticized severely. He regarded the Christian not as a person who shirked duties by becoming a religious hermit, but as someone who played a full part in the life of society. People who did not do this, however 'spiritual' their motive, should be disciplined by the church. It was not very often that Paul instructed a church

The Arch of Galerius, an impressive Roman structure, straddled the Egnatian Way at Thessalonica. Modern Thessaloniki is the second largest city of Greece.

to take disciplinary action against one of its members, but this was one such case. Of course, the other Christians were to do this in a way that brought glory to the Lord whom they were serving: 'Do not look on him as an enemy, but warn him as a brother' (3:15).

Even with all their problems, however, the Thessalonian Christians had learned the true secret of the Christian way of life that Paul had shown them. They were rapidly becoming the kind of congregation of which Paul could be proud: 'your faith is growing abundantly, and the love of every one of you for one another is increasing' (1:3).

Did Paul write 2 Thessalonians?

In our analysis of 1 and 2 Thessalonians, we have assumed that Paul wrote them both, the second one in response to problems that had arisen subsequent to his first letter. But it has occasionally been suggested that the two letters are so individually distinctive that if Paul wrote one of them, he cannot have written the other. Since 2 Thessalonians is the shorter and less comprehensive, this one has most often been questioned, for a number of reasons.

A different eschatology In 1 Thessalonians 4:13–5:11, Paul writes of the coming of Jesus as an imminent event. Christians are warned not to be taken by surprise when it comes. But in 2 Thessalonians 2:1–12, Paul lists a sequence of events that will take place before the *parousia* – and this, it is argued, removes the element of immediacy from it. Paul can hardly have held both views at once. But this argument is not as impressive as it seems:

● Though 'signs of the end' are not listed in 1 Thessalonians, they are implied in 5:1, where Paul writes, 'There is no need to write to you, brothers, about the times and occasions when these things will happen.' This statement seems to suggest that Paul thought they already knew about such matters, and when he proceeds to warn his readers not to be taken by surprise, it is precisely because they, of all people, should be able to recognize when Jesus is about to return.

● The two letters deal with different issues. In the first place, Paul had been asked a personal question about the fate of Christians who died – and he gave his answer on an appropriate personal level. But the question behind 2 Thessalonians is quite different, and concerns people who were saying that the 'day of the Lord' was here already. This was a quite different kind of argument, and it demanded a different sort of answer – not this time from a personal perspective, but on a broader cosmic level.

A different tone 2 Thessalonians is said to be more formal than 1 Thessalonians. Here again, the alleged differences are nothing like as great as some seem to think. The writer of 2 Thessalonians still has a deep concern for his readers. And if, as we have suggested, 1 Thessalonians had been wilfully misunderstood by some people, it is hardly surprising that Paul should have been sterner with them the second time. We can see exactly the same change of tone in the later correspondence between Paul and the church at Corinth – and for the same reasons.

Too many similarities This is almost the opposite argument – not that the two letters are different, but that they are too much alike! Some similar words and phrases are used in both, and according to some this indicates that 2 Thessalonians is just a rewritten form of 1 Thessalonians – rewritten, presumably, by someone else later than the time of Paul.

Here again, this is a very slender basis on which to reach such a conclusion:

● Why would anyone wish to produce such a 'rewritten' version of one of Paul's letters? The only plausible possibility would be to try and contradict, or correct, what was later seen as an erroneous idea in 1 Thessalonians. If the eschatological perspective of 1 and 2 Thessalonians was different, then that could perhaps provide an explanation. But we have already seen that this is not the case.

● In any case, why should an author not repeat himself? Even today, if we engage in a long correspondence we will often refer to previous letters as we write later ones – and there is no reason to suppose that Paul could not have done the same. We certainly know that was the practice among other Greek letter writers. Especially when giving personal advice in a continuing situation, it is often necessary to say the same things more than once.

● In any case, the actual verbal similarities between 1 and 2 Thessalonians are not very extensive. At least two thirds of 2 Thessalonians is quite new; and much of the rest consists of standardised terminology which was part of the stock-in-trade of the letter writer – the equivalent of our 'Dear sir', or 'Cordially yours'.

All these problems are more apparent than real. The kind of distinctions that some have found may seem to be significant to the scholar in the detachment of a study. But they are the kind of variations and repetitions that happen every day in real life, especially in dealing with situations such as these letters presuppose.

It was in Thessalonica that Paul had been accused of 'turning the world upside down'. The congregation of Christians that he left behind him there continued this activity. As we read the letters Paul wrote to them, it is easy to conclude that the Thessalonian church was in serious difficulties. But we must not allow a few trivial criticisms to blind us to the fact that this is one of the very few congregations that Paul commends so warmly for their Christ-like character. The encouragement he received from this church must have been a great help to him as he faced the next big test of his life's work.

Paul's strategy for evangelism

Paul was perhaps the most successful Christian missionary there has ever been. In less than a generation he travelled the length and breadth of the Mediterranean world, establishing growing and active Christian communities wherever he went.

What was his secret? Paul, of course, was always conscious that he was only a messenger, and that what really brought a change to the lives of those whom he met was the power of God's Holy Spirit. As he considered the many hardships that he had to endure, he described himself as a 'common clay pot', just a temporary container for the renewing power of God himself (2 Corinthians 4:7).

But Paul was also a sophisticated strategist. His route was never haphazard, and his methods of communication were based on considerable insight into the ways people think and take decisions.

Paul was a frontier evangelist, but he himself never visited a geographical frontier! He could have spent months, even years, trekking through uncharted territory, or making his way laboriously across country paths to reach remote places. He did neither of these things. Instead, he took advantage of the major highways the Romans had built across their empire. Combined with regular sea routes, they gave ready access to all the major centres of population, and these were the places Paul visited. He knew that he could never personally take the gospel to every man and woman throughout the empire. But if he could establish enthusiastic groups of Christians in some of the key cities, then they in turn could spread the good news into the more remote areas. Moreover, visitors from rural districts often had to visit the nearest city, and they too could be reached with the gospel, which they could then take home to their own people. This is what had happened on the Day of Pentecost in Jerusalem, and Paul was well aware of the great potential that such a strategy offered. At least one of the churches to which Paul later wrote a letter – Colossae – was founded like this.

Paul was also aware of the need for variety in his presentation of the Christian message. A cynic once described a sermon as 'A set of answers to questions that nobody is asking'. Some modern sermons may be like that. But not Paul's. The great secret of Jesus' success had been his ability to speak to people wherever he found them. When he was in the fields, he spoke of growing crops (Mark 4:1–9). With families, he spoke of children (Matthew 19:13–15). With fishermen, the subject was fish (Mark 1:14–18). Paul was the same. He went to people wherever they would listen – in the Jewish synagogues, in the market places, even in the pagan temples. In the synagogue at Thessalonica, he began with the Old Testament (Acts 17:2–3). At Athens, he started from the 'unknown god' for whom the Greeks were searching (Acts 17:22–31). In Ephesus, he was prepared to engage in public debates about the meaning of the Christian gospel (Acts 19:9).

Modern readers of Paul's letters may think they can reduce his message to a collection of abstract ideas on subjects like sin, or justification, or expiation. But that was not how Paul preached. He began where his hearers were, and was prepared to address himself to their needs. Sometimes preaching itself was the wrong method of approach – and in that case, Paul and his helpers were always ready to get alongside people to help them in the everyday difficulties of living. This was part of the secret of success in Thessalonica: 'we were gentle when we were with you, like a mother taking care of her children ... ready to share with you not only the Good News from God but even our own lives' (1 Thessalonians 2:7–8).

It was this sensitivity to people, and flexibility in his evangelism, that Paul was later to encapsulate in saying, 'I make myself everybody's slave in order to win as many people as possible ... all things to all men, that I may save some of them by whatever means are possible' (1 Corinthians 9:19–22).

Chapter 18 Paul the pastor

Acts 18:18–21

Acts 18:22

Ancient Ephesus was an impressive city with baths, libraries, a theatre and market-place. The streets were paved with marble. At a lecture hall called the 'Hall of Tyrannus' Paul rented rooms to teach people his message. The harbour, long-since silted up, lies in the distance here.

When Paul left Corinth he paid a short visit to Ephesus, and then returned direct to Caesarea in Palestine. From there he went straight to Antioch in Syria. After a short stay there he began what is often called his 'third missionary journey', which was not really a missionary expedition at all in the same way as his two earlier tours had been.

This third expedition was more in the nature of a pastor's ministry centred on two main places, Ephesus and Corinth. Paul began by a short trip through Galatia and Phrygia (the districts where he had been during his second expedition), but instead of going north to Troas, as before, he went direct to Ephesus.

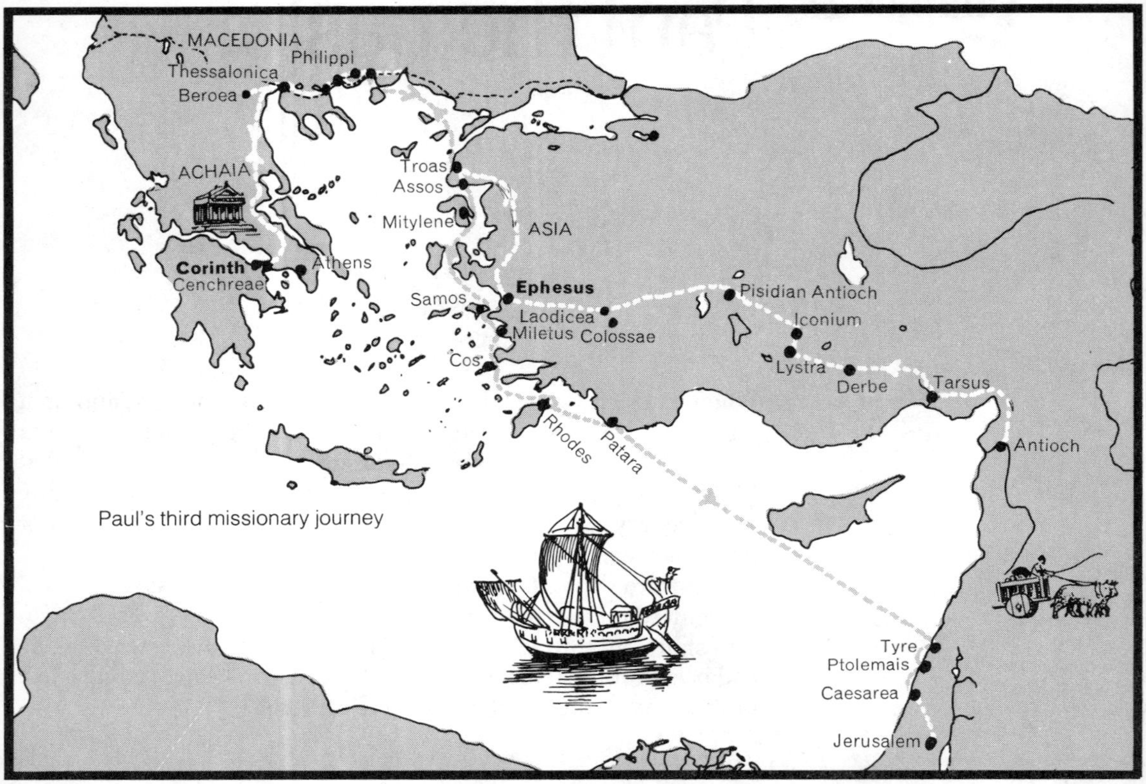

Paul's third missionary journey

Ephesus

Ephesus was the capital of the Roman province of Asia. It was a centre from which, by road or sea, Paul could easily keep in touch with most of the young churches he had already established in Asia Minor and in Europe. It was also a centre from which he and his colleagues could reach out into the whole province of Asia. His stay there resulted in churches being established in such places as Colossae and Laodicea, which Paul himself had not yet visited.

In the course of his three years' stay at Ephesus, Paul seems to have paid a short visit to Corinth. When he finally left Ephesus he went on to revisit the churches in Macedonia – probably Philippi, Thessalonica and Beroea. This may have been the occasion on which he went 'as far round as Illyricum', the region of Greece on the Dalmatian coast of the Adriatic Sea. For a further three months he stayed in Achaia (probably mostly in Corinth), then went back to Macedonia. There representatives of several churches, including Luke, joined him to take a gift from the Gentile congregations to the church in Jerusalem.

Acts 20:1–2

Romans 15:19

Acts 20:3

Acts 20:4–6

The impact of the gospel

Paul's long stay in Ephesus was undoubtedly the most important part of this period of his ministry – perhaps even the most important part of his whole life's work. Besides being the geographical centre of all the places Paul had previously visited, Ephesus was also a prominent centre of pagan religion. In it was to be found the great temple of Artemis (Diana) which was renowned as one of the wonders of the ancient world.

Paul's ministry in Ephesus was so successful that the two mainstays of Ephesian religious life were soon in danger of serious collapse. One of the things for which Ephesus was well known was its great number of magicians and sorcerers. Many of them became Christians and actually burnt their books of magic spells. The silversmiths of the city found that their trade in small replicas of the temple of Artemis for pilgrims began to decline, which led Demetrius and some others to start a riot against the Christians in the city.

Acts 19:19

Acts 19:23–41

Prison again?

1 Corinthians 15:32

In spite of such successes, however, Paul had great hardships at Ephesus – something he had come to expect when his ministry led to large-scale conversions to Christ. He states that he fought with wild beasts there, which may suggest he was thrown into the Roman arena, though it is probably a figure of speech. In 2 Corinthians 1:8 Paul speaks of the afflictions he endured in Asia; while in Romans 16:7, written probably just after he had left Ephesus, he writes of Andronicus and Junias as 'my fellow prisoners'. References such as these are often taken to indicate that Paul was imprisoned during this stay in Ephesus. The evidence for such an imprisonment is considered in more detail in chapter 20.

er the riots protesting at Paul's aching, the citizens of Ephesus thered at the theatre, which could ld 25,000 people.

The Temple of Artemis (Diana) at
Ephesus was four times the size of
the Parthenon. This larger than
life-sized Roman statue of the
goddess is in white marble. It is
based on the many-breasted
mother-goddess figure of the earlier
religion of this area.

Advising the churches

This third period of Paul's ministry is of most interest to us because it is the period when three of Paul's greatest letters were written: 1 and 2 Corinthians and Romans. The fact that these letters later came to be accepted as Holy Scripture and admitted to a central place in the New Testament often tends to obscure for us the fact that they were originally real letters. They are not simply theological tracts written in the form of letters. Like Paul's earliest letters they follow the normal pattern of ancient letters, and each arose out of a specific historical situation.

The great Temple of Artemis lay 1½ miles outside Ephesus. Today it is merely a great rectangular swamp, littered with broken columns.

Paul and the church at Corinth

The letters to Corinth in particular confront us with one of the most complicated historical puzzles of the entire New Testament. Galatians and 1 and 2 Thessalonians were fairly easy to fit into the picture of Paul's activities recorded in Acts. But in the case of 1 and 2 Corinthians we have no information at all from Acts. In order to piece together the historical situation behind this correspondence we depend entirely on the vague hints and allusions which Paul made as he wrote. It was not his main purpose to give a historical account of his own movements or of the state of the Corinthian church, so any reconstruction of what was going on must be more or less imaginative. But there is general agreement among most scholars that Paul's dealings with the church in Corinth at this time can be summarized in six stages:

Bad news from Corinth

During his three years' stay at Ephesus, Paul received bad news of the state of the Corinth church. So he wrote a letter warning them of the dangers of immorality. This is the letter referred to in 1 Corinthians 5:11, where Paul says: 'I wrote to you not to associate with any one who bears the name of brother if he is guilty of immorality ...' Some scholars think that part of this letter could be preserved in what we now call 2 Corinthians – in 6:14–7:1 – since this section seems to be out of character with its context in 2 Corinthians, and it begins 'Do not be mismated with unbelievers ...'

Paul writes 1 Corinthians

Members of Chloe's household also brought reports that the Corinthian church was dividing into different parties. Paul's own authority as an apostle was being challenged (1 Corinthians 1:11). These reports had later been confirmed by Stephanas and two others (1 Corinthians 16:17) who brought with them a letter from Corinth asking certain definite questions. 1 Corinthians was probably Paul's reply to this letter.

Paul visits Corinth

After this, Paul learned, perhaps from Timothy who had returned from Corinth to Ephesus, that his letter was having no effect. At this point he decided to pay a short visit to Corinth to see for himself what was happening. No such visit is mentioned in Acts, but it is certainly implied in 2 Corinthians 2:1; 12:14 and 13:1. On this visit he must have come, as he had threatened in 1 Corinthians 4:21, 'with a rod', for it could be called a 'painful visit' (2 Corinthians 2:1).

Another letter

After his return to Ephesus Paul sent Titus with a much stronger letter, written 'out of much affliction and anguish of heart', as he tells us in 2 Corinthians 2:4. Some think this letter is now preserved in our 2 Corinthians chapters 10–13, where Paul vigorously dismisses attacks made on his apostolic authority, which was almost certainly the subject of this third letter.

Good news from Corinth

Paul then left for Macedonia, having been driven away from Ephesus (Acts 20:1). In Macedonia he met Titus again, who brought welcome news of a change of attitude in the Corinthian church. He also carried an invitation for Paul to go to Corinth (2 Corinthians 7:5–16).

Paul writes 2 Corinthians

Paul sent back to Corinth with Titus a more compassionate letter, expressing his great joy. This letter is probably what we now know as 2 Corinthians chapters 1–9. He also took this opportunity to write on other subjects: the relation of preachers and hearers; the hope of a life after death; the general theme of salvation; and the collection which he was organizing for the Jerusalem church. If 2 Corinthians 10–13 belongs to this same letter, Paul must have heard news of a further revolt against his authority at Corinth while he was actually writing to them, which led him to defend his own position as an accredited apostle of Christ. Some scholars think that 2 Corinthians 10–13, rather than being earlier than 2 Corinthians 1–9 or written at the same time, was actually a letter sent later, when Paul's authority was again being undermined.

So much for the 'mechanics' of how these letters came to be written. But what was Paul actually saying to these Christians? In trying to answer that question, it will be best for us to pick out certain features of what Paul said, from which we can gain a picture of the situation in the church at Corinth. It is in **1 Corinthians** that we find most information about this situation. Paul's argument there falls conveniently into three sections, which may be given the titles: **Life in Christ; Life in the World;** and **Life in the Church.**

1 Corinthians

Life in Christ
(1 Corinthians 1:10–4:21)

One of the things that characterized the city of Corinth was the varied nature of its society. Its position as an important sea port on one of the busiest routes in the Mediterranean ensured this. In the streets of Corinth military men from Rome, mystics from the east and Jews from Palestine continually rubbed shoulders with the philosophers of Greece. When Paul had preached the good news about Jesus in this city, it was a cross-section of this cosmopolitan society that responded and formed the Christian church in Corinth.

Not surprisingly, men and women from such different spiritual and intellectual backgrounds brought with them into the church some very different concepts and ideas. While Paul was with them the various sections of the young congregation were held together. But on his departure these new Christians began to work out for themselves the implications of their Christian faith, and naturally began to produce different answers.

A divided church. As a result the church at Corinth had for all practical purposes been divided into four different groups, of which Paul speaks in 1 Corinthians 1:10–17. Some were claiming that their spiritual allegiance was to Paul, others to Apollos, others to Cephas, while yet others claimed only to belong to Christ (1:12–13). These four parties clearly reflect the diverse backgrounds of the Corinthian Christians:

● The 'Paul Party' would consist of libertines. They were people who had heard Paul's original preaching on the freedom of the Christian and concluded from it that, once they had responded to the Christian gospel, they could live as they liked. This was exactly what the Judaizers who opposed Paul in Galatia had said would happen when the Christian message was declared without making people obey the Old Testament Law. Paul in fact always emphasized that, far from relieving Christians of moral obligations, his message actually made deeper demands on them. But this danger of lawlessness ('anti-nomianism') was always present in his churches.

● The 'Cephas Party' were undoubtedly legalists. They were people like the Judaizers in Jerusalem, who believed that the Christian life meant the strict observance of the Jewish Law, both ritual and moral. Many of them had probably been Jews or Gentile 'God-fearers' before they were converted to the Christian faith.

● The 'Apollos Party' were probably devotees of the classical Greek outlook. Apollos is mentioned in Acts 18:24–28, where we learn that he was a Jew from Alexandria, 'an eloquent man, well versed in the scriptures'. Alexandria in Egypt had a large Jewish population, and several influential and gifted teachers lived and worked there both before and after the New Testament period. Best known among these was Philo (about 20 BC–AD 45), a Jew who specialized in interpreting the Old Testament in accordance with the concepts of Greek philosophy. He was trying to show that all that was in the Greek philosophers had actually been foreshadowed by Moses and other Old Testament writers. As an educated Alexandrian Jew, Apollos would be steeped in this kind of scriptural interpretation. He would naturally be an acceptable teacher to those Christians at Corinth with a Greek philosophical background.

● The 'Christ Party' probably consisted of a group of men and women who considered themselves to be above the groups that had developed around the personalities of ordinary men. They wanted a direct contact with Christ himself, in the same way as they had experienced direct mystical contacts with gods in the pagan eastern Mystery Religions. If Serapis could be called 'lord', so could Christ. But Paul made it clear to them that in fact, 'no one can say "Jesus is Lord" except by the Holy Spirit' (1 Corinthians 12:3). What they were trying to do was to exchange one mystery god for another. Since this kind of belief often led to libertinism in practice, these people may well have found themselves siding with the 'Paul Party' on some important ethical issues.

The confusion at Corinth. As we read through 1 Corinthians we can see how each of these groups was at work, spreading its own ideas and emphases. *The libertines*, who claimed to follow Paul, encouraged the whole church not to worry about open immorality (5:1–13). *The legalists*, claiming to follow Cephas' example, raised the old question of what kind of food Christians should eat. But this time the argument was over food that had been offered in pagan temples before being sold to the public (chapters 8–9). *The philosophers*, followers of Apollos, were insisting that they had a form of wisdom that was superior to anything

Paul had proclaimed (1:18–25). *The mystics*, claiming they were following Christ, were inclined to argue that the sacraments of the church acted in a supernatural way. They claimed they did not have to worry about the natural results of their immoral activities (10:1–13). The resurrection had already come, they claimed, for they had been raised in a mystical way with Christ (15:12–19). They claimed they were now living on a super-spiritual level of existence, far beyond the grasp of the followers of Paul, Cephas or Apollos (see also 4:8).

The combination of these different types of extremism led in the second century to the formation of a heretical movement known as 'Gnosticism'. We can probably see here in Corinth the first stirrings in this direction. But at the time, Paul was not concerned with giving a name to this movement. All he saw was one of his largest churches thrown into utter confusion by fanatics operating from four different directions.

This was totally against all that he understood the Christian message to be. He had told the Galatians that belief in Christ created a new fellowship of equality and freedom for all Christians, something that he had himself experienced as he moved from city to city and found new friends among the unlikeliest of people simply because they had been united in Christ.

Corinth was a city placed at a major junction of trade-routes. Its cosmopolitan character made it a byword for moral permissiveness. The first Christians there had to work out their faith against that background.

The answer in Christ. He knew therefore that the answer to the Corinthian situation must be found in Christ. Neither Paul himself, nor Cephas, nor Apollos, nor the kind of 'Christ' that was being followed in Corinth, could achieve any lasting result. When he first visited Corinth Paul had declared the cross of Christ and his resurrection to be 'of first importance' in the understanding of the Christian faith (1 Corinthians 15:3–7; 1:18–25). This was the only basis on which men and women of diverse cultures could be reunited. Whatever Paul, Apollos or Cephas had done in their own name was of no consequence. So Paul repeated his basic message as the answer to the problems of the Corinthian church: 'No other foundation can anyone lay than that which is laid, which is Jesus Christ' (3:11).

Having set out his own starting-point, Paul went on to look at some of the specific problems of the church at Corinth; problems concerned with their attitudes to non-Christian standards and institutions, and with their attitudes to one another in the gatherings of the church.

Life in the world
(1 Corinthians 5:1–11:1)

Though Christians enjoyed new privileges by virtue of their new life in Christ, they still had to live in a non-Christian world. In Corinth, three main areas posed problems concerning the Christian's relationships with non-Christians:

Christian behaviour. At least two of the 'parties' in the Corinth church claimed to have a theological reason for ignoring the accepted Christian standards of morality. In the central part of his letter Paul mentions three specific matters which had come to his attention.

● Permissiveness. One thing that particularly worried him was the report that 'there is immorality among you ... of a kind that is not found even among pagans; for a man is living with his father's wife' (5:1). Paul was never one for taking drastic action against people with whom he disagreed. But this kind of behaviour was so serious that he felt he had no alternative but to instruct the church members not to associate with the person concerned until he had repented of his sin. He told them: 'When you are assembled, and my spirit is present, with the power of our Lord Jesus, you are to deliver this man to Satan for the destruction of the flesh, that his spirit may be saved in the day of the Lord Jesus' (5:4–5). Some parts of this instruction are difficult for us to understand. But the main point is clear: this kind of sin was so serious that it must be completely destroyed. The person concerned must leave the Christian fellowship – though his final spiritual fate is not the business of the local church but will be revealed 'in the day of the Lord Jesus'.

● Freedom. Once again Paul had to emphasize that freedom in Christ does not mean the freedom to be immoral (6:12–20). Christians are not free to do as they please, but free to serve God, to whom they belong (6:19–20).

● Marriage. One of the questions which the Corinthians had asked Paul was also concerned with marriage and divorce (7:1–40). In replying Paul permits Christians to marry (7:1–9), though he himself was not married and he could 'wish that all were as I myself am' (7:7). He forbids divorce (7:10–11), except in a case where a heathen partner deserts a Christian (7:12–16). And he recommends that the Corinthian Christians should remain in their present condition, either married or single (7:17–24), though he recommends celibacy as the preferable state (7:25–40).

This was clearly advice given for a specific situation that had arisen in Corinth. It is interesting to note the way Paul separates his own advice and opinion from what he believed to be the will of his Master. He felt that he had Jesus' authority for saying there should be no divorce among Christians (7:10–11). But on the other issues with which he deals, in one case he makes it plain that it is 'not the Lord' who is speaking (7:12), and in another he merely says, 'I think that I have the Spirit of God' (7:40).

Some of the things Paul says seem odd to us, to put it mildly. Scholars down the ages have made various suggestions as to why Paul should appear to run down the institution of marriage here. No doubt he had been jilted when young, they tell us, or even perhaps unhappily married! But such explanations fail to take account of the historical context in which he wrote these things. He was aware that the situation of the Corinthian church was extremely serious (7:26), and there were many more important things to be done than making arrangements for weddings.

Was it not something like this that Jesus himself had said? 'If any one comes to me and does not hate his own father and mother and wife and children and brothers and sisters, yes, and even his own life, he cannot be my disciple' (Luke 14:26). There is a striking similarity between this and what Paul says (7:29–31). Yet no one seriously suggests that Jesus was against marriage and family life. Quite the opposite; for it is widely supposed that he raised the whole issue to a much higher level. Examination of the other passages in Paul's writings where he treats the same subject will show that he held marriage in the same high regard as Jesus did (see Ephesians 5:22–33). In 1 Corinthians he was addressing himself to Christians in a desperate situation, and in such a case drastic action was called for.

Christians and the civil law. Another thing that concerned Paul was the way Christians in Corinth were quarrelling with each other, and then going to the civil law courts to sort out their grievances. Paul had to condemn this practice out of hand. For one thing, it was quite absurd that Christians, who claimed to be brothers and sisters, should go to pagan courts at all. When a quarrel arises in a family, it should not be necessary to go to court with it. Surely some member of the church fellowship was wise enough to sort the problem out (6:1–6).

But what disturbed Paul was that quarrels should arise at all. Christians ought to follow the example set to them by Christ, and 'suffer wrong' rather than create division in the Christian fellowship (6:7–8). In the light of what God has done for them in Christ, their petty bickerings fade into insignificance (6:9–11).

Everyday life. It was possible for Christians to live independently of the pagan courts. But they could not help getting involved in other aspects of pagan life in a city like Corinth. Take, for example, the question of food. In our modern world, if we want meat we go to the shop and buy it. Unless we are vegetarians, there are no moral problems involved.

But in Corinth there were no butcher's shops. The purchase of meat was a religious activity. The only meat available for sale was from the carcasses of the animals offered in sacrifice at the various pagan temples. Other meat may have been available in the Jewish community of a Roman city, but that was no help to Christians. They did not want to conform to the Jewish food regulations, nor did Jews want to supply Christians with meat.

So the only alternative appeared to be to buy meat that had been offered to pagan gods, which the Christians knew did not really exist anyway. But this was just the problem. For some of the church members felt that by buying meat of this kind they were somehow encouraging and sharing in the worship of pagan gods. What then was the Christian to do? Paul takes up the matter in 1 Corinthians 8:1–11:1, where he makes the following four points:

● The Christian is free to eat food that had been offered to pagan gods, since such gods do not exist. But the Christian who understands this must also have a brotherly concern for those who see the matter differently. So the 'enlightened' Christian should occasionally be prepared to forgo the freedom to eat food bought from the pagan temples out of consideration for other people (8:1–13).

● This was the kind of concession that Paul himself had made, in a different sphere. As God's messenger Paul had the right to be supported by God's people: 'the Lord commanded that those who proclaim the gospel should get their living by the gospel' (9:14). Paul had given up his right to be maintained in this way, and instead practised self-discipline (9:1–27). He had been willing to place himself under restrictions so that his message might be accepted by all kinds of people: 'though I am free from all men, I have made myself a slave to all, that I might win the more' (9:19).

● Christians should also recognize that there could be real dangers in participating in heathen festivals (10:1–22). Some of the Corinthian Christians had the idea that the Christian sacraments gave them a sort of magical immunity from pagan rituals, so that they could take part without being truly spiritually involved. Paul points out from the history of Israel that this was not so. It was quite impossible to share in the Lord's Supper one day and a heathen feast the next and escape without harm.

● The general principle to be followed in reaching practical decisions on these ethical questions is not to do anything that would lead others astray, even things that are right in themselves, but to 'do all to the glory of God' (10:23–11:1).

Life in the church
(1 Corinthians 11:2–15:58)

Paul had been asked the answer to several specific questions that were puzzling the church at Corinth. Some of them we have already considered, questions concerning marriage and divorce, and food bought from pagan temples. But there were others, concerned with the church's worship (11:2–14:40) and beliefs (15:1–58).

The church's worship
(1 Corinthians 11:2–14:40)

As the church at Corinth met for worship, trying to put into practice what Paul had taught them, three practical difficulties had arisen:

● Freedom in worship. Paul had taught the Christians at Corinth the same things as he had taught the churches of Galatia. Two of the basic points of this message had been that in Christ there is to be no distinction of race, class or sex (Galatians 3:28); and that Christ has given Christians a new freedom (Galatians 5:1). In practical terms of the church's worship, this meant that Paul, contrary to the Jewish custom of the day, allowed women to play a full part in the Christian ministry. He had passed on 'traditions' to that effect to the Corinthian church (1 Corinthians 11:2), traditions which the church members had observed. But they misunderstood the character of Christian freedom. Women who were taking a leading part in the church's services were doing in God's presence things they would not have done in front of their neighbours.

The prevailing social custom of the time laid down that respectable, modest women did not appear in public with their heads uncovered. The Corinthian Christians, however, argued that the Christian was set free even from the normal rules of society, and was able to express this freedom before God in the church. Paul could see that this was a similar situation to the one which had arisen in the church over food bought in pagan temples. But in this case the women in the church were offending the non-Christian society which they were trying to evangelize. So he suggested that women taking a public part in the church's worship ought to follow the prevailing social custom and do so with their heads veiled (11:2–16).

● Morals and worship. The way the church was observing the Lord's Supper (communion) also gave cause for concern (11:17–34). Instead of carrying out the instructions which Jesus himself gave, and which Paul had delivered to them at an earlier stage (11:23–26), the Corinthian Christians were making the service into an occasion for feasting and merriment. They were all bringing along their own food, and having private feasts – feasts which they ought to have held in their own homes (11:22).

The party divisions that Paul was so much against were rearing their ugly heads even at the Lord's table (11:18–19). All this division, and the accompanying revelry and drunkenness in the church, was dishonouring both to the purpose of their gathering and also to the Christians themselves. They were giving no thought to what they were

Both Paul's letters to the Corinthians contain instructions about regular collections for the Christians in Judea who were facing hard times. The call was to express practically their partnership in the gospel.

Prominent among the ruins of ancient Corinth is the Temple of Apollo, behind which rises the rock of Acrocorinth.

doing, and some of them had brought upon themselves the judgement which they deserved (11:29–32).

● Gifts and worship. Another very important feature in the Corinthian church was the exercise of spiritual gifts.

Basic to Christian experience in the apostolic churches was the conviction that Christians were motivated by the Holy Spirit. They were 'charismatics', people with *charismata*, spiritual gifts: speaking in ecstatic tongues (glossolalia), interpretation of such tongues, prophecy (as in Acts 13:1–2), and the working of miracles by the

apostles (Acts 19:11–12).

The Corinthian church possessed all of these gifts and many more in abundance, and they were so eager to exercise them that several people could be taking part in church worship at the same time. This was clearly an unsatisfactory way of going on. Paul had to remind them that 'God is not a God of confusion but of peace' (1 Corinthians 14:33). This meant that when the gifts were exercised in the church, it could be taken for granted that if God was truly inspiring them, they would occur in a way that would lead to the building up of the whole church (12:7).

Paul recognized the validity of all the gifts that had appeared in Corinth. He emphasized that every one of them was God-given and therefore had its rightful place in gatherings of the congregation. Just as the human body has different parts, each of which must make its contribution to the smooth operation of the body, so it is in the church. Each of the gifts possessed by different members of the church should contribute to the smooth running of the whole (12:14–31).

Not every Christian would be given one of the more spectacular gifts, such as tongues, but all had their part to play. One gift should be common to all: the gift of love. Love, for fellow-Christians and other people in general, was the basis on which Christians ought to desire and seek after the other gifts (14:1–2).

The church's belief
(1 Corinthians 15:1–58)

Finally, Paul deals with what he regarded as the core of essential Christian belief. It was also one of the main elements in the problems of the Corinthian church: the resurrection of Christ.

Some members of the church were claiming that in their mystical experiences they had already been raised to a new spiritual level above that achieved by the more ordinary church members. This belief was linked with a misunderstanding about the resurrection of Jesus, and Paul deals with it in two ways.

First he reminds the Corinthians of the firm historical foundation on which belief in the resurrection of Jesus is based (15:3–11). In doing this he gives us the earliest account in the New Testament of the resurrection of Jesus. Secondly he goes on to show how, if the resurrection of Jesus happened historically (as he and the other apostles believed it did), this must be a guarantee that Christians also will be raised at the last day in the same way as Jesus was raised from the dead. Because of the centrality of Jesus' resurrection for the whole of Christian belief, anyone who denied this by spiritualizing it into mystical experiences was in fact denying the basis of the Christian faith: 'if the dead are not raised, then Christ has not been raised. If Christ has not been raised, your faith is futile and you are still in your sins ... we are of all men most to be pitied' (15:16–18).

More arguments in Corinth

2 Corinthians 11:1–15

2 Corinthians 2:1

This was not the end of Paul's correspondence with the Christians at Corinth. He must have been at least partly successful in persuading them to change their minds, for we hear nothing more of questions about the resurrection, or marriage, or things like food bought in the pagan temples. But there were still problems, this time especially connected with the arrival of messengers – 'apostles' as they called themselves – probably from the church in Jerusalem. Paul had already dealt with people like this in the churches of Galatia. But those who came to Corinth were not 'Judaizers' in the strict sense. They were not trying to persuade the Corinthians to become Jews by accepting circumcision and the Old Testament Law. They were aiming to persuade them to transfer their allegiance away from Paul to the Jewish leaders of the original church in Jerusalem.

Paul had apparently chosen to visit the church at Corinth while these people were in residence there – and this is the 'painful visit' to which he refers. It was certainly painful for Paul, for he was insulted by these false apostles and their claims that his authority was questionable. He left in a hurry – something he was later to

2 Corinthians 1:12–22

regret, for it seemed to confirm what his opponents were saying about him.

As a result the Corinthian Christians were left in a turmoil. Who were the real apostles, and how could they tell the difference between true and false? Their loyalty swung from one to the other, and in order to clarify the issues Paul wrote to them yet again. The letter he wrote this time was our 2 Corinthians.

2 Corinthians

1 Corinthians has a clear line of argument from beginning to end. But 2 Corinthians often reads more like an anthology of Paul's advice on different subjects. Some think this is just what it is: a collection of two or three letters that were originally written quite independently, and later joined together by an editor. This would be a standard procedure in the ancient world, and in principle anyone collecting Paul's letters together would be quite likely to fit more than one of them into the same standard length book.

Paul's thought certainly does seem to change subjects rather abruptly at several points in 2 Corinthians.

● 2:14–7:4 is quite different from what precedes and follows it. Moreover, 7:5 makes quite good sense if we place it immediately after 2:13. Then even within this section, 6:14–7:1 seems to break the sense of what goes before and after it. Could it be then that we have here separate letters, perhaps some of those which we know Paul wrote to Corinth but which apparently are not in the New Testament?

● Chapters 8 and 9 seem to deal with the same topic (the collection for the church in Jerusalem), but with no reference to each other. In particular, chapter 9 seems to introduce the subject quite independently of what has already been said about it in the previous chapter. Could 2 Corinthians 9:1–15 be another separate letter – this time written before the troubles began, to recommend Titus and some others to the church at Corinth and to encourage them to give generously for Jerusalem?

● Chapters 10–13 contrast sharply with chapters 1–9. At the end of chapter 9, Paul expresses satisfaction that the Corinthians have sorted out their problems – but at the beginning of chapter 10 he is on the offensive again. So were chapters 10–13 originally written as a separate letter at a time when the situation was more desperate?

Only one of these suggestions seems at all likely. Chapters 10–13 may well represent a different and later letter than chapters 1–9. The change in tone

from 9:15 to 10:1 is so marked that we must certainly suppose that something had happened between the two: either that Paul received information about yet another change of heart in Corinth while he was actually in the process of writing, or that he heard the same news later.

But it is less likely that the other apparent dislocations in 2 Corinthians are to be explained in this way. A collector of Paul's letters would most naturally have copied them out one after the other, rather than inserting separate letters halfway through longer letters in such a way as to disrupt the sense of both. For this reason, it is more satisfactory to account for the apparent change of subject between 2:13 to 7:4 and 8:1–24 and 9:1–15 as digressions in Paul's own thinking as he wrote.

What, then, does 2 Corinthians have to say about these fresh problems faced by Paul and the Corinthian Christians? The letter falls naturally into four main sections:

1. Facing up to problems
(2 Corinthians 1:3–2:13)

Paul knew that he needed to explain the turbulent nature of his relationship with the Corinthian church. But there was also the question of true and false apostleship. Paul clarifies his thinking on these two topics in his opening thanksgiving section (1:3–11). He draws attention not only to his affection for the church in Corinth, but also to his conviction that suffering and weakness are in some way an inevitable part of the true service of God. To cope with persecution, Paul needs to trust wholeheartedly in God. But he also needs the prayerful support of his readers. His relationship with them is not all one-sided: he needs their prayers just as much as they need his guidance.

Paul also needed to reassure the Corinthians that he could be trusted. His unexpected visits and letters, and last minute changes of plan had given them the impression that he was unstable (1:12–2:4). They had concluded that he was afraid to visit them because he knew at heart that the claims of the 'false apostles' were true. Paul obviously felt these criticisms deeply, and defends himself against the charge that he was acting selfishly. Nothing could be further from the truth: he wrote them a letter rather than making a visit because he hoped that would be a less painful way of correcting them: 'my purpose was not to make you sad, but to make you realize how much I love you all' (2:4).

Personal animosities must also be put right – and both Paul and the church should be prepared to forgive those who have been particularly offensive (2:5–11). Paul obviously refers here to a specific person. According to some, perhaps the man mentioned in 1 Corinthians 5:5 who was sleeping with his own step mother. But more likely, someone else who had been specially abusive to Paul himself.

2. What is an apostle?
(2 Corinthians 2:14–7:4)

The major point at issue was Paul's authority as an apostle. Paul introduces this subject with an expression of his own gratitude to God for what he has done in his life. Because of his experience of the living Christ, he is a part of 'Christ's victory procession' (2:14). As such, he is in a close personal relationship to Christ himself. But that does not allow him to boast in a

Paul's travels were by no means always straightforward. He tells the Corinthian Christians that he has been 'in three shipwrecks, and once I spent twenty-four hours in the water'

triumphalist way about his own abilities. Quite the opposite, for endowment with God's Holy Spirit brings great responsibilities, and it is the recognition of this that makes Paul different from the other so-called 'apostles' who had arrived in Corinth: 'We are not like so many others, who handle God's message as if it were cheap merchandise; but because God has sent us, we speak with sincerity in his presence, as servants of Christ' (2:17).

Unlike those who had come from Jerusalem, Paul did not depend on official letters to establish his credentials. He was content for the validity of his work to be judged by its results – the changed lives of his converts, and his own personal lifestyle (3:1–18). If Christians are truly serving God, then God's presence and power should be visible for all to see: 'All of us ... reflect the glory of the Lord ... and that same glory, coming from the Lord, who is the Spirit, transforms us into his likeness in an ever greater degree of glory' (3:18). This was the great benefit that the Christian gospel had brought him over against his previous allegiance to Judaism (3:4–17).

But did this mean that Christian apostles would not be living a super-spiritual sort of existence, in which all the ordinary problems of everyday human life had vanished? Not at all, asserts Paul (4:1–15). Though the gospel is a powerful, life-giving message, God in his wisdom has entrusted it to 'common clay pots'. No one takes special care of everyday crockery, and it will inevitably be chipped and cracked in the course of ordinary use. This is exactly what true servants of Christ can expect: 'We are often troubled ... sometimes in doubt ... badly hurt ... always in danger of death for Jesus' sake ...' (4:7–11). This of course had been Jesus' own experience, culminating in the agonising despair of the cross. But after the cross had come the resurrection – and for Paul, this provided the key to the Christian life. In Galatians (2:19–20) he had emphasised that the secret of his faith was the presence of the living Christ within him. And he repeats the same theme here: 'we are always in danger of death for Jesus' sake, *in order that his life may be seen in this mortal body of ours*' (4:11).

This, says Paul, is where the emphasis ought to be. The messengers of the gospel must not be confused with the message itself. The fact that the 'spiritual treasure' is in 'common clay pots' draws attention to the fact that 'the supreme power belongs to God, not to us' (4:7).

Thinking about the physical dangers that he had faced led Paul onto the subject of life after death. This had already been a major subject of 1 Corinthians. But now his perspective has changed. He asks different questions here – no doubt as a result of his recent narrow escapes from death (presumably in Ephesus, 2 Corinthians 1:9). What he says is one of the most complex passages in all his letters (5:1–10). But two things are quite clear: (i) he is still opposed to the views of those Corinthians (and later Gnostics) who had been claiming that 'resurrection' was a matter of a person's inner spiritual experience; and (ii) he still clings to the Jewish belief in a bodily existence after death, rather than resorting to the Greek view of an immortal soul that would survive the disposable body. Not that he thinks in strictly materialistic terms, for he writes of replacing 'this tent we live in – our body here on earth' by 'a house in heaven ... a home God himself has made, which will last for ever' (5:1).

Even this however was only the final outworking of what was already happening in the lives of Christian people. Like Jesus, Paul saw a tension between what God would do in the future when his kingdom comes in all its perfection, and what he is doing now in the lives of those who accept his sovereignty. The way Christians think, the way they behave, and their standards and values, should reflect here and now the reality of God's living presence: 'No longer, then, do we judge anyone by human standards ... When anyone is joined to Christ, he is a new being; the old is gone, the new has come' (5:16–17). This reached to the very heart of Paul's understanding of the death and resurrection of Jesus, and was the basis of all his work as an evangelist: 'God was in Christ, reconciling the world to himself' (5:19).

In this light, Paul's sufferings in no way contradict his claim to be an apostle. On the contrary, they are the clearest possible demonstration of the truth of that claim (6:1–10). Perhaps Paul felt that he had given a more detailed defence of himself than was really necessary, for he concludes this section by an appeal for his readers to show the same honesty with him as he has shown with them (6:11–13).

He then turns to warn them that the Christian lifestyle should be wholly different from a secular lifestyle. Christians must reflect the values and standards of God himself (6:14–7:1). Modern readers of this passage often suppose that Paul writes about personal morality, especially marriage relationships. No doubt that would be covered by what he says, but his advice is far more wide ranging than that. There is something fundamentally incompatible between the accepted standards of the pagan world and the standards of the Christian gospel – and believers must be prepared to put God first in every area of life, not just where they find it convenient. Jesus had said as much himself: 'No one can be a slave of two masters ... You cannot serve God and money' (Matthew 6:24).

3. Looking to the future
(2 Corinthians 7:5–9:15)

Paul now moves on to the effects of his 'painful letter', which had apparently led to a change of heart on the part of the Corinthians – a change which Titus had reported (7:5–16). It was no doubt on that basis that Paul felt it was now appropriate to invite them to make a contribution to the collection he was organizing for the financial relief of the church in Jerusalem (8:1–9:15). This was not the first time the Corinthians had heard of this (1 Corinthians 16:1–4). But their stormy relationship with Paul had prevented anything being done about it until now.

Paul urges them to be generous not simply out of a sense of duty, but as a loving response to what God had done for them. The coming of Jesus into their lives had been an unmerited act of God's goodness – and they should meet the needs of others in the same attitude: 'You know the grace of our Lord Jesus Christ; rich as he was, he made himself poor for your sake, in order to make you rich by means of his poverty' (8:9). He also believed that such an act of generosity would improve relations between the purely Gentile churches which he had established and the Jewish congregations back in Palestine (9:1–15).

4. Authority and charisma
(2 Corinthians 10:1–13:10)

In this section Paul again takes the offensive. Perhaps he had heard of yet further challenges to his authority even while he was in the process of writing. This time it seems he was being criticized because of his personality. 'Paul's letters are severe and strong', his Corinthians opponents were saying, 'but when he is with us in person, he is weak, and his words are nothing'

(10:10). Clearly, he lacked the charismatic appeal of the 'false apostles' who had come to Corinth. They did not suffer from doubt and persecution as he did. They were always boasting about their own mystical experiences and spiritual maturity. Paul does not answer these charges comprehensively here. He has already done so in his previous discussion of the relationship between weakness and power in the lives of God's servants. He tackles the subject less systematically here, suggesting that these others only seem so impressive because 'They make up their own standards to measure themselves by, and they judge themselves by their own standards' (10:12). Indeed, worse than that. For he accuses the Corinthians of accepting 'anyone who comes to you and preaches a different Jesus, not the one we preached; and you accept a spirit and a gospel completely different from the Spirit and the gospel you received from us' (11:4).

Paul then launches into a wide-ranging attack on those who were questioning his own credentials on this spurious basis – dealing in turn with his relationship to the Corinthian church (11:1–6), his style of life (11:7–11), and the ultimate source of his authority (11:12–15). Far from showing him to be second rate, his suffering and persecution actually demonstrate the reality of his calling (11:16–33).

The 'false apostles' also seem to have been claiming more spectacular manifestations of the Holy Spirit's gifts than Paul. We certainly know that was a perennial difficulty in Corinthian church life (1 Corinthians 12—14). Paul recognized that boasting about such things does no good – but he needed to set the record straight and point out that he too had 'visions and revelations given me by the Lord' (12:1). But he still returns to the theme of suffering and weakness as the cornerstone of his apostolic status: it is only as people recognize their own weakness and trust entirely in God that they can speak of being truly Christian (12:7–10).

Finally, Paul reminds them that he will be visiting Corinth again, and they would do well to put their lives in order before he arrives. Despite what his opponents have claimed, he is prepared to denounce them face to face. But it would be so much happier for everyone if they would get back to the basis of the gospel first, and recognize that it is only when they each acknowledge their human weakness that God's power can work effectively in their lives (13:1–10).

Some of the Christians at Corinth had scruples about eating the meat available, since it had been offered at pagan temples. This inscription is from the meat market (*macellum* in Corinth.

So Paul came to the end of the most complicated letter he ever wrote. Like Galatians, the Corinthian letters were written in the white heat of controversy, which only adds to our difficulties in understanding them. Paul was under attack by his friends as well as his enemies. This must have given him considerable reason to pause and think out his gospel again. He wanted to avoid the pitfalls of the past without in any sense compromising his basic position that in Christ all barriers of race, sex and social standing are removed, and all men and women stand equal in the freedom given to them by the Holy Spirit. It was probably thoughts of this kind that dictated the form of Paul's next major letter, which is quite different from any of those we have looked at so far.

Paul's goal

Rome was naturally Paul's ultimate goal in spreading the good news about Jesus throughout the empire. But Rome had already been evangelized, and had a flourishing church. Many of the Christians in Rome were probably of Jewish origin, and Paul realized that some of them may have been influenced against him. Christians from Judea may well have been there saying it was necessary for all Gentile converts to observe the Law of the Old Testament. If they had heard of what was happening in Corinth they could have been confirmed in their false impression of his message.

Acts 20:2–3
Romans 15:25–27
Romans 1:11
Romans 15:24

Towards the end of his dealings with the Corinthian church, Paul visited the area of Corinth, and spent some three months there. After this he intended to go to Jerusalem with delegates from the Gentile churches who were taking a gift to the Jewish church. Later he hoped to visit Rome and then go on into Spain.

Rome was of crucial importance in the evangelization of the empire. And there was also the need to re-state his own gospel in a form that was not open to misinterpretation, either by sympathisers or by opponents. So Paul decided to prepare for his visit to the capital by writing a letter to the church there, containing a reasoned statement of his own beliefs. This was the letter to the Romans.

Romans

Some regard Romans as a comprehensive summary of the whole of Paul's theology. But this is a misleading and unhelpful assumption. Paul was certainly in a more reflective mood when he wrote Romans than when he penned Galatians or any of the Corinthian letters. But there are several important aspects of his thinking that do not feature here at all – not least his belief in the future return of Jesus (*parousia*) and about life after death. What he says on the nature of the church in Romans is also very limited when compared with his fuller exposition of the theme in 1 Corinthians.

Romans is best understood as a more carefully articulated account of some of the major themes of Galatians and 1–2 Corinthians (1 Corinthians in particular). The great nineteenth century scholar J.B. Lightfoot once wrote that 'the Epistle to the Galatians stands in relation to the Roman letter, as the rough model to the finished statue'. This strikes the right note, except that the Corinthian situation also cannot have been far from Paul's mind at the time. Perhaps it is more accurate to describe Romans as the argument of

Galatians when viewed through the spectacles of what happened in Corinth.

In Romans, Paul was not only preparing for his visit to the capital city of the empire: he was also refining some aspects of his own thinking that had proved to be open to misinterpretation. This was a top priority at the time, for he knew that on his arrival in Jerusalem with the collection he would need to give a satisfactory account of himself to the Jewish Christians there. Perhaps Romans was a draft of some of the things he intended to say to them.

Because Romans is so closely based on Paul's previous letters to the Galatians and to the Corinthians we do not need to summarise it in such great detail here.

The letter falls into three major sections:

How Christians know God

The first part of Romans, chapters 1–8, is one long theological argument starting from a text in the prophet Habakkuk: 'the just shall live by faith' (Habakkuk 2:4). Here Paul argues in a way very familiar to us from Galatians;

indeed many of the points he makes are the same. Everyone, both Jews and Gentiles, is under the power of sin. Apart from Christ there is no way of escape from God's condemnation of sin (1:18–3:20). Yet it is possible to receive 'the righteousness of God', that is, release from God's sentence of condemnation and the power to share in God's own goodness. This is something that can be obtained only through faith in Christ, and not by good works (3:21–4:25).

As in Galatians, Paul illustrates his theme from the life of Abraham (4:1–25). He then goes on (5:1–8:39) to describe the results of this new relationship with God: freedom from the wrath of God; freedom from slavery to sin; freedom from the Law; and freedom from death through the working of the Spirit of God in Christ. 'In all these things we are more than conquerors through him who loved us' (8:37).

These are all themes that Paul had dealt with before in either Galatians or Corinthians. But here we find several new elements. They are all clearly a result of Paul's experience as he had seen his message misunderstood and misapplied in the churches. Paul deals directly with the problem of antinomianism in 6:1–8:39. He makes it clear that though Christians are set free from the rule of all external law for gaining an acceptable standing before God, they have in fact entered into a new kind of service. No longer are they 'slaves of sin' (6:17); they are now 'slaves of God' (6:22). Christians have been set free not to do as they please, but that by the work of the Holy Spirit within them they might be 'conformed to the image of his Son' (8:29). This is the teaching of Galatians as seen by Paul after his experiences in Corinth.

Israel and salvation

In chapters 9–11 Paul moves on. He is concerned with the fact of Israel's rejection of this salvation which he has been describing. He points out that God's apparent rejection of the Jews does not contradict either his promises in the Old Testament or his justice. It is Israel's own fault. She chose the way of 'works' rather than the way of faith. But Paul was still convinced that God's rejection of Israel was not final. Even in the midst of such unfaithfulness, there was a faithful remnant (11:1–10). The present rejection of the Jews was in fact fully part of God's plan for the ultimate salvation of people from all races (11:11–36).

How Christians should behave

Paul then moves away from strictly theological statements to write about the practical application of God's righteousness in Christian living (12:1–15:13). Here he deals with the Christian's relationship to the church (12:1–8), to other people (12:9–21) and to the state (13:1–10). He sums up Christian duty as a whole in the words 'love is the fulfilling of the Law' (13:10). He emphasizes again that standards of Christian morality are to be produced not by an artificial set of rules and regulations imposed from outside, but by the power of the Holy Spirit working within the believer. But the end result of the Spirit's work will be that the Law of God is in fact observed, and the key idea of this law is love. Paul illustrates this by reference to two live issues: the eating of vegetables in preference to meat (14:1–15:6; a similar case to the question of meat bought from pagan temples), and the general attitude of Jews and Gentiles towards one another within the church (15:7–13).

In this letter we have a mature statement of the gospel as Paul understood it. It was a gospel that did not depend on keeping rules and regulations. It was rather a revolutionary message, the message of the living Lord who wanted to be in control of the lives of his followers. Under his direction they would discover a way of living that would be pleasing to God and beneficial to other people. This was something that no one liked, whether Jew or Gentile. But all the same Paul was convinced that it was 'the power of God for salvation'. It was obtained through faith in Christ. But the Christian faith also demanded submission to Christ as Lord, and openness to the power of the Holy Spirit working in the believer's life.

Romans 1:16

Chapter 19 Paul reaches Rome

Romans 15:23
At the end of his letter to the Roman church, Paul made the extraordinary statement: 'I no longer have any room for work in these regions.' Yet we know it would be quite foolish to suppose that by this time the whole of Asia Minor and the Balkan peninsula, where Paul had been working, had been evangelized with the Christian message.

Paul's missionary strategy

But Paul viewed his own missionary task in a slightly different way. He saw his job to be the formation of Christian congregations at strategic points throughout the Roman Empire. From these the surrounding regions could be reached. At this point in his ministry he had completed that kind of work in the areas where he had been operating. He had founded thriving and growing churches in all the main centres of population. The business of establishing other churches in the surrounding areas was now the responsibility of the new Christian converts.

Paul had his sights set on a higher goal. His own special responsibility was to ensure that during the course of his lifetime the gospel would be spread throughout the whole civilized world, which for him meant the Roman Empire. Italy already had churches at its most important centres, including Rome, and so Paul saw Spain as his next objective. Yet at the same time he believed that, as the 'apostle to the Gentiles', he had something to contribute to the church in the most strategic position of all: Rome the capital of the empire. Even though he was normally reluctant to enter what had previously been the sphere of other missionaries, one of his main ambitions was to visit the city of Rome. But before this, he had other problems to face.

Paul and his own people

Romans 15:31

Acts 21:20–21
In writing to the Roman Christians Paul had made what seems to have been almost a prophetic statement. He asked them to pray for him, 'that I may be delivered from the unbelievers in Judea, and that my service for Jerusalem may be acceptable to the saints'. Paul was hated in Judea more than anywhere else, even by some of those who called themselves Christians. In their eyes, he was

nothing less than a traitor to the Jewish faith. As a Pharisee he had been entrusted with the priceless privilege of interpreting the Old Testament Law. As a Christian, they said, he had despised his privilege, declaring the Law to be inadequate as a means of salvation, and powerless as a source of moral inspiration.

This was something that troubled Paul very much. Contrary to what his opponents thought, he held his own Jewish heritage to be very valuable. He was reluctant to think that God had altogether rejected the Jewish people. He believed that they had misun-

Erastus, City Treasurer in Corinth, sent his greetings to fellow-Christians in Rome, at the end of Paul's letter (Romans 16:23). He is probably the same man as is named in this inscription from Corinth: 'Erastus laid this pavement at his own expense, in appreciation of his appointment as *aedile*.'

derstood the whole point of the Old Testament while he, Paul, now saw its full meaning because of his new relationship with Jesus Christ, who was its true fulfilment.

As a sign of his own continuing care for his people, Paul had organized in the Gentile congregations a collection for the Jewish church at Jerusalem. Surely this would show that, whatever theological differences might exist between the Jewish and Gentile Christian churches, they were united in a practical way.

Paul set off for Jerusalem in the company of Christians from Beroea, Thessalonica, Derbe and Ephesus, along with Luke and Timothy. He must have known that in some ways he was taking a foolhardy step, for on the journey he stopped off at Miletus and sent for the elders of the Ephesian church. In the course of his talk with them he made it clear that he did not expect to see them again. He knew that all he could expect at the hands of the Jews was 'imprisonment and afflictions'. But, as on previous occasions, he put the glory of his Lord and Master before his own safety: 'I do not account my life of any value nor as precious to myself, if only I may accomplish my course and the ministry which I received from

Acts 20:4–6

Acts 20:23

Acts 20:24

the Lord Jesus, to testify to the gospel of the grace of God.'

When he arrived in Jerusalem, Paul's fears and expectations were fully realized. Reports brought to Judea by foreign Jews had contained exaggerated accounts of Paul's break with Judaism. They made no mention of those concessions Paul had sometimes made to Jewish prejudices. James, who was now the leader of the church in Jerusalem, explained the situation to him more fully: 'You see, brother, how many thousands there are among the Jews of those who have believed; they are all zealous for the law, and they have been told about you that you teach all the Jews who are among the Gentiles to forsake Moses, telling them not to circumcise their children or observe the customs.'

Acts 21:20–21

James, like Paul himself, hoped the collection brought by Paul and his friends would pacify these hostile Jewish Christians. He also advised Paul to make a peace gesture to the Jews themselves, by paying the expenses involved in a ritual vow taken by four Jewish Christians, and by sharing in their fast. Paul agreed to do this. His policy had always been one of fitting in with all kinds of people: 'I have become all things to all men, that I might by all means save some.'

Acts 21:23–24

1 Corinthians 9:22

Towards the end of this fast, some Jews from the province of Asia spotted Paul in the Temple. They worked themselves up into believing that he had defiled the Temple by taking some of his Gentile companions into its inner court.

Acts 21:27–29

To do this was a very serious crime. It was one of the very few crimes carrying the death penalty that the Romans allowed the Jews to try and punish themselves. To ensure that no one committed this crime unknowingly, an inscription stood over the main gate of the Temple in Paul's day. It read, in three languages: 'No foreigner may enter within the barricade which surrounds the Temple and its enclosure. Anyone who is caught doing so will have himself to blame for his ensuing death.' Two such inscriptions, in Greek, have been found by archaeologists on the Temple site in Jerusalem.

A prisoner for Jesus

Acts 21:30–36

The Jews who saw Paul in the Temple wanted to act without the decision of a court by killing him there and then. But the Roman commander arrived and rescued Paul – not because of any sympathy for the apostle, but probably in the hope of avoiding a riot. This Roman commander assumed that Paul must be some sort of political agitator. He was about to have him flogged to get the truth from him when Paul claimed the immunity from such treatment which was his right as a Roman citizen.

Acts 22:22–29

The next step was to call a meeting of the Jewish supreme council, the Sanhedrin. The accusation against Paul was clearly a religious matter concerned with the Jewish Law, and the Sanhedrin was the proper body to deal with such a question. But the meeting ended in uproar when Paul started a quarrel between the Pharisees and Sadducees by stating that he was still a good Pharisee and believed in the resurrection of the dead.

Acts 23:1–10

Anyone could enter the outer court of the Temple in Jerusalem; but Gentiles were forbidden to enter the inner courts on pain of death. Inscriptions in Greek (like this one) and Latin warned visitors of this penalty.

Paul was kept prisoner for two years at Caesarea, the centre of Roman administration in Judea. The city was a Mediterranean port and commercial centre. A few Roman pillars, later used by the Crusaders in their own building work, can still be seen on the sea shore.

Jerusalem had always been a dangerous place for the Romans. When it was learned that a plan was afoot to kill Paul he was taken under strong guard to Caesarea, the Roman headquarters on the coast of Palestine. There he would escape the direct notice of the Jewish authorities.

Acts 23:12–24

At Caesarea Paul was again tried before the Roman procurator Felix. This time the charge was not only that of defiling the Temple, but also of provoking civil disorder wherever he went. There is a clear parallel here between the trials of Paul and the earlier trials of Jesus. In Jesus' case the original accusation of the Jews was a religious one, which was altered to a political one before the Roman judge, so that a definite charge could be brought under Roman law.

Though Felix, like every other Roman official, disliked anything that might cause disorder, he was convinced of Paul's innocence. He postponed his decision on the case, partly in the hope of receiving a bribe from Paul and partly for fear of arousing yet more trouble among the Jews if Paul was found innocent.

Acts 24:1–26

Paul's voyage to Rome

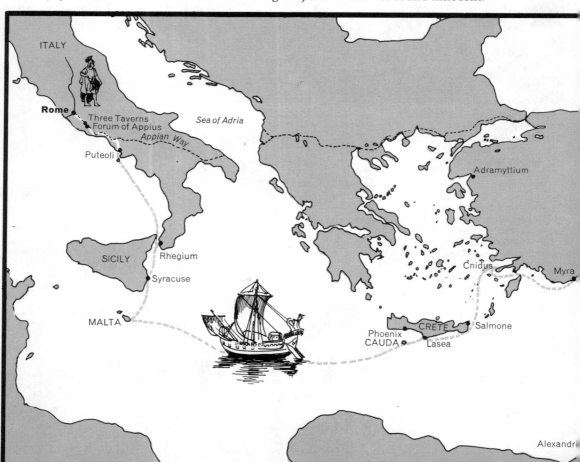

At this point (about AD 59) Felix himself was recalled to Rome to give account of his behaviour in other affairs. The new procurator was a man called Porcius Festus, who heard Paul's case again. He suggested another trial in Jerusalem, something that was quite unthinkable to Paul. He knew the risk of assassination there, and he could also foresee further delays. His imprisonment had already lasted two years. Paul knew that he must reach his ultimate goal, Rome. If he had to go there as a prisoner, so it would have to be. So he decided to exercise his right of appeal to the supreme court of the Roman Empire: the emperor himself in Rome.

Acts 25:1–12

Festus was completely unsettled by Paul's appeal to Rome, for he realized the weakness of the case against Paul and was at a loss to know what to write to the emperor. When Herod Agrippa II visited Caesarea, Paul was again called to appear before both men in the hope that Agrippa, who knew more about Jewish affairs, would be able to suggest a solution. Both rulers appear to have been very impressed with Paul's message, though they tried to pass it off by joking about it.

Acts 26:1–32

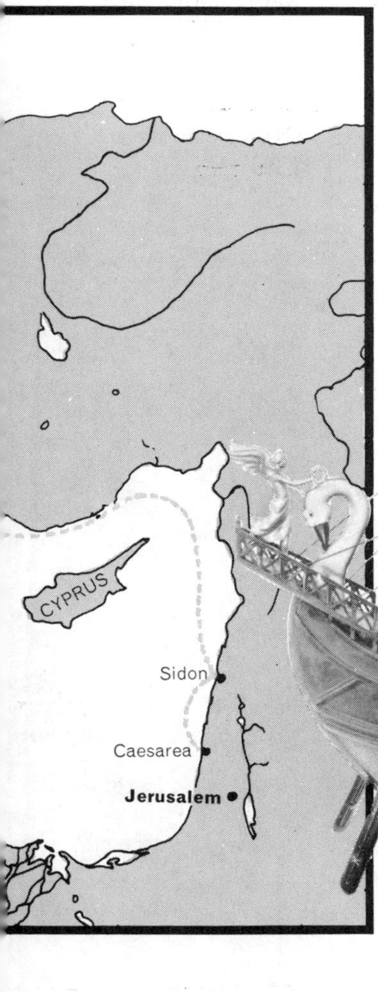

For his voyage to Rome Paul travelled in two of the great grain ships plying between Egypt and Italy. The vessel he started out in, which was wrecked off Malta, evidently carried 276 crew and passengers. It would probably have had a central mast with long yard-arms supporting a large square sail, together with a small top-sail. It probably also had a small foremast with a foresail. Large oars in the stern served as rudders.

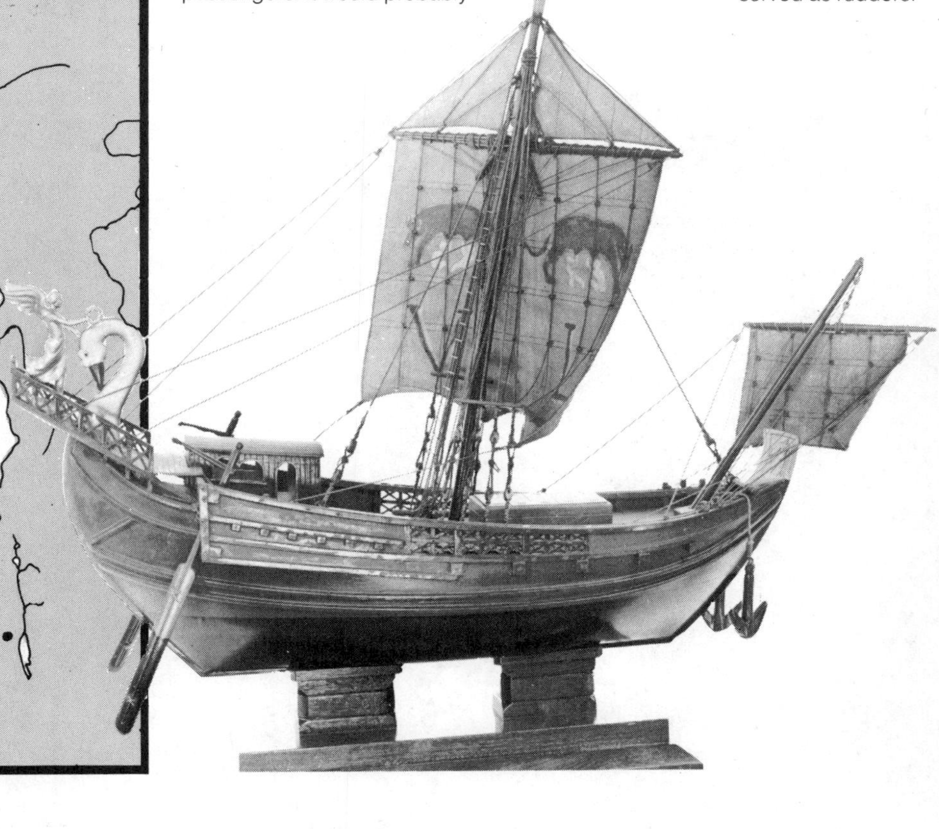

CYPRUS

Sidon

Caesarea

Jerusalem

Destination Rome

At last Paul got his heart's desire, and he was sent off to Rome accompanied by Luke and another of his friends, Aristarchus. He travelled on a ship full of convicted criminals. Such 'prison ships' were making regular voyages from Palestine to Rome at this time. The Romans kept the amphitheatres in Rome operating by the import of wretched criminals from elsewhere in the empire. The criminals probably preferred a 'heroic' death with gladiators or wild animals in the arena to the slow and painful process of crucifixion.

Paul seems to have been treated as a special case. The fact that he had two companions with him suggests he was travelling in the style of a well-to-do Roman, accompanied by two of his slaves. The fact that he could be consulted about details of the voyage also suggests that Paul had a special position. The voyage to Rome, with its storms and shipwrecks, is one of the most graphic descriptions of such an experience in all ancient literature, and is obviously a first-hand account of the journey.

After many adventures on the way, Paul eventually landed at Puteoli in southern Italy, where he was warmly welcomed by the

Acts 27:9–12

Acts 27:1–28:13

Acts 28:14

St Paul's Bay, Malta, ties in with the description of the site of Paul's shipwreck in Acts 27:39–41. A shallow sandbank runs out and is probably where the ship struck and began breaking up. The crew and passengers used timber from the ship to float ashore on the calmer water inside the spit. Paul continued his journey to Rome in the Alexandrian ship Castor and Pollux.

Opposite. After Paul landed in Italy Christians came out from Rome to meet him at the Forum of Appius on the Appian Way. This famous Roman road is still lined with Roman monuments.

Acts 28:15

local Christians. As he got nearer Rome some of the Christians even came out some distance along the road to meet him. For two years Paul remained a prisoner. But he was permitted to live in a house rented by himself along with some Roman guards, whom he would also have had to pay.

Even in such unusual circumstances, however, Paul still did not lose sight of the commission given to him by the risen Lord. He knew that it was not really the Jews or the Romans who had sent him to Rome: it was God. Paul had planned to come to the capital city and, although he could hardly have foreseen the nature of his

It is unclear how the Christian church in Rome came into existence. It included people from Greek, Roman and Jewish backgrounds, and some from the Emperor's household. The Forum, seen here, stood with the other major public buildings at the city centre. Rome at this time had a population of over one million.

Acts 23:11

arrival, he knew that Christ had specifically instructed him to 'bear witness also at Rome'.

Accordingly, Paul soon got in contact with the leaders of the Jewish community there. As in other places, when they heard his message some of them believed but the majority rejected it. So Paul again turned to the Gentiles. In spite of the limitations imposed by his house arrest, the last picture we see of him is of a man still living in complete obedience to the call he had been given so many years before. He was at last in the centre of the empire, 'preaching the

Acts 28:31

kingdom of God and teaching about the Lord Jesus Christ quite openly and unhindered'.

Acts 26:18

Paul had achieved his objective. The risen Lord had sent him out as the apostle to the Gentiles. His job was 'to open their eyes, that they may turn from darkness to light and from the power of Satan to God, that they may receive forgiveness of sins and a place among those who are sanctified by faith in me'. As Paul reached Rome, he knew that he had fulfilled the terms of his commission. He approached the 'eternal city' with the satisfaction of knowing that in every strategic centre throughout the whole of the then-known world there was a group of people who had experienced the enlightenment brought by the Christian message; people whose lives were directed, as his had been, by the risen Christ.

When did Paul die?

The story in Acts ends at the point where Paul arrived in Rome. Luke was more interested in recounting the progress of the Christian message from Jerusalem to Rome than in the messengers whom God chose to spread the good news. But all the traditions of the early church say that Paul met a martyr's death at Rome during the persecution ordered by Nero in AD 64. We may suppose that, despite the long delays, he was ultimately brought to trial at Rome. Perhaps he was sentenced to death immediately after this, though in view of the reluctance of Felix and Festus even to send him for trial it is unlikely that he could have been found guilty on the charges under which he was sent to the emperor's court.

Since this trial would take place about AD 62, Paul presumably engaged in other activities until his final trial and death under Nero in AD 64. This is certainly the view taken by early church tradition. Eusebius, one of the early church historians, tells us that 'after defending himself the apostle was sent again on his ministry of preaching, and coming a second time to the same city, suffered martyrdom under Nero' (*Ecclesiastical History*, 2.22). There are two possibilities for his further activities:

● One is that Paul fulfilled his intention of going on to Spain. There is no biblical evidence to support this. But

there are traditions in Spain itself to this effect, and also a statement that he did so in *1 Clement* 5 (a letter written about AD 95 by Clement of Rome to the church at Corinth). But it is more likely that the originators of these traditions based their statements on what Paul said in Romans 15:24, and assumed that since he wanted to visit Spain he must actually have done so.

● The other possibility concerning what Paul did after his supposed release arises from the references to Paul's travels in the Pastoral Epistles (1 and 2 Timothy and Titus). These letters may suggest that Paul again revisited some of the places he had been to earlier in Asia Minor and Greece, and also some others of which there is no mention in Acts or in the earlier letters, such as Colossae, Crete and Nicopolis.

It is not essential to assume that such visits took place towards the end of Paul's life, for Acts by no means gives us a complete account of all Paul's earlier travels. In 2 Corinthians 11:23–27 he speaks of many incidents not mentioned in Acts, but which had presumably occurred in the course of his pastoral ministry in Ephesus and the surrounding areas. Nevertheless, it would take a considerable amount of ingenuity to fit the travel references of the Pastoral Epistles into the Acts narrative. It is certainly easier to suppose that they represent further missionary exploits after his first visit to Rome. But even then it is by no means easy to fit all these references into a plausible journey. There are also other difficulties involved in understanding the Pastoral Epistles, which are dealt with in the next chapter.

Chapter 20 Letters from prison

In four of his letters (apart from 2 Timothy) Paul refers to himself as a prisoner. So it is generally assumed that they were written during his period of imprisonment at Rome from AD 60–62. These are the letters to the churches at Colossae, Philippi and Ephesus, and the personal letter to Philemon, who lived at Colossae.

The church at Colossae

Colossians and Philemon were written at the same time as each other, the former to the church and the latter to one member of it. Timothy is associated with Paul as the author of them both, and there are greetings in both from the same five people. Aristarchus,

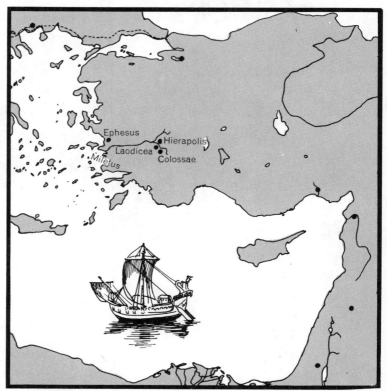

Towns of the Lycus Valley. Several of Paul's later letters were written to Christians in this area (Colossians, Ephesians and Philemon).

Mark, Demas, Epaphras, Luke and Archippus of Colossae are mentioned in both, and so is Philemon's runaway slave, Onesimus.

Though Colossae was not too far from Ephesus, where Paul had worked for three years, he had never visited the town. The church at Colossae had probably been founded by Epaphras, who may have been one of Paul's converts in Ephesus. The fact that such a thriving church had been established at Colossae by this time is striking proof of the wisdom of Paul's missionary strategy of establishing his own work in a central place from which other Christians could reach out to the surrounding areas.

Colossae stood in the broad fertile valley of the Lycus, near Laodicea. The ancient town is now buried beneath a mound – in the background in this picture of modern Turkey.

Epaphras visited Paul during his imprisonment in Rome, and gave him a generally encouraging report of the Colossian church. But one thing was causing him real concern. This was the spread of a false teaching which today we often call 'the Colossian heresy'. It was a combination of the practices Paul was opposing when he wrote Galatians with the sort of beliefs held by the 'Christ party' in Corinth. The racial exclusivism of people like the Judaizers had been combined with the intellectual exclusivism common in many pagan religious cults of the day. As a result a group of people in the Colossian church considered themselves better Christians than the rest of the church members. These people held that a complete and lasting salvation could not be achieved simply by faith in Christ, as Paul had taught. In addition to having faith in Christ, it was also necessary to obtain an insight into divine things through a secret knowledge given in a mystical way.

Such knowledge could be acquired by taking part in various ritual practices, such as circumcision, not eating certain foods, and observing Jewish festivals and sabbaths. We can see that in practice the Colossian heretics must have seemed very similar to the Judaizers who led astray Paul's converts in Galatia. For they were also wanting to impose circumcision and other Jewish rituals. But the keeping of Old Testament principles among the Colossian Christians was in fact quite different from the teaching of the Judaizers. The Galatians had been tempted to observe the Old Testament Law as an integral part of keeping the religious covenants of the Old Testament. The Judaizers had told them they could not be a part of God's people unless they first became Jews, by accepting the claims of the Old Testament Law.

Colossians 2:23

But here in Colossae the heretics were keeping such rules for quite different reasons. They were 'ascetics'; what they wanted was something that would help them to check 'the indulgence of the flesh'. They were not 'legalists' like the Judaizers; the fact that they chose to achieve their asceticism by using certain parts of the Old Testament Law was only coincidence. This is very clear from Paul's reply to them. He deals not with the issues of law and grace (as in Galatians), but with the basic moral issues raised by any kind of ascetic practice.

Colossians

In his letter to the Colossian church, Paul deals with this false teaching by emphasizing again that in Christ believers can find all they need. Like the later Gnostics, some of the Colossians had been suggesting that they needed other supernatural agencies, and that Jesus was just one of several possible manifestations of God. Against this, Paul firmly asserts that 'In Christ all the fulness of God was pleased to dwell' (Colossians 1:19). Indeed, he went further than this by reminding his readers that in Jesus 'the whole fulness of deity dwells *bodily*' (2:9).

The Colossians claimed they needed to experience something deep and mysterious if they were to find full salvation, and Paul agreed with them. His own job could be described as the presentation of 'the mystery'. But far from being something deep and hidden, this 'mystery' was the very thing that lay at the heart of all Paul's preaching: the simple fact of Christ's own life within them (1:27). Whatever the Christian may need, it can all be found in Christ, for in him 'are hid all the treasures of wisdom and knowledge' (2:3).

Paul then went on to remind his

readers of all the things they had as Christians, some of which they were now trying to achieve by other, mystical means.

● Were some of them claiming to be super-spiritual because they were circumcised? All Christians, says Paul, have received 'a circumcision made without hands' (2:11) when they fulfilled the true meaning of the old ceremony by 'putting off the body of flesh', that is their old sinful lives, that they might live a new life in the power of the Holy Spirit given to them by Christ.

● Were some claiming to have a new kind of life that other Christians did not have? Then they should recognize that all Christians have been made alive by God through what Christ did on the cross (2:13–15).

● What about ritual observances, designed to keep 'the flesh' in subjection? These also are of no real value. Even in terms of their own original purpose they have been superseded. They were but 'a shadow of what is to come'. Since the reality has now come in Christ, they are no longer valid. In practice they were a waste of time. For though they may have 'an appearance of wisdom in promoting rigour of devotion and self-abasement and severity to the body ... they are of no value in checking the indulgence of the flesh' (2:23).

Instead of fixing their attention on these things, the Colossians ought to live up to their true position in Christ. Whoever they are, and whatever experiences they claim to have, all Christians stand equal before God. All have the same temptations to face (3:5–11), and there is only one way for all of them to overcome such temptations: 'Set your minds on things that are above, not on things that are on earth. For you have died, and your life is hid with Christ in God ... Hence there cannot be Greek and Jew, circumcised and uncircumcised, barbarian, Scythian, slave, free man, but Christ is all, and in all' (3:2–3, 11).

Instead of following a false set of values based on their own worthless speculations, the Colossians ought again to remind themselves that the true ambition of the Christian must be to become like Christ (3:12–17): 'Whatever you do, in word or deed, do everything in the name of the Lord Jesus, giving thanks to God the Father through him' (3:17).

By their emphasis on asceticism and speculation the Colossian heretics had taken the Christian faith out of real life. But Paul was convinced, as always, that the Christian faith must be a faith for realistic living. So he ends his letter by showing how the power of Christ that lives in the Christian (1:27) works itself out in the family (3:18–21), at work (3:22–4:1), in the church (4:2–4), and in life in general (4:5–6).

Philemon

Along with the letter to the church in Colossae, Paul also sent a personal note to one of its leading members: Philemon. He must have been quite affluent, for the Christians met for their regular meetings in his house (verse 2). Like everyone else in his position in the Roman empire, Philemon had a number of slaves. One of them, Onesimus, had run away from Colossae, perhaps taking some of Philemon's possessions with him (verses 18–19). But he had met Paul, and as a result he became a Christian himself.

Paul knew it was his duty – both as a citizen and as a Christian – to return Onesimus to his master. There were legal penalties in the Roman empire for anyone harbouring runaway slaves – and in addition, Paul could see that any other course of action would threaten the bonds of Christian friendship that existed between himself and Onesimus. It was for these practical reasons that Paul therefore sent Onesimus back to Colossae, along with

this short personal letter. Of course Paul's action in doing this raises other questions about his attitudes to slavery as an institution. In particular, modern readers will wish to ask how this episode fits in with Paul's categorical statements elsewhere that freedom is at the very heart of the Christian gospel (eg Galatians 3:28).

We shall deal with this and related issues in chapter 22. Here we should notice that Paul does explicitly express the hope that he is not returning Onesimus to exactly the same position as he was in before. He sends him back as 'not just a slave, but much more than a slave: he is a dear brother in Christ' (verse 16). And he tells Philemon to 'welcome him back just as you would welcome me' (verse 17). Indeed, more than that. For many scholars think that Paul was actually asking for Onesimus to be released from his service so that he could return to work full-time with Paul as a Christian missionary (verses 11–14).

We have no certain knowledge of what happened when Onesimus got back to Colossae. He may have been set free and returned to Paul, to become a leading figure in the Christian churches of the area. At the beginning of the second century, Ignatius mentions an Onesimus who was leader of the church at Ephesus, describing him as 'a man of inexpressible love' and 'an excellent bishop' (Ignatius, *To the Ephesians* 1). It has been suggested that if this was the same person, it could explain why a short personal letter to Philemon had been preserved and included in the official collection of Paul's letters to churches. Depending on the date we give to Paul's imprisonment when he wrote, this is perhaps just possible. But we can certainly assume that Philemon must have complied with Paul's request – otherwise this note would undoubtedly have been quickly forgotten.

This Roman slave badge reads, 'Seize me if I should try to escape and send me back to my master' Onesimus' escape was a very risky venture.

The church at Ephesus

Colossians 4:16

There is in Colossians a reference to another letter: 'When this letter has been read among you, have it read also in the church of the Laodiceans; and see that you read also the letter from Laodicea.' Laodicea was another town quite near to Colossae, and Paul wanted the churches to exchange letters.

There is, of course, no 'letter to the Laodiceans' contained in our New Testament. Noting this omission, the church of the early centuries lost no time in producing such a letter. We know a Latin version; it may also have been available in Greek. There is every reason to suppose that this letter (which is almost impossible to date accurately) is a forgery. It contains no theology, and consists of a series of bits and pieces from Paul's other letters strung together in an aimless way.

Many modern scholars believe we do in fact possess a copy of 'the letter from Laodicea' to which Paul referred – namely the letter in our New Testament known as Ephesians. This letter contains in a fuller and more carefully argued form the same kind of teaching about the person of Christ as in Colossians, but without the pointed references to the local Colossian heresy.

Three other things also suggest that this letter to the Ephesians was probably intended for other churches in the area as well as for the Christians at Ephesus:

● The words 'at Ephesus' in Ephesians 1:1 (the only indication that the letter was destined for that city) are not found in our best and oldest manuscripts of this letter. Some modern versions of the New Testament put the words 'at Ephesus' in the margin.

● There are no personal greetings in this letter, though Paul probably had more friends in Ephesus than anywhere else.

● The second-century heretic Marcion called our Ephesians 'the letter to the Laodiceans'.

We may therefore suggest that Ephesians was a circular letter addressed to a number of different congregations. The words 'at Ephesus' in Ephesians 1:1 would be found in the copy that went to that city, while the copy referred to in Colossians 4:16 would have the words 'at Laodicea' instead.

Ephesians

In Ephesians, Paul again emphasizes the central place of Christ in the plan of God and in the life of the Christian believer. He begins by reminding his readers of the great privileges they possess in Christ. Though the people to whom he was writing had previously 'lived in the passions of their flesh' (Ephesians 2:3), God had put them in a new position. They had been 'made ... alive together with Christ ... and raised ... up with him, and made to sit with him in the heavenly places' (2:5–6). Every individual Christian had become a part of God's new creation in which he planned 'to unite all things in Christ, things in heaven and things on earth' (1:10).

Some of the people who read Paul's letter had been told these things before by Paul himself. For this was his special ministry: 'to preach to the Gentiles the unsearchable riches of Christ' (3:8); and to demonstrate how those 'riches' could be received and enjoyed in real life. Some of his readers may have been influenced by false teaching like the Colossian heresy. They would find the true satisfaction they desired only if they were willing to be 'filled with all the fullness of God' (3:19), which is found nowhere else but in Christ.

After setting out this profound description of Christ as Saviour of the world and as the source of all physical, mental and spiritual knowledge and activity, Paul went on to draw out the practical implications of all this. If his

readers were indeed members of Christ's body, new people and children of God, they must show by their actions who they really are:

● In the church they should be 'eager to maintain the unity of the Spirit in the bond of peace' (4:3). As in 1 Corinthians 12, Paul again says that they could expect the unity of the Spirit to be displayed by the giving of 'gifts' to 'the body' for its growth and development (4:7–16). Because Christians are united with one another in the church fellowship, any wrong done by one member will inevitably affect the others. This would 'grieve the Holy Spirit of God' (4:30). In view of what God had done for them in Christ, Christians ought to 'be kind to one another, tenderhearted, forgiving one another, as God in Christ forgave' them (4:32). Paul could even advise them to 'be imitators of God' (5:1), by showing in their dealings with one another the same self-sacrificing love as God had shown to them in Christ.

● In personal morality Christians should 'take no part in the unfruitful works of darkness' (5:11). What ought to characterize them is that they are 'filled with the Spirit' (5:18), the results of which Paul had listed in Galatians 5:22–23.

● In their social life Christians must again be ruled by the principle of self-giving love, whether the matter at issue is in the family (5:21–6:4) or at work (6:5–9).

This coin was minted at Ephesus, the leading city of the Roman province of Asia.

The Christian church was and is made up of people, not of an organization primarily or buildings. These people learn an entirely new way of relating together, based on the love Jesus taught.

Finally, Paul reminded his readers that in their life as Christians they would encounter opposition, 'the wiles of the devil', against which they must 'put on the whole armour of God' (6:11).

As an ethical theory, what Paul had put forward here would be impossible to carry out. How could a man or woman be ruled by self-sacrificing love of the same kind that God had shown in Christ? Paul knew from his own personal experience and his knowledge of the experience of others, that it was possible in only one way: if the Christian was 'strong in the Lord and in the strength of his might' (6:10). This was a lesson that Paul had emphasized in the first letter he wrote, and a lifetime of work for Christ had only strengthened his belief that 'if we live by the Spirit', we ought also to 'walk by the Spirit' (Galatians 5:25).

Did Paul write Ephesians?

In most of Paul's letters we are always close to the heartbeat of the apostle, and usually not far from controversy. It takes little imagination to envisage the furious arguments that led to the writing of Galatians or 1–2 Corinthians, for example. But in Ephesians things are different. The discussion is much more serene and settled, and seems to progress independently of any direct involvement with opponents, or indeed any specific readers.

A number of other arguments can also be presented, which together support the suggestion that perhaps Paul never actually wrote this letter:

● **Language** A number of words found in Ephesians are not used elsewhere in Paul's writings. This includes some prominent features, such as the references to 'the heavenly world' (1:3; 1:20; 2:6; 3:10; 6:12) – a key term here, but never used in Paul's other writings.

● **Style** The way Ephesians is put together is also distinctive. Instead of the unplanned – and largely unrestrained – language of the other letters, Ephesians moves from one theme to another in more sedate fashion, generally using more complex sentence structures in the process.

● **Colossians** Ephesians has a close resemblance to Colossians. More than a third of the words of Colossians also occur in Ephesians. And since Coloss-ians has more of Paul's usual personal touch about it, many think that must have been the original letter, which was subsequently copied and adapted by the later author of Ephesians.

● **Doctrine and Theology** At a number of points, Ephesians seems to reflect concerns that we know were especially typical of church life later than the time of Paul. For example, the use of the term 'church' to describe a universal movement, including all Christians everywhere (eg 1:22–23). Paul generally writes only of local groups of Christians ('the church in Corinth', etc.). Then there is the position of 'apostles and prophets' as 'the foundation stone' of this church (2:20): does this (along with the list of church officers in 4:11) point to a time when church structures were more fully developed? There is also the apparent absence of any reference to the *parousia* of Jesus, and to the theme of 'justification by faith'.

So was Ephesians written not by Paul himself, but perhaps by one of his close friends, or a later admirer who wished to commend Paul's work to a wider readership? It has been suggested that Ephesians is a compendium of Paul's teaching, written as a concise introduction to the major themes of his theology, perhaps at a time when his letters were being collected together. But Ephesians is not really a summary of the whole of Paul's teaching. It is precisely the absence of some characteristic themes that has cast doubt on its genuineness as a letter by Paul himself – and the same criticism applies if we regard Ephesians as a synopsis of Paul's theology.

It has also been suggested that both the differences and similarities between Paul's other letters and Ephesians can be explained by his use of a secretary. We know that Paul regularly asked others to actually put pen to paper, only signing his own name to validate what had been written (eg Galatians 6:11) – and it may be that Luke, or some other person, was responsible for the final forms of expression in this letter. There are certainly a number of striking linguistic similarities between Ephesians and Luke-Acts.

Whatever we conclude about the person who actually wrote the words down, we should certainly not miss the weakness of the other arguments put forward against Paul's authorship. The close relationship between Colossians and Ephesians really proves nothing. A modern author writing about theology will quite often base one book on something that has been written previously – and Paul had certainly done this before. The relationship between Galatians and Romans is a useful model here, and is in many significant respects similar to the relationship between Colossians and Ephesians. Both Romans and Ephesians take up points that had previously been made in the heat of debate, while refining them and making them more universally applicable to a wider readership.

Viewed in this light, many of the apparent theological differences between Ephesians and earlier letters also appear in a different perspective. Nothing in Ephesians actually contradicts previous statements by Paul, and much of it is a logical development of things he had said elsewhere. It is true, for example, that nowhere else does Paul use the term 'church' to describe all Christians everywhere. But the very fact that he can talk of Christians in Rome, or Corinth, or wherever, as being 'the church' implies that there must be some distinguishing factor that binds them all together. Paul clearly had a great

In Paul's time many books came in the form of a scroll – a long roll of parchment or papyrus. The reader would unroll one end and roll up the other while reading.

sense of solidarity existing between the various churches, or he would not have organized the collection for Jerusalem – and to talk of all these groups together as 'the church' simply gives theological expression to that reality.

Many of the other alleged doctrinal discrepancies are not as impressive as they can be made to look. It may be true that the *parousia* does not feature in Ephesians (though it must surely be implied in 4:30 and 5:26–27) – but it is not mentioned in Romans either! And 'justification by faith' would only need to be central if it was the foundational core of Paul's thinking, as some have claimed. In point of fact, however, one of the major themes of Ephesians is the work of the Holy Spirit in the lives of Christians – and this almost certainly has a far stronger claim to be the real centre of Paul's theology anyway.

Ephesians is certainly different. But there is nothing in it that cannot legitimately be seen as the product of further reflection by Paul himself on some of the significant themes of his other prison letters. Just as his earlier handling of the controversy in Galatia had led him to articulate his thinking more carefully in his later letter to Rome, so his argument with the Colossian heretics perhaps led to a similar process which culminated in the writing of Ephesians. And in the context of a restriction of his liberty, he must have had plenty of time and opportunity for such further reflection!

The church at Philippi

Paul brought out the same lesson in the other letter he wrote from prison: Philippians. With the exception of Philemon, this is the most personal of Paul's letters. It was written to acknowledge a gift that the Philippian church had sent to Paul to help him financially while in Rome. One of the Philippian Christians, a man called Epaphroditus, had brought the gift from Philippi and had been a great help to Paul during his short stay in Rome. Most of Paul's letter, which was sent back to Philippi with Epaphroditus, is concerned with personal matters affecting Paul's possible release, and expressing his warm affection for the Philippian Christians.

Philippians

Paul had always been especially close to the Christians in Philippi. It was his first church on European soil – and it was also apparently one of the few that had not been torn apart by damaging arguments about Christian faith and behaviour.

Paul begins with an appreciative expression of thanks to God for all that these Christians had meant to him (1:3–11). Unlike some others, they had consistently 'helped me in the work of the gospel from the very first day until now' (1:5). This is why he was able to accept their financial generosity (1:7) – something that he felt unwise in the case of more volatile congregations such as that in Corinth (1 Corinthians 9:8–18). Because of their open and friendly attitude, he can be confident that their Christian living will be marked by 'the truly good qualities which only Jesus Christ can produce, for the glory and praise of God' (1:11).

He continues to sound this note as he brings them up to date with his own situation in prison (1:12–30). His main ambition in life has always been to bring glory to Jesus – and even his imprisonment is doing that (1:12). Since Christians already have Jesus Christ living within them, Paul knows that physical death would only deepen that experience (1:21). Death may be preferable to prison for Paul, but he can see good reasons why God will probably allow him to live a little longer: 'to add to your progress and joy in the faith' (1:25). To suffer for the cause of the Christian gospel is not a sign of defeat, but of triumph. So they should neither be sorry for his present plight, nor afraid of persecution themselves (1:27–30).

But there was one thing that bothered Paul about the church at Philippi. Some of the Christians were quarrelling with each other. Paul later names two argumentative women, Euodia and Syntyche (4:2–3) – but they were not the only ones. In urging them to 'look out for one another's interests, not just for your own' (2:4), Paul quotes from an early hymn that was no doubt familiar to his readers, and probably to Christians in other churches as well (2:6–11). It is obvious that this passage is a quotation: it interrupts the flow of Paul's language; and it has the style of a hymn, with a definite rhythm, carefully balanced lines, and the 'parallelism' that was characteristic of Hebrew poetry. This 'Christ hymn' has been the subject of much scholarly debate. Who wrote it? Where did Paul get it from? How did he use it? And what did it mean? There is no agreed answer to all those questions. But it is clear enough why Paul inserts it here.

This is the only place in Paul's letters where he gives the example of Jesus as a pattern for Christian behaviour (2 Corinthians 8:9–10 is very similar). Modern Christian preachers who tell their listeners to follow Jesus' example usually have in mind the kind of things that Jesus did during his ministry. The Gospels give us many examples of his compassion, care and good works. But it is quite striking that Paul never urges Christians to follow this example. In those places where he does give Jesus as an example for Christians to follow, the

Paul summons the Philippian Christians to 'run straight towards the goal in order to win the prize, which is God's call through Christ Jesus to the life above'.

example he chooses is his giving up all that was his when he became a human person. This idea was very important for Paul, and lay at the heart of much of his thinking. In order to be a Christian at all, people must be prepared to give up themselves and all that they are completely to Christ. This was the lesson he had learned on the road to Damascus, when he himself responded in faith to the demands of the risen Jesus. It runs like a golden thread through the fabric of all his letters.

Paul now moves on to explain in greater practical detail what it means for a Christian's life to be infused with the life of the risen Jesus himself. For his readers, it means a lifestyle that is distinctively Christian, shining like stars in a dark sky (2:12–16). For himself, it would eventually lead to a martyr's death. But that too was a privilege: 'If that is so, I am glad and share my joy with you all' (2:17–18). Epaphroditus (himself a member of the Philippian church) had recently experienced the same feelings, for he too 'risked his life and nearly died for the sake of the work of Christ'. He and Timothy would soon be going to Philippi to encourage the Christians there, and perhaps even to prepare the way for a visit by Paul himself (2:19–30).

At this point, Paul seems to digress and to write about troublemakers who were operating in Philippi (3:1–4:4). Some have argued that this section was originally a separate letter altogether. If so, it is hard to see why a later editor would have inserted it at such an odd point in Paul's writing. We know that Paul wrote impulsively, and would often change subjects quite unexpectedly – and this is what has happened here. The people he writes about are 'those who insist on cutting the body' (3:2) – circumcisers. Paul does not spell out whether they were Judaizers (as in Galatia), or ascetics (as in Colossae). But the former seems more likely, for he replies by reminding them of his own achievements in keeping the Jewish Law (3:1–11). He had more justification than most in sticking to Judaism: 'As far as a person can be righteous by obeying the commands of the Law, I was without fault' (3:6). But he had now discovered a more satisfying way of relating to God.

Even the very best that Pharisaic piety could offer was 'complete loss for the sake of what is so much more valuable, the knowledge of Christ Jesus my lord' (3:8). This knowledge consisted not primarily in knowing facts about Jesus, but in enjoying a close personal relationship with him, in which the resurrection life of Jesus himself gave Paul a new and meaningful dynamic for his own daily life: 'All I want is to know Christ and to experience the power of his resurrection, to share in his sufferings and become like him in his death' (3:10).

This did not mean that Paul had 'arrived' spiritually – as some of his opponents in Corinth and Colossae believed they had. He was still on his way, like a marathon runner moving steadily towards the finishing line. Those who wanted to be spiritually mature should follow his example (3:12–21).

Finally, he closes this most joyful of all his letters with advice on a number of topics. He reminds his readers that, like him, they can have 'the strength to face all conditions by the power that Christ gives' (4:13), for 'my God will supply all your needs' (4:19).

When was Paul imprisoned?

In our consideration of Paul's life and letters, we have assumed that those letters which indicate Paul was a prisoner when he wrote them were written from Rome between AD 60 and AD 62. This is the only imprisonment recorded in Acts, and it has been natural for readers of Paul's letters from the earliest times to assume that they were written at this time.

Following the lead given by Professor G.S. Duncan, some scholars now think that at least one or two of these four letters were written not from Rome but during an unrecorded imprisonment at Ephesus, which took place during Paul's three-year stay there. There is a considerable amount of evidence that makes such an imprisonment likely.

2 Corinthians 11:23, written towards the end of Paul's stay in Ephesus, informs us that by comparison with other Christian workers he had experienced 'far greater labours, far more imprisonments, with countless beatings, and often near death'. In 1 Corinthians 15:32 Paul wrote that he 'fought with beasts at Ephesus', a phrase which we saw to be a figure of speech and could probably describe a trial preceding imprisonment. Again, 2 Corinthians 1:8 speaks of 'the affliction we experienced in Asia', the Roman province of which Ephesus was the capital. In addition Romans 16:7, written shortly after he left Ephesus,

refers to two people as 'my fellow prisoners'.

Other evidence that Paul was imprisoned at Ephesus is to be found in the Latin introductions to New Testament books that were written in the second century under the influence of the Gnostic Marcion. Also the fictitious second-century *Acts of Paul* tells of an imprisonment of Paul at Ephesus, followed by an encounter with lions in the arena, from which he was delivered by supernatural intervention.

Arguments for an imprisonment at Ephesus

The combination of this kind of evidence with the clues in Paul's own writings makes it fairly probable that he did suffer a period of imprisonment during his three-year stay in Ephesus. The fact that Paul may have been imprisoned there does not, of course, make it necessary to believe that he wrote the 'prison letters' from Ephesus. But more positive arguments have been put forward to support this view:

● It is claimed that the friends of Paul who are mentioned as having made contact with him during this imprisonment would be more likely to have been in Ephesus than in Rome, which was a long way from their homes. Against this must be set the fact that we know next to nothing about most of these associates of Paul. The one of whom we know most, Luke, was certainly with Paul in Rome though, according to Acts, not in Ephesus.

● It is argued that Philemon's slave Onesimus would be more likely to run away to Ephesus, which was only about eighty miles from his home in Colossae than to Rome, which would be almost 800 miles away. This again is not a convincing argument; for at that time all roads literally did lead to Rome. A runaway slave would be more likely to try to disappear in the capital of the empire than in a provincial town the size of Ephesus.

● In Philippians we get the impression that there was much travelling to and from Paul's prison; and Ephesus was much nearer to Philippi than Rome. This is often taken to be a strong argument for supposing that Philippians at least must have been written from Ephesus.

● The strongest argument for an Ephesian origin of these letters is that in them Paul was looking forward to an early release, after which he intended visiting his friends in both Philippi and Colossae. In Romans 15:28, however, he had made it plain that after his visit to Jerusalem his intention was not to revisit churches he had founded before, but to go west to Spain.

What then can we conclude from these facts? It is almost certain that Paul did have a period of imprisonment during his stay in Ephesus. It is quite possible that Philippians at least, with its mention of frequent journeys between Philippi and Paul's prison, may have been written at this time. If this was the case, we would need to date the letter to the Philippians about AD 55 instead of AD 62.

In his first letter, the key to much of Paul's argument was found in his conviction that 'I have been crucified with Christ; it is no longer I who live, but Christ who lives in me...'. As he lived

Galatians 2:20

under house arrest in Rome, writing to the Philippian church, Paul again set the dominant note by his simple yet profound

Philippians 1:21

statement, just five words in Greek, 'For to me to live is Christ.' Between these two statements lay a lifetime of Christian experience. Paul had seen what the risen Christ could do with a person's life and talents if they were submitted to the supreme lordship of Christ.

No wonder then that Paul laid such an emphasis on the power that was available to him through the work of the risen Christ in his own life. It had revolutionized the whole course of his career. He knew that it would do the same for all his converts if they were

Philippians 3:8

willing to say with him, 'I count everything as loss because of the surpassing worth of knowing Christ Jesus my Lord.'

It was something of this sort that Paul was saying in all the letters he wrote from prison.

Timothy and Titus

The 'pastoral epistles' (1–2 Timothy and Titus) are quite different in both style and content from Paul's other letters. They were written to advise other leaders of the early church. Both Timothy and Titus are mentioned elsewhere as Paul's companions, though they also worked independently of Paul: Titus in Crete, and Timothy in Ephesus.

These three letters are very similar to each other, and were probably written at about the same time. They deal with four main subjects:

False teachers

Many of Paul's letters were written in response to threats from various opponents: Judaizers in Galatia, ascetics in Colossae, and Jewish Gnostics of a sort in Corinth. Timothy and Titus were facing similar problems, and were under pressure to abandon the gospel message as Paul had delivered it to them.

This false teaching consisted of several elements that we have met before. The Old Testament Law was certainly involved, for some of the troublemakers are identified as 'converts from Judaism, who rebel and deceive others with their nonsense'. It seems that these people were using the Old Testament for their own ends. For Timothy is reminded that 'the Law is good if it is used as it should be used'. The specific argument seems to have been about sex and food. Some were claiming that true spiritual enlightenment could only come by a life of asceticism in which material bodily existence was denied as far as possible. But Timothy is urged to remember that 'Everything that God has created is good; nothing is to be rejected ...'

These people probably had leanings towards a Jewish form of Gnosticism. There is indeed a specific mention of 'the profane talk and foolish arguments of what some people wrongly call "knowledge" (Greek *gnosis*)'. Like the later Gnostics of the second century, they wanted to deny that this world is really God's world – and so the sooner they could escape from it, the better. The fact that Timothy's opponents were arguing about 'myths and endless genealogies which promote speculation ...' and had 'lost their faith in foolish discussions' supports this identification. But of course there was more than one way to belittle bodily existence. Asceticism was not the only option: extreme permissiveness was another. And at least one group mentioned here seems to have chosen this alternative: 'they will hold to the outward form of our religion, but reject its real power'. For Paul, the Christian gospel had always been about changing lifestyles, not about provoking arguments.

Titus 1:10

1 Timothy 1:8

1 Timothy 4:4

1 Timothy 6:20

1 Timothy 1:4–6

2 Timothy 3:5

True belief

In response to all this, Timothy and Titus are encouraged to reaffirm the basic elements of true Christian faith. They must continue to deny the idea that God does not care about the world we live in. The fact that Jesus himself was both truly human and truly divine clearly contradicted such a notion.

Not only did Jesus come into this world to share God's love: he became personally involved with sinful people. The essence of

1 Timothy 3:14–16

1 Timothy 1:15–17

1 Timothy 6:3–10

salvation therefore is not to be found in philosophical speculation, but in humble acceptance of God's love and mercy as demonstrated in the life, death and resurrection of Jesus. Those who have their theological priorities right will show it in the way they live – not motivated by money, but by 'the true words of our Lord Jesus Christ'.

Christian behaviour

1 Timothy 6:1–2; Titus 2:1–5
1 Timothy 5:1–6:2
Titus 3:1–7

Titus 2:5

This theme keeps coming up throughout these three letters. Several passages spell out in more detail how Christians ought to behave. Family relationships, relationships in the church, and attitudes to secular governments should all reflect the best aspirations of the ancient world, 'so that no one will speak evil of the message that comes from God'.

Christian leadership

1 Timothy 6:11–21; Titus 1:5–9
2 Timothy 2:1–26
2 Timothy 3:10–4:8

1 Timothy 3:1–13; 4:6–16

As we might expect, there is much advice here to Titus and Timothy about their own conduct. They are to be examples of good behaviour to all whom they serve. But they must also have courage to stand firm for the truth, recognising that the gospel depends not on personal opinions but on God himself. They must also ensure that those whom they appoint to serve in leadership capacities in their churches also have the same qualities, and are the sort of people whom others can admire.

Did Paul write the Pastoral Epistles?

In the Pastoral letters, each age-group within the church is called to live a life of holiness.

The three letters which we refer to under the combined title 'the Pastoral Epistles' (1 and 2 Timothy and Titus) are very different from Paul's other letters. They were written not to churches, but to two individuals who were working among groups of young Christians: Timothy at Ephesus and Titus in Crete. In form, subject-matter and style these three letters are very similar to each other. But in all these respects they are quite distinct from Paul's other letters. The differences are so striking that many scholars today say that these three letters could not have been written by Paul himself.

In considering this question, four main points need to be taken into consideration:

Paul's movements

It is difficult to fit the movements of Paul shown in these letters into the story of his doings in Acts. Three main reasons have therefore been given to explain the historical references made in these letters:

● First, that *Paul was released after the imprisonment recorded in Acts*. He continued his missionary work for a period of about two years before meeting his death in Rome. No such release is recorded in Acts. But that is no real stumbling-block since Luke's

purpose was not to write a biography of Paul but to tell how the Christian message had spread from small beginnings in Jerusalem to the centre of the empire in Rome. The view that Paul was released and carried on further work has been the traditional view since the earliest days of the church, and is still held today by some scholars. But even working on this assumption, it is still very difficult to string together all the travel references made in the Pastoral Epistles to produce any sensible sort of 'journey'.

● Secondly, noting this, radical nineteenth-century scholars such as F.C. Baur made the suggestion that *these letters were second-century writings* by people who were trying to reinterpret Paul at a time when he had fallen out of favour with the church. These people simply invented the travel references of the Pastorals to give a touch of realism to their own work. The difficulty with this view is that the historical references contained in these letters are not the kind of thing that anyone would invent. Take, for instance, 2 Timothy 4:13, 'When you come, bring the cloak that I left with Carpus at Troas, also the books, and above all the parchments.' This is not the kind of detail that a later 'Paulinist' would invent. It has no theological content and tells us nothing essential

about Paul himself. It is far more likely that it originated in some real-life situation.

● Thirdly, other scholars, recognizing this difficulty, have suggested that, though the letters in their present form were written in the second century by someone who was trying to reassert the authority of Paul in the church, they do *contain genuine Pauline fragments*, such as the piece to which we have referred. Dr P.N. Harrison suggested that five genuine scraps of Paul's writings can be discovered in 2 Timothy and Titus, and that these were fitted into his own work by a second-century writer. Many modern scholars accept this view.

But it is difficult to see how or why five such fragments should have had an independent existence from the time of Paul in the middle of the first century to the time of his imitator almost a hundred years later. Since they contain nothing more than scraps of personal information, it is hard to think that anyone would have been interested in preserving them intact, had they been isolated from other more theological teaching.

Church organization

Attention is often drawn to the fact that the type of church organization shown in these letters is much more developed than the organization seen in Paul's earlier letters. Therefore the Pastoral Epistles reflect something like the second-century church with its ruling bishops and complicated organization. But things are not quite so simple:

● In Paul's earlier letters he was not writing directly about the duties of church officers. So we need not be surprised to find that letters which deal with this subject give the appearance of a more organized kind of church.

● No church officers are mentioned in the Pastoral Epistles that are not mentioned either in Acts or in Paul's earlier letters.

● The position of Timothy and Titus is not that of the 'monarchical' or ruling bishop. Rather are they Paul's personal messengers. Their authority stems from the fact that he was an apostle, and they had been sent as his representatives.

● This whole argument has usually been based on the suggestion that some sort of Gnostic heresy was in view in the Pastoral Epistles and so they must be second-century works. But it is now widely recognized by all scholars that the kind of Gnosticism found in the second century *cannot* be found in these letters. What Timothy and Titus

were opposing was not too different from the kind of thing that Paul faced earlier in Corinth and Colossae.

Doctrinal teaching

Some scholars say that the Pastoral Epistles contain very little of Paul's characteristic doctrinal teaching, except for a few statements called 'faithful sayings' (for example 1 Timothy 1:15). The doctrine of the Holy Spirit is not mentioned here, and whereas in Paul's day the life of the church was directed by the Spirit, or 'charismatic', in the Pastorals it seems to be organizational. Therefore it must reflect a later stage of church development. Two things can be said here:

● We must beware of thinking that Paul's 'charismatic' doctrine led to a free-for-all in the church. Far from it. When Paul spoke of the spiritual gifts (*charismata*) in 1 Corinthians 12–14 he clearly meant to imply that there should be order and position within the church. Not every man and woman would be equipped by the Spirit to perform the same work. Philippians 1:1 and 1 Thessalonians 5:12 show that Paul approved of formal leadership in the church, and according to Acts 14:23 he himself appointed elders. Such men and women ought to be Spirit-directed and empowered. But that did not mean there was no formal or visible order about the way in which they operated.

● It is not true to say that the Holy Spirit has no part to play in the Pastoral Epistles. We find here the same emphasis on the working of the Holy Spirit in the life of believers (2 Timothy 1:14). Timothy himself is said to have been appointed as God's servant by means of prophecy, which was one of the most characteristic ways of the Spirit's working (1 Timothy 1:18).

Style and vocabulary

The real strength of the suggestion that the Pastoral Epistles were not written by Paul lies in the style and vocabulary of the letters. There are about 175 words here which are not found in Paul's other letters. Dr Harrison has argued that all of these are more characteristic of second-century Christian writers than of first-century writers. In addition to these words, there is a difference of style in what might be called the 'connecting tissue' of these letters, that is the arrangement of 'ands' and 'buts' and other conjunctions. This is rather different from Paul's other letters, and 112 of his favourite particles and

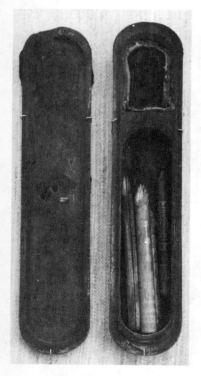

Paul dictated his letters to a secretary, sometimes adding a personal greeting at the end. This wooden pen-case contains reed-pens and an inkwell half-full of black ink, and dates from Paul's time.

prepositions are missing.

These facts are impressive, and should not be set aside lightly. Nevertheless, we may doubt whether they decide the question. Some linguistic experts think that the Pastoral Epistles are too short to provide us with enough material to carry out a trustworthy literary analysis of this kind. And even if the method is valid, both style and vocabulary are very often affected by the subject-matter that is being discussed. Even the argument from the use of typical connecting particles is not wholly convincing, for Colossians and 2 Thessalonians both have considerably fewer of these than Paul's other letters.

What Dr Harrison has shown is that there are differences between the language of the Pastorals and Paul's earlier letters. These differences could perhaps be explained by reference to the different subject-matter, to the fact that Paul was now an older man, or even to the fact that he was using a different secretary. It is also possible that the style of a letter written by Paul himself may have been revised later to make it into better Greek.

These questions are very finely balanced. All the evidence of the early church fathers supports the view that Paul had some connection with these letters – and certainly, they do not reflect life in the church at a period much later than his lifetime. Some have drawn attention to many similarities between the Pastoral Epistles and Luke-Acts, and have suggested that Paul's friend and companion Luke could have written them in their present form after the apostle's death, using Paul's rough drafts as his starting point.

7. Paul and the Christian message

Chapter 21 What does it mean to be a Christian?

The story of Paul's life makes exciting reading. By any standards he was a remarkable person. His courage and perseverance were outstanding. He was one of the great visionaries of his age, and his determination to share the Christian message with the whole of the Roman world was surpassed only by his own fervent commitment to Jesus Christ as Lord and Saviour of his own life. As a writer, he was both prolific and perceptive, and his letters have given us an intimate understanding of the joys and trials of life in the earliest Christian churches.

But Paul was much more than just a brilliant missionary strategist and a devoted disciple of Jesus. He was also one of the church's greatest theologians. His influence was extensive enough during his lifetime. But his writings have inspired many great spiritual movements in every generation since. From the fourth century Augustine of Hippo, to the theologians of liberation in modern South America, men and women of many times and places would affirm that Paul's writings have spoken to their own situations in new and challenging ways. Historically, Paul stands second only to Jesus himself as an innovative thinker in the developing life of the early Christian communities.

From letters to theology

What then was Paul's understanding of the Christian message? It is easier to ask that question than it is to answer it. Paul's writings account for almost one third of the whole of the New Testament, but not a single one of them can reasonably be regarded as a book of theology explaining how Paul would articulate his Christian beliefs in a systematic form.

When we try to produce a comprehensive account of Paul's thinking, then, we need to remember that we are doing something he never attempted for himself. Or, if he did, he has left no written account of it. Moreover, the nature of the writings we do have – as letters – only increases our own difficulties.

For centuries, writers have used the literary form of a letter as an attractive way of presenting a message. Poets and philosophers writing in Greek and Latin often presented their work in the form of such 'literary epistles', just to make their books more interesting to

This priest visiting in a Latin American shanty town is acting in the 'true spirit of the apostle Paul, who became all things to all men, that I might by all means save some'.

read. There are modern examples of the same thing. In *The Screwtape Letters*, C.S. Lewis recorded an imaginary correspondence between various devils and their master. But we all know that these 'letters' were never really written by their alleged authors. They are just an imaginative way of presenting arguments about an important philosophical and theological question. Because of this, we can read them as they stand and discover at once what Lewis thought about the problem of evil.

But Paul's letters are quite different. They are not books of theology dressed up to look like letters. They were all real letters, written to real people to deal with real life situations. If Paul had not come up against the Judaizers in the Galatian churches, we should not have had the letter to the Galatians with its explanation of the relationship of the Christian to the Old Testament Law. If there had been no 'parties' in Corinth, we would not have the equally important teaching of 1 and 2 Corinthians. And if Paul had not been involved in these arguments then perhaps he would never have written Romans in precisely the way he did. Paul's letters were not the product of reflective thinking behind closed doors in the comfort and relative isolation of a study. They emerged out of his experience as a church pioneer, and their contents inevitably reflect that experience.

When we read Paul's letters today, we need to be sensitive to all this. Paul never intended them – either separately or all together –

to be a comprehensive account of the Christian faith. Nor did he generally expect them to be read by anyone other than those to whom they were addressed. Some were detailed replies to other letters that had been sent to him – letters that no longer exist for us to consult. So reading what Paul wrote can be like overhearing one half of a telephone conversation. When that happens, we can often grasp the general meaning of what is being said. But unless we know the people talking to each other very well indeed, the details of their conversation will usually remain obscure. If that is the case with people whose lifestyle and general culture are the same as ours, then it should be no surprise that it is a complex business to come to a full understanding of a person whose letters reflect conditions in a world that was quite different from our own.

To derive a clear and coherent account of Paul's thinking from occasional letters, we need to give special attention to the context in which they were written. In Galatians, for example, Paul argues that it is not necessary to be a Jew first in order to be a Christian. Most of us today would never have thought it might be – and as a result, his long arguments about Abraham, Moses, and the Old Testament Law can often leave us somewhat mystified. Even ideas we think we know quite well can pose similar problems. When we read the word 'church', modern people most naturally think of a particular style of building, or a religious organization. But it meant something altogether different for Paul, and referred neither to buildings nor to bureaucratic structures, but to the quality of relationships that could be found among a particular group of people.

Paul's letters were just as real as this one written by a man to his brother. A previous letter had been eaten by mice, so this letter needs a quick reply!

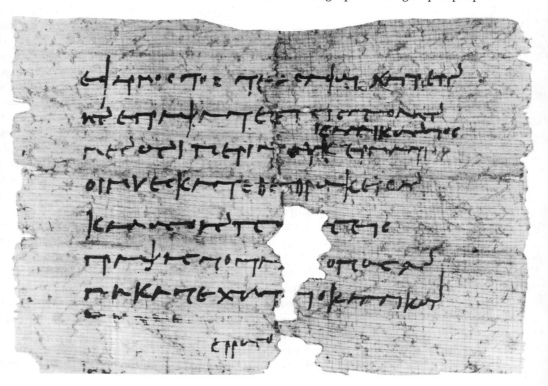

The problems are far from insoluble, however. We have already seen how much agreement there is about the readers and general background of most of Paul's letters. Inevitably, the real significance of some details will elude us. But in spite of all this, it is not difficult to identify the things that formed the central core of Paul's Christian beliefs.

Back to the Damascus road

Acts 9:1–19; 22:6–16; 26:12–18

The foundation stone of Paul's Christian faith was his experience of the risen Christ on the road to Damascus. The events of that day had changed the whole course of his life. We have already seen what that meant for Paul, as he gave himself wholeheartedly to the service of the One whom he met so unexpectedly. This surprise encounter inspired Paul to share with others the living message of Jesus, who had so radically changed his own life. But his meeting with the risen Jesus was more than just an internal experience that affected his personal behaviour. It was also the source of his thinking as a Christian evangelist and theologian. He was converted intellectually, as well as emotionally and spiritually.

When Paul left Jerusalem in hot pursuit of the Christians who had fled to Damascus, he was a convinced Jew. He was quite certain that the most important facts in the world were to be found in the ancient faith of his people, as that was described in the Old Testament and interpreted by the Pharisees. Paul had no doubt listened with attention to the arguments of people like Stephen. But he believed they were mistaken. The claim that Jesus had in some way superseded the Old Testament – still more the idea that he was alive after his shameful death on the cross – was just incredible. This was why Paul was so energetic in his opposition to the Christians. He was convinced that their message was not true. Obeying the Old Testament, not following Jesus, was the only way to please God – and Paul was determined to use every means possible to demonstrate the truth of that.

By all accounts, Paul's own moral and spiritual achievements seemed to back up his thinking. For he later wrote of how 'I was ahead of most fellow Jews of my age in my practice of the Jewish religion, and was much more devoted to the traditions of our ancestors ... As far as a person can be righteous by obeying the commands of the law, I was without fault ...'. It has sometimes been supposed that by the time he met the risen Christ, Paul was already convinced of the moral bankruptcy of Judaism. But there is no evidence at all for this. On the contrary, it was an expression of his fierce pride in his religion that motivated him to persecute the Christians, who to him were the arch-enemies of his beloved Law.

Galatians 1:14; Philippians 3:6

What followed therefore was totally unexpected. For by the time he reached Damascus, he had changed his mind. As a result of his encounter with the risen Jesus, he knew that he had been wrong, and the Christians were right. It is hard to grasp the full impact that this experience must have had on Paul. But it was natural for him that such a radical about-turn should form the starting point for his subsequent reflections on what it meant to be a Christian. He made that clear when he wrote to the Galatians that 'the gospel I preach is not of human origin. I did not receive it from any man, nor did anyone teach it to me. It was Jesus Christ himself who revealed it to me ...'

Galatians 1:11–12

We have seen in an earlier chapter that Paul's understanding of the gospel was in all essentials continuous with the message of Jesus, and consistent with the beliefs of those who were Christians before him. But he certainly had an original way of expressing it – and all the most distinctive aspects of his thinking can be traced directly back to his Damascus road experience.

Who is Jesus?

As a Jew – and a Pharisee – Paul was looking for the arrival of God's new society. Like others of his generation, he was praying for the coming of the Messiah who would inaugurate a new age of justice and peace in which God's will would most truly be done. He no doubt shared the common expectation that when he came the Messiah would be a conquering, all-powerful king, at least part of whose achievements would be to return the land of Israel to the Jewish people and get rid of the Roman troops of occupation. Paul therefore had no time for Jesus. Despite the great claims he had

On the road to Jerusalem from Damascus, Paul had a vivid encounter with the risen Jesus. It completely turned him round, from an enemy of Jesus' followers to a fiery supporter of faith in Jesus.

made for himself, the course of events had proved quite conclusively that he was nothing but a discredited and disreputable messianic pretender. The nature of his death, on the cross, only served to underline that, for the Old Testament had declared that anyone suffering such an end 'brings God's curse on the land'.

Deuteronomy 21:23

But all that was before his conversion. For on the Damascus road, Paul learned not only that Jesus was indeed the expected Messiah – but that he was also the 'Son of God'. This discovery had such an impact on his thinking that it was the major subject of his first Christian preaching in Damascus itself. And when Paul himself later described his experience he recalled that it was on the Damascus road that God had 'decided to reveal his Son in me'. Before that, he could never have entertained the idea that anyone else could stand alongside God. As a Christian, he still believed in only one God, of course. But now he knew that God could only be fully known through Jesus.

Acts 9:20

Galatians 1:15–16

2 Corinthians 4:6

More than that, for throughout his writings he gave to Jesus the title that the Old Testament had reserved exclusively for God himself: Jesus was now 'the Lord'. Paul emphasized more than once that no one could be a Christian without believing that. In doing so, of course, he was following the beliefs of the earliest Christians in

Romans 10:9;
1 Corinthians 12:3; 16:22

Jerusalem, who had also expressed their convictions in the simple confession that 'Jesus is Lord'. Paul discovered that later, and in one place he quotes an Aramaic slogan that the first believers had used. But for Paul himself, it was a fact that he first learned on the Damascus road.

1 Corinthians 16:22

What is the gospel?

How had Paul arrived at this point? What had he done to enable God to break into his life in this way? The answer was: nothing. Paul became a Christian for no other reason than God's loving concern for him, which had led to his unexpected meeting with the risen Jesus: 'God has shown us how much he loves us – it was while we were still sinners that Christ died for us!' On the Damascus road, Paul appreciated that his own salvation depended neither on his privilege as a Jew, nor on his ability to make himself morally acceptable to God. It happened solely because of God's love – love that Paul had never deserved. It was an act of pure 'grace'.

Romans 5:8

Of course, Paul had done something in response to God's undeserved love. He believed it. 'Belief', or 'faith', is a key word in Paul's understanding of the Christian life. But what did he mean by it? The queen in *Alice in Wonderland* told Alice that believing needs practice: 'When I was your age, I always did it for half an hour every day. Why, sometimes I've believed as many as six impossible things before breakfast!' People today often think of Christian faith like this. The Danish thinker Søren Kierkegaard (1813–1855) called faith 'a leap in the dark'. But Paul could never have said that, for two reasons:

● Paul's word 'faith' does not imply 'blind faith' in impossible things. 'Faith' or 'belief' was a way of describing Paul's response to the revelation of God's love in his life. Today, we might more often refer to it as 'commitment'.

● But it was not commitment in a vacuum – nor in the private world of Paul's internal spirituality. Some people think that mystery and irrationality is an inevitable part of religious experience. If something is easy to understand and seems to make sense, then they doubt whether it can be the real thing! But Paul was not like that. His response to God was based on facts. We have already discussed the relation between Christian faith and the facts of history (chapter 12). There were people in Paul's day who imagined that feelings were the all-important criterion of true belief. But Paul firmly dissociated himself from such a view. If it was to have any ultimate meaning at all, then faith must be a rational faith – founded on a bedrock of facts that were true, foremost among them the fact of Jesus' resurrection from the dead.

1 Corinthians 15:1–8

These then were the key features in Paul's gospel: God's undeserved love (his grace) shown to men and women through Jesus, to which people must respond in faith – making a commitment of their lives to God that was based not on feelings or on wishful thinking, but on the absolute facts of Jesus' life, death, and resurrection, and the arrival of God's new society. This was the message that Paul spread so successfully throughout the Mediterranean world. The reason he did that was also related to his conversion. For he discovered that God's grace was not for him only, but was to be shared with others – even those who were not Jews. So without seeking the advice of anyone else, he went off almost immediately to 'Arabia' to share the good news about Jesus with the Gentiles he found there.

Galatians 1:15–17

A social gospel

Just as Paul's new-found faith motivated him to share the good news with others by preaching, so it also gave him new insights into the nature of human relationships. As his ministry developed, the gospel's impact on such relationships became one of the keynotes of his entire teaching. Commitment for Paul was never just a theoretical thing. It was important that his belief should be based on hard facts – but he also knew that it must have some practical outworking in the real world of everyday life.

Paul had discovered the reality of this shortly after he arrived in Damascus. The Christians there knew he was on his way – and no doubt viewed him with apprehension. But in spite of his reputation, they also received him as a brother in Christ and a friend. The warmth of their reception challenged all Paul's preconceptions.

Christians share their faith most effectively when they take time to build relationships with others.

For the entire structure of Roman and Jewish society depended for its stability and survival on the maintenance of inequalities between various groups of people. Jews despised Gentiles. Roman citizens had little appreciation for those whom they thought 'barbarians'. Masters were implacably opposed to slaves – and even in the family it was taken for granted that men would exploit their women. But Paul discovered that the gospel had the power to change all that.

If God could accept people and restore them to fellowship with himself with no preconditions, then those who were Christians must show the same openness in their relationships with others. This became a major theme of Paul's understanding of the Christian faith. It is not a coincidence that he could summarize the message of one of his major letters in social terms: 'there is no difference between Jews and Gentiles, between slaves and free men, between men and women, for you are all one in union with Christ Jesus'. The full meaning of that led Paul to his distinctive understanding of the nature of the church. Our next chapter will deal with this in greater detail. But it was something that Paul first learned on the Damascus road and in what happened immediately after that.

Galatians 3:28

What about the Law?

The relevance of the Old Testament Law for Christian believers is a major subject in many of Paul's letters. As a Jew Paul believed it was possible to please God only by keeping the Old Testament Law. It was because of his loyalty to the Old Testament faith that he found it so difficult to believe that Jesus could be the Messiah. The Law said, 'Anyone who is hanged on a tree is under God's curse'. Since Jesus had been crucified on a cross, he could not have been the Messiah.

Deuteronomy 21:23; Galatians 3:13

When Paul set off for Damascus he was motivated only by loyalty to the Old Testament Law. His hatred of the followers of Jesus was provoked only by a desire to uphold what he knew to be God's standards. So when Paul encountered the risen Christ and discovered that he was wrong, a large question mark was placed against the whole structure of the Jewish religion.

From that moment onwards, he knew that the Old Testament Law was no longer the way to please God – for in the very act of keeping it most meticulously, Paul had clearly found himself on the opposite side to God! Paul's Christian life began with the realization that the way to please God was no longer through faithful observance of the Law – and that anything smacking of legalism was not only irrelevant, but actually contrary to the will of God.

Living the Christian life

So how was the Christian life to be lived? Quite simply, said Paul: not by keeping the Law, but by trusting Jesus. Previously the Law had been the centre of Paul's life. Now Jesus was at the centre. Before, Paul had tried to be good by keeping rules and regulations. Now, he knew he could be truly good by allowing God to change his life. This was a major shift in Paul's moral motivation. He could write of it as a crucifixion and resurrection: a point at which he gave up trying to improve himself, and experienced a power greater than any other that could actually make his life what God wanted it to be.

This was not just a theological theory for Paul. Everywhere in his letters he makes it plain that he had an intense awareness of the power and presence of the living Jesus working in his life to give him victory over sin and to renew his personality: 'it is no longer I who live, but it is Christ who lives in me'. From the moment when he met the risen Christ on the Damascus road, Paul knew that his entire life was to be ruled, guided and directed by this living Lord. And his subsequent experience showed that Jesus could be trusted to do that. Elsewhere, Paul describes the Christian life as a life 'in Christ'. It was by being 'in Christ' that a person could effectively 'die' to a life of sin and receive the power of a new life, reconciled to God. Being 'in Christ' meant that the Christian was filled by Christ, so that at every point the believer could say 'to me to live is Christ ... to know him and the power of his resurrection'.

Paul used such language in a very literal sense. It was God's will for Christians that they all should 'become like his Son'. Jesus himself had been the only one ever to do God's will perfectly – and Christians could do the same by the presence of the risen Lord living within them. The way this would happen was by the operation of the Holy Spirit.

It was as if Paul thought of his life as a blank canvas, on which a picture could be painted by one of two means. He could try and paint it himself – but that was doomed to failure, for it assumed that people were capable of making themselves good enough for God. Alternatively, he could allow God to paint the picture. That involved an admission of his own moral failure, and a recognition of the presence of God's grace. But when the picture is completed, it will bear a perfect image of Jesus. This too was a lesson Paul learned in the moment of his conversion. Looking back to it some time later, he wrote: 'All of us then reflect the glory of the Lord with uncovered faces; and that same glory, coming from the Lord, who is the Spirit, transforms us into his likeness in an ever greater degree of glory.'

Galatians 2:20

1 Corinthians 12:2

Philippians 1:21; 3:10

Romans 8:29

2 Corinthians 3:18

Explaining the faith

Paul's conversion gave him a new understanding of the relationship between people and God. But Paul was a great thinker, and he soon needed to explain these new beliefs in relation to other aspects of his life. What exactly was it that happened to him on the Damascus road – and what did it all mean?

To answer those questions, Paul naturally began with his own roots in Judaism. If the Old Testament was truly God's word, then how could it be understood in the light of what God was now doing through Jesus? That was an important question for Paul, and for many of those with whom he came into contact. But as he took the good news about Jesus into the wider Gentile world, the same questions needed to be answered in other ways. How did the Christian gospel impinge on the social and moral concerns which had dominated much of the religious and philosophical literature of the Roman world? Paul's thinking on both these matters is clearly reflected in his letters.

The Old Testament

The Old Testament must have been Paul's biggest headache. Through Jesus God had accepted him and changed his life, and had asked only for Paul's wholehearted commitment in return. But the Old Testament said that was impossible: pleasing God must include keeping the Law. So if Jesus was God's Son and the Old Testament was God's Law, how could this contradiction be resolved? This was a big question not only for Paul but for every other devoted Jewish person who became a Christian. It was one of the most urgent issues in the life of the early church, which explains why so many of Paul's letters are concerned with it. In looking at Galatians and Romans, we have already noticed briefly how Paul dealt with it.

In effect, he argued that the Jewish view and his new Christian understanding were both true, but not at the same time as each other. The Old Testament *was* God's word, and Jesus *was* God's Son. But the Old Testament was only a temporary word from God, 'our custodian until Christ came, in order that we might then be put right with God through faith'. God's gracious love, accepted in faith, had always been the real basis of salvation, as far back as the time of Abraham himself.

Galatians 3:24

Galatians 3:6–9

Galatians 3:10–12

Human experience had shown that even scrupulous law-keeping could not deliver people from guilt. But Jesus could – and did. How then did he do it? This led Paul to the central facts of Jesus' whole existence: the cross and resurrection. The cross was always at the heart of Paul's preaching, because it explained the relationship between Christian faith and the Old Testament Law.

1 Corinthians 1:18–2:5

To be in the right with God, a person must be a part of the covenant family of Abraham. And that included keeping the Old Testament Law. Human experience, however, showed this to be an impractical ideal. In spite of all his claims to near-perfection, Paul himself was not flawless, and as he thought honestly about the kind of person he was he realized that he was not the kind of person he claimed to be.

On the face of it, therefore, no one could ever hope to please God. Except for Jesus, that is. He voluntarily took upon himself the 'curse' of human failure, by his death on the cross. There, he suffered the alienation from God which was the result not of his own wrongdoing, but of the wrongdoing of others. On the cross, he invalidated the effects of human sin, and his subsequent resurrection made the benefits of that available to any who would commit themselves to him. Paul never tried to explain exactly how this could happen. But he was quite certain of its outcome: 'We were God's enemies, but he made us his friends through the death of his Son'.

Galatians 3:13–14

Romans 5:10

The world of experience

Such arguments made sense to people who were steeped in the Old Testament Law. But Paul took the Christian message to non-Jewish people, and for them there were more appropriate ways of explaining the impact of Jesus' coming.

In doing so, Paul began from an idea that was familiar to both Jews and Gentiles. Our present experience of life is not the only one possible, he said. Certainly it is not a total presentation of the ultimate truth about the world, and God, and people. We have already come across one version of this idea in the beliefs of the Gnostics. For them, the truth was to be discovered in a proper distinction between two worlds: the material world where we live now, and the spiritual world where God is. For them, salvation consisted in escaping from the one to the other. Paul sometimes used their

The good news of Jesus was meant to affect ordinary people in their everyday lives. It was not about abstract ideas but concrete, life-changing power.

language, but his conceptual framework was provided by a Jewish idea of 'two ages'.

These 'two ages' are mentioned in many Jewish apocalyptic writings, and also in the teachings of some rabbis. But the distinction between them was an ethical one, and not a cosmological one like the two worlds of the Gnostics. Jewish thinkers had spoken of life in 'this age' as under the domination of sin or the devil, while life in 'the age to come' would be lived under the direction of God himself, or the Messiah. In that context, evil would be defeated and God's will would be supreme. Paul took this notion as a useful starting point to explain how God through Jesus could be related to ordinary everyday life.

Most people's experience suggests that life as we know it is somehow dominated by evil. However high our ideals may be, it is a simple fact that most of us for much of the time will not actually act in accordance with them. Justice, fairness and equality may seem to be desirable things, but in general the world is not organized that way. On balance, the world seems to be controlled by wrong rather than right. Paul accepted this diagnosis, and recognized that because they are human Christians are a part of 'this present evil age'.

Galatians 1:4

But alongside that, the Christian gospel presented an alternative possibility. Jesus himself had spoken of the new society which would reflect God's standards: 'the kingdom of God'. That society would be ruled not by evil but by God himself, and its values would be the opposite of those which seem to characterize the world as we know it: 'The Spirit of the Lord is upon me, because he has chosen me to bring good news to the poor. He has sent me to proclaim liberty to the captives and recovery of sight to the blind; to set free the oppressed and announce that the time has come when the Lord will save his people.' It is in this rather different world that the true destiny of Christians should be found: they are 'citizens of heaven'.

Luke 4:18–19
Philippians 3:20

All this was good Jewish thinking. But Paul's new Christian perspective enabled him to see it in a different light.

● For Jews, 'the age to come', or 'kingdom of God', was in the future, perhaps a far distant future. But Jesus had announced its arrival. He claimed it was present in his own life and ministry, for he himself was the Messiah and Son of God. He told his disciples that 'there are some here who will not die until they have seen the kingdom of God come with power'. And as the earliest Christians looked back at Jesus' life, death, resurrection and coming of the Holy Spirit at Pentecost, they were certain that this promise had indeed come true. Paul agreed with them. He did not often use the terminology of 'kingdom of God'. But he was conscious of the fact that becoming a Christian meant the transfer of one's allegiance from the standards of the fallen world to the values of God's new creation: 'When anyone is joined to Christ, he is a new being; the old is gone, the new has come ... God rescued us from the power of darkness and brought us safe into the kingdom of his dear Son, by whom we are set free ...'

Mark 9:1

2 Corinthians 5:17
Colossians 1:13–14

To be sure, Christians still live in the world that is dominated by sin. But the prevailing influence in their lives must be God's kingdom, and their behaviour should reflect his will. This formed the basis of Paul's ethical advice to his readers: 'Do not conform yourselves to the standards of this world, but let God transform you inwardly by a complete change of your mind. Then you will be able to know the will of God ...'

Romans 12:2

That did not imply Christians were already perfect. Like Jesus before him, Paul maintained an eschatological tension between the present operation of God's sovereignty in the lives of Christian people and its full and final unveiling at some point in the future. But the presence of the Holy Spirit in the lives of Christians represented the invasion of this world by God's kingdom – and meant that Christians should live accordingly.

Jesus had spelled out the implications of this both in his teaching and by his way of life. Paul expected his readers to do the same: 'let the Spirit direct your lives ... the Spirit produces love, joy, peace, patience, kindness, goodness, faithfulness, humility, and self-control'. Paul also believed that God's standards of justice and fairness must apply to the corporate life of society as well as to personal morality. This is why he could declare so boldly that the barriers of the fallen world were meaningless in the presence of God's new creation.

Galatians 5:16, 22–23

Galatians 3:28; Ephesians 2:11–22

Paul knew well enough that the Christian life would therefore be a life of constant tension, in which the values of the fallen world would be seeking to obliterate the standards of God's new creation. But he believed it was possible for Christians to triumph over sin and live as God intended, provided they recognised the impossibility of doing so by their own best efforts, and were prepared to trust God to breathe new life into them by the operation of his Holy Spirit. This was the true meaning of Christian baptism, which for Paul was a symbolic expression of a moral and spiritual change that took place in a person's life when they had been committed to Christ.

Romans 7:14–25

Galatians 5:25

Romans 6:1–4

● Paul also altered the traditional Jewish 'two worlds' scheme by suggesting that human experience really encompasses not two worlds, but three. Unlike some of his fellow rabbis, Paul was well aware of the fact that the behaviour of people outside the orbit of Judaism could on occasion reflect God's will. Many Jews wrote off the Gentiles as being quite incapable of pleasing God. But Paul's upbringing in the Hellenistic world showed him that this was wide of the mark. Greek and Roman moralists at their best had expressed the highest ideals, some of them apparently similar to the principles announced by Jesus himself.

The same question often plagues Christians today. Why is it that secular humanists can sometimes share the ideals and values of Christians? Paul found the answer by referring back to the Old Testament's teaching that all people are created 'in God's image'. One aspect of the meaning of that phrase is that to be human automatically gives a person a built-in capacity for understanding

Genesis 1:27

God's will. Of course, in the fallen world that capacity has been limited by the impact of evil. But in spite of that, people do instinctively know the difference between right and wrong – whether alerted to it by conscience or by some other internal moral mechanism.

This has often been referred to as the 'natural law' by theologians, and it undoubtedly played an important part in Paul's thinking. It enabled him to explain the relationship between the world as God originally made it, the world in its fallen state as we all know it, and

Romans 1:18–2:16

Renewing God's World

Through the Son, then, God decided to bring the whole universe back to himself. God made peace through his Son's sacrificial death on the cross and so brought back to himself all things, both on earth and in heaven.
Colossians 1:20

	CREATION WORLD: 'IN GOD'S IM (Genesis 1:26-27) PERFECT RELATIONSHIPS: FREE TO SERVE GOD AND ONE ANOTH
THE PHYSICAL WORLD	**PERFECT CREATION** Genesis 1:1-2:4, Colossians 1:15-17
SOCIAL RELATIONSHIPS	NO BARRIERS PEACE MUTUAL SHARING
PARTNERSHIPS	**EQUALITY OF MEN AND WOMEN** Genesis 1:26-31, 2:18 **PERMANENT MARRIAGE** Genesis 1:27, 2:24 **SEX IS GOD'S GIFT** Genesis 1:28, 2:25
PEOPLE AND GOD	**'IN GOD'S IMAGE'** Genesis 1:26-27, Romans 1:18-23 **OPEN RELATIONSHIPS** Genesis 3:8

the new creation that God has inaugurated through the life, death and resurrection of Jesus. Christians understand the character of God's new society because they themselves are a part of it. Non-Christians have a dimmer view of God's standards because they are a part of the world God has made. And both are a part of the fallen world, with its tendency to prevent people from actually carrying out God's will.

The diagram below shows how Paul could relate all this to the concerns of everyday life.

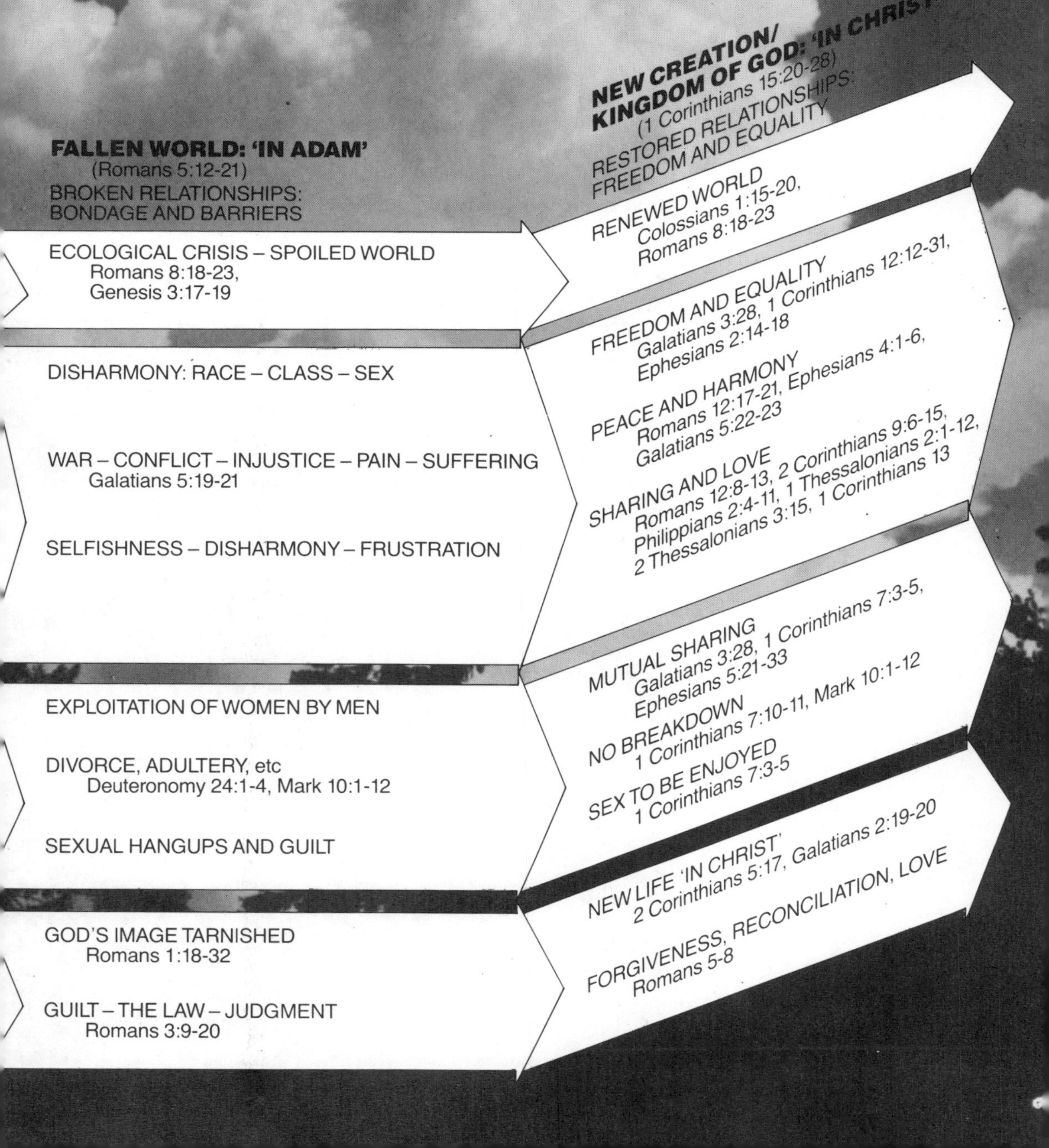

NEW CREATION/ KINGDOM OF GOD: 'IN CHRIST'
(1 Corinthians 15:20-28)
RESTORED RELATIONSHIPS:
FREEDOM AND EQUALITY

FALLEN WORLD: 'IN ADAM'
(Romans 5:12-21)
BROKEN RELATIONSHIPS:
BONDAGE AND BARRIERS

RENEWED WORLD
Colossians 1:15-20,
Romans 8:18-23

ECOLOGICAL CRISIS – SPOILED WORLD
Romans 8:18-23,
Genesis 3:17-19

FREEDOM AND EQUALITY
Galatians 3:28, 1 Corinthians 12:12-31,
Ephesians 2:14-18

DISHARMONY: RACE – CLASS – SEX

PEACE AND HARMONY
Romans 12:17-21, Ephesians 4:1-6,
Galatians 5:22-23

WAR – CONFLICT – INJUSTICE – PAIN – SUFFERING
Galatians 5:19-21

SHARING AND LOVE
Romans 12:8-13, 2 Corinthians 9:6-15,
Philippians 2:4-11, 1 Thessalonians 2:1-12,
2 Thessalonians 3:15, 1 Corinthians 13

SELFISHNESS – DISHARMONY – FRUSTRATION

MUTUAL SHARING
Galatians 3:28, 1 Corinthians 7:3-5,
Ephesians 5:21-33

EXPLOITATION OF WOMEN BY MEN

NO BREAKDOWN
1 Corinthians 7:10-11, Mark 10:1-12

DIVORCE, ADULTERY, etc
Deuteronomy 24:1-4, Mark 10:1-12

SEX TO BE ENJOYED
1 Corinthians 7:3-5

SEXUAL HANGUPS AND GUILT

NEW LIFE 'IN CHRIST'
2 Corinthians 5:17, Galatians 2:19-20

GOD'S IMAGE TARNISHED
Romans 1:18-32

FORGIVENESS, RECONCILIATION, LOVE
Romans 5-8

GUILT – THE LAW – JUDGMENT
Romans 3:9-20

We can see from this that Paul had a very comprehensive definition of the meaning of Christian salvation. He has often been criticized for being narrow-minded and introspective. Some of his greatest admirers have often been both. But nothing could be further from the truth so far as Paul himself is concerned.

For Paul, the whole world – indeed, the whole universe – was the stage on which the drama of redemption was to be played out. Personal and individual salvation was important. But it could never be separated from social and cosmic salvation. The life, death and resurrrection of Jesus was the hinge on which the whole of world history turned. It was the beginning of God's 'new creation'. Like Jesus, Paul looked to a future time when God's new society would arrive in its fullness. But Paul never saw the Christian faith as merely a hope for a better future. On the Damascus road, he had experienced the renewing power of God's forgiving Spirit at work in his own life here and now – and he saw all those who committed themselves to Jesus Christ as a channel through which the life of God's kingdom can be directed into life as we know it in the present fallen world.

Paul taught a 'resurrection faith'. Jesus had been raised from death, and his followers would also be raised to eternal life with God.

Romans 8:18—25

Through the behaviour of such 'kingdom people', God can demonstrate the meaning of the true freedom for which both the physical world and its people are crying out. Christians must show this by the way they handle the world of plants and animals, as well as in their own personal spirituality. But for Paul, the greatest opportunity for demonstrating the reality of life in God's new society was through the new relationships which came into being in the church, and we must now turn our attention more specifically to that.

Paul's view of death

The background

Paul's thinking is dominated by eschatology, just as the teaching of Jesus had been before him. Jesus and Paul both declared that the new society for which devoted Jews had long been waiting had now arrived. Because of the events of Jesus' life, death and resurrection – and, more especially, his own encounter with the living Christ on the Damascus road – Paul was certain that the future had now burst into the present, and Christians were truly living in God's kingdom, despite still being a part of the fallen world which so desperately needed salvation.

So is the present spiritual experience of Christians the only thing that really matters? That was the obvious conclusion reached by some members of the church in Corinth (1 Corinthians

4:6, 15:12). It seemed to be the logical outcome of Paul's own teaching, for he had already written of the Christian life as a sort of 'resurrection' (Galatians 2:20). But Paul was unhappy with this idea – and went to great lengths to show why he thought it was mistaken. The present experience of Christians, he claimed, is but a foretaste of the much greater glory that will transform everything when God's kingdom is established in its fullness. Like Jesus, Paul declared the new age to be inaugurated, but not yet fully perfected. And that meant his faith must always have a future goal, as well as an immediate objective. For Paul, the future meant the return of Jesus himself in glory (the *parousia*), and the transformation of Christians finally and fully to be like Christ (Philippians 3:20–21).

It has sometimes been suggested that all this was no more than an unhelpful hangover from Paul's Jewish past – and that, in any case, he eventually abandoned such a view. It is certainly true that Paul seems to have retained enough of his Pharisaic theology at this point for him to have been able to use the fact to his own advantage when the opportunity arose (Acts 23:6–9; 26:6–8). But the resemblance was limited to the bare fact that both Paul and the Pharisees (as distinct from Sadducees and Greeks) believed that death would be followed by a future life, beginning with resurrection. In fact, Paul's view of God's kingdom as 'present but still to come' followed Jesus' own teaching very closely – and belief in a life after death was a necessary and logical outcome of that.

Further developments

But did Paul's view change as he got older? In view of the intensity of Paul's ministry, it is unlikely that his thinking remained absolutely static throughout his Christian life, and so in principle we can expect to find variations in his letters. Some, however, have claimed to be able to detect at this point not simply the natural changes of growing maturity, but quite striking contradictions in his thoughts on Christians' and physical death.

It has been argued that to start with Paul held a fervent apocalyptic view, and expected all Christians to live until the *parousia* of Jesus. This expectation was challenged by the Thessalonian Christians, some of whose number had actually died – and in response to that, Paul declared they would be raised to life at the *parousia* (1 Thessalonians

4:13–18). Subsequently, he added that the living would also be transformed at the same instant (1 Corinthians 15:51–54) – but then only a short time later, he described this transformation as a gradual change, beginning with conversion and ending with death, which would lead directly into a new existence in a 'spiritual body', without the need for the *parousia* (2 Corinthians 3:17–18; 4:16–5:4). Paul had therefore moved from an original unrefined Jewish view to a more sophisticated position that owed a lot to the thinking of Greek philosophy.

This argument draws attention to some important features of Paul's thinking. But it cannot be accepted as it stands:

● Paul's conversion demonstrated to him that his Jewish beliefs were wrong, and it is therefore unlikely that he ever held a pure Jewish expectation as a Christian. No doubt he used familiar concepts from his past to explain his new Christian faith, but we have no evidence to suggest that such concepts were unaltered by his new perspective.

● In dealing with the fate of the dead in 1 Thessalonians, Paul certainly identified himself with those who would be alive at the time of the *parousia*. But the fact that Paul (like Jesus, Matthew 24:43; Luke 12:39) added that the *parousia* would come 'as a thief comes at night' (by definition, unknowable) hardly suggests that he had some kind of detailed timetable in his mind (1 Thessalonians 5:1–11). We should also remember that when Jewish people discussed the future, central themes were often described as 'near' to emphasise their importance rather than to make chronological predictions.

● It is in any case inaccurate to assert that Paul lost his belief in a direct future intervention by God, and viewed the life of the new age in purely individual and spiritual terms. In Philippians, he could still write of Christian dying in terms similar to those of 1 Corinthians (Philippians 3:20–21), while at the same time retaining a clear expectation of the *parousia* (Philippians 4:5).

How then can we understand this apparent diversity in Paul's statements about death? Two factors are especially relevant:

● Paul certainly continued to think creatively about this question when once it had been raised, and we can expect to see the evidence of that in his letters. The passage of time brings change in the way most people contemplate their own death – and in addition, Paul seems to suggest that he received fresh revelations about the subject from Christ himself (1 Corinthians 15:51–57).

● Between the writing of 1 and 2 Corinthians, Paul had an experience which shook him more than most. We do not know what it was, but he writes of feeling that 'the death sentence had been passed on us' (2 Corinthians 1:9). If he was literally sentenced to death, then questions about life after death would inevitably become more urgent – hence his more detailed teaching on the subject in 2 Corinthians 5.

Paul's thinking never changed on the basic issues. He remained convinced that the coming of the new age was not just an internal experience in the lives of Christian people, but something that would come in power, as God transformed not only the world of people but the world of nature too. And since Jesus was God's Son and Messiah, this great 'day of the Lord' must also be the day of Jesus' return in glory.

Chapter 22

Freedom and fellowship

What is the church?

According to my dictionary, a church is 'a building for Christian worship'. We are all familiar with such places. Some are splendid and ornate, others are plain and simple – but just as easy to recognize. Of course the church today is more than just buildings. It is also an organization – indeed, a whole series of organizations. There are thousands of different 'churches' throughout the world today: the Roman Catholic church, the Episcopal church, the Methodist church, and many more.

If Paul was here today, he would find all this very mystifying. To him 'the church' was neither a building nor a sect. When he wrote of 'the church' he was thinking of people – God's people, followers of Jesus, who were showing by their lifestyle that they were a part of the new society which Jesus had first announced and which Paul believed had now arrived. 'The church' was not something dreamed up by men and women. It was the work of God, founded on the Day of Pentecost when the Holy Spirit had breathed new life into a group of disillusioned disciples. Paul himself had shared in that experience on the Damascus road. His conversion brought a consciousness of personal reconciliation with God. But it also introduced him to a new fellowship of love and joy as he found himself part of a large group of Jesus' followers: the church.

Theologically, the church was a microcosm of the transformation that God's new order would bring for the whole world. To be in the church was to have a foretaste of life in God's kingdom. Socially, the church in the Roman empire was an alternative society. It was based not on selfishness and greed and exploitation, but on the new freedom and fellowship that Jesus had announced: freedom to love God, and to love and serve others.

Mark 12:29–31

This is why the earliest Christians had such enormous success. When men and women asked for proof that God's society had truly arrived, Paul and the other apostles could point to the church. Life in the church was indeed a new society – a context in which men, women and children of diverse social, racial and religious backgrounds had been brought together in a new and radical friendship. Because they had been reconciled to God, they found themselves reconciled to each other. Their whole style of living was totally transformed, and to the honest observer there could be no doubt that something of world-changing proportions had happened.

Jesus had always resisted the temptation to depict God's new society as merely a promise of better things to come in the future. From the very start of his ministry he declared that it was here now – and offered the prospect of renewed lives in the present. In explaining his message in his home town of Nazareth, Jesus made its social dimension unmistakably clear: 'The Spirit of the Lord is upon me ... to bring good news to the poor ... to proclaim liberty to the captives ... recovery of sight to the blind; to set free the oppressed and announce that the time has come when the Lord will save his

Luke 4:18–19 people.' Jesus himself put this into practice, as his own relationships with people demonstrated the reality of God's power to break down the barriers that so often mar human relationships. And the earliest disciples in Jerusalem followed his example.

A major reason for the phenomenal growth rate of the early church was the simple fact that the Christian communities offered

Christians in the United Kingdom send relief supplies to needy Christians in Poland. Right from its beginning, the church was aware of being a partnership in which all the parts belonged together.

a plausible alternative way of life that had the power to fulfil the deepest aspirations of the human personality. As men and women committed their lives to Jesus Christ, they found they were set free to serve God, and incorporated into a new relationship with others who shared their commitment.

Paul had discovered this at the start of his own Christian life. When he arrived in Damascus after his conversion, he found himself united in a new fellowship of love and trust with the very people whom he had sworn to outlaw. After his baptism, Paul spent some time with the Christians in Damascus – and realised that the Christian gospel had within it the power to transform relationships. When he later wrote to the churches in Galatia, he emphasised that faith in Christ should produce reconciliation amongst people as

Galatians 3:28–29 well as peace with God. And he could be certain of that only because he had experienced it in his own life, as the ignorant and uneducated people whom he was determined to hound to death now became his closest friends.

The body of Christ

Ephesians 1:23; 4:12–16
Romans 12:3–8; Colossians 2:18–19

One of Paul's favourite terms to describe the church is 'the body of Christ'. Sometimes he applies it to a particular local group of Christians, like 'the church in Corinth'. At other times, it can refer to the sum total of all Christians throughout the world. In yet other places, Paul seems to have both in mind.

His readers would not be surprised to find Paul using this language to describe groups of people. The Stoics in particular had often used similar concepts. For them, the universe itself could be thought of as a 'body', characterized by a great diversity in its various parts, and yet all of it working together in harmony, sometimes directed by a supreme god as its 'head'. Others had written of the ideal democracy in the same terms, envisaging a community which could accept the diverse individuals who were its citizens, yet at the same time enabling them all to work together for the common good.

When Paul wrote of the church as 'the body of Christ' he was using imagery that many of his readers would readily understand. But it was not the Stoics who had taught him to think of the Christian church in this way. As with other dominant aspects of

Christians, in Paul's language, are 'the body of Christ'. Each is different, yet each has a part to play in the whole organic unity of the Christian community.

his thinking, this too was a lesson Paul first learned at the time of his conversion. As he travelled from Jerusalem to Damascus, he was pursuing Christians to put them in prison. But when the voice spoke to him, it asked 'Saul, Saul! Why do you persecute *me*?' The 'me' was none other than Jesus himself, and Paul was taken aback to learn that in persecuting Christians he was also persecuting Jesus. But he was, and to injure Christians was to afflict their Lord. For they were 'the body of Christ' – living extensions of his personality and influence wherever they went in the fallen world.

Acts 9:4; 22:7; 26:14

One of Paul's most comprehensive explanations of all this is found in his correspondence with the church at Corinth. The precise terms in which the subject is expounded naturally owe a good deal to the specific questions which were being answered. But we have no reason to suppose that Paul's basic message would have been any different in another less contentious context. The idea that Christians are a part of 'the body of Christ' must have been a basic element in Paul's initial preaching of the Christian message, for that is what the Corinthians were arguing about. Paul had spoken to them of 'the body of Christ'. But what exactly did he mean by it – and how should Christians behave in order to demonstrate the new freedom that Paul declared they had within the fellowship of 'the body'?

We have examined the Corinthian letters in some detail in a previous chapter. One of the problems in Corinth was a misunderstanding of the nature of true freedom. If Christ has set us free, some were saying, then we must be free to do as we please, unrestricted by the inhibitions and hang-ups of others. As a result, the life of that particular church had come to be dominated by selfishness and discord rather than the mutual sharing and harmony which were the real signs of the presence of the new age. Their community gatherings were dominated by individuals and small groups who insisted on doing as they pleased. The rich spread social disharmony by having feasts from which the poor were excluded. Even their worship had become a spiritual wasteland, as those with the ability to do relatively spectacular things like speaking in tongues insisted on their 'freedom' to do so, even when it rendered the proceedings meaningless for everyone else.

1 Corinthians 11:17–22

1 Corinthians 14:1–4

There was no way in which Paul could accept all this as a true consequence of his own understanding of Christian freedom. The church at Corinth had become a denial of the gospel. Its worship was incomprehensible, with meetings that Paul said 'actually do more harm than good'. And its evangelism was ineffective, for such behaviour merely made the church a laughing-stock to ordinary people.

1 Corinthians 11:13
1 Corinthians 14:23

Paul was clearly distressed by what was happening in Corinth. But he was also convinced that in the church true freedom must not be only a subject for discussion: it should also characterize the way the church lives. So he set out not so much to contradict as to correct the Corinthians, and in the process he gave us a unique insight into some of the more distinctive aspects of his own thinking.

Life in the body

1 Corinthians 12:1–11

1 Corinthians 12:12–31

1 Corinthians 12:14–20

1 Corinthians 14:26–33

Romans 8:9

1 Corinthians 12:7

1 Corinthians 12:4–11, 27–28

The precise point about which Paul had been questioned was the function of 'spiritual gifts' in the church, and it is in the process of answering that question that he explains his understanding of how Christians should relate to one another in the life of the local church.

In doing so, he uses the image of 'the body' in its simplest possible form. Even with our modern understanding of physiology, it is not difficult to see the way Paul's mind worked. He thinks of our own human bodies as a complex piece of machinery, with parts of different size, shape and constitution, all required to work together in different locations and in different ways to ensure the smooth operation of the whole body. A body without an ear or an eye would be impaired – just as would a body with no hands or feet. To ask whether a hand is more attractive than an eye is an absurd question – for both are required as they are if the human body is to work properly. The unity within diversity that is the key to health in the human body is also a fundamental requirement for proper relationships in the church. Individual Christians are comparable to ears, or hands, or feet, or whatever. They are all different personalities. But they are all vital parts of the whole – and if they are not working properly, then the corporate life of the church will be impaired.

This simple picture introduces us to four decisive aspects of Paul's thinking on the church and its members:

● **All members are indispensable** Everyone has a part to play in Paul's understanding of the church. When Christians meet together for worship or fellowship, everyone has something to offer and must be given the opportunity to do so. This is the opposite of what happens in most churches today. Our modern structures generally allow participation only by a minority (the priest or lay leaders), while the majority are either silent spectators or only occasionally allowed to join in at the specific invitation and under the strict control of the leadership. But this was not Paul's expectation. If every Christian was motivated by the Holy Spirit, and if the church was the sphere in which God's Spirit was working to demonstrate the reality of God's kingdom, then it was only logical to suppose that all Christians should have a part to play in the life of the church. As a result, Paul asserts that every Christian has a ministry to perform – a ministry that is not restricted by either ordination or some other special experience, but which is given to all by the work of the Spirit in the lives of believers.

● **All members are different** Paul's understanding of the work of the Holy Spirit in the lives of Christians never becomes mysticism, in which individuals are swamped by a force outside of themselves. Paul affirms in the strongest possible terms that God always respects the individual personalities of people. This comes out quite clearly in Paul's description of the various functions which different people may be able to perform in order to enhance the life and spiritual development of the church. The list he gives here is by no means exhaustive, and no doubt was determined by the nature of the arguments that were going on in Corinth. Elsewhere he lists

Romans 12:6–21

rather different functions as 'gifts from the Holy Spirit'.

●**All members are equal** Though individual Christians are not identical in either personality or ability, they are all of equal importance. Some, such as those who speak in tongues or those who teach, may seem to be more important. But they are not – and if some wish to have other functions than those God has given them, they should remember that they can only receive what the Spirit gives them. Any attempt to try and obtain particular gifts for themselves will only lead to the destruction of the whole church – presumably because it undermines the basis of mutual trust and respect on which real spiritual freedom is based.

1 Corinthians 12:27–31

● **All members are responsible** Paul has a dynamic concept of the church, not a static one. It is not an organization that holds meetings from time to time – it is an outpost of God's kingdom. This means that Christians do not 'go to church' – they *are* the church, wherever they are and whatever they happen to be doing. Their responsibility for the condition of the church does not end while they are at work or at home. Everything that happens to them has its effect on the whole body. This is true of the human body, of course: an injury to one part will inevitably bring discomfort, or worse, to the whole organism.

The churches of the New Testament were very mixed communities: different races, slaves and free people, men and women, Jews and Gentiles – all joined together in worshipping Jesus Christ and serving the world.

Paul discovered at his conversion that the church is no different: when one Christian suffers, the whole church is injured. But the opposite is also true: 'if one part is praised, all the other parts share its happiness'. For a Christian to be able to opt out of the church was unthinkable for Paul. It only makes sense in a modern church context, where 'joining the church' is a matter of enrolling in a particular sort of organization. But for Paul the church was not a club that could be joined or left: it was a living organism, in which Christians were inescapably related to and responsible for one another because of their new relationship with God through Christ.

1 Corinthians 12:26

Leadership in the body

No matter what the theory may be, every social grouping needs adequate leadership. And the church is no exception. So how did Paul cope with the needs for competent leaders, while still retaining the flexibility and freedom which are the bedrock on which his thinking about the church was founded?

It is clear that Paul never imagined the church could do without proper leadership. According to the book of Acts, wherever he founded a new Christian community it was his regular practice to appoint leaders in it – a fact that is confirmed by references in his letters to 'the bishops and deacons' at Philippi and to 'those who ... are over you' in Thessalonica. Paul himself clearly believed that he had a special position by virtue of being an apostle, and he was quite prepared to recognize the God-given authority of others in similar positions.

Acts 14:23; 20:17–35
Philippians 1:1
1 Thessalonians 5:12
Galatians 1:15–19; 2 Corinthians 11

Acts 15:4; Romans 16:1–15

The really distinctive element in Paul's thinking was the model of leadership which he used to explain the functions of these different people. Nowadays almost all local Christian congregations – and many denominations too – operate with what we might call a 'business' model of leadership. Just as a commercial enterprise will have its chairman at the top, together with a board of directors, followed further down the line by the shareholders, and eventually the prospective consumers – so in the church we often find the clergyman, with his parish council or board of elders, followed by the membership, who in turn may or may not overlap with the 'consumers' (those who attend church services). In this model, authority is passed on from one layer of bureaucracy to the next, and is validated at the top level by various rituals which ensure that what happens there will always be more important than what takes place lower down the structure. Paul however saw leadership in rather different terms. He was working with a 'charismatic' model. Today, this term has been hijacked by those who talk of glossolalia and other strange phenomena as 'charismatic gifts'. But this is an unhelpful restriction of Paul's much wider use of the word. For him, a 'charismatic gift' was not concerned only with the personal experience of individuals: it was a gift that God had given to the whole church, and that had far-reaching repercussions on the whole of its life and relationships.

The centre of authority here is to be found outside the members of the church altogether, and rests with God working through the Holy Spirit. Those who lead are not those who have been appointed to an office by a vote of the congregation, but those who have been equipped to lead by God himself, and whose gifts the other members of the body have recognised. Since God's choice depends on nothing other than his own freely given gifts of grace, every single Christian could be the potential recipient of leadership functions.

Several statements made by Paul in writing to Corinth help to explain this concept further.

● **The Head of the Body** A good deal of debate has been generated by the fact that in 1 Corinthians 12 Paul does not differentiate between the whole body and its head. In later letters, he clearly identifies Christ as 'the head ... from whom the whole body ...

Ephesians 4:15–16

makes bodily growth and upbuilds itself in love'. But even earlier he never thought of Christ as just the sum total of all Christians. He affirms that the whole basis of the church's existence is the con-

1 Corinthians 12:3

fession that 'Jesus is Lord', and in another passage, using a different metaphor, he describes him as 'the one and only foundation' of the

1 Corinthians 3:11

church. The church does not belong to people – not even to its members. It belongs to God, and Christ is its head. He alone is its true leader, and the ultimate authority belongs to him.

● **Led by the Spirit** This is why Paul can expect things to happen 'in a proper and orderly way' even without any apparent hierarchi-

1 Corinthians 14:40

cal leadership to enforce rules and regulations. If all Christians are guided by the Spirit, he reasons, and if it is God's will that 'harmony

1 Corinthians 14:33

and peace' should be the hallmarks of the church, then God will not only equip Christians for different ministries, but he will also give others the grace to recognize and accept such Spirit-led leadership where it emerges. Common experience suggests that this is perhaps a counsel of perfection. It is certainly not easy for fallen human nature to cope with such open structures, and at the very least demands extraordinary sensitivity and spiritual discipline. But Paul simply observed that for people whose lives had been transformed by the power of God, that should be no problem!

● **Partners in Ministry** One reason for Paul's optimistic expectations at this point is the fact that he never supposed just one person would emerge as the sole leader of any given congregation. In the church worldwide, he envisaged the emergence of a number of complementary leaders: 'some to be apostles, others to be prophets,

Ephesians 4:11

others to be evangelists, others to be pastors and teachers'. But he also saw such diversity of leadership operating in the context of local congregations too. In his advice to the Corinthians he mentions apostles, prophets, teachers and several others all working

1 Corinthians 12:27–31

alongside one another in order to build up the whole church. He never for a moment imagined that one person could have a monopoly on the gifts of God's Spirit in the church. It would take the whole church fully to express the greatness of God. For Paul the only thing that determined a person's function in the church was the endowment of God's Spirit. In God's new society sex, race, and social class – all barriers of the fallen world – were quite irrelevant.

This is Paul at his most radical. Even those who have found his understanding of personal salvation most congenial have not often followed him in his thinking on the nature and operation of the church. Yet for Paul the two were inseparable. The heart of the gospel was freedom: freedom from guilt, freedom from the Law, freedom from sin, and freedom from all that would inhibit the development of the human personality to become what God intended it to be. To be set free by Christ was to be released into a new world in which people could find their own true identity, relating to each other in freedom and fellowship because they were related to Christ himself. That final transformation was yet in the future, when 'the glorious freedom of the children of God' would be fully realized. But in the meantime, the church stands as a testimony to that future hope, and as the context in which men and women can serve one another most truly as they love and serve God himself.

Romans 8:18–25

Did Paul really believe in freedom?

If not quite the heart of Paul's gospel, 'freedom' is certainly one of its leading motifs. It features prominently in all his major letters, whether he is dealing in a theological way with the nature of salvation (as in Galatians and Romans) or with its practical outworking in the Christian community (as in 1–2 Corinthians). But what sort of freedom was Paul talking about? In Galatians, he asserts quite categorically that a true understanding of Christian freedom would lead to the abolition of the major social divisions of the ancient world. Prejudice and discrimination based on race, social class and sex were quite incompatible with the Christian gospel: 'there is no difference between Jews and Gentiles, between slaves and free men, between men and women; you are all one in union with Christ Jesus' (Galatians 3:28). Yet when we look elsewhere in Paul's writings, especially where he gives practical advice to his readers, his specific instructions do not always seem to be consistent with his general statements of policy. This is especially true of his statements about the place of women in the church, and his handling of the issue of slavery. But in order to set these in their proper perspective, we must also see them alongside his attitude to racial issues.

Racism

Some interpreters have argued that the freedom Paul talks of in Galatians is some kind of 'spiritual' freedom, with no social implications at all. On this

view, Galatians 3:28 refers to the way God sees people, rather than how people ought to view one another. But this is unlikely to be Paul's meaning. Throughout his writings he makes it plain that his Christian faith was not segregated from the rest of his life. What he believed must affect his style of living. Moreover, his entire life was dominated by his absolute determination that racial prejudice would have no part in the Christian community. His determination to prove that Jews and non-Jews were all equal became almost an obsession with him. He was even prepared to disagree publicly with Peter over it (Galatians 2:11–14), and it was the immediate cause of his final arrest and transportation to Rome (Acts 21:17–36).

It is impossible to believe that Paul thought racism would be abolished only in some ideal world, when he spent most of his life opposing it in human relationships wherever he found it. In principle, therefore, we can only conclude that he *did* see Christian freedom as defined in Galatians and Romans as something that would affect relationships between people here and now.

Sexism

When we come to Paul's statements about the place of women in the church's life, we find exactly the same emphasis. In describing the various 'gifts of grace' in 1 Corinthians and Ephesians, he never suggests that God will give these gifts only to men. In principle, all positions in the Pauline church were open to all Christians, regardless of sex. Paul himself was happy to work alongside women, some of whom were close friends. His most extensive list of greetings to Christian leaders includes many women (Romans 16:1–15), and at least one to whom he refers as an 'apostle' (Junias, Romans 16:7). Furthermore, when he gives advice to the church at Corinth about the appropriate way to behave, he takes it for granted that both men and women should 'pray and prophesy' in public worship (1 Corinthians 11:4–5). Indeed he reminds them that he had delivered 'traditions' to that effect as part of his initial teaching to them – in much the same way as he had passed on information about the resurrection (1 Corinthians 11:2; 15:1–8 – using the same Greek words in each case). There are certainly some complex statements made in these contexts, but the whole frame of reference is determined by Paul's insistence that men and women have the same freedom and opportunity to play a full part in the life of the church.

The same point also comes out clearly when he discusses marriage. Here again, some of what he writes is a little obscure, no doubt because of its specific reference to details of the Corinthian situation. But the general principle is clear: men and women relate to each other not in a context of male (or female) domination, but in a life of mutual love and service: 'A man should fulfil his duty ... a woman should fulfil her duty ... A wife is not the master of her own body ... a husband is not the master of his own body...' (1 Corinthians 7:3–4).

All this is but the logical outcome of Paul's teaching on the freedom which the gospel brings. The only apparent problem is the fact that in 1 Corinthians 14:33b–35, Paul appears to undermine it by writing that 'the women should keep silence in the churches. For they are not permitted to speak'. Some have solved this riddle by suggesting that these verses are not a part of Paul's original letter, but were added later by someone who wished to find Pauline authority for silencing troublesome women. There is a little evidence for this in the ancient manuscripts of the New Testament, but not enough to justify such a conclusion. There are however a number of other clues in Paul's letters that will help us to see the real meaning of what he says here:

● If *we* can see a contradiction between Paul's advice in 1 Corinthians 11:2–16 and 14:33b–35, then we can be sure Paul would not have missed it. Presumably he did not think there was a contradiction here. But he may well have thought that in one passage he was

As Paul saw it, women had a vital role alongside men in the church's life and ministry.

stating a general principle, while in another he was giving specific advice to deal with a very particular situation. The whole of the Corinthian correspondence is shot through with this kind of tension: the volatile nature of the church almost demanded it. In this particular case, 1 Corinthians 11:2–16, with its appeal to creation, has every appearance of being the general principle.

● In 1 Corinthians 14 it is not only women who are told to be quiet: the whole chapter is full of instructions to various people in the church (some of them certainly men), telling them when it is appropriate to speak and when they should be silent. Worship in Corinth was being continually disrupted by groups of people competing with each other to gain the attention of the rest. No doubt a group of women was one of them. It is instructive that as an alternative to speaking in church, Paul here tells them to 'ask their husbands at home'. This strongly suggests that the 'speaking' in question was irreverent chattering, that had no real connection with the worship of the church.

● In dealing with the church at Corinth, we have suggested that there was something like what later came to be known as 'Gnosticism' lurking in the background. If so, this could also give us a possible clue to the meaning of this passage. The only other New Testament book which contains similar instructions to 1 Corinthians 14:33b–35 was probably written against a similar background of church life (1 Timothy 2:8–15). In the Gnostic heresies of the second century, women often played a conspicuous part that amounted to 'female chauvinism' – and some groups in Corinth may even at this early period have had theological reasons for wanting to assert such female supremacy. If so, it is consistent with Paul's teaching that he should have wanted to put them down. To him, exploitation of men was just as abhorrent as prejudice against women, and both would be a denial of the true meaning of Christian freedom.

Slavery

But what about Paul's attitude to slaves? Was Paul committed to the abolition of slavery too? There is less material available for us to give a precise answer to that question, for nowhere does Paul actually write about the future of slavery as an institution. Of course, Galatians 3:28 implies the end

Slavery was a fact of life in New Testament times, as it was in many places until little over a century ago. Paul did not directly challenge slavery as an institution, but he taught that slaves and free people are 'all one in Christ Jesus'.

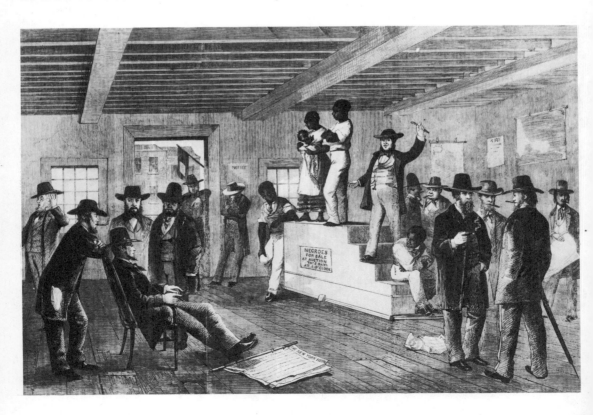

of slavery, just as it spelled out the end of racism and sexism. But there are only one or two hints in Paul's letters of how he would deal with this particular matter:

● In Colossians (3:22–4:1) and Ephesians (6:5–9) Paul gives advice to his readers on how to cope with different family circumstances, one of which is the master/slave relationship. Here, he simply takes it for granted that slavery will continue to exist, though his advice contains certain distinctive elements when he reminds masters that they have a personal responsibility for the welfare of their slaves, and for that reason they should treat them generously.

● In Philemon, we have a personal letter sent by Paul with a runaway slave whom he was returning to his master. Here again, his precise intention is ambivalent, as we saw when we discussed that letter in detail. On the one hand, he seems to be asking Philemon to release the slave Onesimus – yet, paradoxically, he sends him back at the same time!

The Onesimus episode seems to suggest that though Paul wanted the slave released, he was not prepared to go outside the law to achieve it – and this perhaps gives us a clue to Paul's thinking on the matter. We cannot reasonably think that Paul would not have realised that the gospel demanded an end to slavery. But his attitude to it was probably influenced by two further considerations:

● In the Roman empire, slavery was the foundation stone on which the whole economic structure of society rested. To abolish slavery would have been like introducing capitalism to the Soviet Union, or Marxism to the United States: it would have meant all-out revolution against the state. But neither Paul nor the other Christians were in a strong position politically: 'from the human point of view few of you were wise or powerful or of high social standing' (1 Corinthians 1:26). In any case, the Roman slave revolts of the first century BC had shown that such attempts were doomed to failure. Paul had to make a difficult choice: either challenge the vested interests of the Roman state and perish in the process, or accept the situation and seek to exert whatever influence could be achieved through the establishment of a counter-culture in the church. Paul made the second choice – and we have no reason to suppose that he did not invite slaves and masters to demonstrate their new-found Christian freedom within the Christian community, even though he was forced to recognise his inability to change things in the wider world.

● Paul's personal experience of Roman slaves probably helped him to reach this decision. Today, we tend to think of slavery in terms of the American experience in the eighteenth and nineteenth centuries. There were of course many pathetic souls who found themselves under the power of such tyranny in Rome – mostly because they were either criminals or belonged to races that had been conquered by the imperial armies. But the majority of slaves in Roman society were 'household slaves', whole groups of servants who lived in the homes of their masters in a more or less harmonious extended family. Socially, they were the equivalent of today's ordinary workers, except that their employers gave them the security of housing as well as employment. Onesimus was this sort of slave, and he was probably typical of thousands of the early Christians. This was the type of slavery Paul knew about, and he could no doubt see that unless it was accompanied by a radical revision of the entire Roman economic system, the 'emancipation' of such household slaves would lead not to greater freedom, but less, with homelessness and destitution being the inevitable outcome.

Paul's attitude to slavery is perhaps less liberal than some of his modern readers would like. But Paul was also a pragmatist, and realised that there must be a limit to the extent of social reform that one person with no influence can bring about single-handed. His gospel demanded that slavery should go, and where Paul could achieve this – in the church – he sought to do so. But it was left to later generations of Christians, in changed political circumstances, to realise the full significance of his gospel of freedom, and to act in accordance with it.

8. Unity in diversity

Chapter 23 The Spirit and the letter

The charismatic church

In the previous chapter, we examined at some length Paul's understanding of the nature of the church. But this view was not unique to him. The story of the earliest church in Jerusalem shows that it too began with a charismatic understanding of its own life. These early followers of Jesus were dominated by their experience of the Holy Spirit at work among them. At the very beginning they gave little thought to the problems of organizing the infant church. It never occurred to them to appoint officials or write a constitution. Nor did they find it necessary to establish an army of bureaucrats to direct their worldwide mission from some central headquarters. They believed they already had the only organizing force they needed, in the guidance of the Holy Spirit himself.

Acts 4:8; 5:32
Acts 4:31

The Spirit told them what to say in their preaching, and gave them the boldness to say it. When Ananias and Sapphira tried to deceive the church, Peter had no doubt that this was a direct

Acts 5:9

challenge not to himself, but to the Holy Spirit. For the church did not belong to the apostles. It had come into being with the arrival of the Spirit, and the ultimate responsibility of its members was to God. We find the same emphasis throughout the later chapters of Acts. When the church at Antioch in Syria sent Paul and Barnabas off as missionaries, it was acting on the instructions of the Holy Spirit, who spoke directly to the congregation through certain

Acts 13:1–3

Spirit-filled individuals within it. And this sense of dependence on the Spirit's guidance is perhaps the main characteristic of Paul's work, both in the stories of Acts and in his own writings. This emphasis is so strong in Acts that some readers of the New Testament have preferred to regard it not so much as the 'Acts of the Apostles', but rather 'The Acts of the Holy Spirit'.

Many of us today would regard all this as rather naive. It is certainly not the way that we would go about things. If we wanted to establish some new church today, we would first write a constitution and appoint leaders and an organizing committee, together with all the bureaucratic paraphernalia that seems indispensable to the modern mentality. But this difference of approach underlines a fundamental distinction that must be drawn between the life of the earliest church and what most of us know of the Christian church today.

The start of it all

Luke 24:13–24

For at the beginning, nobody ever sat down and planned to start the church. When Jesus died on the cross, his disciples were for the most part disillusioned and perplexed. This was not what they had expected. Even after the resurrection, they were still apprehensive. The church was not the brain-child of the disciples: it was the work of God. On the Day of Pentecost, God spoke to its founder members and worked among them in such power that they had no option but to respond to his orders. Into the deadness of their own frustration, the Spirit breathed the life of God himself. And as individual disciples experienced the compelling power of the Holy Spirit for themselves, they were drawn together in a fellowship of love and friendship – love for God, love for one another, and love for the non-Christian world. Their educational, social, economic and political backgrounds were quite diverse, and the only thing they had in common was the fact that through the Spirit, God had changed their lives.

They were bound together as a group not by the fact that they all belonged to the same organization but because they were all inspired by the same Holy Spirit. It is at this point that we can locate the distinctive self-understanding of the early church. To many people today, the Christian church is a kind of religious business enterprise. And like all such secular enterprises, it needs a bureaucracy to make it work. These first Christians, however, saw themselves not as an organization, but as a living organism. Paul expressed this idea most fully when he called the church 'the body of Christ'. What unites Christians, he said, is not the fact that they are all shareholders in the same religious business but the fact that each and every one shares in the life and power of Jesus himself, through the operation of the Holy Spirit in their lives. The Spirit himself was the 'organizing principle' of the church's life, and because of that it was unnecessary for the believers to organize the church themselves. The same kind of argument is used by Jesus when he describes the relationship between Christians and Christ using the imagery of a living plant, with the same source of life

Romans 12:4–8; 1 Corinthians 12:12–31

Meeting together in homes was a feature of the life of the early church; Christians today also find that this kind of informal setting is important and helpful for sharing their faith.

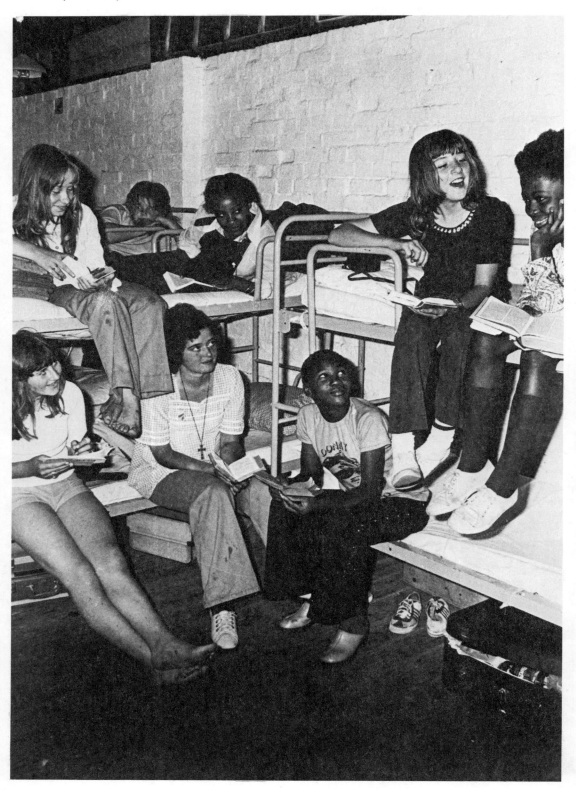

John 15:1–10

filling and energizing all its parts.

We have already seen how this understanding of Christian fellowship became central for Paul, and we have no reason to doubt that it was the view of other apostles, including Peter. The authentic picture of a church in the New Testament is of groups of Christians acting together in a spirit of mutual love and friendship. When Paul wrote to the church at Rome some twenty years after the events of Pentecost, there seems to have been no organized hierarchy. In the final chapter of his letter he seems to imply that there were several groups of Christians there, meeting together in the homes of different individuals in an informal way. Paul mentions a number of people known to him, together with the names of the people in

Romans 16:3–15

whose homes these house churches met. But he makes no suggestion that any of them had any sort of 'official' position among the Christians. Instead, they are all 'Christian brothers and sisters' – just as the followers of Jesus had always been, not only from the Day

Mark 3:33–35

of Pentecost, but even from the time of Jesus' own ministry.

The institutional church

Within another forty years, all this had changed quite dramatically. Our next piece of evidence from the church at Rome is the early Christian document called 1 Clement. This was a letter sent from the church at Rome to the church at Corinth in about AD 95. It is an especially interesting document, for it lets us see what was going on at that time in two churches that we know about from the New Testament. The church in Corinth had not changed much at all; it was still being torn apart by controversies and arguments of one sort and another. But the church at Rome used a new argument to try to put things right.

Leadership and organization

It suggested that certain of its leaders had special authority, which was vested in them by their position as accredited officials in a church hierarchy: 'The apostles have received the gospel for us from the Lord Jesus Christ. Christ was sent forth by God, and the apostles by Christ. Both these appointments were made in an orderly way, according to the will of God ... The apostles appointed the first-fruits of their labours to be bishops and deacons for those who would believe. Nor was this a new fashion, for indeed it had been written concerning bishops and deacons from very

1 Clement 42

ancient times :..'

We can reasonably conclude that by AD 95, these local 'bishops and deacons' in the church at Rome were being thought of as the successors of the apostles – not just metaphorically, but quite literally, for they had the confidence to try and exercise the supreme authority of the apostles, even over the church in the Greek city of Corinth. This impression is reinforced when we notice that in an earlier chapter of 1 Clement, two groups of people are distinguished within the congregation. No longer are they all equal as brothers and sisters in Christ. Instead, we find the notion of 'clergy'

A shared faith in Jesus Christ cuts across barriers of age, sex, class and race.

1 Clement 40

and 'laity'. Indeed, there even seem to be two groups of clergy: 'His own peculiar services are assigned to the high priest, and their own proper place is prescribed to the priests, and their own special ministrations devolve on the Levites. But the layman is bound by the layman's ordinances.'

Of course, 1 Clement can only tell us how things were moving in the church at Rome. There is no guarantee that the church in Corinth actually accepted all this when it received the letter, still less that it was itself organized in the same way. But as we look at other Christian literature from the same period, we cannot fail to discern a significant change in the church's self-understanding. There was still a certain degree of admiration for the idea that the church could and should be led by the guidance of the Holy Spirit. But Christians were coming more and more to feel that the church must be organized along more institutional lines.

Ignatius, the bishop of Antioch in Syria at the beginning of the second century, also had something to say on this subject. While he was on his last journey to Rome to face execution, he wrote seven letters to various churches. One of the subjects that he discussed was the relationship between a church and its leaders – and it is clear that, in his view at least, the leaders of the church had a special authority that distinguished them from ordinary church members. There are three distinct types of clergy: the elders or presbyters, the deacons, and over them both, the bishop. The word 'presbyter' has given us the modern word 'priest'. But at that stage there was no thought of sacrifice on behalf of the people in the Old Testament

It has become the practice for many Christian churches to ordain ministers. This ceremony often includes the laying-on of hands, which was a custom by which the early Christians identified themselves with people who were called to special service.

sense. Both bishop and elders should be given great respect, for a person's attitude to them is a reflection of his attitude to God. Indeed, in another letter, Ignatius declares that anyone who agrees with the bishop is a friend of God, while those who disagree with him are God's enemies: '... as many as are of God and of Jesus Christ, they are also with the bishop ... but if any man follows one who makes a division, he shall not inherit the kingdom of God.'

To the Magnesians 3

To the Philadelphians 3

Again, we must remember that Ignatius was speaking for himself. Many modern readers of his letters have pointed out that he goes to such lengths to defend the status of these religious offices that their significance must have been in some dispute. But nevertheless, it was not long before Christians throughout the world came to accept that this was what the church should be. Instead of the community of the Spirit that it had originally been, the church came to be seen as a vast organization. Instead of relying on the Spirit's direct guidance, it was controlled by a hierarchy of ordained men, following strict rules and regulations which covered every conceivable aspect of belief and behaviour.

By the middle of the second century, the change was complete. At the beginning, the only qualification for membership of the church had been a life changed by the power of the Holy Spirit. Indeed, at the very start there had been no real concept of 'church membership' at all. On the Day of Pentecost, all believers in Jesus were automatically members of the church. There was no need for them to apply to get in, nor could they have opted out, even had they wished to do so. But by the end of the first century things were rather different. Now the key to membership of the church was not to be found in inspiration by the Spirit, but in acceptance of ecclesiastical dogma and discipline. And to make sure that all new members had a good grasp of what that meant, baptism itself was no longer the spontaneous expression of faith in Jesus, as it had originally been. Now it was the culmination of a more or less extended period of formal teaching and instruction about the Christian faith. And in all this, we can see how the life of the Spirit was being gradually squeezed out of the Body of Christ, to be replaced as the church's driving force by the more predictable if less exciting movement of organized ecclesiastical machinery.

Acts 2:40–42

Didache 7

The changing church

But why did this happen? Was it just an accident? Or was it a part of some ancient anti-charismatic plot by subversive elements in the church? Or was it perhaps just a good example of the way that any new movement founded by a dynamic leader will eventually become yet another settled institution in its second generation?

We may trace four main reasons for this change in the style of the early church.

Church growth

One of the most impressive features of the early church is the amazing rate at which it grew. Beginning from a handful of people in rural Palestine, within twenty years or less it spread through the whole of the civilized world. All this was achieved with no real organization at all – and yet the very success of this spontaneous world mission was itself to demand some integrated scheme of operation.

At first, no one gave much thought to organization. They already had all the organization they needed. Most of those who became Christians on the Day of Pentecost had been Jews or Gentile converts to Judaism, and they simply accepted and continued in the forms of worship that they already knew and loved. The early chapters of Acts tell how they met with fellow-believers in Jesus, but that was an extra, for they also worshipped in the local synagogues, and even in the temple itself.

Acts 2:46

But it was not long before the need arose for some kind of organization, however primitive. Stephen came to prominence as a leader among the Hellenist Christians of Jerusalem because they felt they were not getting a fair share in the distribution of church funds. The nature of their complaint implies that the Hebrew Christians were not suffering the same disadvantage – and the fact that the response to the complaint was the establishment of a group of seven men to supervise the distribution of funds to the Hellenists suggests very strongly that there was already in existence a similar group dealing with the needs of the Hebrew Christians.

Acts 6:1–6

We should perhaps not be surprised that these first church 'officials' were appointed to deal with such a practical matter, for the only 'office' known to us in the small group of Jesus' twelve disciples was that of treasurer – a function carried out by Judas Iscariot, sometimes with less than complete honesty. And it is not accidental that the very first stirrings of 'organization' within the early church should be concerned with the same subject. Had not Jesus himself taught that after love to God, love to one's neighbour was the next most important thing? It was certainly one aspect of his message that the early church took very seriously indeed. Its members even sold their goods and property and pooled the proceeds. They were determined to be united with their fellow-believers not only spiritually, but in other more tangible respects too. They all shared one common purse, as well as serving the same Lord.

John 12:4–6; 13:29

Matthew 19:19; 22:39; Mark 12:31, 33; Luke 10:27

Acts 2:44–45; 4:32, 34–35

The 'communism' of the early Jerusalem church

Some scholars, however, have questioned whether this picture of life among the first Christians is authentic. They point out that in Acts 2:44 and 4:32, the believers are said to have shared all their possessions – and yet in a later episode, both Barnabas and Ananias still have property to sell (4:36–5:11). But there is no real contradiction here. The earlier passages themselves make it clear that the members of the Jerusalem church did not dispose of everything at once. Instead, they sold things as the need arose, and then shared the profits with the rest of the Christian community (2:45).

There are no good reasons for doubting the general accuracy of Luke's account at this point. The sharing of goods was nothing new, and was regarded as an ideal by Greek writers, while the Jews were well aware of the need to be charitable. The commune living by the shores of the Dead Sea at Qumran practised a similar sharing of resources, though in this case a convert did not hand over all his possessions until a year after joining the sect.

The distinguishing mark of the

Christian 'communism' was its spontaneity. At Qumran, such sharing was carefully regulated by rules, as was the distribution of charity among Jews in general. But Jesus had laid down no hard and fast economic policy for his disciples to follow. Admittedly, he himself lived in relative poverty, and his immediate followers left all they had to join him. When a rich man wanted to become a disciple, he was told, 'Go and sell all you have and give the money to the poor' (Mark 10:21) – and it is difficult not to conclude that

after its humble proletariat beginnings, the church soon moved into the middle classes of society, and here the ideals of communistic life were not so attractive. It is certainly true that as the church moved into the wider Roman world, some of its converts came from the higher social classes. But this was not the case in Palestine. Everything we know of the church in Jerusalem suggests that it continued to be poor throughout its existence. The church at Antioch in Syria sent a gift to Jerusalem (Acts 11:27–30), as did Paul's Gentile

The excavated buildings of the Essene monastery at Qumran give a flavour of the communal life-style which this religious group sought to put into practice.

Jesus believed a rich person would find it harder to follow him than a poor one (Matthew 19:24). But even the poor could become obsessed with riches, and they too were expected to give away their last coin in the service of God (Mark 12:41–44).

So it is not difficult to understand why these early Christians wanted to share their resources with one another. Yet it does not seem to have been an altogether successful enterprise, for we hear nothing more of such whole-hearted sharing, either in Jerusalem or elsewhere. According to the Marxist historian Karl Kautsky, this is because,

churches (Romans 15:22–29). Paul twice refers to the Jerusalem church as 'poor' (Romans 15:26; Galatians 2:10), and later Jewish Christians in Palestine called themselves 'Ebionites', which meant simply 'the poor'.

It is more likely that this early experiment in community living broke down simply because the Christians ran out of money. In their enthusiasm, perhaps they had forgotten to balance a sharing of goods with a sharing of labour, with the result that they disposed of the resources they already had, but could find no way of replenishing them.

Though this primitive kind of communism was not to be typical of the church when it spread to other parts of the Roman Empire, the sharing of goods to a greater or lesser degree was always part and parcel of the Christian gospel. We have already noticed the generosity of the church at Antioch and the Gentile Christians of Greece and Asia Minor. Jesus' emphasis on loving one's neighbour was taken seriously throughout early Christianity. The New Testament is full of exhortations to do just that in many detailed ways –

Acts 11:27–30; Romans 15:26

Didache 12

while by the end of the first century, the church was also acting as an employment agency for unemployed Christians.

Obviously, as the church got bigger, the demand for such services increased enormously – and as a result, the co-ordination of aid began to demand more organization than it had required at first. Of course, people performing these jobs were not doing the work of the later 'clergy'. They had no control over worship, and their very existence was more a matter of convenience than anything else. Some translations of the New Testament confuse their role by calling them 'deacons'. But they were not 'deacons' in any modern sense of the word. They had no authoritative position in the church. Quite the opposite: they were the church's servants (the real meaning of the Greek word from which 'deacon' is derived).

But were there others who were formally recognized leaders with responsibility for the regulation of worship and belief in the early churches? This is a highly debatable question. Professor Ernst Käsemann has done more than any other modern scholar to enlighten us on Paul's understanding of church order, and he concludes in effect that there was none. At least, there was no bureaucracy as such. Instead, an individual's usefulness in the church was determined directly by his or her endowment with the Spirit. Even the apostles, he claims, had no authority just because they were apostles. They had authority only in so far as the Holy Spirit gave it to them. So even Paul himself was just 'one charismatic among many', and the whole notion of people being specially appointed to a position of authority was quite foreign to Paul's thinking. Instead, all those who had received the Holy Spirit – and it was impossible to be a Christian without that – were 'office-bearers' in the church. The radical Roman Catholic theologian, Hans Küng, accepts much of what Käsemann has to say at this point, as also does the more conservative Dutch theologian Hendricus Berkhof. Applying all this to the modern scene, he writes: 'taking the charismatic structure of the church seriously would put an end to clericalism and a church ruled by ministers.'

There is a great deal of truth in all this, and Professor Käsemann has undoubtedly penetrated to the radical centre of Paul's thinking in a way that few other students of the New Testament have been able to do. At the same time, we need to remember that Paul's charismatic understanding of leadership did not lead to a free-for-all in the church. Paul makes it quite clear that a Spirit-directed leadership will itself involve a certain limitation of the work of any given individual within a church, for not every Christian is equipped by the Spirit to perform the same tasks. When Christians are prepared together to obey the Spirit, he himself will produce a situation in which 'everything must be done in a proper and orderly way'.

It is not inconsistent with this for Paul to refer elsewhere to specific leadership functions within various churches. The church at Philippi has its church leaders and helpers, while Paul's letter to the Thessalonians also mentions 'those who work among you, who

1 Corinthians 12

1 Corinthians 14:40

Philippians 1:1

1 Thessalonians 5:12

guide and instruct you in the Christian life'. But it is certain that such people owed their position not to some formal act of ordination (as later), but simply to their endowment with the Spirit.

When we turn to the church in Jerusalem, we get a slightly different picture. There, James seems to be very much a man in charge of the church, though no doubt he was guided and assisted by others ('the apostles and elders'). Later Christian traditions credit him with having been the first 'bishop' of Jerusalem, and though they may well be exaggerated it seems likely that he owed his position to some sort of hierarchical arrangement.

Acts 15:6, 22

In the tradition of many 'heresies' down the years, Sun Myung Moon, founder and leader of the Unification Church or 'Moonies', claims to have received special revelations from God, though his teaching directly contradicts the Bible.

We know very little of the formal organization of other churches during the New Testament period. Even the church at Rome is something of a mystery. When Paul wrote to it, he mentioned no leaders at all, though his list of house churches tends to suggest that its organization was much more like the earliest churches in Jerusalem than the later congregation led by James. Books like 2 Peter, 1 John and Jude mention no leaders at all, while others speak vaguely of 'leaders', 'elders' or 'shepherds' but without explaining their functions.

Romans 16:3–15

Acts 20:17; Hebrews 13:7, 17, 24; James 5:14; 1 Peter 5:1–5

Walter Bauer has suggested that churches in different parts of the Roman Empire developed in different ways and at different speeds, and no doubt this applied to their forms of organization just as much as to their theological development. But we can be quite sure of two things. In the first century, the Christian churches had a very loose and diverse form of organization. And that 'of official Christian priests we must honestly admit that there is in the New Testament not the faintest whisper' (R.P.C. Hanson).

Heresy

The single most important factor that led to the development of a well-organized and disciplined church in the second century was the emergence of heresy of various kinds.

The charismatic view that we find in the early chapters of Acts and in Paul had always been open to abuse. That was clearly part of the trouble that Paul had to deal with in the church at Corinth. As

The early Christians had to meet the challenge posed by heretics by defining more precisely what they believed and by basing their everyday lives on those beliefs.

Galatians 5:22–26
Romans 13:8–10; 1 Corinthians 13

long as Christians were truly led by the Spirit, then things could be expected to work smoothly. But the unscrupulous could easily manipulate such a situation for their own ends. It was all too easy for a person's own ideas and selfish motives to be put forward as the Spirit's guidance – and it was correspondingly difficult for others to prove that someone claiming the Spirit's guidance did not actually have it. Paul believed that the Holy Spirit would lead Christians to do only those things that were compatible with the way Jesus himself had lived – producing the 'fruits of the Spirit', especially that supremely Christian virtue, love. But even this was not enough

2 Corinthians 11:1–15

1 John 4:7–21
1 John 4:1–6

to control the 'pseudo-charismatics' in Corinth. Paul's own position as an apostle was itself called into question, for others were claiming that by the power of the Spirit they were 'super apostles', and their revelations were more spectacular than his.

Similar arguments are to be found in the background of the letters of John. Wandering teachers claiming the inspiration of the Holy Spirit were not only scandalizing other Christians by their behaviour, but were also putting forward theological ideas that the church and its leaders found unacceptable. But how could Christians deal with such people? In the earlier period the apostles had been the final authority. But as they died, the problem became more difficult. Fringe groups such as the Gnostics were gaining ever more ground, and it soon became clear to those in the mainstream of the church that it was no longer sufficient just to assert that they had the

Holy Spirit – for their opponents were making exactly the same claim. Faced with such problems, the church had no alternative but to begin a radical rethinking of its position. What did it believe? How could it be sure of knowing where to get authoritative guidance? And how could it ensure that the church in the second century would follow the guide-lines laid down by Jesus and his apostles at the very beginning? To try and find the answers to these questions, the church began to reassess its life in three main areas:

● **Beliefs** The Christians of whom we read in the early chapters of Acts had not been too concerned to set out their beliefs in any sort of systematic way. That is not to say they had no theology. Jesus himself had claimed the title 'Son of Man', and in the early chapters of Acts we find him identified as the 'Servant of God' as well as 'the Messiah'. Because of their own experience of the coming of the Holy Spirit, they had no hesitation in associating Jesus with God, and giving him the title 'Lord', the name of God in the Old Testament. Of course, they also knew that Jesus had been a real person who lived in Galilee and died on a Roman cross. But they were not concerned with defining their beliefs about Jesus more precisely. The kind of theological reflection that later led to dogmas about Jesus' 'divinity' or 'humanity' seemed both irrelevant and unnecessary.

However, when other people came along with claims that Jesus had been only partly divine, or not really divine at all, the church was faced with a challenge. It was not a new challenge, for Paul had already met something of the sort in Corinth. Perhaps that is one reason why he wrote his letter to Rome not long after that – as a kind of summary and exposition of his own Christian thinking. But after Paul's death, the problem became more acute. 1 John was written to counteract views of this kind, and we shall examine the precise nature of these Gnostic or Docetic beliefs in chapter 25. The fact that there were people who called themselves followers of Jesus but had distinctive ideas about his significance meant that everyone in the church had to do some hard thinking, to try and define more precisely what they really believed.

But where could they find their beliefs? The Gnostics and their associates had their own books, and many of their documents are still known to us today – books such as the *Gospel of Thomas*, the *Gospel of Philip*, the *Gospel of Truth* and many others allegedly containing secret teaching given by Jesus to some of his disciples. Up to this point, much of the church's teaching had been passed on by word of mouth. Though most of the New Testament books were in existence by the end of the first century, almost all of them had been written for specific situations in particular churches, and, with the possible exception of the letters of Paul, they had not been gathered together in any sort of permanent collection. Some church leaders, like Papias, still preferred the spoken word to what they could read in books. But the majority felt that the time had come to try and decide exactly what they did and did not believe.

● **Worship** In the earliest days, the Christians met together every

Acts 3:13, 26; 4:27, 30
Acts 2:31, 36; 3:18, 20; 5:42; 8:5

Acts 2:36; 7:59–60;
1 Corinthians 16:22

Eusebius, *Ecclesiastical History*, III.39

1 Corinthians 14:26–33

day, and their worship was spontaneous. This seems to have been regarded as the ideal, for when Paul describes how a church meeting should proceed, he depicts a Spirit-led participation in worship by many, if not all members of the church. No doubt this was the natural way to proceed at a time when the church generally met in someone's house. But as churches got bigger it was no longer possible for Christians to meet in this informal setting.

Then there was also the fact that anyone had the freedom to participate in such worship. In the ideal situation when everyone was truly inspired by the Holy Spirit, this was the perfect expression of Christian freedom. But it was also accompanied by the danger that those who were out of harmony with the church's beliefs and outlook could also use this freedom to pervert the faith of the church. Because of this it became necessary to ensure that those who led the church's worship could be relied upon to be faithful to the Christian message as it had been delivered by Jesus and the apostles. By the end of the first century a fixed form of service was in existence for the Lord's Supper, and other forms of Christian

The uninhibited style of worship of a 'charismatic' congregation aims to recapture the Spirit-led freedom of expression in the early church.

Didache 9, 10, 14

worship were also becoming less open than they had been. Not everyone welcomed this. Indeed, the *Didache* itself asserts that the ministry of Spirit-inspired speakers should not be curtailed in the interests of a formal church order. But in the face of growing threats from fringe groups in the church it was inevitable that this should happen eventually, in order to preserve the integrity of the Christian faith.

●**Authority** If the conduct of worship is to be controlled so as to exclude undesirable elements, two groups must be created within the church: those with the authority to conduct its worship, and those without such authority. It is important to realize that the movement towards a more authoritarian church hierarchy also originated in the fight against unacceptable beliefs. At a time when Gnostics were claiming a special authority because of their alleged endowment with the Spirit, it was important for the mainstream church to have its own clear source of power. It was of little practical use for the church's leaders to claim – even if it may have been true – that they, rather than their opponents, were truly inspired by the Spirit. They needed something more than that – and they found it in the apostles. In the earliest period, supreme authority had rested with them. So, they reasoned, anyone with recognized authority in the church must be succeeding to the position once held by the apostles. They were the apostles' successors, and could trace their office back in a clear line of descent from the very earliest times. They stood in an 'apostolic succession'.

Church growth and heresy were undoubtedly the major reasons for the changing pattern of church life at the end of the first century. But others have claimed to find different reasons for this change, and we must give some consideration to two of their suggestions:

Social change

The sociologist Max Weber has argued that any group started by an inspiring leader will inevitably change after his death. As his followers try to adapt his charismatic life-style to the normal concerns of everyday life, the structures they create will inevitably become more institutionalized. This happens for a number of reasons, according to Weber, but economic interests are the most significant. The original leader's close associates subsequently become his official representatives. They therefore have a vested interest in developing an organization, and setting themselves up as a privileged hierarchy with the main job of other members of the movement being to pay their wages.

In the course of this process, the dynamic inspiration of the original leader is lost, and his charisma is changed into a more tangible quality that can be handed on from one holder of an office to another.

There can be no doubt that this is what has happened in the church. Hans Küng has criticized the church and its structures for precisely these reasons. And they are not entirely absent from the New Testament. For example, in 1 Timothy we find the reception

1 Timothy 4:14 of spiritual gifts identified with the act of ordination to an office – and that is a notion that has been widely held in the church ever since. But the odd thing is that it should have taken so long for this new development to happen. The early church became fully institutionalized not in the first generation after Jesus, but in the second and third generations.

Up to that point, the experience of the church runs contrary to what we would expect on Weber's sociological theory. Though Jesus was undoubtedly what we would call a 'charismatic leader', the church also had elements of institutionalism from the start. For example, it observed the Lord's Supper as an exclusive community meal. It practised baptism of its converts, and it was conscious of having traditions to hand on to future generations. Its leaders had great authority, and were, at least on some occasions, paid by other church members. But there was one conviction that prevented the church developing into an organization existing for the sole benefit of its leaders. This was the universally-held belief that Jesus was not in fact dead, but alive – and continuing to work among his followers through the power of the Holy Spirit.

For as long as the church saw itself as the community founded by the Holy Spirit, this state of affairs could continue. But once it became suspicious of the exercise of charismatic gifts (because of their misuse), the living presence of Jesus became more of a dogma than a living reality – and it was a short step from that to the institutionalized church. There is no doubt that sociological analysis is helpful in explaining the course of later church history, and also certain aspects of the life of the earliest churches. But when we look for an explanation of the change from a charismatic to an institutional church, the main reasons lie elsewhere.

Frustrated hope

It has also been argued that the loss of the hope in the future return of Jesus (*parousia*) led to this change in the church's structure. Professor Käsemann has laid great emphasis on this. Jesus and the first Christians, he claims, had a vivid expectation of God's coming Mark 9:1 intervention in history. Jesus himself declared that God's new society would soon come with power, and after his resurrection the disciples lived in daily expectation of the return of Jesus himself in glory. But of course, nothing happened – and so they had to come to terms with the fact that the world was going to continue as it had always been. As a result, they needed a visible and tangible form of organization.

Others, of course, have argued that when Jesus spoke of the coming new society he was speaking of a spiritual experience that his disciples could enjoy here and now. We have already examined this whole issue in considerable detail in chapter 6. We suggested there that both these elements can be found in the teaching of Jesus: God's new society had already arrived in the person of Jesus himself, but its complete fulfilment was yet to come in the future.

Naturally, different groups in the early church found different parts of this message more attractive than others. The Christians in the Greek city of Thessalonica became so excited about the fact that Jesus was to return that they gave up work in order to concentrate

1 Thessalonians 4:13–5:11

on preparing for this great event. But Paul rebuked them for this. Though he shared their sense of anticipation, he was quite sure that scaremongering and imaginative speculation were not the way Christians should behave. He reminded them in the words of Jesus himself that 'the day of the Lord will come as a thief comes at

1 Thessalonians 5:2

night'. In the meantime, Christians should be good citizens, work for their living and encourage and help other people. That is the way they will be ready for the coming of Christ.

Despite Paul's reticence in making pronouncements on such matters, many people still find it possible to believe that he was obsessed with nothing but the supposedly imminent end of the world. Professor Käsemann describes Paul quite unjustifiably as 'a possessed man pursuing a feverish dream'. Paul was nothing of the kind, nor were the other leaders of the early church. Of course they believed that Jesus would return one day. But they were also quite sure that in an important sense, Jesus was already with them: in the person of the Holy Spirit.

Romans 8:18–27;
2 Corinthians 5:1–5

In other words, we find exactly the same tension in Paul between present and future as we have already seen in Jesus. In every letter he wrote, Paul gave instructions for Christian behaviour in a settled period of church life. Had he supposed that it was all to come to an abrupt end, such instructions would have been quite unnecessary.

Ephesians 2:1–5; Colossians 2:13

He describes the *present* experience of Christians as 'eternal life', and John uses the same expression. For him, 'eternal life' is not just a life that goes on forever in the future. More significantly, it is the life of God as it can be experienced by Christians here and now in

John 4:23; 17:3

the present.

With this kind of outlook, the non-occurrence of the second coming of Jesus would hardly be a problem. But there is one New Testament writing where it seems to be taken more seriously. This is 2 Peter. Here, the writer explains the apparently unexpected delay in the coming of Jesus by the observation that 'there is no difference in the Lord's sight between one day and a thousand

2 Peter 3:8

years'. But we ought to note that the problem had occurred here because unbelievers had raised it, mocking the church by saying,

2 Peter 3:4

'He promised to come, didn't he? Where is he?'

Perhaps the issue would never have arisen otherwise – though it certainly became more important to Christians at a later period. Eventually the prospect of a future return of Jesus was lost altogether, and theologians were content to think of the church itself as the new society which Jesus had promised. But this was long after the New Testament period, and the disappearance of a future hope was not the cause of the church's institutionalization, but was one of its results.

In the final analysis, the church became an institution not out of conviction but out of practical necessity. It is easy to look back with hindsight and to imagine that the problems of heresy and church

The early church recognizes the New Testament

AD 100

All dates approximate

Different parts of our New Testament were written by this time, but not yet collected and defined as 'Scripture'. Early Christian writers (for example Polycarp and Ignatius) quote from the Gospels and Paul's letters, as well as from other Christian writings and oral sources.

Paul's letters were collected late in the first century. Matthew, Mark and Luke were brought together by AD 150.

AD 200

New Testament used in the church at Rome (the 'Muratorian Canon')

Four Gospels
Acts
Paul's letters:
   Romans
   1 & 2 Corinthians
   Galatians
   Ephesians
   Philippians
   Colossians
   1 & 2 Thessalonians
   1 & 2 Timothy
   Titus
   Philemon

James

1 & 2 John
Jude
Revelation of John
Revelation of Peter
Wisdom of Solomon

To be used in private, but not public, worship
The Shepherd of Hermas

AD 250

New Testament used by Origen

Four Gospels
Acts
Paul's letters:
   Romans
   1 & 2 Corinthians
   Galatians
   Ephesians
   Philippians
   Colossians
   1 & 2 Thessalonians
   1 & 2 Timothy
   Titus
   Philemon

1 Peter
1 John

Revelation of John

Disputed
Hebrews
James
2 Peter
2 & 3 John
Jude
The Shepherd of Hermas
Letter of Barnabas
Teaching of Twelve Apostles
Gospel of the Hebrews

AD 300

**New Testament used
by Eusebius**

Four Gospels
Acts
Paul's letters:
  Romans
  1 & 2 Corinthians
  Galatians
  Ephesians
  Philippians
  Colossians
  1 & 2 Thessalonians
  1 & 2 Timothy
  Titus
  Philemon

1 Peter
1 John

Revelation of John
(authorship in doubt)

AD 400

**New Testament fixed
for the West by the
Council of Carthage**

Four Gospels
Acts
Paul's letters:
  Romans
  1 & 2 Corinthians
  Galatians
  Ephesians
  Philippians
  Colossians
  1 & 2 Thessalonians
  1 & 2 Timothy
  Titus
  Philemon
Hebrews
James
1 & 2 Peter
1, 2 & 3 John
Jude
Revelation

**Disputed but
well known**
James
2 Peter
2 & 3 John
Jude
To be excluded
The Shepherd of Hermas
Letter of Barnabas
Gospel of the Hebrews
Revelation of Peter
Acts of Peter
Didache

Part of the last chapter of John's Gospel in Greek, from the fourth-century *Codex Sinaiticus* growth could have been tackled in some other way that would have been less inhibiting to further development. But there can be no doubt of the sincerity of the second-century church leaders, nor of their genuine regret that because of excess and abuse, the charismatic ideal was no longer a practical way forward.

Putting the New Testament together

To establish their position, Christians had to decide which books contained an authoritative statement of the church's beliefs, and it was thinking on this subject that eventually led to the collection of our twenty-seven New Testament books as having supreme

Testament writers. And the sayings of Jesus also had a special place in their thinking. But in the very earliest times we find no fixed and clearly-defined body of such teaching. We can see this from the fact that the New Testament occasionally refers to sayings of Jesus

Through the centuries, as with this 'chained Bible', the Bible has had a place of great importance in the lives of Christians: it is the source-book for belief and behaviour.

authority. This collection is often called the 'canon' of the New Testament. The word 'canon' here comes from a similar Greek word meaning 'a measuring stick': the New Testament was to be an accurate measure by which all theological and doctrinal viewpoints could be tested.

From our modern perspective, we might suppose that somebody in the early church actually sat down and decided which books would form a part of this special collection. But it did not happen like that. The books of the New Testament were not accorded a special authority overnight, and in fact it was well into the fourth century before an actual list of books was drawn up. We can trace four stages in this process:

● Right from the earliest times, Christians gave special authority to certain collections of teaching. The Old Testament, for example, was regarded as sacred Scripture by the New

that are not contained in the Gospels (see Acts 20:35), and then we also have to take account of the second-century collections of sayings of Jesus, some of which are almost certainly genuine. The fact that there are four Gospels in the New Testament instead of just one also shows that there was no idea of a fixed and exclusive collection of Jesus' teaching, and John 21:25 mentions many other sayings and deeds of Jesus not included in his Gospel, but no doubt known to some of his readers in one form or another.

The apostles themselves had considerable authority, and their writings were highly respected. We must remember that all the letters of the New Testament were written to specific people for specific purposes, but they do nevertheless contain indications that their authors felt a special authority attached to their words (see, for example, Galatians 1:7–9). By the time 2 Peter was written, Paul's letters at least were regarded very highly, and could be classed as 'Scripture' (2 Peter 3:16).

● When we move beyond the first century, into the period of the so-called 'Apostolic Fathers' (people like Ignatius, Clement of Rome and Polycarp), we find a similar situation. These writers clearly respect many of the New Testament books. But they do not regard them as 'Scripture'; in addition, they also valued many other Jewish and Christian writings.

● This state of affairs received a serious challenge from Marcion. In about AD 150, this individual left the church at Rome and declared that he had found a new message. This message had allegedly been given in secret by Jesus to the twelve disciples. But they had not preserved it intact, and so its secret was given to Paul. To prove all this, Marcion made a list of sacred books. This list included only one Gospel (identical with none of the New Testament Gospels, but not too different from Luke), together with ten letters of Paul.

At about the same time there was an explosion of other heretical groups, all of which had their own sacred books. And it was not long before the leaders of the church began to write their own lists. Towards the end of the second century, Irenaeus, Bishop of Lyons in France, had a kind of 'canon' of New Testament books. He also laid down a rough test for deciding the relative value of different Christian books, suggesting that those of most value were connected with the apostles themselves (*Against Heresies* 3.11.8). This principle, applied by Irenaeus to the Gospels, was refined and extended in the years that followed, and in the third century the church historian Eusebius listed in his *Ecclesiastical History* 3.25.1–7 three different categories of Christian writings: those that were certainly authoritative (the four Gospels, Acts, the letters of Paul, 1 Peter, 1 John and Revelation); those that were certainly not (*Acts of Paul, Shepherd of Hermas, Apocalypse of Peter, Epistle of Barnabas, Didache, Gospel according to the Hebrews*); and those whose status was disputed (James, Jude, 2 Peter, 2 and 3 John).

● Eventually in the fourth century, we find an actual list of authoritative scriptural books, from Athanasius in the eastern section of the church (AD 367), and from the Council of Carthage in the western part of the church (AD 397), and the books they listed are the twenty-seven books of our New Testament. But, of course, they did not gain their authority then. These books had already been widely used and highly regarded for centuries by then, and the decisions made in the fourth century were simply the formal acceptance of a state of affairs that had existed for practical purposes for many years before that.

Chapter 24 The church and its Jewish origins

We shall never fully understand the story of the early church if we forget that the Christian movement had its origins in the Jewish religion. Jesus was a Jew, as were all his original disciples. Most if not all of the converts on the Day of Pentecost were Jews, but even in the earliest days of the Jerusalem church people like Stephen were asking whether Christianity was a part of Judaism, or whether it was something distinctive and new. These questions became more pressing once Paul and others had moved out into the wider world to take the good news about Jesus to people with no Jewish connections. Yet, though he regarded himself as the 'apostle to the Gentiles', wherever Paul went he always took his message first to the Jewish synagogue. As a result, many of the issues dealt with in his letters have a distinctively Jewish flavour – questions about the

Romans 11:13
Acts 13:14; 14:1; 17:1–2

The first Christians had to wrestle with the problem of carrying over Jewish traditions into the life of the early church. In modern times, synagogue worship conducted according to ancient traditions helps to reinforce the strong sense of Jewish identity and their links with the past.

Old Testament Law, and the nature of Christian belief and behaviour over against Jewish traditions.

These issues were to become increasingly important for every aspect of the life of the early church, as Christians took over the Jewish scriptures (the Old Testament) as a part of their own authoritative writings. They naturally needed to know what relationship there might be between the message of God in the Old Testament and their own new experience of Jesus and the Holy Spirit. Paul's answer to this question has already been explored in previous chapters. But there are other writings in the New Testament which show us how other Christians were tackling these issues. These writings are generally shorter in length than Paul's letters, and they are also for the most part considerably less complex. But they are no less valuable for that, for they give us direct access to areas of the church's life and thinking that are mentioned nowhere else in the New Testament.

Four books in particular can help us to understand the Jewish dimension in the life of the church: James, Hebrews, 1 Peter and Revelation. They all have a clear orientation towards Jewish interests, but they are not identical. Indeed their very diversity makes them the more useful, for they give us an insight into at least four different aspects of Jewish thought that were taken over and further developed among the first Christians.

Christians disassociated themselves from the excesses and debauchery of the Roman festivals.

Christians and Jewish morality

Judaism had always been deeply concerned with behaviour. In the Roman world, Jewish people were often distinguished not so much by what they thought as by what they did. They circumcised their male children, kept the sabbath day apart and observed complicated laws about food. These were the things that announced to the Romans that the Jews were different. But they were not the only things. For the Jewish people also had a comprehensive code of moral behaviour. Many of the things that were taken for granted in a pagan life-style were avoided by Jews – not just because they were un-Jewish, but because they seemed to be against the Law of God. As Jewish people in different parts of the Roman Empire explained their ancestral faith to other people, they often found that Gentiles were attracted by their moral standards. After the self-indulgence of Greek and Roman life, many Gentiles found the Jewish way refreshingly simple and disciplined. There must have been many Romans like Cornelius, who actually became adherents to the Jewish religion ('proselytes') – while many more followed the Jewish way of life without necessarily taking up the full burden of the Torah.

Acts 10:1–2

The foundation of Jewish morality had been laid many centuries before in the Old Testament. Besides its concern with matters of religious ritual, the Torah has a strong moral core, in the Ten Commandments and elsewhere (especially Deuteronomy). It was concerned to ensure that worshippers in ancient Israel should carry their religious beliefs over into the affairs of everyday life. As Amos and other Old Testament prophets never tired of pointing out, it was a waste of time to make high-sounding religious affirmations in the temple if they meant nothing in the market-place.

Exodus 20:1–17

Amos 5:21–24; Micah 6:6–8

James

The message of Jesus was largely concerned with this theme, and the letter of James is very similar: it emphasizes that religious belief is worthless if it does not affect the way we live. Devotion to God does not end at the door of the church. It only begins there: 'What God the Father considers to be pure and genuine religion is this: to take care of orphans and widows in their suffering and to keep oneself from being corrupted by the world.' The heart of real devotion to God is to love one's neighbour as oneself – and without deeds that will put such sentiments into action, religious faith is worthless.

James 1:27
James 2:1–13

James 2:14–26

Like Jesus, James uses many illustrations to deliver his message. He draws a vivid verbal picture of the apparent splendour of a rich person. Like the flowers whose beauty he tries to copy, his day will soon be over: 'The sun rises with its blazing heat and burns the plant; its flower falls off, and its beauty is destroyed. In the same way the rich man will be destroyed ...' James also turns his attention to the dangers of thoughtless talk. The tongue is just like a rudder, which can steer a ship many times larger than itself; its influence is out of all proportion to its size – and if we are not careful it can make trouble for ourselves and other people. Once a person loses control of his tongue, it can create conditions like a forest fire, which

James 1:10–11; 5:1–6 and Matthew 6:28–30

is started by just one small spark but is very difficult to put
out.

James 3:1–12

James takes many illustrations from the familiar world of
Palestinian agriculture. He condemns the selfishness of the master
who refuses to pay his servants a proper wage for a day's work.
Jesus had used a similar story to make a rather different point. He
told of a master who hired men to work in his vineyard. They
started work at different times of the day, so that when the time
came for them to receive their wages some of them had only worked
for an hour, while others had worked the whole day. But the master
gave them all the same wages! Jesus' hearers must have rubbed their
eyes with amazement when they heard that, for in their experience
employers were more likely to treat them in the way James
describes. But, of course, Jesus was speaking of a different master:

James 5:1–6

Matthew 20:1–16

Having faith is a waste of time, James
wrote, unless it influences our
day-to-day lives and the way we treat
other people.

God himself, who is overwhelmingly generous in all his dealings
with men and women.

The book of James has no coherent 'argument', any more than
Jesus' Sermon on the Mount has a consistent theme. But its
message would not be lost on its readers. These people were
suffering the kind of discrimination that James mentions, and they
are urged to be patient and to trust in God for deliverance. God will
keep his promises to his people, and they will be vindicated in the
end.

Matthew 5–7

James 5:7–20

A Christian book?

There are many unsolved problems with the letter of James. But two
things are quite clear: it is an intensely Jewish writing, and it is concerned above everything else with correct behaviour. Some have
thought it so Jewish that they have doubted whether it is really
Christian. Martin Luther had no time for it at all, and he regretted
that it had ever been included among the books of the New

James 1:1; 2:1

James 2:21–24; 5:11, 17; 2:25

Testament. By comparison with the other New Testament writings it was, he said, 'a right strawy epistle ... for it has no evangelical manner about it'. Others have pointed out that James mentions the name of Jesus in only two places, and that when he gives examples for his readers to follow, he chooses Old Testament figures like Abraham, Job, Elijah and even the prostitute Rahab rather than Jesus. No significant facts about Jesus are mentioned anywhere in the book – not even his death and resurrection. Indeed, if we were to look for other books of a similar kind, we would most easily find them in books like Proverbs in the Old Testament and other so-called 'Wisdom' books that were popular with Jewish readers in the time of Jesus.

Some have therefore suggested that James was not written by a Christian at all, and that the two references to Jesus were inserted at some later date when Christians became embarrassed by the existence of this apparently Jewish book in their scriptures. But there is no evidence to support this idea. If a later Christian editor had set out to change a Jewish book into a Christian one, he would surely have inserted far more references to specifically Christian ideas than just two mentions of the name of Jesus.

James and Jesus

The message of James is in general very much in harmony with the teaching of Jesus. But there is more than just a superficial similarity between them. For there are many detailed points at which James's advice corresponds closely to specific aspects of Jesus' teaching.

Similarities between the teaching of Jesus and James.	
God is the source and giver of all good gifts	Matthew 7:7–11 James 1:17
Christians must pay attention to God's word but also be prepared to put it into practice	Matthew 7:24–27 James 1:22
Christians should share God's mercy with others	Matthew 5:7 James 2:13
Christians should endeavour to make peace in the world	Matthew 5:9 James 3:18
'Love your neighbour as you love yourself'	Matthew 22:39 James 2:8
If this teaching is followed, the true nature of the Christian will be impossible to hide	Matthew 7:16–18 James 3:12
Followers of Jesus can pray to God in the knowledge that he will answer	Mark 11:22–24 James 1:6
God is the only judge and Christians too will have to give an account of their deeds to him	Matthew 7:1–2 James 4:11–12
Christians should make promises that others can accept and trust, because they intend to keep them, instead of trying to emphasize their sincerity by using unnecessary oaths	Matthew 5:33–37 James 5:12

The words of James and the words of Jesus are not *identical* in any of these passages. But the language used and the sentiments expressed are so similar that we can hardly deny there is a connection. The most likely explanation of this is that the writer of James knew these sayings of Jesus in a slightly different form from that now incorporated into the New Testament Gospels. We know that the Gospel materials circulated by word of mouth for some time before they were written down, and the fact that some of this teaching has a more primitive form in James than it does in Matthew suggests that James had access to it at an earlier stage than the writers of the Gospels.

The letter of James

But all this begs an important question. Who wrote the letter of James? And who were its first readers? Most other New Testament books contain some clues that enable us to answer such questions. But in the case of James, we have virtually nothing to go on.

Who was James?

Apart from the mention of a person called James in the opening sentence, the book tells us nothing about its writer, readers or any other event or person. There is no hint as to where James and his readers lived, nor are we told who James actually was. This was a very common name among Jewish people, and a James who is described as 'a servant of God and of the Lord Jesus Christ' could have been any Christian of that name. Similarly, the way the book describes people and their behaviour could apply to many different situations not only in the ancient world, but even today too. It is as pointless to look for the identity of the rich man (James 2:1–4) as it would be to try and find out who the Good Samaritan was (Luke 10:25–37).

Early church traditions give us no more real help. There is no trace of this letter of James in other Christian literature until the end of the second century. Eusebius, the fourth-century church historian, listed it as one of the New Testament books whose value was disputed (*Ecclesiastical History* 3.25.3). But he also added that the same disputed books 'have been produced publicly with the rest in most churches', and then he links it with James, the brother of Jesus and leader of the church in Jerusalem (*Ecclesiastical History* 2.23.25). A number of modern scholars believe that, though this statement in Eusebius is much later than the writing of the book of James, it nevertheless contains some truth, and so they regard the book as the work of James of Jerusalem.

If it is necessary to link it with some person by the name of James who is mentioned elsewhere in the New Testament, then there are only two possible candidates: James the disciple and brother of John, and James the brother of Jesus. Of these two, most scholars choose the second, on the ground that James the apostle was martyred in AD 44 (Acts 12:1–3). It is assumed that this date would be too early for the writing of any of the New Testament books, though there is really no evidence to support such an assertion. At the same time, James the disciple does not figure prominently in the stories of the early church in Acts, whereas James of Jerusalem obviously became well-known: he is a central figure in Acts, and also in Paul's writings, and would therefore be in a better position to write to other Christians with no more introduction than his name.

But a number of arguments have been put forward against this idea that James of Jerusalem wrote the letter of James:

● It is written in very good Greek, in an elegant style that shows some acquaintance with Greek literature. But would this be likely if it was the work of a Galilean countryman? This argument once carried considerable weight, because it was believed that Palestine was not so heavily influenced by Greek culture as other parts of the Roman Empire. But we now know that this was not the case, and in an area such as Galilee with a large non-Jewish population a person like James could easily have learned a good deal about the Greek language. At a number of places in the book, the idiom and style of the Semitic languages Hebrew and Aramaic seem to have influenced his writing (2:7; 3:12; 4:13–15; 5:17), which suggests that the writer also spoke one or both of these languages.

● If this book was written by James the brother of Jesus, we might have expected him to make more specific

James draws on imagery from rural life and agriculture for many of his illustrations.

mention of his brother. Since James was not a disciple during Jesus' lifetime, we might even have expected some account of his conversion (1 Corinthians 15:7). But the writer seems to go out of his way to avoid mentioning Jesus directly. There is some weight in this argument, but it really depends on guesswork. If we are not sure of the identity of an ancient author, we can hardly be in a position to judge what he may or may not have been expected to write!

● In James 2:14–26 we have a passage which contrasts faith and actions as the basis of true commitment. Paul also draws the same contrast, especially in his letters to the Galatians and to the Romans, and some scholars have seen in James a deliberate reply to and correction of Paul's viewpoint. If this is the case, then James must have been written after Paul's time, and probably after his views had become a source of controversy – and on any account this must have been long after the death of James of Jerusalem. But

there is no reason to suppose either that James knew Paul's writings, or, as some have suggested, that Paul knew of James. Certainly they use the same terminology, but their concerns are different.

● The strongest reason of all for doubting that James of Jerusalem could have written this book is its conviction that true belief should be described in purely ethical terms. We know that James had faced this question over the admission of Gentile converts to the church. Were they to obey the whole of the Old Testament Law or not? While James did not go along with those extremists who insisted that Gentile Christians should become Jews by being circumcised, he did agree that they should observe not only the moral laws of the Old Testament, but also some of the ritual and food laws as well (Acts 15:13–21). Is it therefore likely that he would have written that the 'law of the Kingdom' could be kept by loving one's neighbour (2:8)? There is a fundamental difference between what

we know of James from Acts and Galatians (and what we learn from Josephus and other historians) and what we read in the book that bears the same name. In the view of many people, this difference is so crucial that it alone must cast doubt on the alleged connection between the two.

The date

Though this book may well have no connection with James of Jerusalem, a number of facts suggest very strongly that it belongs to an early period of the church's life rather than a later one:

● In its opening sentence, it addresses itself to 'the twelve tribes in the Dispersion' (1:1). Taken literally, of course, that could mean the whole of the Jewish people scattered throughout the world. But it is probably to be seen in the same light as the similar address in 1 Peter 1:1 or Paul's designation of his Galatian readers as 'the Israel of God' (Galatians 6:16). From an early time, Christians saw themselves as the heirs and successors of the people of God in

the Old Testament, and it was natural to apply to themselves language that had previously been used of Israel. But, of course, the only period in the church's history when anyone could write to the whole of God's people in this way (as contrasted with 1 Peter, which was addressed only to certain areas) was at the very beginning of its history – when the church was still essentially Jewish and centred on Jerusalem. Theodor Zahn argues that this points unmistakably to the time after the death of Stephen, but before Paul's travels had begun.

● This is further supported by the fact that there is no sign anywhere in James of a break between Judaism and Christianity. The well-to-do oppressors of the poor (2:6–7) were almost certainly Jews but they are not condemned because of that. All the attention is focussed on their basic selfishness. Moreover, the gathering so vividly described in James 2:1–4 is said to be in 'the synagogue' (2:2). Dr John Robinson believes that this situation is

very similar to that described in Acts 4–5 when Jewish aristocrats were oppressing a lower-class proletarian Christian movement.

● The background to much of the imagery of James is clearly Palestinian. The 'autumn and spring rains' of 5:7 meant nothing in other parts of the Roman Empire, while the agricultural practices mentioned in the previous verses are of a type that disappeared for good in Palestine after AD 70, but which were widespread in the days of Jesus.

● There is no evidence anywhere in James of the later practices and problems of the church. Not only is the Jewish/Gentile controversy unknown, but there is no mention of heresy, and no reference to the organization of the church or to doctrinal arguments. Its moral teaching does not include later ethical concerns over the introduction of pagan moral standards into the church. Instead, it is almost exclusively directed to the kind of problems that would occur in a Jewish environment.

Origins

It has been suggested that the writer of James spoke both Hebrew and Aramaic. This Hebrew text from the Pentateuch is accompanied by an Aramaic paraphrase (or *Targum*).

We seem to be faced with two main conclusions. On the one hand, the evidence for associating this book with James of Jerusalem is not all that compelling; but on the other, there are strong reasons for placing it in a very early period of the church's life. So where did it come from, and what was its purpose?

We must recognize that we do not have enough information to give a full answer to that question. But the kind of teaching that we find in James is so similar to that of Jesus himself, and uses so much of the same rural imagery, that it is not unreasonable to suppose it has a similar background. It is not inconceivable that it had its origins among those followers of Jesus who remained in Galilee after the main centre of the church moved to Jerusalem. It is impossible to prove this, of course, for we know next to nothing about such Galilean believers. But the message of James would certainly be especially appropriate to those who were worshipping in the Jewish synagogues of rural Palestine, and at the same time were trying to put into practice what Jesus had taught them. Such people must have been tempted to substitute religious formality for the spiritual realities of which Jesus had spoken – and, as a relative minority, they would also be open to the kind of persecution that James mentions.

If the book originated in such a context, this may also explain why it went unrecognized in the wider church for so long. Its eventual association with an important person like James of Jerusalem would then have been a means of justifying its inclusion in the canon of the New Testament. It could also reflect the possibility that the church in Jerusalem was included in 'God's people in the Dispersion', to whom James was originally despatched at an early stage in the history of the church.

'Faith' and 'works' in Paul and James

When Martin Luther called James 'an epistle of straw', his main reason for doing so was that he believed James's theology was fundamentally different from Paul's – and, since Paul was his hero, he was forced to relegate James to a secondary position. If we compare James 2:24 with Romans 3:28, we can soon see what led him to this conclusion:

● **James 2:24**: You see that a man is justified by works and not by faith alone.

● **Romans 3:28**: For we hold that a man is justified by faith apart from works of the law.

These two statements have every appearance of being mutually contradictory. Not only do they seem to be saying opposite things from each other: they also use exactly the same Greek words to do so! But when we examine them more carefully, and especially when we place them in their proper contexts, this alleged contradiction becomes much less obvious:

● Though they both speak of 'faith', James and Paul seem to mean rather different things by this word. For Paul, it has almost a technical sense, referring specifically to that belief and commitment to Jesus that characterize the Christian life. In James, however, 'faith' has a much broader meaning. No doubt specifically Christian faith is not excluded, but it is not the main emphasis. This is on 'faith' as belief in God, as opposed to atheism. James is more concerned with the intellectual acceptance of theological propositions, whereas Paul is exclusively concerned with commitment.

● There is a similar distinction in the way they use the term 'works'. When James mentions 'works', he is referring to the kind of behaviour that naturally stems from commitment to

Christ (1:25; 2:8). But the 'works' that Paul writes about are the actions and rituals that were prescribed in the Old Testament Law. Paul refers to things that a person would do in order to gain God's approval. James refers to the things a person will do because he or she already has a living relationship with God through Christ.

● Paul and James were addressing themselves to different practical problems, and this inevitably affected the way they expressed themselves. In Galatians and Romans, Paul was contending against the self-righteousness of people who thought that by keeping the Old Testament Law they could commend themselves to God. So he condemns the keeping of the Law – and in doing so, he echoes the teaching of Jesus (Luke 18:9–14). James, on the other hand, was fighting against the temptation to suppose that right belief is all that matters – and he accordingly emphasizes that doctrines with no practical effect are worthless. Again, he also echoes the teaching of Jesus (Matthew 7:21–23).

Christians and Jewish ritual

1 Kings 8:20–21

Jeremiah 21:1–23:32

Ezra, Nehemiah

Overleaf: The temple in Jerusalem occupied a site with a long-established tradition of sacrifice. Temple worship came to an end in AD 70 when the Romans sacked the city; the Moslem Dome of the Rock was built in 691–92 on the same site.

The temple in Jerusalem had always held a special place in the life and thinking of Jewish people. Built originally in the time of Solomon, at the height of Israel's political expansion, the temple and all that it represented came to have an almost mystical significance. Even in the dark days just before its destruction by Nebuchadnezzar, king of Babylon, the people of Jerusalem had believed against all the odds that the presence of the temple in their city would somehow save them from invasion. They were wrong, of course, as the prophet Jeremiah was quick to remind them – for they were pinning their hope on an outward form of religious activity instead of a personal relationship with God himself.

Almost 150 years after Nebuchadnezzar had plundered Solomon's temple, it was eventually patched up and brought back into regular use under the influence of Ezra and Nehemiah. But by the New Testament period it was in the process of being replaced with a structure even more splendid than the original had been. In 20 BC, Herod the Great decided that he would build a temple that would be as impressive as any building anywhere in the Roman world. But he did not live to see it finished. The work was so ambitious and costly that it went on for something like eighty years. The new temple was eventually completed – only to be destroyed shortly afterwards by the Roman general Titus in AD 70.

This was the temple that Jesus and the first Christians knew, and it was a centre of devotion for Jewish believers from all over the Roman Empire. By New Testament times Jewish synagogues had been established in every town or city where there was a Jewish

population of any size. But worship in the synagogue was not the same as worship in the temple. The synagogue had originated as a social convenience for Jews living in lands far removed from Palestine. But it was at the temple in Jerusalem that Israel's religious past could be seen in true focus. The worship of the synagogue could incorporate some of the ancient rituals such as circumcision and the old food laws. But it was only in the temple that the rites prescribed in the Old Testament could be carried out in their entirety. Here, the priests still offered sacrifices as they had done for generations past, and the great religious festivals had special significance when celebrated in the temple at Jerusalem. Jews from all over the empire had the ambition to go there and worship in its holy places. The crowds who gathered to hear Peter on the Day of Pentecost were not at all unusual: Jerusalem was the one place that every pious Jew must visit at least once in his lifetime.

But what were the new Christians to think about all this? Gentile believers with no previous connection with the Jewish faith had never thought of the temple at Jerusalem at all. But those who had been Jews before becoming Christians saw it as an important question. For the Torah was not just a compendium of moral instructions. It also contained detailed regulations for the proper conduct of worship. No one seems to have questioned the acceptance of Jewish standards of behaviour in the church. But what was to be done with the ritual of the Jewish religion?

This was a more complex question, for it included not only the role of the temple in Jerusalem, but also the vexed problem of circumcision. That was ultimately solved in favour of those who, like Paul, believed that the Old Testament Law was not directly relevant to the Christian life. But there were many Jewish Christians who not only continued with practices like circumcision but also felt a special affection for the priesthood and ritual of the Old Testament. The first followers of Jesus in Jerusalem had participated freely in the services at the temple: it never occurred to them not to do so, and in any case that was where they would find others willing to listen to their new message about Jesus. But as time passed, things soon changed. Many Hellenist Christians felt, like Stephen, that the day of the temple and its rituals was finished altogether. The death of Jesus had now made repeated sacrifices for sin a thing of the past. But the church in Jerusalem seems to have continued to worship in the temple, and was allowed to do so because of its relatively conservative stance on the issue of Gentile Christians. And there were many others who wished to join them. After all, these Hellenist Christians had been born Jews. No one could change that. In addition, their non-Christian compatriots were naturally eager to know where they stood. Did they support and approve of the Jewish way of doing things – or did they, like Stephen, believe that even the temple was now redundant?

Acts 2:46; 3:1

Hebrews This is the kind of question that seems to lie behind the New Testament book of Hebrews. The way the author encourages and advises his readers seems to suggest that they were being persecuted in some way. This may explain why the question of Jewish worship had become so important to them: if they were prepared to conform to Jewish practices, life could be a lot easier. The early chapters of Acts show how antagonistic Jews could make life difficult for Christian believers, and some scholars believe a similar situation is envisaged here. On the other hand, Christians throughout the Roman Empire must have been tempted to try and link themselves to Judaism in some way, especially in times of persecution. For Judaism was a permitted religion under Roman law, whereas Christianity was not.

Acts 13:50; 14:5, 19

The writer of Hebrews was quite sure that it was both pointless and unnecessary for Christians to keep the ritual requirements of the Old Testament Law. The message of Jesus is God's final word to men and women. The prophets and others in ancient Israel had spoken in God's name to the people of their own time, but they were all now superseded by Jesus. Even Moses and Joshua were insignificant compared to Jesus, not to mention the angels who according to Jewish tradition had been connected with the giving of the Torah. Jesus was also far greater than Aaron, the archetype of every Jewish priest. Aaron was only an ordinary man, as great a sinner as the rest of people. But Jesus was the Son of God. Because of his human experience, he understood how people felt when faced with the power of evil. But he was not affected by it, and he could therefore be thought of as 'a great high priest', who has provided 'eternal salvation for all those who obey him'.

Hebrews 1:1–3
Hebrews 3:1–4:13

Hebrews 1:4–2:18

Hebrews 2:17–18; 4:14–15

Hebrews 4:14–5:10

Continuing to write of Jesus under the imagery of the Jewish priesthood, Hebrews goes on to suggest that a more suitable Old Testament illustration of what Jesus had done may be found in the figure of Melchizedek. He is a shadowy figure of whom we know next to nothing. In one of the psalms, the king in Jerusalem is called 'a priest for ever in the line of succession to Melchizedek', and many Christians have applied this description to Jesus. He also appears briefly in a story about Abraham. But the writer of Hebrews uses the obscurity of the Old Testament record to his own advantage. Since 'there is no record of Melchizedek's father or mother or of any of his ancestors; no record of his birth or of his death', he must be 'like the Son of God', who is similarly timeless. He also draws attention to the fact that Abraham had recognized the greatness of this priestly figure, long before Aaron and his descendants had ever been heard of. If the great ancestor of the Jewish nation had himself paid homage to Melchizedek, then that in itself was enough to demonstrate the superiority of his position over the later priestly line descended from Aaron. For since Aaron was as yet unborn, he was at least potentially present in Abraham's body when he met Melchizedek. If further proof of Jesus' supremacy was needed, there was always the fact that the Old Testament priests died and were succeeded by others, while Jesus, like Melchizedek apparently, lived for ever.

Hebrews 5:11–7:28

Psalm 110:4

Gensis 14:17–20

Hebrews 7:3

The sacrifice of Jesus

The precise form of the author's argument may elude most of us today. But for him the point of it all is simple: 'we have such a High Priest, who sits at the right of the throne of the Divine Majesty in heaven. He serves as High Priest in the Most Holy Place, that is, in the real tent which was put up by the Lord, not by man.' Everything that had been achieved on a temporary basis through the rituals of Old Testament worship – first in the 'tent' (or tabernacle), then in the temple – had now been achieved permanently by Jesus. The sacrifices offered by the Old Testament priesthood had to be repeated, because they could only account for past wrongdoing. But the sacrifice of Jesus (himself, on the cross) had more far-reaching consequences. Not only was it the basis on which men and women could be forgiven and accepted by God, but the divine power released by it could also set them free from 'useless rituals, so that we may serve the living God'.

Hebrews 8:1–2

Hebrews 9:25–28

Hebrews 9:14

Now, 'God does away with all the old sacrifices and puts the sacrifice of Christ in their place'. Because of that, those who are tempted to go back and take part in the old rituals of Judaism are actually denying the effectiveness of what God has done in Jesus. They are 'despising the Son of God', and insulting the Holy Spirit. They have effectively joined with those who reject Jesus, and God has no time for such people. To turn back to Jewish ways is to be lost, but those who trust in God and accept what he has done for them in Jesus will find true and lasting salvation.

Hebrews 10:9

Hebrews 10:29

Hebrews 6:4–8

Hebrews 10:39

All this is strong stuff. But our author was convinced that it was nothing new, for he goes on to list a 'large crowd of witnesses' taken from the Old Testament and Jewish history, whose experience of God can bear this out. These people will receive the same reward as faithful Christians, and their story should be a lasting encouragement to Christians to get their priorities right and to keep their eyes firmly fixed on Jesus alone as their example and inspiration. To do this, they must live at peace with others and show love for their fellow-Christians, as well as members of their own families. By doing so, they will please God and he himself will 'provide you with every good thing you need in order to do his will'.

Hebrews 11:1–38
Hebrews 11:39–40

Hebrews 12:1–11

Hebrews 12:14; 13:1–21

Hebrews 13:21

Hebrews: author, readers and date

According to Eusebius, the third-century Church Father Origen wrote of this book, 'only God knows the truth as to who actually wrote this epistle' (*Ecclesiastical History* 6.25.14). Some translations and versions of the Bible give it the title, 'The epistle of Paul to the Hebrews'. But these words are not original, and it is highly unlikely that this book has anything to do with Paul:

● For one thing, it is not really an epistle at all. When Paul wrote letters he always followed the normal practice of Greek letter-writers (see chapter 16). He also leaves us in no doubt as to who his readers were and what has caused him to write to them. But Hebrews is not addressed directly to anyone, and the only possible reason for supposing it to be a letter of some sort is the inclusion of what appears to be a personal greeting after the benediction with which the book closes (13:22–25). Some have suggested that this section was added later, to make Hebrews look like one of Paul's letters. It has even been suggested that Paul himself added the news of Timothy given in 13:23 to a book that Timothy had originally written. But there is nothing to support either of these conjectures.

● The language and style of Hebrews is in any case totally different from that of Paul's writings. Hebrews has just about the best Greek style of any New

Testament book, and reaches a far higher literary standard than Paul could ever aspire to. Even Origen noticed this: 'The character of the diction of the epistle entitled "To the Hebrews" has not the apostle's rudeness in speech ... that is, in style. But that the epistle is better Greek in the framing of its diction, will be admitted by everyone who is able to discern differences of style' (Eusebius, *Ecclesiastical History* 6.25.11–12).

● The concerns of Hebrews are also quite different from Paul's interests. If, as many believe, it was written primarily for the benefit of Jewish Christians, then Paul is unlikely to have written it in any case. But even if it was written for Gentiles, its interest in the Torah is quite different from Paul's. Above all else, Paul emphasized the *moral* demands of the Old Testament Law. The ritual of tabernacle, priests and sacrifices which is so important in Hebrews did not concern Paul.

We can be quite sure that Paul did not write Hebrews. But it is not easy to decide who did. There is so little specific reference to people and events that the most diverse characters have been suggested, all with more or less equal plausibility: Barnabas, Apollos,

The book of Hebrews was concerned to explain how Jesus related to the story of the Old Testament. Here a Jewish family celebrates the Feast of Tabernacles, or Booths – a reminder of the time Israel spent in tents in the desert after the exodus from Egypt.

Opposite: Suffering for the Christian faith is not a thing of the past; these Christians in Russia have to meet in secret for fear of persecution by the atheistic authorities.

Timothy, Aquila and Priscilla, and Luke have all been put forward as possible candidates. In reality, we are no nearer to a solution than Origen was. But we can discover a number of facts about the unknown author from what he has written:

● He did not belong to the same group as the apostles. Explaining how the Christian message had reached him, the writer comments: 'The Lord himself first announced this salvation, and those who heard him proved to us that it is true' (2:3). Some scholars have drawn inferences from this about the possible date of the book. But this statement does not necessarily imply that the writer belonged to a different generation from the apostles – only that he was not among their number. A person like Stephen would fit this description just as easily as a much later character.

● The author was clearly well-educated. He knew how to write Greek, and he was well versed in the literary and rhetorical conventions of the Hellenistic age. He also seems to have had some acquaintance with ideas that were common among Greek thinkers. The way he contrasts the heavenly world, where Christ is, and the material world in which the Jewish ritual system exists, is not all that different from Plato's notion about the world of forms, or ideas, that gives meaning to the world we know through our senses.

●At the same time, the author's real background seems to be in Judaism. It has been argued that his knowledge of Plato's system came not through direct acquaintance with Greek thinking, but through knowledge of the work of a Hellenistic Jewish philosopher like Philo, who flourished in the early years of the Christian era at Alexandria in Egypt. But he also seems to have been familiar with the way the Jewish teachers in Palestine interpreted the Old Testament. In addition to that, some of his most distinctive imagery was very popular in various groups on the fringes of Judaism. The people from Qumran, who wrote the Dead Sea Scrolls, were expecting a Messiah who, like Jesus in Hebrews, would also be a high priest. They also had considerable interest in the Old Testament figure of Melchizedek and, like the writer of Hebrews, had a particular fascination with the rituals of the Day of Atonement. This has led some scholars to suggest that Hebrews was written to Christians who had come under the influence of the commune at Qumran. But some of these ideas are found in other Jewish documents like the

Testaments of the Twelve Patriarchs, while purification ceremonies such as those mentioned in Hebrews 6:2 were observed by many groups in the Jewish community.

The readers

Since we cannot identify the author of Hebrews, we cannot expect to be certain who its first readers were. But there are a number of indications in the book itself that can help us to gain quite an accurate impression of the kind of people they were.

● Most modern readers have concluded that they were Jewish Christians. This is implied in the title, 'To the Hebrews'. But the author himself did not give the book this title: it was added for convenience in later centuries (like all the titles of our New Testament books). It could therefore be misleading. Some prefer to think of Gentile Christians as its recipients. But it is not easy to see why non-Jewish Christians should have had such a detailed interest in the sacrificial system of ancient Israel. Jewish Christians, of course, would want to know what they were to make of it all, for to them the Old Testament and its rituals had been given by God. What was its status now? Had God somehow changed his mind with the coming of Jesus? These questions would certainly have more point for Jewish Christians than for Gentiles. They would be of greatest interest for Jewish Christians living in Jerusalem itself, and some have suggested that this is where Hebrews originated. But a number of facts speak against this:

i. The church at Jerusalem was always a poor church, whereas the readers of Hebrews seem to have been reasonably well off (6:10, 10:34).

ii. The temple is not actually mentioned in Hebrews. Instead, the author describes in great detail the worship associated with the tent of worship used by Moses and the Israelites in their desert journey from Egypt to Canaan. This suggests that his readers did not have firsthand experience of the temple, and their only direct access to rituals like sacrifice and priesthood was through what they could read for themselves in the books of Leviticus and Numbers. This would obviously suit the situation of Hellenist Jewish Christians living elsewhere in the Roman Empire.

● The readers of Hebrews also seem to have been involved in persecution. Not long after they became Christians, they had 'suffered many things, yet

were not defeated by the struggle. You were at times publicly insulted and ill-treated, and at other times you were ready to join those who were being treated in this way. You shared the sufferings of prisoners, and when all your belongings were seized, you endured your loss gladly' (10:32–34). But the author then goes on to encourage his readers not to evade further persecution. Up to the time of writing, they had 'not yet had to resist to the point of being killed' (12:4), like some of the early Jerusalem Christians, but they should not shrink even from that.

● The book of Hebrews gives the impression that it is not addressed to an entire church, but to a group within a church. In 5:12–14 they are criticized because they have not yet realized their God-given potential to be teachers – a function that not every Christian would expect to have. Then 10:25 could be taken to suggest that they were reluctant to meet with other Christians – while 13:24 asks them to convey 'greetings to all your leaders and to all God's people'. It has been suggested that Hebrews may have been addressed to some sectarian group mentioned elsewhere in the New Testament – perhaps the Colossian heretics, who were opposed by Paul in his letter to the church at Colossae. These people were certainly interested in the role of angels, and in some aspects of Jewish ritual practices. But they had no Jewish convictions. They saw the Old Testament rules as a useful way to achieve quite different objectives, and that would seem to distinguish them from the concerns of Hebrews.

● The recipients of Hebrews lived in Italy, perhaps in Rome. This is made clear in 13:24: 'The believers from Italy send you their greetings'. Whoever the author was, he was in the company of a group of Italian Christians who wished to be remembered by their friends at home. If this was in fact in Rome, the circumstances of the church there have some interesting similarities to the situation envisaged in Hebrews. The last chapter of Romans shows that in the late fifties the Roman church was not one unified congregation, but a collection of separate, though not unrelated 'house churches' (Romans 16:3–15). Other evidence from the Jewish community in Rome suggests that as the Christian gospel was proclaimed in different synagogues, they made different responses to it and formed Christian congregations distinguished by their various viewpoints on questions connected with Jewish observances. We also know that the Jews of Rome had a close interest in the kind of ideas that Hebrews shares with some fringe sects within Judaism.

The date

So when was Hebrews written? Various dates have been suggested, ranging from the early sixties to the end of the first century. On no account can it have been written later than about AD 90, for it is referred to in 1 Clement which was written in Rome no later than AD 96. A number of arguments are involved in fixing a more precise date:

● Some have pointed to the statement in 2:3 that 'The Lord himself first announced this salvation, and those who heard him proved to us that it is true'. They argue that this shows the author was a second- or third-generation Christian, and would date Hebrews between AD 80 and 90. But we have already seen that this is not a necessary inference from that verse.

● It has also been pointed out that the book seems to emphasize the human character of Jesus, perhaps because this was the subject of controversy. This in turn would take us to the arguments about Jesus' humanity and divinity ('Docetism') that emerged towards the end of the first century. But when we examine such references closely, many of them are seen to be based on the outline of Jesus' life that we find in the Gospels, and they are used in Hebrews to provoke a specific recollection of Jesus' behaviour and actions as an example and encouragement (2:14; 4:15; 5:7–9; 13:12). If we compare this with the way 1 John opposes heresy (see chapter 25 below), we will find significant differences.

● In fact there are few signs of the interests of the institutional church in Hebrews. The tension between present experience (1:2; 6:5) and future hope (9:28; 10:34–38) that was so characteristic of the age of the apostles is still found – and there is no more church hierarchy in view than may be suggested by the vague title 'leaders' (13:24).

● The writer of Hebrews seems to suppose that the kind of worship described in the Old Testament was still in existence. 'The same sacrifices are offered for ever, year after year ... the sacrifices serve year after year to remind people of their sins ...' (10:1–3). These, and other similar statements, suggest that the temple in Jerusalem was still standing, and if that is the case then the book can be dated before AD 70. It may be objected that Hebrews refers not to the temple, but to the tent of worship in the desert. But the Old Testament regulations are the same in each case, and may indeed have the same origin if modern Old Testament scholars are to be believed. In fact there are no temple regulations as such in the Old Testament. Solomon's temple is just assumed to have taken over the pattern of worship already laid down in the Torah. If the temple had ceased to function when Hebrews was written, it is impossible to believe that the author would not have mentioned the fact, for the literal destruction of the Old Testament ritual in AD 70 was the final confirmation of the whole argument of his book.

● If Hebrews was directed to readers in Rome, then the statement that they had not yet given their lives for the gospel would seem to point to a time before Nero's persecution came to a climax in AD 64. The earlier persecution that they had suffered could then have been connected with the disturbances that led Claudius to expel the Jewish people from Rome for a time in AD 48.

Origins

We may tentatively conclude that Hebrews was written by an unknown author in the period leading up to Nero's persecution. Its first readers were a group of Hellenist Jewish Christians in Rome who were trying to escape the consequences of being known as Christians by lapsing back into the practices of Judaism. They wanted the protection that the empire gave to Jews. But they also wished to enjoy the privileges of being Christians. The author of Hebrews deplored such a selfish attitude. They were betraying their fellow-Christians, and their acquiescence in Jewish rituals was in effect a denial of what Jesus had done for them. If they truly wished to serve him, they must be prepared to stand up and be counted as his followers, whatever the cost might be.

Hebrews and the Old Testament

The most distinctive feature of the book of Hebrews is the way that it uses the Old Testament to back up its arguments. Taking up Old Testament figures like Aaron or Melchizedek, and Old Testament rituals like the Day of Atonement, the author suggests that these things were a kind of symbolic preview of the work of Jesus. Just as Aaron was a high priest, so is Jesus – though with significantly greater effect. His position is more directly comparable to that of Melchizedek, and the sacrifice he offers has more lasting benefits than the Old Testament ritual of the Day of Atonement.

If we ever think about the Old Testament at all today, this is not the way we generally approach it. We may ask questions about its morality or its picture of God, but we would not expect to find detailed descriptions of the person of Jesus hidden within its pages. Yet our modern concerns are basically the same as those that concerned the author of Hebrews: namely, in what sense is the Old Testament a 'Christian' book? It was not written by Christians, of course, but the author of Hebrews shared the conviction of the early church (and of later Christians) that the God of whom the Old Testament speaks is the same God as Jesus revealed. Since God is unchangeable, it is therefore legitimate to look for some sort of unity between the Old Testament and the New Testament.

The author of Hebrews found this unity by supposing that, since the same God is involved in both parts of our Bible, his activities in the earlier stages of its story can be taken as a pattern or visual aid for his activity in the later stages. It is in this light that we can understand the way the writer uses the Old Testament. He is not suggesting that the people of Old Testament times understood their history and priestly rituals as a kind of glimpse into the unknown future. To them, these things were the facts of everyday life. But when Christians looked back with the benefit of hindsight, they could see how the life, death and resurrection of Jesus could appropriately be described as the fulfilment of the Old Testament. Peter, for example, described Jesus as 'the Servant of God' (Acts 3:13, 26; 4:25–30), no doubt referring to those passages in the book of Isaiah that we call 'the Servant Songs' (Isaiah 42:1–4; 49:1–6; 50:4–9; 52:13–53:12). For Isaiah and his contemporaries, the Servant was a real person or persons – the whole nation of Israel, or perhaps the prophet himself. But as Peter looked back, he saw that these passages summed up Jesus' ministry in a special way. Hebrews is doing the same thing with other Old Testament people (Moses, Joshua, Aaron, Melchizedek) and things (the Day of Atonement and the rituals of the tent of worship in the desert).

This interpretation of the Old Testament was not unknown in Judaism. Philo of Alexandria had elevated it to an art, arguing that the apparently 'historical' events of the Old Testament were a symbol of Greek philosophy, at least as he understood it from his own Jewish background. Many of the Church Fathers later read not only the Old Testament but also the New Testament in this way, ignoring the reality of its stories and regarding them instead as complex symbols of theological truths. This is how the fourth-century writer Hilary of Poitiers described the reasoning behind this: 'Every work contained in the sacred volume announces by word, explains by facts, and corroborates by examples the coming of our Lord Jesus Christ ... From the beginning of the world Christ, by authentic and absolute prefigurations in the person of the Patriarchs, gives birth to the Church, washes it clean, sanctifies it, chooses it, places it apart and redeems it: by the sleep of Adam, by the deluge in the days of Noah, by the blessing of Melchizedek, by Abraham's justification, by the birth of Isaac, by the capitivity of Jacob ... The purpose of this work, is to show that in each personage, in every age, and in every act, the image of his coming, of his teaching, of his resurrection, and of our church is reflected as in a mirror.'

But Hebrews is not like that. It takes the Old Testament story seriously, and does not ignore its historical reality. It does not treat the Old Testament like an ancient *Pilgrim's Progress*. It is not a story with no meaning apart from what it may be held to symbolize. On the contrary, it records the actions of God in real history – and, in an important sense, when Hebrews compares Old and New Testaments, it concentrates not so much on their specific details as on the person of God himself. It is at pains to emphasize that what God has done in Jesus is continuous with – indeed grows out of – his revelation in the Old Testament.

Scholars have traditionally called this method of interpretation 'typology'. But this tells us little, for the same term is also used to describe the work of Philo and the Church Fathers, and Hebrews is certainly different from them. Hebrews draws attention to correspondences between Old and New Testaments, showing how God's work in one period of time was fulfilled and superseded by God's work in Jesus.

This method of expounding the Christian message is not found in any comprehensive form anywhere else in the New Testament. Its main appeal would obviously be to Christians with Jewish connections. It is far removed from the questions that modern Christians ask about the Old Testament, but its essential message is not irrelevant, for it is a reminder of the faithfulness and consistency of God's dealings with men and women at all times and in all places (Hebrews 13:8).

It was on Mt Sinai that God gave Moses the Ten Commandments and other laws for the Israelites.

Christians and the Old Testament covenant

Genesis 12:1–3; 15; 17; 22:16–18;
Exodus 19:5–8; 20–24

The debates in the early church about Jewish morality and ritual were the symptoms of a much more fundamental problem. In Old Testament times, to be a member of the people of God was not simply a matter of behaving in the same way as other like-minded people. It also involved inclusion in the covenant relationship that God had established with Israel's ancestor Abraham, and with Moses at Mt Sinai. This relationship had started with God's concern and care for his people. Abraham was called from Mesopotamia and given a new homeland not because of any moral or spiritual superiority that he may have possessed, but simply because God's affection was centred on him. His descendants later emerged from the shattering experience of the exodus not because of their own moral perfection but simply through the care of a loving God.

Genesis 15:1–6

On the basis of these undeserved acts of kindness, God had made certain demands of his people. Abraham and his family were promised a great and prosperous future. In response to God's goodness, Abraham had accepted that both he and his descendants should give tangible and lasting expression to this new covenant relationship that existed between them and God: 'You and your descendants must all agree to circumcise every male among you ...

Genesis 17:9–14

Any male who has not been circumcised will no longer be considered one of my people, because he has not kept the covenant with me.'

We find the same elements in the covenant relationship established between God and Israel through Moses at Mt Sinai. God had rescued his people from slavery in Egypt, and they were to

Exodus 19:4–8; 20; Leviticus; Numbers

respond with obedience to his laws – moral laws like the Ten Commandments, and also the ritual regulations that we find in Leviticus and Numbers.

When Christians claimed that Jesus had come to fulfil what God had promised in the Old Testament, these were the promises the Jewish people would inevitably recall. And the Christians themselves believed that what they were experiencing through the presence of Jesus and the power of the Holy Spirit made them the heirs of Abraham himself. This is why the Old Testament Law and circumcision became such important issues in the church. For on a plain reading of the Old Testament, this was the only way that a person (whether born as a Jew or a Gentile) could ever be a part of God's covenant people. At the beginning, all Christians paid due attention to this, for they were all followers of the Jewish religion. But when Paul and others accepted into the church Gentiles who had not been circumcised and saw no reason for keeping the Old Testament Law, the basic theological argument between Jews and Christians was transformed into a burning practical issue. Traditional Jewish thinking suggested that people who would not obey the Torah could not expect God to work in their lives. But the activity of the Holy Spirit among these pagan Gentiles seemed to

Acts 10:44–48

be no less spectacular than his work in the lives of those Christians who were also faithful Jews.

Paul was one of the first Christian preachers to be faced with this problem. He was quite sure that circumcision and keeping the Old Testament Law should not be required of Gentile Christians. But the Old Testament had made it perfectly clear that to share in the blessings promised by God a person must become a member of Abraham's family. Paul did not wish to deny that the Old Testament was the word of God – and his opponents were not slow to remind him that being a member of Abraham's family meant circumcision and obedience to the Law.

Paul tackled this problem in his letter to the Galatians. He argued that the blessings promised by God to Abraham did not come to fruition because he kept the Law. That did not even exist in his day. But, Paul argued, the relationship that Abraham enjoyed with God was a matter of faith. 'Abraham believed and was blessed; so all who believe are blessed as he was.' Circumcision was just an external sign to confirm that a person was trying to keep the Old Testament Law. But if the Law was now redundant, then circumcision had also lost its value. What should matter to the Christian is 'faith that works through love'. We have already dealt with Paul's argument. The question is important to us here because we can trace the same issues in Peter's first letter.

Galatians 3:17

Galatians 3:9

Galatians 5:2–12
Galatians 5:6

1 Peter Many of the same themes are found here, though in a different form. Abraham is mentioned only in passing, and in a different context altogether – and there is no sign of the complex theological arguments that Paul brings forward in Galatians and Romans. But 1 Peter conveys the clear conviction that Gentile Christians are now the true successors to the people of God in Old Testament times. It also asserts that they have achieved this position as a result of their response in faith to what God has done for them. Like the family of Abraham, Christians owe their knowledge of God not to their own piety or insight, but to God's gracious action in showing his love for them. In the case of Israel, this had been demonstrated particularly in the exodus. For the Christian, 'it was the costly sacrifice of Christ, who was like a lamb without defect or flaw'.

1 Peter 3:6

1 Peter 2:9–10

1 Peter 1:1–19

The relationship of Christians to the Jewish covenants is the main subject of Paul's letter to the Galatians. 1 Peter was not written in the same controversial context. But that only makes more striking its emphasis on the fact that Christians are now the true 'family of Abraham' without compulsory obedience to the Old Testament Law. For it shows how this issue was soon settled in the church along the lines that Paul suggested.

● **The Christian's status** These themes appear in the very first verse, where we are told that the letter is written 'To God's chosen people in the Dispersion throughout the provinces of Pontus, Galatia, Cappadocia, Asia, and Bithynia'. This opening is similar to the book of James. We noticed there that 'God's people in the Dispersion' could indicate Jewish people. But it is more likely to refer to the church. In the case of 1 Peter, there can be no doubt at all that Gentile Christian readers are in view.

1 Peter 1:1–12

1 Peter 1:14, 18; 2:9–10; 4:3

This initial greeting is followed by a thanksgiving to God, but this soon turns to an exhortation. Peter's readers are encouraged to praise God for his goodness to them, 'even though for a little while 1 Peter 1:6 you may have to suffer various trials'. He tells them that such trials are insignificant when set against God's power. Christians already know something of this in the new life that they enjoy through Jesus. They can also look forward to 'the Day when Jesus Christ is 1 Peter 1:7 revealed', when they will meet him face to face. Simple Gentile

Peter uses the word-picture of 'living stones' to describe how Christians are built together into the fabric of a 'living temple' which rests on the foundation of the work of Jesus Christ.
1 Peter 1:13–2:10

believers may find this difficult to understand – even the angels cannot fully do so – but what is happening to them now, and the destiny that is waiting for them in the future, is all a part of God's plan that was first revealed in the Old Testament.

● **Christian development** The writer then goes on to remind his readers that acceptance of the good news about Jesus imposes responsibilities as well as bestowing privileges. They must never forget that they are called to share their faith with others, both in word and in deed. Christ's death and resurrection has 'set you free from the worthless manner of life handed down by your ancestors', and the recollection of all that this means should lead Christians to obey God, and share his love with their fellow-citizens.

1 Peter 1:18

They should also grow and develop in their Christian experience, being as eager for spiritual nourishment as a baby is for its mother's milk. This is how they will grow as Christians, so they can 'come as living stones, and let yourselves be used in building the spiritual temple, where you will serve as holy priests to offer spiritual and acceptable sacrifices to God through Jesus Christ'. As Christians mature in this way, they will demonstrate how they are 'the chosen race, the King's priests, the holy nation, God's own people'.

1 Peter 2:5–9

There is not another passage of comparable length in the whole New Testament where more Old Testament imagery that was originally applied to Abraham and his descendants is taken over and applied to the Christian church, the 'new Israel'. But there are also some interesting connections here with Paul's thinking. The picture of the church as a building constructed out of living stones (one of which, the 'cornerstone', is Jesus himself) is not dissimilar to Paul's description of the church as a living body made up of many parts, 'Christ's body'. Indeed, Paul may well have thought in the same terms himself, for in Romans he writes of Christians offering 'a living sacrifice' that will bring glory to God. So, when Peter says that all Christians are 'priests', he is saying the same thing as Paul when he declares that all Christians have a God-given ability that they must share with the church at large. But they use entirely different language from each other.

1 Corinthians 12:12–31

Romans 12:1–2

1 Peter 2:11–4:19

● **Christian behaviour** Peter goes on to remind his readers that, as God's people, they have different standards from non-Christians. They are as much at home in pagan society as 'strangers and refugees'. Their only true allegiance is to God himself and so everything they do should be intended to glorify him alone. Even when they have to 'endure the pain of undeserved suffering', they can look to the example of Jesus. For 'when he was insulted, he did not answer back with an insult; when he suffered, he did not threaten, but placed his hopes in God, the righteous Judge'.

1 Peter 2:11

1 Peter 2:19

1 Peter 2:23

Exactly the same principles should determine how the Christian behaves at home. Christian wives should be ready to share the love of Christ with their husbands – and they for their part must treat their wives with respect and understanding. In a word, every believer should follow the advice of Jesus: 'Love one another ... and be kind and humble with one another. Do not pay back evil with evil or cursing with cursing; instead, pay back with a blessing.'

1 Peter 3:8–9

Peter knew that it is never easy to behave like this, especially when Christians are suffering unjust persecution. It involves putting God first so that a Christian's life is controlled not by whims and fancies, but by God himself. But it is always worthwhile in the end. 'The end of all things is near', and God's people should be especially careful how they behave. Suffering is just a temporary thing, and Christians must look beyond it to the judgement of God.

1 Peter 4:7

1 Peter 4:19

They can trust themselves to his care, for he 'always keeps his promise'.

1 Peter 5:1–14

● **Serving Christ** Finally, Peter gives advice to those who are, like himself, 'elders' or 'shepherds' in the church. They must not be

1 Peter 5:3

domineering in any way, but should be 'examples to the flock', recognizing that the church will flourish only when all its members

1 Peter 5:5

have 'put on the apron of humility' to serve one another. They would not be the first to do that, for Jesus himself had worn the

John 13:1–17

apron of a slave in order to wash his disciples' feet. But above all, they must not lose their trust in God in the midst of persecution. Even this is a part of God's plan for his covenant people: 'After you have suffered for a little while, the God of all grace, who calls you to share his eternal glory in union with Christ, will himself perfect

1 Peter 5:10

you and give you firmness, strength, and a sure foundation.'

Who wrote 1 Peter?

1 Peter was well-known and widely read in the church from quite early times. 1 Clement refers to it (AD 96), as also does Polycarp (AD 70–155), while Irenaeus stated towards the end of the second century that it was written by the apostle Peter himself. There are good reasons to accept this view of its authorship:

● Much of its teaching is exactly what we would expect from a disciple of Jesus. Many aspects seem to echo the teaching of Jesus himself, sometimes following it quite closely.

The author seems to contrast the readers' knowledge of Jesus, which was second-hand, with his own firsthand knowledge, and he seems to have witnessed both the trials (2:21–24) and the crucifixion of Jesus (5:1). Some scholars also believe that certain passages contain allusions to Gospel stories in which Peter was particularly involved. Others have claimed that if this letter was the work of Peter, then we would expect to read much more about Jesus. But this argument depends on the mistaken assumption that an

---

Similarities between the teaching of Jesus and Peter

Christians should have an alert and watchful attitude	Luke 12:35 1 Peter 1:13
Christians have the privilege of calling God 'Father'	Luke 11:2 1 Peter 1:17
Christian conduct should cause non-believers to praise God	Matthew 5:16 1 Peter 2:12
Christians should not pay back evil for evil	Luke 6:28 1 Peter 3:9
There is joy to be had when the Christian is being persecuted for doing what God wants	Matthew 5:10 1 Peter 3:14
We will all have to give an account of ourselves to God on Judgement Day	Matthew 12:36 1 Peter 4:5
If Christians are insulted because they are followers of Jesus, they should be glad	Matthew 5:11 1 Peter 4:14
Christians should be characterized by humility, and God will make them great	Luke 14:11 1 Peter 5:6
Because God is caring from them, Christians should not be worried or anxious	Matthew 6:25–27 1 Peter 5:7

Peter encourages his readers not to give up their faith when times become hard, but to endure trials with patience, knowing that they are following Jesus' example and that they will receive God's blessing.

author must write everything he knows in everything he writes. We should also remember that Peter's reminiscences of the life and teaching of Jesus may well have been recorded in a comprehensive way already, in the Gospel of Mark.

● There are also a number of connections between 1 Peter and the speeches of Peter in the book of Acts. Jesus' cross is called 'the tree' in Peter's speech to the Jewish rulers (Acts 5:30) and in his sermon to Cornelius (10:39), and also in 1 Peter (2:24). In 1 Peter 2:22–24 Jesus is referred to in the language of the 'Servant Songs' of the book of Isaiah, and according to Acts, Peter consistently called Jesus 'the Servant of God' in his earliest preaching (Acts 3:13, 26; 4:25–30). Jesus is also linked with the stone mentioned in Psalm 118:22 by Peter in his defence before the Jewish authorities, and again in 1 Peter 2:4 – and the emphasis on the fulfilment of Old Testament promises in Acts 3:18–24 is very similar to 1 Peter 1:10–12.

● There is no sign in 1 Peter of the concerns and interests of the later institutional church. There is still a tension between what God has done in the life of his people already (1:8–9, 23) and what will be accomplished in the future with the return of Jesus himself (1:3–5, 7, 13; 4:13; 5:4). Nor is there any evidence of a developed hierarchy in church organization. The leaders of the church are simply 'elders' or 'shepherds' (5:1–4).

There are therefore good reasons for accepting the ancient view that Peter was the author of this letter. But a number of modern scholars have drawn attention to three other facts which may point in a different direction:

● Like Hebrews, 1 Peter is written in an exceptionally fine Greek literary style, and it is suggested that a Galilean fisherman would not be capable of this – especially one who was described as 'uneducated and common' (Acts 4:13). We have already seen that the Galilean origins of Peter, far from disqualifying him from knowing Greek, would actually point in the opposite direction. Nor can the statement in Acts mean that Peter was illiterate. The point is just the opposite, for the Jewish leaders were expressing their amazement at the *eloquence* of men who had come from the remote hillsides of Galilee. Some wish to associate Peter with the letter itself, but not with its written form, and they have suggested that since Silas acted as Peter's secretary (5:12), the Greek style is really his and not Peter's.

● Why would Peter have written a letter to Gentile Christians living in Asia Minor when according to Galatians 2:8 he was 'an apostle to the Jews'? This question is often raised, but it is scarcely relevant. For one thing, Paul's statement was not intended as a hard and fast rule. Paul himself never kept it, for he preached the gospel to many Jews even though he described himself as 'apostle to the Gentiles'. In addition, we have already seen how Peter moved into the Gentile world at a relatively early date. Paul mentions Peter's extensive travels (1 Corinthians 9:5), and there is no good reason why he could not have visited some of the places to which this letter was sent. Many think that Paul himself was forbidden to go to this area precisely because Peter was already working there (Acts 16:6–10). On the other hand, we need to take seriously the statement about 'the messengers who announced the Good News' in 1 Peter 1:12, which seems to suggest that the writer of the letter had not been the one who first brought the Christian message to this area.

● It has also been argued that 1 Peter is too similar to Paul's letters to have been written by Peter. But this is hardly convincing. It presupposes that Paul was the odd man out in the early church, saying entirely different things from anyone else. We have already argued that this is an unrealistic way to look at Paul – and we also noted good reasons for believing that he and Peter saw eye to eye on most issues. So why should 1 Peter be entirely different from Paul's writings? In any case, the two are not identical. It is significant that though Peter's teaching on the church and the Old Testament covenants is so similar to Paul's, he uses altogether different language and imagery. The closest parallels between them are all in the ethical instructions. But these can be found in a similar form not only in Paul's writings, but elsewhere in the New Testament – and this suggests that both Paul and Peter were passing on moral advice that was widely accepted throughout the early church.

Date and origin

If Peter did indeed write this letter, then obviously we must date it before his death, which took place in the persecution of Christians begun by Nero in AD 64 or 65. But dating it more precisely than that depends on our interpretation of the various references to persecution that occur throughout the letter. We can make a number of observations about this:

● In all the organized persecutions of Christians that took place towards the end of the first century, obedience to the emperor – even worship of him – was a crucial test of Christian allegiance. But this was clearly *not* the case in the persecutions envisaged in 1 Peter. Christians are encouraged to 'respect

the Emperor', and to accept his authority – even though it must come second to the authority of God (2:13–17).

● The readers of 1 Peter seem to have been surprised to be persecuted (4:12) – and after the persecutions of Nero, we might have expected them to accept suffering as the norm.

● The descriptions of persecution in 5:8 ('Your enemy, the Devil, roams round like a roaring lion, looking for someone to devour') and 1:7 (testing by fire) could well refer to the events of Nero's persecution itself. According to the Roman historian Tacitus, the hated Christians 'were covered with wild beasts' skins and torn to death by dogs; or they were fastened on crosses, and, when daylight failed, were burned to serve as lamps by night' (*Annals* 15.44).

1 Peter 5:13

It may therefore be suggested that 1 Peter was written as the Neronic persecution of the Christians was in its early stages. We have no certain evidence that it eventually spread to Asia Minor. But even if it did not, the official persecution in Rome would certainly have encouraged people elsewhere to despise the Christians in their own cities. We do know that Peter was in Rome at the time. The term 'Babylon' was frequently used by the early Christians and others as a sort of code word for Rome. As Peter saw what was happening there, he felt that it would only be a matter of time before such a great evil must spread to other parts of the empire. He wanted his fellow-Christians to be assured that when the trial came, they were not alone in their suffering. Others were suffering too. But most important of all, God had them all in his care, for they were his covenant people.

Elders in the church should be like shepherds, says Peter: leaders who guide, tend and care for the people who are in their charge.

The theme of baptism in 1 Peter

On the surface, 1 Peter appears to be an ordinary letter, written to encourage Christians who were being persecuted. But some scholars have suggested that there is more to it than this. They have argued that the central part of 1 Peter (1:3–4:11) is not a letter at all, but an account of a service of baptism in the early church. They draw attention to a number of its features:

● This passage seems to be a self-contained section of the letter. The words of 4:11 would certainly make a suitable conclusion, for they contain a fuller benediction than we actually find at the end of chapter five. Peter also says in 5:12 that he is writing a 'brief letter', and since the whole of 1 Peter is hardly 'brief', the actual letter that he wrote may only run from 4:12 to 5:14, while the rest of the book is an account of the church's worship.

● Baptism is mentioned only in one obscure passage (3:18–22). This may be thought a good reason for doubting its importance. But in this passage, Noah's deliverance in the Old Testament is said to be 'a symbol pointing to baptism, which now saves you'. The emphasis on 'now' suggests to some that those addressed had only just been baptised. Others have claimed to be able to

discern subtle changes in the language towards the end of the first chapter, and they argue that the act of baptism had actually taken place between 1:21 and 1:22. On this understanding, this part of 1 Peter is regarded as a kind of account of the service of baptism, complete with hymns, responses, prayers, a sermon and a benediction. Other evidence for this is drawn from the exhortation to 'Be like new-born babies, always thirsty for the pure spiritual milk' (2:2). Evidence from the *Apostolic Tradition* ascribed to Hippolytus describes how towards the end of the second century a cup of milk and honey was given to Christians who had just been baptized, to remind them of the land promised to Israel ('a land flowing with milk and honey', Exodus 3:8). But 1 Peter mentions neither the honey nor the land, and the milk is described as 'pure and spiritual', which suggests it should be understood metaphorically rather than literally. Another link with the *Apostolic Tradition* has been found in 1 Peter 3:3. Here Christian women are reminded that a person's character has nothing to do with 'the way you do your hair, or the jewellery you put on, or the dresses you wear'. In later customs, women removed jewellery and clothing and rearranged

Baptism of both adult converts and children is practised today by Christians as a sign of their faith and a public expression of their intention to follow and serve Christ.

their hair before being baptized. But the emphasis in 1 Peter is not so much on this, as on the positive moral virtues that should be found in the Christian.

● There are a number of places where Peter uses language and imagery taken from the Passover story in the Old Testament. He says, for example, that Christ is 'a lamb without defect or flaw' (1:19), just as the Passover lambs had been (Exodus 12:5). Christians are told to 'gird up your minds' (1:13), in the same way as the Israelites fastened up their clothing on Passover night (Exodus 12:11). And 2:1–10 has many connections with the Old Testament books of Exodus, Leviticus and Numbers. The relevance of this Passover connection is found in the fact that Tertullian, writing at the end of the second century, says that the ideal time for Christians to be baptized was at Easter (Passover).

These arguments are very weak, and there is no compelling reason to think that 1 Peter contains an account of a service of baptism:

● We have no way of recognizing a first-century baptismal service, for we have no real idea how baptism was carried out in the earliest churches. Where the New Testament mentions it, baptism seems to have taken place at the same time as a person's initial commitment to Christianity. There is certainly no indication in the New Testament that baptism was an important event in the organized worship. No doubt Christians soon developed their own preferred ways of conducting worship. But it is highly unlikely that these were as stereotyped in the New Testament period as they were in the days of Hippolytus and Tertullian.

● It is also difficult to reconcile this theory with the plain evidence of 1 Peter. There is no indication at all that

the section 1:3–4:11 has originated in a different context from the rest. It is written in exactly the same style, and the same arguments seem to carry over from one section to the other.

● This baptismal theory has no way of explaining how a baptismal liturgy for the church at Rome could have got mixed up with a letter to Christians in Asia Minor. On the face of it, 1 Peter is a letter to persecuted Christians, and we must make sense of it in that light.

The evidence that has been claimed in support of this theory could no doubt carry some weight if we had other reasons to connect 1 Peter with Christian baptism. But they are hardly sufficient in themselves to establish such a connection. In addition, there are important differences between the accounts of Hippolytus and what we read in 1 Peter. Later, the service of baptism included exorcism, anointing and the laying-on of hands – and there are no hints of any of these in 1 Peter.

The occurrence of themes that seem relevant to newly-baptized Christians is probably due to the fact that Peter, like Paul, wanted to remind his readers of what was involved in being a Christian. To do this, he needed to recall the commitment they had made when they first came to faith in Christ. Quite possibly he would repeat the sort of things that he was in the habit of saying to new converts. But that does not lead to the conclusion that he was giving an eyewitness report of an actual church service.

Once a preacher has worked out an effective way of expressing something, he will always tend to repeat the same ideas in different contexts. The author of this book has regularly expounded themes found in these pages in many a sermon – but that hardly justifies the conclusion that the whole book is some kind of worship manual for the services of the church!

Peter and the church in Rome

After the stories of the early chapters of Acts, the course of the rest of Peter's life is unknown to us. Apart from Paul's reference to his missionary activity (1 Corinthians 9:5), and what is perhaps a cryptic mention of his death in John 21:18–19, the New Testament tells us nothing more about him. 1 Peter, of course, is evidence that he was at one time in Rome – but it gives us no further personal details.

It was not long, however, before Christians began to enquire about Peter more specifically. Just as they wanted to know about Andrew, Matthew, Philip and other disciples of Jesus, so they

wanted to know what had become of the disciple whom Jesus had once called 'the Rock', on whose foundation he said the church would be built (Matthew 16:17–19).

The second-century Acts of Peter purport to tell of how Peter came at an early stage to the city of Rome and there established a large and thriving Christian community. Like his Master before him, he performed many miracles, though his progress was continuously hindered by a pagan magician called Simon – who, among other things, had the power to fly. According to this document, Peter's mission to Rome was cut short by the events of Nero's persecution. His Christian friends advised him to leave the city and escape martyrdom. In that way he would be free for yet greater exploits in proclaiming the Christian message. But as he was leaving the city in disguise, Peter saw Jesus himself entering Rome. He asked Jesus where he was going (in Latin *Quo vadis?*). 'And the Lord said to him, "I am coming to Rome to be crucified." ... And Peter came to himself; ... he returned to Rome rejoicing and giving praise to the Lord.' As a result of his return, Peter himself was crucified, insisting that he should be hung upside-down on the cross.

Like the stories about the other disciples, all this is mostly fiction. But, like them, it probably reflects some facts. For there is no reason to doubt either that Peter visited Rome and played an important part in the work of the church there, or that he was put to death in the persecution started by Nero. 1 Clement 5 connects the deaths of both Peter and Paul with this period, and before the end of the second century the graves of these apostles were a place of pilgrimage (Eusebius, *Ecclesiastical History* 2.25.5–7). At a later date, when Constantine became a Christian, he erected a more elaborate shrine at the spot (probably in about AD 333), and today the Basilica of St Peter stands on the same site. All of this has been confirmed in recent investigations by archaeologists working beneath the Vatican. Not only has Constantine's monument been discovered, but traces of the second-century edifice have also been found. Further remains of bones and early graves, some going back to the first century, have also been discovered. But there is considerable disagreement among archaeologists about the significance of them. Some believe that the actual grave of Peter himself has been laid bare, while others argue that these graves are not even Christian. This is a genuine argument about the evidence: many Roman Catholic scholars do not believe that the grave of Peter is here, while some Protestants are quite convinced that it is. It is worth observing that the argument is unlikely to be resolved: even if we had the bones of Peter in front of us, no one could prove conclusively that they were his.

But we may be sure that Peter did die as a martyr in Rome during the persecution of Nero – and we can be reasonably certain that his grave lies somewhere on the site of St Peter's Basilica. But we have no evidence to show that he was the founder of the Roman church – though (along with Paul) he must have been the most important Christian leader to be connected with it, and it is therefore not surprising that he soon became its patron saint.

This 'graffiti wall' under St Peter's Basilica in Rome is said to contain the relics of the apostle Peter.

Hope for the future

Peter was not the first writer to face the problem of unjust suffering. It was a question that had come to be increasingly important to Jewish writers in the centuries just before the birth of Jesus.

The Old Testament had never understood God's relationship with men and women in exclusively personal and individual terms. Those who knew God best in ancient Israel found him not through isolated, mystical experiences, but in the events of everyday life. They believed that God was guiding and directing the history of their entire nation, and this meant that his people must express the meaning of their worship in the social institutions of national life. The Old Testament prophets went so far as to suggest that the whole course of Israel's history somehow depended on their

Isaiah 1:15–20; Jeremiah 8:4–12;
Ezekiel 7:3–4

attitude to God. If the people were obedient to him, they prospered; if not, they could expect hard times.

These hard times had reached a climax when Jerusalem was captured by the Babylonian king Nebuchadnezzar in 586 BC. Not only did he invade the country, but he also took many of the people Jeremiah 52 to live in exile in Babylon. After only a short time there, the Jews had been allowed to return to their homeland – and those who Ezra, Nehemiah returned were determined not to repeat the mistakes of the past. They went out of their way to try and keep every detail of the Old Testament laws. But as things turned out, they did not prosper either. As time went on, the real way to prosperity seemed to lie more in collaboration with outsiders like the Romans than in remaining faithful to their own religion. Those who tried to keep the Old Testament faith alive found themselves more and more in a minority, and those who prospered often did so by sitting loosely to their fathers' faith, or even abandoning it altogether.

All this clearly demanded an explanation. Why did faithfulness not now lead to prosperity? Why were the faithful suffering? And why did God not put an end to the power of evil forces? Was there some contradiction between all this and the confident teaching of the Old Testament?

In the period from about 100 BC to AD 100, many Jewish writers put forward their own solution to these problems. Their books are so similar to one another that many modern scholars think of them as a distinct movement in Palestinian society. They have come to be known as 'apocalyptists'. We have already met them in discussing the teaching of Jesus. These books have a number of distinctive features:

● They are almost always pessimistic about the world and its history. Unlike the Old Testament prophets, the apocalyptists despaired of God ever being able to work in the world. The forces of evil seemed too strong for that, and they saw the world running headlong to a final and tragic end. Since there was no point in trying to discover God at work in the midst of such apparent evil, the apocalyptic writers concentrated their attention on affairs in another, heavenly world. One of them stated that 'the Most High 2 Esdras 7:50 has made not one world but two', and many others shared his viewpoint. The apocalyptists believed that their job was to reveal events in God's world, and to assure their pious readers that, however much they may have been suffering, they still had a central place in God's plans.

● Their concern with the heavenly world led the apocalyptic writers to emphasize things like dreams, visions and communications by angels. If God was remote in his own world, he would naturally need to use go-betweens to communicate with people in our own world. So the typical apocalypse contains extensive reports of how its writer had received speculative visions and messages telling him what was going on in heaven.

● Along with this, they used a distinctive literary form. For apocalyptic visions were not described in straightforward terms.

Instead, they used a special kind of coded language. Mythological beasts and symbolic numbers feature prominently, usually accompanied by obscure quotations from other apocalyptic books.

● Apocalypses were also usually written under the name of some great figure from the past. Enoch, Noah, Adam, Moses, Ezra and various other Old Testament characters had apocalyptic works attributed to them. This may have been necessary because the Jews believed that the time of genuine prophecy had passed. But it is more likely that in times of persecution such authors wished to obscure their real identity for fear of reprisals.

On the face of it, this kind of escapism seems to be quite foreign to the outlook of the New Testament. But there is one New Testament book that has clearly been profoundly influenced by the style, if not the thinking, of the Jewish apocalyptists.

Revelation   Probably no book in the entire New Testament is less read and less understood than this one. All the great interpreters of the past had

The apocalyptic writings were full of strange and intricate symbolism, mysterious creatures and messages from angels. The German artist Albrecht Dürer captured the mood of these prophetic visions in his woodcut 'The Four Horsemen of the Apocalypse'.

difficulty with it. Martin Luther found it an offensive piece of work, with very little to say about Christ – and John Calvin also had grave doubts about its value. Many modern readers feel the same way, and see its message as a return to the worst of Jewish thinking, and by implication a denial of the message of Jesus himself.

It is not surprising that we should find Revelation a difficult book. We do not think in the same terms as Jewish apocalyptists. For us, their secret language and visions are both meaningless and bizarre. Many of us are uneasy with their conviction that God has no relevance to the world in which we live, and we find it difficult to imagine that his sole intention is to destroy human society and set up some sort of other-worldly kingdom instead. At the same time, there are others for whom the book of Revelation assumes far greater importance than many other books of the New Testament. They claim that it gives an insight into God's ultimate plans for humanity – even down to the details of how our present world will come to an end. So what can we make of it? Does it have any lasting significance, or is it to be dismissed as an unfortunate mistake by the early church, which should never have been included among the books of the New Testament?

A Christian book?

There can be no doubt that despair and pessimism about human history is fundamentally at odds with the outlook not only of the New Testament, but of the Old Testament as well. The biblical writers face up to the tragic realities of much of our human experience, but they have no doubt that God can and does meet men and women in the everyday events of normal life. God is not remote. How could he be, when through Jesus he has himself shared in our human existence? The writer of Hebrews, for instance, was quite sure that this was precisely why God can and does understand even the most trying aspects of life in this world.

Hebrews 4:14–16

When we look at the book of Revelation in detail, it is clear that its author shares this positive Christian emphasis on God's involvement in human affairs. Though the language and imagery in which he writes is apocalyptic in form, his message has a distinctive Christian emphasis.

● Unlike every other apocalyptic book, Revelation names both its author and its first readers. It was written by a person called John, and was sent 'From John to the seven churches in the province of Asia', in the towns of Ephesus, Smyrna, Pergamum, Thyatira, Sardis, Philadelphia and Laodicea. These churches are addressed in quite specific terms, and incidents and individuals are mentioned by name. This kind of self-confidence was never shared by the Jewish apocalyptic writers. On the contrary, they were generally so afraid of their persecutors that to have identified themselves in this way would have led to certain death. Of course, this is what it led to for some members of these churches. But that was no reason for disguising the true nature of their Christian faith.

Revelation 1:4

● Even in those parts of the book which are most similar to Jewish writings, John's visions are always closely linked to his

Revelation 1:10

Revelation 1:5–6; 12:10–12; 19:5–8;
22:13; 7:10, 12; 11:15, 17–18;
4:8, 11; 5:9–10; 15:3–4; 19:1–2

Isaiah 2:6–22; Hosea 2:14–23;
Joel 2:28–3:21

One of the letters to the seven
churches in Revelation was written to
Christians in Ephesus, the leading
city of the Roman province of Asia. In
Paul's day, Ephesus was a centre for
the worship of the goddess Diana
(Artemis), and later became known
for emperor-worship. The Temple of
Hadrian shown here dates from the
second century AD.

experience of life in the church. His vision comes to him 'on the Lord's day', perhaps in the course of Christian worship, and the contents of his visions have many references to the worship of the church: its confessions of faith, prayers and hymns.

● Revelation looks forward to a future intervention of God in the affairs of this world. But its understanding of this is different from that of the Jewish apocalyptists. Without exception, they regarded this world and all its affairs as irretrievably evil. History was a meaningless enigma, and the sooner its course was stopped, the better. This had not been the view of the Old Testament writers. Some of the prophets had looked forward to the coming of a 'Day of the Lord', when God would intervene in a final and decisive way in the affairs of the world. But they believed that this would be the continuation of what God was already doing in the present order of things: the God who would inaugurate a new world order in the future was also the God who could be known here and now in the events of human life.

The apocalyptic writers rejected this view, because they could make no sense of their own present experience. But like the Old Testament, the book of Revelation makes a clear link between what

Revelation 5

Revelation 12:10–12

God is doing in history now, and what he will do in the future. Indeed, the entire meaning of God's plan for the future of humanity is to be found in a historical event – the life, death and resurrection of Jesus himself, 'the Lamb of God'. And far from the sufferings of Christians being a meaningless interlude, John declares that it is one of the most powerful responses against all forms of evil.

Revelation therefore does not follow slavishly the pattern of the Jewish apocalyptic books. It presents a distinctive and positive

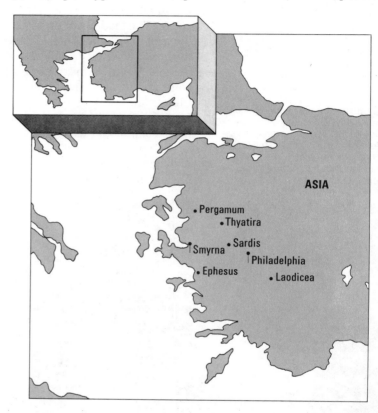

The seven churches of Revelation.

Christian explanation of the presence of evil in the affairs of human life. Its message is expressed through conventional Jewish language and vivid Old Testament imagery, but its content goes beyond the literary form of apocalyptic writing.

The book and its message

Revelation 1–3

The first three chapters of Revelation are similar to many other New Testament writings: they contain seven letters to seven churches in the Roman province of Asia. They are not real letters like those written by Paul, for they purport to come from the risen Jesus himself. John says that their content was given to him in a vision, just like the rest of the book. But they deal with very down-to-earth matters, and show a detailed knowledge of these people and their environment. Their churches were involved in disputes over Christian beliefs. Their commitment to Christ was wavering, and as a result they were in no position to face up to the challenge of state persecution. To do that, they needed to be whole-heartedly committed. This is a message that we find many times in the New Testament, and it is not significantly different from the message of 1 Peter.

Revelation 4–22

But the second part of the book is quite different. Here we come face to face with the language and imagery of apocalyptic writings. No longer do the visions seem to relate to real events and people. Instead, they introduce monsters and dragons in a quick succession of terrifying events. The whole section is introduced in chapters

Revelation 4–5

four and five by a vision of heaven. This sets the scene for what fol-lows. Here the author sets out the basic way in which he under-stands God's workings in history. God is the one who is 'high

Isaiah 6:1; Revelation 4:2
Revelation 4:4

and exalted' in absolute majesty and holiness. Men and women (represented by the twenty-four elders in the divine court) fifid their true significance as they worship and serve God. But they are quite incapable of reflecting every aspect of God's personality. When a sealed scroll is produced, containing God's revelation to the world, the elders are unable to open it to reveal its contents. After an angel has searched unsuccessfully in heaven, on earth and in the underworld, God's own heavenly deliverer appears on the

Revelation 5:1–8

scene – the Lamb of God, Jesus Christ.

This is a powerful and impressive presentation of the central importance of the life, death and resurrection of Jesus in the Chris-tian understanding of life and its meaning. It is significant that at the very beginning of his visions, John links the future destiny of the world and its inhabitants with God's revelation of himself in the historical events of the life of Jesus.

The chapters that follow then present a series of visions describ-ing how God judges all those forces that are implacably opposed to

Revelation 6:1–21:4

him. Many of the descriptions here are quite horrific, and much of the language in which God's judgement is described comes from the story of the plagues in Egypt in the Old Testament book of

Exodus 6:28–12:36

Exodus. This gives us a clue to the point that John is making. For in the exodus story, God's main purpose had not been the plagues. They were merely a prelude to the salvation that God had planned for his people – and through them, for the whole world. So too in Revelation, the main point of the book is not to be found in God's judgement upon evil, but in the conviction that God is now in the process of making a new world from which evil will be completely banished. In this new world, men and women will enjoy a new and unfettered freedom to know God in a direct way: 'God himself will be with them ... He will wipe away all tears from their eyes. There will be no more death, no more grief or crying or pain. The old

Revelation 21:3–4

things have disappeared...'

There have been many attempts to arrange the visions of Revelation according to some sort of outline. One of the most attrac-tive suggestions was first put forward by the German scholar Ernst Lohmeyer. He suggested that, with the exception of chapters four

Revelation 21:5–22:21

and five, and the description of the new heavens and earth, the whole book is arranged in a pattern of seven sections of sevens:

● Seven seals (6:1–8:1)
● Seven trumpets (8:2–11:19)
● Seven visions of the dragon and his kingdom (12:1–13:18)
● Seven visions of the Lamb of God and his coming (14:1–20)
● Seven bowls of God's anger against evil (15:1–16:21)
● Seven visions of the fall of 'Babylon' (17:1–19:10)
● Seven visions of the end (19:11–21:4)

What we have in these visions is a kaleidoscopic picture of how God will finally overcome the powers of evil. It is the work not of a self-conscious theologian but of a great artist, and like a good artist John depicts the same subject from a number of different perspectives, in order to reinforce the overall impression that he wants to create.

Making sense of the message

It is difficult for us today to appreciate fully every detail of these visions. But we can readily understand their impact on the original readers of the book of Revelation. John assured his Christian readers that their present suffering was only temporary. Their great enemy 'Babylon' – a term which John, like Peter, used to refer to Rome – would ultimately come under the judgement of God. God would not allow injustice and evil to win the day, for he alone is the Lord of history. He has the destiny not only of nations, but of every one of his children in his personal control.

Revelation 2:10; 3:10

Revelation 18

This view of Revelation is consistent with the way we have tried to appreciate the other New Testament books. It is sometimes called the 'Preterist' view of Revelation (from the Latin word *praeteritum*, 'referring to the past'), and it is a widely-held view.

But over the centuries, other readers of the New Testament, fascinated by the seemingly mysterious character of Revelation's message, have refused to accept that its significance can be exhausted just by seeing what it meant for those Christians to whom it was first addressed. Some of the Church Fathers regarded it as a symbol of some of the great truths of the Christian faith. Origen and Augustine thought of its imagery as a symbolic account of the principles of God's working throughout history. They saw its weird descriptions of persons and battles and beasts not as real events, but as a dramatic presentation of the age-long opposition between God and the forces of evil. There is no doubt that this way of understanding Revelation can be very helpful. It makes sense of many of the most difficult passages in the book, and it also succeeds in relating it to the needs of its first readers – for they needed to be assured of the successful outcome of the struggle in which they were engaged.

But in the last 100 years or so, a large body of popular opinion has come to look at Revelation in a different way. The so-called 'futurists' argue that its real meaning is connected with events that are still in the future even now, and its full significance will become plain only to that generation which finds itself living in 'the last days'. Some have even suggested that the seven letters with which the book opens are not real letters at all, but part of a detailed clairvoyant insight given to John. They see them as detailed descriptions of seven successive ages of church history, reaching from the first century up to the end of time. Many of these so-called 'Dispensationalists' also believe that we today have reached the stage of the seventh and final letter (to Laodicea); so, they claim, our own generation is living at the very end of world history. There are many difficulties with views like this.

● There is of course the plain fact that several generations have believed themselves to be living in the last days – some even putting a date on the end of the world. But they have all been wrong.

● More serious is the fact that Jesus himself explicitly warned his disciples not to indulge in this kind of speculation: 'No one knows ... when that day and hour will come – neither the angels in heaven, nor the Son; the Father alone knows.' If that is true, it is hardly likely that God would have given the information only to a select band of modern readers of the book of Revelation!

Matthew 24:36

● Another serious objection is that according to this view, the book of Revelation must have been totally meaningless and irrelevant to the people for whom it was ostensibly written. If the letters to the churches of Asia were not real letters, related to the concerns of real people, that would make Revelation quite different from every other book in the whole of the Bible. It also shares the general pessimism about existence in this world that we have seen to be the hallmark of Jewish apocalyptic literature – but something that is quite foreign to New Testament thinking. The God of the early church was not offering 'pie in the sky', but a living relationship with himself through Jesus Christ here and now in this present life.

There is no justification for regarding either Revelation or any other book of the Bible as a kind of blueprint for the future course of world events. That is not to suggest that the Christian faith has no expectation of a better world at some future date. The whole New Testament presents the clear conviction that there will be a point at which God must deal decisively with the forces of evil – and then, the new society of peace and justice announced by Jesus will become a lasting and tangible reality.

The book of Revelation confirms that conviction. It assures us that this world belongs to God and not to the forces of evil. It reminds us in vivid and powerful imagery that God will act to put things right, no matter how long his action may seem to be delayed. And when he acts, men and women will not simply be able to make a new start: they will have a part in the new world, where sin, misery and evil have no further place. Those who prefer to serve evil rather than God will have no part in the new world, just as Jesus himself had said. But God's intention is that no one should be excluded. The new living relationship established between God and humanity through the life, death and resurrection of Jesus is freely available to all those who will accept it, and the book of Revelation underlines that message: 'Come, whoever is thirsty: accept the water of life as a gift, whoever wants it.'

Revelation 21:27
Matthew 25:31–46

Revelation 22:17

The author and date of Revelation

The Roman emperor Domitian
(AD 81–96).

Revelation is the only New Testament book that was dated by the Church Fathers. Irenaeus states that John saw his vision 'not long ago, but almost in our own generation, towards the end of Domitian's reign' (*Against Heresies* 5.30.3).

This corresponds quite closely with what we can see from the concerns of the book. Domitian (AD 81–96) demanded that all citizens should offer worship to him as a test of their political allegiance. Naturally, Christians did not want to be disloyal citizens – but they were not prepared to offer worship to the emperor. As a result, many of them were persecuted and hounded to death as enemies of the state.

A handful of scholars, however, do not accept this dating. Dr John Robinson, for example, argues that Revelation is to be set earlier, in the days just after the persecution of Christians by Nero. But Nero's persecution did not, so far as we know, involve the demand for emperor-worship. Robinson avoids this objection by suggesting that the author of Revelation had been in Rome during Nero's time, and saw worse to come. So he wrote his book to the Christians of Asia Minor not so much as an encouragement in the face of actual persecution, but as a warning of what they could expect soon. He also claims that careful analysis of the possible identities of the seven emperors listed in 17:9–11 leads to the time of Nero or his successor Galba (AD 68–69). But this (and other efforts to identify these characters) assumes that John had actual historical figures in mind at this point. It is just as likely that the seven emperors were not meant to be real people, but just the sum total of all the evil that is opposed to God.

On balance, there seems no compelling reason to reject the traditional date for Revelation of about AD 95.

The author of Revelation was a person called John. Justin Martyr states that this same John was 'one of the apostles of Christ' (*Dialogue with Trypho the Jew* 91). But many students of the New Testament find that hard to accept. The writer of Revelation seems to mention 'the twelve apostles of the Lamb' as a group that was quite separate from his own experience (21:14), and the way he writes of himself as 'your brother ... a follower of Jesus ... your partner' (1:9) hardly suggests he was a person of great authority in the church. But he was clearly steeped in the imagery of Jewish apocalyptic writings, and we may therefore suppose he was a Jew.

At the same time, there are a number of unusual connections between Revelation and the Gospel of John – and that document should almost certainly be linked with the apostle of that name. Both John and Revelation refer to Jesus as 'the word [*logos*] of God' (John 1:1–14; 1 John 1:1–4; Revelation 19:11–16). Both of them also call Jesus 'the Lamb of God', though they use different Greek words to do so (John 1:29; Revelation 5:6–14). Then we have the further fact that both the Gospel and the letters of John seem to have had some connection with the city of Ephesus – and that was one of the churches addressed in Revelation.

In view of all this, some have suggested that there was at Ephesus a 'school' of Christian thinkers established and inspired by John the apostle – and perhaps different members of this group, including John himself, were responsible for the final form of the various books which now go under his name.

Chapter 25

The enemies within

The most influential factor in the changing pattern of life in the early church was the emergence of various groups of people who came to be regarded as 'heretics' by the majority of Christian believers. But who were these people? We know a great deal about the heretical groups that prospered in the second century and later – Montanists, Gnostics, and others – but our information from the New Testament period is much less comprehensive. In the first century, the tensions that led to the eventual formation of separate sects were only just beginning to surface in church life, and the battle-lines that emerged towards the end of the second century were much more loosely drawn. Despite this, there are clear signs of moral and theological arguments in many of the New Testament books.

These arguments go back at least as far as the time of Paul. In his letter to the churches of Galatia, he wrote to counteract the influence of people whom he believed to be proclaiming 'another gospel'. Then, a few years later, in the church at Corinth he was again opposed by people with a fundamentally different understanding of the Christian message. Probably none of these people were 'heretics' in the later, technical sense. Paul certainly never went so far as the second-century church leaders, by suggesting that they should be excluded from the church. Most of them seem to have been personal opponents of Paul, who sprang up spontaneously in a number of his churches, rather than the local representatives of any sort of organized group within the church at large.

Galatians 1:6

2 Corinthians 11:1–4

But it is clear that Paul was not wholly successful in despatching them altogether. For as we read some of the later New Testament books, we can see how the teachers opposed by Paul on a piecemeal basis were beginning to organize themselves into distinctive movements within the church.

The book of Revelation

Revelation 2:1–7, 12–17, 18–29

We have already looked at the message of much of the book of Revelation. But in its first three chapters, this book reflects the conditions of the seven churches in Asia Minor to which it was addressed. The advice given by the risen Jesus to three of these churches (Ephesus, Pergamum and Thyatira) is about their attitude to various false teachers.

The church at Ephesus is commended because it has 'tested those who say they are apostles but are not, and have found out that they are liars'. In addition, its members are said to 'hate what the Nicolaitans do'. In Pergamum, some church members had actually followed the teaching of these 'Nicolaitans'. Others were following 'the teaching of Balaam'. The church at Thyatira had also come under the influence of false teaching – in this case from 'that woman Jezebel, who calls herself a messenger of God'. According to John, this person was actually teaching about 'the deep secrets of Satan'.

There is some debate as to the precise identity of all these people. But they were probably all connected with each other, rather than being separate groups in different cities. The Nicolaitans are certainly mentioned in both Ephesus and Pergamum, and in the message to Pergamum the followers of Balaam appear to be the same people. Though neither of these names is applied to the heretics in Thyatira, the activities of the Nicolaitans/Balaamites in Pergamum are the same as those practised by 'Jezebel' and her devotees there: they all eat food offered to idols and indulge in immoral practices.

Revelation 2:2, 6
Revelation 2:15, 14

Revelation 2:20

Revelation 2:24

The Gnostics laid great stress on mystical knowledge communicated to them alone. Members of the Aetherius Society, founded in 1954, listen to revelations from the skies. They claim that the secret knowledge imparted to them by extra-terrestrial beings enables them to contribute to world peace and survival.

Paul had dealt with both these issues at an earlier period, though he never suggested that those involved in such activities were 'heretics' in the strict sense. Paul certainly denounced immorality, but he declared that eating food offered to idols was a matter of indifference to Christian believers. Things must have changed in the interim. In Paul's time, these things were mainly practical issues – an understandable hangover from the pagan past of many of his converts. But they had now become theological and doctrinal issues. The book of Revelation gives no real indication of the kind of beliefs that led to such activities. But a number of considerations suggest that these sects were an early form of what was later known as Gnosticism:

● One of the prominent Gnostic groups of the second century actually called themselves 'Nicolaitans'. They traced their origins back to a man called Nicolaus, who according to Acts was one of Stephen's Hellenist colleagues in the early Jerusalem church. It is unlikely that they had any real connection with this person. But some of their practices were not dissimilar from what we read about in the book of Revelation.

● Though the heretics opposed in Revelation were undoubtedly less sophisticated and less well-organized than these later groups,

1 Corinthians 8

Acts 6:5

Revelation 2:24

The ruins of ancient Pergamum rise high above the modern Turkish town of Bergama. Pergamum was, according to Revelation, 'where Satan has his throne', possibly referring to the Altar of Zeus which was situated between the two trees, overlooking the town. Pergamum also became a centre of the official cult of emperor-worship.

there are some signs of Gnostic terminology and ideas here. For instance, Jezebel's teaching in Thyatira is referred to as 'the deep secrets of Satan', and this phrase is found among later Gnostic groups as a description of their own beliefs. Then the very fact that a woman should have been so prominent in this movement also suggests a Gnostic type of thinking. For in the Gnostic heresies of the second century, certain women played a large and conspicuous part. Indeed, this was one reason why the church after the New Testament period officially excluded women from any form of public service.

● The evidence of other New Testament books points in the same direction. The letters of John, as well as the letter of Jude and

2 Peter, all seem to have originated in the same area as Revelation, and in all of them we meet wandering teachers operating in the same way as those mentioned in Revelation. 1 John explains their theology in considerable detail, and we can see from that how clearly these heretics were moving towards classical Gnosticism.

The letters of John

1 John 5:13
John 20:31

Part of the *Pistis Sophia*, a Gnostic manuscript which circulated in the late fourth or early fifth century.

Like the Gospel of John, 1 John tells us why it was written. In chapter five, the writer says, 'I am writing this to you so that you may know that you have eternal life – you that believe in the Son of God'. The Gospel of John was written to demonstrate that Jesus was Messiah and Son of God – and to win people to faith in him. By contrast, 1 John was written to people who were already Christian believers. But they clearly needed to be reassured of the truth of what they believed.

In his first letter, John emphasizes that 'God is light and in him is no darkness at all'. His readers, surrounded by people advocating a pantheistic mysticism, needed reassuring of the clarity of God's truth.

The heretics

1 John 4:1

1 John 2:19

1 John 2:4; 4:8
1 John 4:1

1 John 1:6, 8, 10
1 John 1:5; 2:9
1 John 1:6, 8, 10; 2:4; 3:7–12; 4:20

1 Corinthians 10:1–13

1 Corinthians 4:7–8

1 Corinthians 15:12–19

2 Timothy 2:17–18

It is not difficult to see why they needed such reassurance. Like the churches mentioned in Revelation, the church to which they belonged was suffering from the activities of 'false prophets'. These false prophets had originally been church members themselves. But they had left its fellowship, and they were now trying to subvert it from the outside. Of course, that was not how the false teachers saw things. They believed they had received special revelations that were not given to the ordinary church members. They spoke of 'knowing' God in an intimate way, through the special operation of the Holy Spirit in their lives. They also believed that this enabled them to live on a different plane from ordinary Christians. They were already spiritually 'perfect', living in full appreciation of the 'light' which was God himself – and so the normal earth-bound rules of Christian morality no longer applied to them.

All this sounds remarkably similar to the claims of Paul's opponents in Corinth. They too were claiming that because of their remarkable mystical experiences, they were no longer bound by the normal constraints of human existence. They believed that through these mystical experiences they had already been raised to a new spiritual level far above that enjoyed by ordinary Christians. It was, they said, just as if the resurrection had already come. They might seem to be living in this world, but really they had been totally liberated from it, and so they no longer shared its concerns.

People with similar views are also mentioned in Paul's second letter to Timothy. 1 John does not actually say that these false teachers also believed that the resurrection had already come in their own mystical experiences, but it is likely that they held this view too.

Docetism

1 John 2:22–23; 4:2, 15; 5:1–5, 10–12

1 John 4:1–3

But there is a new element in 1 John. For the 'false prophets' mentioned here had a distinctive understanding of the person and significance of Jesus himself. It is clear from what he says that John's opponents were denying that Jesus was the Messiah and the Son of God. It was not that they denied that Jesus had revealed the power of God. But they found it difficult to see how an ordinary human person could reveal the character of the eternal God. So they asserted that Jesus was not truly human at all.

In Greek thinking there had always been a strong conviction that this world in which we live is quite separate from God's heavenly world. The Old Testament prophets had always believed that God's activity could be seen in the affairs of human experience. But Greek thinkers had regarded life in this world as a miserable existence. The true destiny of men and women, they claimed, was not here, but in the spiritual world inhabited by God. True salvation, therefore, could only consist in the escape of a person from the 'prison' of this world into the life of the supernatural world. There were many theories to explain precisely how this could be accomplished, and it is obvious that the desire for such liberation was what motivated both Paul's opponents in Corinth, and the false teachers of the church to which 1 John was addressed.

At the beginning, Christians were interested in such ideas mainly because they were attracted by the promise of exciting mystical experiences. But as these mystics began to think out the theological implications of their experience, they inevitably found it hard to cope with the church's belief that Jesus had come from God himself. For if God was a part of this mystical, supernatural world, then there was no way in which he could also be a real human person. For the all-powerful God to be imprisoned in the life of a human being would be a contradiction in terms.

One way out of the dilemma was to suggest that Jesus had only *seemed* to be the Messiah or Son of God. This view is called 'Docetism' (from the Greek word *dokeō,* 'to seem'), and this is the view that is opposed in 1 John. Many of the early Church Fathers mention people with such beliefs. Irenaeus tells how the apostle John once went to a public bath-house in Ephesus. But when he got there, John refused to take a bath because Cerinthus, who was himself a prominent Docetist, was also there.

Against Heresies 3.3.4

Some have suggested that 1 John was a direct reply to Cerinthus himself. He argued that the 'divine essence', or 'Christ', came into the human Jesus at his baptism, and left him before the crucifixion – and 1 John includes a statement that can be seen as a reply to this: 'Jesus Christ is the one who came with the water of his baptism and the blood of his death. He came not only with the water, but with both the water and the blood.' But Cerinthus had many other ideas not mentioned at all in 1 John, and the problems dealt with in this letter are undoubtedly less complex than the theology of Cerinthus and his followers. Indeed, with the exception of their speculation about the person of Christ, the heretics of 1 John have much more in common with Paul's opponents in Corinth, and it is probably more accurate to regard them as an intermediate stage between the Corinthian heretics and the fully-developed Gnostic systems of the second century.

1 John 5:6

1 John

The author of 1 John clearly had no time for these people. He denounced their beliefs and opposed their practices in every section of his letter. He realized all too well the strong pressure that they were placing on the members of the church, and he went out of his way to assure them that they, and not the heretics, were the ones who had the truth.

But it is not easy to find any logical argument here. Some scholars have tried to rearrange John's letter to make it fit together more logically. Others have explained what they regard as inconsistencies by supposing that the letter went through more than one edition and is therefore the work of more than one writer. But none of these suggestions is particularly convincing. The book contains not just the author's response to the heretics. It is also a part of his own theological reflection on the situation which he faced, and for that reason it is more a work of art than a book of theology. It can usefully be compared to a musical composition, in which the main theme is first expounded, and then is taken up and developed and elaborated as the composer moves on to other themes and ideas yet always returning to his first thought.

The message

'Our love should not be just words and talk; it must be true love, which shows itself in action', wrote John. Relief supplies for Kampuchea, provided by an international relief Christian agency, are a demonstration of Christian concern to show the love of God in action.

1 John 1

1 John 2:1–6

1 John 2:7–16
1 John 2:15–17

John 2:18–19

Whatever the form of the argument, the message of 1 John is crystal clear. Like every other New Testament writer, John is convinced that mystical experiences, however elevated, are totally irrelevant to Christian faith unless they affect the way people behave. It is no use talking about being liberated into the world of light, unless God's light truly informs and inspires our behaviour. To say that mystical experiences actually release men and women from the power of evil is unrealistic and untrue. Anyone who claims to be perfect and free from the influence of sin is fooling himself.

True Christians must 'live just as Jesus Christ did' – but they must also accept the reality of their moral poverty, and accept the forgiveness which only Jesus can give. Living like Jesus is a practical affair: it is a matter of loving other people, and this means that anyone who despises others (as did the Docetists) can hardly claim to be doing God's will. In reality, they are just indulging their own selfishness.

The fact that such people could ever have been a part of the church should serve to emphasize that the day of judgement is not far off. The others must not be intimidated by them. Whatever the

1 John 2:20–29

heretics may claim, those in the church are the true recipients of the Holy Spirit, and they are the ones who have been accepted by God. Not that they have done anything to deserve that love. But having been adopted as God's children, they should ensure that they continue to do as he wants. Just as Christ loved them, so they must love one another – then they can be sure that they are truly living in harmony with the Holy Spirit, and in union with God himself.

1 John 3:1–10
1 John 3:11–18
1 John 3:19–24

But telling the true from the false is not just a matter of human judgement. There is a test of belief that can distinguish the heretics from the true believers: 'Anyone who acknowledges that Jesus Christ came as a human being has the Spirit who comes from God. But anyone who denies this about Jesus does not have the Spirit from God.' Having God's Spirit naturally leads to love, just as God himself is love. It also leads to obedience to God's commands, and to final victory over all that is opposed to his will. With this assurance, true Christians can be certain that they will know and understand God in a way that the Docetists never could.

1 John 4:1–6
1 John 4:7–21
1 John 5:1–5

1 John 5:6–21

The books by John

We cannot consider 1 John independently from the other letters of John, and John's Gospel. 2 and 3 John are related very closely to 1 John, though they are quite different types of literature. Unlike 1 John, they are short,

the church, and because of this many scholars think that 2 John must have been written before 1 John. For in 1 John the heretics had already been excluded from the church (1 John 2:19).

3 John advises Gaius about a man by

Hierapolis was situated about 6 miles/10km north of Laodicea in the Lycus Valley in what is now Turkey. It was a centre of pagan cults and became important because of the healing powers of its hot springs, from which came pools and rock channels. There is a reference to their 'lukewarm' water in the letter to Laodicea in the book of Revelation.

personal letters, one addressed to a church and the other to an individual called Gaius. Their author calls himself 'the Elder'. In 2 John he warns his readers against wandering teachers 'who do not acknowledge that Jesus Christ came as a human being' (2 John 7–11). He was concerned that these people should not be welcomed into

the name of Diotrephes. He was aspiring to be the leader of the church, and 'the Elder' says that he intends to pay a short visit to correct 'the terrible things he says about us and the lies he tells' (3 John 9–10). Professor Ernst Käsemann has suggested that the way 'the Elder' writes here indicates that he himself was the heretic, and that it was

Diotrephes who was trying to preserve the integrity and faith of the church. But there is no evidence to support this view. The little that is said in 3 John does not suggest that there was any theological disagreement between 'the Elder' and Diotrephes – while 2 John (quite apart from John and 1 John) hardly suggests that its author held a Docetic theology.

It is more likely that 3 John reflects a stage when new patterns of church leadership were beginning to emerge. As the apostles and their representatives died, the corporate leadership of the earliest churches began to disappear, and new leaders were trying to assert themselves. This process eventually led to the formal appointment of just one authoritative leader in each local church. Perhaps 'the Elder' represented the older form of church organization, and that may explain his concern about the emergence of just one person claiming to be the church's leader. In the second century, anyone with the title of 'Elder' would himself have been a part of the organized hierarchy of the church. But the writer of these letters clearly does not belong in that context. He was obviously highly respected by his readers, but he does not seem to have had absolute authority over them. He can only appeal to them to do what he believed to be right.

The majority of scholars believe that 'the Elder' who wrote 2 and 3 John also wrote 1 John. There are many connections between the three letters in vocabulary and style, and certain statements in 2 and 3 John seem to presuppose some knowledge of the issues dealt with in the first letter. So if we can decide the identity of 'the Elder', we can presumably identify the writer of all three letters.

But this is easier said than done. Scholars have often turned for guidance to a statement attributed to Papias. He was bishop of Hierapolis in the early second century, and wrote five books entitled *The Interpretation of the Oracles of the Lord*. Unfortunately, these are all now lost, and our only knowledge of them comes through a few scattered quotations in the works of Irenaeus and Eusebius. Eusebius quotes a statement in which Papias tells how he obtained his information about the earliest days of the church: 'If ever anyone came who had followed the elders, I inquired into the words of the elders, what Andrew or Peter or Philip or Thomas or James or John or Matthew, or any other of the Lord's disciples, had said, and what Aristion and the elder

John, the Lord's disciples, were saying.' Eusebius goes on to observe that 'It is here worth noting that he twice counts the name of John, and reckons the first John with ... the other Apostles ... but places the second with the others outside the number of the apostles ... This confirms the truth of the story of those who have said that there were two of the same name in Asia, and that there are two tombs at Ephesus both still called John's' (Eusebius, *Ecclesiastical History* 3.39.4–6).

If the 'elder John' to whom Eusebius refers was the same person as 'the Elder' who wrote 2 and 3 John, then presumably this second-generation Christian was also the author of 1 John (and perhaps of the Gospel of John). But some scholars have pointed out that Papias's statement is ambiguous, for he also appears to call the disciples themselves 'elders'. Eusebius may therefore be wrong to infer that Papias was referring to two different Johns.

Of course, this whole argument assumes that Papias had access to reliable information. But we must treat the statements of the Church Fathers with caution, especially when we only have second-hand knowledge of what Papias actually wrote. So far as the writings of John are concerned, it is more helpful to begin with the documents themselves.

There is a certain amount of debate about the precise relationship between 1, 2 and 3 John, and the Gospel of John. There are considerable and close similarities between the Gospel and 1 John. Both use the same language in the same way. The contrasts between light and darkness, life and death, truth and error, and the emphasis on love – not to mention the description of Jesus as the Word or *Logos* – are all found in both Gospel and letter. Both of them also use the same techniques for conveying their message, initially stating an idea in a simple and easily-remembered way, and then examining its implications from a number of different angles.

But there are also a number of differences. 1 John has a more restricted vocabulary than the Gospel. Its emphasis is also slightly different at some points. For instance, while the Gospel lays most emphasis on the present experience of the Christian (so-called 'realized eschatology'), the letter has much more emphasis on the future hope. The letter also has a stronger emphasis on the church and its sacraments – though here again, these things are not entirely absent from the Gospel.

Rudolf Bultmann suggested that the

Gospel was edited by the writer of the letter, to bring it into line with his own thinking on these points. There is certainly some evidence that the Gospel contains the work of more than one person. But it is unlikely that the original form of the Gospel has been revised by someone who found it theologically unacceptable. An explanation of the complex connections between the various books connected with the name of John is the suggestion that there was in Ephesus a 'school' of Christian thinking associated with and growing out of the work of John, the disciple of Jesus. He served as the theological mentor of a whole group of Christians, and was the source of the information contained in the fourth Gospel (see John 21:24). But the literature as we know it now was the product of this 'school' rather than of just one individual.

In chapter 11, I have suggested that the Gospel of John was first written in what we might called a 'Palestinian edition'. If so, then the Gospel would possibly be the first of these books to be edited and reissued from the school in Ephesus. Perhaps its message was subsequently misunderstood and misapplied by its new readers. In a Jewish context, the contrasts between darkness and light, truth and error, life and death were ethical contrasts. But the same terms had always been used by Greek thinkers to describe the cosmological distinction between the divine world of spirit, in which God lives, and the evil world of matter,

where we live. Some Greek readers of the Gospel could easily have been misled by these terms – and that misunderstanding ultimately led them to the position adopted by the Docetists. The way the Gospel emphasizes the present reality of the resurrection in the life of Christian believers would also lend colour to such speculations.

In response to this growing threat, 'the Elder' (presumably a prominent member of the Johannine school – perhaps John himself) wrote 2 John to warn against such false teaching. But things went from bad to worse, the false teachers broke away from the church to form their own sect and 1 John was written as a more theological response to the problem. Not only was the Docetic view of Jesus challenged, but it was now emphasized that the resurrection hope was very much something tangible and future, and not just a part of the present spiritual experience of Christians.

If this reconstruction is correct, the date we give to these letters will depend on the date we give to the Gospel. The kind of teaching opposed in 1 John is certainly more advanced than that opposed by Paul in Corinth. There is a clear idea of 'heresy' in 1 John, but it is not as complex as we find in the second century. Since the heretics opposed in 1 John seem to have a number of features in common with those mentioned in Revelation, a date sometime towards the end of the first century is perhaps the nearest guess we can make.

Jude and 2 Peter

The influence of false teachers is also the subject of two of the most obscure books of the New Testament: Jude and 2 Peter. These books clearly belong together, for almost the whole of Jude (in a slightly modified form) is contained in 2 Peter. But otherwise, neither book contains any information to help us identify their original readers.

The heresy

The way in which Jude and 2 Peter oppose false teachers suggests that they originated in a situation quite similar to that dealt with in the opening chapters of the book of Revelation. The term 'gnosis' (knowledge) is not actually mentioned, but they are described as

Jude 19

'psychics' ('controlled by their natural desires'), and we know that this was a technical term used by the Gnostics. These people

Jude 8

certainly laid a great emphasis on their own spiritual experiences, and they argued that because they themselves had been 'raised' to a new level of spiritual life, they had also been released from the

Jude 12–13; 16, 18, 23

normal constraints of Christian morality. But all this was unacceptable to those in the mainstream of the church. Jude reminds them that even in Old Testament times God had punished people for the same kind of wrongdoing – and unless his readers were prepared to repent, they could expect to share the same fate.

2 Peter also suggests that these people were denying the reality of the future coming of Jesus. No doubt they argued that since they themselves had already been spiritually 'raised' to heaven, there would be no further need for the kind of literal resurrection hope held by the majority of the early Christians. In any case, they said, nothing had happened, even though the church had fervently expected Jesus to return in glory. This argument had first been put forward by Paul's opponents in Corinth. But 2 Peter introduces a new answer to it, by asserting that God's time-scale is not the same as ours: 'There is no difference in the Lord's sight between one day and a thousand years...' The fact that the end has not yet arrived does not mean that God has failed to fulfil his promises. Quite the opposite is true, for the delay in the coming of Jesus is itself an expression of God's patience in allowing men and women more time to repent.

Jude does not describe the beliefs of these heretics so precisely. He simply asserts that they 'reject Jesus Christ, our only Master and Lord'. It seems likely that these false teachers had not gone quite as far as those who were opposed in 1 John. They had not challenged the church's beliefs on a theological level, by declaring that Jesus was not the Son of God come in the flesh. Instead, like the heretics mentioned in Revelation, they had 'given themselves over to the error that Balaam committed' – and, as we have already seen, that was more of a moral and practical problem.

Jude 8–16

2 Peter 3:1–18

1 Corinthians 15:1–34

2 Peter 3:8

Jude 4

Numbers 22:1–35; Jude 11;
Revelation 2:14

Authors and dates

Neither Jude nor 2 Peter contains any information at all that might link them to specific events or people in the early church. The only way we can understand their background is by trying to fit them into what we know about the development of the early churches in general. A number of indications seem to suggest that both these books belong to the end of the New Testament period, rather than the time of the apostles themselves:

● Unlike Paul (and 1 John), Jude does not set out to argue with his opponents. He simply denounces them, and asserts that the answer to their problems is a return to 'the faith which once and for all God has given to his people' (Jude 3). We have seen in a previous chapter that the development of a standard form of belief like this was one of the things that characterized the emerging institutional church at the end of the first century.

● Jude 17 also indicates a date later than the age of the apostles, when the writer refers to 'what you were told in the past by the apostles of our Lord

Jesus Christ'. Of course, that might refer to some occasion on which the readers had actually met the apostles themselves. But the same cannot be said of the reference to Paul in 2 Peter 3:14–16. Here, Paul's letters are mentioned as a recognized and well-known collection of writings, and they are also classed as 'scripture'. Paul's letters were probably not gathered together in a collection until after his death, and we can be sure that it would take a little longer again for them to be regarded as 'scripture' in any authoritative sense.

Most modern scholars interpret these facts to indicate that both these books must be dated sometime in the second century. Some would place them as late as AD 150. But there are difficulties about such a late date:

● It seems quite likely that 2 Peter was used (along with other New Testament books) by the unknown author of a work called *The Apocalypse of Peter*. But this is commonly dated sometime in the period between AD 100 and 135, and so 2 Peter can hardly be later than that.

● There is also the fact that the description of the false teachers in Jude and 2 Peter is quite different from any known second-century heresy. There is no hint even of a Docetic view of Jesus, let alone of the more complex theories of the classical Gnostic systems.

● There is also no trace of much of the apparatus of the second-century church. There is a consciousness of a fixed body of Christian doctrine, but there is no indication of an organized ministry in the church. Both Jude and 2 Peter appeal to their readers on a moral basis rather than on an authoritarian one.

A minority of scholars therefore have tried to explain the origin of these books by recourse to their opening sentences. For both of them appear to be claiming to be the work of people who flourished in the age of the apostles themselves. 'Jude, servant of Jesus Christ, and brother of James' (Jude 1) is almost certainly meant to be that Jude who is named in the Gospels as a brother of Jesus and of James in Mark 6:3; while 'Simon Peter' is clearly intended to identify the author of 2 Peter as the apostle himself (2 Peter 1:1). But there are other problems involved here:

● The early church had a number of doubts about both these books. Jude is mentioned occasionally by the early Church Fathers, but 2 Peter is mentioned nowhere before the works of Origen (AD 185–254), and as late as the fourth century both of them were regarded either as spurious or of doubtful value. This at the very least must suggest that they were not generally supposed to be the writings of leaders of the first generation of Christians.

Christians in Uganda know what it means to suffer for their faith; nevertheless, they are enthusiastic to share the good news about Jesus. Here, members of a mission team in Kigezi hold up copies of the Gospels before setting out on an evangelistic visit.

● Coupled with this, there is general agreement among scholars of all opinions that if 1 Peter is the work of Peter, the disciple of Jesus, then 2 Peter is not. Many writers in the early church were perplexed by the differences between the two, for in style of writing, theological emphasis and general outlook they are so different that it is impossible to think the same person wrote them both. So if we are correct to connect 1 Peter with Peter himself, then we must look elsewhere for an explanation of 2 Peter.

An ingenious solution to this problem has been put forward by Dr John Robinson. He points out that the writer of Jude tells us that he was in the process of writing a letter to his readers, when he suddenly realized a more urgent need to communicate with them immediately – and in response to that, he wrote the letter of Jude (Jude 3). But what was the original letter that he was busy writing? In view of the close connections between them, could it have been 2 Peter? And could it be that the earlier letter that is referred to in 2 Peter 3:1 was not 1 Peter, as most people have thought, but Jude? Dr Robinson goes on to suggest that Jude may well have been writing as Peter's representative, and he points out that according to Acts 15:14, the leaders of the Jewish church commonly referred to Peter as 'Simon', which could explain the unusual use of that name in the opening sentence of 2 Peter.

Of course, the problem with this is that we know nothing at all about the activities of the Jude who was the brother of James and of Jesus. But there is nevertheless a good deal to commend this suggestion. It is more difficult to go along with Dr Robinson and date the writing of both these books sometime between AD 60 and 62. If, as we have suggested, the heresy being opposed here is similar to that found in the seven churches of the book of Revelation, then we must look for a date nearer the end of the first century. The other pointers indicating a late date must also be taken seriously, and we know that the kind of practical immorality mentioned in Jude was much more common around AD 100 than it was in the middle of the first century.

Despite attack and opposition, persecution and heresy, the Christian church has shown an amazing ability to survive through the centuries. It often grows most vigorously when conditions seem at their bleakest.

2 Peter 1:16–18

It may well be that Jude and 2 Peter both originate from a group of Peter's disciples, in much the same way as we suggested the Johannine letters originated from a 'school' of John's disciples. This could explain both the similarities and the differences between 1 and 2 Peter. It could also explain why certain sections of 2 Peter (like the description of the transfiguration of Jesus in chapter one) have struck many readers as authentic reminiscences of Peter himself. Perhaps what we have in both these short letters is a fresh application of the teaching of Peter to the concerns and interests of a Hellenistic Jewish Christian congregation somewhere in Asia Minor towards the end of the first century.

As the years passed, the church had to change and adapt itself to deal with new threats and take advantage of new opportunities. But it never forgot that its thinking and behaviour must always be firmly anchored in the experiences and outlook of those first followers who had actually known Jesus. Had it not been for the continuing commitment of a small group of Palestinian peasants, the wider world would never have heard this life-changing message. It was not easy for them. Their courage and boldness were rewarded with persecution, and even death. But their own experience of Jesus was such that they had no thought of turning back. They knew that Jesus was not dead, but alive – and working in power in their own lives through the presence of his Spirit. Not only did he inspire them to great exploits, but he also strengthened them in their trials. And it is no coincidence that one of the latest New Testament writings should sum up their deepest conviction in some of the most striking language of the entire Bible: 'To him who is able to keep you from falling, and to bring you faultless and joyful before his glorious presence – to the only God our Saviour, through Jesus Christ our Lord, be glory, majesty, might and authority, from all ages past, and now, and for ever and ever!'

Jude 24–25

Other books on the New Testament

*Books marked with an asterisk are recommended for more advanced study

General

G. Bornkamm, *The New Testament: a guide to its writings*, Fortress, 1973/SPCK, 1974. A helpful elementary introduction to the study of the New Testament.

*J. D. G. Dunn, *Unity & Diversity in the New Testament*, SCM/Westminster, 1977. A study of the social and theological variety of the early churches, and the implications for New Testament study.

F. V. Filson, *A New Testament History*, Westminster, 1964/SCM, 1965. A broad perspective on the whole New Testament story.

L. Goppelt, *Theology of the New Testament*, Eerdmans, 1981/82 (2 vols). A comprehensive presentation of the meaning of the New Testament writings.

R. M. Grant, *Early Christianity & Society*, Harper & Row, 1977/Collins, 1978. The relationship between early Christians and various aspects of life in the Roman empire.

D. Guthrie, *New Testament Introduction*, IVP, 1970/InterVarsity, 1971. An encyclopedic treatment of all the New Testament books and their background.

D. J. Harrington, *Interpreting the New Testament*, Michael Glazier/Veritas, 1979. A practical handbook, illustrating and explaining the modern study of the New Testament.

W. G. Kümmel, *Introduction to the New Testament*, Abingdon, 1975/SCM, 1977 (2nd ed.). Similar to Guthrie's book, though written from a different perspective.

W. G. Kümmel, *Theology of the New Testament*, Abingdon, 1973/SCM, 1974. A lucid discussion of the whole of the New Testament, with many helpful insights on the message of Jesus, as well as Paul and John.

E. Lohse, *The First Christians*, Fortress, 1983. A short examination of some major aspects of the life of the early church.

A. J. Malherbe, *Social Aspects of Early Christianity*, Fortress, 1983 (2nd ed.). An important book, exploring the way the church fitted into Roman society.

J. A. T. Robinson, *Redating the New Testament*, SCM/Westminster, 1976. A provocative and radical examination of the dates given to New Testament books. An especially lucid analysis of the problems involved.

Section One. Setting the scene

Chapter 1. The world of the first Christians

J. Dart, *The Laughing Savior*, Harper & Row, 1976. A readable account of the Nag Hammadi Gnostic library, and of the significance of Gnosticism for early Christianity.

M. Hengel, *Jews, Greeks & Barbarians*, SCM/Fortress, 1980. Jewish history immediately prior to the New Testament period.

W. S. LaSor, *The Dead Sea Scrolls & the New Testament*, Eerdmans, 1972. A judicious and thorough survey of the subject.

E. Lohse, *The New Testament Environment*, Abingdon/SCM, 1976. A readable and comprehensive account of the religious background to the New Testament.

J. Neusner, *Judaism in the beginning of Christianity*, Fortress/SPCK, 1984. A reliable account of what can be known of Jesus' Jewish contemporaries.

F. W. Walbank, *The Hellenistic World*, Fontana/Humanities, 1981. A wide-ranging account of the world of the first Christians.

Section Two. Jesus: God's promised deliverer

Chapter 2. Jesus' birth & early years

*R. E. Brown, *The Birth of the Messiah*, Macmillan/Chapman, 1977. An encyclopedic exposition of the birth stories in Matthew and Luke.

C. H. H. Scobie, *John the Baptist*, SCM, 1964. A survey of all that is known of John, and analysis of his significance.

H. Hendrickx, *Infancy Narratives*, Chapman/Winston, 1984. A commentary-like study of its subject.

Chapter 3. Who was Jesus?

*O. Cullmann, *The Christology of the New Testament*, SCM, 1959/Westminster, 1964. Discusses the various titles applied to Jesus throughout the New Testament.

*J. D. G. Dunn, *Christology in the Making*, SCM/Westminster, 1980. Discussion of the titles Son of Man, Son of God, and the emergence of belief in the incarnation.

M. Hengel, *The Son of God*, SCM/Fortress, 1976. A succinct account of the meaning of this title.

*M. D. Hooker, *Jesus & the Servant*, SPCK, 1959. The importance for Jesus of the Old Testament concept of the Servant of the Lord.

*B. Lindars, *Jesus, Son of Man*, SPCK, 1983/Eerdmans, 1984. Latest in a long line of attempts to explain the precise meaning of this title in the Gospels.

I. H. Marshall, *The Origins of New Testament Christology*, IVP, 1977. Discusses the relation between the church's beliefs about Jesus and his beliefs about himself.

*C. F. D. Moule, *The Origin of Christology*, CUP, 1977. Similar in scope to Marshall, though more detailed.

G. O'Collins, *Interpreting Jesus*, Paulist/Chapman, 1983. Uses all the Gospel materials to explain the significance of Jesus.

C. Tuckett, *The Messianic Secret*, SPCK/Fortress, 1983. A series of essays exploring the concepts first proposed in W. Wrede's classic book (*The Messianic Secret*, CUP, 1971).

Chapter 4. Why did Jesus die?

On Jesus' trials

J. Blinzler, *The Trial of Jesus*, 1959. A helpful guide to the complexities of the Gospel stories.

*A. N. Sherwin-White, *Roman Society & Roman Law in the New Testament*, OUP, 1963, pp. 24–47. A legal study of the trials.

The Last Supper

*J. Jeremias, *The Eucharistic Words of Jesus*, SCM/Allenson, 1955. A comprehensive study of the meaning and significance of the Last Supper, arguing that it was the Passover.

I. H. Marshall, *Last Supper and Lord's Supper*, Paternoster, 1980/Eerdmans, 1981. A helpful study of Jesus' last night with his disciples, and the church's sacrament.

The Cross

H. Hendrickx, *Passion Narratives*, Chapman/Winston, 1984. An exegetical study of the Gospel stories.

M. Hengel, *Crucifixion*, Fortress/SCM, 1977. The cross in historical and social perspective.

M. Hengel, *The Atonement*, Fortress/SCM, 1981. The cross and its meaning in the early church.

Chapter 5. The resurrection

H. Hendrickx, *Resurrection Narratives*, Chapman/Winston, 1984. Study of the Gospel stories, and the issues raised.

S. H. Hooke, *The Resurrection of Christ*, Darton Longman & Todd, 1967. Helpful discussion of the background of the concept, the Gospel stories, and their relevance to New Testament theology.

G. O'Collins, *The Easter Jesus*, Darton Longman & Todd/Judson, 1973. Readable discussion of the New Testament evidence.

*T. F. Torrance, *Space, Time & Resurrection*, Handsel/Eerdmans, 1976. Discussion of the philosophical and scientific questions raised by the resurrection stories.

Section Three. The Kingdom is here

Chapter 6. What is God's Kingdom?

B. D. Chilton, *The Kingdom of God*, SPCK/Fortress, 1984. Essays on various aspects of the subject.

C. H. Dodd, *The Parables of the Kingdom*, Fount, 1978/Harper & Row, 1981. Dodd's classic study of 'realized eschatology' (originally published in 1935).

*W.G. Kümmel, *Promise & Fulfilment*, SCM/OUP, 1961 (2nd ed.). Argues that Jesus had an eschatology 'in the process of being realized'.

G. E. Ladd, *The Presence of the Future*, Eerdmans, 1974/SPCK, 1980 (2nd ed.). A survey of the various approaches to Jesus' eschatology.

N. Perrin, *The Kingdom of God in the Teaching of Jesus*, SCM/Westminster, 1963. An account of various views on the subject.

*J. Riches, *Jesus & the Transformation of Judaism*, Darton Longman & Todd, 1980/Winston, 1982. Original study of the ways Jesus used familiar language with new meanings.

Chapter 7. Pictures of the Kingdom

*J Jeremias, *The Parables of Jesus*, SCM/Scribner, 1972 (3rd ed.). Survey of the parables and their meaning, against their historical background and in the life of the church.

G. V. Jones, *The Art & Truth of the Parables*, SPCK/Allenson, 1964. Looks at the parables as art forms, emphasizing their direct appeal to the human situation.

W. S. Kissinger, *The Parables of Jesus*, Scarecrow, 1979. A comprehensive history of their interpretation.

*T. W. Manson, *The Sayings of Jesus*, SCM/Allenson, 1949. An older exposition of the non-Marcan material in the Gospels of Matthew and Luke.

R. H. Stein, *The Method & Message of Jesus' Teachings*, Westminster, 1978. A helpful study of Jesus' teaching methods, and the substance of his message.

Chapter 8. The Power of the Kingdom

R. H. Fuller, *Interpreting the Miracles*, SCM/Allenson, 1963. The meaning of the miracles in the New Testament, and their value to Christians today.

C. S. Lewis, *Miracles*, 1947 (& many reprints). A readable study of the problem of what we mean by miracles.

*H. van der Loos, *The Miracles of Jesus*, Leiden, 1968. An encyclopedic examination of the Gospel narratives and the issues raised by them.

Chapter 9. God's Kingdom in Action

*W. D. Davies, *The Setting of the Sermon on the Mount*, CUP, 1964. A scholarly study of the meaning of the Sermon in its first-century context.

A. M. Hunter, *Design for Life*, SCM, 1965 (2nd ed.). A clear, concise and helpful exposition of the meaning of the Sermon on the Mount.

H. Hendrickx, *The Sermon on the Mount*, Chapman/Winston, 1984. A helpful study of the Sermon and its meaning.

*R. Schnackenburg, *The Moral Teaching of the New Testament*, Search/Seabury, 1975. Includes a section on Jesus, as well as the rest of the New Testament.

Section Four. Knowing about Jesus

Chapter 10. Understanding the Gospels

*M. Dibelius, *From Tradition to Gospel*, CUP, 1971 (originally in German, 1919). A pioneering work on form criticism.

C. H. Dodd, *The Apostolic Preaching & its Developments*, Hodder/Harper & Row, 1963 (3rd ed.). Dodd's classic study of the form of the *kerygma*.

*W. R. Farmer, *The Synoptic Problem*, Western North Carolina Press, 1976. A solution based on the Griesbach theory.

I. H. Marshall, *New Testament Interpretation*, Paternoster/Eerdmans, 1977. Articles on source, form, redaction criticism, as well as other aspects of New Testament study.

K. F. Nickle, *The Synoptic Gospels*, John Knox, 1981/SCM, 1982. A useful introductory handbook to the Gospels.

*B. H. Streeter, *The Four Gospels*, Macmillan, 1924. The classic study of the origins of the Gospels.

W. B. Tatum, *In Quest of Jesus*, John Knox, 1982/SCM, 1983. Elementary introduction to the issues involved in modern study of the Gospels and the life of Jesus.

Chapter 11. Four portraits of Jesus

Matthew

*B. W. Bacon, *Studies in Matthew*, Macmillan, 1930. Suggests the five-fold division of the Gospel, paralleling the five books of the Pentateuch.

*D. Hill, *The Gospel of St Matthew*, Oliphants/Eerdmans, 1972.

P. S. Minear, *Matthew: the Teacher's Gospel*, Pilgrim, 1982/Darton Longman & Todd, 1984. A useful short study.

E. Schweizer, *The Good News according to Matthew*, John Knox, 1975/SPCK, 1976. Readable and helpful commentary by a noted German scholar.

G. N. Stanton, *The Interpretation of Matthew*, Fortress/SPCK, 1983. Essays on major issues in understanding Matthew.

Mark

M. D. Hooker, *The Message of Mark*, Epworth, 1983. A short introduction to recent study of Mark.

D. E. Nineham, *St Mark*, Penguin, 1963. Takes full account of the work of form criticism.

E. Schweizer, *The Good News according to Mark*, SPCK, 1971/John Knox, 1976. A companion volume to the author's work on Matthew.

Luke

E. E. Ellis, *The Gospel according to Luke*, Oliphants/Eerdmans, 1974 (2nd ed.).

*I. H. Marshall, *The Gospel of Luke*, Paternoster/Eerdmans, 1978. Massive and scholarly commentary.

John

C. H. Dodd, *Historical Tradition in the Fourth Gospel*, CUP, 1965. Scholarly study of John, arguing that it contains reliable independent information about Jesus.

L. Morris, *The Gospel according to John*, Eerdmans, 1971. Good all-round commentary.

J. A. T. Robinson, *The Priority of John*, SCM, 1985. Argues for an early date and independent value for John.

*R. Schnackenburg, *The Gospel according to St John*, Crossroad/Burns & Oates, 3 vols, 1980–82. Enormous encyclopedic commentary.

Chapter 12. Can we trust the Gospels?

R. S. Barbour, *Tradition-Historical Criticism of the Gospels*, SPCK/Allenson, 1972. Critique of the various techniques used for discovering the authentic words of Jesus in the Gospels.

F. F. Bruce, *Jesus & Christian Origins outside the New Testament*, Hodder, 1984 (2nd ed.). Comprehensive discussion of apocryphal gospels, gnostic traditions, and Jesus in Islam and Judaism.

J. D. G. Dunn, *The Evidence for Jesus*, SCM, 1985. Looks at the historical trustworthiness of the Gospel stories.

B. Gerhardsson, *The Origins of the Gospel Traditions*, SCM/Fortress, 1979. Argues for the essential reliability of the Gospels, when seen in a Jewish context.

*H. Palmer, *The Logic of Gospel Criticism*, Macmillan, 1968. Critical analysis by a philosopher of the methods used by New Testament scholars. Helpful for clarifying the issues involved in the historical Jesus debate.

H. Riesenfeld, *The Gospel Tradition*, Blackwell, 1970, pp. 1–29. Claims that Jesus himself took care to ensure that his teachings were reliably handed on to future generations.

Section Five. Into all the world

Chapter 13. Confronting the ancient world

F. F. Bruce, *Men & Movements in the Primitive Church*, Paternoster, 1979 (*Peter, Stephen, James & John*, Eerdmans, 1980). A brief readable account of the life and work of selected personalities in the early church.

F. F. Bruce, *The Speeches in the Acts of the Apostles*, Tyndale, 1942. Still a useful discussion of the nature of the sermons of Acts.

L. E. Elliott-Binns, *Galilean Christianity*, SCM/Allenson, 1956. Examination of what can be known of the early churches in Galilee.

*F.J. Foakes-Jackson & K. Lake, *The Beginnings of Christianity, Part I. The Acts of the Apostles*, Baker, 1979. A huge work in five volumes (first published 1942), giving a comprehensive study of Acts.

M. Hengel, *Acts & the History of earliest Christianity*, SCM/Fortress, 1980. An eminent German scholar argues for the authenticity of Acts.

M. Hengel, *Between Jesus & Paul*, SCM/Fortress, 1983. An important study of this period of church history.

I. H. Marshall, *The Acts of the Apostles*, IVP/Eerdmans, 1980. Concise and helpful commentary.

Section Six. Paul: evangelist extraordinary

Chapter 14. Who was Paul?

G. Bornkamm, *Paul*, Hodder/Harper & Row, 1971. Good general introduction to Paul's life and thinking.

F. F. Bruce, *Paul and Jesus*, Baker, 1974/SPCK, 1975. Examines all aspects of its subject.

F. F. Bruce, *Paul, Apostle of the Free Spirit*, Paternoster, 1977 (*Paul, Apostle of the Heart set Free*, Eerdmans). A comprehensive account of most aspects of Paul's life and letters.

F. F. Bruce, *The Pauline Circle*, Paternoster/Eerdmans, 1985. Studies of some of Paul's friends and helpers.

*W. D. Davies, *Paul & Rabbinic Judaism*, SPCK/Harper & Row, 1970. Detailed comparison of Paul's theology with his background in Judaism.

R. F. Hock, *The Social Context of Paul's Ministry*, Fortress, 1980. Sets Paul in the context of life in the Roman empire.

*B. Holmberg, *Paul and Power*, Gleerup, 1978. Original study of Paul's relations with other early church leaders.

A. M. Hunter, *Paul & his Predecessors*, SCM, 1961 (2nd ed.). Original and important study of Paul's attitude to those who were Christians before him.

J. G. Machen, *The Origin of Paul's Religion*, Eerdmans, 1973, pp. 211–317. Out of date in some ways (first published 1921), but still useful on Paul and the mystery religions.

C. J. Roetzel, *The Letters of Paul*, John Knox, 1982/SCM, 1983 (2nd ed.). Helpful introduction to studying Paul.

Chapter 15. Paul the persecutor

*R. Jewett, *Dating Paul's Life*, Fortress/SCM, 1979. Clear analysis of the issues involved.

W. M. Ramsay, *St Paul the Traveller and the Roman citizen*, Hodder, 1920 (14th ed.). Expounds the view adopted in this book.

Chapter 16. Into all the world

W. G. Doty, *Letters in Primitive Christianity*, Fortress, 1973. Sets Paul's writings in a wider literary context.

K. Lake, *The Earlier Epistles of St Paul*, Rivingtons, 1911. An older book, but still unsurpassed in its clear presentation of the issues involved in Paul's early career.

Galatians

C. K. Barrett, *Freedom & Obligation*, SPCK, 1985. Not quite a commentary, but an extended and helpful discussion of the message of Galatians.

J. Bligh, *Galatians*, St Paul, 1969. Good all-round commentary.

*F. F. Bruce, *The Epistle to the Galatians*, Paternoster/Eerdmans, 1982.

Chapter 17. Paul the missionary
Missionary strategy

F. Hahn, *Mission in the New Testament*, SCM/Allenson, 1965. Covers Paul as well as the rest of the New Testament.

*J. Munck, *Paul & the Salvation of Mankind*, John Knox/SCM, 1959. How did Paul think his work fitted into the broad sweep of salvation history?

1 & 2 Thessalonians

E. Best, *A Commentary on the First and Second Epistles to the Thessalonians*, Black/Harper & Row, 1972.

*F. F. Bruce, *1 & 2 Thessalonians*, Word, 1982.

Chapter 18. Paul the pastor
1 & 2 Corinthians

*C. K. Barrett, *A Commentary on the First Epistle to the Corinthians*, and *A Commentary on the Second Epistle to the Corinthians*, Black/Harper & Row, 1968 & 1973.

F. F. Bruce, *1 & 2 Corinthians*, Marshalls/Eerdmans, 1971. A good general commentary on these letters.

J. Murphy-O'Connor, *St Paul's Corinth*, Michael Glazier, 1983. A very useful study of ancient Corinthian society, and of Paul's relationship to it.

Romans

*C. K. Barrett, *A Commentary on the Epistle to the Romans*, Black/Harper & Row, 1962.

C. E. B. Cranfield, *Romans: a shorter commentary*, Clark/Eerdmans, 1985. An abbreviated version of the larger (and excellent) *Romans* (2 vols), Clark, 1975 & 1979.

*K. P. Donfried, *The Romans Debate*, Augsburg, 1977. Essays on the background and origin of the letter.

E. Käsemann, *Commentary on Romans*, SCM/Eerdmans, 1980. Especially helpful on Paul's theology.

J. A. T. Robinson, *Wrestling with Romans*, SCM/Westminster, 1979. Good short introduction to the letter.

Chapter 19. Paul reaches Rome

K. F. Nickle, *The Collection*, SCM/Allenson, 1966. Paul's strategy in this final stage of his ministry.

Chapter 20. Letters from prison
Colossians & Philemon

R. P. Martin, *Colossians & Philemon*, Marshalls/Eerdmans, 1974.

E. Schweizer, *The Letter to the Colossians*, Augsburg/SPCK, 1982. One of the best recent commentaries on the letter.

Ephesians

F. F. Bruce, *The Epistle to the Ephesians*, Pickering/Revell, 1961. Simple but helpful exposition.

C. L. Mitton, *Ephesians*, Marshalls/Eerdmans, 1976. Good commentary with comprehensive discussion of authorship.

Philippians

*G. F. Hawthorne, *Philippians*, Word, 1983.

R. P. Martin, *Philippians*, IVP/Eerdmans, 1959.

Pastoral epistles

*P. N. Harrison, *The Problem of the Pastoral Epistles*, OUP, 1921. Argues they were composed from scraps written by Paul.

C. K. Barrett, *The Pastoral Epistles*, OUP, 1963. Good short commentary, taking a view similar to Harrison.

J. N. D. Kelly, *A Commentary on the Pastoral Epistles*, Black/Harper & Row, 1963. Argues for authorship by Paul.

Paul's imprisonments

G. S. Duncan, *St Paul's Ephesian Ministry*, Hodder, 1929.

Section Seven. Paul and the Christian message

Chapter 21. What does it mean to be a Christian?

*E. E. Ellis, *Paul's use of the Old Testament*, Baker, 1981 (originally 1957). Original study of Paul's quotations.

M. J. Harris, *Raised Immortal*, Marshalls/Eerdmans, 1985. Study of resurrection and immortality in the whole New Testament, but based on Paul.

M. D. Hooker, *Pauline Pieces*, Epworth, 1979 (*A Preface to Paul*, OUP, 1980). Helpful introductory explanation of Paul's theology.

*E. Käsemann, *Essays on New Testament Themes*, SCM/Allenson, 1964; and *New Testament Questions of Today*, SCM/Fortress, 1969. Some of the most penetrating and original work on Paul in recent years. Hard going for beginners!

L. E. Keck, *Paul and his Letters*, Fortress, 1979. Short introduction to Paul's thinking.

*S. Kim, *The Origin of Paul's Gospel*, Mohr, 1981/Eerdmans, 1982. Original study of its subject, laying particular emphasis on the importance of Paul's conversion.

*H. N. Ridderbos, *Paul*, Eerdmans, 1975/SPCK, 1977. Exhaustive analysis of Paul's theology.

D. E. H. Whiteley, *The Theology of St Paul*, Blackwell, 1964. Comprehensive survey of its subject.

J. A. Ziesler, *Pauline Christianity*, OUP, 1983. A helpful study of Paul's major themes.

Chapter 22. Freedom and fellowship

R. Banks, *Paul's Idea of Community*, Paternoster/Eerdmans, 1980.

V. P. Furnish, *The Moral Teaching of Paul*, Abingdon, 1979. An excellent book, trying to discover how Paul's teaching can be applied today.

R. N. Longenecker, *New Testament Social Ethics for Today*, Eerdmans, 1984. Takes its starting point from Galatians, and explores the meaning of Paul's idea of freedom.

R. P. Martin, *The Spirit and the Congregation*, Eerdmans, 1984. A careful exposition of 1 Corinthians 12–14.

P. Richardson, *Paul's Ethic of Freedom*, Westminster, 1979.

J. P. Sampley, *Pauline Partners in Christ*, Fortress, 1980. Explores the meaning of Paul's thinking in terms of its social and legal context in the Roman empire.

Section Eight. Unity in diversity

Chapter 23. The Spirit and the letter

C. K. Barrett, *Church, Ministry & Sacraments in the New Testament*, Paternoster, 1985. Valuable study of changing patterns.

*H. von Campenhausen, *Tradition and Life in the Church*, Collins/Fortress, 1968.

J. D. G. Dunn, *Jesus & the Spirit*, SCM/Westminster, 1975. A classic exposition of the charismatic church, including extensive discussion of Paul.

E. Lohse, *The Formation of the New Testament*, Abingdon, 1981. The history of the New Testament canon.

E. Schweizer, *Church Order in the New Testament*, SCM/OUP, 1961. A standard book on its subject.

M. Warkentin, *Ordination*, Eerdmans, 1982. A historical and theological critique of the practice of the church in the period after the New Testament.

Chapter 24. The Church and its Jewish origins

E. Best, *1 Peter*, Marshalls/Eerdmans, 1971.

R. E. Brown, K. P. Donfried, J. Reumann, *Peter in the New Testament*, Augsburg, 1973. Ecumenical essays on a contentious subject.

F. F. Bruce, *The Epistle to the Hebrews*, Eerdmans, 1964.

G. B. Caird, *A Commentary on the Revelation of St John the Divine*, Black/Harper & Row, 1985 (2nd ed.).

*F. L. Cross, *1 Peter, a Paschal Liturgy*, Mowbrays, 1954. Argues that 1 Peter originated as a baptismal homily.

*P. H. Davids, *The Epistle of James*, Eerdmans/Paternoster, 1982.

E. S. Fiorenza, *The Book of Revelation – Justice & Judgment*, Fortress, 1985. Sets Revelation in the context of the other Johannine writings, as well as exploring its message.

S. Laws, *A Commentary on the Epistle of James*, Black/Harper & Row, 1980.

Chapter 25. The enemies within

*R. E. Brown, *The Community of the Beloved Disciple*, Paulist/Chapman, 1979. An imaginative (and generally plausible) reconstruction of the Christian community which produced the Johannine writings.

E. E. Ellis, *The World of St John*, Eerdmans, 1984. Useful short account of its subject.

J. N. D. Kelly, *A Commentary on the Epistles of Peter and of Jude*, Black/Harper & Row, 1969.

I. H. Marshall, *The Epistles of John*, Eerdmans, 1978.

W. M. Ramsay, *The Letters to the Seven Churches*, Baker, 1985 (originally 1904). Classic exposition of the first three chapters of Revelation, showing how the letters to the churches reflect the situation of their readers.

*S. S. Smalley, *1, 2, 3 John*, Word, 1984. A judicious commentary based on original work.

Index

SOURCES OF QUOTATIONS & OTHER REFERENCES

Bible texts are always quoted from either the Revised Standard Version or the Good News Bible.

Chapter 4   Page 97   L. Morris, *The Gospel according to John,* Eerdmans, 1971, page 785 (New International Commentary on the New Testament)

Chapter 6   Page 114   W. G. Kümmel, *The Theology of the New Testament,* Abingdon Press, 1973/SCM Press, 1974, page 35

Chapter 9   Page 150   A. M. Hunter, *Design for Life,* SCM Press, 1965 (2nd ed.), pages 67–68

Page 157   T. W. Manson, *The Sayings of Jesus,* SCM Press, 1949, page 37

Chapter 10   Page 178   E. Käsemann, *Essays on New Testament Themes,* SCM Press/Allenson, 1963, page 15

Pages 178–79   F. F. Bruce, *The New Testament Documents,* IVP/Inter-Varsity 1960 (2nd ed.), pages 32–33

Chapter 11   Page 192   B. H. Streeter, *The Four Gospels,* Macmillan, 1924, page 385

Chapter 12   Page 198   R. Bultmann, *Jesus and the Word,* Scribner's, 1934, page 8

Page 202   N. Perrin, *Rediscovering the Teaching of Jesus,* SCM Press, 1967, page 15

Page 212   J. Jeremias, *Unknown Sayings of Jesus,* SPCK/Allenson, 1964 (2nd ed.), page 121

Chapter 13   Page 241   N. Perrin, *The New Testament: an introduction,* Harcourt, Brace, Jovanovich, 1974, page 204.

Ph. Vielhauer, 'On the "Paulinism" of Acts', *Studies in Luke-Acts,* ed. L. E. Keck & J. L. Martyn, Abingdon Press, 1966/SPCK, 1968, pages 33–50

Chapter 18   Page 326   J. B. Lightfoot, *Saint Paul's Epistle to the Galatians,* Macmillan, 1865, page 48

Chapter 23   Page 399   Karl Kautsky, *The Foundations of Christianity,* Allen & Unwin/International Publishers, 1925

Page 400   E. Käsemann, *Essays on New Testament Themes,* SCM Press/Allenson, 1963, page 81.

Hans Küng, *On Being a Christian,* Doubleday/Collins, 1977; *The Church,* Burns & Oates, 1967/Sheed & Ward, 1968.

H. Berkhof, *Christian Faith,* Eerdmans, 1979/T. & T. Clark, 1980, page 400.

Page 401   W. Bauer, *Orthodoxy and Heresy in Earliest Christianity,* Fortress Press, 1971/SCM Press, 1972

Page 402   R. P. C. Hanson, *Christian Priesthood Examined,* Lutterworth, 1979, page 32

Pages 405–406   Max Weber, *Economy and Society,* Bedminster Press, 1968; *On Charisma and Institution Building,* Chicago University Press, 1968.

Page 407   E. Käsemann, *New Testament Questions of Today,* SCM Press/Fortress Press, 1969, page 241

Chapter 24   Page 419   Th. Zahn, *Introduction to the New Testament,* volume 1, Scribner's/T. & T. Clark, 1909

Pages 449–50   E. Lohmeyer, 'Die Offenbarung des Johannes 1920–1934', *Theologische Rundschau* 6 (1934), pages 269–314 and 7 (1935), pages 2–62

Chapter 25   Pages 461–62   E. Käsemann, *The Testament of Jesus,* SCM Press/Fortress Press, 1968

Pages 462–63   R. Bultmann, *The Johannine Epistles,* Fortress Press, 1973

The photographs in this book are reproduced by permission of the following photographers and organizations:

J. Allan Cash: 36, 53, 62, 74, 97, 142, 153, 166, 168, 172
American School of Classical Studies, Athens: 100, 298–99, 325, 329
Andes Press Agency: Carlos Reyes 359, 374–75
BBC Hulton Picture Library: 62 (background), 128,152
Barnaby's Picture Library: 27, 63, 80, 88, 154–55 (background), 165, 215, 235, 239, 261, 402, 410, 412, 415, 427, 438–39, 457 (right)/Don Long 179
British Library: 360
British Museum: 17, 48, 177, 303, 344, 409, 420, 457 (left)
Camera Press: 89, 140, 279
Tony Cantale Graphics: 206
Church Missionary Society: 464–65
K.W. Coates: 119, 147
Bruce Coleman: 149
Ecole Française d'Archaeologie, Athens: 302
Keith Ellis: 396
Fritz Fankhauser: 55 (middle inset), 68, 113, 135, 187, 211
Gordon Gray: 219, 365
W.B. Grunbaum: 379
Haifa Maritime Museum: 92
Sonia Halliday Photographs: Sonia Halliday 15, 23, 41, 46, 55 (left inset), 58, 62 (inset above left), 75 (inset below), 95, 106–107, 125, 126, 139, 144–45, 156, 171, 183, 197, 224, 232-33 (background), 272, 316, 319, 323, 362–63, 369, 372–73, 447/Jane Taylor 31, 73, 133, 148, 231, 422–23, 432, 435, 440/Laura Lushington 131, 199
Michael Holford: 343
Alan Howard: 345
Lion Publishing: David Alexander 19, 34, 52, 82, 102, 108, 115, 137 (left), 160, 163, 181, 191, 193, 196, 200 (both), 218, 226 (below), 233 (inset), 248, 249, 253, 254, 255, 262, 264, 268–69, 270, 273, 275, 276, 278, 282 (both), 283, 284, 286, 287, 294, 297 (both), 298 (right and left inset), 299 (inset above and below), 300, 306, 309, 311, 312, 313, 320, 331 (both), 334, 335, 336, 340, 347, 354, 399, 418–19, 456, 461/David Alexander/Haifa Maritime Museum 333/Jon Willcocks 348/Jennie Karrach 383
London City Mission: Peter Trainer 365
Ake Lundberg: 243
Martin Lynch: 353
Phil Manning: 75 (middle left inset)
Mansell Collection: 25, 47, 194 (both), 195 (both), 226 (above), 234, 237, 240, 242, 301, 388, 413, 452
MEPhA: 40, 59, 104, 120
Museum of London: 257, 259
Open Doors: 429
Ivor Philip: 466
Picturepoint: 441
Popperfoto: 51, 55 (background), 62 (middle and right inset), 67, 70, 75 (top and middle right inset), 117, 118, 123, 154 (both), 155 (both), 205, 209, 401
John Rylands Library: 203
Clifford Shirley: 393, 394, 404
TEAR Fund: 55 (right inset), 137 (right), 189
Topham: 454–55
John Twinning: 380
World Council of Churches: 387
World Vision: 460
Wycliffe Bible Translators: 271

Design and graphics by Tony Cantale Graphics